Register Now for Online Access to Your Book!

SPRINGER PUBLISHING
C⏻NNECT™

Your print purchase of *Research Design for the Behavioral Sciences: An Applied Approach* **includes online access to the contents of your book**—increasing accessibility, portability, and searchability!

Access today at:
http://connect.springerpub.com/content/book/978-0-8261-4385-3
or scan the QR code at the right with your smartphone
and enter the access code below.

5W241PDG

Scan here for quick access.

If you are experiencing problems accessing the digital component of this product, please contact our customer service department at cs@springerpub.com

The online access with your print purchase is available at the publisher's discretion and may be removed at any time without notice.

Publisher's Note: New and used products purchased from third-party sellers are not guaranteed for quality, authenticity, or access to any included digital components.

SPRINGER PUBLISHING
View all our products at springerpub.com

D1376676

RESEARCH DESIGN FOR THE BEHAVIORAL SCIENCES

Stephen V. Flynn, PhD, LPC, LMFT-S, NCC, ACS, earned his MA degree from Rowan University and his PhD from the University of Northern Colorado. Dr. Flynn is an associate professor of counselor education and is a research fellow in the Center of Research and Innovation at Plymouth State University, Plymouth, New Hampshire. He teaches research, clinical, and writing courses for the Counselor Education, Marriage and Family Therapy, and Educational Leadership graduate programs at Plymouth State University. He is a licensed professional counselor (Colorado), licensed marriage and family therapist (Colorado and New Hampshire), national certified counselor, approved clinical supervisor, American Association of Marriage and Family Therapy (AAMFT) Clinical Fellow, and an AAMFT Approved supervisor. Dr. Flynn has published numerous research articles using diverse methodological frameworks, including qualitative, quantitative, and mixed methods. His research and scholarship interests include five areas (a) research methodology and processes, (b) the relationship between altruism and self-interest, (c) multicultural and diversity issues, (d) counselor preparation, and (e) student retention.

RESEARCH DESIGN FOR THE BEHAVIORAL SCIENCES

An Applied Approach

Stephen V. Flynn, PhD, LPC, LMFT-S, NCC, ACS

Editor

 SPRINGER PUBLISHING

Springer Publishing Company, LLC
11 West 42nd Street, New York, NY 10036
www.springerpub.com
connect.springerpub.com/

Acquisitions Editor: Rhonda Dearborn
Compositor: Transforma

ISBN: 978-0-8261-4384-6
ebook ISBN: 978-0-8261-4385-3
DOI: 10.1891/9780826143853

Qualified instructors may request supplements by emailing textbook@springerpub.com
Instructor's Manual: 978-0-8261-4387-7
PowerPoint: 978-0-8261-4388-4
Test Bank: 978-0-8261-4386-0 (Available on Respondus®)
Sample Syllabus: 978-0-8261-4389-1

21 22 23 24 25 / 5 4 3 2 1

The author and the publisher of this Work have made every effort to use sources believed to be reliable to provide information that is accurate and compatible with the standards generally accepted at the time of publication. The author and publisher shall not be liable for any special, consequential, or exemplary damages resulting, in whole or in part, from the readers' use of, or reliance on, the information contained in this book. The publisher has no responsibility for the persistence or accuracy of URLs for external or third-party Internet websites referred to in this publication and does not guarantee that any content on such websites is, or will remain, accurate or appropriate.

Library of Congress Cataloging-in-Publication Data

Names: Flynn, Stephen V., editor.
Title: Research design for the behavioral sciences : an applied approach / Stephen V. Flynn, PhD., LPC, LMFT-S, NCC, ACS, editor.
Description: New York, NY : Springer Publishing Company, [2022] | Includes index.
Identifiers: LCCN 2020043730 (print) | LCCN 2020043731 (ebook) | ISBN 9780826143846 (paperback) |
   ISBN 9780826143853 (ebook)
Subjects: LCSH: Psychology—Research. | Experiential research. | Psychology—Statistical methods.
Classification: LCC BF76.5 .R45 2022 (print) | LCC BF76.5 (ebook) | DDC 150.72—dc23
LC record available at https://lccn.loc.gov/2020043730
LC ebook record available at https://lccn.loc.gov/2020043731

Contact sales@springerpub.com to receive discount rates on bulk purchases.

Publisher's Note: **New and used products purchased from third-party sellers are not guaranteed for quality, authenticity, or access to any included digital components.**

Printed in the United States of America.

To Dr. Linda Black, my first research mentor, the open atmosphere, empowerment, and attention to research standards you provided have always inspired me; and to Meredith and all of our children, whose love and support provide the foundation on which amazing things can be created.

CONTENTS

PART II. QUANTITATIVE RESEARCH

5. Experimental Research   *125*
Kristin L. K. Koskey and Ingrid K. Weigold

9. Content Analysis Research   251
Cassandra A. Storlie and Hongryun Woo

PART III. QUALITATIVE RESEARCH

PART IV. MIXED METHODS RESEARCH

CONTRIBUTORS

Ania Bartkowiak, MS, Doctoral Student, Counseling Program, Oregon State University, Corvallis, Oregon

Ashley J. Blount, PhD, Assistant Professor, Department of Counseling, University of Nebraska Omaha, Omaha, Nebraska

Nicole V. Brady, MEd, Certified School Counselor, Jobs for America's Graduates (NH-JAG) Youth Specialist, Laconia High School, Laconia, New Hampshire

Joshua J. Castleberry, PhD, NCC, Assistant Professor, Counselor Education Department, Kent State University, Kent, Ohio

Robert J. Cox, MS, Graduate Student, Counseling Program, Oregon State University, Corvallis, Oregon

Heather Dahl, PhD, Assistant Professor, Department of Counselor Education, School Psychology, and Human Services, University of Nevada, Las Vegas, Las Vegas, Nevada

Yue Dang, PhD, Assistant Professor of Instruction, School of Counseling College of Health Professions, The University of Akron, Akron, Ohio

Cody Dickson, PhD, LPC-S, LMHP, NCC, Licensed Professional Counselor Supervisor and Consultant, Private Practice, Lubbock, Texas

Stephen V. Flynn, PhD, LPC, LMFT-S, NCC, ACS, Associate Professor, Innovation and Entrepreneurship Cluster, Plymouth State University, Plymouth, New Hampshire

Shelby K. Gonzales, EdS, Doctoral Student, Department of Educational Studies, University of South Carolina, Columbia, South Carolina

Jessie D. Guest, PhD, Adjunct Instructor, Department of Educational Studies, University of South Carolina, Columbia, South Carolina

Natoya Hill Haskins, PhD, LPC, NCC, Associate Professor, School Psychology and Counselor Education and Supervision, College of William and Mary, Williamsburg, Virginia

Wendy Hoskins, PhD, Associate Professor, Department of Counselor Education, School Psychology, and Human Services, University of Nevada, Las Vegas, Las Vegas, Nevada

Kim Lee Hughes, PhD, Assistant Professor, Counselor Education, Clark Atlanta University, Atlanta, Georgia

Tynisha I. Ingerson, MS, Graduate Student, Marriage and Family Therapy Program, Innovation and Entrepreneurship Cluster, Plymouth State University, Plymouth, New Hampshire

James S. Korcuska, PhD, LPC, NCC, Professor, School of Education, North Dakota State University, Fargo, North Dakota

Kristin L. K. Koskey, PhD, Associate Professor, Educational Foundations & Leadership, The University of Akron, Akron, Ohio

Amanda C. La Guardia, PhD, LPCC-S, Associate Professor, University of Cincinnati School of Human Services, Cincinnati, Ohio

Michael S. Leeman, PhD, LPCC-S, Assistant Professor, Department of Health and Human Services, Southeastern Louisiana University, Hammond, Louisiana

Dodie Limberg, PhD, Associate Professor, Department of Educational Studies, University of South Carolina, Columbia, South Carolina

Hailey Martinez, PhD, Online Full Time Core Faculty, College of Humanities and Social Sciences, Grand Canyon University, Phoenix, Arizona

Ann McCaughan, PhD, Associate Professor, University of Illinois Springfield, Human Development Counseling Department, Springfield, Illinois

W. Bradley McKibben, PhD, IMH (FL), NCC, Assistant Professor, Department of Counseling, Nova Southeastern University, Fort Lauderdale, Florida

Katherine M. Murphy, PhD, LPC, LMHC, LIMHP, University of South Dakota, Vermillion, South Dakota

Tiffany Nielson, PhD, Assistant Professor, University of Illinois Springfield, Human Development Counseling Department, Springfield, Illinois

Janise Parker, PhD, LP, NCSP, Assistant Professor, School Psychology and Counselor Education and Supervision, College of William and Mary, Williamsburg, Virginia

Deborah J. Rubel, PhD, Associate Professor, Counseling Program, Oregon State University, Corvallis, Oregon

Varunee Faii Sangganjanavanich, PhD, Professor & Director, School of Counseling College of Health Professions, The University of Akron, Akron, Ohio

Jeremy D. Shain, EdS, Doctoral Student, Counseling Program, Oregon State University, Corvallis, Oregon

Cassandra A. Storlie, PhD, Associate Professor, Counselor Education & Supervision, Kent State University, Kent, Ohio

Emily J. Sturn, MEd, LPC, NCC, Doctoral Student, North Dakota State University, Fargo, North Dakota

Dalena Dillman Taylor, PhD, Associate Professor, Counselor Education and School Psychology, University of Central Florida, Orlando, Florida

Eric S. Thompson, PhD, Assistant Professor, Department of Counseling, Nova Southeastern University, Fort Lauderdale, Florida

Danielle Render Turmaud, MS, NCC, Doctoral Student, Counseling Program, Oregon State University, Portland, Oregon

Lindsey K. Umstead, PhD, LPCA (NC), NCC, Visiting Assistant Professor, Department of Counseling and Educational Development, The University of North Carolina at Greensboro, Greensboro, North Carolina

Clarissa M. Uttley, PhD, Professor, Democracy, and Social Change Cluster, Plymouth State University, Plymouth, New Hampshire

Unity Walker, MEd, Doctoral Student, Counselor Education, College of William and Mary, Williamsburg, Virginia

Samantha Waterhouse, BS, Graduate Student, Marriage and Family Therapy Program, Innovation and Entrepreneurship Cluster, Plymouth State University, Plymouth, New Hampshire

Ingrid K. Weigold, PhD, Professor, Department of Psychology, The University of Akron, Akron, Ohio

Hongryun Woo, PhD, Associate Professor, Department of Counseling and Human Development, University of Louisville, Louisville, Kentucky

FOREWORD

When I worked full-time as a mental health counselor, one of my clients was a heterosexual, African American woman in her mid 20s. I can still see her face and remember her name, despite the fact that I have not seen her in almost two decades. I recall she presented for counseling with symptoms of depression, and she was struggling to finish her college degree. We began our work together focused primarily on her symptoms and coping strategies. As our counseling relationship grew, she disclosed that she had an emergency hysterectomy the year prior to entering counseling. She was also in an abusive relationship at that time, although she did not define it as such immediately. In this relationship, I learned about her intense grief and loss related to not being able to have children, the lack of support she felt from her partner as well as her family and friends, and her questioning of her faith as a Christian. Through our work together—and the relationship we built—we deconstructed and reconstructed what it meant to be a woman absent the role of being a biological mother. We navigated grief, loss, spirituality, relationship violence, and race, and how these constructs weave together to form experiences that both united us and distinguished us from one another.

I share this story because this client was an impetus for my questioning of what I learned in my training from textbooks, research articles, and course lectures. Her presentation of depression, intimate partner violence, career development, support system needs, and racial, feminist, and spiritual identities was different from what I had learned. It was also different from what I had personally experienced. The knowledge gaps were so pronounced for me. This counseling relationship was a turning point in my professional counselor identity development and taught me valuable lessons. First, to be an effective counselor, I needed to be a critical consumer of research and "best practices" offered by my profession. I was accountable to my clients and their communities to question what I have learned about them and to intensively search for how their voices are missing from counseling-related constructs and practices. Furthermore, I needed to collaborate with them to continually deconstruct and reconstruct knowledge, so that underrepresented communities are meaningfully included to produce better client outcomes. To this end, gaining tools for engaging in research was required to grow my professional identity as a counselor.

Counselor trainees and those new to the profession have a wonderful opportunity, and responsibility, to integrate a strong research identity within their emerging professional counselor identity. The American Counseling Association (n.d.) defines counseling as "a professional relationship that empowers diverse individuals, families, and groups to accomplish mental health, wellness, education, and career goals." Through consuming and expanding our counseling research base, and partnering with clients and communities in those efforts, we facilitate accomplishing these counseling goals.

Counselors have the power, if intentional and inclusive, to advance our profession; to expand definitions and examples of mental health, resilience, privilege and oppression, and new or revised ways of knowing within diverse communities. As they gain research knowledge and experience, counselors expand their understanding and ability to describe and explain phenomena that impact clients' lives (Fassinger & Morrow, 2013; Snow et al., 2016). Counselor growth requires stretching and pushing boundaries regarding what has been known to be "true" about social, psychological, and systemic phenomena. As effective, critical researchers, they are more effective counselors. Research *is* practice.

I wholeheartedly invite counselor trainees and counselors into this journey of growing the research component of their professional identity. To be effective and competent researchers, counselors must be flexible and creative, develop collaborative relationships and diverse research teams, gain (and continually question) knowledge of previous scholarship as well as historical and contemporary counseling practices, understand the mechanics of the research process itself, and ethically and professionally conduct and integrate research in applied settings (Wester & Borders, 2014).

Flynn and his colleagues prepare counselor trainees and counselors for this journey well and guide them carefully toward researcher competency. In an approachable and developmentally appropriate manner, they highlight for the profession the value of research and how it can be conducted. They provide a treasured and diverse toolbox of research methods; their historical, ethical, legal, and cultural uses and limitations; the foundational nature of counselor–client relationships; and strategies counselors can (and should) employ to partner with clients and communities to advance the counseling profession.

The text begins with three foundational chapters to contextualize for readers the research tools that follow; these introductory chapters are often missing in research texts in counseling and counseling-related texts, focusing on philosophical assumptions, research rigor, ethical principles, paradigmatic influences, literature review and writing strategies, and pioneers and research trends across the helping professions. Throughout the remaining chapters of the text, Flynn and his colleagues provide balanced and varied methodological tools for quantitative, qualitative, and mixed-methods research approaches. Within the chapters of this text, they infuse cultural and ethical considerations, apply concepts in case studies and other examples, suggest practice exercises, and offer software options and other resources for further learning.

Welcome to the journey. Let's begin.

Danica G. Hays, PhD
American Counseling Fellow
Professor and Executive Associate Dean
University of Nevada, Las Vegas, Nevada

REFERENCES

American Counseling Association. (n.d.). *20/20: A vision for the future of counseling.* Retrieved from https://www.counseling.org/about-us/about-aca/20-20-a-vision-for-the-future-of-counseling

Fassinger, R., & Morrow, S. L. (2013). Toward best practices in quantitative, qualitative, and mixed-method research: A social justice perspective. *Journal for Social Action in Counseling & Psychology*, 5, 69–83. https://doi.org/10.33043/JSACP.5.2.69-83

Snow, K. C., Hays, D. G., Caliwagan, G., Ford, Jr., D. J., Mariotti, D., Mwendwa, J. M., & Scott, W. E. (2016). Guiding principles for indigenous research practices. *Action Research*, 14, 357–375. https://doi.org/10.1177/1476750315622542

Wester, K. L., & Borders, L. D. (2014). Research competencies in counseling: A Delphi study. *Journal of Counseling & Development*, 92(4), 447–458. https://doi.org/10.1002/j.1556-6676.2014.00171.x

PREFACE

"It is the unknown that excites the ardor of scholars, who, in the known alone, would shrivel up with boredom."

— *Wallace Stevens*

This first edition of *Research Design for the Behavioral Sciences: An Applied Approach* symbolizes a comprehensive scholarly journey emphasizing the philosophy, science, and practice of research and scholarly based pursuits. The behavioral sciences should be erupting with curiosity, innovation, and rigor as its practitioners endeavor to understand human behavior in all of its complexity. The success and rigor of our research, not to mention the outcomes of this work, are important to the continued growth of our respective professions. Although empirical research has brought much awareness to our collective understanding of human behavior, emotion, cognition, and consciousness there is still much left to be discovered. The gaps in understanding human behavior captivate our imaginations and serve as a motivator to take action in the exploration of various phenomena. *Research Design for the Behavioral Sciences: An Applied Approach* provides researchers with the philosophies and methods that will allow them to bring their scholarly interests to life.

GOAL OF THIS TEXTBOOK

The overall goal of this textbook is centered on informing students enrolled in doctoral and advanced master's degree programs about (a) the foundations of behavioral science research, (b) the nuances and procedures associated with the major research traditions, (c) the philosophical integration that sits behind each research methodology, (d) instructions on how to increase the rigor of each approach to research, and (e) the integration of multicultural and social justice principles into scholarly pursuits. Each chapter that emphasizes a research tradition concludes with an applied case study that puts the tradition into action.

Through providing clear and in-depth blueprints for how to use distinct research methodology and methods, *Research Design for the Behavioral Sciences: An Applied Approach* provides both an in-depth and pragmatic understanding of the standards and procedures for specific research traditions. After reading this textbook, students will increase their research self-efficacy;enhance their ability to accurately match their research interests with the appropriate tradition; increase their understanding of qualitative, quantitative, and mixed methods standards of rigor; and build a foundation for an emerging research identity.

This work offers chapters dedicated to topics and traditions that are often not included in behavioral science research-based textbooks. There are entire chapters that are dedicated to history and philosophy of social science research, various forms of content analysis designs, consensual qualitative research, and three chapters that review six separate mixed methods research traditions. In addition, included in this textbook is a comprehensive statistics chapter, entitled "Descriptive, Inferential, and Bayesian Statistics." These chapters are listed below:

- Chapter 2: History of Research in the Social Sciences
- Chapter 4: Descriptive, Inferential, and Bayesian Statistics
- Chapter 9: Content Analysis Research
- Chapter 14: Consensual Qualitative Research
- Chapter 16: Mixed Methods Research: Convergent and Embedded Designs
- Chapter 17: Mixed Methods Research: Explanatory and Exploratory Designs
- Chapter 18: Mixed Methods Research: Transformative and Multiphase Designs

INSTRUCTOR RESOURCES

Research Design for the Behavioral Sciences: An Applied Approach is accompanied by an instructor's manual and comprehensive instructor resources, which include PowerPoint slides, classroom exercises, and a test bank. Structurally, all chapters have learning objectives, student exercises, summaries, helpful books, websites, videos, and key references that indicate the most influential resources within each chapter.

This textbook has an easily accessible chapter flow that lends itself nicely to graduate school courses. Educators can direct students' attention to the chapter-based learning exercises, case studies, and encourage further student learning with the suggested web links and readings. Lastly, throughout the textbook we provide clear, detailed, and contextually accurate examples of a variety of writing and quantitative, qualitative, and mixed methods procedures and processes. Incorporating these examples into student learning can greatly enhance and contextualize students' understanding of the material.

INTENDED AUDIENCE

The intended audience for this textbook is doctoral and advanced master's degree programs in the behavioral sciences. While the target audience of this book is doctoral level counselor education programs, it has a secondary audience of doctoral-level social work, psychology, and marriage and family therapy programs. A third audience includes master's level counseling, social work, psychology, and marriage and family therapy programs with a strong research emphasis. The following lists several potential courses in which this textbook could be adopted.

- Research Seminar in Counselor Education and Supervision
- Advanced Research in Counseling
- Foundations of Research in Counseling

Mid and late career professionals who have some experience with research design will also find this book useful for understanding various procedures, philosophical assumptions, and traditions. Professors and seasoned practitioners will hopefully see this textbook as including state-of-the-art methods, descriptions of rigor, philosophical integration, and resources created to provide a foundational level of training.

ORGANIZATION OF THE CONTENT

Research Design for the Behavioral Sciences: An Applied Approach is an introduction as well as an in-depth, detailed synopsis of the practice of research. This 18-chapter textbook begins with informing the reader of the basic building blocks of research and ethics (Chapter 1), provides an overview of the history and philosophy of research in the social sciences (Chapter 2), explores the foundations of scholarly writing and American Psychological Association style (Chapter 3), and presents a chapter that prudently explores descriptive, inferential, and Bayesian statistics (Chapter 4). The remainder of the textbook (Chapters 5–18) explores quantitative, qualitative, and mixed methods research traditions. In total, 17 methodological traditions and their variants are reviewed.

Throughout the textbook authors attempt to highlight the most important, useful, and pragmatic aspects of research design in the behavioral sciences. The authors fold into their writing many examples of basic and advanced research design procedures and processes. To help organize the four distinct yet interrelated sections of this textbook, the chapters are organized into four parts, including: (a) introduction, history, and writing, (b) quantitative research, (c) qualitative research, and (d) mixed methods research.

PART I: INTRODUCTION, HISTORY, AND WRITING

The first three chapters of this textbook thoroughly prepare emerging researchers with relevant information on the foundations of qualitative, quantitative, and mixed methods designs and research ethics. The macro research categories are reviewed in a comprehensive manner that sets the stage for the remainder of the text. Topic areas include (but are not limited to) problem statements, research questions, purpose statement, sampling, methodological sampling, paradigmatic hierarchy, common data collection points, data analysis, methods for the enhancement of rigor, methodological research identity, and the scientist–practitioner model. This section of the textbook also includes a thorough review of the ontology, epistemology, theory, methodology, and methods that underlie the research traditions commonly employed in the behavioral sciences. Students will review the contemporary and historical research trends within the various helping professions. In addition, the textbook will also review information on engaging the scholarly writing process in a meaningful and rigorous manner setting the stage for scholarly inquiry. A few of the writing topics covered include understanding the purpose and structure of the *Publication Manual of the American Psychological Association*, writing mechanics, constructing a literature review, and concept mapping.

PART II: QUANTITATIVE RESEARCH

Chapters 4 through 9 investigate a variety of statistical procedures and quantitative research traditions. This section begins with an overview of measurement, descriptive statistics, inferential statistics, Bayesian statistics, reliability, and validity procedures. Next, the authors review a number of quantitative research traditions, including experimental research, predictive research, single subject design, survey research, and content analysis. This review gives special attention to the paradigmatic hierarchy, procedures, methods for increasing rigor, multicultural issues, and case studies.

PART III: QUALITATIVE RESEARCH

Chapters 10 through 14 review a variety of qualitative research traditions and their variants. The authors explore case study research, phenomenological research, grounded theory research, narrative research, and consensual qualitative research. This review includes the unique procedures for each approach, methods for enhancing qualitative rigor, the philosophical integration relevant to each approach, trustworthiness procedures, multicultural considerations, and case studies.

PART IV: MIXED METHODS RESEARCH

The fourth section of this textbook includes common approaches to mixed methods research and contains Chapters 15 through 18. This section includes six mixed methods research traditions, including action research, convergent designs, embedded designs, explanatory designs, exploratory designs, transformative designs, and multiphase designs. The chapters provide special attention to relevant mixed methods procedures, paradigm decisions, methods for increasing rigor, multicultural considerations, and case studies.

Qualified instructors may obtain access to supplementary material (Instructor's Manual, PowerPoints, Test Bank, and Sample Syllabus) by emailing textbook@springerpub.com.

ACKNOWLEDGMENTS

This textbook and my process have benefited tremendously from many individuals and their contributions. I begin by thanking my Springer Acquisitions Editor, Rhonda Dearborn, for her coordination, encouragement, and support throughout the project. In addition, I would like to thank Springer Assistant Editor, Mehak Massand for all of her help throughout the writing and editing process. I would also like to thank the entire Springer staff for their encouragement and support of the field of research design within the behavioral sciences.

I wish to acknowledge the scholars who contributed their time, expertise, and talent to the completion of their respective book chapters and for advancing the field of research design. I would like to thank the following reviewers for their helpful feedback: Jennifer Preston, Saybrook University; Laura Hayden, University of Massachusetts-Boston; Alexander Fietzer, Hunter College; Stephanie Bell, Delta State University; Cassandra Storlie, Kent State University; Sabina de Vries, Texas A&M University-San Antonio; and Kathleen Palmer, University of Detroit Mercy.

I would like to acknowledge a number of individuals who were important in helping me with the editing and writing of this textbook. None of this would have been possible without my supportive spouse, Meredith Flynn. She has stood by my side through every struggle and success.

I am eternally grateful to my bright, energetic, and delightful children Corrina Flynn, Anelie Flynn, and Eliza Flynn for providing a tremendous amount of inspiration and motivation to complete the first edition of this textbook.

I would like to thank my mother, Joyce Flynn, for her unconditional support during this project and in all aspects of my life. And a very special thanks to my sisters Suzy Ueberroth and Janet Flatley for their unconditional love and support.

PART I

INTRODUCTION, HISTORY, AND WRITING

CHAPTER 1

UNDERSTANDING RESEARCH AND ETHICS

Stephen V. Flynn and Tynisha I. Ingerson

INTRODUCTION TO RESEARCH AND ETHICS IN THE BEHAVIORAL SCIENCES

This chapter is your introduction to social science research and ethical considerations. Early-, mid-, and late-career professionals entering the world of research will likely be surprised by the number of research traditions, methods, and procedures available to them. Because very few textbooks introduce a wide-ranging collection of research methodology, many helping professionals feel ill equipped to understand what approach they want to utilize and how to effectively execute the associated methods. To further confuse adult learners, much of the literature in the behavioral sciences fails to adequately match pragmatic aspects of a research tradition (methods, sampling procedures, trustworthiness procedures) with the overarching research philosophy (ontology, epistemology, theory).

RESEARCH TRADITIONS

This textbook aims to provide a sophisticated overview of 17 unique research traditions and an introduction to the worlds of research ethics, research writing, statistics, and the history of research in the social sciences. Within each chapter, the author(s) provide a concise breakdown of the research tradition's philosophical integration. This philosophical hierarchy encompasses five levels: ontology (i.e., form and nature of reality), epistemology (i.e., theory of knowledge acquisition), theoretical stance (i.e., philosophical stance), methodology (i.e., process for discovering what is knowable), and method (i.e., procedures for gathering and analyzing data (Flynn & Korcuska, 2018a,b; Flynn, Korcuska, Brady, & Hays, 2019). By perusing chapters that outline a coherent methodological blueprint, emerging and seasoned researchers alike can glean an in-depth understanding of the various paradigmatic levels of a research tradition and how these levels inform one another. In other words, a research tradition's philosophical descriptions will demonstrate how your decision to use a particular methodology or method is linked to the manner in which you view reality. In exploring these vantage points, you will have an opportunity to fully consider a research tradition's theoretical blueprints.

In addition to laying out the coherent blueprints of 17 unique research traditions, every chapter will teach you how to increase the rigor of a particular research tradition. Methodological rigor can be determined by the degree to which a researcher uses a systematic and coherent approach in designing a study that exemplifies validity, trustworthiness, diversity, and amount of data collected (Flynn et al., 2019; Kline, 2008). Researchers and reviewers of research place great importance on a study's rigor because it partly determines the nature and the meaning of the findings. Given the unique standards within each research tradition, rigor will not always look the same. For example, using one subject for a survey research project would not be considered rigorous, yet it would be considered normative in case study research.

ACCREDITATION AND IDENTITY DEVELOPMENT

Throughout this textbook, accreditation standards are considered in the context of research design. Accredited institutions are required to meet acceptable levels of quality in research training. Graduate programs accredited through national organizations such as the Council for Accreditation of Counseling and Related Education Programs (CACREP), the American Psychological Association (APA), the Commission on Accreditation for Marriage and Family Therapy Education (COAMFTE), and the Council on Social Work Education (CSWE) emphasize research considerations in the training of mental health practitioners. Accredited programs engage in a continuous review process to meet and maintain research standards, ethics, faculty identity, curriculum, and licensure expectations set by the profession (Black & Flynn, 2020).

It would be an understatement to describe identity development as a major movement in the counseling profession. In fact, counselor education training programs have been tasked with developing a professional counselor identity within trainees (CACREP, 2016; Gibson, Dollarhide, & Moss, 2013) and scholars have described counselor identity development as a national imperative (Spurgeon, 2012). In addition to facilitating overall identity development, training programs have been charged with creating a research culture and identity (Lambie & Vaccaro, 2011). Over the past 15 years, there has been scholarly discourse about other forms of identity in relation to research, including methodological research identity (Flynn et al., 2019), qualitative research identity (Reisetter et al., 2004), counselor education doctoral student research identity (Lamar & Helm, 2017), and master's level counselor research identity (Jorgensen & Duncan, 2015). Given this emphasis on identity, together with the particular applicability of various traditions, this textbook will illuminate certain aspects of the methodological identity of each research tradition through careful articulation of ontology, epistemology, theory, methods, sample size, participant populations, standards of rigor, and multicultural considerations.

RESEARCH ETHICS

Research ethics aims to promote the rights and welfare of participants while pursuing our shared interest in enhancing the world through investigations that fall in line with ethical principles and federal regulations. Most individuals who are completing advanced research courses or going through their university's ethics training program (e.g., Collaborative Institutional Training Initiative [CITI]) as part of the institutional review board (IRB) expectations, will review grievously unethical experiments such as the Tuskegee Syphilis Study, Jewish Chronic Disease Hospital Cancer Cell Injections, Willowbrook Study, and NAZI Medical War Crimes (National Institutes of Health [NIH], 2002). The aforementioned research-based atrocities are important to review for a number of reasons (e.g., to avoid repeating history, to better understand the parameters of ethical research). In addition to repudiating unethical experiments such as these, mid-20th century scholars focused their efforts on creating systems, such as the Belmont Report Principles, that protect human participants from harm.

The importance of protecting research participants in the social sciences is balanced with the need to provide behavioral science scholars with the academic freedom to explore topics that create dissent (Whitney, 2016). Topics sensitive to public opinion such as sexuality, racial discrimination, and participant perception on a variety of constructs (e.g., financial compensation disparities, gun control, homicidal ideation), are most often explored within social science research. With the appropriate procedures in place (e.g., protection of vulnerable populations, informed consent, full disclosure of procedures, assent, opt out), potential subjects can explore such topics with little risk of uninformed psychological, social, physical, cognitive, and/or moral injury. Although some of these topics may be sensitive territory for participants, institutions, and those holding particular political vantage points, researchers have the right to ground contemporary political topics in scholarly evidence. According to the Electronic Code of Federal Regulations (2018), "The IRB should not consider possible long-range effects of applying knowledge gained in the research (e.g., the possible effects of the research on public policy) as among those research risks that fall within the purview of its responsibility" (45 CFR 46.111(a)(2)) (https://www.ecfr.gov/cgi-bin/retrieveECFR?gp=&SID= 83cd09e1c0f5c6937cd9d7513160fc3f&pitd=20180719&n=pt45.1.46&r=PART&ty=HTML).

Some behavioral science practitioners, particularly those who have little interest in conducting research, might ask themselves, "How do research ethics apply to clinical work?" In response to this common question, it is indisputable that clinicians have an ethical imperative to engage in evidenced-based practice (American Counseling Association [ACA], 2014; CACREP, 2016). According to Wester and Hines (2017), evaluating client progress and counselor effectiveness is a method for engaging in evidence-based practice. Analyzing data from symptom checklists, outcome questionnaires, surveys, and inventories at various points in treatment (each session, 3 weeks, 1 month, 3 months) is effective for gathering data on client progress and determining whether a client is ready for the next stage of treatment (e.g., termination). For example, the Outcome Questionnaire 45.2, the most peer-reviewed self-report outcome measure in the world, measures client symptomology on three subscales: symptom distress, interpersonal relations, and social role. These scales, along with various critical items measuring suicidal ideation, violence, and substance abuse, provide clinicians with frequent snapshots of how clients are functioning across a variety of domains. By analyzing changes in the data, clinicians can measure the effects of their interventions along with the symptom disposition of their clients (Lambert et al., 2004).

THE SCIENTIST–PRACTITIONER MODEL

With the increasing demand for evidence-based treatments, the scientist–practitioner (SP) model (also known as the "Boulder model") is gaining increased attention for its emphasis on the personal experiences of clinicians and researchers (Sheperis, 2017). This clinical emphasis leads to more effective treatment and is considered *best practice* within the behavioral sciences. Outlined in 1949, the SP model is based on the belief that trained professional mental health workers (psychologists, counselors, therapists, etc.) should be well versed in both clinical practice and human subjects research (Jones & Mehr, 2007). The SP model is the most widely used training model for graduate students in the behavioral sciences. While the SP model was initially intended for use within clinical psychology, its efficacy extends to training other helping professionals (e.g., counselors, social workers, marriage and family therapists) as well (Sheperis, 2017). The model stresses the importance of developing strong evaluative skills, and clinical researchers are directed to explore topics that are meaningful and relevant to their practice (Alderman & Knight, 2017).

The SP model has provisions that help a therapist ensure that their own biases and opinions are not influencing their practice. It is easy to envision how practitioners might impose their own biases in their work with clients. Simply having a preferred treatment method can be an example of bias. This preference becomes problematic if the practitioner does not have evidence to support the efficacy of the method. For example, it would likely be considered inappropriate and unethical for a therapist to decide to make Eye Movement Desensitization and Reprocessing (EMDR) the primary mode of treatment for a client who has been diagnosed with anorexia nervosa. Perhaps the clinician's thinking is centered on the success they had when conducting EMDR with a client who had been diagnosed with posttraumatic stress disorder (PTSD). The SP model postulates that the therapist must research the efficacy of EMDR for clients diagnosed with anorexia nervosa before implementing the intervention with such clients.

According to Lowman (2012), the SP model requires practitioners to explain to their clients the rationale for a treatment's efficacy. This rationale is often based on the knowledge the clinician has gained from their own review of research, rather than their personal opinion. The importance of knowledge and concern for efficacy, limitations, and liabilities are to be stressed by SPs (Lowman, 2012). Furthermore, the SP model helps to connect diverse therapeutic professions with the promotion of research in clinical practice. The SP model incorporates three parts, together with three assumptions. The three parts assigned to clinicians include becoming producers of new data, engaging in the review of relevant research, and becoming evaluators of effective therapy (Sheperis, 2017). Engaging in the dual roles of practitioner and scientist produces clinicians who are involved in the research process as well as researchers who are more involved in clinical work (Crane & Hafen, 2002). The three assumptions within the SP model include (but are not limited to) the following: (a) clinicians, with an understanding of research methods, will promote effective psychological services; (b) research is crucial to the advancement of scientific databases; and (c) the direct involvement of researchers in therapeutic practice facilitates accurate understanding and treatment of crucial social issues (Jones & Mehr, 2007).

COHERENTLY NESTING RESEARCH METHODS

Throughout this textbook we will label various research paradigms in several ways, including nesting, paradigmatic hierarchy, and philosophical integration. At this point you may be asking, "Why is this information important to understand?" First, it is important to realize that research traditions go beyond qualitative, quantitative, and mixed methods descriptions. Researchers and reviewers of research acknowledge that understanding and showcasing the ontological, epistemological, theoretical, and methodological issues and constructs associated with a research project (a) constitutes a comprehensive analysis of the research process; and (b) justifies the use of specific methods. Understanding the philosophical integration of a research process helps scholars in three additional ways. First, it helps them understand the theoretical assumptions behind their work (e.g., grounded theory's use of inductive reasoning, intersubjectivity of ethnography). Second, it can ensure the accuracy of their research (e.g., statistical analysis standards used in survey research). Third, it provides a unique interpretation of the data. In other words, the knowledge gained by applying various methodological frameworks will differ based on the distinctive assumptions embedded within the philosophical integration (e.g., positivism's accurate and unambiguous interpretation of the world; Crotty, 2003).

QUALITATIVE, QUANTITATIVE, AND MIXED METHODS

To start, we explore definitions of qualitative, quantitative, and mixed methods research. In describing these constructs, it is important that you, the reader, understand that these terms focus on how a researcher approaches data and methods. In other words, while general terms are often used to describe data, these terms alone do not acknowledge that the knowledge produced and interpreted through various methodological frameworks differs based on the integration of ontology, epistemology, and theoretical assumptions (Crotty, 2003). We understand that much of the literature, in various fields, describes these terms as being synonymous with research paradigms (i.e., ontology, epistemology, theoretical stance, methodology, and methods), however, as you have already surmised, the research world extends far beyond a singular worldview such as this (Shannon-Baker, 2016). While it is important to understand why a researcher might choose a particular methodology, these general terms also provide a quick way to ascertain how a researcher is approaching the data that are collected. In addition, due to the proliferation of these terms in the research literature, it is important for all researchers to understand their meaning.

You may also be wondering why qualitative, quantitative, and mixed methods research need separate terms and procedures for ensuring that a study has merit and rigor. For starters, quantitative researchers use the scientific method (i.e., replicability, precision, falsifiability, and parsimony) to investigate research questions. Unlike qualitative research, quantitative studies rely on probability theory. For example, researchers who employ quantitative methodology often use a type of sampling that is based on theories of probability, called probability sampling (e.g., random sampling, stratified sampling, cluster sampling). A probability sampling method is any method of sampling that utilizes some form of random selection of participants. In order to employ a random selection method, you must set up a process or procedure that ensures that different aspects of your population have equal probability of being chosen. When conducting quantitative research, researchers utilize the scientific method to collect measurable statistical evidence in a hypothesized experiment, with the results ultimately supporting or failing to support a theory (Bhattacherjee, 2012).

In comparison, qualitative researchers engage in nonprobability sampling because they are not interested in generalizing their findings to a larger population, and consequently, participants are not selected according to the logic of probability. Qualitative researchers reject the notion that randomized samples equate to truth. Participants are selected because they meet a particular criterion or because of participant convenience and access. A major goal of qualitative research is to purposefully explore in-depth experiences of a specific group, family, or individual in a naturalistic context. As such, qualitative researchers reject the notion that randomized events relate to social life (Merriam, 1998).

The number of qualitative research articles published within counseling and related journals has increased significantly over the past two decades (Arredondo, Rosen, Rice, Perez, & Tovar-Gamero, 2005; Woo & Heo, 2013). This textbook provides an in-depth introduction to five unique qualitative research traditions: case study research, phenomenological research, grounded theory research, narrative research, and consensual qualitative research. In addition, a section within the content analysis chapter covers qualitative content analysis. According to Punch (1998), qualitative research includes traditions that collect and analyze data that are not in the form of numbers. A second, more detailed, definition states that "Qualitative research is multimethod in focus, involving an interpretive, naturalistic approach to its subject matter. This means that qualitative researchers study things in their natural settings, attempting to make sense of, or interpret, phenomena in terms of the meanings people bring to them" (Denzin & Lincoln, 2000, p. 3).

Quantitative research statistically uncovers patterns that are meant to generalize to a larger population. Quantitative researchers gather numerical data to categorize, rank order, and analyze their findings. These patterns, together with associated raw data, are often visually displayed in graphs and tables (McLeod, 2013). This textbook offers an in-depth review of five unique quantitative designs: survey research, experimental research, predictive research, content analysis research, and single-subject design research. In addition to these distinct approaches, Chapter 4 provides an overview of descriptive, inferential, and Bayesian statistics.

According to Johnson, Onwuegbuzie, and Turner (2007), *mixed methods research* is a type of methodology in which a researcher combines elements of qualitative and quantitative research to achieve breadth and depth of understanding and corroboration of the findings. Similar to other research traditions, mixed methods research has philosophical assumptions and tenets that guide researchers in deciding how and when certain data are collected and in what manner results are interpreted. Within this textbook, you will explore the world of mixed methods research in four chapters covering seven unique methodological frameworks: action research, convergent (triangulation) design research, embedded design research, explanatory design research, exploratory design research, transformative design research, and multiphase design research.

Throughout the past 20 years there has been significant growth in the mixed methods literature. Due to the proliferation of this innovative approach, mixed methods has been labeled *the third methodological movement* (following qualitative and quantitative research; Tashakkorie & Teddlie, 2010). Mixed methods research is a process that uses unique configurations of qualitative and quantitative threads and points of interface (i.e., synthesis of qualitative and quantitative information) to create new data and knowledge. This process of cohesively integrating both qualitative and quantitative processes and data is known as *commensurability legitimation*. During the commensurability legitimation process mixed methods researchers explore unique thread configurations, including exploratory (i.e., larger initial qualitative thread smaller secondary quantitative thread), explanatory (i.e., larger initial quantitative thread smaller secondary qualitative thread), convergent (i.e., simultaneous use of full qualitative and quantitative threads), and embedded (i.e., main thread and an embedded secondary thread) and multiple sequences (e.g., concurrent, sequential, and single phase). Next, mixed methods researchers focus on integrating threads at various point-of-interface (e.g., sampling, data collection, data analysis, conclusion) and the eventual creation of meta-inferences (i.e., integrated qualitative and quantitative results). While the new meta-inferences produced by the mixing of methods are important, mixed methods researchers also ensure the valid and trustworthy application of the separate qualitative and quantitative threads prior to the mixing process (i.e., *multiple validities legitimation*; Onwuegbuzie & Johnson, 2006).

Since the split between qualitative and quantitative research is primarily at the data level, the most accurate way to discuss philosophical integration is to refer to the epistemological split between constructionism/subjectivism and objectivism. Most qualitative research has either a constructionist or subjectivist epistemological approach. Similarly, most quantitative research has an objectivist epistemology. Sound research requires the researcher to determine an appropriate philosophical integration that warrants merit in the eyes of observers. Most researchers do not embark on a project with their overarching philosophical integration already in place. Instead, they begin with a question or a series of questions they would like to answer. After identifying these questions, it is the researcher's responsibility to create a process through which to answer the questions. The process should include ontology, epistemology, theoretical stance, methodology, and methods (Crotty, 2003). In addition, while the philosophical integration is recommended for most qualitative and quantitative approaches, many mixed methods approaches direct scholars to nest their methodology and methods within the paradigm of pragmatism (Hanson, Plano-Clark, Petska, Creswell, & Creswell, 2005) or to meet the philosophical integration expectations of both qualitative and quantitative approaches within a singular investigation.

RESEARCH PROBLEMS AND QUESTIONS

Selecting your *research problem* will be the first step in your research process and is one of the most important (Salkind, 2010). The research problem is the topic that the researcher intends to investigate, and it is usually a concern or issue that the researcher wants to explore. When selecting the research problem, investigators will review literature related to the topic and consult with peers in the field (Sheperis, 2017). This preliminary work is done in hopes of finding a gap in the literature and undertaking research that will help to narrow the scope of the research problem. The research problem starts with a concept that, through investigation, discussion, and refinement, becomes the research problem. An example of a research problem in the behavioral sciences could be the following: There are moral and ethical implications involved in the treatment of refugee families who are separated and detained at the southern border of the United States.

Following the identification of the research problem, the *research question* will begin to form. The research question is used to guide an investigation and pursue philosophical integration, and it is a fundamental step toward creating a viable research plan. Examples of research questions include the following: "Does frequency of exercise, for incarcerated males, influence their participation in support groups?" or "How does the carbohydrate intake of school-aged children with a diagnosis of attention deficit/hyperactivity disorder impact the child's ability to pay attention during homework time?"

Utilizing Resources to Explore Possible Research Problem(s) and Question(s)

To identify the research problem and create the research question, researchers consult with colleagues and review existing literature related to the topic. Reviewing previous research provides a better understanding of related subject matter and previous research. It also helps the researcher identify potential gaps in the research. From here, the researcher develops a clearer understanding of the research problem and begins to formulate the research question. It is not uncommon for researchers to write a short section at the end of their article explaining how their research could be taken a step further or even describe additional research questions that emerged during the project.

Narrowing and Clarifying the Research Problem and Question

Three steps help the researcher to narrow and clarify the research question (Geher, 2019). Step one involves creating the research question from a theoretical perspective. Step two requires the researcher to magnify variables. Step three takes place as the researcher operationally defines each of the variables identified in step two.

Variations of Research Questions

Below are eight variations of research questions. To decide which type will best suit your project, it is necessary to first understand the unique attributes of each variation (Meltzoff & Cooper, 2018).

- *Existence questions* involve observing whether something exists or occurs. For example, can signs of dementia be detected in MRI brain scans?
- *Description and classification questions* ask what characteristics something has. For example, what are the most common personality traits of a stay-at-home father?
- *Composition questions* ask what something consists of. For example, what factors are considered when preparing to teach a special needs class?
- *Descriptive-comparative questions* compare group X to group Y. For example, are single mothers or single fathers more likely to be seeking a romantic partner?
- *Relationship questions* ask whether there is a relationship between X and Y. For example, do commute times affect job performance?
- *Causal questions* ask whether X changes, halts change, or creates Y. For example, does father involvement affect a female child's self-esteem?
- *Causal-comparative questions* compare the level of change that Y and Z evoke in X. For example, are male or female teachers more effective in defusing potential conflict among high school students?
- *Causal-comparative interactional questions* seek to determine whether X evokes more change in Y than Z does, given certain circumstances. For example, do the daughters of stay-at-home fathers have more secure self-esteem than the daughters of stay-at-home mothers?

METHODOLOGICAL RESEARCH QUESTION

You may understand that your research question will guide your investigation and your philosophical integration, yet you may be asking yourself, "How do I know whether I am asking a qualitative, qualitative, or mixed methods research question?" Qualitatively, you are usually starting with an open-ended question beginning with the words "what" or "how." Next, you would present the phenomenon being explored. In addition to the central question under investigation, sub-questions are often utilized to further analyze the construct. Qualitative research questions often avoid using the word "why" or setting up a direct comparison. For example, qualitative researchers avoid questions with certain verbs, such as "relate," "influence," "affect," or "cause." Questions of this ilk often describe a direct comparison or a cause-and-effect relationship and are more in line with quantitative investigations (Hurlburt, 2017).

Quantitative research questions contain an independent variable (x; i.e., a characteristic that is changed or controlled) and a dependent variable (y) or variables (i.e., outcomes that occur when the independent variable changes). The researcher measures, manipulates, and controls variables to look for descriptions, relationships, and/or comparisons. The overarching research question, in quantitative research, typically starts with words like "how," "what," or "why." Similarly, quantitative hypotheses, which are tested statistically, are guesses the researcher makes about the probable associations among variables. Quantitative researchers have something specific they are attempting to research and are careful to keep the research clear and focused by not asking participants open-ended questions (Sheperis, Young, & Daniels, 2017).

Researchers who are looking to create a study that has both qualitative and quantitative dimensions will likely be using a mixed methods approach. The research question style and format should match the nature of the questions. The overarching mixed methods approach will guide the researcher on how to create the research questions. For example, certain mixed methods investigations (e.g., explanatory research design) have a large quantitative thread and small qualitative thread, while other traditions (e.g., exploratory research design) have a major qualitative thread and minor quantitative thread. The research questions should fully incorporate the threads the researcher is aiming to uncover and should also address the mixing of threads (Creswell & Plano Clark, 2017).

THE PURPOSE STATEMENT

During the process of developing your research problem and researcher questions, you have been consciously or unconsciously developing your purpose statement. Alternatively, you may have developed your purpose statement prior to developing your research questions. According to Hays and Singh (2012), "The point of a purpose statement is to anchor the proposal or study; it is where the conceptual framework and research design meet" (p. 127). Researchers use a declarative purpose statement to capture the main goals of their project. The purpose statement is different from the action-oriented research questions and should stimulate the readers' interest in the overall topic. On the other hand, it is similar to a research question because the purpose needs to be very specific and detailed. A benefit of creating a well-crafted purpose statement is that, in writing the statement, you will simultaneously enhance, clarify, and formulate your research questions.

While variability exists, the research purpose statement is often placed at the beginning of the methodology section of the manuscript or at the end of the manuscript's literature review section. There are some common steps to keep in mind when developing your purpose statement. First, the researcher(s) engaging in the project must be reasonably certain that no major investigations have already fulfilled the stated purpose. For this step to be successful, it is essential for the researchers to be well versed in the relevant research and literature on the topic. Second, the purpose of any research study should relate directly to the previously identified research problem. Third, researchers should be clear and concise regarding what they are investigating while avoiding stating any potential outcomes. Lastly, the purpose statement should inform the reader if the investigation is qualitative, quantitative, or mixed methods in nature (Hays & Singh, 2012).

Whether you are using a qualitative, quantitative, or mixed methods tradition there are certain tradition-specific issues to keep in mind. There are certain factors that you must consider when creating a qualitative purpose statement. Haverkamp and Young (2007) described the essence of the purpose statements of specific qualitative research traditions. For example, a grounded theory purpose statement is centered on exploring underlying processes while a phenomenological purpose statement is aimed at describing the lived experience of a construct. Similarly, quantitative researchers provide the reader information on their procedures within the purpose statement. For example, if researchers plan to test a theory, it would be stated in very clearly within the purpose statement along with the independent and dependent variables. Shoonenboom and Johnson (2017) described a common purpose for incorporating any mixed methods framework: to expand, strengthen, and corroborate the analysis and results of an investigation with complementary qualitative and quantitative threads. Similar to qualitative and quantitative traditions, specific mixed methods design (e.g., embedded, convergent, exploratory, explanatory, transformative, multiphase) have their own specific purpose requirements. Greene, Caracelli, and Graham (1989) described five common purposes for mixing methods, including triangulation, complementarity, development, initiation, and expansion (see Chapter 17 for a review of these factors).

OVERVIEW OF PHILOSOPHICAL INTEGRATION IN RESEARCH

Scholars refer to the philosophical integration of a research tradition as a *paradigm*. Paradigms, or world views, are a series of constructed entities about how problems should be considered and addressed (Kuhn, 1962). It is important for you to know that there is a tremendous amount of literature in the scholarly and philosophical worlds about the notion of a research paradigm and nuances of a paradigm; however, this book will provide an introduction to the most common elements of a paradigm. These elements include serving as a theoretical umbrella for unique configurations of ontology, epistemology, theory, methodology, and methods. Figure 1.1 displays the nature of a research paradigm. The double-sided arrow under the word *paradigm* indicates that the paradigm encompasses this unique philosophical integration. The philosophical integration itself (i.e., ontology, epistemology, theoretical stance, methodology, and methods) is hierarchical, yet the arrows indicate interaction on every level. Finally, the combination of unique philosophical and pragmatic aspects of a research project interact with the original research problem, research question(s), and purpose statement.

Ontology is the study of being. The ontological perspective in social science research essentially involves trying to answer the question "What is the nature of existence?" Within a research tradition's philosophical integration, there exists a particular manner in which the approach acknowledges the nature of being. While there are quite a few ontological positions in philosophy (see Effingham, 2013), two common research-based ontological positions include realism (i.e., some positivist and objectivist positions) and relativism (i.e., some constructionist and postmodern positions). The ontological position of realism is the view that objects exist outside of being perceived (Phillips, 1987). Authors suggest that realism has been the leading ontological view in social science research (Maxwell, 2008). According to Guba and Lincoln (1994), a research methodology promoting a relativist ontology postulates a finite number of subjective experiences of a phenomenon. From a relativistic perspective, reality cannot be distinguished from one's subjective experience.

Epistemology informs us of the nature of knowledge. It asks the question, "How do you know something?" (Crotty, 2003). In the context of a research paradigm, epistemology informs the

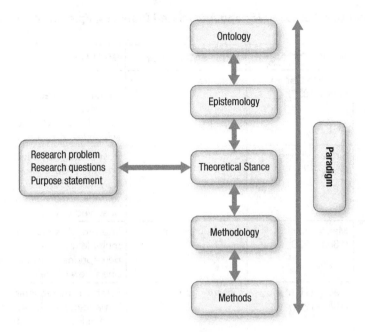

FIGURE 1.1 The Nature of a Research Paradigm in Behavioral Science Research.

NOTE: Double-ended arrows = interaction; large vertical double-ended arrow underneath the word *paradigm* demonstrates that the paradigm encompasses ontology, epistemology, theoretical stance, methodology, and methods.

theoretical perspective through apprising a researcher on what kind of knowledge is possible and legitimate (Maynard, 1994). Similar to philosophical ontology positions, there are many philosophical epistemologies (see Audi, 2010). Common epistemologies used in social science research include objectivism, constructionism, and subjectivism. From an objectivist vantage point, knowledge exists apart from any conscious individual or group meaning construction. Things have an intrinsic meaning outside of subjective or collective thought. Constructionism implies that knowledge is constructed through the interaction of realities. Various individuals and groups can construct knowledge in different ways and the interaction of these knowledges can create meaning. The subjectivist vantage point postulates that knowledge about a construct is created subjectively by an individual. Whether it is through introspection, a dream, or a passing thought, knowledge is created within the individual and placed on the object of study.

A research theoretical perspective is a series of assumptions that inform the research methodology and process. The theoretical perspective is essentially a philosophical stance that answers the question, "What theoretical perspective lies behind the methodological framework?" (Crotty, 2003). Two common theoretical frameworks include positivism and critical inquiry. Positivism is a theoretical position that posits information taken from sensory experiences, filtered through logic, and creates knowledge. An assumption of this approach is that truth is only discovered through experience and empirical knowledge (Johnson, 2014). In comparison, the assumptions grounded in critical inquiry include the inherent connection between values, knowledge, and politics. This vantage point assumes that truth emerges through speech and discussion (Fui, Khin, Khin, & Ying, 2011). Table 1.1 provides a cohesive overview of the major research-based theoretical perspectives, a selected theoretical pioneer, influencing epistemology, and snapshot of the theory's view on

TABLE 1.1 Theoretical Perspectives and Associated Pioneers, Epistemologies, and Views on Reality

THEORY	EARLY PIONEER	EPISTEMOLOGY	REALITY IS BASED ON
Positivism	Auguste Comte (1798–1857)	Objectivism	Positivists believe reality is based on what is observed scientifically through empirical methods. Positivists believe everything can be explained using the scientific method.
Post-Positivism	Sir Karl Popper (1902–1994)	Objectivism	Post-positivists believe reality is based on what is observed scientifically; however, post-positivists acknowledge that the researcher can influence the observed object.
Interpretivism	Max Weber (1864–1920)	Constructionism	Interpretivists believe there are multiple realities due to different perceptions. Meaning is derived from one's view of reality.
Symbolic Interactionism	George H. Mead (1863–1931)	Constructionism	Symbolic interactionists believe reality is made comprehendible through human interaction with symbols and language.
Constructivism	John Dewey (1933–1998)	Constructionism	Constructivists believe individuals construct their own understandings through the interaction of what they already know and the ideas with which they come into contact.
Critical Inquiry	Karl Marx (1818–1883)	Subjectivism	Critical Inquiry views reality as shaped by social, political, cultural, economic, ethnic, and gender values formed over time in individuals' lives.
Phenomenology	Edmund Husserl (1859–1938)	Subjectivism	Phenomenological reality is shaped through individual's lived experiences within the world.
Feminism	Elizabeth C. Stanton (1815–1902)	Subjectivism	Feminist reality is based on lived experiences and the belief in human equality, and that old systems of oppression must change.
Post-Modernism	Jacques Derrida (1930–2004)	Subjectivism	Objectivity and reality are individually or socially constructed, everything is perspective, there is no such thing as objective fact.

NOTE: Each theory has multiple pioneers, however, only one is listed; Given a research configuration, the influencing epistemology could change.

reality (Crotty, 2003). Chapter 2 provides a more thorough review of relevant behavioral science research theories and theorists.

Methodology provides a plan and procedure for discovering new knowledge. This level of nesting also provides the blueprints for what methods might be used to uncover the information. Methodology is a more pragmatic aspect of the paradigm that answers the question, "What methodology governs the choice in methods?" (Crotty, 2003). Examples of methodological frameworks include survey research and phenomenological research. These along with 11

TABLE 1.2 **The Components of a Paradigm**

ONTOLOGY	EPISTEMOLOGY	THEORETICAL STANCE	METHODOLOGY	METHODS
What is the nature of existence?	How do we know something?	What theory lies behind the methodological framework?	What methodology governs the choice in methods?	What are the techniques and procedures used to gather and analyze data?

NOTE: The name of paradigm element is highlighted in black as the column heading; the question symbolizing the paradigm component is beneath name of paradigm element.

additional research methodologies are thoroughly explored within this book; however, let's analyze how a methodology could inform a method of researching. Two conventions embedded within the phenomenological research methodology include: (a) the importance of understanding the lived experience of individuals who have an understanding of the phenomenon, and (b) the researcher bracketing their understanding of the world in order to reduce the bias when observing the phenomenon in question. These standards for understanding participants' lived experiences could be realized if the researcher were to conduct semi-structured individual interviews with a group of people who have experienced the phenomenon in question. The bracketing of bias could partly be enacted if the researcher were to write down their bias and intra- and interpersonal experiences in a research journal at the beginning and end of each interview (Hays & Singh, 2012).

Research methods are techniques and activities used to gather and analyze data. When considering research methods, one must ask, "What are the techniques or procedures used to gather and analyze data?" (Crotty, 2003). While this is the most pragmatic aspect of philosophical integration, it is our belief that this is the area of research design that helping professionals spend the most time formally learning about. As we create a detailed breakdown of the methods we will be using to uncover the information in question, it is vital that we have a direct connection with the overarching methodology and theory of the approach. Examples of methods can include those techniques used for data collection (e.g., survey, focus group, observation); data analysis (e.g., statistical analysis, open coding, textural description); sampling (e.g., random sampling, purposeful sampling, convenience sampling); trustworthiness (e.g., triangulation, data saturation, cross-validation); validity (e.g., content validity, criterion validity, discriminant validity); and reliability (e.g., test-retest, internal consistency, interrater reliability). Table 1.2 breaks down the major components of a research paradigm and provides an accompanying question that symbolizes the element.

AXIOLOGY

As you explore any given research paradigm, examining both the merit of your approach and the ethical decision-making procedure is central to every phase of your work. As a researcher, how do you know if what you are doing has value or worth? According to Heron and Reason (1997) axiology has to do with the nature of value and philosophically captures the notion of what is intrinsically worthwhile. In the world of research, axiology is centered on using aesthetics and ethics to shape the creative decision-making effort. Viega (2016) adds that axiology informs the ethical and visual decision-making process in the evaluation and design of qualitative research. According to Lincoln and Guba (2013), a researcher may ask the axiology-oriented question,

"Given all of the data provided to me, what is the most valuable?" Another question might be, "Given the research problem and purpose, how can I strictly adhere to the ethical decision-making tenets of beneficence, justice, and respect?" (National Commission for the Protection of Human Subjects of Biomedical and Behavioral Research, 1978).

QUALITATIVE PHILOSOPHICAL INTEGRATION

There are many nuances to creating an appropriate qualitative philosophical integration. Schreier (2012) aptly describes this nuanced and diverse process: "Qualitative researchers are comfortable with the idea that there can be multiple meanings, multiple interpretations, and that these can shift over time and across different people" (pp. 20–21). Ontologically, realism and relativism often inform qualitative research design and constructionism and subjectivism are often the epistemological positions informing the qualitative theoretical stances of symbolic interactionism, phenomenology, feminism, post-modernism, and critical inquiry. There are numerous qualitative methodological frameworks (e.g., grounded theory, phenomenological research, narrative inquiry, ethnography); unique qualitative methodological stances within each methodology (e.g., Glaserian, Straussian, and constructivist grounded theory); and a host of data collection, analysis, sampling, and trustworthiness methods tailored to each approach. As you can see, there is no shortcut to having deep and widespread knowledge of these issues prior to conducting research. Developing expertise in a particular approach to research design often includes formal education (e.g., course work, reading scholarly publications); research mentorship (e.g., dissertation, thesis mentoring); and developing one's expertise through consulting and collaborating with colleagues who have diverse and in-depth expertise of the research framework.

You may be wondering how you will know if you are doing your philosophical integration correctly. Depending on the nuances and specifics of one's research study, there is variability regarding what should be nested with what. Ultimately, the expertise and judgment of the researcher are appraised and depended upon. It is the researcher's responsibility to provide the rationale and justification for creating a research paradigm. Researchers with a strong command of their research design will undoubtedly find this process easier than individuals who are new to a research approach. Those who have expertise in a particular methodology will thoroughly understand the differences and idiosyncrasies of each approach within that framework. While variability exists, there are inappropriate combinations; for example, it would be incorrect if a researcher were to combine the following: realism (ontology), objectivism (epistemology), post-modernism (theory), phenomenological research (methodology), and statistical analysis (methods). Within the aforementioned example, the theoretical stance of post-modernism would most likely not reside under the epistemology of objectivism, and a phenomenological methodology would not typically support statistical analysis as a method. Due to the core differences in these elements, this sequence would seem incompatible; however, as scientist practitioners, we always leave room for individuals to justify their rationale. Table 1.3 provides a concise breakdown of four (i.e., two qualitative, two quantitative) research paradigm possibilities. Following Table 1.3 we expand on common qualitative methods.

QUALITATIVE SAMPLING METHODS

Each chapter that promotes a particular research tradition, will provide for you a review of the sampling procedure(s) native to the particular methodological framework being explored.

TABLE 1.3 **Four Examples of Possible Research-Based Paradigms**

PARADIGM	ONTOLOGY	EPISTEMOLOGY	THEORY	METHODOLOGY	METHOD
Qualitative	Relativism	Constructionism	Symbolic interactionism	Grounded theory research	Focus group
Qualitative	Relativism	Subjectivism	Phenomenology	Phenomenological research	Interview
Quantitative	Realism	Objectivism	Post-positivism	Survey research	Statistical analysis
Quantitative	Realism	Objectivism	Post-positivism	Experimental research	Testable hypothesis

NOTE: Each column provides only one possibility, there are other relevant possibilities. The method column provides only one example, however, there are many different methods (e.g., validity, reliability, trustworthiness, data analysis, sampling) relevant to each tradition.

Qualitative researchers engage in non-probability sampling. As described earlier in this chapter, qualitative researchers believe randomized events are irrelevant to social life and humans are not predictable like objects (Merriam, 1998). Furthermore, because qualitative investigations are not centered on generalizing the results to a particular population, researchers are not concerned that each member of the population has a certain probability of being selected for the sample. Consequently, qualitative research participants are often selected because they are familiar (often deeply familiar) with the phenomenon under investigation. In the following, we briefly review a few of the most common purposeful and convenient qualitative non-probability sampling methods.

Purposeful Sampling

Qualitative purposeful sampling is an umbrella term to describe sampling strategies used to recruit individuals who have experienced the phenomenon or the construct being studied. The composition of the sample population can be based on the researcher's judgment, or it could be solicited through expert judges. Purposeful sampling strategies are often used on rare populations (Hays & Singh, 2012; Schwandt, 2001).

Criterion Sampling

Criterion sampling is a form of purposeful sampling that ensures all participants are selected based on the fact that they meet a particular criterion. This form of sampling can be a helpful quality assurance method (Hays & Singh, 2012; Schwandt, 2001). For example, a researcher may be interested in the parenting beliefs of African American fathers between the ages of 30 and 40. The researcher might use racial identity, parent status, and age as the criteria to participate.

Maximal Variation Sampling

Maximal variation is a form of purposeful sampling where the researchers intentionally recruit diverse individuals who are likely to hold different perspectives on the phenomenon in question. The idiosyncratic nature of the investigation dictates the amount to which the sample is maximized. The essence of this sampling approach is to diversify the findings as much as possible, thereby enriching the findings (Hays & Singh, 2012; Schwandt, 2001). Using the same example, the researcher could further maximize the sample by adding groups of White fathers, Hispanic fathers, and older African American fathers.

Theoretical Sampling

Theoretical sampling is a third purposeful sampling method that uses a systematic process to sample a population in order to determine an emergent theory. Theoretical sampling begins with a particular criterion for recruitment, however this can change as the theory emerges. Once no new information presents itself, saturation has been achieved and data collection can stop (Hays & Singh, 2012; Schwandt, 2001). For example, an initial sample criterion could be African American fathers between the ages of 30 and 40, however, after 15 semi-structured individual interviews, the researcher (or research team) may decide that a focus group of eight African American children should be conducted. After the focus group meets, the researcher may again decide to conduct a document analysis regarding research on parenting practices.

Convenience Sampling

Convenience sampling is an umbrella term used to describe sampling methods that are based on the researcher's ability to easily access a particular population. A clear benefit to this form of sampling is the ease in accessibility regarding the resources needed for the study (Hays & Singh, 2012; Schwandt, 2001).

Snowball Sampling

Snowball sampling is a form of convenience sampling that depends on the research participant's relationships with individuals who have experienced the same or a similar phenomenon. The researcher inquires about these relationships to grow the sample size. As the name suggests, once the researcher finds a participant that meets the criterion, they will ask for references of other individuals who may have experienced the phenomenon. Snowball sampling is helpful if the participants in an investigation are difficult to locate (e.g., non-cooperative groups; Hays & Singh, 2012; Schwandt, 2001). For example, if the researcher is exploring the post-war culture for veterans, they could use a single participant's personal references to increase their sample size.

QUALITATIVE DATA COLLECTION PROCEDURES

When qualitative researchers are collecting data, they are not interested in the generalizability, validity, and reliability of their findings. Instead, they are often concerned with the thickness and richness of the data collected and the naturalistic nature (studying people in their natural setting) of the inquiry. Thick data descriptions emerge when a researcher (or team of researchers) makes a detailed account of the data that are collected in the field. In addition, thickness refers to the amount of data that is collected (e.g., number of interviews). When researchers engage in an in-depth account of a phenomenon, they do not want it to be thin. Thin (i.e., vague, shallow, and lacking consensus) qualitative data can lack the credibility and confirmability that partly ensures the trustworthiness of the findings. It would not be uncommon for qualitative researchers to describe the thickness of their data by acknowledging the number of transcribed pages produced during a series of interviews. They also provide evidence of thickness within their in-depth description of the contextual factors (e.g., cultural patterns, social relationships) involved in a particular participant or group of participants (Holloway, 1997). This ensures the data collected are rich and demonstrates the complexities and intricacies of the data being explored. Rich data almost always demonstrate the researcher has intimate knowledge of the interpersonal and intrapersonal aspects of the participant's life (Given, 2008). Researchers seeking to enhance the richness of their data may develop the interview questions to have follow-up probes or can add a different form of data collection (e.g., focus group) to the overall analysis.

Qualitative researchers are highly concerned with the *quality* of their methods, analysis, and findings. Therefore, researchers engaging in qualitative research go to great lengths to describe, in detail, the various data collection methods (e.g., in-depth, semi-structured, individual interviews); the coordination of the data collection (e.g., participants were contacted individually via email); the environment where the data are being collected (e.g., the focus group took place in a confidential conference room); individuals involved (without identifying the participant); the date; and the length of time the researcher took in collecting the data (e.g., interviews ranged from 10 to 65 minutes in length). While the diversity and differences in the forms of data collection are clear, most qualitative traditions expect the data to be placed in tandem with other data collection points prior to analysis. In the following we review a few common qualitative data collection procedures.

Individual Interview

Individual interviews are the most common form of data collection in counseling qualitative research (Flynn, et al., 2019). Qualitative interviews are exploratory in nature and are used to discover social phenomenon. Most qualitative interviews use open ended questions and are semi-structured and/or in-depth, however, structured interview questions and questionnaires are certainly supported qualitative methods. Similar to other data collection methods, qualitative researchers are sure to provide maximum details regarding the interview. For example, it would be common to see the time range of the interviews, date the interview was conducted, demographics of the participants, multiple examples of participant quotes, and a breakdown of the number of transcribed pages.

Focus Group

A focus group is when a collection of participants and a researcher explore a phenomenon in a group format. This dynamic interaction between participants and a researcher creates a new form of data (Hays & Singh, 2012). This form of data collection gathers the subjective experiences of the participants, however there is an interaction between participants and the researcher that creates an original and nuanced data. When compared to individual interviews, the same level of detail is applied to focus group interviews, however the researcher must ensure that they have gathered data on every participant (e.g., screening, demographic, and contextual data).

Artifacts

Artifacts are often presented to the researcher in the form of a drawing, symbol, or a picture. Researchers are interested in collecting and analyzing the actual artifact and the participant's description of the artifact. During the data collection process, researchers will ask questions and probes about the artifact and its relevance to the investigation (Hays & Singh, 2012). For example, in a qualitative research study on the dynamic interaction of altruism and self-interest, participants were asked to provide and describe a self-interest and altruistic artifact (Flynn & Black, 2011).

Document and Journal Analysis

Document analysis is a data collection method that centers on reviewing documents relevant to the investigation. This form of data can be helpful in corroborating findings across data collection points (Hays & Singh, 2012). Common examples include ethical codes, mission statements, annual reports, emails, blogs, list serves, and agendas. A journal analysis is a data collection method in which the researcher collects data through choosing relevant journal(s) and analyzing the articles that fall within a specified time-period (e.g., past 15 years). Similar to the analysis of an interview transcript, documents and journal articles are analyzed, coded, and added to the emergent themes.

QUALITATIVE DATA ANALYSIS PROCEDURES

The qualitative data analysis procedure that is incorporated into an investigation is dependent on the methodology being used. All major qualitative traditions have unique data analysis processes that are recommended; however, authors frequently augment their data analysis framework with unique procedures (e.g., coding scheme) and theories (e.g., feminism; see Flynn, et al., 2019). Examples of unique qualitative research data analysis frameworks include Colaizzi's (1978) seven-step approach (phenomenology), Van Manen's (1990) six-step approach (phenomenology), constant comparison analysis (grounded theory), and open, axial, and selective coding framework (grounded theory). While there are many unique elements within each data analysis framework, all of the qualitative data analysis procedures that we reviewed share three common factors: coding (i.e., condensing data into small units); categorizing (i.e., clusters of coded data that share a theme); theming (i.e., higher level abstract categories that interrelate); and systematic connection of themes (i.e., depiction of the interrelation of themes; Jorgensen, 1989).

In a general sense, qualitative data analysis has to do with the researcher noticing, sorting, and thinking. When the researcher is at the *noticing* phase of any investigation, they may be making observations, writing field notes, recording interviews, and/or gathering documents. While the researcher is reviewing the information, they will notice something within the data that has an underlying meaning. They will code this information and place the information within a codebook. Next, the researcher will begin *sorting* the coded data into clusters of information that share some commonality. Once the data become somewhat manageable (i.e., a large number of clusters), the researcher will begin breaking up, separating, and re-organizing the clusters into meaningful themes. At this point the researcher will attempt to *think* about the emergent themes and try to refine and make sense of the information. The researcher will look for patterns and relationships across the data set. Once the finalized themes and secondary themes are in place, the researcher will attempt to determine how the data systematically work across themes and determine the relationships between themes and larger domains (Seidel, 1998).

TRUSTWORTHINESS PROCEDURES

According to Schwandt (2001), qualitative trustworthiness is the description given to a set of criteria that appraises the quality of qualitative research. Trustworthiness has to do with a qualitative study's rigor and reliability of the data, methods, and interpretations. While there is no prescribed procedure that ensures 100% trustworthiness, the researcher works to establish criteria necessary for a study to have legitimacy (Polit & Beck, 2014). Lincoln and Guba (1985) created criteria for ensuring trustworthiness. These criteria include credibility, dependability, confirmability, and transferability; they later added authenticity (Guba & Lincoln, 1994). In the following we provide descriptions of Guba and Lincoln's criteria and provide one example of how to execute a procedure during qualitative research study.

The credibility of an investigation is the confidence in the accuracy of the study procedures and findings. This form of qualitative trustworthiness is similar to the quantitative research process of internal validity. The use of a reflective journal, member checking, and peer debriefing are all techniques used to establish the credibility of an investigation (Polit & Beck, 2014). Member checking is when a researcher sends participants a copy of the interview transcript, a breakdown of the emergent themes and secondary themes, and examples of the emergent themes within the interview transcript. Participants are then invited to engage in a dialogue regarding the researcher's interpretation of the interview. Participant perceptions are taken into consideration and themes are further refined.

According to Schwandt (2001), confirmability demonstrates qualitative objectivity and the neutrality of the findings. In other words, it is important to demonstrate that the conclusions derived from a study were not developed by the researcher. Methods for ensuring confirmability include memos, audit trail, and triangulation (i.e., examining data from multiple perspectives). Triangulation is a process that, in theory, should take data from a variety of sources and eventually converge on some level of certainty. Krefting (1991) found data methods to be the most common type of triangulation. An example of this form of confirmability would be to examine a construct (e.g., the psychology of carpet color) through several data collection methods. For instance, the researcher's explored carpet color's effect on mood through 15 in depth semi-structured interviews, two focus groups, and participant artifact reviews. Results were triangulated among these three data collection points and the findings confirmed the emergent themes.

Dependability requires qualitative research to be traceable, logical, and documented. This ensures the data are stable over time and are similar to the quantitative construct of reliability. Examples of dependability include process logs, dependability audits, and peer debriefings (Polit & Becker, 2014). Peer debriefing is beneficial in creating a reliable understanding of the phenomenon. This method would require the researcher to seek multiple peers who hold impartial views of the topic. Peers would be sent the transcripts, emergent themes and secondary themes, and directions on how to provide peer feedback. The peer feedback is funneled into the analysis to enhance the dependability of the findings.

Transferability is the qualitative version of external validity and attempts to see if phenomena can be transferred from case to case. This is not to say that the qualitative data will generalize to a larger population; however, it does attempt to ensure that the individuals involved in the study did have data transfer from and among cases (Schwandt, 2001). Transferability can be ensured through detailed, rich, and thick descriptions of the findings, procedures, and research setting. One aspect of providing rich and thick descriptions of the phenomena can include thoroughly defining a theme, including secondary themes, and providing multiple quotes that symbolize the themes.

Lastly, authenticity is the degree the researcher accurately portrays the participant's life (Polit & Beck, 2014). Deep and contextually accurate descriptions of all elements of the research process convey authenticity. An example of authenticity could be a clear statement indicating the rationale for the sample size.

QUANTITATIVE PHILOSOPHICAL INTEGRATION

Quantitative researchers tend to have a consistent philosophical integration. Ontologically, realism informs their research philosophy, while objectivism is the primary epistemological position informing the quantitative theoretical stances of positivism and post-positivism. There are a plethora of quantitative methodological frameworks, including (but not limited to) experimental research, survey research, predictive designs, single subject design, and certain content analysis traditions. Within each methodological framework are methods centered on enhancing the generalizability of the findings through statistical formulations. Quantitative researchers aim to create rules, so they can ascertain the framework for generalizability and prediction. The essence of most quantitative frameworks is a deductive approach to data, and correlation and experimentation are used to deduce complex social constructs (Crotty, 2003; Scotland, 2012). Scotland (2012) provides a clear and concise description of the essence of quantitative procedures.

> [Quantitative]Research is deemed good if its results are due to the independent variable (internal validity), can be generalized/transferred to other populations or situations (external validity), and different researchers can record the same data in the same way and arrive at the same conclusions (replicable and reliable). Additionally, research needs to be as objective as possible and robust to empirical refutation (p. 11).

Unlike the appreciation of multiple realities or a subjective reality that is embedded within the qualitative philosophical integration, objectivists believe that there is absolute knowledge and truth in the world. The objectivist knowledge is outside of one's subjective perceptions, and the cultural/perceptual lens one touts plays very little in the construction of reality. Consequently, a goal of the quantitative researcher is to impartially discover the meaning objects in the world (Scotland, 2012). These objects are knowledge and facts and are free of subjective values and biases. Theoretically, most quantitative research conducted in the social science is centered on a post-positivistic framework. Post-positivists believe that the knowledge produced in research is not absolute truth; it is the researcher's belief in the tested hypothesis (Popper, 1959). Furthermore, post-positivists believe that scientific results are not truth; they are tentatively accepted statements. This tentative acceptability of knowledge is based on the philosophy of the principle of falsification. Falsification suggests that for things to be scientific they must be able to be proven false (Popper, 1959).

Quantitative researchers investigate variables. A variable is an event or object that is liable to change (https://techterms.com/definition/variable). A variable could refer to a wide variety of things (e.g., level of depression, climate change, hair growth). In algebraic equations, variables are often symbolized as "x" or "y" and one variable is often dependent on the value of another variable. Similarly, quantitatively oriented researchers are interested in the relationship between independent and dependent variables. Independent variables are objects that are manipulated by researchers and the effects are measured or compared. Dependent variables are what measures the effect of the independent variable(s). Dependent variables are dependent on independent variables. For example, if you decided to research the effects of daily vitamin C consumption on level of persistent depressive disorder among a sample of middle-aged persistently depressed women, your independent variable would be daily vitamin C consumption and your dependent variable would be level of depression. In this example, you would measure the independent and dependent variable with an approved quantitative data collection method (e.g., survey, observation, experiment) so the information produced would be numerical and eventually statistical.

QUANTITATIVE SAMPLING METHODS

The sampling methods that most individuals hear and know about are quantitative in nature. Please recall the previous description of probability theory and the notion that quantitative researchers are interested in the nature of randomness. Consider that just about every statistical test relies on probability concepts and researchers are very attentive to the level of uncertainty any research process has (Hurlburt, 2017). Quantitative researchers are interested in every member of a population having an equal chance of being selected to participate in a given study. They are typically attentive to developing procedures that create a representative sample of a larger population of interest. A population is the group that is the focus of the researcher and a sample is some subset of that group. This subset is not chosen in a purposeful or convenient manner; rather, it is chosen by chance because it represents, in some way, the larger population. Quantitative researchers make great efforts to reduce any bias that might sneak into their choice of sample. In other words, they focus on setting aside their personal preferences of a sample's composition in favor of a purely chance method of selecting a population (Hurlburt, 2017). In the following we briefly review a few of the most common quantitative probability sampling methods.

Simple Random Sampling

Simple random sampling is a frequently used method of sampling in which a subset of individuals, from a population of interest, is statistically selected in a manner that is random and completely by chance. In a simple random sample, every individual in the population has an equal probability of being chosen (Hurlburt, 2017). For example, if a researcher wants to investigate the outcomes of dissociative fugue treatment in the United States, they might start by making a list of all inpatient psychiatric units in the United States. Next, they develop a sampling frame by giving a number to each psychiatric unit. They would then determine the right sample size. Lastly, using a random number generator, the researcher(s) would select a sample.

Stratified Random Sampling

Stratified random sampling is a method of random sampling that divides the population of interest in strata (i.e., small subgroupings) that reflect the shared demographics (e.g., education, gender, income) of the population of interest. An important difference between simple and stratified random sampling is that stratified sampling is used to draw attention between sub-groups (i.e., strata). In comparison, simple random sampling is centered on the equal probability of being sampled. For example, if a researcher wanted to conduct a study on incarcerated U.S. males, the researcher could use a stratified random sample. They would initially look up the population demographics of American male prisoners. Next, they would use statistics to divide their participants into strata based on the population demographics (e.g., race, ethnicity, socioeconomic status). The strata can either be a proportional stratified sample (i.e., size of strata proportionate to the population) or a disproportional stratified sample (i.e., size of the strata is not proportionate to the population).

Cluster Random Sampling

Cluster random sampling is a method where a sample of various groupings, based on a population of interest, is comprised of all or close to all members of a population. An important difference between stratified and cluster random sampling is cluster sampling does not need to have equal selection from each subgroup of the population within the sample; however, with cluster sampling, the entire population of interest should be involved (Hurlburt, 2017). In addition, cluster sampling cannot have participant cross-over. In other words, each participant should only have membership in one cluster sample. Lastly, while stratified sampling is used with demographics, cluster sampling can be based on any categorization (e.g., interests, astrological sign, hobbies, opinions; https://study.com/academy/lesson/cluster-random-samples-definition-selection-examples.html).   For example, a researcher would like to know the political views of a local high school. The researcher wants information from the different grade levels (freshman, sophomores, juniors, and seniors). In this example, none of the students are members of more than one grade and all of the students are members of a particular grade.

Multistage Random Sampling

Multistage random sampling involves the grouping of mini clusters of a population of interest. The researcher chooses one of the clusters at random to sample, and sampling units become progressively smaller at each stage. Multistage random sampling is often a combination of random, stratified, and cluster sampling methods (https://www.statisticshowto.datasciencecentral.com/multistage-sampling/). For example, a researcher wants to explore which color American school children prefer. The first stage could include the researcher dividing the population into states and taking simple random samples from each state. Next, the researcher could take a simple random sample of schools within each state. For last stage, the researcher could conduct a simple random sample of the children within each school.

QUANTITATIVE DATA COLLECTION PROCEDURES

When quantitative researchers are collecting data, they are interested in the generalizability, validity, and reliability of their results. Instead of the open-ended and exploratory nature that embodies the essence of qualitative data collection procedures, quantitative data collection is centered on answering a hypothesis through tools (e.g., survey) that capture a numerical value (e.g., Likert scale). Quantitative data can be considered objective and conclusive because it is numerical in nature. Statistical computations turn the numbers gathered into comprehendible knowledge (often with help of graphs, tables, and charts). In the following we describe a few of the most common quantitative data collection procedures.

Survey

Survey data collection approaches are systematic methods for collecting data on a population of interest. The direct nature of survey research gives it an edge with determining trends within populations, relationships among variables, and comparison groups. Survey researchers take great care that the ordering and wording of questions does not create biased results. The methods used for survey research includes (but are not limited to) online survey, paper-and-pencil survey, computer assisted interviewing, face-to-face surveys, and mail surveys. Questionnaires are often self-administered, and interviews are delivered in a consistent manner by the interviewer. Decisions on whether or not to use questionnaires or interviews can be partly determined by the survey design (longitudinal, cross-sectional; Creswell & Plano Clark, 2017).

Observation

A controlled observational study has to do with quantitatively observing the participant(s) (i.e., variables of interest), and gathering data on them in a controlled setting. Researchers agree on behaviors to observe and a scale to measure the behavior. Researchers will then observe the controlled participant(s) and code their interaction and behaviors based on the agreed upon items and scale. The discrete categories on the scale are used to turn the observation into numbers and later into statistics (Hurlburt, 2017).

Experiment

Experimental research (i.e., true experiment) is conducted with a clear understanding of the variables the researcher wants to test and then measure. In addition, there is a random assignment or preselection of participants to groups. In an experiment, a researcher will create a treatment group and observe the response on the participants. In addition, the researcher may also create a control group. The control group does not receive the treatment or will receive a placebo. Comparisons can be made between these two groups. A related form of research is the quasi experiment. This form of research is often used in the behavioral sciences. The researcher(s) do not use a random assignment with this form of research. Instead, the researcher manipulates something within the participant group to observe the consequences (Hurlburt, 2017).

QUANTITATIVE DATA ANALYSIS PROCEDURES

You may be wondering what happens once the quantitative data are collected. A researcher will turn their attention to the analysis of data. Similar to qualitative traditions, quantitative data analysis procedures are in line and dependent on the quantitative methodology being employed. All major quantitative traditions have unique data analysis procedures that are recommended. In a general sense, quantitative data analysis is a systematic method that transforms what was collected or observed into numerical data and the numerical data is then categorized in some comprehendible way. Quantitative analysis is the analytic aspect of the investigation that gets to the core of whether or not a researcher(s) findings support or fail to support an idea or a hypothesis. While quantitative data can be analyzed in a variety of different ways, the general essence involves measuring quantities that answer the "why," "what, and "how many" questions a researcher may have about something.

In regard to statistical analysis, there are two broad classifications: descriptive statistics and inferential statistics. Descriptive statistics is centered on describing a data set and avoids making conclusions. Typically, this description of the data involves the measures of central tendency (e.g., mean, median, mode) and measures of dispersion (e.g., variance, standard deviation). The essence of inferential statistics is using a sample to test a hypothesis in order to make inferences about a population. Since inferential statistics is aimed at making inferences about a larger population, it is very important to attain a representative and large sample. While some error is inevitable in any statistical computation, it is significantly improved through sample size and representation (https://www.mymarketresearchmethods.com/descriptive-inferential-statistics-difference/). Inferential statistics usually include sophisticated tests, including (but not limited to) T-Test, Chi-Squared, ANOVA, two-way-ANOVA, ANCOVA, MANOVA, and regression (Hurlburt, 2017). These concepts are thoroughly reviewed in Chapter 4.

VALIDITY AND RELIABILITY

The quantitative constructs of validity and reliability are covered thoroughly in Chapter 4; however, given their importance in quantitative research, we will briefly describe each here. Validity has to do with the degree you are measuring what you are supposed to be measuring. Cook and Campbell (1979) define validity as the "best available approximation to the truth or falsity of a given inference, proposition or conclusion" (p. 37). For example, a depression inventory should measure depression. The degree to which it does measure the construct of depression, and not something else, is its level of validity.

While there are a variety of validation procedures used to assess the validity of a test (e.g., criterion validity, construct validity, predictive validity, concurrent validity), an important distinction that we will make in this chapter is between internal and external validity. Internal validity is the estimate of a causal relationship between the independent variable(s) (i.e., the variable(s) being manipulated) and dependent variable(s) (i.e., what is being measured). In a general sense, the level of internal validity refers to whether the effects of the research are due to the manipulation of the independent variable and not some other external factor (e.g., loss of job, sudden death in the family). Researchers are investigating the strength of the causal relationship between the independent and dependent variable(s), and, through controlling extraneous variables (i.e., variables not deliberately studied), they attempt to improve internal validity. Comparably, the level of external validity refers to the level of positivity that a study's results can be generalized to diverse settings, people, and over times. Researchers work to improve the external validity of their work through random sampling and conducting research in a more natural setting (Hurlburt, 2017).

Reliability, on the other hand, approximates the consistency of your estimates. In other words, reliability is the degree to which an instrument produces the same results when used more than once. An assessment is considered to be reliable if its use on the same sample/object consistently produces the same results (Hurlburt, 2017). Similar to validity, there are a variety of procedures used to assess the reliability of a test (e.g., test re-test reliability, parallel forms reliability, inter-rater reliability, internal consistency reliability). These concepts, and much more, will be explored in Chapter 4.

MIXED METHODS PHILOSOPHICAL INTEGRATION

The third behavioral science methodological movement, following quantitative and qualitative research, is mixed methods research (Tashakkori & Teddlie, 2003). In comparison to quantitative and qualitative methodology, mixed methods methodology is very new to the world of research. While the first known mixed methods research project may have been Campbell and Fiske's (1959) model of multitrait-multimethod matrix (MTMM), during the 1980s the combination of qualitative and quantitative methods began to gather a lot of attention in the world of research (see Greene, Caracelli, & Graham, 1989). In a general sense, mixed methods research design is the notion that qualitative and quantitative methods can be combined, in a complementary manner, to produce unique knowledge beyond what one methodological framework could do alone.

You may be asking yourself, "How do the previously discussed philosophical integration models fit in with a methodological framework that can combine qualitative and quantitative methods?" That is a great question. Truly, from a paradigm perspective, mixed methods research is an iterative and inductive moving target. One approach has a primarily quantitative thread and a smaller qualitative aspect, while another approach touts a main qualitative component and a less significant quantitative element. This mixing of methods does not fit neatly into a paradigmatic hierarchy. Consequently, the philosophy of *pragmatism* often guides mixed methods research (Biesta, 2010; Maxcy, 2003). Instead of the creation of paradigmatic camps (i.e., qualitative and quantitative), mixed methods often purport that whatever works should guide research processes (i.e., pragmatism). In short, to echo Johnson and Onwuegbuzie (2004), mixed methods research takes a pragmatic and pluralistic position that provides the flexibility to further advance the discovery of knowledge.

Pragmatism does not fall into the traditional philosophical integration (ontology, epistemology, theory, methodology) that qualitative and quantitative traditions are centered on. Fitting pragmatism into the paradigmatic hierarchies that govern other research traditions would be antithetical (Dewey, 1929). According to Hall (2013) pragmatism, as a paradigm, directs researchers to take action and experience a situation prior to making meaning of it. Consequently, the notion of pluralism becomes relevant if the situation is deemed to need such action. An example of pluralism (i.e., two or more systems co-existing) can be seen when combining both qualitative and quantitative methods to a research process (Morgan, 2014).

MIXED METHODS SAMPLING AND DATA COLLECTION METHODS

Mixed methods sampling and data collection possibilities are dictated by the researcher(s) belief in what will maximize the understanding of a phenomenon. Mixed methods research design has at least two points (qualitative and quantitative) in which data are collected. Chapters 15 through 18 of this textbook cover major mixed methods research traditions, including the sampling and data collection methods native to each approach. Within each chapter, the order of operations native to the particular mixed methods research approach are discussed. For example, in an explanatory mixed methods design, the researcher first collects quantitative data, and after analyzing the quantitative data, will follow up with qualitative data collection. Within these mixed methods approaches, a combination of qualitative and quantitative sampling procedures, previously reviewed, will either be combined or used at various points (e.g., first phase is *quantitative*, and second phase is *qualitative*) in the research process. Within this example, the researcher(s) could use a simple random sample within the first phase of the project and a criterion sample within the second phase. See Table 1.4 for a quick review of the common probability (quantitative) and non-probability (qualitative) sampling methods that mixed methods researchers can choose from. Similarly, mixed methods researchers use a combination of data collection methods; usually both quantitative (e.g., survey) and qualitative (e.g., individual interviews) methods will be combined to converge on a better understanding of the phenomenon. Lastly, validation and trustworthiness procedures are used, within the appropriate phase, to ensure results are trustworthy, valid, and reliable.

RIGOR

Many beginning researchers have been disappointed and discouraged by the research process because they have been rejected by a journal or their dissertation/thesis committee has slowed down or, in some cases, prohibited their progress toward fulfilling their degree requirements (Flynn, Chasek, Harper, Murphy, & Jorgensen, 2012). Oftentimes, these research-based

TABLE 1.4 Common Probability and Non-Probability Sampling Methods

	NAME OF SAMPLING METHOD	PROBABILITY OR NON-PROBABILITY	DESCRIPTION
1	Simple Random Sampling	Probability	This method of sampling is randomized. Randomization could involve using a randomized number generator in order to select numbers.
2	Stratified Random Sampling	Probability	This method of sampling divides population into smaller sub-groups and then uses simple random sampling to choose subjects from the groups to select the sample.
3	Systemic Sampling	Probability	This method of sampling required selecting every "nth" participant from the population to complete your sample.
4	Cluster Random Sampling	Probability	In cluster random sampling, the researchers select a cluster to sample from instead of the entire population.
5	Multi-Stage Random Sampling	Probability	This method of sampling uses a mixture of all sampling techniques.
6	Convenience Sampling	Non-probability	This method of sampling uses participants that are conveniently accessible to the researcher.
7	Purposive Sampling	Non-probability	This method of sampling uses the researcher's own judgment to select what they feel will be the most suitable sample for the study.
8	Expert Sampling	Non-probability	This method of sampling uses experts from the field related to the study, selected by the researcher.
9	Heterogeneity Sampling	Non-probability	This method of sampling purposefully selects participants to represent all perspectives in the sample.
10	Modal Instance Sampling	Non-probability	This method of sampling takes the most "common" participants for the sample.
11	Quota Sampling	Non-probability	This method of sampling represents demographics proportionally.
12	Snowball Sampling	Non-probability	This method of sampling allows participants to recruit further participants for the sample.
13	Maximum Variation Sampling	Non-probability	This method of sampling allows for the selection of individual, group, and setting to maximize the diversity of perspective.
14	Theory-Based Sampling	Non-probability	This method of sampling allows for the inclusion of participants that help a theory develop.
15	Extreme Case	Non-probability	This method of sampling allows for the selection of outlying cases.

NOTE: This table contains 15 concise sampling descriptions. Further reading is necessary to fully understand each approach.

rejections are centered on design flaws, including (but not limited to) poorly formulated research questions, non-optimal instrumentation, and/or unreliable and weak methods. In addition, there are instances where the researcher simply is not doing enough. It could be that the research is not adding enough originality to our collective scholarly knowledge. These projects are often labeled unoriginal, predictable, lacking implications, and/or trivial. Furthermore, research can seem thin and unsubstantial if the number of participants is low and the results cannot be generalized to a particular population (quantitative research), or if the methods being used lack depth and diversity (qualitative research; Flynn et al., 2019; Laher, 2016). In many of the aforementioned circumstances, the research can be made acceptable and appropriate if additional rigor is added.

QUANTITATIVE RIGOR

One important way this textbook enhances your understanding of each research tradition is through describing how to increase the rigor of each approach. Rigor, in research, generally refers to the processes followed to ensure integrity, soundness, and legitimacy of a project (Laher, 2016). Quantitative rigor is centered on the development of the project, how clear and objective the methods are, how detailed the research design is described, and how well the researcher(s) adhere to the rules of the particular research tradition (Laher, 2016). In addition, quantitative researchers, who are interested in increasing the rigor of their investigation, pay scrupulous attention to the systematic design of the approach as it relates to answering the research question(s), choosing the most optimal method or design for the problem and population being investigated, large and appropriate chosen sample size and/or design, and ensuring the data are both complete and reliable.

While there a variety of factors that contribute to the rigor of quantitative research, internal validity, external validity, and replicability are at the core. Understanding eliminating the various threats to internal validity and external validity can greatly enhance a study's rigor. Five main threats to internal validity include: history (i.e., environmental changes pre/post-test); maturation (i.e., changes that take place over the time of an experiment); attrition (i.e., effect of dropout rates); selection bias (i.e., unequal number of participants have similar attributes); and diffusion (i.e., when the comparison group learns about the experiment group; Babbie & Mouton, 2004). External validity evaluates the generalizability of results to and across individuals (population validity), settings (ecological validity), and time. Threats to external validity can come in the form of an interaction effect of testing. In these instances, results may not generalize because pre-testing interacts with the experimental treatment group. A second threat to external validity could be in the form of reactive effects of the experimental arrangements. For example, the Hawthorne effect can change participant's natural behavior due to the novelty of experiencing the research process. Lastly, replicability refers to the extent to which the same or similar results would be obtained if the same study was conducted somewhere else. Issues that are common threats to replicability include research with low statistical power and poorly described methods sections (Coryn, 2007).

QUALITATIVE RIGOR

Qualitative rigor refers to the extent to which an investigation presents a rigorous methodology, analysis, and trustworthiness. Anyone conducting an article review on the rigor associated with qualitative and quantitative research will quickly realize that there are far more articles concerning qualitative rigor. Why is there a greater focus on establishing rigor in qualitative research? According to Guba (1981) the constant efforts aimed at understanding and enhancing qualitative rigor is due to the nonexperimental nature of qualitative research. As we mentioned earlier in the chapter, Lincoln and Guba (1985) attempted to enhance qualitative research through developing criteria to ensure rigor (i.e., credibility, confirmability, dependability, transferability, and authenticity). In addition to these criteria and the associated trustworthiness strategies, qualitative rigor can be ensured through the use of diversity in data collection methods (e.g., individual interviews, focus groups, document analysis, and artifact analysis) and engaging in multiple iterations of the same data collection method (e.g., multiple individual interviews with the same participants; Flynn, et al., 2019). These diverse and in-depth methods help to ensure thick and rich descriptions, greater understanding of the phenomenon, and create an in-depth triangulation of data (see Figure 1.2).

Qualitative trustworthiness procedures are designed, in part, to enhance the rigor of an investigation. Most trustworthiness procedures are centered on the researcher completing tasks to enhance the rigor of the investigation. Examples of researcher-centered trustworthiness procedures include prolonged engagement (i.e., spending time observing and developing rapport with participants); thick description (i.e., a detailed account of field-based context); the reflection of researcher bias (i.e., exploring and bracketing bias to ensure trustworthiness); negative case analysis (i.e., analyzing data to demonstrate the opposite of a theme); reflexivity (i.e., constantly examining perceptions and its connection with research decisions); epoche (i.e., internally suspending judgment); and triangulation (i.e., exploring the same topic with multiple methods). Two additional trustworthiness strategies that are non-researcher centered include member checking and auditing (i.e., dependability audit, inquiry audit, and confirmability audit). Member checking is conducted with the participants to confirm the credibility of the findings. Audits are conducted with an auditor after the completion of an aspect or the entirety of the research process to confirm the credibility and dependability of the investigation (Creswell, 2012; Hays and Singh, 2012). While there are very few standards addressing how to use various trustworthiness strategies, there is evidence suggesting that qualitative researchers should use at least two strategies in any study (Creswell, 2012).

MIXED METHODS RIGOR

As you probably guessed, qualitative and quantitative standards of rigor both apply to mixed methods research. Qualitative standards of rigor (e.g., credibility, confirmability, dependability, transferability, authenticity) apply to the qualitative methods and quantitative standards (e.g., validity, reliability, replicability, generalizability) apply to the quantitative methods. Researchers implement qualitative and quantitative components either concurrently or sequentially, with the same sample or with different samples. In addition, mixed methods research adds the element of *mixing* to rigor. Mixing is the process of the qualitative and quantitative phases interacting to produce a dynamic and enhanced account of the research (Zhang & Creswell, 2013). In addition to mixing data appropriate to each method's tradition, researchers must both plan and justify their integration.

Once the separate qualitative and quantitative threads are demonstrating appropriate rigor and merit, mixed methods researchers ensure the mixing phase is rigorous. When mixing qualitative and quantitative results, mixed methods researchers often use the process of qualitatizing of quantitative data or the quantitizing of qualitative data to create meta-inferences (Onwuebuzie & Johnson, 2006). From a rigor perspective, mixed methods researchers are focused on both the design quality and interpretive quality. Design quality has to do with ensuring the mixed methods tradition was appropriately applied and interpretive quality is centered on the mixing interpretation (Tashakkori & Teddlie, 2003).

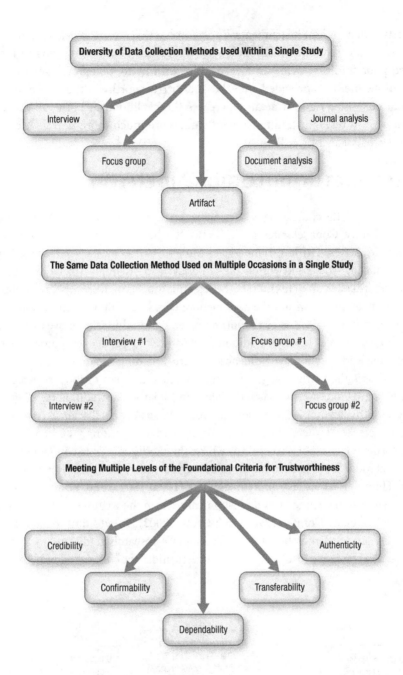

FIGURE 1.2 Three Strategies for Attaining Qualitative Rigor.

NOTE: Each representation symbolically demonstrates a unique way to achieve qualitative rigor.

PILOT STUDY

Pilot studies are a final area of inquiry that qualitative, quantitative, and mixed methods traditions use to create higher levels of investigatory rigor (Ismail, Kinchin, & Edwards, 2017). The essence of a pilot study or feasibility study is to conduct a smaller investigation that provides feedback to a larger research project. Pilot studies include conducting smaller forms of a full research study and the pretesting of appraisal instruments. The nature of this feedback helps the researcher(s) to make adjustments and refine the methodology and methods prior to engaging in the full study. Well-executed pilot studies provide an investigation with methodological rigor by ensuring the study itself and the methods provided are valid and/or trustworthy. Although conducting a pilot study does not guarantee rigor, it greatly increases the likelihood of both validity and success. While common in all research traditions, pilot studies are much more prevalent in quantitative investigations (Ismail, Kinchin, & Edwards, 2017).

RESEARCH METHODOLOGICAL IDENTITY

As previously discussed, the counseling profession has been placing a lot of attention on the construct of professional identity. Counselor research identity has been promoted within doctoral training programs (Lambie, Hayes, Griffith, Limberg, & Mullen, 2014), master's level training programs (Jorgensen & Duncan, 2015), and within the American Counseling Association (ACA) Code of Ethics, counselors are called upon to embrace the scientific aspects of the counseling profession (ACA, 2014). This identity emphasis within the aforementioned scholarship and professional standards is centered on the development of the counselor; however, within this section, we turn your attention to the identity of a particular research tradition. The nature of a particular approach has a lot to do with its history, the leaders who have influenced the creation of the tradition, the manner in which a particular field uses the methodology to better understand topics of interest, which groups are sampled, and what methods are emphasized when using a particular tradition (see Figure 1.3).

In Chapter 2 of this textbook, we explore the foundations of social science research, including philosophy, pioneers, and legacies. The unique history and foundation that each research tradition has greatly informs the manner and style in which the methodology is conducted. For example, the philosophical roots of phenomenology has its origins in the writings of René Descartes (1596–1650), David Hume (1711–1776), Immanuel Kant (1724–1804), and Edmund Husserl (1859–1938), while positivism has some of its philosophical roots in the writings of Pierre-Simon Laplace (1749–1827) and Auguste Comte (1798–1857; Crotty, 2003). In addition to the vast legacies of foundational scholars, different helping professions use research traditions to uncover unique information. According to the results of a recent investigation, the counseling profession most often

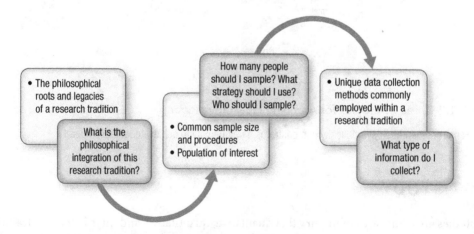

FIGURE 1.3 The Nature of Methodological Identity.

NOTE: Each white rectangle represents a unique aspect of methodological identity. The dark rectangles include questions indicateing what the researchers are asking themselves.

explored the topics of multiculturalism when using the research traditions of phenomenology and consensual qualitative research, and pedagogy when using grounded theory (Flynn et al., 2019). While the philosophy and topic patterns are only two aspects of methodological identity, they start to paint a distinct picture of the character of each approach.

Best Approach for Problem Versus Best Approach for a Researcher

There can be a considerable amount of dissonance with the manner in which individuals conceptualize research approaches and their own identity. We have heard a number of early career professionals and colleagues claim to be a qualitative researcher or a quantitative researcher. It is our belief that much of this identification with a type of research has to do with the developmental stage of the scholar, the methodological leanings of their mentor(s), comfort or discomfort with particular approaches, and/or incomplete and inadequate research training. Developmentally speaking, it is important to remember that the researcher development process is long, intensive, and multi-stepped. Oftentimes, trainees leave a training program with a few research courses and a thorough capstone experience (e.g., thesis, dissertation) with one particular approach to research (e.g., survey research, case study). Naturally, it is normal to identify with the research approach one understands, however, it is important that trainees develop a foundational understanding that one approach is not the answer for all research problems/questions. While one might not know much during the formative years of research training, it is essential to have an understanding that research methodology and methods are tools within a belt of sorts, and depending on the research question/problem, a different tool can and should be used.

Most researchers have a mentor who was key in their development of competency in the research tradition they used to conduct their capstone research project. This mentor may have noticed a particular skillset the trainee brought to a research project. For example, competency and interest in statistics may have served as an antecedent for the mentor to encourage the trainee to conduct a quantitative investigation. Another possibility is the mentor encouraged the trainee to conduct research in an area in which the mentor has competency. While often not the intention of any party, this in-depth grounding in a particular research paradigm (i.e., mentoring) can have the unintended effect of creating camps. Instead of the aforementioned tool belt metaphor, early career professionals may start feeling they are only a quantitative or qualitative researcher. Furthermore, they can start to see the other types of research traditions as incompatible with their identity and capability as a researcher, or they may conceptualize their approach to research as being compatible with all research-based questions. To thwart these potential negative outcomes, trainees should be encouraged to engage in diverse trainings and experiences (e.g., research projects, thesis and dissertation, and case study reviews). Expanding one's repertoire would most likely have the result of increased self-efficacy in multiple approaches and viewing research methodology as the approach that best answers the research question or solves the research problem and not only one's personal interest (e.g., "I really like to provide in-depth interviews").

Attaining Competence

Can you imagine how absurd it would sound if someone said they were going to gain full competence as a cognitive behavioral therapist through reading one book chapter? To truly develop the therapeutic competency in any modality, a trainee would need formal education, required readings, years of practice, and frequent supervision. The same can be said for the attainment of research competency. No one piece of scholarship can provide trainees the necessary education, experience, and mentoring to thoroughly understand and efficiently execute a particular methodology. Reviewing a foundational graduate level research text can be a great starting place in terms of understanding a research tradition and, if written thoroughly, foundational readings can create a sense of awareness and understanding of the steps required to achieve research competency.

Prior to any formal education, it is important to remember that most early career professionals come to graduate school with research-based knowledge gained in previous courses and other educational and life experiences. Depending on the level of previous exposure, students will start to connect earlier knowledge to the new material being explored (Ambrose, Bridges, DiPietro, Lovett, & Norman, 2010). In a general sense, the more connections one makes to the research world, the more research-based self-efficacy. The classroom is one place to enhance and foster growth within these research-based connections. Vygotsky (1978) described the classroom as a socially constructed environment that fosters collaboration through conversation and interaction with peers and instructors. Through the simultaneous learning of material and instructor-driven elaboration of particular, developmentally appropriate learning points, students are able to transfer theoretical and philosophical notions into pragmatic application in unique contexts. Similarly, Bain (2004) described how the best university instructors create effective learning experiences. One of his key areas was entitled *structuring intentional learning experiences*.

When instructing early career professionals in the area of research-based competency, it is helpful to intentionally scaffold deeper levels of review with hands-on application (e.g., team learning, case studies, and engaging in the research process). For example, upon entering a training program, a graduate student will take a foundational research course. During this course, there may be a variety of educational experiences. The experiences could be in the form of research-based discussions, case studies, exams, presentations, and/or peer critiques. Once a basic understanding of research has been achieved, students could collaborate with a faculty member or peer on the creation of a research project. This project would be supervised by a faculty member (required by most institutional review boards (IRBs), and would provide an initial opportunity to hone valuable research skills. Finally, most doctoral level programs have a capstone research experience (i.e., dissertation). Through the dissertation experience, students are mentored and supported in gaining in-depth research-based competency. Through engaging in the research process and thoroughly being mentored in a methodology, one may begin to identify with a particular tradition (i.e., research identity).

Research competency is significantly increased when early career professionals experience initial success with scholarly tasks (Järvelä & Renninger, 2014). Having a passionate and committed research mentor who is open to collaborating with early career professionals on initial research experiences is akin to having a knowledgeable tutor at one's service. When novice researchers witness their efforts culminating in the creation of new knowledge and a scholarly publication, the consequence is often an increase in research self-efficacy and a sense of motivation. The aforementioned motivation affects early career professionals because the research project reflects a combination of the high value the professional has placed on the project and their outcome expectancies regarding the research experience (Ambrose et al., 2010). Early mentoring and successful research experiences are often in the form of independent studies, collegial collaboration, mentor and mentee work, and turning one's dissertation or thesis into a refereed publication.

HUMAN SUBJECTS RESEARCH

Numerous ethical considerations surface when working with human research participants. As a community of scholars, we have learned a tremendous amount about the treatment of human participants from unethical and ethically questionable research studies (e.g., The Milgram Experiment, Stanford Prison Experiment). As researchers, we must consider how human subjects might be affected by the requirements of a study. Sheperis (2017) described 12 ethical areas where researchers can consider the implications for their work. These areas include: the research question, design of the study, methodology selected, data collection instruments, possible risks for participants, steps taken to minimize risks, data collection processes, presentation of informed consent, data analysis processes, confidentiality procedures, the processes in which results are shared (e.g., publications, discussions, presentations and workshops), and the researcher's decision to protect the participant's rights throughout the study (Sheperis, 2017).

When research involves human beings, certain ethical considerations must be taken into account. Throughout history, there have been numerous egregiously unethical experiments that have significantly impacted the lives of participants. Thankfully, the research community has made great strides toward ethical treatment of participants. The Belmont Report was the first official ethical code of conduct for researchers. Following the Belmont Report's ethical stipulations, the importance of informed consent was incorporated into the research community, and today it is an ethical requirement for researchers whom are members of the ACA, American Association for Marriage and Family Therapy (AAMFT), National Association of Social Workers (NASW), and APA to follow their codes of ethics.

The Belmont Report

The Tuskegee Syphilis Study generated a great deal of public outrage (Privitera, 2014), leading Congress to establish a National Commission for the Protection of Human Subjects in Biomedical and Behavioral Research in 1974, just 2 years after the study concluded (Privitera, 2014). The objective of the Commission was to identify and develop ethical guidelines for research involving human participation. In 1979, the Commission drafted and published the Belmont Report, which consisted of three principles for ethical research.

The three principles for ethical research, as determined by the Commission, are respect for others, beneficence, and justice (Wright, 2013). The principle of *respect for others* is comprised of two components: the moral obligation to respect and acknowledge autonomy, and to protect individuals who have decreased autonomy. *Beneficence* also had two elements; first to do no harm, and second to minimize all possible risk factors for the participants. The final principle of the Belmont Report, *justice*, stressed the importance and need to make certain that groups or classes of participants are going to benefit equally, as well as burdened equally, by the research project. For example, if conducting an experimental/control group research study on the efficacy of a mindfulness meditation group as an intervention to help manage anxiety, if the intervention proves successful, the same intervention must be given to the control group.

Informed Consent

Research participants should be viewed as volunteers and volunteers should enter into participation without coercion or improper reward for their participation (Wright, 2013). Participants, ethically, must clearly understand the risks of the study and understand their right to leave a study at any point. All of this information is covered in an informed consent agreement. The informed consent is a verbal and signed/confirmed process, where the description of the study, risks and rewards, confidentiality, compensation, and so forth are discussed and understood by the participant. The participant is informed to make a decision whether to participate in the study or not (Privitera, 2014). It is important to note that consent must be obtained prior to research starting and the informed consent does not relieve researchers from answering all of the participant's questions (Wright, 2013).

HISTORY OF RESEARCH-BASED CONCERNS

There have been numerous unethical studies performed throughout history, including (but not limited to) the Tuskegee Syphilis Study, Jewish Chronic Disease Hospital Cancer Cell Injections, Willowbrook Study, and Nazi Medical War Crimes (National Institutes of Health [NIH], 2002). As horrendous as these studies were, it is important to understand and reflect on the context, outcomes, procedures, and motivation behind these investigations. While focusing on the egregious ethical issues is important, it is also extremely helpful to consider why the policies, originating in the Belmont Report, were initially developed.

Tuskegee Syphilis Study

The Tuskegee Syphilis Study lasted a total of 40 years, beginning in 1932 and is one of the longest running studies to occur in the United States (Wester & Hines, 2017). The intention of this study was to investigate the impact of syphilis in human beings and the researchers' sample consisted of 600 Black men, 399 infected with syphilis and 201 men without syphilis (Privitera, 2014). The participants were given misinformation and not given an informed consent. Participants were told they would be receiving treatment for "bad blood," although the men did not receive proper treatment.

Four years after the study began, the researchers understood that participants infected with syphilis had an increased number of, and more serious, complications than the non-infected population (Wester & Hines, 2017). Despite this understanding the study continued. Ten years into the study, researchers observed that the risk of death doubled for participants with syphilis when compared to those without. Around the same time in the 1940s penicillin was acknowledged as an effective treatment for the disease, however participants were not notified or given treatment. This study continued for another 30 years after this, until a researcher expressed concern over the ethics of the study in 1968, leading to the study concluding in 1972 (Privitera, 2014).

Jewish Chronic Disease Hospital Cancer Cell Injections

In 1963, Dr. Chester Southam, at the Jewish Chronic Disease Hospital, was interested in researching if a healthy person could fight off cancer cells. This interest came from the idea that perhaps individuals suffering from cancer do not have enough antibodies and their bodies are unsuccessful in fighting off cancer cells due to another debilitation, therefore a human with an increased amount of antibodies was thought to be able to fight off the cancer cells. Southam and his team of researchers, at the Jewish Chronic Disease Hospital, were able to find participants for this study although they neglected to inform them what they would be injected with, nor were the participants provided an informed consent (Wester & Hines, 2017). Later, Southam and his research team explained they did not feel it necessary to inform their participants of the risks involved with the study or tell them they were going to be injecting participants with cancer cells, as researchers feared this information could frighten potential participants. As a result of this study some patients did develop cancer. In an interview with the *New York Post*'s Allen Hornblum, Southam was asked what would happen when the participants contracted the disease, to this Southam answered "If they did, we'd just cut it out" (Hornblum, 2013).

Willowbrook Study

The Willowbrook Study took place in a significantly overcrowded and understaffed school on Staten Island, New York, in 1963 (Wright, 2013). The researchers infected healthy children with intellectual disabilities with the live hepatitis virus. Some were infected orally, while others were injected with the virus (Wright, 2013). Parents were coerced into consenting to this treatment by the Willowbrook State School. Officials from the school stated that the children would only be admitted if they took part in the study. They added that even if a child were not to participate in the study, the child would still be infected with the virus simply from being at the school, due to the overcrowding and general lack of cleanliness (Wester & Hines, 2017). As a result of this research, many children became very ill. This study went on for 14 years, and ultimately, some children were treated while others were not.

Nazi Medical War Crimes

In concentration camps, Nazi physicians preformed numerous studies on their prisoners during World War II (Wester & Hines, 2017). The treatment the prisoners received during this time include injections with gasoline and live viruses. In addition to these injections, many prisoners were immersed in ice water or were forced to consume poison. Unsurprisingly, these studies often resulted in the death of the prisoner or in disease and suffering. The Nazi party was eventually tried and convicted for crimes against humanity due to the monstrosities that occurred in the concentration camps.

INSTITUTIONAL REVIEW BOARDS AND FEDERAL GUIDELINES

With the same intention of the Belmont Report's three principles—respect for others, beneficence, and justice—the IRB was created. IRBs are organizations with a minimum of five members (e.g., scientist, non-scientist, prisoner advocate, chairperson, and a member who is not otherwise affiliated with the institution), one of which must come from outside the institution (Privitera, 2014). All institutions receiving federal funding have an IRB, including universities, schools, hospitals, and some community agencies (Wester & Hines, 2017). The IRB's purpose is to review the protocols of research, weigh the risks and benefits of the research, and determine the level of risk involved; no risk, minimal risk, or greater-than-minimal risk.

In addition to the aforementioned IRB guidelines, there are federal regulations that must be upheld as well. Federal regulations for research with human participants, 45 CFR part 46, is broken into four subparts (Office of Human Research Protections, 2016). Subpart A defines federal policies for working with human participants, this is also called the common rule. Subpart B describes the additional protections needed for research involving pregnant women, fetuses, and neonates. Subpart C clarifies the additional protections required for prisoners. Lastly, Subpart D explains additional protection required when working with children. Information about the federal regulations and the Electronic Code of Federal Regulations can be found on the Department of Health and Human Services website at https://www.hhs.gov/ohrp/regulations-and-policy/regulations/common-rule/index.html. All emerging and seasoned researchers should review these guidelines regularly.

MULTICULTURAL ISSUES

Minority populations, low income populations, confined populations, and women who are single or pregnant are considered to be more vulnerable to unethical research practices (Wester & Hines, 2017). Given this information, it is important to assess, as the researcher, one's own understanding of work with multicultural populations. Investigators must continually remain culturally competent throughout the entire research process. Wester and Hines (2017) describe three competencies, recognized by the ACA, which guide researchers in their work with multicultural backgrounds.

The first competency requires the investigator to be aware of their own values and biases. For example, if a researcher is a happily married woman and she is doing research on the effectiveness of an intervention for married couples considering divorce, she may strongly value marriage and have negative thoughts about divorce, which could set the stage for her being biased toward the efficacy of the intervention and the research in general. The second competency states that researchers must have an understanding of the participants' world view. It is important for researchers to acknowledge that everyone has a unique world view. Thus, researchers must gain some understanding of the lens from which their participants view the world (e.g., demographic questionnaire, reflective journal, processing probes). Lastly, the third competency requires that interventions be appropriate with the understanding gained from the prior two competencies. For example, it is very important for researchers not to generalize their findings to unexplored populations. If an intervention has proven effective for homeless African American women, this does not mean researchers can assume it will be successful for homeless Mexican American women.

SUMMARY

Throughout this chapter you were introduced to the philosophical and pragmatic aspects of research traditions, research ethics, and information on the importance of scholarly rigor and identity. As you continue your journey through the remainder of this textbook, you will review the way specific research traditions use the general concepts and topics discussed in Chapter 1. Specifically, the contributing authors will review each tradition's philosophical integration, rigor, and history. Given that the nature of this textbook is centered on future producers of research, it is our hope that information presented within each chapter will create a sense of motivation to start initiating research projects and self-efficacy in understanding the essence of research. Through reading this chapter, you learned the basic blueprints of qualitative, quantitative, and mixed methods research. Good luck in your future work as researchers, we hope you will contribute, in your own way, to our shared intellectual community.

STUDENT ACTIVITIES

Exercise 1: The Scientific Method

Directions: Consider the scientific method described herein. The scientific method is a standardized way of gathering data, testing predictions, and interpreting results. Conduct an Internet search on the terms replicability, precision, falsifiability, and parsimony as they relate to the scientific method. Following this search answer the following questions.

- What is Ockham's razor and how does it relate to parsimony?
- Review the following link and describe how the work of Karl Popper impacted the notion of falsification. https://plato.stanford.edu/entries/popper/
- Given the information you just learned on the scientific method, how can one know something scientifically? How is this knowledge best obtained?

Exercise 2: Writing a Research Question

Directions: Review all of the variations and example research questions herein. Consider research problems/topics that are of interest to you. Practice writing your own research question for each of these different variations of research questions.

Exercise 3: Developing a Tradition-Based Purpose Statement

Directions: Review the following qualitative, quantitative, and mixed methods purpose statement frameworks. Creatively, fill in the blanks with the appropriate nomenclature.

QUALITATIVE PURPOSE STATEMENT

The purpose of the present study was to _____ (explore, uncover, etc.) how _____ (counselors, psychologists, etc.) can help in the _____(construct being explored) of _____ (particular participants being explored) and to propose a _____ (grounded theory, phenomenon, etc.) of the _____ (name of the construct being explored) of _____(particular demographic being explored).

QUANTITATIVE PURPOSE STATEMENT

The purpose of this investigation was to test _____ intervention (independent variable) by comparing _____ (group 1) and _____ (group 2) in terms of the _____ (dependent variable) for _____ (participants) at _____ (research site)

MIXED METHODS PURPOSE STATEMENT

The purpose of this mixed methods study was to explore the use of _____ (construct of interest) with _____(participants of interest) to enhance their understanding of the predicting relationship between _____(independent variable) and _____ (dependent variable), via mixed methods analysis.

Exercise 4: Gaining Research Expertise

Directions: Gaining competence in a research design is no simple task, however it is something that is achievable. Respond to the following prompts: Describe one methodological framework that is interesting to you. Where can you find a mentor in this area (e.g., faculty at your university, professor at a different institution, book author, etc.)? Reach out to this individual and ask them if you could consult with them and/or collaborate with them on a project. Review the scholarly literature and find two books or articles describing your methodology of interest. Now you are starting your scholarly journey in gaining research competence.

Exercise 5: Writing the Informed Consent

Directions: Go to your university's IRB website. Find the requirements for the informed consent document. Now consider a research study that you would like to conduct during your time in graduate school. Complete the entire informed consent document based on your research interest.

ADDITIONAL RESOURCES

Software Recommendations

NVivo Software (https://www.qsrinternational.com)
CAQDAS Software (https://www.maxqda.com)
ATLAS ti (https://atlasti.com)
MaxQDA (https://maxda.com)
Statistical Package for the Social Sciences (SPSS): (https://www.ibm.com/analytics/spss-statistics-software)
R: (https://www.r-project.org/)
SAS: (https://www.sas.com/en_us/software/stat.html)
Mplus: (https://www.statmodel.com/)

Helpful Links

- https://www.ecfr.gov/cgi-bin/retrieveECFR?gp=&SID=83cd09e1c0f5c-6937cd9d7513160fc3f&pitd=20180719&n=pt45.1.46&r=PART&ty=HTML

- https://people.uwec.edu/piercech/ResearchMethods/Data%20collection%20methods/DATA%20COLLECTION%20METHODS.htm

- https://towardsdatascience.com/sampling-techniques-a4e34111d808

- https://www.healthknowledge.org.uk/public-health-textbook/research-methods/1a-epidemiology/methods-of-sampling-population

- https://www.wikihow.com/Understand-and-Use-Basic-Statistics

- https://www.statisticshowto.datasciencecentral.com/reliability-validity-definitions-examples/

- https://nursekey.com/trustworthiness-and-integrity-in-qualitative-research/

- https://cirt.gcu.edu/research/developmentresources/research_ready/mixed_methods/choosing_design

Helpful Books

Audi, R. (2010). *Epistemology: A contemporary introduction to the theory of knowledge* (3rd ed.). Routledge.
Creswell, J. W. (2017). *Research design: Qualitative, quantitative, and mixed methods approaches* (5th ed.). SAGE.

Crotty, M. (2003). *The foundations of social research: Meaning and perspective in the research process* (2nd ed.). SAGE.

Effingham, N. (2013). *An introduction to ontology.* Polity Press.

Hays, D. G., & Singh, A. A. (2012). *Qualitative inquiry in clinical and educational settings.* Guilford.

Hurlburt, R. T. (2017). *Comprehending behavioral statistics* (6th ed.). Kendall Hunt.

Lincoln, Y. S., & Guba, E. G. (1985). *Naturalistic inquiry.* SAGE.

Meltzoff, J., & Cooper, H. (2018). *Critical thinking about research: Psychology and related fields* (2nd ed.). American Psychological Association.

Sheperis, C. J., Young, J. S., & Daniels, M. H. (2017). *Counseling research: Quantitative, qualitative, and mixed methods.* Pearson.

Helpful Videos

- https://www.khanacademy.org/math/cc-sixth-grade-math/cc-6th-data-statistics/cc-6-statistical-questions/v/understanding-statistical-questions

- https://www.youtube.com/watch?v=wbdN_sLWl88

- https://www.youtube.com/watch?v=IsAUNs-IoSQ

- https://www.youtube.com/watch?v=JHNNNW97ssI

KEY REFERENCES

Only key references appear in the print edition. The full reference list appears in the digital product found on http://connect.springerpub.com/content/book/978-0-8261-4385-3/part/part01/chapter/ch01

Alderman, N., & Knight, C. (2017). Keeping the "scientist-practitioner" model alive and kicking through service-based evaluation and research: Examples from neurobehavioural rehabilitation. *The Neuropsychologist, 3,* 25–31.

Audi, R. (2010). *Epistemology: A contemporary introduction to the theory of knowledge* (3rd Ed.). Routledge.

Babbie, E., & Mouton, J. (2010). *The practice of social research* (10th ed.). Oxford University Press.

Biesta, G. (2010). Pragmatism and the philosophical foundations of mixed methods research. In A. Tashakkori & C. Teddlie (Eds.), *SAGE handbook of mixed methods in social and behavioral research* (2nd ed., pp. 95–118). SAGE.

Bhattacherjee, A. (2012). *Social science research: Principles, methods, and practices.* Textbooks Collection. Book 3.

Creswell, J., & Plano Clark, V. (2017). *Designing and conducting mixed methods research* (3rd ed.). SAGE.

Crotty, M. (2003). *The foundations of social research: Meaning and perspective in the research process.* SAGE.

Flynn, S. V., & Korcuska, J. S. (2018a). Credible phenomenological research: A mixed methods study. *Counselor Education & Supervision, 57,* 34–50. doi:10.1002/ceas.12092

Flynn, S. V., & Korcuska, J. S. (2018b). Grounded theory research design: An investigation into practices and procedures. *Counseling Outcome Research and Evaluation, 9,* 102–116. doi:10.1080/21501378.20 17.1403849

Flynn, S. V., Korcuska, J. S., Brady, N. V., & Hays, D. G. (2019). A 15-year content analysis of three qualitative research traditions. *Counselor Education & Supervision, 58,* 49–63. doi:10.1002/ceas.12123

Hays, D. G., & Singh, A. A. (2012). *Qualitative inquiry in clinical and educational settings.* Guilford.

Office of Human Research Protections. (2016). Federal policy for the protection of human subjects ("Common Rule"). Retrieved July 6, 2019, from https://www.hhs.gov/ohrp/regulations-and-policy/regulations/common-rule/index.html

Onwuegbuzie, A. J., & Johnson, R. B. (2006). The validity issue in mixed research. *Research in the Schools, 13,* 48–63.

Scotland, J. (2012). Exploring the philosophical underpinnings of research: Relating ontology and epistemology to the methodology and methods of the scientific, interpretive, and critical research paradigms. *English Language Teaching, 5*(9), 9–16. doi:10.5539/elt.v5n9p9

CHAPTER 2

HISTORY OF RESEARCH IN THE SOCIAL SCIENCES

Dodie Limberg, Jessie D. Guest, and Shelby K. Gonzales

LEARNING OBJECTIVES

After reading this chapter, you will be able to:

- Understand the two main types of ontology (realism and relativism) in social science research
- Recognize the differences and similarities between research epistemologies
- Understand the differences and similarities between research theoretical positions
- Comprehend the history of research trends in the helping professions
- Identify ways in which helping professions intertwine and are influenced by one another

AN INTRODUCTION TO THE HISTORY OF RESEARCH IN THE SOCIAL SCIENCES

Understanding the various epistemological and ontological approaches and reflecting on your own beliefs about the nature of existence and truths is paramount as these views assist in guiding your research paradigm selection. A research paradigm acts as a web that holds a system of ideas or assumptions about existence and truth, research theories, research strategies, and research methodologies (Fossey et al., 2002). The paradigm you select for your research often indicates your view of the world and the question you are trying to answer. The essence of a strong research design is the congruence between the researcher's beliefs about the nature of existence and its relationship to creation of new knowledge with a particular research. As a review, a traditional research paradigm includes five components: ontology (i.e., form and nature of reality); epistemology (i.e., theory of knowledge acquisition); theoretical stance (i.e., philosophical stance); methodology (i.e., process for discovering what is knowable); and method (i.e., procedures for gathering and analyzing data; Flynn & Korcuska, 2018a, 2018b; Flynn et al., 2019). In this chapter, we explain all the different forms of each of the components. It is important that your research paradigm is congruent with your research approach. For example, if you are interested in learning more about the experiences of professionals in your field to better understand a particular phenomenon, a positivism or post-positivism theoretical stance might *not* fit your research question or your research methodologies. Instead, your paradigm would likely be based in a relativist ontology using a theoretical stance within the constructionism epistemology. However, if you wanted to examine the impact of a specific intervention on a particular client population then you would be functioning from a realism ontology using a theoretical stance within the objectivist epistemology.

ONTOLOGY IN SOCIAL SCIENCE RESEARCH

As mentioned in Chapter 1, ontology shapes or informs researchers' epistemological approaches and research methods as it focuses on one's beliefs about reality or existence; often asking the question, "Does the world exist and if so, in what form?" (Potter, 1996). Although there are many philosophical viewpoints explaining and understanding reality and existence (Heppner et al., 2016), the two primary ontological positions among research perspectives are realism and relativism. For example, you may view the world as concrete or tangible; things you can observe or measure. Alternatively, you may view the world through various lenses of perception and experiences guided by your thoughts, values, and interpretations of various sensations. The debate between realism and relativism is one of a single reality versus multiple realities and is often the diverging point between the objectivists' deductive research inquiries (e.g., What is the effect of an intervention on clients' self-harming behaviors?) and subjectivists' inductive research inquiries (e.g., What are the experiences of clients who engage in self-harming behaviors?).

REALISM

Realism is the epistemological belief or position that true existence and reality are independent from our consciousness, mind, and experiences (Levers, 2013). The realism position is closely related to scientific inquiry, objectivity, and universal truths, as it focuses directly on objects and matter rather than perceptions and personal experiences. Additionally, the role of the researcher within the realism position is strictly concerned with data and facts and does not believe that the person of the researcher has any influence on the data and vice versa. The realist's goal is to separate the person of the researcher while engaging in research to ensure there is no influence on the data. In order to uphold the strict adherence to data and facts, realists make every effort to conduct studies that isolate the independent variable removing or reducing all possible influences of extraneous variables during data collection and analysis. Thus, using valid, reliable, and objective measures to collect data as well as using concrete or statistical analysis to analyze data are paramount to the realist's research values. However, even among the realism position there are competing forms of realism—direct realism and critical realism.

Direct realism is viewed as more rigid and naïve as it strictly views existence and truth as being completely centered on what our senses can show us (i.e., what we can see, touch, hear, taste, and smell; Levers, 2013). Direct realism is not influenced by our perceptions or interpretations and essentially breaks down to "what you see is what you get," alluding that our senses provide an accurate depiction of the world and reality (Saunders et al., 2009). Based on this position, reality is consistent and does not change across people, cultures, or contexts. Critical realism, on the other hand, is a bit more contemporary compared to the direct perspective as it adds an additional condition. The critical realism position offers that reality does exist independent and outside of the human mind regardless if it can be fully or directly experienced. Similar to direct realism, critical realists believe that reality is held independently from our minds and perceptions; however, the critical realist adds that since we do not have access to the world in its entirety and we only understand reality through fragments or smaller parts, truth about the whole is based on reasoning about its observable parts (Bergen et al., 2010). An example of this would be studying the influence of an intervention to increase self-esteem among middle school students. Since we do not have access to every middle school student in the world, we can study a smaller sample of middle school students to make generalizations about the whole (i.e., all middle school students). Additionally, critical realists also believe that we experience our sensations about the world (e.g., how we see, hear, smell, feel, and taste is dependent on the individual and not the actual object), which are representations of the world and not the actual world directly (e.g., watching a football game on television). If taken blindly and without reason, our senses can often be deceptive and do not accurately portray the real world (Novikov & Novikov, 2013). For example, optical illusions are created to deceive our senses into thinking what we see is real (i.e., direct realism) instead of some kind of distortion of the senses. However, once we are provided time for reason or an explanation how or why the optical illusion worked, we have a new understanding of reality (i.e., critical realism). Therefore, from the critical realist perspective, truth about whether an entity exists can be derived through observation and reasoning of the fragments of an entity, rather than strict observation of the whole entity without reasoning (Clark et al., 2007).

RELATIVISM

Relativism differs from realism in that truth and reality are determined through our experiences and the belief that nothing exists outside of our thoughts (Denzin & Lincoln, 2005). Just as realism most closely aligns with objectivism, relativism most closely aligns with subjectivism. Unlike realism, relativism does not "take things as they are" but looks at the world from a variety of different perspectives that may change or illuminate certain aspects of the world. Through this perspective, all existence and knowledge are filtered through the multiple lenses (e.g., culture, language, gender, age, social class, religion, ethnicity, sexual orientation) that provide as many truths and realities as there are people. Not only does everyone experience life differently but everyone's world is different, thus creating multiple truths and realities (Stajduhar et al., 2001). For example, sticking with the optical illusion references, many people are familiar with the duck or bunny illusion or the old lady and young woman, black and white illusion. Based on your perspective, focal point, angle, or even preconceptions of what the picture is supposed to look like, some people see one picture while the others see another. Neither perspective is wrong and both groups are right. This is the idea of subjective reality and multiple truths. The goal of the research and knowledge created under the relativism perspective is to better understand the subjective experience of reality and truth of others (Denzin & Lincoln, 2005), while simultaneously recognizing that the person of the researcher influences their observations just as the observations influence the researcher.

EPISTEMOLOGY AND THEORETICAL STANCE IN SOCIAL SCIENCE RESEARCH

Two major components of a research paradigm are epistemology and theoretical stance. Epistemology is the theory of knowledge acquisition and a theoretical stance is a researcher's philosophical stance. We describe three major epistemologies in social science research: objectivism, constructionism, and subjectivism. Additionally, we explain the theoretical stances within each epistemology and present the key pioneers of each. The theoretical stances we discuss are: positivism, post-positivism, constructivism, interpretivism, critical inquiry, feminism, and post-modernism.

THE HISTORY OF OBJECTIVISM

Objectivism, defined by Crotty (2003), is the belief that reality, truth, and meaning exist outside of social factors or human subjectivity. Individuals that hold this belief seek to understand objects or various phenomena as they exist outside of contextual factors and human biases. Objectivists believe that knowledge is not a social product but that it already exists and is waiting to be discovered, not created. Thus, the goal of science is to uncover universal laws of truth (Nicholls, 2009) and the purpose is to explain, predict, and control phenomena being observed or studied. Individuals adhering to an objectivist epistemology do not believe that researchers are influenced by what they are observing or studying, and the researchers do not influence what they are observing or studying. Therefore, according to this philosophy knowledge is universal and can be applied across contexts, cultures, and situations because the essence of an object or phenomenon does not change and will not change when studied by others. Positivism and post-positivism are two common theoretical stances that draw from the objectivist epistemology.

POSITIVISM

The term positivism, or also called empiricism, holds the belief that scientific knowledge is the only authentic knowledge; therefore, positivism is most closely connected to the scientific method (Crotty, 2003). Positivism is a general attempt to use the methods from the natural sciences to identify causal relationships among the social sciences. Since the positivist theoretical stance relies heavily on the scientific method, it rejects all concepts from religion or metaphysics (i.e., explanation of reality through elements that exist beyond the physical world) and theorizes researchers can be "positive" or certain about knowing. There are five guiding principles of the positivist theoretical stance: (a) phenomenalism or knowledge verified by the senses (i.e., observation) is considered truth; (b) deductivism, theories are used to generate hypotheses to test and confirm laws; (c) inductivism, gathering facts or observations provides the foundation of knowledge; (d) objectivism, science and knowledge are value free; and (e) scientific statements, declarations of cause and effect (Bryman, 2008). The founding principle of positivism is that knowledge and truth already exist and, therefore, can be observed, studied, and measured objectively. According to positivist thought, knowledge is gained or discovered through objective measurement, observation, and experimentation on phenomena identified by our senses (i.e., things we can touch, taste, see, hear, or smell). Positivists believe that everything can be proven by science and that knowledge or truth comes from positive affirmations of theories or hypotheses tested through strict, rigorous adherence to the scientific method (Heppner et al., 2016). According to positivists, the world operates in terms of cause and effect and can appear to be mechanical in nature. The task of positivism is to describe and explain objects as well as to predict and prescribe relationships between phenomena.

The primary goal of a researcher viewing the world from a positivist theoretical stance is to uncover the universal laws or truths that govern every object and their relationship to one another. Similar to the objectivist epistemological viewpoint, the researcher is independent from the object and vice versa. The researchers are expected to remain value free and, in fact, the researcher's thoughts, values, or perspectives on the phenomena under investigation are not important for discovery of existing knowledge. The only role of the researcher in this paradigm is to provide material for testing theories and developing laws (Bryman, 2008). The researchers are expected to remain objective, focus only on what the senses can experience, and utilize valid and reliable measurements. Since the researcher is independent and does not influence the phenomena being examined, researchers are considered to be interchangeable as the experiment or study should render the same findings regardless of who is conducting the study. This does not mean that all researchers are the same as each researcher has their own strengths; however, the positivist belief is that researchers do not yield results, the experiments yield results. This concept of strict adherence to the scientific method leading to confidence in results regardless of the researcher, indirectly indicates the idea and importance of replication in research. For example, if a study is done with integrity (e.g., isolating the independent variable as best as possible, using valid and reliable measurement instruments, utilizing appropriate statistical analyses) and with close adherence to the research methodology utilized, then the study should yield similar findings when conducted by other researchers.

Research paradigms often encapsulate many beliefs or theories about existence, truth, knowledge, and how knowledge is found, created, or determined. However, research paradigms also include other characteristics that include what we study, how we study it, and what our findings mean. Positivism is often associated with highly structured research methodologies that facilitate replication and statistical analysis such as quantitative research. For example, the Asch Conformity Study was conducted by Solomon Asch (1907–1996), a Polish-American social psychologist, in 1951 and tested an individual's choice to conform to the group even when the individual knows the group is incorrect. All participants in the study were given a "vision" test to determine which line on a card was longer. Asch assigned 50 male college students to either the control or experimental group, in which the experimental group included majority actors purposely choosing the incorrect answer, while the control group did not have any actors. Over 12 trials, Asch found that in the experimental group, one third of the participants conformed to the incorrect majority and 25% never conformed at all; while in the control group, less than one third of the participants chose the incorrect answer, thus illustrating that individuals are more likely to conform to groups to fit in. Not all phenomena studied in the social sciences fit the positivist paradigm and the associated methodologies, but the use of a positivist paradigm in social sciences can increase credibility among "hard" or natural sciences. Although positivism provides structure, objectivity, and reliable measurement systems, it often falls under criticism as positivist theories are viewed as static, it does not account for structural change, and the strict adherence to the value-free, independent researchers often leads to researchers overlooking how their own biases and assumptions influence their findings.

Pioneers of Positivism

Auguste Comte (1798–1857), a nineteenth-century French philosopher, is known as the founder of positivism and greatly advanced research among the social sciences. Comte believed that research used in the natural sciences should be used in the social sciences to ensure "positivity" in achieving reliable, concrete knowledge that could be used to enact social change for the better. Comte is most noted for his Law of Three Stages. He believed that every society goes through three stages of development and progressing through such stages is inevitable. The Law of Three Stages includes the Theological Stage, Metaphysical Stage, and the Scientific or Positive Stage (Crotty, 2003). In the Theological Stage, knowledge is considered to stem from religion; gods, goddesses, and spirits create knowledge and are the cause for all natural events. During this stage, knowledge is strictly focused on religion without any scientific basis. The Metaphysical Stage consists of abstract power guiding the world, with religion providing the foundation and structure but combines it with a scientific mindset. This stage identifies universal laws that are grounded in abstract principles. The last stage, the Scientific or Positive Stage, focuses on observation, the use of the scientific method to discover knowledge, and disregards the metaphysical and religious explanations of the world. During this stage, Comte postulated that not everything in the world could be explained or made sense of but the only things that mattered were the things we could measure, observe, and experience with our senses. As society progresses through the three stages, the reliance on religion for explanations decreases while the reliance on science increases (Crotty, 2003).

In addition to Comte, there was a group of philosophers who also valued the scientific method and rigorous investigations, and viewed science as the only meaningful source of knowledge. This group, led by Moritz Schlick (1882–1936), was known as the Vienna Circle. The group was comprised of a social philosopher, mathematician, and a physicist. This group was considered to be radical in their views and beliefs about the philosophy of science. The members of the Vienna Circle criticized the mechanistic nature of positivism and created their own movement entitled, *Logical Positivism* (Crotty, 2003), also the name of a salient book edited by A. J. Ayer (1959). Logical positivists believed that information experienced through the senses and had "meaning" was considered science. The only statements deemed meaningful by this group were statements that could be verified by observation or math. All metaphysical elements or knowledge were considered to be meaningless. Logical positivism operated out of the verificationist theory that later came to be highly criticized by post-positivists, Sir Karl Popper (1902–1994) and Thomas Kuhn (1922–1996).

POST-POSITIVISM

Since positivism was viewed as rigid and strict, post-positivism or post-empiricism as it is sometimes referred to, was created as a response to the multiple criticisms of the positivist theoretical stance. Post-positivism is considered to be a more contemporary stance as it is more adaptive. Post-positivists maintain many of the foundational elements of the positivist beliefs such as knowledge is discovered not created, the belief in one truth versus multiple truths, the use of rigor, precision, objectivity, and the use of the scientific method for such discovery (Crossan, 2003). However, post-positivists amended the traditional positivists' views to be more expansive and inclusive. For example, although post-positivists strive for objective measurement, they also acknowledge that objective measurement is not totally possible as the researcher's background, culture, values, and theoretical perspective does influence their observations or perceptions of the phenomena under investigation. They believe that researchers are the ones who determine the legitimacy of conclusions or findings and determine what findings add value to the knowledge base in a field, not strictly algorithms or statistics. Additionally, post-positivists do not believe in absolute or universal truths as researchers do not have direct access to everything or all populations, but they do have access to samples or pieces of reality (Guba, 1994). Therefore, post-positivists believe in an approximate reality, in hypotheses or conjectures not absolute truths, and that measurement can be both direct and indirect as we may only have access to phenomena indirectly.

The goal of post-positivistic research is to make generalizations about a whole, provide explanations about causes, and make predictions with closer approximations to the truth. According to post-positivists, truth is based on perceptions of pieces of reality since we cannot fully know something;

therefore, approximations or probabilistic statements are made about truth. These approximations or probabilities are also known as *p*-values in statistical analysis as it asserts that there is truth, but we cannot be absolutely certain, as there is always a small probability that the researcher is wrong (Heppner et al., 2016). This belief leads to the foundational difference between positivists and post-positivists; the Theory of Falsifiability. Falsifiability is the capacity for a hypothesis or theory to be proven wrong. Additionally, the Theory of Falsifiability states that conclusions about a whole cannot be made from a simple observation but from multiple observations through rigorous testing in attempts to negate the hypothesis or conclusion. Ultimately, since we do not have access to everything and cannot observe anything absolutely or directly, the scientific method should be used to search for evidence to refute the hypothesis, not confirm it. The black swan example is often used to describe this theory. A man stated all swans are white after only ever observing white swans in the town in which he lived (positivist statement). Although this is all he has ever seen, his conclusions are false as there are black swans in different parts of the world. Therefore, just because he did not see a black swan does not mean they do not exist. Similarly, from a counseling context, mental illness is often viewed differently across the world as certain parts of the world believe mental illness does exist while other areas do not believe mental illness exists. According to post-positivists and the Theory of Falsification, science is about making hypotheses and not testing to prove them right but testing them rigorously to prove them wrong. It is only when the hypotheses cannot be proven wrong or broken that truth and knowledge are discovered (Crotty, 2003). Thus, the post-positivists accept that knowledge is imperfect because the researchers influence it, but through scientific rigor and objective testing, we are closer to understanding the truth.

Pioneers of Post-Positivism

Although there were many influential people during the 20th-century studying the philosophy around scientific inquiry, there are two pioneers that were significant in our current conceptualization of science and how we understand the philosophy behind it. Sir Karl Popper and Thomas Kuhn were integral in the creation of the post-positivism paradigm and its advancement. Sir Karl Popper (1902–1994), born in Vienna and an economics professor and philosopher in London, was one of the first to challenge positivists' views. He is known for his writing and many books but one of his most famous, *The Logic of Scientific Discovery*, focused on contrasting and clearly differentiating scientific work and pseudo-sciences (Crotty, 2003). Popper spent his time confronting the positivist use of the scientific method on induction and using scientific testing to confirm general laws as opposed to challenging them. He was concerned that making claims about a phenomenon and only searching for evidence to support such claims led to irrefutable pseudoscience. He believed if we do not critically investigate science or our beliefs, we can always find what we want. Therefore, Popper believed in using the scientific method to test hypotheses searching for evidence to refute theories. He believed science is about falsification, not confirmation; thus, coining the term and creating the Theory of Falsification. An example of this in our current quantitative research methodologies is the idea of hypotheses and null hypotheses. As researchers, we are not conducting a study to prove the hypothesis is true (i.e., a specific intervention causes a particular outcome) but we are attempting to reject or disprove the null hypotheses (i.e., there is not a difference or impact on various behaviors due to the specific intervention) as our results are written as "fail to reject or reject the null hypothesis."

Another pioneer of science philosophy is Thomas Kuhn (1922–1996), an American Philosopher of Science with a PhD in Physics from Harvard University. Kuhn wrote one of the most influential books of modern-day science, *The Structure of Scientific Revolutions,* encapsulating historical and sociological perspectives of science questioning the objectivity and value-free neutrality of researchers (Crotty, 2003). Kuhn believed that researchers conducted their investigations and observed the world in and out of contexts and theories. According to Kuhn, the package of beliefs and theories that the researchers operate from form a *paradigm.* Kuhn coined the term *paradigm* to describe the ways researchers view and make sense of the world. Paradigms allow researchers to have assumptions about existence, reality, and truth so that they are able to investigate other phenomena based on those assumptions. Kuhn believed that without paradigms or assumptions, science would not advance. However, there are times in which the paradigm cannot explain findings; therefore, a *paradigm shift* needs to occur. According to Kuhn, it is in this new way of viewing reality that a scientific revolution occurs. Kuhn's beliefs strongly contrast the beliefs of objective, value-free, and detached researchers through asserting that scientific endeavors include human interests and values.

THE HISTORY OF CONSTRUCTIONISM

The epistemology of constructionism was developed by Seymour Papert (1928–2016), who studied under Piaget (the major contributor to constructivism). Papert describes constructionism as a method of education as opposed to an action in education (i.e., constructivism). Constructionism includes three major theoretical stances: constructivism, interpretivisvm, and critical inquiry. Constructivism is the idea that one's worldview is based on their own beliefs and perceptions of an experience. It differs from constructionism, because constructivism functions more as an action of understanding a construct as opposed to constructionism being the development of the construct. For example, using the construct of altruism, applying constructionism is understanding how it came to be (e.g., innate, learned) and applying constructivism is how one understands or defines it (e.g., doing something for someone without expecting anything in return). Interpretivism is examining data in a subjective way and interpreting the depth that it represents. Critical inquiry is understanding the influence of societal factors on values and knowledge.

CONSTRUCTIVISM

Constructivism is the idea that one's worldview is based on their own beliefs and perceptions of an experience. Constructivists believe that people "construct" their world based on the influence of several factors including (a) the physical environment, (b) the social environment, (c) their culture, and (d) prior experiences. The "truth" within constructivism is in the individual's description of an event and how they make sense and meaning of an experience. Two people can experience the same event, but the reality of what happened is based on each individual's view; therefore, their descriptions could be very different but are very true for each person. A process exists within constructivism, meaning the way something begins may be very different at the end. This process is based on the transfer of information and the influence of place, society, culture, and experiences. A simplified description of constructivism is the childhood game of telephone. Although there is a right and wrong, from what the word started as to what it "should" end as, each child hears the word in their own way based on what they believe they heard. A researcher who utilizes a constructivist theoretical stance wants to answer their research question based on the experiences and perceptions of the participants involved in the study, instead of the results of a psychometric measurement.

Pioneers of Constructivism

Constructivism is rooted in educational learning theory and development. Jean Piaget (1896–1980) is the pioneer of constructivism. He was a Swiss psychologist who focused on child cognitive development. His theory of development consists of four stages: the sensorimotor stage, the preoperational stage, the concrete operational stage, and the formal operational stage. He valued play throughout the lifespan and recognized that children obtained knowledge and meaning from their experiences—more specifically, through assimilation (i.e., connecting new experiences to previous ones) and accommodation (i.e., changing views of previous experiences and gaining new ideas based on new experiences). Another important contributor to constructivism is Lev Vygotsky (1896–1934), a Russian psychologist who established the Social Development Theory, which is foundational to constructivism (Daniels, 1996). Unlike Piaget, he believed that social learning came before development. Vygotsky examined the impact of society on a person's language and thoughts. He believed that cognitive development was influenced by social interactions and peoples' beliefs and perceptions were based on these exchanges. Another pioneer of constructivism was an American philosopher and educator, John Dewey (1859–1952). Dewey developed progressive education in North America, which went against the traditional lecture and rote memorization approach to teaching. Instead, Dewey suggested that children should have hands-on experiences when learning and be active participants. He believed that people gained knowledge from experiences they find important and meaningful (Neubert & Reich, 2009).

INTERPRETIVISM

Interpretivism relies on researchers interpreting the data in a subjective way and examining the depth that data represent. Interpretivism is the opposite of positivism (i.e., that truth is found in direct observation and measurement). The foundation of interpretivism is in hermeneutics, which is the science of interpretation. The intent of interpretive research is to examine how people come to understand or interpret, not to identify a specific process for understanding (McManus Holroyd, 2007). Interpretivism is based on the idea that people are complex beings and that they understand and experience reality in individual ways. Researchers function as interpretivists to examine and make sense of the differences between participants in a study. Additionally, interpretivist researchers are aware that they cannot be separated from their own knowledge and experiences. Therefore, they acknowledge the connection between them and their participants and the topic of the study and are keenly aware of their bias. Interpretivists believe that truth consists of multiple interpretations and is measured by understanding experiences of participants. Instead of directly measuring constructs in a quantitative manner, interpretivists use qualitative data collection methods (e.g., interviews, reflective journaling) to explore phenomena. More specifically interpretivists are not interested in what can be directly observed, instead they probe to understand the subjective view of people and truly seek to understand the values, prejudices, feelings, and perspectives (Wellington & Szczerbinski, 2007).

Pioneers of Interpretivism

As mentioned, interpretivism is rooted in hermeneutics. Friedrich Schleiermacher (1778–1834) was a German biblical scholar, who focused on hermeneutics, specifically related to interpreting the Bible. He wanted to know *how* people understood communication (i.e., text and verbal) not just *if* they understood it. At the German Historical School during the 1880s, scholars were beginning to value the "many sciences" view, which supported the idea that there were multiple ways to conduct and understand research. Wilhelm Dilthey (1833–1911) and Max Weber (1864–1920) were both philosophers and idealists who believed that truth is a combination of peoples' ideas and the physical world and that the two ways of experiencing truth cannot be separated (Glesne, 2011). Dilthey focused on human sciences by applying Schleiermacher's hermeneutics to understand peoples' lived experiences and how they interpreted social-historical contexts. Weber's work centered around religion and culture. He developed the Social Action Theory, which focuses on the social actions of people and, more importantly, interpreting the meaning behind the actions. He emphasized the importance of understanding or "verstahen" of the whole person rather solely focusing on just the immediate situation. Dilthey and Weber introduced the concept of how defining social institutions (e.g., marriage) is based on the interpretation of the person involved rather than what society "says" it should be. Therefore, according to interpretivists, one's interpretation of a situation is their truth and meaning, regardless if others see it as the truth (Chowdhury, 2014).

CRITICAL INQUIRY

Critical inquiry supports that one's truth is socially constructed by values and knowledge and influenced by societal factors such as media and politics. Critical inquiry acknowledges the importance of power and agency of individuals (Mack, 2010) and the interaction of race, class, gender, sexuality, and religion. More specifically, "critical researchers intentionally adopt the ethical, moral, political standards to judge the situation and practice their research with consideration of social, economic, political and cultural context for specific research's objects or events" (Hammersely, 2013, p. 30). As previously stated, researchers seek truth through direct communication (i.e., speech, discussion) with participants (Fui, Khin, Khin, & Ying, 2011) and critical inquiry emphasizes the influence of language and how it impacts our reality. According to Horkheimer (1982), one of the leading critical inquiry theorists, critical inquiry should include three criteria: (a) identify what is wrong with social reality currently, (b) identify an action-oriented way to change it, and (c) provide a framework for criticism and transformation.

Pioneers of Critical Inquiry

Pioneers of critical inquiry include Max Horkheimer (1895–1973), Theodor Adorno (1903–1969), and Herbert Marcuse (1898-1979), who were all part of the Frankfurt School. Additionally, although not considered among the pioneers of critical theory, it is important to acknowledge Paulo Freire's (1921–1997) contributions to critical pedagogy, specifically his publication of the *Pedagogy of the Oppressed* (Freire, 1970). The Frankfurt School was not an actual school, it was a school of thought centered on the development of critical theory and a collaboration of scholars who were associated with the Institute for Social Research at the University of Frankfurt in Germany. The Frankfurt School of thought is centered around how oppression is caused by social factors such as politics, culture, consumerism, and economics, and that peoples' awareness of this process is crucial to changing it. Horkheimer was the director of the Frankfurt School, and he believed that advancements in technology were influencing culture and persuading people to have a unified view instead of allowing them to have their own ideas. Marcuse focused on consumerism and believed that the people were convinced they needed something, instead of actually needing it. Adorno studied self-destruction and human suffering. He believed peoples' thoughts and beliefs were influenced by media and their workplace, therefore, they were unable to have their own individual thoughts. All contributors to the Frankfurt School, emphasized the importance of people's ability to be critical of "what is" and more focused on "what could be" (Glesne, 2011).

THE HISTORY OF SUBJECTIVISM

René Descartes (1596–1650), a French philosopher and known as the father of modern philosophy, developed the epistemology of subjectivism. Subjectivism centers on the idea that truth is found in a person's experience. Subjectivism includes two major theoretical stances: feminism and post-modernism. Feminism is focused on the influence of the perception of women's roles on social norms. Post-modernism is based on the idea that all truth and knowledge should be challenged because it is created by those it benefits.

FEMINISM

Feminist theory is aligned with critical inquiry, but it is more rooted in the concept that traditional roles of females and males have been socially constructed and that they are based on power that was assigned to men. Feminist theorists view gender as a social construct that impacts and determines the function of our lives and, in regard to research, gender influences how we gain and share knowledge (Maynard, 2004). Feminist theory supports the idea that social norms can be reconstructed if people identify the historical context in which these norms were created. The foundation of feminist theory is based on three core beliefs: (a) traditionally, society is set up to prioritize men and is patriarchal; (b) historically, the subordination of women is supported; and (c) identifying ways to achieve equality for all should be prioritized (Tong, 2001). Creswell (2013) stated that researchers utilizing feminist theory "center on and make problematic women's diverse situations and the institutions that frame those situations" (p. 29).

Pioneers of Feminism

There are three waves of feminism and each had its own focus and pioneers. Susan B. Anthony (1820–1906) and Mary Wollstonecraft (1759–1797) were pioneers of the first wave; they focused on women's lack of legal rights and the impact it had on their oppression. Betty Fiedan (1921–2006) and Andrea Dworkin (1946–2005) were pioneers of the second wave; they concentrated on women's reproduction rights and sexual identity. The third wave was pioneered by Judith Butler (1956–) and Gayatri Spivak (1942–1977), who recognized the need to be aware and appreciate the differences among women (Krolokke & Sorensen, 2006).

POST-MODERNISM

Post-modernism is based on the idea that all truth and knowledge should be challenged because it is created by those it benefits. Post-modernism emphasizes multiple ways of knowing and deconstructing traditional ways of knowing. The focus of post-modernism is to question the approach to inquiry within social science, and to be more accepting to other forms of inquiry (e.g., literature and arts; Gall et al., 2007). Post-modernism researchers do not align with traditional scientific research methods, and challenge power and authority. Within post-modernism, there are several continuums of philosophical beliefs: (a) progressive to conservative, (b) reaction and resistance, and (c) reform to the disruption of status quo. Additionally, post-modernism challenges the value of research for all people and recognizes that the approach and findings are not universal and are ethnocentric. Scheurich (2013, p. 1), a post-modern researcher, stated that:

> *even though we researchers think or assume we are doing good works or creating useful knowledge or helping people or critiquing the status quo or opposing injustice, we are unknowingly enacting or being enacted by "deep" civilizational or cultural biases, biases that are damaging to other cultures and to other people who are unable to make us hear them because they do not "speak" in our cultural "languages."*

Pioneers of Post-Modernism

Jean-Francois Lyotard (1924–1998), a French philosopher, was a major contributor to post-modernism in the 1980s; he authored the book *The Postmodern Condition*. Jacques Derrida (1930–2004) was also a pioneer of post-modernism. His work centered on the theory of deconstruction, which focused on challenging the traditional Western thought and is closely related to post-modernism. Fredric Jameson (1934–) is a Marxist political theorist and authored *Postmodernism, or the Cultural Logic of Late Capitalism* (1991), in which he emphasized the influence of media and capitalism on people's beliefs and ways of living.

RESEARCH TRENDS IN THE HELPING PROFESSIONS

Helping professions have a long history of working with and for people to improve individuals' lives and the world around them. The work of early philosophers, like Plato (428 BCE–347 BCE) and Aristotle (384 BCE–322 BCE), laid the foundation for the curious, paving the way for future trail blazers to research and develop the fields of counseling, psychology, social work, and marriage and family therapy. As a student of Plato and a product of his moral philosophy and moral thinking, Aristotle was among the first to write about ethics (Kraut, 2018). Some of Aristotle's work was centered on the golden mean (i.e., the concept that moral behavior can be found in the middle, or the mean, of the two extremes of excess and deficiency). Aristotle believed that discussing one's *eudaimonia* (happiness) leads to an examination of their nature of *arete* (virtue or excellence), allowing human beings to explore the character traits that lead to them living their best life (Kraut, 2018), indirectly channeling the work that many helping professionals do today. Found in many ancient cultures, the chanting or reciting of mantras are connected to work done within the helping professions such as mindfulness and meditation. Furthermore, during the age of enlightenment (late 17th century to late 18th century), individuals began to intellectually challenge cultural norms, placing emphasis on reason, individualism, and skepticism and finding ways to provide support, financial or otherwise, for those who were in need. Although these professions overlap in many ways, they all address different needs and provide unique services to individuals and society. Additionally, each profession has evolved and continues to grow using research to enhance the legitimacy of their professions and better serve society. The history and development of each of these helping professions could easily be elaborated further through an in-depth review; however, this section serves as a brief overview of key pioneers and the influence of research over time in each field (Table 2.1).

TABLE 2.1 Helping Professions, Relevant Degrees and Licensure, Pioneers, and Research Trends

HELPING PROFESSION	DEGREES AND LICENSES	PIONEERS	TRENDS IN RESEARCH
Counseling Counselors have training in ethical practice, social and cultural diversity, human growth and development, career development, helping relationships, group work, assessment, and program evaluation.	**Degrees** Master's, Education Specialist (EdS), or Doctorate (PhD) degree **Licenses** School Counseling, Clinical Mental Health, and Clinical Rehabilitation	Frank Parsons (1854–1908) Carl Rogers (1902–1987)	• Parsons pioneered the vocational guidance movement • Carl Rogers defined the role of a counselor by creating core conditions, expressing genuineness, empathy, and unconditional positive regard • Group therapy grew rapidly along with assessments and data collection on counseling practices • Development of data and implementation of valid and reliable research methods
Psychology Psychiatrists are board certified medical doctors, trained in therapeutic relationships, psychopathology, diagnosis, and human development and psychological and biological theories of behavior.	**Degrees** Medical doctor (MD) or Doctor of Osteopathic Medicine (DO) **Licenses** Psychiatry	Sigmund Freud (1856–1939) Wilhelm Wundt (1832-1920) William James (1842–1910) B. F.Skinner (1904–1990)	• Began with Freud • Wundt and James opened the first laboratories • Pavlov, Watson, and Skinner researched behaviors in a laboratory setting • Notable trends in psychology include structuralism, functionalism, psychodynamic, behaviorism, cognitive, and social-cultural
Social Work A social worker is trained in understanding an individual's environment, social and economic influences and can identify beneficial social agencies and community resources to support clients.	**Degrees** Bachelor of social work (BSW), master of social work (MSW), and doctor of social work (DSW) **Licenses** Administrative MSW and clinical social worker	Jane Addams (1860–1935) Frances Perkins (1880–1965) Whitney M Young Jr. (1921–1971)	• The Poor Law was put into place to support individuals facing starvation • Charity Organization Society was formed in 1869 • Jane Addams established Hull House in Chicago, Illinois, in 1898 • Research in the field of social work was lacking • Currently research in the field is still relatively new but is now more reinforced by the Counseling on Social Work Education accrediting body
Marriage and Family Therapists Marriage and family therapists work with families and couples to address issues as a whole.	**Degrees** Master's degree, Education Specialist (EdS), or Doctorate (PhD) **License** Marriage and family therapists and couples and family counseling	Gregory Bateson (1904-1980) Murray Bowen (1913–1990) Jay Haley (1923–2007) Nathan Ackerman (1908–1971) Carl Whitaker (1912–1995) Virginia Satir (1916–1988) Salvador Minuchin (1921–2017)	• Exploration into marriage and family therapy began following World War II • Soldiers returning impacted family dynamics and changes in the workforce • Looking for insight into schizophrenia, therapists began looking into family systems and dynamics • Group therapy stemmed from work that therapists did in family counseling • Many theories addressing family stressors and dynamics have developed from the work of marriage and family therapists

COUNSELING

Pioneers and Legacies. Although the counseling profession is considered to be young in relation to the psychology and social work fields, there are a number of influential counselors who paved the way for new ways of thinking about human behavior, treating individuals, and evaluating effective treatments. In the late 1800s, the first forms of contemporary counselors emerged. Beesley (2004) described school-based professionals like primary and secondary teachers as such, using their position to guide school children in their academic and social development. Following the USSR's 1957 launch of the Sputnik satellite, the demand for counseling professionals significantly increased. As Russian technology advanced, the United States Congress passed the National Defense Education Act of 1958 (NDEA) which provided support for guidance program in school and training for guidance counselors (Bradley & Cox, 2001). The counseling profession was greatly influenced by the field of psychology; however, it began to take its own form with the emergence of the guidance movement in response to increased mental health and guidance needs for those facing developmental milestones. Frank Parsons (1854–1908) is often referred to as the Father of Vocational Guidance (Blocher, 2000). Parsons began his career as an engineer and a lawyer, but he found himself exhausted and uninterested in the career he had initially pursued. Parsons sought out many other career opportunities including teaching art at a public school, working in publishing, laboring in an iron mill, and working as a college professor in both social sciences and in law. Following many attempts at a number of jobs, he considered his own career explorations to be a series of mistakes. This belief led him to call a meeting of local neighborhood boys that were on track to graduate. Parsons inquired about their knowledge of the world of work. After discovering that their knowledge was both lacking and uniformed, he began advising them and others, leading him to establish the Vocation Bureau. Throughout his late career in vocational guidance, Parsons wrote 14 books, developed the first self-inventory or questionnaire for interests, aptitudes, and personality to match work environments, and designed the first counseling agency. Parson's creation of the first counseling agency sparked the development of vocational guidance in schools. He was the first to frame counseling as a mutual process involving cooperation between an expert and client. As stated, Parsons not only became known as the Father of Vocational Guidance but was also considered an activist and advocate for clients (Granello & Young, 2012).

Another key figure and a true pioneer for counseling practice and research was Carl Rogers (1902–1987). His idea of counseling became a foundational staple in the development of the counseling profession and the establishment of new counseling theories. Rogers's emphasis on the counseling relationship and the role of the counselor was vastly different than the current theoretical approaches to working with clients at that time. He believed that the counselor must create the "core conditions" of genuineness, empathy, and unconditional positive regard and the therapeutic relationship was the vehicle of change for positive client change. Not only was Rogers a gifted counselor, he was a strong researcher and writer. Rogers's book, *Counseling and Psychotherapy* (1942) was a collection of his innovative concepts and research on the helping relationship. Additionally, he published *Client-Centered Therapy* in 1951, a major work for the counseling profession that not only became a major counseling theory that is still widely used today but it also ignited the humanistic movement among his fellow clinicians (Granello & Young, 2012).

Trends. Soon after Rogers's impact and the explosion of the humanistic movement in the early 1970s, a wave of group therapy took the United States by storm. Many of these therapeutic groups were conducted by clinicians and other individuals who were not licensed and were considered to be paraprofessionals. Though groups were seemingly beneficial, there were practices conducted by nonprofessionals that pushed boundaries without grounds in effectiveness for group participants (Granello & Young, 2012). Consequently, counselors began noticing an increased need for research and data to support the practices conducted in therapy and provide data about effective treatments. Although research was always a part of the counseling profession as counseling theories were derived through systematic and careful examinations of client change over time, the heightened awareness for scientific support among the counseling profession erupted as America was expanding its industry. During this time, science began to take hold partly because of the work being done by Thomas Edison, opening new doors and inquiries into the reliance of scientific findings and how data can be used to validate counseling practices and ideas peaked. Many counselors were interested and began using data and research to inform their practice; however, due to the interest of using data and research to inform practices, some members of the profession felt appraisal or use of testing on clients clashed with the core values of counseling (Granello & Young, 2012), causing a discussion surrounding best practices to evaluate and work with clients. Additionally, counselors struggled with creating and using valid assessments and measurements; therefore, test scores were not as reliable. Over time, the development of appropriate data collection methods, assessments, and evaluations increased, and therefore the implementation of valid and reliable research methods progressed.

Another notable trend within counseling is the concept of wellness. Throughout history, the concept of wellness can be found woven within ancient civilizations, ethical codes and foundational tenets of counseling and medical fields (Blount et al., 2016). However, in the field of counseling, practitioners have placed emphasis on taking a holistic and wellness-oriented approach. Though a variety of wellness models have been proposed, many of those versions being based in the physical health professions or in the positive psychology movement, there is one current model that is grounded within counseling theory, The Individual Self or IS-WEL Model. This model stemmed from the early works of Sweeny and Witmer (1991) and Witmer and Sweeney (1992) when they originally developed the Wheel of Wellness Model based on Individual Psychology (Sweeney, 1998). Those models were later expanded into a new, evidence-based wellness model called The Indivisible Self (Myers & Sweeney, 2004). For mental health and counseling practitioners, the IS-WEL Model gives a strength and evidence-based approach that can be integrated into counseling practices.

Building off of the work done by Piaget (1954) surrounding the developmental stages of children, there is consideration of the developmental perspective in the work that counselors do with their clients. In the early 1960s psychologists like Kohlberg (1968) and Loevinger (1966) explored ways in which adults develop from an infant that has tendencies of self-centered needs to an adult with mature approaches with meaningful actions (Cook-Greuter & Soulen, 2007). By linking what developmental psychologists know about human development, counselors can assist their clients in their personal growth as they navigate the different aspects of their lives. However, just as counselors can utilize and consider the insights about development in their work with clients, counselors follow their own developmental process in their skills as a clinician (MacCluskie & Perera-Diltz, 2012). According to MacCluskie and Perera-Diltz (2013), almost all counseling skill instructional models attend to four components: exposure to helping skills knowledge and information which includes theoretical knowledge; an observation of learned counseling skills in action, practice, and experience; and finally, feedback and supervision. A developmental perspective can be seen throughout the field of counseling in the ways in which clients are conceptualized as well as through the development of counselors themselves.

The emphasis on multicultural counseling competency (MCC) has emerged as a crucial aspect in the work that counselors do with their clients. The MCC movement can be tracked back to articles published in the 1950s (Abreu, Chung, & Atkinson, 2000) that called for the need to address the counseling needs of Black Americans, and in the 1960s when the Civil Rights Movement gained traction and there was an increase in racial and ethnic diversity among counselors and psychologists, pressing the American Psychological Association to take note and action within the mental health professions. During the Vail Conference of 1973, the discussion of psychological practice and cultural diversity materialized. It became apparent after this conference that providing professional services to individuals who come from a culturally diverse background is unethical if the counselor is not competent in that area and, in response to this conclusion, it is necessary for graduate training programs to teach appropriate cultural content. In a summary statement, Korman (1973) defined cultural competence as a matter of ethical practice and recommended that issues of cultural diversity be included in education and preparation programs. Work done by Sue and Sue (1977) pioneered this early discussion of multicultural competence. This early literature aimed to define what MCC is while working to identify ways for counselors to learn how to become competent in multicultural counseling. In 1982, Sue et al. published the *Position Paper: Cross-Cultural Counseling Competencies*. The competencies outlined in this paper included beliefs and attitudes, knowledge, and skills that a counselor needs to practice with MCC. This · paper has served as a foundational element for MCC investigations to come as well as led to a call in 1992 from Sue et al. for the profession to implement multicultural counseling competencies and standards in counseling practice and education. Professional accrediting bodies such as the APA's Accreditation Handbook (APA, 1986) and Guidelines for Providers of Psychological Services to Ethnic, Linguistic, and Culturally Diverse Populations (APA, 1993), are mandated to promote MCC. Following suit, counselor preparation programs that are accredited by the Council for Accreditation of Counseling and Related Educational Programs (CACREP) must integrate and teach multicultural competencies to their students.

As research in counseling continues to grow, there has been more of a shift from practice-based evidence to evidence-based practice. Practice-based evidence is evidence developed by doing or evidence developed in session. It is typically more anecdotal but can also include quantitative measures or quantitative engagement with clients; however, practice-based evidence is strictly based on what works for a particular counselor and what the counselor sees in practice with clients. Measures often used in practice-based evidence are client outcome measures or process measures, most often completed by clients themselves. Although practice-based evidence is more subjective, it often is used to inform evidence-based practices. Evidence-based practice uses systematic, empirical research to inform treatments and then implementing those treatments clinically. The focus becomes more specific and often focuses on what treatments are effective for what diagnosis or populations. Rigorous research and growth in evidence-based practices not only demonstrate the validity of counseling, but also help gain funding for the profession. Furthermore, the increase in research and evidence-based practice increases the availability of counseling services to as many people as possible, increases trust and faith in our profession, and maintains counselors' ethical responsibility to clients to use therapeutic practices that are effective for their best care. Therefore, the training of future counselors and counselor educators have research integrated into their curriculum as required by the Council for Accreditation of Counseling and Related Educational Programs (CACREP, 2016).

PSYCHOLOGY

Pioneers and Legacies. Before the rise of contemporary applied psychology, research of the human mind can be attributed to work done by Franz Anton Mesmer (1734–1815) and Franz Josef Gall

(1758–1828). Gall was a German neuroanatomist who created phrenology in the 19th century which is the idea that the brain in a human being was the center of thought and will power, and that by examining the bumps on an individual's head, you can judge their character (Aston, 2013). Now viewed as a pseudoscience, phrenology was an initial emergence of the examination of the human mind (Aston, 2013). Mesmer began studying a practice known as animal magnetism. Mesmer believed that every individual had magnetic fluid flowing through channels throughout their body; if there were blockages in the flow of the fluid, this would cause emotional or physical disease. In some cases, certain individuals had more or less animal magnetism. Mesmer would sit facing patients, with their knees touching as he would move his hands over different parts of their bodies in sessions that could last hours. Mesmerism shifted toward what we now view as modern hypnosis with the work of Marquis de Puysegur (1751–1825) and was continued by Dr. James Braid (1795–1860), a Scottish medical doctor (Kappas, 2012). At the end of the 19th century, mesmerism, hypnosis, and phrenology took a back seat to the emerging works of psychology. The field of psychology has a vast research history and began to gain global attention in the late 1800s. Early researchers like Sigmund Freud, Wilhelm Wundt, William James, and B. F. Skinner began to explore the intricacies of the human mind and behavior. Sigmund Freud began as a Viennese physician when his own research led him to develop and then apply methods of hypnosis, free association, and dream interpretation that was aimed to reveal a person's unconscious beliefs and desires. Freud would work intensely with clients to examine their thoughts, both conscious and unconscious, while attempting to diagnose the causes of distress or conflict the patient was experiencing (Prochaska & Norcross, 2014). Though Freud's work was foundational in the field of psychology, Wilhelm Wundt opened the Institute for Experimental Psychology at the University of Leipzig in 1879. Wundt, a German physician, philosopher, and professor, was among the first to separate psychology from philosophy to analyze the workings of the mind in a more structured and calculated way. The development of this laboratory was the first of its kind dedicated to psychology and is thought to be the beginning of modern psychology. Paralleling Wundt's work, an American physiology instructor, William James opened a small experimental psychology laboratory at Harvard University. James's most notable contribution to psychology was his role in developing the field of functionalism. As a whole, functionalism countered the existing field of structuralism. Functionalism focused more on the objective aspects of the mind and the influence of the environment, while structuralism focused more on the processes of thought and introspection (Stangor & Walinga, 2014).

As the field of psychology continued to grow, different branches of psychology were developed, and more pioneers of the field paved the way to new insights of human behavior. The early works of Ivan Pavlov (1849–1936) studied a branch of learning behavior called a conditioned reflex and his theory of classical conditioning was born. Following Pavlov, Max Wertheimer, Kurt Koffka, and Wolfgang Kohler, German psychologists who immigrated to the United States looking to escape Nazi Germany, were the founders of Gestalt psychology. Gestalt psychology focused on how individuals experienced and organized their perceptions (Saber, 2013). Another influential American psychologist, John B. Watson, furthered Pavlov's work examining human behavior. Although, Watson's work with "Little Albert" sparked discussion due to his controversial experiment, both he and Pavlov were instrumental in developing the field of behavioral psychology (Bergmann, 1956). In addition to Pavlov and Watson, according to Brennan and Houde (2017), the work done by B. F. Skinner spiked advances in the field of behavioral psychology by harnessing the knowledge of operant conditioning. Initially influenced by the work of Pavlov (Woody & Viney, 2014), Skinner continued to advocate for the need to examine and explore behavior in an experimental way by using environmental and reinforcement contingencies in his research (Brennan & Houde, 2017).

Trends. Within the field of psychology, there were evolutions and different branches that grew from the development of modern psychology. Some of the most impactful and notable trends include structuralism, functionalism, psychodynamic, behaviorism, cognitive, and social-cultural. Each of these individual branches aimed to explain and explore different elements of what we know about human behavior. The role of research and the use of empirical data are foundational elements in the field of psychology. However, this too had a progression over time. Psychology began as a branch of philosophy, but its tenets do not lend itself to objective or rigorous evaluation. The field of psychology moved to a more experimental psychology context in the early 1880s, which led to the creation of a variety of applied psychology applications (e.g., clinical psychology, counseling psychology, sport psychology; Prochaska & Norcross, 2014). Over time, psychology moved from more philosophical theories to the study of unconsciousness and consciousness, to behaviors, cognitions, and interdisciplinary approaches to studying the human mind including evolutionary psychology, linguistics, and neurobiology. It is through the growth of experimentation and the emphasis on empirical data that psychologists adhere to the scientific method for evaluation and assessment. Additionally, psychological research tends to focus on correlational research, descriptive research, and experimental research. Reliance on quantitative measures and naturalistic, objective observation has been, and continues to be, a consistent research trend throughout the psychological field. Condensing the foundations of research of psychology into a brief section is a feat that leaves many influential people without mention. It is important to remember that psychology acts as a founding field to the helping professions while still standing alone and thriving today. The individuals who began to study human behavior and the human mind have paved the way for all of us in the helping professions to continue to research and explore the ever-evolving world and the people in it. Today, there are a few contemporary research trends in applied psychology that include the impact of climate change, growth of drug-free pain management, a demand for more sports psychologists, and understanding how nutrition impacts mental health (APA, 2018).

SOCIAL WORK

Pioneers and Legacies. Social work as a profession began to take shape in the 19th century as a response to the fear of poverty or the impoverished becoming a social threat in the United States and United Kingdom. As a result of the mass migration where many Europeans voluntary migrated to the Americas, overcrowding in various eastern American cities ensued causing social problems and healthcare needs to rise. To address these needs, the first professional social workers in America were trained by Richard Clarke Cabot, in 1905 at Massachusetts General Hospital. Mirroring the Americas, the United Kingdom was facing its own societal needs where poverty was viewed as menace to social order. In the United Kingdom a societal intervention was put into place to address poverty known as the "Poor Law" in 1834. Under this law, support from that individuals' own parish would be provided to people who were completely destitute and facing starvation (Pierson, 2011). Though this law was flawed, the new "Poor Law" was one of the first to establish a welfare system that would support and care for individuals who were living in poverty. Throughout the mid-19th century, there was an increase in volunteer activity as various associations set out to address a new social reality, mass urban poverty. Formally known as the Society for the Organization of Charitable Relief and Repressing Mendicity, the Charity Organization Society (COS) was formed in 1869 with sights set on validating and coordinating charitable giving. The COS is recognized as a significant development of social work, realizing that when coordinating with charities and leading by example, their reach could extend further (Pierson, 2011). One of the earliest influential professionals in social work was Jane Addams (1860–936). Addams was considered an activist, community organizer, international peace advocate and a social philosopher in the United States. Though she is well known for the work she did in the social settlement movement, Addams was one to challenge and explore conventional gender understandings alongside male philosophers like John Dewey and William James (Hamington, 2019). As the creator of the U.S. Settlement House Movement, she led the charge to establish settlement houses in areas of urban poverty. Focusing on the root causes of poverty, she used research to educate middle-class social workers to provide education, legal, and health services to those in need. She established the Hull House in 1898 in Chicago, Illinois, which, according to Schneiderhan (2015), served as an incubator for many ideas that would become the foundation of modern social work. Other notable social workers include Frances Perkins who was the first woman to be appointed to the cabinet of a U.S. president and Whitney M. Young Jr. (1921–1971) who was the executive director of the National Urban League while he worked as the Dean at the Atlanta School of Social Work (Schneiderhan, 2015). Developed in 1910, the National Urban League is a civil rights organization that dedicates itself to the economic empowerment, equality, and social justice on behalf of African Americans and other historically underserved groups. The National Urban League can be found in 36 different states along with the District of Columbia; has 90 affiliates serving 300 communities targeting the development of social programs and public policy research; and provides advocacy for policies and services that close the equality gap (National Urban League, 2020).

    Trends. Similar to other helping professions, the legitimacy of social work as profession was questioned. It was often argued that since social work lacked application of theoretical knowledge to solving human issues, it was a semi-profession (Carr-Saunders & Wilson, 1936). Therefore, in the early 20th century there was an increase in effort by social work professionals to focus on casework and the scientific method to boost educational opportunities in social work. After World War II, social work professionals provided services for military veterans and became leaders in promoting social justice for those in need. Although the social work profession made great strides in increasing educational opportunities and creating professional standards of practice, they were still lacking in the use of research. Therefore, a new generation of post-war social workers wanted to transform the training and practice in the profession to be more research driven. Rosen and Proctor (2003) state that social work is distally related to research because using research in the field is still relatively new. Founded in 1952, the Council on Social Work Education (CSWE) was created as a national association that would represent social work education in the United States. Social workers began engaging in research to solve practical problems in social practice and social policy. Currently, the CSWE is the accrediting body for social work programs and built within its accreditation competencies, social workers are to understand and engage in practice-informed research and research-informed practice, working to advance the science of social work (CSWE, 2015). Through increased use of research, enhanced educational opportunities, structured training, and consistent competencies, social work has emerged as a top profession in social justice advocacy and social policies.

MARRIAGE AND FAMILY THERAPY

Pioneers and Legacies. Although it may be difficult to pin-point the exact time or the first person to create a movement, the initiation of marriage and family therapy can be traced back to the decade following World War II when practitioners realized that there is something to be said about the family's role in creating and stabilizing psychological disturbance in one or more family members. In light of sudden family reunions after the war, there were a number of problems that arose in family dynamics on the spectrum of social, interpersonal, cultural, and situational instances (Goldenberg & Goldenberg, 2016). Therapists were tasked with handling the influx of mental health needs of individuals returning home from war while families were experiencing an array of problems. Some of these problems consisted of new job transitions and educational opportunities for soldiers returning home, an influx of immigration due to war-time conflict, and changing gender roles due to women in the workplace deciding to either return home or to continue working. Conflicts arose because the world was trying to return to the pre-war era in a post-war world. As needs grew and more individuals within family systems were affected, psychologists, psychiatrists, social workers, and counselors started to investigate family relationships and the interactions between members (Goldenberg & Goldenberg, 2016).

In Freud's early work, he acknowledged that families play an influential part in an individual's life. When conflict occurs within the family system, Freud assumed that the individual would internalize the issue. This belief caused him to concentrate on treating the person engaged in the conflict rather than trying to address the system that was causing the problem (Goldenberg & Goldenberg, 2016). Although Freud did not treat the family unit, his awareness of the influence of the family on an individual led others to examine the family influences on people. Initially, setting out to explore schizophrenia and the pathogenic role of the family environment, researchers, such as Frieda Fromm-Reichmann, began to explore early mother–child relationships in adults diagnosed with schizophrenia. In the mid-1950s, a major demand for family research in the area of schizophrenia presented itself, leading researchers like Gregory Bateson, Theodore Lidz, and Murray Bowen to investigate the presentation of schizophrenia separately, not connecting their research until later. Before work done by Bateson, Lidz, and Bowen, counselors and psychologists did not work with the whole family, just the individual. Bowen's realized that solely treating the individual was not producing long-lasting outcomes for his patients, which led him to examine the relationships of patients that he worked with (Metcalf, 2011). Therefore, family therapy was initially created and carried out for specific scientific research purposes. It should also be noted that Gregory Bateson was one of the initial individuals who was able to recognize the complexities of the social and behavioral sciences, therefore placing emphasis on understanding how human interactive systems work (Goldenberg & Goldenberg, 2016). In 1956, Bateson and his colleagues, Don Jackson, Jay Haley, and John Weakland, developed the double bind theory of schizophrenia which hypothesized the cause of schizophrenia was linked to an individual who consistently receives equal disapproval for doing something or not doing it (Corsini, 2002). For instance, if a child is told that they are messy but when they make an effort to clean, their actions are dismissed, they are basically in a lose–lose situation. Forming his own theory, after working with his own patients that were clinically admitted to the hospital that he oversaw, Bowen moved to working with the whole family unit for therapy, coining the term "emotional divorce," which described the patterns of interaction between parents, which could lead to the development of schizophrenia (Waring, 1978). While the conclusions drawn by both Bowen and Bateson were found to be neither objective, repeatable, or controlled (Waring, 1978), these pioneers did serve as the catalyst for the exploration of family and family systems in therapy.

As more helpers began noticing and valuing the impact of families on individuals and vice versa, a number of key pioneers in the family therapy field emerged. Nathan Ackerman, a child psychoanalyst, is credited with having written the first paper addressing the treatment of the entire family. This article confronted the norm of treating the child and parent separately (Akerman, 1937). Years following Ackerman's work, John Bell, a psychologist working in academia, was another notable creator in the development of family therapy. Bell applied group therapy techniques to working with entire families and, unlike his colleagues, he worked with families who did not have members of their family diagnosed with schizophrenia. Similarly, Don Jackson developed a set of descriptive constructs for insight into communication structures within families like family rules (Goldenberg & Goldenberg, 2008). Additionally, Carl Whitaker integrated the use of a co-therapist and the intergenerational family members in a patient's therapy resulting in a highly active style with patients which was considered innovative for this time period. Following Carl Whitaker, Salavodor Minuchin expanded family work to include environmental contexts and influences. He is most noted for his work on the Minuchin's Wiltwyck School Project (Minuchin, Montalvo, Guerney, Roasman, & Schumer, 1967) where he assembled researchers and therapists to reform the institutional setting for youth in a correctional facility to a family-oriented approach. As well, Minuchin developed structural family therapy, which was a systemic approach focusing on problem resolution while being mindful of the social environment or context from which the family problems emerged and were maintained (Goldenberg & Goldenberg, 2016). Minuchin also recruited Braulio Montalvo and Jay Haley to train clinic staff and minority paraprofessionals to work with families at the Philadelphia Child Guidance Clinic in 1967 after he was appointed as the director. The clinic went on to adopt working with families in the treatment of diabetes, asthma, and anorexia (The Minuchin Center for the Family, 2020). Lastly, Virginia Satir is a major notable individual in development of family therapy. Satir published *Conjoint Family Therapy* in 1964, which was crucial in popularizing the family approach when working with individuals. Satir was a captivating presenter as she was highly emotional, experiential, and engaging at meetings and workshops all over the world. Though most of the foundational years of marriage and family therapy can be linked to the 1950s and the work done by Nathan Akerman, John Bell, Don Jackson, Murray Bowen, and Carl Whitaker, the expansion and further development of the field can be attributed to work done by Jay Haley, Salvador Minuchin, and Virginia Satir.

Stemming from the work of the pioneers just described, marriage therapists emerged looking at the dynamics within couples and the life experiences individuals bring into relationships. Marriage and pre-marriage counseling are based on the concept that psychological disturbances come to the surface when there is a conflict between two individuals. Focusing on the particular struggles that come with marriage, early marital counselors included social workers, psychologist, college professors who worked as family-life specialists, physicians, and even lawyers, as they were all assumed to be "experts" and would offer their advisements when people needed answers through sexual and marital difficulties (Broderick & Schrader, 1991). It was not until Emily Mudd initiated the creation of the American Association of Marriage Counselors (AAMC) that any unity in the marriage and counseling field was established. The AAMC brought together professionals who had stake in the new field of marriage counseling and created a formal professional code of ethics for the discipline (Broderick & Schrader, 1991).

Trends. As mentioned earlier in this section, many of the foundations of family therapy stem from the research that was done early on in the field surrounding schizophrenia, leading to expansion in the discipline including family group therapy and the child guidance movement. Research in marriage and family therapy began examining families of individuals with specific diagnoses and then transitioned to examining family structures, communication patterns, and more proactive treatment to reduce psychological disturbances and enhance individual and family functioning. In terms of research, marriage and family therapists continue to strive for more empirical data to inform treatments and enhance the field. However, research has always been an important element to the marriage and family profession as Akerman and Jackson established the first research journal for family therapy, entitled, *Family Process*, with Jay Haley as the first editor. The journal's purpose was to enable researchers and practitioners to network their ideas and eventually led to the planning and organizing of national conferences. The creation of research journals not only disseminates innovative work to those in the field but also increases the legitimacy of the profession and promotes research and data to inform treatment.

Today, much of the work that was started by Bateson, Akerman, and other pioneers in the field continues. Contemporary trends such as medical family therapy and marital therapy can be found within marriage and family therapy. Medical family therapy emerged in the 1980s to address the shortcomings within the healthcare system. The sub-field of family medical therapy (MedFT) aimed to address to the lack of communication and collaboration between mental health and medical professionals and added a holistic approach to patient care that bridged the gap between mind and body, creating a clear lapse in care that needed to be addressed (Tyndall et al., 2012). Though MedFT has been defined by McDaniel et al. (1992), as a "biopsychosocial systems model and actively encourages collaborations between therapists and other health professionals" (p. 2), Linville et al. (2007) expanded that definition to "an approach to healthcare from a biopsychosocial-spiritual perspective, informed by systems theory" (p. 86). Over time, MedFT has evolved from a clinical orientation or framework to an area that makes contributions to and enlightens research surrounding the work that clinicians, mental health and medical professionals do with families and can often be found in training programs for family therapy (Marlowe, 2011).

As similar but slightly different areas, martial and couples therapy emerged to meet the needs of individuals in different stages in their romantic relationships. Around the 1930s marriage counseling centers began to establish themselves, but at the time, they were not managed by counselors but by other professionals like clergy and gynecologists. According to Gurman and Fraenkel (2002), there have been differing views on whether or not couple therapy should be addressed within family counseling but until the 1960s, all couples counseling took place in separate sessions with the individuals working separately rather than together. Gurman and Fraenkel (2004) describe the history of couple therapy in four phases: (a) Theoretical Marriage Counseling Formation (1930–1963); (b) Psychoanalytic Experimentation (and reemergence) (1931–1966 and 1985– present); (c) Family Therapy Incorporation (1963–1985); and (d) Refinement, Extension, Diversification, and Integration (1986– present). Attesting to the value of couples therapy, Gurman and Fraenkel state that couples therapy is both reparative and preventive which has greatly contributed to the understanding that we as counselors have surrounding intimate relationships. There are a multitude of theories that aim to address family stressors and dynamics, similar to the counseling profession. Research and data continue to drive innovative practices and determination of efficacy among current treatments. As the trend for increased empirical support for the marriage and family profession continues, research competencies have been integrated into marriage and family curricula as required by the Council for Accreditation of Counseling and Related Educational Programs (CACREP, 2016).

Case Study Example

Nick is a first-year doctoral student in a counselor education program. As a new doctoral student, Nick is working on transitioning from his work as a school counselor to becoming a scholar and a researcher. Over the course of his program, Nick will continue to develop his new researcher identity and begin to integrate his clinical identity and expertise with his researcher and scholar identity. As a part of his first semester in the doctoral program, Nick is tasked with an assignment to create his own research study with future plans of implementation. Unsure of where to start, Nick decides to begin to integrate his school counseling experience into his research by focusing on an area of interest that relates to his previous work as a school counselor. Nick is interested in the school counselors' experiences with school shootings or school violence and its impact on school counselors' personal and professional wellness. Still learning about quantitative and qualitative research methodologies, Nick is unsure which methodology would be best to examine his interest; he decides he needs to take a closer look into how he believes knowledge or truth is determined. Reading more about the *realism* and *relativism* ontologies, he decides that he isn't 100% on board with either perspective but believes that there are times in which both realist and relativist ontologies provide an accurate understanding of knowledge and truth. Since Nick is struggling with which ontology best represents his beliefs on reality, he decides to allow his research question to guide him through the process of selecting and aligning his research ontology, epistemology, theoretical stance, and methodology. Based on Nick's professional experience and interest, his primary research question is, "What are the lived experiences of school counselors who have endured a school shooting or threats of other mass violence in their school?"

Based on Nick's research question and the main emphasis on school counselors' *experiences,* Nick is led to accept the *relativist* ontology that truth and reality are determined through our experiences. Now that Nick chose the relativist ontology, his next step is to decide on his *epistemology* or his theory of how knowledge is acquired. Under the relativism ontology umbrella, Nick has a choice between *constructionism* (i.e., reality is created by individuals/groups) or *subjectivism* (i.e., reality is perception) as his epistemological perspective. After much deliberation and reflection on how he believes knowledge is acquired and what he believes his research question is really asking, Nick decides that constructionism best fits his views and his research aim for this study. As Nick continues to move through his research paradigm, he is constantly reflecting on his views and beliefs as well as checking back to his research question ensuring that all the components (ontology, epistemology, theoretical stance, methodology, and methods) align and fit together. The alignment of all paradigm components leads to increased strength and validity in his research design and study. Next, Nick has to decide between the two key *theoretical stances* under the constructionist epistemology: *constructivism* (i.e., knowledge is constructed through interactions with others) and *interpretivism* (i.e., knowledge is interpreted based on lived experiences). Since his research question clearly emphasizes his interest in the *lived experiences* of school counselors and how they have interpreted school violence, Nick chooses interpretivism as his theoretical stance for this study. Now that Nick has an integrated understanding of the ontology, epistemology, and theoretical stance driving his investigation, he can now decide on the best methodology or means to study this phenomenon. Nick's paradigm pathways led him toward a *qualitative design* and a choice between phenomenological research, grounded theory, narrative research, consensual qualitative research, and possibly mixed Methods research. Although Nick's research question could fit several different qualitative methodologies, the best fit falls under the *phenomenological research methodology.*

SUMMARY

In Chapter 2, you learned about the history of social science research. More specifically, you learned about the components of a research paradigm. You now know that realism and relativism are the two major ontologies in social science research. Additionally, you are aware that there are three major epistemologies: objectivism, constructionism, and subjectivism. Within each epistemology there are theoretical stances that provide the foundation for scientific inquiry. Objectivism includes positivism and post-positivism. Constructivism, interpretivism, and critical inquiry are all theoretical stances of constructionism. Subjectivism is comprised of feminism and post-modernism. Whether you are conducting qualitative or quantitative research, it is important to approach your research utilizing a paradigm to help you navigate the process. Additionally, now you can recognize who generated each theory within research paradigms. Finally, now you have a clearer understanding of the history and trends in the helping professions; specifically, counseling, psychology, social work, and marriage and family therapy. All of the information from Chapter 2 will help you understand the paradigms of each research tradition presented in the rest of the chapters. Understanding a research paradigm is often a missed step of the research process, but it is an important one! Now you have the tools to conceptualize your paradigm of your research approach using a series of constructed entities about how problems should be considered and addressed.

SUMMARY POINTS

- Two types of ontology in social science research are: realism and relativism
- Positivism and post-positivism are theoretical stances within objectivism
- Constructivism, interpretivism, and clinical inquiry are theoretical stances within constructionism
- Feminism and post-modernism are theoretical stances with subjectivism
- Each helping profession has research trends that highlight the changes within social science research

STUDENT ACTIVITIES

Exercise 1: Your Paradigm

Directions: Using Figure 2.1 and reflecting on your personal beliefs on existence and knowledge and your professional experiences, describe each component (i.e., ontology, epistemology, theoretical stance, methodology) of the paradigm that best aligns with your beliefs and views of the world. Based on the paradigm you most closely align with, what does this mean about the focus of your future research? Which components of a paradigm are the hardest to accept or understand?

Exercise 2: Theoretical Stance

Directions: Choose two theoretical stances discussed in this chapter and write a research question on a topic of interest to you and your profession that would align with the tenets of that theoretical stance.

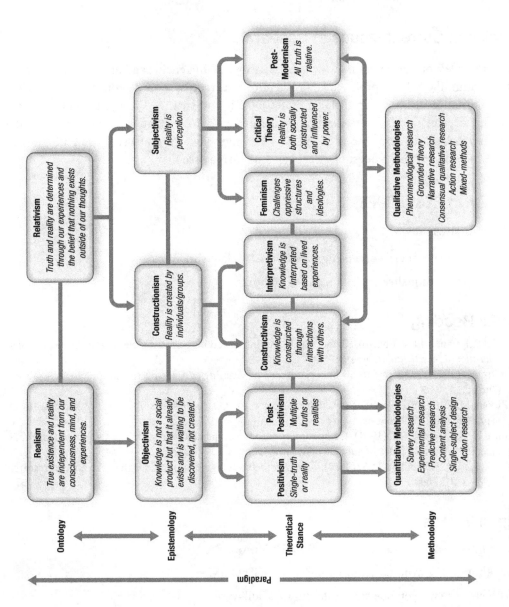

FIGURE 2.1 A closer Look at Research Paradigms.

Exercise 3: Identifying Trends

Directions: Consider the helping professions of counseling, psychology, social work, and marriage and family therapy. What are trends that you notice within each profession? Where do they align, differ, and intertwine with one another?

Exercise 4: Current Issues in Research

Directions: Reflect on current issues which have a history of influencing and inspiring the research interests within the helping professions. (a) Identify a current issue or need in society. (b) How does the current issue impact the helping professions? (c) In what ways can your future research impact that need or trend? After reflecting on these questions complete the following: Using the relativism ontology, develop a research question related to your current issue. Using the realism ontology, develop a research question related to your current issue.

ADDITIONAL RESOURCES

Helpful Links

- https://www.socialworkers.org/News/Facts/Social-Work-History
- http://www.qualres.org/HomePhil-3514.html

Helpful Reading

Abdul Rehman, Adil & Alharthi, Khalid. (2016). An introduction to research paradigms. *International of Educational Investigations, 3*(8), 51–59.

Crotty, M. (2003). The foundations of social research: Meaning and perspective in the research process (2nd ed.). SAGE

Glicken, M. D. (2005). *Improving the effectiveness of the helping professions: An evidence-based approach to practice.* Sage Publications.

Guba, E., & Lincoln, Y. S. (1994). Competing paradigms in qualitative research. In N. K. Denzin & Y.S. Lincoln (Eds.), *Handbook of qualitative research* (pp. 105–117). Sage.

Novikov, A.M. & Novikov, D.A. (2013). Research methodology: from philosophy of science to research design. CRC Press.

Helpful Videos

- https://www.youtube.com/watch?v=zUh5mAekUfA
- https://www.youtube.com/watch?v=v0T4GSgOiqM&t=519s
- https://www.youtube.com/watch?v=wf-sGqBsWv4
- https://youtu.be/a4VzRSnksmA

KEY REFERENCES

Only key references appear in the print edition. The full reference list appears in the digital product found on http://connect.springerpub.com/content/book/978-0-8261-4385-3/part/part01/chapter/ch02

Creswell, J. W. (2013). *Qualitative inquiry amd research design: Choosing among the five approaches.* SAGE.

Crotty, M. (2003). The foundations of social research: Meaning and perspective in the research process (2nd ed.). SAGE.

Freire, P. (1970). *Pedagogy of the oppressed (MB Ramos, Trans.)*. Continuum, 2007.

Heppner, P. P., Wampold, B. E., Owen, J., Thompson, M. N., & Wang, K.T. (2016). *Research design in counseling* (4th ed.). Cengage.

Novikov, A.M. &Novikov, D.A. (2013). *Research methodology: from philosophy of science to research design*. CRC Press.

Woody, W. D., & Viney, W. (2017). *A history of psychology: The emergence of science and applications*. Routledge, Taylor & Francis Group.

CHAPTER 3

A GUIDE TO THE LITERATURE REVIEW AND AMERICAN PSYCHOLOGICAL ASSOCIATION STYLE

James S. Korcuska, Amanda C. La Guardia, and Emily J. Sturn

LEARNING OBJECTIVES

After reading this chapter, you will be able to:

- Identify the four tools of effective academic writing
- Create concept maps to support theory development and research criteria for literature reviews
- Address multicultural context in academic writing including employing bias-free writing
- Describe the purpose and structure of the *Publication Manual of the American Psychological Association (7th ed.)* as a tool for successful academic writing
- Understand the basics of preparing a manuscript for publication

INTRODUCTION TO THE LITERATURE REVIEW AND AMERICAN PSYCHOLOGICAL ASSOCIATION STYLE

Successful academic writers effectively use four tools for discovering and disseminating research. The first tool, the concept map and literature review, plays a key role in the process of discovery, as it illuminates and directs the focus of the research by identifying where the research has been and the potential for where the research may go. The second tool is precise and credible writing, which showcases the writer's ability to present clear and well-founded approaches to knowledge construction. The third tool is an approach to research and writing incorporating intersecting multicultural contexts, diversity, and strategies to reduce bias. The fourth and final tool is the *Publication Manual of the American Psychological Association (APA), Seventh Edition*, which is essential for disseminating research.

The purpose of the *Publication Manual* is to standardize scholarly communication. Standardization aids readers to assess a manuscript's content efficiently and accurately. Standardization also ensures readers have the essential information to determine the quality of a paper or manuscript. Academic writing is the art of "precision" (APA, 2019; p. 132). Precision and standardization, however, can be at odds with approaching academic research and writing from an inclusive and culturally humble mindset. Scientific language constrains what is researched and published (Matías-Guiu & García-Ramos, 2011). In short, the very production of scientific knowledge excludes other ways of knowing. Excluding other ways of knowing, such as indigenous research methodologies (e.g., Tuhiwai Smith, 2012), limits the precision, complexity, and breadth of the knowledge bases revealed through scientific writing.

No wonder, given the complexity of research and writing tasks, graduate students in the social sciences find academic writing difficult to learn, let alone master. Our goal in this chapter is to identify the purpose of each and to offer guidance for using them to improve your skills as an academic writer and researcher. We also explore the connection between writing and thinking by way of an approach for researching and writing a literature review, which includes creating concept maps to support the theoretical foundation of a literature review and addressing multicultural issues in academic writing. You will also learn how to use the *Publication Manual of the American Psychological Association, Seventh Edition,* to improve your academic writing and avoid common errors of APA style. Finally, we offer suggestions on translating the paper, thesis, or dissertation into a manuscript ready for submission to a publication.

MULTICULTURAL AND SOCIAL JUSTICE—COMPETENCY (SECTION 5)

We begin with the multicultural and social justice–competency as a framework for the remainder of the chapter. Cultural considerations in writing are expansive and can include the mechanics of language through to the context by which information is framed and communicated to an audience. Transcultural research includes a consideration of the context by which information is gathered, engagement practices, supra-cultural consideration in the intersectional and transformative nature of scholarly work, as well the method by which findings are distributed (König & Rakow, 2016). A scholar must consider not only the cultural context of participants but those of stakeholders and potential consumers of the research. The first step is to think about your own racial and ethnic identity and relationship with the dominant culture (Table 3.1). What aspects of your identity fit with the dominant narrative and what identities seem to be marginalized with regard to cultural expectations of said identity?

Reflections about identity can move into diversity issues, beyond culture, race, and ethnicity. An introspective process will assist in becoming aware of, evaluating, and checking your own bias as a researcher. We are all influenced by cultural messaging and expectations; thus, this reflective process is important for each of us to engage in when developing our research design, analyzing data, and ultimately presenting results. Poe (2013), building on Huot (2002), suggested using a *Frame for Race* in writing that focuses on situating race locally (populations and needs) and in a context-specific way, identifying expectations of stakeholders and potential stereotyping in both your assumptions of them and their stated interests, and making connections between language and race (linguistic diversity). While this process is specific to race, ethnicity, and cultural linguistic diversity, the concepts extend beyond into other realms of diversity. Thus, attention to issues of race are expansive and serve as a useful first step when attempting to conceptualize intersections of diverse identities (gender, sexual and affectional orientation, ability, social economic status/experience, etc.). Engaging in a reflective process that challenges your experiential lens will assist you as you expand your knowledge about yourself, others, and the topic you're researching.

TABLE 3.1 **Becoming Anti-Racist and Multicultural Responsive in Writing**

AREAS OF BECOMING	SELF-REFLECTION	LOCAL REFLECTION	STEREOTYPING OF EXPECTATIONS	LINGUISTIC INTERSECTIONS
Fear	• Am I striving for comfort/ease? • Do I avoid hard questions? • Do I tend to consult people who think and look like me?	What is my willingness to use inclusive perspectives and language in my writing? How do I label populations that may be impacted by my scholarship?	What stereotypes do I ascribe to? Am I open to perspectives of others when they challenge my own? What identity groups do I interact with?	What is my position on grammar and use of language in technical writing? How do I recognize language use in context?
Learning	• How can I be vulnerable about my own biases and knowledge gaps? • When do I listen to people who think and look differently than me? • Have I sought questions that make me uncomfortable?	Who does my research serve? How am I creating specificity and context to honor participants? How can my research design better address the needs of the population of focus?	Have I sought to interact with identity groups that I don't typically engage? How is has my writing and research been contextually inclusive of race and ethnicity?	What are my racialized assumptions of linguistic diversity? What is my awareness of how language patterns are codified and taught?
Growth	• How do I unknowingly benefit from racism? • How do I educate my peers through my writing about how racism harms our profession? • How am I willing to yield my power or use it to advocate for those otherwise marginalized?	What is the historical legacy of the terminology I use in my writing? How is my research designed and written in a way that is multi-leveled and meaningful to participants and readers alike?	How does my writing challenge stereotypes? How does my research address social constructions of identity? How are potential stereotyped expectations of others influencing my writing?	How can writing be a cultural practice and the diversity of language a cultural resource? How is your language use tied to your cultural and racial identity?

NOTE: Based on Ibrahim's Model (@AndrewMIbrahim, Twitter, 6 June 2020) and Poe (2013)

THE LITERATURE REVIEW

Graduate students often struggle researching and writing a literature review. The literature review is more than gathering articles on a topic area and summarizing them. Writing a literature review is akin to putting together pieces of a jigsaw puzzle (Western Sydney University Library, 2017). It fuels discovery and research. Academic writing promotes critical thinking about research (Parker,

1985), as well as the craft of writing. Writing about what we have read for a review of the literature facilitates critical thinking. Thus, writing promotes critical thinking about research (Meyer, 1997; Parker, 1985), as well as growth as a writer. Thus, we first write to learn and then to communicate what we have learned (Parker & Goodkin, 1987).

A literature review is an examination and synthesis of information relevant to an identified topic and is most often presented in a narrative format. The complexity of the literature review process is influenced by the varying types of literature, the distinctive types of literature reviews, and the method used in the review process. The type of information included in the review is contingent on the topic in question, the goal of the review, the depth and breadth of information available, access to information, and the criteria established by the review method and research question. One tool to aid in the process of defining a topic and determining the goal of a review is to create a concept map.

CONCEPT MAPPING

A concept map is a tool to clarify the theoretical development of a topic. Using a concept map to support the formation of new ideas and organize what is known about a topic can provide direction and serve as a guide for the literature review process. Concept maps are a visual and external expressed model of the internal representation of knowledge (Chang, 2007; *How to Make a Concept Map*, 2018). When thinking about a topic, everyone has a cognitive structure or mental model that represents what is known about that topic (Novak & Cañas, 2007). Concept mapping creates a visual map of mental constructs to help make sense of the information, understand theory, and connect interrelated concepts (Alias & Suradi, 2008). When applying them to literature review topics or research questions, concept maps promote meaningful learning, knowledge creation, and theory development (Novak & Cañas, 2007). There are many ways to construct concept maps. In the following we describe one way (Figure 3.1 offers a visual representation; it is not intended to convey content).

The first step in creating a concept map is to write a focus question that the map will explain. For example, if you are creating a concept map that explained the process of writing a literature review, a focus question might be: What encompasses a literature review? Once a focus question has been established, a single domain, that is, topic under review, should become evident. (Continuing with the same example, the selected domain is *literature review*.) Next, pinpoint three to six key concepts that are most significant in that domain. Key concepts are represented by a new shape and color, as using differing shapes and colors to denote levels can highlight the hierarchical structure of the concepts. When developing concepts within domains, consider the context in which those concepts occur and how intersections of diversity and culture influence those domains (e.g., linguistic access to potentially relevant research).

Then, arrange the domain and key concepts in a top-down fashion, with the domain at the top of the map and the key concepts evenly spaced underneath. Connected lines, arrows, and enclosed boxes define the space and relationships (Daley et al., 2010). Each connection is linked in a meaningful way with a propositional word or phrase, such as, generate, identify, develop, or support. Move horizontally and vertically on the map, further identifying and linking main ideas related to each key concept through words or phrases and visual lines. These main ideas can also be broken down into subsequent connected components that link to other main ideas in the same or differing key concepts. Through this process, a network of complex relationships will emerge. Some relationships will connect to more than one key concept, indicating interrelationships and the intricacy of the representation and construction of knowledge. To reiterate, the colors, shapes, and sizes of shapes all support the hierarchical structure of concepts composing the construction of the domain.

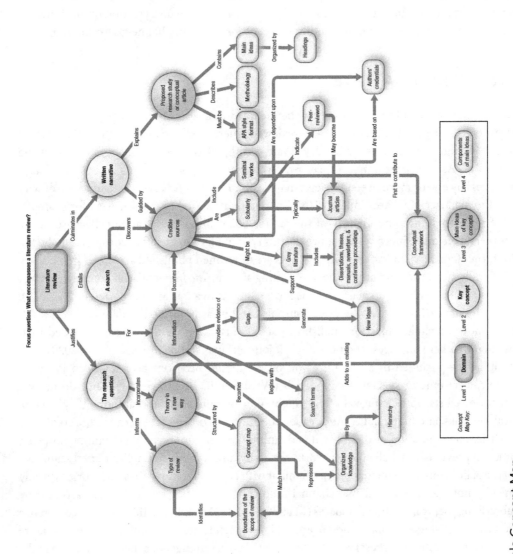

FIGURE 3.1 Example Concept Map.

NOTE: This is a visual and not intended to convey content.

Because of the cross-links and interrelated concepts, concept maps are dynamic and continually evolving as new knowledge is created and relationships become more empirically focused and validated (Novak & Cañas, 2007). Before diving into the literature, an initial construction of a concept map may provide insight into the aims of the review and can assist in reflection on any initial conceptions or assumptions, potential stereotypes, and biases associated with a topic. Once the literature has been explored, revisions to the concept map may generate a new understanding and conceptualization of the topic. This can lead to the organization and creation of the literature review narrative or provide insight into another facet of the literature that needs exploration.

TYPES OF LITERATURE

There are various kinds of literature that may be included in a review. The purpose and scope of the review dictates the kind of literature to be reviewed. There are three distinct types of literature: peer-reviewed, non-peer reviewed, and grey (Ward-Smith, 2016). Peer-reviewed literature is the most common. As the name implies, peer-reviewed manuscripts have undergone a thorough review process by one or more peers. Reviews may be blinded. A blind reviewer is unaware of who authored the manuscript (Ward-Smith, 2016). There are unblinded reviews as well; for example, where the reviewer knows the identity of the author but is blind to the author. Because of the rigorous review process of peer-review journals, this type of literature is often considered to be the superior form of quality publications. These works are most often published as articles in scholarly journals. Scholarly journals are also subject to a rating system, *The Impact Factor*, and high impact scholarly journals or frontier journals have the most citations in a 2-year time period (APA, 2019). Not all articles appearing in peer-reviewed journals can be easily located in databases, however. Databases show a language bias for English in part because they are more easily accessed than those written in other languages, and non-English journals may not be indexed (Hays, 2020).

Not all articles included in a literature will be, or should be, from peer-reviewed journals, for example, electronic or special issue journals (Ward-Smith, 2016). Although they do not get the peer-reviewed stamp of approval often sought after by publishers and authors, they may be empirical, rigorous, and high quality. As a reader, the burden is on you to determine the credibility of the article. The reputation of the journal and author are other markers of credibility; however, as mentioned previously, not all credible works are easily discoverable in English biased searches.

The type of literature that you may be least familiar with is grey literature. These are works typically published by nontraditional academic channels and can be easily disseminated and accessed by non-subscribing users on Internet databases (Marsolek et al.,2018). Dissertations, theses, conference proceedings, newsletters, manuals, and government documents are all examples of grey literature and are now discoverable and preserved in Internet repositories. Indigenous literature may be in the form of stories, metaphors, and songs, for example (Hays, 2020) Securing this form of literature may involve directly speaking with participants. The internet and search engines allow online material related to a topic to be easily explored and obtained, though it's important to note that grey literature does not refer to online-only material and printed copies of works are also considered to be under this umbrella. Systematic literature reviews are typically the most common type of review that utilizes grey literature, as this type of review is often comprehensive and integrative in nature; however, any type of literature review may contain grey literature (Cronin et al., 2008; Marsolek et al., 2018).

The date of publication is also important. Typically, inclusion criteria are typically set for the last 5 to 10 years of published studies (Paré et al., 2015). You may search outside this timeframe based on your topic or purpose. For example, you may wonder about evolution of the kinds of research methods used by counselors over the past 20 years. This would be a reason to move beyond the typical period. Additionally, some works stand the test of time. These are known as seminal works. Seminal works have a standing in the literature, for example, most citations, on the current topic of interest (Bornmann et al., 2016; Cronin, et al., 2008). They may have a place in your paper or manuscript. For example, if you were reviewing the literature to assess current trends in psychoanalysis, you would likely include content written by Freud as it establishes a historical context needed to understand the current study.

TYPES OF LITERATURE REVIEWS

The kinds of literature, for example, peer-reviewed, included in the review is influenced by the type of review selected and subsequent search and analyses processes unique to that review. There are at least nine different types of literature reviews: argumentative, critical, historical, integrative, methodological, narrative/traditional, scoping/mapping, systematic (subtypes: meta-analysis, meta-synthesis, and umbrella), and theoretical. These are summarized in Table 3.2. The type of review used is determined by the review's goal and research question. Determining the type of review to implement often involves identifying the goal and purpose of the review.

DESIGN THE REVIEW

Consider the research question, the participants, the audience, and the purpose before conducting a review (Pautasso, 2013). Authors at the Joanna Briggs Institute (JBI, 2014) offer two strategies for organizing the review. The first strategy—Population, Intervention, Comparison, Outcome (PICO)—is used with quantitative studies. Recent revisions to the JBI (2019) method for reviews have amended PICO to Population, Exposure of Interest (independent variable), and Outcome (dependent variable; PEO). The second—Participants, Phenomenon of Interest, Context/Setting (PICo) is used for qualitative studies.

The first step in defining a research question for your study is to identify the who (Population/Participants). In the second step identify the what (Intervention/Phenomenon of Interest). For quantitative studies, this usually involves the participants being exposed to an intervention of some sort; whereas in qualitative studies, the goal is not to act upon the participants, but to observe and understand them in a certain context.

The context leads to the third and final step in qualitative research. Identification of the where (Context/Setting) the observation took place. What context are the participants going to be in? An example would be…How do new teachers at the local community elementary schools experience connectedness? *Participants* are new teachers; the *phenomenon of interest* is connectedness; and the *context* is in the school and in the community. For a quantitative study, following the PEO method, the third step refers to either the *Outcome* or how did the exposure influence the participants? However, if the PICO method is applied, there is an additional step which includes identifying a *Comparison* group to which to compare the intervention. This also includes having a specific way to measure the final step, or *Outcome*. Were there significant differences in outcome between the groups because of the intervention? An example of this using the previous example content would be: Are there significant differences in perceived connectedness in the school between new teachers who were part of an ongoing welcome group compared to new teachers who were not part of the

TABLE 3.2 **Types of Literature Reviews**

TYPE OF REVIEW	BRIEF DESCRIPTION	PURPOSE	STRENGTHS	LIMITATIONS
Argumentative (Grant & Booth, 2009; Rowe, 2014)	Identify literature that either supports or refutes a specific argument	Provide strong evidence for one position; persuade others	Extensive research and presentation of material for a specific topic or viewpoint	Problems of bias
Critical (Grant & Booth, 2009; Paré et al., 2015)	Assess the trustworthiness of the source and findings. Primary focus is to find weaknesses, discrepancies, and holes in research	To analyze the quality of the research	Quality control	Subjective
Historical (Grant & Booth, 2009)	Follow the historical evolution of a topic, theory, or phenomenon during a specific time period or specified dates	To see the evolution of a topic and to understand where existing theories have come from	Puts the topic of research within a historical context so as to see the developments and provide insight into where future research might be justified	Not always necessary to know the origins of a topic and could be quite extensive if there is a long history
Integrative (Grant & Booth, 2009; Ward-Smith, 2016)	Integrates and synthesizes research findings from all relevant sources, literature typologies, and research methodologies. This review serves as rationale for the generation of new ideas and perspectives for research and theoretical frameworks	Primary aim is to synthesize all relevant research on topic of interest	Comprehensive and exhaustive	May include research from non-peer–reviewed sources, which are not always quality controlled
Methodological (Grant & Booth, 2009; Munn et al., 2018)	Examines the methodologies used by researchers to study a research topic. Concerned with understanding how the data have been analyzed in the literature and focuses less on what was studied	Concerned with the quality of the research methods being used. To study effectiveness of methodology	Allows for quality assurance and identifying optimal methods, as well as relevant criteria for establishing significance	Time consuming. Still might need to have another literature review to support the topic
Narrative/Traditional (Cronin et al., 2008; Grant & Booth, 2009; Paré et al., 2015)	Summation of literature on a topic typically with no clear process or system to the search. The researcher selects sources based on ease of access and relatively general knowledge of the topic of interest	To get a general idea of what is known about a topic to assist in establishing a research question	Quick and efficient, literature is easily accessible	Subjective, hard to replicate, and not necessarily representative of all empirical research on the topic

TYPE OF REVIEW	BRIEF DESCRIPTION	PURPOSE	STRENGTHS	LIMITATIONS
Scoping/Mapping (Arskey & O'Malley, 2005; Grant & Booth, 2009; Khalil et al., 2016; Levac et al., 2010; Paré, 2010; Tricco et al., 2015).	Introductory search of all literature available on the topic of interest; including ongoing research. Aim is to identify what is known about the topic and the extent of information already available regarding the research interest. Research questions are broad. May be systematic or not	Collect preliminary account of activity for a specific research topic or area of interest and identify gaps in the literature	Rapid review. Gives an overview of the breadth of literature available and possible directions for future research and assists in narrowing the research question	Extensiveness of information is dependent on time and resources available to the reviewer. Shortcuts might be taken and quality appraisal may not be included
Systematic (Boell & Cecez-Kecmanovic, 2015; Grant & Booth, 2009; Onwuegbuzie et al., 2012; Munn et al., 2014; Paré, 2010; Rowe, 2014).	Pre-determined method of reviewing the research is decided prior to beginning the review. A well-defined hypothesis or question of interest is at the forefront of the review and the fixed method allows for a critical and standardized way of accumulating, evaluating, and describing the studies under review. The method of collection and analysis must be described in detail with complete transparency regarding process, including protocols to reduce bias	Graphical presentation of findings	Reduces bias and provides standardization of how the research is used and presented	Time consuming and little flexibility in analysis once the method of review has been established
Three Subtypes: Meta-analysis	Evaluates variability between results, effect sizes, potential sources of bias, and predicting relationships among variables	Statistically descriptive. Sets up rationale for theory testing in quantitative research	Uses statistical analysis to recognize and analytically evaluate the literature	
Meta-synthesis	Review of literature using non-statistical methods, with predetermined inclusion and exclusion criteria. Analysis and synthesis of the findings from many qualitative studies using a specific coding system	Qualitative research. Derive literature from many sources, including interviews, photos, observations, drawings, video, etc. (sometimes referred to as grey literature)		

(continued)

TABLE 3.2 (continued)

TYPE OF REVIEW	BRIEF DESCRIPTION	PURPOSE	STRENGTHS	LIMITATIONS
Umbrella	A review of reviews	Allows for the collection of a wide range of information that has already been reviewed	Efficient. Identify gaps in the reviews	
Theoretical (Grant & Booth, 2009; Onwuegbuzie et al., 2012; Paré, 2010; Tungpunkom, 2015)	Synthesizing the literature on a specific theory, issue, concept, or phenomenon by recognizing what themes or constructs already exist, identifying relationships between the existing theories, analyzing to what extent the offered theories have been explored, and creating new hypotheses that could be investigated in future studies or the current proposed study	Offers evidence for the use of a new or revised conceptual framework. Included in qualitative and quantitative research to introduce a hypothesis and create rationale for the research study. Typically presented in a narrative format	Exhaustive and comprehensive	Time consuming. Demands quality writing and synthesis of information in a cohesive, clear manner, and relevant to overarching topic

group? In this example, the population is still the teachers; the intervention or exposure of interest is the welcome group; the comparator is perceived connectedness (which is likely measured using a survey or assessment); and the outcome is if there were differences in perceived connectedness between the new teachers who received the intervention compared to the teachers who received no intervention.

The next step in a systematic review is to identify inclusion and exclusion criteria for sources, methodologies utilized in studies, and types of literature. In an integrative design, all types of literature would be utilized, and less emphasis would be placed on when the information was published. Any type of review should have basic parameters around the search to prevent it from becoming overwhelming or spending too much time on it because of no clear end point to stop. Generally speaking, it is preferable to start with a narrow focus and then expand the limits later if necessary (Paré et al., 2015). For this literature review, we used the past 10 years as a barometer; however, if we found an article older than 10 years that was mentioned consistently in the current research, we considered it a seminal work (Bornmann et al., 2016). Seminal works have a standing in the literature; for example, most citations, on the current topic of interest. For example, the Arskey and O'Malley published their method for a scoping review in 2005, but because it was mentioned in subsequent other articles, we included it.

CONDUCT THE SEARCH

When conducting the search, the best first place to start is on an online academic database search site. Most universities have this feature on their library's directory. For example, the database used in conducting the literature review for this book chapter is EBSCO host, which is affiliated and accessed through my university's library website. Academic journals and online databases typically require subscriptions to access the entire article.

When searching an online database, use keywords or phrases to secure the most robust results. Trying different combinations of words can also be helpful. Using the rules of Boolean searching assist in specific searches and generating relevant results. When researching keywords, think about alternative definitions. For example, the word "connectedness" could refer to connection, relationship, or belonging. Adding those keywords to your search might yield larger results. Therefore, it is important to clearly define the research question and set boundaries around exact search criteria. Perhaps you are meaning connectedness in a different way than relationship or belonging, then it becomes important to define what is meant by connectedness and how that differs from those other similar concepts, as well as the rationale for using the definition you have chosen. Research the data again to identify areas that may have been missed upon the first search and to solidify the existing sources as consistent with other search attempts and databases. When the same authors and articles continue to reappear in the search, this is a good indication that the search has been exhaustive and inclusive of all relevant data available.

ANALYZE THE LITERATURE

The next step is to analyze the literature. Typically, you will not read each article upon discovery and determine inclusion or exclusion from the review at that point. The researcher does a preliminary scan of an article, title, author, journal, abstract to get a baseline for judging if the article is worth a more in-depth exploration. You will need to develop your own system for organizing potential sources, often utilizing tables and categories to sort the sources and information. The system you use may be contingent on the review being conducted and the inclusion criteria set forth at the beginning of the process.

The next step is to determine if and how the article relates to and supports the research question. Identify the most pertinent articles and make decisions about their relevance and credibility while including potential intersections of culture and diversity. This analysis can be time consuming; however, employing an effective and organized method for reviewing each article can save time and energy. One of the methods cited in the literature on conducting literature reviews includes the acronym, PQRS, Preview, Question, Read, Summarize (Cronin et al., 2008). Preview or scan the article by first reading the abstract and keywords and then identifying questions that you have about the article content before reading it in its entirety. Some of those questions might include further inquiry into the method, outcome, or theoretical basis for the study in question.

The final step is to analyze the findings. Begin by taking notes and highlighting significant findings and elements (Pautasso, 2013). Then, summarize the main points—the research question, the method, and the outcome of the study⌧and compare these main points against the interest area defined for the review. The abstract, summary, and reference are all key elements to record in a table and are used in the categorization of the literature based on a decided upon organizational system, which may include keyword, topic, method, theory, themes, or chronology.

WRITING THE RESULTS/FINDINGS

There are seven steps to writing a literature review. First, clearly define the research question and the purpose of the review. This includes identifying which type or types of review were conducted; for example, scoping. Second, establish clear boundaries for inclusion and exclusion criteria while evaluating the reasoning for those boundaries. This is especially pertinent for systematic reviews. Third, search the literature; for example, online database searches using keywords and Boolean search terms. Fourth, use the Preview, Question, Read, and Summarize (PQRS) method to analyze research and determine categorization procedures to organize sources. Fifth, sort the data into a table or spreadsheet using predetermined categories based on themes, chronology, sources, outcomes, methodology, or other characteristics of the literature. Sixth, use the table or spreadsheet and summaries to start synthesizing information and constructing the narrative of the review. Finally, solicit feedback.

The organizing structure of a literature review narrative for a publication includes an introduction, body, and conclusion (Cronin et al., 2013). Introducing the topic and methods utilized in conducting the review provides the reader with the purpose and subsequent organization of the synthesis of the literature. The body then becomes the main section for expanding upon the rationale for the publication and justifying the thought and decision-making process that informed the formation of the research question. The conclusion provides the reader with a brief summary of the purpose and research question, and it also serves to highlight any limitations in the search and review of the literature.

The final step in writing a quality literature review is to get feedback from peers, professors, or experts on the subject matter. These individuals will hopefully provide helpful criticism that enhances the readability and overall understanding of the review and the publication. As mentioned in the section on types of literature, peer-reviewed literature is indicative of a higher quality publication. This step also increases trustworthiness and can be included in the description of methods for conducting the review.

ACADEMIC WRITING

There are many styles of writing. They range from informal, for example, writing an email to a friend, to formal, for example, writing a manuscript for publication. You will use an academic writing style for the literature review. The *Publication Manual of the American Psychological Association, Seventh Edition,* is the academic writing style guide for the social sciences. You most likely followed it in your undergraduate psychology or sociology classes. A purpose of the *Publication Manual* is to make scientific work easier to read (APA, xvii) for a specific audience by standardizing such elements as format and giving credit where it is due. Successful writers keep their audience in mind, engaging them in an imaginary conversation (Singh & Lukkarila, 2017).

Standardization of style assists the writer to place proper and expected elements into proper and expected places ("The Works of the Rev. Jonathan Swift/Volume 5/A Letter to a Young Clergyman—Wikisource, the free online library," n.d.). Writing to an audience's expectations improves their predictions of what is to come and where they will find it (Singh & Lukkarila, 2017). APA style, then, is primarily a tool for academic writers to help them meet the expectations of an audience in the social sciences.

The *Publication Manual* was developed and continues to be revised to aid academic writers to realize four goals: speak to an academic audience, write clearly and concisely, give credit where credit is due, and use standardized formatting. Furthermore, the *Publication Manual* outlines the structure of papers and manuscripts, which aids in reader predication. There are eight sections: title page, abstract, introduction, method, results (quantitative research) or findings (qualitative research), discussion, references, and appendices. You will want to become familiar with the latest edition. The goal of the *Publication Manual* is to improve the quality and accessibility of research to an audience in the social sciences, including professors.

CREDIBILE WRITING

In addition to making papers and articles easier to read, the style guide fosters the appearance of neutrality and scientific objectivity (Almeida, 2012). The first *Publication Manual* appeared as a seven-page journal article in 1929, but not before a struggle between advocates for scientific objectivity and those for originality ("The History of APA Style," 2014). Thus, the *Publication Manual* embodies a set of explicit and implicit professional values (Madigan, Johnson, & Linton, 1995). One of the most explicit values to appear in recent iterations of the *Publication Manual* is attending to how language perpetuates inequities in persons and groups (Section 7). This is especially true for words that concern "race and ethnicity, sexual orientation, socioeconomic status, and intersectionality" (pp. 131–132). The value of reducing bias in our writing is related to another explicit value of research which is credibility or "believability" (Lincoln & Guba, 1985). Readers determine the veracity and utility of a study's findings to the extent they make sense. Singh and Lukkarila (2017) identify eight criteria for credible writing (see Table 3.3.).

The credibility of a paper or manuscript depends upon the credibility of the writing. Manuscripts that are poorly organized, contain errors of grammar and syntax, and fraught with APA style errors are less likely to be accepted for publication because they raise questions about the credibility of the study (Onwuegbuzie et al., 2010). There is also a link between familiarity with APA style and undergraduate psychology student grades, as adherence to the psychological manual is crucial in academic writing in the social sciences (Smith & Eggleston, 2001). Whether writing a paper for a class or for publication, your work will be viewed through the lens of APA style and how successfully you adhere to it.

TABLE 3.3 **Singh and Lukkarila (2017): Eight Criteria for Credible Writing**

CRITERION	GOAL	TIPS
Academic audience	Expected to share common knowledge bases in a discipline or course	• Read articles from that journal and author guidelines • Know course content, assignment requirements, and the professor's preferences
Argumentative purpose	Persuade the audience that you are adding something new to the literature	• Support your argument with facts, logic, credible sources • Avoid the research paper trap which provides information
Problematizing approach	Develop a rationale and problem statement for knowledge-based gaps and weaknesses in existing knowledge bases	• Use concept mapping • Analyzing findings from a search of literature review to reveal gaps
Rational tone	Creates a logical and evidence-based argument	• Connect to audience using a logical, impersonal tone • Using hedging language to signal the reader that they make the decision about your claim (Hyland, 1998), for example, "seems"
Relevant content	Builds an argument on academically credible information	• Use credible sources • Use grey sources minimally
Coherent structure	Use the principles of argumentation to order and link propositions and ideas from general to specific	• Use an effective introduction to set up coherent structure (Crossley & McNamara, 2011) • Develop a thesis that makes a claim and offers initial support for the assertion
Cohesive style	Offer the reader what they need to know and understand; establish connections between and among ideas	• Use topic sentences and transitions between paragraphs that continually connect the reader back to the thesis (Crossley & McNamara, 2011)
Specific and precise language	Convey complex ideas by using precise language and proper grammar, vocabulary, and mechanics	• Minimize long sentences • Use complex language only when there is no alternative

REDUCING ERRORS OF APA STYLE

Knowing where errors are likely to occur keys you into areas needing concentrated attention. Using proven methods to learn and apply APA style will reduce the time spent on searching for correct information. By one count, there are 60 common errors of APA style found in a study of published manuscripts (Onwuegbuzie et al., 2010). Expectedly, 65% of the common errors found by these authors were APA style specific. Over 57% of these errors were improper use of numbers, for example, not using figures for numbers 10 and above. The incorrect use of headings (e.g., not capitalizing heading words properly) represented 44.5% of the 60 common errors. Incorrect formatting of tables and figures (e.g., repeating information in the table or figure in the text). Knowing common errors of APA style can alert you these errors in your own writing.

NUMBERS (APA 6.32–6.52)

As noted, the proper use of numbers represents a significant portion of common APA errors. The main source of confusion seems to be when and how to use figures (e.g., 12) and numbers (e.g., two). There are few general rules to keep in mind. Use figures for all numbers 10 and above. This rule, however, does not apply when starting a sentence with a number (e.g., "Twelve participants…"). If the number is large (e.g., One hundred twenty-five participants…), consider rewriting the sentence so you can use a figure instead (e.g., There were 125 participants…). Another rule to keep in mind is to use figures to represent time, dates, ages, sample, subsample, population size, and a numbered series. Finally, avoid combining numerals and words to express numbers.

CITATIONS (APA SECTION 8) AND REFERENCES (APA SECTION 9)

Properly crediting sources accounts for 20% of the errors found by Onwuegbuzie, Combs, Slate, and Frels (2010). Correctly crediting sources is critical for establishing your credibility as a scholar. Problems with proper citation of sources often begin well before a manuscript reaches publication. One source is lack of knowledge of APA style. Studies with undergraduate students indicated they struggled to know how to cite sources (Head & Eisenberg, 2010; Miller, 2013). The second source of problems are organizational, for example, not keeping references in one place. Managing your references at the onset of your research is critical to avoiding sourcing errors. This requires a means to manage citations and references. The tool you select depends upon the task. Citation managers are the most robust and aid with writing; citation builders are dedicated to doing the single task of creating a reference.

Electronic citation managers are multi-purpose tools. They effectively aid data collection and organization. Plugins or add-ons compatible with software programs such as word processors can improve writing workflow. A plugin adds a feature to an existing software program such as Microsoft Word. For example, citation managers such as Zotero, have plug-ins to Word that insert citations and references into your text with a few keystrokes. They are imperfect, however. There are choices, some which entail cost unless your school or library provides them, for example, EndNote. There are several workflow considerations when selecting an electronic citation manager. Will you work from multiple computers or computer platforms or locations or need to work offline? Is this a group project requiring multiple users to share the same database? Will it import citations from other databases or webpages?

Electronic citation managers have a learning curve, so sticking with one long enough to learn its strengths and weaknesses is important. We rely on Zotero, for example. After trying EndNote and Mendeley, Zotero works for us because it is free, facilitates teamwork, integrates into our preferred browser, and works with our writing workflow (e.g., creates a reference page when a citation is inserted into the text). In the end, it is a matter of personal choice.

For all they do well, there are problems associated with citation management tools. Like their human counterparts, they are error prone. EndNote and Zotero have similar error rates for citations,

TABLE 3.4 APA Seventh Edition: Five-Level Heading Format (Section 2.18)

LEVEL	FORMATTING
1	**Centered, Bold, Title Case Heading** Text begins as a new paragraph.
2	**Flush Left, Bold, Title Case Heading** Text begins as a new paragraph.
3	***Flush Left, Bold Italic, Title Case Heading*** Text begins as a new paragraph.
4	**Indented, Bold, Title Case Heading, Ending with a Period.** Text begins on the same line and continues as a regular paragraph.
5	***Indented, Bold Italic, Title Case Heading, Ending with a Period.*** Text begins on the same line and continues as a regular paragraph

NOTE: See APA section 7.14 for guidance on creating table notes.

averaging around 2.35 (Homol, 2014). Choosing one over the other should be a matter of cost and preferences rather than accuracy. Both tools struggle to capitalize references accurately, correctly format issue numbers, and to manage digital object identifiers (DOIs; Homol, 2014). When using a citation manager, pay attention to these areas. To partially address this issue, we use citation builders to cross-check for the accuracy of the citation. Crossref is a citation builder dedicated to check for DOIs. In the end, verifying the accuracy of citations and references is your responsibility.

HEADINGS (SECTION 2.18)

The incorrect use of headings (e.g., not capitalizing heading words properly) represented 44.5% of the 60 common errors found by (Onwuegbuzie et al. 2010). Incorrect formatting of tables and figures was also indicated as a common error (e.g., repeating information in the table or figure in the text). Academic writing emphasizes a cohesive style of organization. This is reflected in the hierarchical five-level heading format of the *Publication Manual.* Global ideas are placed at the highest level and subsequent, related ideas next. Table 3.4 provides a quick reference.

TABLES AND FIGURES (APA SECTION 7)

Tables and figures are information dense, that is, they pack a large amount of information into a compressed space. They save space by not duplicating information in the text. Simply refer the reader to the table or figure, adding in text information to clarify or expand on the information in the table or figure. Instruct the reader to Table X or Figure X for more information. Templates of properly formatted tables and figures are useful in reducing errors. The type of formatting, however, depends upon the kind of information presented. Use the table feature of your word processing program to create a table template. Tables and figures have titles at the top and notes at the bottom.

In general, tables have more than one column and row. Although one page is preferred, tables may span multiple pages. If a table spans multiple pages, repeat the header row and add "(continued)" on the second and subsequent pages. Portrait or landscape orientation is permissible. Regardless of the orientation of the table, format them with at least one-inch margins. Tables should be readable; thus, 12-point type, double-spacing, and 1-inch margins are preferred. Fonts down to eight-point may be used, however. Refer to tables (or figures) in the text by number, for example, "Table 3" or "Figure 2" and do not refer to them by the position relative to the text, for example, "see bottom of the page."Figures give readers a visual aid to understanding. They contain some form of nontextual, visual element, for example, a line graph. When creating a figure, minimize the use of color in figures; use grayscale shading or cross-hatching when necessary. If you are using data from a source in your figure, be sure to cite the source after the figure description. Section 7 of the *Publication Manual* provides a table checklist.

MINIMIZING APA ERRORS

Proficiency in APA style requires practice. Assessing manuscripts or papers for errors of APA style has been shown to reduce subsequent errors (Smith & Eggleston, 2001). One way to practice is to review the work of others rather than our own, since we tend to see what we expect to see, that is, correctly formatted work. Templates or checklists (Franz & Spitzer, 2006) are another aid. Instructors may provide an APA-focused rubric. Using such rubrics can improve adherence to APA style, especially after using it to evaluate another student's work (Greenberg, 2015). A word of caution, however. Not all templates and checklists are correct, nor may they be updated to reflect the shift from the sixth to the seventh edition. This, however, can be used to your advantage by checking the template, checklist, or rubric against the seventh edition of the *Publication Manual* which will likely increase your grasp of the latest edition.

MINIMIZE ERRORS: PROOFREAD

Critically proofreading your work is worth the time and effort it takes to do it well. Effective proofreading requires that we trick our brains into seeing the manuscript or paper as if for the first time. Otherwise we risk reading what we thought we have written. There are a few ways to address this problem, all which require intentionally changing what we attend to and how we attend to it. They are time, attention, different formats, and focusing on a single aspect at a time. See APA sections 4.27 to 4.30 in the *Publication Manual* for added guidance.

Proofreading requires time, an attention-focusing environment, and different formats of the text. Although deadlines for papers and manuscript are known, too little time for proofreading is budgeted. Attention-focusing environments can mean a quiet place for some, and for others, it may mean the chatter and clatter of a coffee shop. There are various ways to proofread utilizing different text formats. Reading your work aloud is perhaps the single most effective way to catch errors. If time is short, this might be your best option. Read aloud and read slowly. Note items needing further attention. Examine the document for correct verb tense. Changing the look of the document can be accomplished by converting the document into a PDF, changing the font, viewing it on a different screen size than the one on which it was created (smaller or larger), and printing a hard copy. Proofing from the end to the beginning is another strategy allowing the brain to see the work anew. Finally, have a peer or person unfamiliar with your topic or discipline proofread your paper, perhaps focusing on a single aspect, for example, APA style. Using templates, checklists, and rubrics as discussed previously can reduce the occurrence of APA errors. We use all these strategies for proofing parts of or the entire document.

Reverse outlining is a useful strategy to examine the organizational structure of a manuscript at the global and paragraph levels. The reverse outline is created after the early drafts are completed.

It may be done multiple times. Constructing a reverse outline is uncomplicated but requires critical thinking about your goal(s) for the manuscript. In the side margin (comment boxes are useful here) of the draft, create the main idea conveyed by each paragraph. You may also find it helpful to use the outline feature in Word or Google Docs to start the process of identifying main ideas. This main idea may become or refine the paragraph's topic sentence. A topic sentence introduces the main idea of the paragraph. Consider if each paragraph connects to the main idea and whether ideas are presented in a logical order. Furthermore, review paragraphs to ensure they present only one idea and are neither too short nor too long. If a paragraph is short (e.g., three or fewer sentences, consider lengthening or eliminating it). Long paragraphs (and sentences) are difficult to read. Long paragraphs often contain more than one idea. If they do, create an additional paragraph or paragraphs. Long paragraphs can contain redundant information, which can be deleted. For more on reverse outlining, see Homol (2014).

CREATING MANUSCRIPTS FROM THESES AND DISSERTATIONS

Conveying the results of research to others is an important part of the scholarly process. To advance any field, research must be completed to address gaps in knowledge or support current theory. In doing this important work, researchers must be knowledgeable in the process of design, implementation, and promulgation of their work. Becoming proficient in all three areas of research is a career-long journey. In this section we focus on how to translate empirical results for qualitative, quantitative, and mixed methods research within the confines of typical publication limits (i.e., page number, table, and figure restrictions). In addition to discussing logistical limits of writing research, we will also review how to attend to your writing style in relation to the different types of empirical manuscripts so as to allow your results to be more easily understood by interdisciplinary and within discipline audiences to ensure your work is accessible to the widest professional audience. When developing research for publication, the mechanics of writing can sometimes present barriers when authors are trying to determine the best way to convey both their research process, their thoughts regarding that process, and the resultant information. Writing can look very different depending on the venue the information is being displayed through (e.g., peer reviewed journal, book, dissertation, newsletter). In this section, we will also discuss common writing errors within the frame of different types of publications to include both conceptual and empirical writing.

QUALITATIVE AND QUANTITATIVE WRITING

When writing empirical research articles, be they qualitative or quantitative, there are several aspects of writing an author must keep in mind during development and editing that go beyond the design itself. In this section, we will review the appropriate use of quotes, limitations of writing (e.g., page length and inclusion of tables and figures), and how to present findings in a concise way relevant to the journal's scope and readership. When developing your manuscript, it is important to think about what message you would like to send to the reader that is fully reflective of the context and implications of your study as well as who your intended audience is. For information on writing of research specific for the *Journal of Counseling and Development* and other professional counseling journals, we call your attention to volume 89, issue three published in 2011. This issue included a number of articles focused on how to present empirical research as well as conceptual writing. Reading this entire volume of articles is an excellent place for any counseling or other helping professional to start when getting oriented to formal, professional writing expectations in the field (see Student Activity 6). As you write a thesis and dissertation, we encourage you to begin developing the manuscript for publication in an identified journal as you complete each chapter or step in your writing process. Identifying a journal for publication assists in ensuring the manuscript is developed in a way that will align with author guidelines. Ultimately, staying engaged and embedded in your topic supports the writing process. The further from your work you become, the harder and more time consuming it will be to get your research distributed to a wider readership.

Qualitative Technical Writing

Translating a dissertation or thesis written in a five-chapter format into a 20–30 page journal article can be extremely difficult. The reason many take a qualitative approach is to be able to tell a contextual, nuanced story related to a phenomenon of interest. This usually makes for a longer dissertation or thesis, longer than you might see for a quantitative study. Results are framed from the perspective of the participants. Trustworthiness and credibility come in the varied types of data collected, participant engagement, and the thoughtfulness/reflectiveness of the researcher. While it is important to address all of these areas in a journal article, the information must be presented far more concisely.

Thinking about the central findings and implications for the field will help shape how methods, results, and implications are presented. Focus on what is most important for the readership to know, what participant voices speak to the core of the themes or story being presented, and what limitations and delimitations are important to note so the study can be replicated or appropriately integrated into a counselor's decision-making. Methods need to include a specific naming of the design, the theoretical lens influencing the approach to the design, researcher bias/assumptions, and similar contextual information for participants along with typical sections on sampling, measures (interview protocols), and the approach to analysis. Delimitations are often dispersed in the sampling method, researcher bias or assumptions, and suggestions for future research. Remember, you can always cite your own dissertation or thesis as a source to expand on the information presented in the article (as well as past research you've published). You'll need to remember to blind any references to your own work when submitting for review. It may be important to note that these tips translate to any writing of qualitative research, whether it is being translated from a dissertation or summarized from the trail of data collected as part of a qualitative research endeavor. Being concise and focused can be a challenge for qualitative researchers attempting to clearly communicate their findings and a skill that can be developed through reading the work of others, working with experienced research partners, and being consistently engaged in qualitative work over time.

Quantitative Technical Writing

Quantitative writing tends to be more prescriptive than both conceptual and qualitative writing. Any study involving statistical analysis will need to be presented in a particular way consistent with that analysis. In translating dissertation or thesis manuscripts, there are several areas that tend to be presented with more brevity when written for journal publication. The most obvious of these is discussion of processes associated with data cleaning, outlier management, and statistical assumptions. While these areas need to be addressed, often a sentence or two is devoted to each. Any cases removed need to be mentioned with a reasoning consistent with expected practice (you'll need to cite a source or sources that communicate said practice and support your reasoning). Methods should include a power analysis. Results presented need to include both statistical significance and effect size. Any effect size results should be explained in practical terms as they relate to the measures either in the results section or in the initial paragraph of the discussion.

Keep in mind that not all readers will be familiar with the statistical analysis you use to evaluate resultant data, thus practical explanations of findings are important in the discussion prior to highlighting potential implications. Often, dissertations and theses contain a number of tables to display results. For journals, these tables will typically need to be consolidated. Assume you will only be able to present two tables and think about how you might present findings within that restriction. Typically, one table will focus on demographic summaries and the other will focus on the results of analysis, including means, standard deviations, statistical test values, p-values, and effect size. Other output may be included depending on the type of analysis (e.g., factor analysis would include quite different information in the table presented). Precision and factual conclusions that draw directly from findings are essential components of any presentation of data. When presenting findings, a common error is an overgeneralization of results (which can also be true of qualitative studies). Make sure that any implications are derived directly from and are supported by the data. Any potential applications need to be presented tentatively as they relate to areas for future research illuminated by results and the context of your findings.

Conceptual Writing

Writing conceptual work can be theoretical in nature, process/practice oriented, or serve as a presentation of a body of literature on a particular issue. The goal of any conceptual writing should be to guide future developments in practice or research design around a particular phenomenon of importance to the field. One common error in conceptual writing is a lack of solutions. Often, ideas are presented, theories discussed or critiqued, and research summarized without a clear direction forward or identification of an evidenced use for any proposed professional actions, models, or practices. Any conceptual work should provide a path forward and serve to encourage growth within the field regarding the identified topic.

THE PEER REVIEW PROCESS

Peer review involves the evaluation of your work by colleagues or other professionals within your field of work or a related field of study. Peer review can be both formal and informal and is most often engaged in through formal processes linked to journal publication. Formalized peer review is fairly common, and preferred, in the process of producing research for public consumption, be it a lay or professional audience. It is important to engage in informal review, prior to seeking publication, and formal review to ensure research is robust enough for consideration by a wider professional audience.

Informal Review

Informal review is typically a process that could be undertaken by an outside person not involved in the development of the manuscript or implementation of research connected with it (e.g., auditors for qualitative research). Informal review might also involve critique by subject matter experts. Soliciting an informal review provides an opportunity to find out if your writing is easily understood by your intended audience, if your logic makes sense, and if you've missed any important contextual literature that could improve the presentation of your work. Encourage an informal reviewer to question your approach, your reasoning, and your conclusions and offer other potential explanations for your findings. In doing so, you will make your manuscript stronger and better positioned for peer review.

Professional Journals and Formal Review

When you submit an article for review by a professional journal, your work will likely be subject to formal review by other professionals and subject matter experts in your field. Sometimes these professionals will be chosen by the journal editor or editorial staff or you may be asked to provide names of potential reviewers. The purpose of this process is to ensure the soundness of your arguments, methods, analysis, and interpretation of results. Formal review ensures not only the credibility of your work, but the credibility of the work the future research is built upon. Typically, you will encounter double blind review, which means you will not know who your reviewers are and reviewers will not be aware of the identity of authors. This approach is used to help prevent bias in the review process that might both unfairly benefit or inhibit publication.

SUMMARY

In this chapter we introduced four tools to effectively research and write in the academic style. The literature review is the first tool, along with its companion the concept map. The literature review is the cornerstone of research, revealing gaps and problem areas in existing knowledge. Writing in the academic style, the second tool, makes your work easier to read and to be seen as credible. Precise and credible writing shows that the writer is attuned to multicultural sensitivity and striving for bias-free writing. This is the third tool. The fourth and final tool, the *Publication Manual of the American Psychological Association, Seventh Edition*, is a critical resource for successful academic writing and bias-free writing.

STUDENT ACTIVITIES

Exercise 1: Creating a Concept Map

Directions:

1. Think of a broad topic that interests you in your prospective profession (e.g., child rearing practices).
2. Identify a focus question that relates to the topic and provides direction for the subsequent concept map (e.g., how do parents decide on child rearing practices?). Do not be too specific with your question.
3. Create a concept map breaking down the topic into the four levels: Domain, Key Concepts, Main Ideas, and Components. Keep in mind that you are also seeking to answer your focus question.
4. Connect all levels using words, phrases, and lines with corresponding arrows indicating directional flow of the map. Remember that all concepts connect to another concept and may have multiple, multi-level connections. Follow the hierarchical structure as best you can, continuing to narrow each concept further as each new connection is added.

Exercise 2: Identifying the Three Types of Literature

Directions: Using your previously generated concept map, find an example of each type of literature, peer-reviewed, non-peer reviewed, and grey, on your topic of interest. Also describe how you found the example, (e.g., what steps did you take in your search process to find it?) and provide justification for the example being identified under that type of literature.

Exercise 3: Summarizing Literature Content and Determining Source Inclusion

Directions: Go back to your three pieces of literature that you found in Exercise 2. Summarize each piece and determine whether it would be included in your final written review. Provide justification for your decision, including which type of review you would conduct if you were to conduct a complete literature review and how the piece does or does not fit into that type of review.

Exercise 4: Avoiding Common APA Errors

Directions: Using the Seventh Edition of the APA Publication Manual, locate and review the pages on how to avoid the four common APA errors. Make note of them; for example, use colored tabs mark their location in the *Publication Manual*.

Exercise 5: Proofreading

Directions: Find a partner and share with each other a recent paper that you are about to submit. Proofread your partner's paper. Use track changes and comments to edit the paper. Examine the paper for bias-free language. If you wish to take this a step further, proofread your own paper before seeing your partner's feedback on your paper.

Exercise 6: Comparing Approaches to Writing

Directions: Find four articles, two qualitative and two quantitative, using similar methodologies. Select one article from a professional counseling journal and one from another helping profession's journal (e.g., *Journal of Counseling and Development* and the *Developmental Psychology* journal). Compare how methods, results, and implications are presented and discuss how this review will inform your approach to writing both qualitative and quantitative research.

ADDITIONAL RESOURCES

Helpful Links

APA STYLE

- APA Style Blog. https://blog.apastyle.org/apastyle/apa-style-blog-6th-edition-archive.html
- Citation Machine. https://www.citationmachine.net/apa/cite-a-website
- Creating a Concept Map. *Creately.* https://app.creately.com/manage/recent
- Purdue OWL. https://owl.purdue.edu/owl/purdue_owl.html

▨   Resources for Learning English. https://languages.oup.com/

▨   Zotero. https://www.zotero.org/

Helpful Books
APA Style and Writing

Cooper, H. M. (2020). *Reporting quantitative research in psychology: How to meet APA style journal article reporting standards* (2nd ed., revised). APA.

Howe, S., & Henriksson, K. (2007). *Phrasebook for writing papers and research in English* (4th ed.). The Whole World Company.

Levitt, H. M. (2020). *Reporting qualitative research in psychology: How to meet APA style journal article reporting standards* (2nd ed., revised). American Psychological Association.

Concept Mapping and the Literature Review

Machi, L. A., & McEvoy, B. T. (2008). *The literature review: Six steps to success.* Corwin Press.

Helpful Videos

▨   Creating a Concept Map for a Literature Review. https://libguides.williams.edu/literature-review/concept-maps

▨   An introduction to concept mapping. *How to Make a Concept Map* (2018, May 31). https://www.youtube.com/watch?v=8XGQGhli0I0&vl=en

▨   Reverse Outlining. https://writingcenter.unc.edu/tips-and-tools/reverse-outline/

KEY REFERENCES

Only key references appear in the print edition. The full reference list appears in the digital product found on http://connect.springerpub.com/content/book/978-0-8261-4385-3/part/part01/chapter/ch03

Bornmann, L., Thor, A., Marx, W., & Leydesdorff, L. (2016). Identifying seminal works most important for research fields: Software for the Reference Publication Year Spectroscopy (RPYS). *COLLNET Journal of Scientometrics and Information Management*, 10(1), 125–140. https://doi.org/10.1080/09737766.2016.1177948

Cronin, P., Ryan, F., & Coughlan, M. (2008). Undertaking a literature review: A step-by-step approach. *British Journal of Nursing*, 17(1), 38–43. https://10.12968/bjon.2008.17.1.28059

Hays, D. G. (2020). Multicultural and social justice counseling competency research: Opportunities for innovation. *Journal of Counseling & Development*, 98(3), 331–344. https://doi.org/10.1002/jcad.12327

Onwuegbuzie, A. J., Combs, J. P., Slate, J. R., & Frels, R. K. (2010). Evidence-based guidelines for avoiding the most common APA errors in journal article submissions. *Research in the Schools*, 16(2), ix–xxxvi.

Singh, A. A., & Lukkarila, L. (2017). *Successful academic writing: A complete guide for social and behavioral scientists.* Guilford Press.

PART II

QUANTITATIVE RESEARCH

CHAPTER 4

DESCRIPTIVE, INFERENTIAL, AND BAYESIAN STATISTICS

W. Bradley McKibben and Lindsey K. Umstead

LEARNING OBJECTIVES

After reading this chapter, you will be able to:

- Categorize levels of quantitative measurement
- Explain descriptive statistical concepts
- Apply and interpret inferential statistical tests
- Describe key concepts from Bayesian statistics
- Summarize reliability and validity concepts
- Evaluate multicultural issues in measurement and statistics

INTRODUCTION

In this chapter, we cover some of the important foundational concepts to understanding research design, including measurement of variables, descriptive and inferential statistics, Bayesian statistics, and validity and reliability. We also address important multicultural issues in quantitative measurement and underscore the importance of facilitating research through a multiculturally competent lens.

MEASUREMENT

As a precursor to discussing measurement and accompanying statistical concepts, it is important to define what exactly a researcher is measuring when utilizing the tools and concepts in this chapter. When dealing with statistics, a researcher is measuring variables and the changes that occur in variables, either naturally or as a result of the influence of other relevant variables. In its most basic form, the measurement of variables is the basis of quantitative scientific investigation. For example, a speed radar detector (i.e., "radar gun") allows a person to measure a car's speed as it is being driven down the road. The speed of the car as detected by the radar detector is a variable, and the researcher can opt to measure speed alone or to examine other variables that might influence the speed being detected. The extent to which the driver of the car presses the gas pedal, or perhaps applies the brake, can each influence the speed detected by the radar device.

A variable can be just about anything that varies in some way, either within a group (e.g., variation in biological sex, gender, race, weight, or height within a given group of people at a given point in time) or within a person over time (e.g., change in a person's weight over time). Submitting a variable to statistical analysis requires the researcher to first quantify how a given variable actually varies, usually by assigning a numerical value, so that the variable can be measured consistently. This process is called operationalizing a variable, or providing an operational definition, meaning that the researcher defines a variable in a way that it can be measured. In the behavioral sciences, researchers often seek to measure psychological variables that do not exist in the physical world, making them potentially difficult to operationally define. For example, it is a common assumption that "depression" varies among individuals in the population, perhaps from non-existent to clinical levels to very severe. Even at clinical levels, the *Diagnostic and Statistical Manual of Mental Disorders, Fifth Edition* (*DSM-5*; American Psychiatric Association, 2013) specifies a range of depressive disorders with varying symptoms, severities, and timelines (e.g., major depressive disorder, persistent depressive disorder, other-specified or unspecified depressive disorders), underscoring that "depression" can have a wide variety of experiences and definitions. Because of this, operationally defining a variable, like depression, so that it can be studied can be a complex task for researchers because what one person considers to comprise depression might be multifaceted and might be different from how others define or experience depression. Additionally, it can be difficult to assign a numerical value that corresponds to changes in the variable depression. In the radar example, the researcher might have a concrete understanding of what it means for the car to go from 30 to 50 mile per hour on the radar detector, but what does it mean to go from a three to a four on a Likert scale survey measuring depression? In sum, variables vary, and capturing the variance, also known as the true score variance, of any given variable can be tricky for even the savviest of researchers.

With the basic goal in mind that measurement and statistics go back to measuring variables and their accompanying change, consider that measurement consists of various levels. Researchers typically measure variables along four levels of scaling: nominal, ordinal, interval, and ratio (Stevens, 1946). These levels, described in detail in the following, refer to the type of information provided by the value assigned to a variable. In other words, when a researcher operationalizes a variable and attempts to measure it numerically, the numerical values assigned to a given variable are either nominal, ordinal, interval, or ratio.

NOMINAL SCALE

A nominal scale refers simply to identification, and as such, the numbers used hold no mathematical value. For example, consider a demographic survey item asking whether or not participants are married, and the participants can answer the question "yes" or "no." The researcher can more easily analyze the yes/no responses by assigning numerical values (i.e., 1 = yes, 2 = no). A response of "no" is not twice as much as "yes"— this makes no sense. These numbers merely identify each participant's categorical response to the survey item, and the numbers can help the researchers more easily classify groups of participants based on a survey response. Any variable that is assigned a numerical value is, at a minimum, considered nominal because it identifies something in relation to the variable being measured. Common nominal-level variables include biological sex (e.g., male, female, intersex), gender identity (e.g., man, woman, transgender, cisgender, nonbinary), race (e.g., White/Caucasian, Black, Asian), ethnicity (e.g., Hispanic, Latino/a/x, African American), and religion (e.g., Christian, Jewish, Hindu, Muslim).

ORDINAL SCALE

A variable measured on an ordinal scale refers to the amount or magnitude of a variable. By extension, ordinal data can be rank-ordered in some way (e.g., highest to lowest, least to most). An important, defining characteristic of an ordinal scale is that the distance between amounts is not necessarily equal, if it is known at all. For example, we could rank order individuals running a 5K race in terms of when they cross the finish line, such as first place, second place, third place, and so on. We would consider first place to be a higher ranking (i.e., a faster runner) than second place, and second place a higher rank/faster runner than third. However, the time it takes each person to finish the race is not necessarily equal for all persons. The first place runner might finish in 13 minutes, second place in 15 minutes, and third place in 18 minutes. In this case, there is a 2-minute difference between first and second place, and a 3-minute difference between second and third. Thus, our rank ordered categories for first, second, third place and so on have unequal intervals of time between the categories.

The same concept from the 5K race applies in behavioral science research. Indeed, ordinal is the most common level of measurement in the behavioral sciences, and it is also the level that most individuals think about when measuring a variable quantitatively. Ordinal-level measurement refers to questions such as "How much of this variable exists?" or "To what extent does a participant agree with this statement?" Answers to such questions refer to amount or magnitude. Commonly utilized scales, such as Likert scales, measure variables at an ordinal level, although many researchers treat such scales as interval-level data as discussed below.

Consider a personality inventory in which participants respond to items using a one to five Likert scale with the following anchors: 1 = strongly disagree, 2 = disagree, 3 = neither agree nor disagree, 4 = agree, 5 = strongly agree. If we were dealing strictly with mathematics, we could assume equal distances between integers: two is one greater than one, three is one greater than two, and so on. However, in the case of a Likert scale on our hypothetical personality inventory, the numbers refer to dichotomous categories that define value, amount, or magnitude, in this case, the extent to which participants agree or disagree with statements assessing personality traits. Because "personality" is a psychological variable that does not exist in the physical world, a researcher cannot state definitively that the distance between one (strongly disagree) and two (disagree) is the same for every participant, nor might it be the same distance between three (neither agree nor disagree) and four (agree). Stated alternatively, what does it mean for a person to move from agreeing with a survey item to strongly agreeing with it? Because each participant subjectively evaluates the item and their response, the researcher cannot assume equal distances between the response categories. The researcher can assume that "strongly agree" is a higher endorsement of the item than "agree," but equal distances cannot be assumed at the ordinal level.

INTERVAL SCALE

Interval-level data are similar to ordinal, but interval scales contain equal distances between values. That is, interval scales identify categories and define a level of amount or magnitude *in equal distances.* An example of interval data is our conceptualization of times and dates. The distance from the year 2000 to 2001 was 364.25 days, which was the same unit of time for 2001 to 2002 and for all years. Thus, the same amount of time lapses between each unit of measurement. The same can be said for measurement of hours in any given day or for months in a given year (but not for days in a month).

To repeat, although almost all surveys measured on a Likert scale are technically ordinal scales, researchers often treat such data as interval, meaning that researchers assume that each category on a scale are equidistant from one another in measuring the underlying construct. Referring back to the ordinal example, treating participant responses to the personality inventory as interval data would be to assume that the distance from "strongly disagree" to "disagree" is the same as the distance from "disagree" to "neither agree nor disagree."

RATIO SCALE

Like interval scales, data points on ratio scales are equidistant, but ratio scales go one step farther in that there is a meaningful zero-point to the scale. A ratio scale can identify categories of variables (nominal), as well as define values/amounts of a variable (ordinal) with equal distances between values (interval) in relation to a meaningful zero. Common examples of ratio-level data include age, weight, income, and temperature. The meaningful zero that distinguishes ratio scales offers a helpful comparison point for referencing data. With age, for example, a child who is 6 years old implies that the child is 6 years (i.e., six equal units of measurement) from the date of their birth, and birth in this case is the meaningful zero-point. Similarly, zero pounds or kilograms implies weightlessness, and each pound or kilogram above zero is evaluated in comparison to this zero-point.

In behavioral science research, survey scale measurement rarely, if ever, yields data at a ratio level because a meaningful zero is nearly impossible to define. Drawing on a previous example, what does it mean to have zero depression? What does it mean to have zero wellness, self-efficacy, intelligence, personality, achievement, or anxiety? Such psychological variables are extremely difficult to define with a meaningful zero.

DESCRIPTIVE STATISTICS

By this point in your academic career, you likely have had some exposure to descriptive statistics. With regard to behavior, descriptive statistics are essential due to their ability to help clinicians and researchers describe the populations they work with or study. Generally speaking, descriptive statistics include methods that allow researchers to organize, simplify, summarize, and make sense of a group of numbers from a dataset. Descriptive statistics are helpful to researchers as they allow direct and precise statements about the data that have been collected and their basic features (Cozby, 2001). These statistics are useful to researchers when they must make sense of large datasets consisting of many variables. In the following, we examine several types of descriptive statistics that researchers use, including measures of central tendency and measures of variability.

MEASURES OF CENTRAL TENDENCY

Central tendency statistics give researchers information about what their sample, or data distribution, is like on the average or as a whole. In other words, measures of central tendency include those values that are the most representative of the center a group of scores. These values are meaningful to researchers because they inform them about where the center of their distribution lies. The three types of central tendency statistics—mean, median, and mode—are discussed.

Mean. The mean, or arithmetic average, of a data distribution is the most commonly used measure of central tendency. The mean is symbolized in two ways: $\bar{X}$ (read "x-bar" and used in equations) and M (used in scientific reports or papers). The mean of a set of scores is computed by dividing the sum of all scores (Σx) in a sample by the number of observations (n) in the sample: $\bar{x} = \frac{\Sigma x}{n}$. Importantly, the mean is considered the best measure of central tendency for datasets that are presumed to be normally distributed and do not contain outliers

Median. The median (Mdn) score of a data distribution divides the group of scores in half, where 50% of the scores fall above the median and the other 50% fall below (Cozby, 2001). Put another way, the median is the middle score when a set of scores is organized in terms of magnitude or rank (i.e., from the lowest value to highest). Due to this definition, the median is also referred to as the 50th percentile (Howell, 2013). When there is an even number of scores in a data set, the median is established by computing the average of the two middle-most scores (i.e., halfway between $\frac{N}{2}$ and $\frac{N+2}{2}$). When there is an odd number of scores in a data set, the median is calculated as: $Mdn = \frac{N+1}{2}$. In the case of skewed distributions (discussed later in the chapter), the median is the most accurate measure of central tendency because it is not impacted by outliers.

Mode. The score that occurs most frequently in a distribution is referred to as the mode. Put another way, the mode is the most common value in a dataset. When viewing a distribution, the mode can be thought of as the peak, or highest point, of the curve. When two non-adjacent values in a dataset occur with equal frequency, the distribution is considered to be *bimodal*—that is, containing two modes (both of which would be reported). Alternatively, for a distribution with two adjacent values that occur with equal frequency, the mode would be computed by taking the average of the two values.

The mode can be calculated for any of the measurement levels noted previously (i.e., nominal, ordinal, interval, ratio). Recall that nominal-level data have no mathematical value, but the mode can still be used to identify the most frequently occurring category within a set of nominal data. Importantly, the mode is the only interpretable descriptive statistic with nominal data; means and medians are meaningless if the numerical data are not ordinal, interval, or ratio.

MEASURES OF VARIABILITY

When researchers obtain a dataset, it is important to determine the degree to which all scores are spread out in the distribution in order to more fully understand respondents' scores. Imagine that a professor decides to collect data on students' levels of anxiety in a research class using the Beck Anxiety Inventory (BAI; Beck, Epstein, Brown, & Steer, 1988). The professor calculates the mean anxiety score at 11 (indicating mild anxiety). Although able to report, "The mean anxiety score for students in my class is 11," the professor is not able to paint a full picture of the data collected and the characteristics of the overall distribution. In other words, the mean alone does not provide information about the spread of data in the distribution. For instance, $M = 11$ because everyone in the professor's class reported the same amount of anxiety and responded to all items the same way? In this case, the data distribution would not be spread out at all; that is, there would be no variability. Or, perhaps the mean score is 11 because half of the class obtained scores of 2 (minimal anxiety) and the other half obtained scores of 20 (moderate anxiety). Here, the distribution is much more dispersed, indicating that there is more variability within the sample. Alternatively, the variability of this distribution might fall somewhere between these extremes, depending on how each individual student scored on the scale.

Variability plays an important role in a data distribution. Specifically, variability refers to the amount of dispersion among all of the scores around the mean value, and it tells researchers the extent to which scores in a distribution deviate from: (a) a measure of central tendency for the distribution, such as the mean; and (b) one another (Vogt & Johnson, 2011). Thus, the variability of a distribution is affected by all of the scores in the dataset. Data distributions that share the same mean can have varying amounts of spread. Similarly, data distributions with different means can have the same amount of spread. In the remainder of this section, we discuss three measures of variability that can be used to characterize the amount of spread among scores in a dataset: variance, standard deviation, and range. We also discuss data distributions, including normal and standardized normal distributions, skewness, and kurtosis. These data distributions help the researcher identify variability of scores within a dataset, which is a vital component in checking an assumption of data normality for inferential statistical hypothesis testing discussed later in the chapter.

Variance. One of the most common measures of variability is variance, or sample variance (s^2). The variance of a distribution is a statistic that measures the spread or dispersion of a data distribution. Variance is calculated by dividing the sum of squares for the distribution by the total number of observations minus one $\left(s^2 = \frac{\Sigma(X_i - \bar{X})^2}{N-1}\right)$. A larger variance value indicates that individual scores are farther from the mean. Conversely, a smaller variance indicates that individual scores are closer to the mean.

Standard Deviation. The variance of a distribution can be used to determine another common measure used to describe variability: standard deviation. For a sample, standard deviation is symbolized as s and sometimes as SD. Standard deviation is defined as the square root of the variance:

$$s = \sqrt{\frac{\Sigma\left(X - \bar{X}\right)^2}{N-1}}$$

The standard deviation of a dataset measures the *average* deviation of scores from the mean. The more dispersed scores are within a distribution, the larger the standard deviation will be. By the same token, a smaller standard deviation value communicates to researchers that scores in their dataset are closer to the mean. The standard deviation is an important value because it is used to calculate other statistics, such as correlations, standard scores, and standard error. Additionally, standard deviation provides information about how many scores in a dataset for a normal or approximately normal distribution are expected to fall within one, two, and three standard deviation units from the mean. Approximately two thirds, or 68%, of scores are expected to fall one standard deviation above and below the mean. About 95% of scores are expected to fall two standard deviations above and below the mean. Finally, over 99% of scores would be expected to fall three standard deviations above or below the mean.

Range. Another measure of variability, range, refers to a measure of distance between the lowest and highest values in a distribution. There are two ways to calculate range. First, exclusive range is determined by subtracting the lowest score from the highest score to obtain a range value. Alternatively, inclusive range is calculated by subtracting the lowest score from the highest score and adding one. Inclusive range, as its name suggests, is a more inclusive measure of range because it takes into account the highest and lowest values in the distribution. While it is a generally simple measure of variability to obtain, range can paint a distorted picture of a distribution's variability by including extreme values, such as outliers. The inclusion of an extreme value may drastically affect the range for a dataset, thereby providing the researcher with an inaccurate measure of variability.

Normal Distribution. Measures of central tendency and variability can aid in the interpretation of data distributions, which graphically depict all possible values of a dataset. Such data distributions assist the researcher in further describing observed data by comparing it to probability distributions, such as a normal distribution. A normal, or Gaussian, distribution is a theoretical probability distribution that plots all possible values of a variable and the probability that any given value will occur (Vogt & Johnson, 2011). A normal distribution is hypothetical and based on the central limit theorem in probability theory, which states that if observations of a variable are randomly drawn from a large number of independent samples, then the distribution of scores from these observations will trend toward a normal distribution (Lyon, 2014). In other words, when a population or sample is sufficiently large enough to yield a large number of observations, then the average of the sampled observations will be normally distributed around the mean. Normal distribution plots are often referred to as a bell curve because of the higher frequency of observations at and around the mean.

Consider a 10-item survey, scored on a one to five Likert scale, measuring self-esteem. The maximum possible survey score would be 50 if someone endorsed fives for all ten items, and the minimum score would be 10. The median, if someone endorsed threes for all items (i.e., the midpoint of the scale), would be 30. If this survey were distributed to a large sample of participants, it is likely that summed survey scores will vary between 10 and 50 as individuals respond in various ways to the 10 items. A normal distribution for this particular survey would plot all potential values (i.e., all possible summed scores for the 10 items) along an x-axis, as well as the probability that all possible values will actually occur along a y-axis. These plots yield a histogram that resembles a bell curve. Recall that the normal distribution in this case is hypothetical and based on the assumption that there are a large number of observations. If a researcher administered the self-esteem survey to a sample of 50 college students and plotted each participant's score, this would yield an observed distribution, which may or may not reflect the hypothetical normal distribution.

An important tenet of normal distributions is that observations at and around the mean occur more frequently than extreme (low or high) observations. This concept is often referred to as regressing to the mean. In fact, in a perfectly normal distribution, the mean and median are equal because the arithmetic average of scores would equal the middle number in the array of scores. Returning to the self-esteem scale example, a normal distribution of scores based on a large sample of observations would imply that most individuals would report an approximately average level of self-esteem. Fewer participants would report very high (e.g., all fives) or very low (e.g., all ones) self-esteem.

Standard Normal Distribution and Standard Scores. In the previous section, we discussed the normal distribution in terms of raw (summed) scores, which can be complicated when it comes to comparison. Recall that Likert scale data are technically ordinal, meaning that the distance between response categories cannot be assumed equal. Thus, when comparing raw scores, we can only rank order them. For example, all we know for certain is that a score of 40 on the self-esteem survey is a higher score than 35, and this interpretation is limited. One way to remedy this is to standardize the scores. Standardized scores allow individual participant scores to be represented relative to the entire set of scores in a distribution (Jones, 2017). In other words, standardizing a raw score provides information about how far a person is from the group mean.

Common standardized scores include z-scores and T-scores, both of which can be easily calculated when mean and standard deviation (SD) are known. A z-score is calculated as $z = \frac{X-\mu}{\sigma}$ in which X is the observed score, μ is the mean, and σ is the SD. Any raw score that equals the mean will always have a z-score of zero. One SD above the mean has a z-score of one, and one SD below the mean has a z-score of negative one. T-scores yield the same information as z-scores, but they eliminate negative SD values by setting the mean at 50 rather than zero ($T = 50 + 10z$). A difference of 10 from the mean (e.g., 40, 60) indicates a difference of one SD.

Skewness. Asymmetrical data distributions can be described in terms of their skewness, a term that refers to where most scores fall on one side of a measure of central tendency. More importantly, skewness provides information about where the tail, or trailing end of a distribution, lies. Asymmetrical distributions can be positively or negatively skewed. Here, "the tail tells the tale"—that is, the side on which the distribution's tail lies determines whether the distribution is positively or negatively skewed. Thus, positive (right) skewness describes distributions in which the tail trails toward greater values. Alternatively, a negatively (left) skewed distribution is one in which the tail trails toward smaller values.

Importantly, greater skewness in a distribution indicates greater variability in scores. Skewness can be calculated statistically and depicted graphically using software programs such as SPSS. Positive measures of skewness indicate a positive skew, whereas negative values indicate a negative skew. For normal distributions, the skewness value is zero. Mode is often used as the best measure of central tendency for skewed distributions as it is not influenced by extreme values.

Kurtosis. Kurtosis is sometimes referred to as a distribution's peakedness or flatness. Although this can help a researcher begin to think about kurtosis, it does not provide the full picture of what kurtosis means. In actuality, kurtosis is used to describe the heaviness or lightness of the tails of a distribution. In other words, kurtosis tells the researcher about outliers or extreme values present in a dataset and how this impacts the overall shape of the distribution based on how many data lie in the tails. Heavily tailed distributions are those with a lot of data in the tails. These distributions are taller and pointier in appearance and are described as being leptokurtic. Alternatively, non-normal distributions with lighter tails have fewer data in the tails and thus appear flatter. These distributions are described as platykurtic (one way to remember this is to think about a platypus, one of nature's flatter mammals). Finally, normal distributions are referred to as mesokurtic and have a value of zero. Like skewness, kurtosis can be expressed numerically and graphically with the help of statistics programs. In general, negative values for kurtosis indicate that the distribution is platykurtic or flatter than normal, and positive values suggest that the distribution is leptokurtic or taller than normal.

INFERENTIAL STATISTICS

Up to this point in the chapter, we have discussed ways to operationalize and measure variables and to describe data obtained from participants. In this section, we discuss common statistical approaches that researchers use to make inferences about data collected from a sample to generalize to a broader population of people. Because a goal of inferential statistics is generalizability from observed data to a population, the ideal sample is randomly sampled from the population, meaning that each individual within the population has an equal chance of being selected to participate in a study. In fact, because the statistical tests in this section are based on the central limit theorem described previously, they are designed to measure the probability of a result in a random sample of participants (Vogt & Johnson, 2011). If a researcher does not employ some form of random participant selection or assignment from a population as part of the study's methodology, then the tests described in this section may be of limited utility.

As a precursor to describing common statistical tests, it is important to highlight what exactly is being evaluated in such a test. Inferential statistical tests based on the central limit theorem typically involve evaluation of statistical significance and practical (or clinical) significance. Statistical significance refers to the probability of rejecting the null hypothesis, and it implies that the measure of a variable is larger or smaller than what would be expected by chance. Tests described in this section assume that the null hypothesis is true, and thus the researcher must weigh the evidence for/against rejecting the null hypothesis. Importantly, with an inferential statistical test, the researcher cannot definitively accept an alternative hypothesis, only that the null can be rejected. A common cutoff for inferring statistical significance is when the p-value is less than or equal to .05, meaning that there is a 95% chance that the observed effects detected by the statistical test are not caused by error or random chance.

Because statistical significance involves probabilities, the researcher needs enough statistical power to run the tests described in this section. Power refers to the probability of rejecting the null hypothesis when the null hypothesis is indeed false. In other words, if there is truly a statistically significant effect that is not due to chance or error, then a researcher needs enough participants to be able to observe the true effect and distinguish it from error. More participants in a study yield more statistical power. There can be "too much of a good thing," however, in that a large sample size will almost always yield a statistically significant finding even if there is not one (i.e., rejecting the null hypothesis when the null hypothesis is true, also known as type I error or a false positive) because power is too high. Researchers often conduct a priori power analyses to determine how many participants would be needed given the minimum α level (often .05) and desired level of power (often .8–.95). G*Power (Faul, Erdfelder, Lang, & Buchner, 2007) is a free, online tool that many researchers find helpful for power analyses.

Effect size refers to the magnitude of the effect between variables (Kelley & Preacher, 2012). Effect size allows the researcher to determine the extent of the impact the independent variables have on the dependent variables. Stated alternatively, effect size refers to the proportion of variance in dependent variable scores accounted for by independent variable scores. This statistic is particularly useful in the behavioral sciences wherein research informs practice. For example, assume a researcher conducted an experiment testing the effects of trauma-informed cognitive behavioral therapy (TF-CBT) for posttraumatic stress disorder (PTSD). An experimental group received six session of TF-CBT, and a comparison group was waitlisted and received treatment as usual. Suppose that the researcher found a statistically significant result, supporting the hypothesis that participants in the experimental group reported lower levels of PTSD than the control group at the conclusion of the trial. Effect size would tell the researcher the extent of the impact of being in the experimental group (i.e., receiving TF-CBT) on the PTSD symptoms. If the effect size was small (e.g., .15), this would suggest that although the difference between groups was statistically significant, the magnitude of difference was not very much. For practitioners who read the study trying to decide whether the TF-CBT approach is worth implementing with their own clients, a small effect may or may not be worth the effort. If the effect size is large (e.g., .8), then not only is there a statistically significant difference between the two groups, but the intervention has a sizeable impact on scores.

Tests for effect size vary based on the statistical test being conducted, and we will address the requisite test as we discuss statistics in this section. A few important notes about effect size are worth noting. First, Cohen (1988) provided broad guidelines for interpreting effect size, which can also vary depending on the statistical test. For example, when evaluating effect size from a Pearson r correlation, Cohen recommended the following: <.5 is a small effect, .5–.79 is a medium effect, and

TABLE 4.1 Inferential Statistical Tests by Variable Type

	IS THE INDEPENDENT VARIABLE CATEGORICAL OR CONTINUOUS?	IS THE DEPENDENT VARIABLE CATEGORICAL OR CONTINUOUS?
Chi-squared	Categorical	Categorical
t-test	Categorical (2 groups)	Continuous
ANOVA/MANOVA	Categorical (3+ groups)	Continuous
ANCOVA/MANCOVA	Categorical (+ covariates)	Continuous
Regression	Continuous	Continuous

>.8 is a large effect. When utilizing Cohen's *d*, he recommended the following: .1–.29 is a small effect, .3–.49 is a medium effect, and >.5 is a large effect. Again, these are broad interpretations that will undoubtedly vary by profession and by context for the study being conducted. It is not uncommon to find smaller effect sizes in behavioral sciences research, though a small effect does not limit the utility of a result. Often researchers, particularly in quantitative studies, can only measure so much at once, and therefore can only account for so much variance in a dependent variable at a time.

Another note about effect sizes is that data from more participants are needed to detect smaller effect sizes. Imagine trying to view something under a microscope. The smaller the object you are trying to view, the stronger the magnification needed on the microscope. The same principle holds true with effect size. The smaller the effect size, the more data you need to detect it, and thus the more participants a researcher will need to sample. Effect size is a vital statistic when evaluating the practicality or utility of the findings. Most journals now require some reporting of effect size prior to publishing inferential quantitative studies.

The remainder of this section focuses on common inferential statistical tests used in the behavioral science. We begin with tests used to investigate group differences. Groups can mean groups of people (i.e., participants) or other nominally defined categories. Such tests include chi-squared tests, *t*-tests, and analysis of variance (ANOVA). We conclude this section by reviewing statistical tests commonly used to investigate relationships between or among continuous variables, such as regressions, as well as analysis of covariance (ANCOVA) in which categorical and continuous variables are simultaneously measured. Table 4.1 summarizes the types of tests and the variables they measure.

CHI-SQUARED ANALYSIS

A chi-squared (χ^2) test measures whether categorical (nominal) variables are independent from one another. Chi-squared can also be used as a goodness of fit test (e.g., in confirmatory factor analysis), but as a test of independence, χ^2 is commonly used to test whether there are significant differences between observed and expected frequencies of categorical variables, which often are represented in a contingency table (Vogt & Johnson, 2011). A good example of χ^2 comes from Avent, Wahesh, Purgason, Borders, and Mobley (2015), who content analyzed peer feedback in triadic clinical supervision pairings to investigate where peers focus their feedback to other peers in supervision. The authors reviewed videotaped triadic supervision sessions and recorded peer feedback content into five nominal categories that defined the type of peer feedback given: counseling performance skills, cognitive counseling skills, self-awareness, professional behaviors, and self-reflection. The authors also created nominal categories defining the participants, which included whether the students were in a counseling practicum, first-semester internship, or second-semester internship. A χ^2 was used to test whether or not there was a significant difference among the five feedback categories and the three supervision groups; in other words, to test whether or not students at various points in practicum or internship differed significantly in the type of feedback they offered to peers during triadic supervision. The χ^2 test was an appropriate test in this case because the authors were comparing two sets of nominal categorical variables.

Like most common inferential statistics, χ^2 is evaluated for statistical significance by consulting the p-value. A χ^2 test is considered statistically significant if $p < .05$. If the test is statistically significant, then the researcher would reject the null hypothesis that observed frequencies for the categorical variables are not statistically significantly different from expected frequency counts. In Avent et al. (2015), the authors found that their χ^2 test was statistically significant ($p < .01$), indicating that the frequencies of feedback across the five categories were not independent from the three participant groups. That is, the frequencies for types of feedback were related in some way to a student being in practicum or internship. Had their test not been statistically significant, then the authors would have concluded that the frequencies of feedback categories were independent from (i.e., unrelated to) the participant groups.

Researchers also are encouraged to further explain the significant findings by reporting effect size and adjusted standardized residuals (ASRs). Recall that effect size refers to the magnitude of the effect between variables. A Phi coefficient can be used to report effect size if two variables are being tested (i.e., 2x2 table), and Cramer's V can be used when there are more than two variables/ levels (e.g., Avent et al. [2015] had a 5x3 table). Either estimate of effect size can be interpreted in accordance with Cohen's (1988) guidelines.

Computation of ASRs (also referred to as adjusted Pearson residuals) is a post hoc analysis for a statistically significant χ^2 that allows the researcher to identify which frequency counts might be driving a statistically significant finding. ASRs are computed for frequency counts of each categorical variable. ASRs follow a standard normal distribution (i.e., $M = 0$), and can thus be interpreted similar to a z-score (Agresti, 2010). A z-score of ±1.96 is associated with a .05 alpha level; thus, an ASR greater than or equal to ±1.96 indicates that an observed frequency count is significantly different (higher or lower) than the expected frequency. For example, Avent et al. (2015) computed ASRs to show that practicum students focused their feedback on counseling performance skills more than expected, and first-semester interns focused their feedback on cognitive counseling skills more than expected and on counseling performance skills less than expected.

Recall that, as a test of independence, a χ^2 is testing for significant differences between observed and expected frequencies of categorical variables. By extension, an assumption of χ^2 is that expected frequency counts should be five or more for at least 80% of the variable categories, and no category should have less than one observation (McHugh, 2013). When there are fewer than five observed frequencies for 20% or more of the nominal categories, then a χ^2 test is contraindicated. In these cases, a researcher might utilize a Fisher-Freeman-Halton (FFH) test, which tests for independence among categorical variables like χ^2, but does not have a lower bound for empty cells (Freeman & Halton, 1951). The caution in using the FFH test is that it provides an exact p-value for inferring statistical significance rather than an estimated p-value as with χ^2. When there is a high frequency of zeros in the observed data or if the data set is large, an exact p-value can be skewed, increasing the possibility of type I or type II error. To overcome this, the researcher can apply a Monte Carlo method, which will provide confidence intervals (CIs) for the p-value. A researcher can infer statistical significance from an FFH test if the exact p-value and the upper-bound p-value CI (95%) are equal to or less than .05. To see an application of an FFH test, see Bledsoe, Logan-McKibben, McKibben, and Cook (2019).

t-TEST

A *t*-test is a test of significance between two group means (Vogt & Johnson, 2011). Specifically, researchers use *t*-tests to investigate the extent to which mean scores on an outcome variable differ between two groups of participants. Whereas a χ^2 is used when both variables are categorical, with a *t*-test, the independent variable is categorical (e.g., gender, race) and consists of two groups, but the dependent variable is continuous (e.g., scores on a wellness survey). The null hypothesis assumes group mean scores are not significantly different for the dependent variable, whereas the alternative hypothesis assumes there is a significant difference in group mean scores.

Assume that a researcher wanted to know if individuals who engage in nonsuicidal self-injury (NSSI; e.g., cutting, scratching, burning) experience a greater number of negative emotions than individuals who do not engage in NSSI. To answer this question, the researcher administered a negative affect survey to 50 participants who engage in NSSI and 50 who do not. After data collection, the researcher used a nominal variable to assign participants to one of two groups (i.e., 1 = engages in NSSI, 0 = does not engage in NSSI). When using a *t*-test to analyze the data, "group" (1/0) is the independent variable, and scores on the negative affect scale are the dependent variable. Results of the *t*-test (i.e., *p*-value) help the researcher infer if there is a statistically significant difference in negative effect between the two groups. Cohen's *d* is the estimate of effect size for a *t*-test.

The *t*-test example described is called an independent samples *t*-test because data were obtained from two separate groups of participants. There is also a paired samples (or dependent) *t*-test, which is commonly used in pretest/posttest designs with a single group of participants. For example, assume that a school counselor wanted to implement a program on social and emotional learning with a class of 30 seventh graders. Before implementing the program, the couselor administered a pretest survey of students' social competence, and then administered the same survey to the same class after the program concluded. The school counselor could use a paired samples *t*-test to see if mean scores on the social competence scale changed significantly from before to after the program was implemented.

There are several key assumptions that should be checked before utilizing a *t*-test. One assumption is that the dependent variable is normally distributed for each observation, either from each group in an independent samples *t*-test or from each data collection in a paired samples *t*-test. This assumption can be checked with a histogram of the dependent variable. Researchers should also screen data for outliers that could bias the results of the *t*-test. A related assumption is that sample sizes are sufficiently large. A small sample size can result in too few observations of the dependent variable. When this occurs, the researcher may not have enough observations (insufficient power) to trend toward a normal distribution, violating the preceding assumption. A final assumption is homogeneity of variance, meaning that the variances of each observation are equal. If this assumption is violated, then a *t*-test can still be utilized if the groups being compared are the same size (Markowski & Markowski, 1990); otherwise, a Welch's *t*-test is advised because this test is less sensitive to unequal variances or sample sizes.

UNIVARIATE AND MULTIVARIATE ANALYSIS OF VARIANCE

Similar to a *t*-test, an analysis of variance (ANOVA) is used to test differences among group means, but ANOVA is used when there are more than two groups being compared. The independent variable in ANOVA is categorical and consists of more than two groups, and the dependent variable is continuous. Also like the t-test, the null hypothesis for ANOVA assumes that group mean scores are not statistically significantly different for the dependent variable, and the alternative hypothesis assumes there is a statistically significant difference among group mean scores.

Think back to the previous example of the school counselor interested in social and emotional learning. Before designing, implementing, and evaluating a comprehensive program in this area, the counselor may wish to see if the sixth, seventh, and eight graders at the middle school differ in social competence, thereby identifying an ideal group with whom to implement the program. The school counselor could administer the social competence survey to a sample of students from each grade level, and then use an ANOVA to test whether there are statistically significant differences in social competence among sampled sixth, seventh, and eighth graders (i.e., three groups).

The test for significance of the overall ANOVA model is the F-test, which is defined as the variance between groups divided by the variance within groups (or explained variance divided by unexplained variance). The statistical significance of F is determined by the p-value ($p < .05$). If the F-test is statistically significant, then the researcher can examine post hoc t-test results for each group within the independent variable to determine which groups are significantly related to the dependent variable. Researchers also commonly report the actual mean scores for each group of participants being compared. In ANOVA, effect size refers to the amount of variance in the dependent variable explained by the independent variable (i.e., the participant groups). Common indicators of effect size in ANOVA are eta-squared (η^2) for standard one-way ANOVAs or partial eta-squared (ηp^2) when there is more than one independent variable. Notably, η^2 and ηp^2 have a biased tendency to overestimate the magnitude of an effect size, which is typically not problematic if a sample size is sufficiently large. However, if a researcher is dealing with a smaller sample size, then omega-squared (ω^2) is a more conservative estimate of effect size.

For the school counselor, let's assume that the survey was administered to 50 each of sixth, seventh, and eighth graders ($N = 150$). The results of the ANOVA might look something like: $F(1,149) = 3.93$, $p = .03$. Because $p < .05$, the counselor has evidence to reject the null hypothesis, meaning that there is some statistically significant difference in mean scores of social competence among the three groups of students. If the counselor were to examine the follow-up t-test results, the counselor could identify which group(s) of students specifically are statistically significantly related to social competence. Effect size tells an additional important component of the story. If, for example, $\eta^2 = .052$, then the counselor could conclude that 5.2% of the variance in social competence is explained by the classification of being a sixth, seventh, or eighth grader. The extent to which this effect is meaningful depends on the setting and circumstances.

The school counselor example represents a one-way ANOVA, meaning that there is one independent variable (with more than two categories) and one continuous dependent variable. One-way ANOVAs are most common, but two-way ANOVAs also are possible when there are two categorical variables and one continuous dependent variable. ANOVAs are a univariate analysis, meaning that there is always one dependent variable included at a time. If a researcher wished to analyze more than one dependent variable, rather than conduct multiple separate ANOVAs (i.e., measuring one dependent variable at a time), the ideal test is a multivariate analysis of variance (MANOVA). With a MANOVA, a researcher can include one or more categorical independent variable(s) with two or more continuous dependent variables. For example, if the school counselor wanted to test whether sixth, seventh, and eight graders significantly differed in their social competence and their academic achievement, the counselor could use a MANOVA to test for statistically significant mean differences in both dependent variables among the three groups of participants.

There are several advantages to using a MANOVA over running several separate ANOVAs. For one, MANOVA offers more statistical power and can thus detect smaller effects than ANOVAs. Recall that more participants are typically required to detect smaller effects, and MANOVA can "squeeze" more power for smaller effects than trying to conduct separate ANOVAs. Additionally, running multiple ANOVAs increases the likelihood of rejecting a true null hypothesis (type I error), but because MANOVA is one robust test of multiple variables, it limits type I error. Finally, MANOVA can detect and account for patterns among the dependent variables. Thus, a MANOVA is particularly useful when two dependent variables are correlated.

As with all inferential statistics, there are important assumptions that should be checked before utilizing ANOVAs. For univariate ANOVAs, there is an assumption that the residuals, defined as the difference between each observed score and the sample mean, are normally distributed for the dependent variable. This assumption can be checked using a Shapiro-Wilk test, but should also be compared visually against a quantile-quantile (Q-Q) plot, which plots the residuals in relation to theoretically expected values. If this assumption of normality is violated, the ANOVA test may still be reliable if the sample size is large, but the researcher should use caution with small sample sizes or if the data are highly non-normal. Alternatively, the researcher could utilize a Kruskal-Wallis H test, a nonparametric test, in lieu of an ANOVA. The researcher also could transform data (e.g., natural logarithm [ln] transformation) to "force" the data to normality.

Another assumption is homogeneity of variance, meaning that the variance in observed scores for the dependent variable is equal across all groups in the independent variable. This assumption can be tested with Bartlett's test. If this assumption is violated, then the researcher should utilize Welch's ANOVA or a Brown-Forsythe test because the classic ANOVA's F-test will not be reliably interpretable when variances are unequal across groups. The researcher might also examine the data for outliers that could be causing the assumption to be violated. Finally, an assumption of ANOVA is independence, meaning that observed scores were taken at random and from samples that are independent from each other. Although the random criterion may not hold in the absence of experimental studies, participant data should not appear in multiple groups of the independent variable.

UNIVARIATE AND MULTIVARIATE REGRESSION

Linear regression conceptually parallels ANOVA; however, with regression, the independent variable(s) is continuous rather than categorical. The dependent variable also is continuous. A simple linear regression involves one independent variable and one dependent variable; in this case, a correlation analysis (r) would yield the same results as a simple regression. More common is a multiple linear regression (MLR), which refers to more than one independent variable and one dependent variable. With MLR, the researcher can test the overall fit of a linearly related model with multiple independent variables. In other words, the researcher can determine the amount of variance in the dependent variable that is explained by all independent variables combined, as well as the amount of variance explained by each independent variable. The null hypothesis for regression assumes that relationships between independent and dependent variables are not statistically significantly related, and the alternative hypothesis assumes there is a statistically significant relationship among variables.

Assume that a licensed clinical social worker (LCSW) at a community mental health center wanted to test whether depression and anxiety were related to psychological well-being among clients seen at the center. The LCSW hypothesized that higher levels of depression and anxiety would statistically significantly relate to lower levels of psychological well-being. Using surveys that measure depression, anxiety, and psychological well-being, the LCSW sampled 100 clients from the center. In this scenario, the LCSW would utilize MLR to test whether higher scores for depression and anxiety (each a continuous, independent variable) were statistically significantly related to lower scores for psychological well-being (a continuous dependent variable).

There are several important metrics to consult in a regression analysis output. The multiple correlation coefficient (R) refers to the strength of the association between the dependent variable and all (combined) independent variables. In the previous example, R would refer to the correlation between [depression + anxiety] and psychological well-being. The statistical significance of R is evaluated with an F-test, which tests the statistical significance of the overall regression model. If F is statistically significant (i.e., $p < .05$), then the researcher can evaluate statistical significance for each individual regression coefficient (i.e., standardized betas [β]) to determine the extent to which each independent variable relates to the dependent variable.

The coefficient of determination (R^2) indicates the proportion of variance in the dependent variable that is explained by all independent variables in the model. R^2 is also considered a measure of effect size. For example, if the LCSW conducted a MLR and found an R^2 of .350, then the LCSW could conclude that, among the sample of clients, 35% of the variance in psychological well-being scores was explained by depression and anxiety scores.

A regression equation is considered a univariate analysis if there is one dependent variable, regardless of the number of independent variables, because the researcher is interested in the probability of a single outcome given the condition of the independent variables. If there is more than one dependent variable, then the researcher would utilize a multivariate regression. For example, if the LCSW wished to test whether depression and anxiety are related to psychological well-being and subjective well-being, then a multivariate regression would be the appropriate statistical test.

Prior to conducting a regression analysis of any sort, the researcher should check several important assumptions. First, regression assumes that there is a linear relationship between each independent variable and the dependent variable(s). This assumption can be tested by examining scatterplots. Another assumption is normality, specifically multivariate normality if using MLR or multivariate regression. Normality can be checked with a Shapiro-Wilk test or a Kolmogorov-Smirnov test, though either test should be compared to Q-Q plots. If the assumptions of linearity and/or normality are violated, then the researcher should consider transforming the data (e.g., ln) or conducting a non-linear regression.

A third assumption in regression is lack of multicollinearity. Multicollinearity occurs when the independent variables in a regression equation are too highly correlated. When this happens, it can be difficult for the researcher to decipher which independent variables are accounting for variance in the dependent variable. To test for multicollinearity, the researcher can run a correlation analysis for each pair of independent variables; if $r \geq .8$ for any pair of independent variables, then the two variables may be too highly related to one another and multicollinearity may be an issue. This assumption can be further tested by examining the tolerance (T) and variance inflation factor (VIF) in the regression analysis output. Tolerance refers to the influence of one independent variable on all other independent variables, and VIF refers to the extent that variance in R is increased due to multicollinearity. General cut scores for each that indicate the likelihood of multicollinearity are T < .1 and VIF > 5–10. Violations of this assumption are trickier to overcome. The researcher may need to remove one or more highly correlated independent variables from the regression model, but only if this decision can be justified in context of the conceptual framework guiding the study and construction of the hypothesized model being tested. Alternatively, the researcher might center the data by subtracting the mean from each individual score for each respective variable. The research could also utilize a principal component analysis in lieu of a regression analysis.

The assumption of homoscedasticity implies that error is the same across all values of the independent variable. When data are heteroscedastic, some participants' scores may have more influence within the data than others, which can bias the findings. An examination of a scatterplot of the residuals can check this assumption. If data are highly skewed/heteroscedastic, then the researcher may need to apply a square root transformation to the data. Finally, regression analyses are sensitive to outliers, so researchers should scan the data for univariate and/or multivariate outliers prior to conducting the regression. Univariate outliers can be identified via box and whisker plots or histograms; multivariate outliers can be identified using Mahalanobis's distances.

UNIVARIATE AND MULTIVARIATE ANALYSIS OF COVARIANCE

Analysis of covariance (ANCOVA) blends elements of ANOVA and regression by testing the extent to which mean scores on a continuous dependent variable differ among groups of a categorical independent variable while also controlling for the influence of other continuous variables (i.e., covariates). That is, ANCOVA involves categorical independent and continuous dependent variables just like ANOVA, but it also controls for possible covariates within the model. Recall the school counselor example in the discussion of ANOVAs who sought to test whether differences in social competence existed among a sample of sixth, seventh, and eighth grade students. Grade level alone may not be particularly meaningful (i.e., may not account for much variance as indicated by a small effect size), but the school counselor may wish to control for potential covariates, such as students' family income or emotional intelligence. In this case, an ANCOVA would allow the school counselor to account for these variables, which may not be directly related to the hypothesized statistical model but that could be potential confounds. Because ANCOVA can control for possible confounding variables, it is a particularly helpful test when conducting experimental and quasi-experimental studies in which the researcher seeks to control for confounds. A multivariate ANCOVA, or MANCOVA, involves another layer of complexity in which the researcher can test the extent to which mean scores on two or more continuous dependent variables differ among groups of one or more categorical independent variables while also controlling for the influence of other continuous variables (i.e., covariates).

Like ANOVA and regression, the test for statistical significance with ANCOVA is an F-test. Post hoc t-tests can identify which groups within the independent variable are statistically significantly related to the dependent variable. Effect size estimates are the same as in ANOVA (i.e., η^2, ηp^2, ω^2). The statistical assumptions that apply to ANOVA also apply to ANCOVA, though there are a few additional assumptions as well, including an assumption of a linear relationship between any covariates and the dependent variable (assessed via scatterplots). There also exists an assumption of homogeneity of the covariate regression coefficients, which essentially implies that the regression equation for any given covariate predicting the dependent variable is the same for any given group within the independent variable. In the school counselor example, this homogeneity assumption would mean that the regression equation for family income (or emotional intelligence) predicting social competence would be equal across sixth, seventh, and eight graders in the study.

CONCLUDING THOUGHTS ON STATISTICAL MODELING

The statistical tests described in this section are widely used in the behavioral sciences, but they are not above critique. Recall that these inferential statistics are based on sample and population distribution probabilities from the central limit theorem. By extension, some tests require large sample sizes in order to have enough power to test for statistical significance, and this raises an important consideration about the translation from research to practice. That is, many helping professionals do not work with large enough groups of clients or students to match the level of statistical power for some of the tests in this section. In addition to feasibility concerns of large sample sizes, large samples can jeopardize the fidelity of how an intervention or program is implemented consistently, which represents a threat to the internal validity of a study (discussed later in the chapter).

A related caution is that many of the tests described in this section assume some level of linearity in the relationships between variables. When it comes to measuring change, either over time or in relation to other variables, the statistical tests in this section "force," for lack of a better word, the researcher to interpret the results in comparison to a linear model of change. However, in reality, most helping professionals can readily attest that change is rarely, if ever, linear. Though beyond the scope of this chapter, it is worthy of note that nonlinear analyses do exist, such as growth curve analysis (Singer & Willett, 2003) or time series analysis (Hamilton, 1994).

It is helpful to keep in mind that statistical models are only as good as the overall methodology driving the study, and the results of a statistical test are meaningless without a clearly articulated conceptual framework guiding a study. In their simplest form, statistics are simply numerical probabilities that tell us about relationships among scores (more numbers) on surveys or observations. Without theory and prior research to make sense of the statistics, the numbers are meaningless. Thus, the inferential statistical tests used in a study should match, and should strive to answer, clearly defined research questions based in a clear review and critique of existing literature and based in a comprehensive conceptual framework. Statistics do not create theories of how things work; they test hypotheses based in a theory.

BAYESIAN STATISTICS

In this section we cover the basics of Bayesian statistics, which is an area of statistics that is rapidly growing in popularity in general, but remains less common within the behavioral sciences. Bayesian statistics, based in Bayes' theorem is a method of hypothesis testing that relies on existing data of some kind to inform the probability modeling that follows. It is Bayesian modeling that allows computers and machines to "learn" and produce more targeted outcomes. For example, email spam filters work by identifying key features (e.g., words) in emails that might classify an email as spam. Over time, as the spam filter algorithm accurately and inaccurately flags spam, the filter becomes more accurate at screening incoming emails. The reason for this is that the spam filter algorithm based in Bayesian modeling utilizes its own data to hone the probability function of accurately flagging new incoming emails (i.e., new data). In this section, we review the key concepts for Bayesian statistics, including Bayes' theorem, Bayesian inference, Bayes factors, and credible intervals and high density intervals.

BAYES' THEOREM

Whereas the central limit theorem proposes that a large sample of independently drawn, random observations will trend toward a normal distribution, Bayes' theorem is a formula for computing conditional probabilities of an observation given previous knowledge about conditions that can cause the observation (Gelman, Carlin, Stern, & Rubin, 1995). This formula is expressed as: $P(H \mid E) = \frac{P(E \mid H)^* P(H)}{P(E)}$. Stated plainly, this formula is calculating the probability (P) of a hypothesis (H) after gathering evidence of its occurrence (E), also called a posterior probability ($P[H \mid E]$). This posterior probability equals the likelihood of the hypothesis and the evidence occurring, which is expressed as a likelihood ratio: $\frac{P(E \mid H)^* P(H)}{P(E)}$. That is, the likelihood ratio equals the probability of the evidence occurring given the hypothesis, multiplied by the probability of the hypothesis occurring ($P[H]$; also considered a prior probability), and then the product is divided by the probability of the evidence occurring.

Consider the probability that someone will smile. This can be difficult to predict, but if we have some evidence that people are more likely to smile when they are happy, then we can factor in happiness as a conditional probability to help us better predict smiling. Such a conditional probability might be: "What is the probability that someone will smile, given that they are happy?" In this question, we want to know the probability of someone smiling, but we can also base this probability on a known condition related to smiling—whether or not someone is happy. In Bayes' formula, the probability of someone smiling (H) given that they are happy (E) is the posterior probability ($P[H \mid E]$), which can be calculated as the probability of happiness being present when someone is smiling ($P[E \mid H]$) multiplied by the probability of someone smiling ($P[H]$), divided by the probability of someone being happy ($P[E]$).

BAYESIAN INFERENCE

Bayes' theorem allows researchers to make more informed inferences about hypotheses, and in fact has spawned a distinct method of statistical inference in which Bayes' theorem is applied to data distributions. By utilizing information that is already known about what is being measured in a study, a researcher can utilize Bayesian inference to hone in and draw conclusions from relatively small data sets (Bolstad, 2007). To do this, Bayes' theorem is applied to data distributions. For example, a prior distribution refers to a researcher's assumptions about data before a construct is measured. This concept parallels a prior probability ($P[H]$). Assume that a marriage and family therapy (MFT) researcher wanted to collect data on marital satisfaction. Prior to collecting any data, the researcher might have some assumptions about how these data might look, perhaps from prior research on this construct (e.g., Do scores tend to be normally distributed? Skewed?) or based on common knowledge about marital satisfaction (e.g., It rarely equals zero). Based on these prior assumptions, a researcher can apply a non-uniform prior distribution. If a researcher has no prior assumptions, then the researcher might assign a uniform prior distribution, meaning that any given outcome is equally likely, though this is rarely the case. Note that a uniform prior distribution is not the same as a normal distribution. A normal distribution implies that observations closer to the mean are more likely than scores farther from the mean; thus, as a prior distribution in

TABLE 4.2 *K*-Values for Interpreting Bayes' Factors in Hypothesis Testing

STRENGTH OF EVIDENCE	K	LOG$_{10}$K
None	0	0–.5
Weak	1–3	
Moderate	3–10	0.5–1
Strong	10–30	1–2
Very strong	30–100	
Decisive	>100	>2

NOTE: Values indicate evidence in support of M_1. No evidence for M_1 indicates support for M_2. For K, see Jeffreys (1961). For log$_{10}K$, see Kass and Raftery (1995).

Bayesian inference, a normal distribution is non-uniform. Because the prior distribution serves a multiplicative (or weighted) function in Bayes' theorem, it can magnify observations that are more likely and diminish observations that are less likely, thus generating a posterior probability distribution of scores that are more honed based on prior knowledge.

BAYES' FACTORS

Building on the concept of Bayesian inference, the use of Bayes' factors is a method of hypothesis testing that differs from the traditional approach (i.e., *p*-values as indicators of statistical significance). Whereas traditional hypothesis testing compares an alternative hypothesis to a null hypothesis with the intent to reject, or fail to reject, the null hypothesis, Bayesian modeling compares the probabilities of two competing statistical models, regardless of which is assumed correct (Ly, Verhagen, & Wagenmakers, 2016). Each model is expressed as a posterior probability ($P[M \mid D]$) in which the probability (P) of a statistical model (M) given observed data (D) equals a likelihood ratio including the probability that some data are produced under the model's assumptions ($P[D \mid M]$). The overall formula for this Bayesian model refers directly back to Bayes' theorem: $P(M \mid D) = \frac{P(D \mid M)*P(M)}{P(D)}$.

A Bayes' factor (K) is derived from the comparison of two Bayesian models (M_1 and M_2). Although the math can be complex, the concept is fairly straightforward. The value of K indicates the weight in favor of M_1 over M_2. The most common indices for interpreting K, reported in Table 4.2, come from Jeffreys (1961) and Kass and Raftery (1995).

CREDIBLE INTERVALS AND HIGH-DENSITY INTERVALS

In Bayesian statistics, a credible interval refers to the bounds within which an unobserved parameter has a given probability. A credible interval conceptually parallels a confidence interval, but a credible interval can build in information from the prior distribution (or prior hypothesis [P (H)] in Bayes' theorem), meaning that the estimated parameter is considered random within a set of fixed, bounded data parameters (Lee, 2012). For example, a 95% credible interval implies that 95% of possible values of a given parameter will fall within the bounded data parameters. One of the most common credible intervals is a high density interval (HDI). An HDI is the narrowest/smallest interval range that contains values of the highest probability. By extension, an HDI always includes the mode, even if the mode is zero, which is not always the case in other credible intervals (e.g., equal-tailed). An HDI can apply to a prior or posterior distribution; when applied to a posterior distribution, it is called a highest posterior density (HPD) interval.

RELIABILITY AND VALIDITY

Behavioral research requires researchers to carefully measure the constructs they are interested in understanding. To do this, researchers must consider two important concepts when determining how they will measure their constructs of interest: reliability and validity. While these are different concepts, both play an important role in the extent to which researchers can accurately measure variables and draw conclusions from their results. We discuss these concepts in more detail in the following.

Before we dive into these concepts, it is important to understand measurement error, or the extent to which error exists in data collection due to poorly constructed instruments and/or human error. Due to the inevitable existence of measurement error, it is difficult, if not impossible, to know an individual's true score on any given test, assessment, or instrument. An individual's observed score on an instrument, then, consists of their true score plus error. Measurement error can be systematic, or consistent across respondents, due to issues with the equipment or instruments used to measure constructs and/or flaws in the research design, or random due to factors out of the researcher's control, such as an individual's mood or anxiety level. Although random error is hard to control for, systematic error can be reduced by utilizing sound research methods and procedures. Importantly, measurement error can be reduced through the use of reliable and valid measures of the variables one seeks to examine through research.

RELIABILITY

In general, reliability refers to the consistency with which a construct or variable is measured. A reliable instrument would yield the same result if it was administered to the same individual repeatedly. Alternatively, an unreliable measure would yield quite different results across administrations. However, because you most likely are collecting data from one individual at a limited number of time points, it is important to have information about an instrument's reliability prior to using it.

Reliability can be assessed using correlation coefficients. Most commonly, Pearson's product-moment correlation coefficient (r) is used as an expression of overall reliability for an instrument. As a reliability coefficient, r can range from zero to one, with values closer to one indicating greater reliability, or stability, of the instrument. In general, measures are considered reliable if their reliability coefficient is .7 or higher. Reliability can be further separated into three types: test-retest, internal consistency, and interrater reliability. We elaborate on these types of reliability further in the following sections.

Test-Retest Reliability. This type of reliability is assessed by taking individuals' scores on an instrument at two time points. For example, if a professor administered a measure of intelligence to everyone in the class tomorrow and again one week later, the professor could then calculate a correlation coefficient using the two scores of all individuals in the class to determine the test-retest reliability. A higher correlation coefficient would suggest that individuals' scores reflect a truer measure of intelligence rather than measurement error. Importantly, test-retest reliability may be affected by individuals' memories or familiarity with the assessment from time one to time two. To rectify this, alternate form reliability can be used by administering different versions of the same assessment to respondents in a sample.

Test-retest reliability is not always the most appropriate form of reliability to utilize depending on the construct a researcher is measuring. For example, a person's mood likely will fluctuate across time, meaning that test-retest reliability will not provide a dependable estimate of an instrument's reliability. Thus, other methods of assessing reliability should be used.

Internal Consistency. An instrument's consistency can be determined by obtaining only one score from an individual by using the instrument's items or statements. This can be accomplished using internal consistency reliability, or the extent to which all items on an instrument are correlated with one another. Accordingly, internal consistency reliability measures the degree to which items on a scale measure the same construct. Cronbach's alpha (α) coefficient is a commonly used measure of this form of reliability and correlates each item in a scale with all other items to obtain a large number of correlation coefficients. The average of these coefficients and the total number of items provides an overall measure of internal consistency. A typical rule suggests that an α of .7 or higher indicates sufficient or strong internal consistency. Importantly, reliability increases with the increasing numbers of items on an instrument (Cozby, 2001).

Interrater Reliability. Some behavioral research entails researchers' observations and ratings of behaviors. In this case, two or more researchers follow instructions about how to rate and score behaviors in order to obtain a measure of a construct under study. For example, if two researchers are interested in measuring aggression in adolescents, they would determine which behaviors qualify as aggressive behaviors and make judgments about behaviors they see the sampled adolescents exhibiting. Although the researchers could rate these behaviors on their own, the measurement might be unreliable. Accordingly, using two or more ratings of aggressive behaviors in adolescents would give the researchers a more reliable measure of aggression. This method would allow them to calculate interrater reliability, or the degree to which multiple raters agree on their observations of behaviors. Cohen's kappa is a commonly used coefficient of interrater reliability and is a percentage-of-agreement measure of reliability that corrects for chance or random agreement among raters. A Cohen's kappa value of one indicates perfect agreement among raters on their judgments of behaviors.

VALIDITY

Reliability is necessary for establishing instruments that are valid, or accurate, in their measurement of a construct. In the context of behavioral research, validity refers to the degree to which an instrument or test accurately measures what it claims to be measuring. For instance, if a researcher were studying depression in college students, that researcher would want to use a valid measure of depression that accurately captures the degree to which the participants experience depression. Alternatively, this measure of depression would not be valid if it were in fact capturing participants' anxiety or stress levels. Using this invalid measure would not allow the researcher to establish accurate results and thus, conclusions, about depression in college students because the researcher did not actually measure depression.

Relatedly, validity refers to the strength of the research design in producing results that accurately answer the research question under examination. Beyond this, validity also refers to the accuracy of inferences or conclusions and thus, actions taken in response to research results. Note that a common word used across these explanations of validity is accuracy. Again, validity matters because it gives the researcher an indication of how true a measure of a variable is and thus, how true the results, inferences, and conclusions drawn from the data are. Given the expansive nature of validity, various subcategories of validity are used to provide support for overall validity. We describe these types of validity in more detail.

Face Validity. The simplest form of evidence for validity, face validity refers to the degree to which an instrument "on the face of it" measures what it is supposed to measure. For example, if the measure of depression the researchers above seek to use appears to include items related to depression symptoms (e.g., hopelessness, loss of interest in activities, sadness, loss of or increase in appetite, decreased or increased sleep, fatigue), they could say that the instrument contains face validity. Thus, the content of the instrument reflects the construct being measured. Face validity is not represented by statistics but is instead up to the discretion of the individual's judgment about the degree to which the instrument looks like it measures what it claims to measure. Importantly, face validity provides only weak evidence of validity. Even poorly developed measures can contain face validity (e.g., think about some of the Internet quizzes you have maybe taken). Because face validity is subjectively determined using one's own judgment, it is not sufficient to use it as sole means of providing evidence for validity.

Content Validity. A similar but different type of validity, content validity assesses the extent to which the items accurately represent the construct being measured. That is, an instrument would be said to have content validity if it measured all facets of the variable one is interested in, not just some of its facets. Returning to the example of a measure of depression, the researchers could say that their instrument contained content validity if it represented all components of depression. This measure would lack content validity if it only measured certain components of depression, such as only focusing on behavioral symptoms as opposed to behavioral, cognitive, and affective components. Another way to think about content validity is in terms of the degree to which the content of the measure captures the universe of content that defines the construct as a whole (Cozby, 2001). Like face validity, content validity is determined using subjective judgment and not statistical properties. Accordingly, content validity should not be used as a singular means of determining an instrument's validity.

Criterion-Related Validity. This type of validity, also called "concrete" validity, refers to a test's ability to make accurate predictions about a criterion, or "gold-standard," measure of a construct. Criterion-related validity, then, is the extent to which a test is related to a specific outcome. Typically, this outcome is something other than a score on another instrument, such as grade point average (GPA) or work performance. Two types of criterion-related validity can be used: concurrent and predictive validity. Concurrent validity examines the degree to which scores on a test are related to a criterion measured at the same time as the test (i.e., concurrently). For example, concurrent validity would be assessed for high school students' scores on an intelligence test and overall GPA. In this example, GPA is the criterion used to establish the validity of the intelligence test. Alternatively, predictive validity measures the extent to which scores on a test predicts a criterion that occurs in the future. An example here includes the degree to which scores on a college entrance exam (e.g., the SAT) predict students' college GPA after the first year. Here, the criterion is college GPA, which is assessed later in time following the collection of SAT scores. Both concurrent and predictive validity are tested statistically, making them more objective measures of validity. However, one issue with this type of validity lies in the lack of "gold standard" criteria that can be used for the questionnaire-based measures that are often used in behavioral research.

Construct Validity. This subtype of validity assesses the extent to which a variable or instrument accurately measures the construct it aims to measure. This concept is very similar to the general idea of validity; however, construct validity differs from validity as a whole by focusing specifically on how well constructs (i.e., the topics, phenomena, variables, or things) are operationalized. That is, how well does the operational definition of a construct of interest truly get at, or capture, the thing a researcher is trying to measure? In general, a variable or instrument is said to have construct validity if it accurately measures a specific construct and not some other construct. For example, say a researcher wished to quantitatively measure the theoretical construct of research self-efficacy to better understand whether a class of master's students enrolled in a statistics course experiences a change in this variable across the semester. The researcher would want to ensure that the operationalization of this construct accurately measures research self-efficacy and not a different topic, such as research interest or researcher identity.

Evidence for construct validity can be evaluated using two different means. The first, convergent validity, looks at the overlap between two different measures of the same or similar construct. To do this, scores from a measure of a construct would be correlated with scores on another instrument looking at a similar construct. The idea here is that these two measures of the construct should converge, or be related, to show that the construct being tested does accurately capture the thing it is meant to capture. Returning to our research self-efficacy example, the researcher might choose to test the operationalization of this construct against an existing measure of research self-efficacy. A strong significant correlation (.70 or higher) would suggest that convergent validity is present, providing some support for construct validity.

Alternatively, discriminant validity, also known as divergent validity, looks at whether a construct differs from constructs with which it should not be related. That is, does a construct differ from conceptually different constructs? If yes, there is evidence for discriminant validity. In the case of discriminant validity, a measure of a construct of interest should not correlate with measures of different construct. For instance, if the measure of research self-efficacy did not correlate with a measure of something theoretically dissimilar, such as mindfulness or avoidant coping, then the researcher would have evidence for discriminant validity. Importantly, convergent and discriminant validity should work together to provide evidence of construct validity. In other words, it is important to demonstrate each of these forms of validity, as relying solely on one or the other is insufficient for showing construct validity.

Construct validity is important because it influences the degree to which a researcher can make inferences about, and draw conclusions from, the operationalized variables in a study to the theoretical concepts they aim to reflect. Thus, construct validity impacts both internal and external validity, which are discussed next.

Internal Validity. Internal validity is concerned with the degree to which the results of a study can be attributed to a trustworthy cause-and-effect relationship established between a treatment and outcome. Thus, internal validity refers to the extent to which a researcher can draw valid conclusions from a study based on how well the researcher designed the study. Several factors can improve internal validity, including random selection and assignment, experimental manipulation, and effective study procedures. On the other hand, several factors can act as threats to internal validity, including confounding variables, maturation and testing effects, historical events, attrition of participants, and researcher bias.

External Validity. This form of validity is used to evaluate the extent to which research findings can be extended beyond the study from which they come. In other words, external validity looks at the degree to which research results can be generalized beyond the study. External validity can be thought about in terms of the degree to which findings can be generalized to the population at large, different settings, across time, and treatment conditions. External validity is important because it provides information about how well study results translate to the world beyond the study and thus, can be applied to practical situations.

CONCLUDING THOUGHTS ON RELIABILITY AND VALIDITY

As mentioned, although an instrument can be reliable without being valid, an instrument cannot be valid without also being reliable. Thus, while validity requires reliability, the opposite is not true. This means that ultimately, a researcher should aim to use a measure that is deemed to have strong validity. One limitation of research is that journals often publish studies that only provide information about an instrument's reliability as opposed to both reliability and validity. Thus, as you begin engaging in your own research, it is important to search diligently for information about a scale's validity as well as reliability.

MULTICULTURAL ISSUES IN STATISTICS

Living in a dynamic and multicultural world necessitates research that is representative of diverse populations. Importantly, a distinct characteristic of some behavior-oriented fields, such as counseling and psychology, includes an increasing emphasis on multiculturalism (Heppner, Kivilighan, & Wampold, 2008). Experts in some of these disciplines have developed standards and competencies for producing research from a multicultural lens in order to recognize the importance of diversity and the need for intentional research practices that account for differences across cultures and identities.

For example, the Association for Assessment and Research in Counseling (AARC) Standards for Multicultural Research (O'Hara et al., 2016) outlined basic standards of practice related to research and multiculturalism in order "to promote cultural intentionality, inclusion, and responsiveness" (p. 1). This document discusses eight standards pertaining to advocacy and the importance of multicultural research; research goals and design; the research process; literature; participants and procedures; measures; data analysis; and findings and applications.

Similarly, the Association for Multicultural Counseling and Development's (AMCD) Multicultural and Social Justice Competencies provided several competency standards about counselors' responsibilities related to multicultural research (AMCD, 2015; Ratts et al., 2016). For example, Section IV, Counseling and Advocacy Interventions, stated that competent multicultural and social justice counselors "...[e]mploy quantitative and qualitative research to highlight inequities present in current counseling literature and practices in order to advocate for systemic changes to the profession" (p. 12) and "[c]onduct multicultural and social justice based research to highlight the inequities that social institutions have on marginalized clients and that benefit privileged clients" (p. 13).

The Association for Lesbian, Gay, Bisexual and Transgender Issues in Counseling (ALGBTIC) has published competencies for counseling lesbian, gay, bisexual, queer, questioning, intersex, and ally (LGBQQIA; Harper et al., 2013) and transgender (Burnes, et al., 2010) clients, and both sets of competencies underscore the importance of research "with" rather than research "on." These competencies also note the historical marginalization and discrimination that has been upheld or advanced by researchers pathologizing LGBQQIA and transgender individuals. A multiculturally competent approach to the concepts in this chapter involves carefully and intentionally thinking through each step of the research process, including how constructs are defined, operationalized, measured, statistically tested, and evaluated in ways that are reflective and respectful of the lived experiences of diverse individuals.

A seemingly small, but important multicultural consideration with measurement and statistics involves measurement of demographic variables. Recall that in the nominal measurement section of the chapter, common nominal variables included demographic items one might see in a survey (e.g., participant race, ethnicity, religion, sex, gender). Such demographic items are not only standard in most studies, both quantitative and qualitative, but also are considered best practice in behavioral science research (American Psychological Association, 2009). Historically, such demographic items have been provided in a "forced choice" format. That is, a survey item might ask, "Which of the following best describes your race?" Participants would then check a box of one of the racial categories provided by the researchers. Rather than creating categories a priori, it is recommended that researchers allow participants to self-identify any relevant demographic items via open-ended response items and then to create nominal categories from the groups that emerge from the data.

Importantly, quantitative methodology is grounded in empiricism and deductive reasoning, which are traditionally Western values. Diverse ways of knowing, particularly perspectives and voices from marginalized groups, can be easily overlooked or dismissed in the name of the scientific method. Multicultural research competencies can and should be used to engage in research practices that are informed by social justice and that center the voices and experiences of underrepresented and marginalized groups. Ultimately, multicultural research competence plays a critical role in your work as a researcher and should be prioritized in order to produce research and thus, knowledge, that is culturally responsive.

SUMMARY

This chapter covered many of the core tenets of descriptive inferential statistics, including how to define and measure variables, how to describe data, how to test relationships among variables with inferential statistics, and how to evaluate reliability and validity. The chapter also discussed Bayesian statistics, a rapidly growing area of statistics with immediate applicability to behavioral sciences research. As behavioral scientists continue to seek new insights and test promising prevention and intervention strategies, we suspect that the Bayesian methods will become increasingly popular in research across helping professions. Likewise, in an ever-increasingly diverse society, researchers using the methods and concepts in this chapter are tasked with reflecting the voices and experiences of diverse groups through the use of multiculturally responsive and competent research practices.

STUDENT ACTIVITIES

Exercise 1: Calculating Central Tendency and Variability

Directions: A mental health counselor has asked clients to complete a brief session satisfaction survey at the end of their sessions. He administered the 5-item survey, scored on a 1 (not at all satisfied) to 5 (very satisfied) Likert scale, to 10 clients in the last week. Summed scores from the 10 clients were as follows: 6, 10, 15, 25, 24, 16, 14, 25, 20, 18. Use these scores to calculate the following measures of central tendency and variability:

- Mean
- Median
- Mode
- Variance
- Standard Deviation
- Range

Exercise 2: Critiquing Inferential Statistical Tests

Directions: Each inferential test involves interpreting key statistical values and checking assumptions. Using your university library website, locate two empirical quantitative studies published in journals in your field of study that utilized one of the statistical tests in this section. Critique the strengths and weaknesses of the authors' use of the statistical test in light of the following:

- What were the variables being measured? Which were categorical or continuous?
- Did the authors select the correct statistical test? Why or why not?
- Did the authors check the assumptions of the test prior to running the statistical analysis? If so, which assumptions were checked and how? If any assumptions were violated, how did the authors address the violation? If the authors did not check assumptions, what concerns do you have about the results of the statistical test?
- What evidence did the authors report for statistical significance and for effect size? Do you agree with the authors' interpretation of these statistics? Why or why not?

Exercise 3: Evaluating Reliability and Validity

Directions: Think about a research interest of yours, and identify a topic or construct that might be measured in this area. Next, using your university library website, locate a published article in which the authors developed a survey/instrument to measure the construct of interest to you (often called "instrument development" or "survey design"). As you read the article, reflect on the following questions:

- What type of reliability evidence (e.g., test-retest, internal consistency) did the authors report? Are there any reliability indices reported that are not covered in this chapter?
- What type of validity evidence (e.g., construct, criterion) did the authors report?
- Do you agree with the authors' assertions about reliability and validity for the survey/instrument that was tested? Why or why not?
- Remember that validity refers to accuracy of the findings based on the measures *and* on the study itself. How might validity be impacted, positively or negatively, by the way the authors set up or conducted the study (beyond the survey itself)?

Exercise 4: Multicultural Competence and Statistics

Directions: Select one of the competency documents listed in this section (i.e., AARC, AMCD, ALGBTIC) and review the sections about research. After reading, reflect upon and respond to the following questions:

- What does it mean to be multiculturally competent when handling statistical data?
- How can statistical research be used to better capture the experiences and voices of diverse individuals and communities and to improve service delivery?
- As a researcher, what does it mean to you to research "with" rather than research "on"?

ADDITIONAL RESOURCES

Software Recommendations

- Statistical Package for the Social Sciences (SPSS): https://www.ibm.com/analytics/spss-statistics-software
- R: https://www.r-project.org/
- SAS: https://www.sas.com/en_us/software/stat.html
- Mplus: https://www.statmodel.com/
- G*Power: http://www.psychologie.hhu.de/arbeitsgruppen/allgemeine-psychologie-und-arbeitspsychologie/gpower.html

Helpful Links

- https://aarc-counseling.org/ https://www.learner.org/series/against-all-odds-inside-statistics/
- https://benlambertdotcom.files.wordpress.com/2018/08/bayesianbook_problemsanswers_final.pdf

Helpful Books

Agresti, A. (2010). *Analysis of ordinal categorical data* (2nd ed.). Wiley.
Cohen, J. (1988). *Statistical power analysis for the behavioral sciences* (2nd ed.). Erlbaum.
Gelman, A., Carlin, J. B., Stern, H. S., & Rubin, D. B. (1995). *Bayesian data analysis*. Chapman and Hall.
Vogt, W. P., & Johnson, R. B. (2011). *Dictionary of statistics and methodology: A nontechnical guide for the social sciences* (4th ed.). SAGE.

Helpful Videos

- https://www.youtube.com/watch?v=g1WpcRAXWf0
- https://www.youtube.com/watch?v=0F0QoMCSKJ4
- https://study.com/academy/lesson/issues-in-psychological-assessment-reliability-validity-and-bias.html

KEY REFERENCES

Only key references appear in the print edition. The full reference list appears in the digital product found on http://connect.springerpub.com/content/book/978-0-8261-4385-3/part/part02/chapter/ch04

Agresti, A. (2010). *Analysis of ordinal categorical data* (2nd ed.). Wiley.

Avent, J. A., Wahesh, E., Purgason, L. L., Borders, L. D., & Mobley, A. K. (2015). Content analysis of peer feedback in triadic supervision. *Counselor Education and Supervision*, 54, 68–80. https://doi.org/10.1002/j.1556-6978.2015.00071.x

Bledsoe, K. G., Logan-McKibben, S., McKibben, W. B., & Cook, R. M. (2019). A content analysis of school counseling supervision. *Professional School Counseling*, 22, 1–8. https://doi.org/10.1177%2F21 56759X19838454

Cohen, J. (1988). *Statistical power analysis for the behavioral sciences* (2nd ed.). Erlbaum.

Jeffreys, H. (1961). *Theory of probability* (3rd ed.). Oxford University Press.

Kass, R. E., & Raftery, A. E. (1995). Bayes factors. *Journal of the American Statistical Association*, 90, 773–795.

Kelley, K, & Preacher, K. J. (2012). On effect size. *Psychological Methods*, 17, 137–152.

Stevens, S. S. (1946). On the theory of scales of measurement. *Science*, 103, 677–680. https://doi.org/10.1126/science.103.2684.677

CHAPTER 5

EXPERIMENTAL RESEARCH

Kristin L. K. Koskey and Ingrid K. Weigold

LEARNING OBJECTIVES

After reading this chapter, you will be able to:

- Distinguish experimental research from other quantitative traditions
- Describe the paradigmatic hierarchy of experimental research
- Compare and contrast experimental laboratory and field experiments
- Recognize data analytic techniques aligned to research questions addressed in experimental research

INTRODUCTION TO EXPERIMENTAL RESEARCH

Have you ever heard the expression: "Correlation does not equal causation?" The major distinction between experimental research and correlation research design is that the purpose of experimental research is to test for causal effects. A causal effect is when a change in one (or more) variables explains the change in another variable, with all other variables being equal or fixed (Heppner et al., 2016). The manipulated variable is the independent variable (x), and the affected variable is the outcome known as the dependent variable (y). In other words, the manipulated independent variable is the *cause*, and the dependent variable is the *effect* being studied. In social science research, experimental designs are commonly used to test the effectiveness of interventions such as treatments and services (Rubin & Babbie, 2016). In this chapter, we use the term intervention interchangeably with condition and treatment. Under the umbrella of experimental research are types of experimental designs, some of which are more or less powerful in determining causal effects. These variations are outlined in more detail later in this chapter.

EXPERIMENTAL RESEARCH AND OTHER QUANTITATIVE TRADITIONS

Experimental research is distinct from other commonly used designs in the profession including single-subject research design, predictive design, and survey research. **Single-subject research design** differs from experimental research in two ways. First, as indicated in the name of the design, only one subject participates in the study. Second, that participant is the control and treatment group through different phases of baseline or non-treatment and treatment. Data are collected longitudinally, before and after each phase. Periods of non-treatment and treatment are systematically tested in a particular sequence to determine the effect of a specified treatment on the outcome(s).

Predictive design differs from experimental design in that the purpose of predictive design is to identify a variable or combination of independent variables that reliably forecast a *future* phenomenon. This future phenomenon is the dependent variable (y). In predictive design, independent variables are referred to as **predictors** and the dependent variable as the **criterion**. Correlation is used to test the strength and direction of the relationship between the predictors and criterion. Prediction design takes it another step further by testing whether the value of one variable can reliably estimate the value of the criterion (Hayes, 2017). A predictor variable might not be manipulated as it is in experimental research. For instance, demographics or baseline psychological measures might be used to test as predictors of a later outcome.

In contrasting experimental research to survey research, it is first important to distinguish between a *survey* and survey *research*. A **survey** is a data collection tool that can be used to collect data from participants. Surveys might be used as a data collection tool in many different designs in human subjects research. **Survey research**, on the other hand, is a type of research design. Survey research differs from experimental research in the study purpose and treatment of the independent variable. The purpose of survey research is to collect data from a representative sample to generalize the results to a larger target population to describe some phenomenon (e.g., perceptions, experiences, needs; Dillman et al., 2014). Surveys can be used in experimental research as a data collection tool, however, the purpose is not to conduct survey research. Also, although relationships between variables can be studied in a survey research design, the independent variable is not controlled or manipulated by the researcher as in experimental research.

TESTING FOR A CAUSAL EFFECT

Regardless of the type of experimental design, specifications need to be met to test for a causal effect, which further distinguish experimental research from other quantitative traditions. We highlight three specifications that must be met at minimum as outlined by Chambliss and Schutt (2014). The first specification relates to the time order of the variables being studied (Chambliss & Schutt, 2014). The independent variable must have **temporal priority** over the dependent variable. In other words, the independent variable needs to occur first to attribute the change in y to a change in x.

The second specification is that the variables share an **empirical relationship**, otherwise referred to as correlation or association (Chambliss & Schutt, 2014). The variables need to co-vary as observed through a positive relationship (as one variable increases/decreases, the other variable increases/decreases at the same time) or a negative relationship (as one variable increases, the other variable decreases at the same time). If the variables do not co-vary, a causal effect is not possible. However, it is important to note that an empirical relationship does *not* equate to a causal effect.

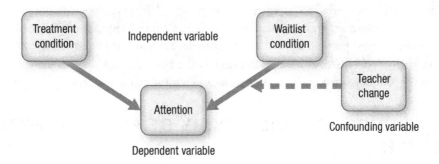

FIGURE 5.1 Example of the Relationship Among Independent, Dependent, and Confounding Variables.

There are many instances where two variables share a strong empirical relationship but not a causal effect. As an example, posttraumatic stress disorder (PTSD) symptom severity and mental illness stigma have been shown to share a strong relationship in veterans (DeViva et al., 2016). However, it is unwarranted to infer that PTSD causes mental illness stigma because PTSD is not a variable manipulated in this research. In other words, just because variables share a relationship does not prove that a causal effect is observed.

The third specification is that this relationship is *nonspurious* in that the change observed in the dependent variable is due to a change in the independent variable and not explained by "other" variables (Chambliss & Schutt, 2014). These "other" variables are referred to as confounding variables, a type of **extraneous variable** for which data are not collected in the study. A **confounding variable** is a variable unaccounted for in the study that influences the relationship between the independent and dependent variable. For instance, Thomas and Atkinson (2015) conducted a randomized control trial to assess the impact of a mindfulness-based intervention (the independent variable) on children's attention (the dependent variable). Students and teachers were randomly assigned to either receive the intervention or be on a waitlist. There was mixed evidence of the effectiveness of the intervention. However, as illustrated in Figure 5.1, the teacher for the students in the waitlist condition changed partway through the study (the confounding variable), and the authors speculated this change may have affected the results.

RANDOM ASSIGNMENT

Experimental researchers use methods to isolate the effect of the independent variable on the dependent variable to increase the likelihood that the relationship is nonspurious and not influenced by confounding variables. Similar to the study on the effect of a mindfulness-based intervention, one method is to establish an experimental and a control group (Rubin & Babbie, 2016). When comparing groups, the control group consists of participants who did not receive any intervention, whereas the experimental group received the intervention.

Random assignment is commonly used in experimental designs in which participants are randomly assigned to the experimental or intervention group, such that all have an equal chance of being in either condition. In the 1920s, R.A. Fisher, an agricultural statistician, outlined the analytical approach for randomization of units to experimental and control conditions. In the

1950s, the use of randomization in experiments escalated in psychology (Underwood, 1957). Although use of random assignment increases the rigor, a control group is not feasible to establish at times. In these cases, participants will serve as their own control by participating in all of the conditions, with their return to baseline serving as the control. This distinction will further be explored in this chapter when outlining between- and within-group experimental designs.

THE PARADIGMATIC HIERARCHY OF EXPERIMENTAL RESEARCH

As discussed in Chapter 1, a research paradigm (the philosophical bedrock on which research designs are based) consists of five components: ontology, epistemology, theoretical stance, methodology, and methods (Crotty, 2003). Listed hierarchically from broadest to most specific, these components interact with one another and the details of specific research studies (e.g., research questions, sample, rigor). Consequently, experimental research studies are all based on the same general research paradigm.

Ontology, the first step in the hierarchy, refers to the essence of reality and how it is understood (Scotland, 2012). Experimental research is based in **realism**, or the belief that there is a true, universal reality existing outside of subjective understanding. This view primarily differs from the relativist perspective in that personal experiences and interpretations do not constitute reality. Relatedly, the epistemological basis of experimental research is **objectivism**, in which researchers are detached from the reality they are studying. Experimental researchers aim to be as impartial as possible and separate themselves from the phenomenon they are studying. In this way, they attempt to describe and make inferences about an objective reality that is not tied to their personal experiences.

The theoretical stance of experimental research is an offshoot of positivism known as **post-positivism** (Kivunja & Kuyini, 2017). Post-positivism states that, although there is a true, objective reality, it is not possible to fully understand a single reality. Consequently, researchers are only able to estimate the essence of reality and make general statements about it, rather than provide definitive conclusions (Heppner et al., 2016). This theoretical stance underlies the tentative language typically used when reporting the findings of experimental studies. For example, researchers often state that results "indicate" or "suggest" certain findings but will not conclude that their results "prove" something definitively. Additionally, researchers often replicate studies using similar samples or procedures to add support for initial findings. Finally, although researchers attempt to be impartial and exact in their methods (stemming from the objectivist epistemology), they recognize that it is not possible for any study to be conducted either without personal bias or under perfect conditions.

Next, as the name suggests, the experimental methodology underlies experimental research (Heppner et al., 2016). Consequently, researchers use the scientific method to systematically examine phenomena of interest. This process includes developing testable hypotheses based on previous knowledge that guides the development and execution of studies. Results of these studies are then used to provide an approximate understanding of objective reality (Kivunja & Kuyini, 2017).

EXPERIMENTAL LABORATORY STUDIES VERSUS FIELD EXPERIMENTS

Given that the purpose of experimental research is to test a causal hypothesis, researchers attempt to isolate the causal effect by conducting **experimental laboratory studies** in a controlled environment. You might be envisioning a laboratory with test tubes. Instead, laboratory refers to conducting the study under highly controlled conditions to minimize the role of extraneous variables (Heppner et al., 2016). Highly controlled conditions coupled with standardized procedures provides for replication of the study (and cause and effect, if observed).

Let us consider a seminal experimental laboratory study on learned helplessness conducted by Seligman and Maier (1967). The researchers assessed the impact of escape possibility (the independent variable) on later escape behavior (the dependent variable). They put dogs into an apparatus that delivered shocks to the dogs' footpads. The dogs were randomly assigned to have a panel in their apparatus that, when pressed by the dog, would either stop the shocks or have no effect. As expected, most of the dogs who had a panel that would stop the shocks quickly learned to push it when the shocks started. However, the dogs that were not able to escape the shocks showed difficulty in learning how to escape, even when they were given mechanisms to do so. In this experiment, all dogs were put in the same apparatus and had the same number and intensity of shocks administered. There was even a panel present in both conditions; the only difference was if the panel stopped the shocks or had no effect on them. This was the controlled aspect of the study that is necessary for an experimental laboratory study. Although this experiment would likely not be conducted today due to problematic ethical issues with harming animals, it does provide a seminal example of a controlled laboratory study.

In the social sciences, however, there are many instances where it is not feasible to study a phenomenon in a laboratory due to access to the target population or nature of the intervention being studied. In these cases, **field experiments** are conducted in which the experiment takes place in the real-world (i.e., natural) setting. For instance, testing an intervention in a school or classroom environment takes place in a real-world setting. While Donald Campbell and Thomas Cook were seminal leaders in applying experimental designs in social science research in the 1950s, use of field experiments increased during the 1960s with the evaluation of the federal government's Great Society social programs under the War on Poverty (Shadish et al., 1991).

Important to note is that field experiments are distinct from field studies. **Field studies** are non-experimental in that the researcher studies behaviors or attitudes *without* manipulating a variable in the natural environment or controlling for potential extraneous variables (Persaud, 2010). In field experiments, the researcher follows the scientific process and can establish randomized controls (Persaud, 2010). Let us consider an example of a field experiment testing the effectiveness of the Helping to Overcome Post-Traumatic Stress Disorder through Empowerment (HOPE) program (Johnson et al., 2016). The researchers tested the impact of HOPE on a number of psychological outcomes for residents of battered women's shelters. After meeting multiple inclusion criteria to participate in the study, women similar on the baseline measures (i.e., Clinician-Administered PTSD Scale; Blake et al., 1995) and in demographics were randomly assigned to the HOPE or control condition. The HOPE condition consisted of completing 10 sessions during their residence at the shelter and six sessions 3 months following their residence at the shelter. The control group received the traditional shelter services. The women completed measures 1 week, 3 months, and 6 months post treatment. Given the target population and the nature of the intervention partially during their residence at a battered women's shelter, a field experiment was necessary.

CONDUCTING LABORATORY OR FIELD EXPERIMENTS

You might be questioning at this point how a researcher decides whether to conduct an experimental laboratory study or field experiment. As with any research study, the research purpose and questions drive the research design. We outline six factors to consider in this decision. These factors are not described in any priority order and are non-exhaustive.

First, consult the federal regulations for research as the regulations might indicate that the research should be conducted in a laboratory to protect the participants. Second, consider whether you are conducting human subjects or animal subjects research. While human subject research might take place in a laboratory or field environment, animal subjects research typically takes place in a laboratory environment. Third, determine the access to the target population. The target population might only be accessible in a real-world context. Fourth, consider how closely the intervention implementation (i.e., treatment fidelity) and data collection needs to be monitored to provide for precise results (e.g., high-stakes medical research). Fifth, consider how closely the response to intervention needs to be monitored for adverse events due to the potential of risk. Sixth, determine what apparatus is needed for data collection. If equipment such as brain imaging or physiological monitoring are used, then a laboratory setting will likely be needed.

STRENGTHS AND LIMITATIONS OF LABORATORY AND FIELD EXPERIMENTS

Experimental laboratory studies and field experiments have different strengths and limitations. Experimental laboratory studies increase the internal validity of the study results through use of highly controlled conditions. In the context of experimental research, **internal validity** refers to what extent the independent variable explains the causal effect (Campbell, 1957; Campbell & Stanley, 1963). Although internal validity is increased, the degree of **external validity** or generalizability is threatened because the research is conducted in an artificial setting. Specifically, the **ecological validity** of the study results is lowered in that the results might not transfer to other contexts or settings (Campbell, 1957; Campbell & Stanley, 1963).

Field experiments, on the other hand, have increased **external validity** in that the study results are more likely to generalize to the real-world setting in the social world where the phenomenon is taking place (Persaud, 2010). However, the internal validity is lowered in a field study in that the experimental researcher is unable to control or account for a number of extraneous variables. Additionally, experimental field studies have higher **participant mortality** (or **attrition**), meaning dropout rates, especially when taking place over an extended period of time. For instance, in the study testing the effect of the HOPE program on PTSD in residents of battered women's shelters, three in the control group and nine in the intervention group were not able to be accessed by the fourth data collection point in the study 6 months post treatment. As a result of lack of a controlled setting, a field experiment is less replicable. In turn, the cause and effect observed in a field study might also be less replicable as compared to an experimental laboratory study.

Figure 5.2 summarizes the relationship between internal and external validity for laboratory and field experiments. Whereas experimental laboratory studies increase the degree of internal validity, external validity is decreased. The inverse is true for field experiments in that while the degree of external validity is increased, internal validity is decreased.

Two specific designs commonly applied in the social sciences that may be conducted as laboratory or field experiments are between-groups and within-groups experimental designs. Before we outline these two designs in detail, complete Exercise 1 to apply your understanding of the (a) main characteristics of experimental research as compared to other quantitative traditions, (b) distinction between laboratory and field experiments, and (c) relationship between internal and external validity.

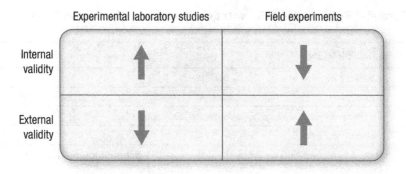

FIGURE 5.2 Relationship Between Internal and External Validity in Laboratory and Field Experiments.

BETWEEN-GROUPS EXPERIMENTAL DESIGNS

Between-groups experimental designs refers to experimental designs addressing research questions comparing the effect of the independent variable across independent groups. The groups being compared are the intervention and control group or different conditions of the intervention. Also, the groups must be independent in that participants are only in one of the groups being compared. For instance, participants are only in the intervention or control group or one of the conditions being compared. Two types of between-groups experimental designs are **true experimental** and **quasi-experimental**. The independent variable is manipulated by the researcher in both types of designs but how the groups are formed differs across the two designs. Let us first consider variations of true experimental designs, which are the most robust type of experimental design.

TRUE EXPERIMENTAL DESIGNS

In **true experimental designs**, the researcher randomly assigns participants to an experimental or a control condition to test for a causal effect. As a review, random assignment is when each participant has an equal probability of being assigned to each condition (Schweigert, 2012). The use of random assignment increases the likelihood that any differences observed between the groups on the dependent variable are accounted for by the independent variable and not extraneous variables. In theory, any systematic individual differences are minimized by being equally distributed across the experimental and control groups (Heppner et al., 2016). As a result of minimizing error variances, the use of random assignment increases the degree of internal validity of the study results.

There are multiple variations of true experimental designs that can be applied depending on the research question. Researchers illustrate the type of design by using a standard notation system. Common symbols used in experimental research are listed in Table 5.1. This notation system provides for researchers to illustrate the design using a common language. It is customary practice to illustrate the design in notation when describing the experimental design in research reports. This notation system is particularly useful when designing complex experimental studies with multiple conditions and time points.

Table 5.2 provides a summary of the major experimental research designs. The notation for the most basic form of each design is listed to easily differentiate among types of experimental designs. Table 5.2 can be a useful resource for deciding which design aligns to your research question.

TABLE 5.1 Common Symbols Used in Notation System for Illustrating Experimental Research Designs

SYMBOL	DESCRIPTION
R	Random assignment
O	Observation
O_1, O_2, O_3	Observation number (e.g., O_1 = baseline, O_2 = posttest)
X	Intervention
X_A, X_B, X_{AB}	Intervention condition whereby the letters denote different intervention conditions (e.g., X_{AB} = combination of intervention A and B).
P	Placebo
_ _ _ _ _	Non-equivalent groups

TABLE 5.2 Summary of Common Between-Groups Experimental Research Designs

EXPERIMENTAL RESEARCH DESIGNS		
DESIGN	DESCRIPTION	NOTATION FOR BASIC DESIGN
Pretest-posttest control group design	Intervention and control group compared on baseline and post measures	$R \quad O_1 \quad X \quad O_2$ $R \quad O_1 \qquad O_2$
Posttest only control group design	Intervention and control group compared on post measures only	$R \quad X \quad O$ $R \qquad O$
Alternative treatment design	Two different intervention conditions with a control group	$R \quad O_1 \quad X_A \quad O_2$ $R \quad O_1 \quad X_B \quad O_2$ $R \quad O_1 \qquad O_2$
Dismantling studies	Multiple intervention conditions including the full intervention and components of the intervention, as well as a control group	$R \quad O_1 \quad X_{AB} \quad O_2$ $R \quad O_1 \quad X_A \quad O_2$ $R \quad O_1 \quad X_B \quad O_2$ $R \quad O_1 \qquad O_2$
Placebo control group design	Intervention group and at least two control groups with one control group receiving no treatment and one control group receiving a placebo treatment	$R \quad O_1 \quad X \quad O_2$ $R \quad O_1 \quad P \quad O_2$ $R \quad O_1 \qquad O_2$
Quasi-Experimental Research Designs		
Equivalent-group research design	Intervention and control groups who are demonstrated to be statistically similar at baseline on the dependent variable(s) and other key variables	$O_1 \quad X \quad O_2$ $O_1 \quad X \quad O_2$
Non-equivalent group research design	Intervention and control (or alternative treatment) groups who differ at baseline on key variables	$O_1 \quad X \quad O_2$ _ _ _ _ _ _ _ $O_1 \quad X \quad O_2$

Pretest-Posttest Control Group Design

A commonly applied experimental design is the **pretest-posttest control group design**, where data are collected at baseline and after the intervention for the experimental and control group. In this design, there is one experimental group and one control group who complete the same measures at both time points. The design is denoted as (Rubin & Babbie, 2016):

$$R \quad O_1 \quad X \quad O_2$$
$$R \quad O_1 \qquad O_2$$

The R indicates each participant was randomly assigned to either the experimental or control group, O_1 is the first point of data collection at baseline, and O_2 is the second data collection point directly after the intervention X was implemented for the experimental group. Data collection points can be extended to include multiple posttests completed by both groups (e.g., $O_{3...}$).

This design is appropriate for addressing research questions testing for a causal effect by comparing whether an experimental and a control group significantly differ on a dependent variable(s). Since data are collected for each individual in the experimental and control groups, this design can be used when testing for differences in growth or change scores between the groups on the dependent variable(s). As an example, Esmaeilian et al. (2018) tested the effect of a 12-week Mindfulness-Based Cognitive Therapy for Children (MBCT-C) on multiple psychological outcomes for children of divorced parents. The research purpose was to test whether children who completed the therapy (the experimental group) had a greater increase in emotional resiliency and mindfulness (the effects) compared to children who did not participate in the therapy (the control group). The independent variable in this study was the variable manipulated by the researcher, the MBCT-C intervention (the cause). Multiple dependent variables were measured in this study to represent emotional resiliency including depression, anxiety, anger symptoms, and mindfulness (the effects).

In Esmaeilian et al.'s (2018) study, the children had to meet **inclusion criteria** to participate in the study. For instance, they had to be between 10 and 13 years old and have no history of clinical or behavior problems on their school record prior to their parents being divorced (Esmaelian et al., 2018). By establishing this inclusion criteria, the researchers were attempting to minimize the influence of pre-existing behavior problems on the dependent variables. Random assignment (R) was used with 16 boys and 26 girls assigned to the experimental group ($n = 42$) and 17 boys and 24 girls assigned to the control group ($n = 41$). Both groups completed the same four pretests prior to the intervention (O_1), the posttest directly after the 12-week intervention (O_2), and again two months following the intervention (O_3). Having both groups complete the pretest and posttests allowed the researchers to (a) establish a baseline, (b) test if any pre-existing differences were observed between the two groups, (c) test for change within each group over time (main effect of time), (d) test for group differences on the posttests (main effect of group membership), and (e) test for an interaction between time and group membership on the dependent variables.

By applying this design, the researchers controlled for or minimized threats to internal validity by use of random assignment, specific inclusion criteria, and assigning relatively equal sample sizes with similar demographic make-up across the two groups. However, potential threats to internal validity remain in the pretest-posttest design. One threat is the **testing effect** in that participants are completing the same measures multiple times (i.e., repeated testing) which might result in error variance. Participants in either group scoring really high (**ceiling effect**) or low (**floor effect**) on the pretests might have **regression toward the mean** on the posttests. As a result of their initial scores, differences on the posttests might be due to this phenomenon of regression toward the mean instead of true differences between the two groups (Schweigert, 2012).

Another threat to internal validity associated with pretest-posttest control group designs, and any design with a repeated measuring, is participant attrition. In the case of Esmaelian et al.'s (2018) MBCT-C intervention study, 90% of the children in the experimental group completed the posttests with two dropping out before participating in the intervention and two dropping out during the intervention due to scheduling conflicts. In the control group, 80% of the children completed the posttests with four dropping out after completing the pretests and another four dropping out before completing the follow-up measures. This attrition can impact whether the groups remain equivalent. **Equivalent** refers to the experimental and control group being the same (or not statistically different) at baseline on the study variables and other key characteristics related to the study variables.

Experimental researchers need to consider whether this attrition was non-systematic or systematic mortality. **Non-systematic mortality** occurs when participant attrition is evenly distributed across the groups and their measures did not differ on the dependent variables compared to those retained in the study (Schweigert, 2012). **Systematic mortality** occurs when the attrition is unevenly distributed or those who dropped out differ on the study variables compared to those who remained in the study (Schweigert, 2012). For instance, systematic mortality would be a threat to internal validity if those who dropped out in the experimental group were those scoring extremely low on the pretests, whereas those dropping out in the control group were those scoring extremely high on the pretests.

Posttest Only Control Group Design

In cases where the testing effect or attrition is a concern, a **posttest only control group design** can be applied. In this design, the experimental and control group complete only posttest measures. The posttest only control group design is denoted as (Rubin & Babbie, 2016):

$$R \quad X \quad O$$
$$R \quad \quad O$$

Similar to all true-experimental designs, R indicates random assignment of participants to the experimental and X represents the intervention implemented in the experimental condition. The O stands for the single data collection point for both groups after the intervention implementation.

This design is appropriate when a researcher has evidence to support that completing the pretest will influence the intervention, a **testing effect** is likely to influence the scores on the posttest, or it is not feasible to collect pretest data. For example, consider a study examining whether therapists' encouragement of self-help resources increases therapy clients' use of such resources. In this case, clients completing a pretest questionnaire about different self-help strategies they might have engaged in prior to therapy could impact interval validity by influencing the intervention. By completing the questionnaire, the clients might learn about self-help interventions of which they were otherwise not aware. Such awareness might lead to some clients making use of self-help resources, regardless of whether they are in the experimental group (receiving therapist encouragement to use self-help resources) or the control group (not receiving this type of encouragement). Consequently, a or gathering retroactive pretests (e.g., asking at posttest which self-help interventions clients used prior to therapy) would minimize the effects of such awareness on the study being conducted.

The assumption in a posttest-only design is that random assignment will yield equivalent groups in regard to their baseline on the dependent variable(s) such that any difference observed on the posttest is due to the independent variable (Rubin & Babbie, 2016). As a result of this assumption and lack of pretest measures, this design is more subject to threats to internal validity compared to a pretest-posttest control design and is thus less robust for claiming a causal effect.

Alternative Treatment Design

If two experimental conditions are being compared on a dependent variable(s) to test for a causal effect, then an **alternative treatment design** with pretest and posttest is appropriate. This design is an extension of the pretest-posttest control group design. In an alternative treatment design, multiple experimental conditions are compared and tested against the control group to establish a causal effect. A key characteristic is that each participant is only exposed to one of the experimental conditions. The most basic notation for this design is (Rubin & Babbie, 2016):

$$R \quad O_1 \quad X_A \quad O_2$$
$$R \quad O_1 \quad X_B \quad O_2$$
$$R \quad O_1 \qquad\; O_2$$

The R indicates random assignment into one of the two experimental conditions or control group with all three independent groups completing the pretest (O_1) and posttest (O_2). X_A represents one experimental condition and X_B represents a different experimental condition.

Researchers might apply this design when comparing treatments or interventions that differ in terms of approaches, cost, invasiveness, or intensity. Imagine that two different treatments designed to target the same outcomes are shown to be equally as effective but one is more costly or invasive than the other. The result would lend support in adopting the less invasive or costly treatment.

Another application of the alternative treatment design is for testing a newly developed treatment over an established treatment. For example, there might be a therapy treatment that was developed 20 years ago that is widely applied in practice. A new and completely different therapy informed by current research and theory is developed by a team of researchers. Let us refer to the two treatments as therapy A (older technique) and therapy B (newly developed technique). Therapy B was designed to target the same diagnosis and outcomes but differs greatly in its approach than therapy A. To test this newly developed therapy against the older but widely used treatment, the researchers can conduct an alternative treatment design study randomly assigning clients to condition A, condition B, or no treatment (control condition).

Dismantling Experimental Design

If comparing interventions that have overlapping components, then a **dismantling experimental design** is more appropriate. The purpose of this design is to test which components of the intervention or combination of components is most effective on the dependent variable(s). A common example is comparing whether medicine (condition A), therapy (condition B), or medicine + therapy (condition C) is most effective compared to the control condition. The most simplistic form of this design can be denoted as (Rubin & Babbie, 2016):

$$R \quad O_1 \quad X_{AB} \quad O_2$$
$$R \quad O_1 \quad X_A \quad O_2$$
$$R \quad O_1 \quad X_B \quad O_2$$
$$R \quad O_1 \qquad \quad O_2$$

Notice that random assignment (R) is used to assign participants to one condition whereby X_{AB} is the condition with the full intervention, X_A is the condition with an element of the full intervention removed, and X_B is a different element of the full intervention removed. Participants across all of the conditions complete the pretests (O_1) and posttests (O_2) to determine which intervention was most effective.

This design is useful when developing treatments to isolate which core component(s) are more or less effective on the dependent variable(s). The condition that yields the largest change in the desired direction on the dependent variable(s) from pretest to posttest is the most effective (Rubin & Babbie, 2016). Let us use the preceding example with three treatment conditions and one control condition to consider the different results that might occur in dismantling studies. The first scenario is that no treatment condition yields a significant change in the desired direction. The second scenario is that all three treatment conditions (X_{AB}, X_A, X_B) are equally as effective and more effective than the control condition. The third scenario is that one treatment condition (e.g., X_{AB}) is more effective over the other two (e.g., X_A and X_B). The fourth scenario is that two of the treatment conditions are more effective over the third treatment condition. However, for a causal effect to be established for any one of the treatment conditions, the effect needs to be greater than for the control group.

Placebo Control Group Design

In cases that research reactivity is a concern when testing the effect of an intervention, the **placebo control group design** can be applied. **Researcher reactivity** is a threat to internal validity in that the effect is cause by a researcher's behavior or the procedures instead of the independent variable (Rubin & Babbie, 2016). Researchers can control for this threat by establishing a placebo condition whereby participants are informed that they are receiving the treatment and are exposed to a similar stimulus but indeed are not receiving the treatment being tested.

A placebo condition can be established through a single-blind or double-blind procedure. In a **single-blind procedure**, either the participant or researcher is unaware what condition the participant was assigned to for the study (Schweigert, 2012). In a **double-blind procedure**, both the participant and researcher are unaware what condition the participant was assigned to for the study (Schweigert, 2012). A double-blind procedure minimizes the threat of research reactivity more than a single-blind procedure by limiting the researchers' **demand characteristics** (i.e., cues) that might influence the participant's response to the treatment.

QUASI-EXPERIMENTAL DESIGNS

When conducting human subject research in the social sciences, it is not always possible to randomly assigned individual participants to an experimental and a control condition, especially when conducting research in natural settings (i.e., field experiments). A **quasi-experimental**

research design is used when testing a causal hypothesis but random assignment is not possible. Before we further define quasi-experimental designs, consider the basic definition of "quasi." *Quasi* is of Latin origin meaning "as if" or "as though." If you research the definition of *quasi*, you will find that it is commonly defined as "having some, but not all of the features" (Dictionary.com, 2019). In this case, quasi-experimental designs resemble some characteristics but not all with true experimental designs.

In quasi-experimental research designs, individual participants are *not* randomly assigned to an experimental or a control condition. The groups in quasi-experimental research are often pre-existing groups, also referred to as pre-formed groups. Examples of existing groups are students nested in a classroom or clients already participating in a type of intervention (or lack of). These groups might be pre-existing based on natural characteristics or artificial characteristics, such as gender, past use of therapy, or cultural background. Because the groups are pre-existing, the control group is more appropriately referred to as a **comparison group** since the researcher did not randomly assign individual participants to this group. Also, more often than not, the comparison group receives the traditional (i.e., treatment as usual) form of services, treatment, or other intervention.

Let us consider four scenarios of pre-existing groups that form the experimental and control condition. In one scenario, the researcher might assign one group to the experimental condition and another group to the control condition. For instance, one classroom of students might be assigned to the intervention (X) condition and another classroom of students assigned to the control group. This scenario is common when conducting research in educational settings where it is not feasible to rearrange classroom assignments. In a second scenario, the researcher might randomly assign which classroom is in the experimental or control condition. However, because the individuals are not randomly assigned, it is still a quasi-experimental design and not a true experimental design. In a third scenario, participants might already be enrolled in the intervention under study or a particular site might be participating in a program and thus by default in the treatment condition.

The use of a control group and manipulation of the independent variable for testing a causal hypothesis results in quasi-experimental research designs and in more robust than correlational designs. However, the lack of random assignment results in these designs being less robust than true experimental research due to threats to internal validity (Cook & Campbell, 1979). Nevertheless, these designs are often applied in the social sciences. Two major types of quasi-experimental designs are **equivalent-group** and **non-equivalent group research designs**. A brief description and the basic notation for these two designs are provided in Table 5.2.

Equivalent-Group Research Design

In an **equivalent-group research design**, the intervention group (or alternative treatment groups) and control group are demonstrated to be statistically similar on key variables including the dependent variable(s) at baseline. This design is denoted as:

$$O_1 \quad X \quad O_2$$
$$O_1 \quad \quad O_2$$

Notice that the lack of R in the notation indicates the researcher did *not* randomly assign individual participants to each condition. This design can be modified to reflect pretest-posttests or posttest only or extended to reflect different conditions being tested such as alternative treatments.

Consider an example of an equivalent group's quasi-experimental design in a study conducted on the effects of a Truancy Intervention Program (TIP) on students' annual daily school attendance rate over time from seventh to tenth grade (McNeely et al., 2019). The program consisted of three levels of interference including a parent meeting, hearing to generate a school attendance agreement, and petition to juvenile court. The intervention group was made up of students who lived in a public school district where TIP was adopted and had a record of six or more unexcused absences. The comparison group was made of students enrolled in a demographically similar school district that did not implement a TIP intervention (matching level 1). Also, a statistical technique was used to identify students for the comparison group who were similar to those in the intervention group (matching level 2). Several variables deemed by the researchers as relevant to the study were used to establish an equivalent comparison group. These variables included absenteeism rate from the prior 3 years, demographic variables, individualized education program status, and history of maltreatment, to name a few. Because the samples were matched at baseline, the researchers could be more confident that the differences observed on school attendance rate were attributed to the TIP intervention.

Non-Equivalent Groups Research Design

In a **non-equivalent groups research design**, the two groups are shown to differ at baseline on the key variable including the dependent variable(s). In this design, matching techniques are not used to establish the comparison group. This design is denoted as (Rubin & Babbie, 2016):

$$O_1 \quad X \quad O_2$$
$$- - - - - -$$
$$O_1 \qquad O_2$$

A dashed line (- - - - -) is used in the notation to indicate the groups are non-equivalent. Matched sampling is not used either because researchers do not have the available data to establish a matched sample or the groups are pre-formed. For these reasons, this design is less robust than equivalent-groups given that the effect of the intervention might be due to pre-existing differences at baseline.

Creating Matched Groups

When random assignment is not possible, multiple statistical techniques are available for creating **matched samples** whereby the intervention and control group are similar on pre-existing variables referred to as **covariates**. Creating matched samples increases the degree of internal validity by reducing the likelihood that differences observed between or among groups on the outcome are due to pre-existing differences or potentially confounding variables. Although the goal is to equate the groups, noteworthy is that these techniques are *not* as robust as using random assignment (Nagengast et al., 2014).

In order to create matched samples, the researcher must identify relevant covariates to use in creating the matched samples. Data on the covariates must be available for a pool of individuals in the intervention group and those not receiving the intervention. For instance, if comparing school climate for year-round schools (the intervention group) and traditional calendar schools (the comparison group), there must be data available on students from the comparison group to generate the matched samples.

Common techniques include Mahalanobis Distance Matching (Rubin, 1980), Propensity Score Matching (Rosenbaum & Rubin, 1983), and Coarsened Exact Matching (Iacus et al., 2009). **Propensity Score Matching** or PSM is one of the more commonly applied matching technique in the social sciences. This technique can be conducted using a variety of statistical packages such as R, SPSS, or SAS. Briefly, a logistic regression approach is adopted to estimate the probability or odds of group membership in the intervention or control group based on a set of baseline covariates (Rosenbaum & Rubin, 1985). The covariates are the independent or predictor variables in the model and the group membership (intervention or control) is the dependent variable. Individuals who have exact or similar **predicted probability** of being in the intervention or control group based on a vector of covariate values are identified as a match. The resultant predicted probability of an individual being in a condition given the covariates is referred to as the **propensity score**, denoted as:

$$p(x) = \Pr(T = 1 \mid X = x)$$

In this equation, $p(x)$ represents the conditional probability that an individual will belong to the treatment group, T is the treatment group, and $X = x$ is the set of covariate scores. The covariates are tested to determine sufficient overlap among the groups on the covariates, providing support that the groups are similar. Multiple different algorithms can be used to generate the matches using different parameters. Depending on the algorithm applied, a 1:1 match might result or the overall sample size might be reduced based on the number of individuals able to be matched. Noteworthy is that this match is based on a *predicted* probability, indicating there is a degree of error associated with each propensity score computed, as with any statistic.

Additional techniques such as the Piecewise Propensity Score Analysis (Bodily et al., 2018) or marginal mean weighting through stratification (Hong, 2010, 2012) can be used for cases where more than three matched samples need to be created. Each technique has its own strengths (e.g., Rosenbaum & Rubin, 1983) and limitations (e.g., King & Nielsen, 2019) that are discussed in-depth in the literature. It is beyond the scope of this chapter to review each technique in depth. Instead, we point the reader to the additional resources listed at the end of the chapter for further readings on the different techniques and procedures for creating matched samples.

WITHIN-GROUPS EXPERIMENTAL DESIGNS

Within-groups experimental designs refer to those designs in which all participants experience both the treatment and control condition(s). In other words, participants are their own controls (Greenwald, 1976). As with other experimental designs, there is a manipulated independent variable and (when applicable) participants are randomly assigned, making within-group designs true experiments (Heppner et al., 2016). Consequently, they use the same symbols to denote the particular designs as shown in Table 5.1. Since the same participants complete all of the conditions, all within-groups designs are **longitudinal**; that is, data are collected at different points in time (Appelbaum et al., 2018).

In this section, we cover two types of designs: **crossover** and **time series**. A crossover design is the major type of within-groups experimental design with many variations depending on the research scenario. Time-series designs are considered quasi-experimental (Phan & Ngu, 2017); however, we have chosen to discuss them here, rather than with the other quasi-experimental designs, as they also share characteristics with within-groups designs, such as examining the same participants over time. These two designs are outlined in Table 5.3 as a quick resource tool.

TABLE 5.3 **Summary of Common Within-Group Experimental Research Designs**

DESIGN	DESCRIPTION	NOTATION FOR BASIC DESIGN
Simple crossover design	All participants in two (or more) intervention conditions	$O_1 \quad X_1 \quad O_2 \quad X_2 \quad O_3$
Counterbalanced crossover design	Two (or more) intervention conditions completed in different orders	$R \quad O_1 \quad X_1 \quad O_2 \quad X_2 \quad O_3$ $R \quad O_1 \quad X_2 \quad O_2 \quad X_1 \quad O_3$
Simple interrupted time series	Multiple observations with one intervention condition	$O_1 \quad O_2 \quad O_3 \quad X \quad O_4 \quad O_5 \quad O_6$
Non-equivalent dependent variable interrupted time series	Multiple observations of more than one dependent variable with one treatment condition	$O_{A1} \quad O_{A2} \quad O_{A3} \quad X \quad O_{A4} \quad O_{A5} \quad O_{A6}$ $O_{B1} \quad O_{B2} \quad O_{B3} \quad X \quad O_{B4} \quad O_{B5} \quad O_{B6}$
Comparative time series design (quasi-experimental)	Multiple observations of more than one dependent variable with one intervention condition compared to a control group not receiving the intervention	$O_1 \quad O_2 \quad O_3 \quad X \quad O_4 \quad O_5 \quad O_6$ $O_1 \quad O_2 \quad O_3 \qquad O_4 \quad O_5 \quad O_6$

CROSSOVER DESIGNS

Simple crossover designs are characterized by participants completing all levels of the independent variable, with observations of the dependent variable before and after each level of the independent variable is administered. This design is denoted as:

$$O_1 \quad X_1 \quad O_2 \quad X_2 \quad O_3$$

Since the same participants complete all of the conditions, it is important to start with an observation of the dependent variable, which can serve as a baseline for comparison after manipulating the independent variable. After the first observation, one level of the independent variable is administered, after which there is another observation of the dependent variable. Next, the second level of the independent variable is given, followed by a final observation of the dependent variable. In this way, the three observations of the dependent variable can be compared (i.e., the baseline observation to each of the later observations; the observation after the first level of the independent variable to the observation after the second level of the independent variable) to determine where effects took place.

For example, a researcher might be interested in determining the effectiveness of two different treatments for anxiety. All participants would first complete a measure of anxiety to determine how high their anxiety is prior to receiving treatments. Next, one of the treatments would be given to all the participants. After giving the first treatment, anxiety levels are measured again. The participants then all receive the second treatment, then their anxiety levels are measured for the last time. The decision which treatment to give first depends on the research; there may be a specific reason (e.g., a standard treatment first followed by a new treatment), or the decision may be arbitrary. Similarly, the time between the observations and treatments can vary. Finally, the design can be extended to include more than two levels of the independent variable and subsequent observations.

This basic type of crossover design is seldom used in practice due to its threats to internal validity, particularly **order effects** and **sequence effects** (Greenwald, 1976; Heppner et al., 2016). Regarding order effects, the order in which the levels of the independent variable are administered might impact all of the following observations of the dependent variable, not just the one immediately following. For instance, in our earlier example, participants were given two treatments for anxiety to determine the effectiveness of each treatment. The second observation of the dependent variable was given after the first treatment, and the third observation was given after the second treatment. However, since all participants had completed both treatments by the time the third observation was given, it is difficult to determine if the results were due to the second treatment or both treatments. If anxiety decreased from the second to the third observation, this might be due to the second treatment, the first treatment, or a combination of both. For instance, participants might have learned skills from the first treatment that they continued to employ while completing the second treatment; this might lead to lower levels of anxiety at the third observation that is due to the first treatment but not the second. Sequence effects are similar to order effects in that the particular order in which treatments are given might impact their effectiveness. For instance, the second treatment might only be useful if participants learned certain skills during the first treatment, yielding low anxiety scores on the final observation; if the order had been reversed, the second treatment might not have had an impact.

Given the issues with order and sequence effects in the simple crossover design, it is much more common for researchers to use the **counterbalanced crossover design**. Like the simple crossover design, all participants receive all levels of the independent variable, with observations of the dependent variable at the start, end, and between each level of the independent variable. However, participants are first randomly assigned to the sequence in which they will be exposed to the levels of the independent variable. This design is denoted as:

$$R \quad O_1 \quad X_1 \quad O_2 \quad X_2 \quad O_3$$
$$R \quad O_1 \quad X_2 \quad O_2 \quad X_1 \quad O_3$$

In this case, participants are randomly assigned to receive both levels of the independent variable, but in different orders. The first group is first administered one level of treatment and then the other, whereas the second group is administered the treatments in the opposite order. This helps to "counterbalance" the potential order effects (as the two groups complete the levels of the independent variables in different orders). Additionally, the observations of the dependent variable can be compared across the groups to determine if there are sequence effects. For instance, if the second treatment appears to have a strong effect for the first group (for whom it was administered second) compared to the second group (for whom it was administered first), it is possible that the second treatment may be more effective when it follows the first treatment (Heppner et al., 2016).

As an example of a counterbalanced crossover design, Swift et al. (2017) examined the impact of student therapists' mindfulness training (the independent variable) on their own mindfulness, their presence during therapy sessions, and their clients' beliefs about session outcomes. They randomly assigned 40 psychology graduate student therapists to one of two groups. The first group completed a 5-week mindfulness training, followed by a 5-week waiting period (the two levels of the independent variable). The second group completed the two levels in the opposite order: they began with a 5-week waiting period, then completed the 5-week mindfulness training. In both groups, the student therapists completed measures of mindfulness and session presence, and their clients completed a measure evaluating their therapy sessions, at the start, end, and between the two conditions of the independent variable. The results showed that the mindfulness training resulted in higher levels of therapist-reported mindfulness and presence during session, although clients' evaluations of sessions did not differ significantly across conditions.

Although the discussion of the counterbalanced crossover design so far has focused on only two levels of the independent variable, it is possible to extend it to three or more levels. However, this is more complex than with the simple crossover design. For the simple crossover design, the additional levels could simply be added at the end, with the appropriate observations of the dependent variable also included. For the counterbalanced crossover design, participants should be randomly assigned to groups in such a way that all levels of the independent variable are in all positions relative to each other (**counterbalancing**). This is relatively simple with two levels but becomes increasingly complex as more levels are added. For example, with two levels of the independent variable (X), only two groups are needed: one group receives the first level (X_1) first and the second level (X_2) second ($X_1 X_2$), and the second group receives them in the opposite order ($X_2 X_1$). However, with three levels of the independent variable, six groups are needed for one group to receive each potential order: (a) $X_1 X_2 X_3$, (b) $X_1 X_3 X_2$, (c) $X_2 X_1 X_3$, (d) $X_2 X_3 X_1$, (e) $X_3 X_1 X_2$, and (f) $X_3 X_2 X_1$. Four levels of the independent variable would require twenty-four groups, and so on. Consequently, studies with more than two or three levels of the independent quickly become impractical to conduct with one group per order.

Given the aforementioned difficulty, researchers have determined a way to practically conduct counterbalanced crossover designs with several levels of the independent variable by using **Latin square designs** (Richardson, 2018). First described by Fisher (1925), in Latin square designs, the number of group participants are randomly assigned equal to the number of levels of the independent variable. Across groups, the levels of the independent variable appear only once in each position. For example, a counterbalanced crossover design using a Latin square design would have three groups denoted as such:

$$
\begin{array}{ccccccc}
R & O_1 & X_1 & O_2 & X_2 & O_3 & X_3 & O_4 \\
R & O_1 & X_3 & O_2 & X_1 & O_3 & X_2 & O_4 \\
R & O_1 & X_2 & O_2 & X_3 & O_3 & X_1 & O_4
\end{array}
$$

In this case, each level of the independent variable is at each possible position: first, middle, and last (Richardson, 2018). An easy way to create a Latin square design order with multiple variable is to list them in order for the first row, then take the last variable and put it first for the second row, then take the last variable for that row and put it first for the third row, and so on until all levels of the independent variable are accounted for. This technique has been done as an example. The treatment order was originally $X_1 X_2 X_3$ for the first row. Moving X_3 to be first for the second row, this would simply move over the other two levels, creating $X_3 X_1 X_2$. Moving X_2 to be first for the third row, this would then move over the other two levels, making $X_2 X_3 X_1$. If X_1 were moved to start a fourth row, the resulting sequence would repeat the first row and is thus unnecessary.

There are known strengths associated with crossover designs (Greenwald, 1976). Since participants are their own controls, this design tends to be powerful statistically, resulting in needing approximately half the number of participants compared to a similar between-groups design. Additionally, **subject variance** (random differences across groups due to individual differences among participants) are minimized, since participants are compared to themselves rather than other groups of people. Finally, in some cases, crossover designs might have higher ecological validity than between-groups designs due to the presence of confounds such as the passage of time.

Such strengths notwithstanding, there are several limitations that researchers should consider when deciding to use crossover designs, in addition to the order and sequence effects already mentioned (Heppner et al., 2016). Due to the longitudinal nature of crossover designs, they are time-consuming, even if fewer participants are required. They are also prone to threats to internal validity associated with longitudinal designs, such as **history** (the occurrence of something in the environment during the course of a study that impacts the results of the study), **maturation** (participants developing and growing older across time), and participant attrition. Consequently, it is important for researchers to carefully consider the aim of their studies when using within-groups designs to determine if the threats are appropriate tradeoffs for the strengths.

TIME-SERIES DESIGNS

As we noted earlier in the chapter, **time-series designs** are considered quasi-experimental (Phan & Ngu, 2017); however, they share characteristics with within-groups designs. Unlike crossover designs, their focus is on collecting many observations of a dependent variable, rather than manipulating an independent variable. Time-series designs can be used with case studies (to assess a single participant) or a group of participants. In this chapter, we will focus on *interrupted time series*, which are used with groups (Heppner et al., 2016). They consist of many observations of the dependent variable that are, at some point, "interrupted" by some type of experimental condition (e.g., treatment, intervention).

In a **simple interrupted time series**, the same participants are observed across time on the dependent variable, with an intervention occurring at one point among the observations. This design is denoted as:

$$O_1 \quad O_2 \quad O_3 \quad X \quad O_4 \quad O_5 \quad O_6$$

Notice that there are many observations given both before and after the intervention. This design can be extended to include many more observations, and the number of observations does not need to be identical on both sides of the intervention (Heppner et al., 2016). Additionally, only one intervention is given, so there is no manipulation of an independent variable. The reason for the multiple dependent variable observations is that it helps control for some of the threats to validity found in other longitudinal designs, such as maturation and history. The presence of both may be indicated by changes across the dependent variable observations that are not situated right after the intervention.

For example, a researcher might be interested if the addition of progressive muscle relaxation to a 10-session therapy treatment would be effective in reducing anxiety for clients. The researcher might assess clients' anxiety levels at each of the first five therapy sessions, then conduct a session in which progressive muscle relaxation is introduced to the clients, then assess clients' anxiety levels again at each of the last four sessions. Changes in anxiety associated with the general therapy treatment may be captured by comparing the first several observations to one another. Additionally, the impact of a crisis occurring for the client on anxiety levels during the course of therapy would likely be reflected in the observations around that time period.

A **non-equivalent dependent variable interrupted time series** is very similar to the simple interrupted time series, except more than one dependent variable is observed across time. The notation is:

$$O_{A1} \quad O_{A2} \quad O_{A3} \quad X \quad O_{A4} \quad O_{A5} \quad O_{A6}$$
$$O_{B1} \quad O_{B2} \quad O_{B3} \quad X \quad O_{B4} \quad O_{B5} \quad O_{B6}$$

In this case, there are two dependent variables being observed, which are denoted by subscripts A and B. The same participants are assessed on each of the dependent variables. Otherwise, it is the same as the simple interrupted time series (Heppner et al., 2016).

Although threats to internal validity, such as history and maturation, might be detected with multiple observations (Heppner et al., 2016), they are not controlled for in the way that they would be if using two conditions. Consequently, researchers might choose to use *comparative interrupted time series* in which there are also participants in a control group that does not receive the intervention (St.Clair et al., 2015). This design is denoted as:

$$O_1 \quad O_2 \quad O_3 \quad X \quad O_4 \quad O_5 \quad O_6$$
$$O_1 \quad O_2 \quad O_3 \qquad O_4 \quad O_5 \quad O_6$$

In a comparative interrupted time series, participants undergo similar observations of the dependent variable (or, in the case of comparative non-equivalent dependent variable interrupted time series, more than one dependent variable), but only one group receives the intervention. Although it is possible to randomly assign participants to groups (Phan & Ngu, 2017), this does not often happen; rather, the control group is either **non-equivalent** (not randomly assigned) or **matched** to the intervention group (chosen due to similarities in specific characteristics). The use of a control condition can reduce threats to internal validity (St.Clair et al., 2015).

As an example of a comparative non-equivalent dependent variable interrupted time series, Booth and colleagues (2015) examined how clinical depression might be affected by bariatric surgery, hypothesizing that the surgery would lead to lower levels of depression across time. They examined the records of individuals who had received bariatric surgery, assessing them yearly from 3 years prior to the surgery to 7 years after the surgery. The authors compared these records to a control group of individuals with similar body mass indexes, ages, and genders who did not receive bariatric surgery during the same time period. The two dependent variables assessed were the diagnosis of depression and prescriptions for antidepressant medication. They found that, overall, those in the intervention condition had higher levels of depression than those in the control condition. Additionally, there was a small reduction in both the diagnosis of depression and antidepressant medication prescriptions for the intervention condition in the years following surgery, although these results did not last past 3 years.

Time-series designs have several strengths and limitations. Compared with other quasi-experimental designs, history and maturation threats are more likely to be spotted (Heppner et al., 2016). Additionally, as different levels of an independent variable are not given to the same participants, there is little chance for order and sequence effects. However, the statistics associated with time-series designs are complex. One issue is **autocorrelation**, or the relationship between each observation of the dependent variable to the observation(s) around it. These observations are likely to be dependent on one another, which is problematic in statistical analyses (Heppner et al., 2016). For example, an individual's depression score at the second observation (prior to treatment) is likely to be strongly related to their depression score at the first observation such that a person scoring in the severe range of depression at the first observation would be much less likely to score in the mild range of depression at the second observation compared with another person who scored in the mild range of depression at the first observation.

DATA ANALYSIS

Common statistical procedures for experimental designs include *t*-tests, analysis of variance (ANOVA), and regression-based techniques. Which statistical approach is appropriate depends on the number of groups compared, number of time points, number of dependent variables,

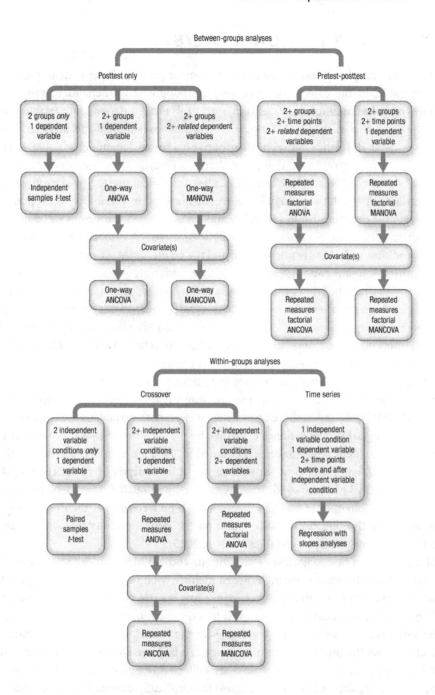

FIGURE 5.3 Common Parametric Inferential Statistical Procedures Used in Experimental Designs for Continuous Level Dependent Variables.

whether including covariates in the model, and whether testing for interaction between variable(s) in explaining the causal effect. Next, we overview common approaches adopted for designs comparing groups on a single time point (posttest only designs), comparing a single group over one or more time points (within-groups designs), and comparing groups over multiple time points (mixed designs). Figure 5.3 illustrates a decision tree including widely applied inferential parametric statistical analyses depending on the experimental design.

POSTTEST-ONLY DESIGN ANALYSES

An **independent samples *t*-test** is used when comparing two independent groups on one dependent variable. In the case of between-subjects designs, an independent samples *t*-test is employed whereby the condition (intervention or control) is the independent variable and posttest measure is the dependent variable. This comparison is the most simplistic because the researcher is only testing the mean difference between two groups on a single dependent variable, as in the case of a posttest only control group design or posttest only equivalent or non-equivalent group design.

Analysis of variance (ANOVA) techniques can be used for comparing two or more groups on a dependent variable in which the ratio of between to within group variability is computed (Cohen, 2013). The larger the between-group variability and smaller the within-group variability, the more likely a significant difference between groups will be observed. A **one-way ANOVA** is conducted treating the condition as the independent factor and the posttest measure as the dependent variable such as in alternative treatment or dismantling studies with only one time point. If an ANOVA is significant, samples *t*-tests or other post hoc analyses can be conducted to determine which specific conditions differ. In cases where the independent and dependent variable are both categorical, a non-parametric **Chi-square test** can be employed to test whether there are significant differences in frequency counts on the outcome variable (e.g., diagnosis, relapsed/did not relapse, retained/not retained) by group membership (e.g., intervention, control).

In some cases, researchers will control for (i.e., hold constant) a variable or set of variables in attempt to isolate the effect of group membership on the dependent variable. **Analysis of covariance (ANCOVA)** is used in these cases where one or more variables are entered as covariates in the model (Cohen, 2013). The variance explained by the control variable(s) is first accounted for in order to determine the unique variance accounted for by condition. In cases where the groups are compared on multiple dependent variables, a **multiple analysis of variance (MANOVA)** or **covariance (MANCOVA)** is employed whereby two or more *related* dependent variables form a composite variable (Cohen, 2013). MANOVA reduces **type I error** (i.e., incorrectly rejecting the null hypothesis) rate through testing differences on the dependent variables in one analysis as compared to conducting multiple ANOVAs (Cohen, 2013).

Control variables can be categorical or continuous and are identified by researchers in one of two ways. First, researchers use prior literature to identify what variables have strong evidence for being related to the outcome in prior research supporting the need to collect data on these variables and build them into the model as covariates. It is important to avoid including "everything but the kitchen sink" as covariates; the more variables in the model, the greater the variance we can likely account for but the interpretation of findings can become convoluted. Second, researchers might test for significant covariates after data are collected (e.g., differences on the outcome by demographic variables, site, or baseline measures) to statistically control for in the model.

WITHIN-GROUP DESIGN REPEATED MEASURES ANALYSES

Repeated measures analyses are used when comparing a single group over multiple time points (Field, 2018). A **paired samples *t*-test** (the repeated measures *t*-test also referred to as matched *t*-test or dependent samples *t*-test) is employed when there are only two observations of the dependent variable being compared (e.g., pretest and posttest). **One-way repeated measures ANOVA** is used when comparing a single group across three or more observations (e.g., baseline, first treatment, second treatment).

Interrupted time series designs involve regression analyses. Regressions are correlation-based techniques that are typically used with quantitative descriptive designs. They examine how much variance in an outcome variable is explained by one or more predictor variables (Field, 2018). One of the assumptions of regressions for interrupted time series is **linearity**, or that the relationship between the outcome and predictor variables can be represented by a straight line. The steepness of the line, or how strongly social support and depression are related, is called the **slope** of the regression line. For example, there is a relationship between social support and depression (see Rueger et al., 2016) such that higher levels of perceived social support are related to lower levels of depression, moderate levels of perceived social support are related to moderate levels of depression, and lower levels of perceived social support are related to higher levels of depression. This relationship could be represented as a line since, as one variable goes up, the other goes down in a linear fashion. The steepness of the line, or how strongly they are related, would be the slope.

In the case of interrupted time series designs, the linear relationship for the observations of the dependent variable are examined at three time points: (a) the observations occurring prior to the intervention, (b) the observations occurring around the intervention (i.e., right before and after), and (c) the observations occurring after the intervention (Kontopantelis et al., 2015). The slopes of these lines are compared to determine if the intervention had an effect. For example, a novel intervention designed to reduce the relationship between social support and depression might be effective if the slope of the line is higher before the intervention than during or after (i.e., the relationship between social support and depression is not as strong during and after the intervention compared to before the intervention). More complex versions of these statistics can also be used to assess other points in time (Kontopantelis et al., 2015), such as several time points after an intervention to determine if there are sustained effects.

MIXED DESIGN ANALYSES

Mixed-design ANOVAs are employed when both between-group and within-group comparisons are done in the same analyses (Cohen, 2013). Between-group experimental designs and crossover designs involving the comparison of two or more independent groups on two or more time points call for mixed design analyses. The between-subjects factor is group membership, while the within-subjects factor is time (pretest-posttest measures). In the most simplistic form, three effects are tested using a mixed-design ANOVA: main effect of time (change over time within each condition), main effect of condition (difference between conditions), and interaction effect (interaction between time x condition). The interaction term is interpreted first to determine whether change on the dependent variable differed as a function of condition (testing for the causal effect). Repeated measures ANOVA can also be extended to include controlling for covariates (**mixed-design ANCOVA**) or comparison of conditions on multiple related dependent variables (**mixed-design MANOVA**).

EXPERIMENTAL VALIDITY AND INCREASING RIGOR

Experimental validity refers to the degree of internal and external validity in an experimental study. An indicator of a rigorous experimental study is evidence of strong internal and external validity and utilization of methods for minimizing threats to validity. As a review, in the context of experimental research, internal validity refers to the extent the causal effect was due to the intervention. External validity, on the other hand, is the extent the results can be generalized to other contexts, settings, and populations beyond the conditions of the specific study. Threats to internal and external validity specific to between-groups and within-groups designs were noted throughout this chapter. In this section, we outline major threats to external and internal validity, as well as methods for addressing these potential limitations to increase the rigor of your experimental study.

EXTERNAL VALIDITY IN EXPERIMENTAL RESEARCH

Two major threats to external validity in experimental research relate to ecological validity and representativeness of the sample to the target population. As discussed earlier in the chapter, field experiments tend to have a higher degree of ecological validity in that the results are more likely to generalize to other settings. As review, field experiments are conducted in real-world or natural settings, whereas experimental laboratory studies are conducted under highly controlled settings. Because the context is highly controlled, laboratory study findings are less likely to transfer to other settings where in reality many variables are not controlled.

Similar to other designs under the quantitative research tradition, the degree of representation of the sample characteristics to the target population the researcher is seeking to generalize the results to and sample size will impact the external validity. Probabilistic sampling techniques can be used or combined with random assignment to increase the degree of external validity. **Stratified sampling** can increase the degree of external validity through drawing a homogeneous sub-sample of participants from different **strata** (i.e., sub-groups) existing in the target population on variables that are relevant to the study (Rubin & Babbie, 2016). This technique can be combined with cluster sampling and proportional sampling to represent each strata in proportion to the distribution in the target population.

INTERNAL VALIDITY IN EXPERIMENTAL RESEARCH

Selection of Participants

A leading threat to internal validity is selection bias. **Selection bias** occurs when participants are assigned to the conditions in such a way that they are not comparable on the dependent variable due to participants in one group being more or less predisposed to a certain response to the treatment (Rubin & Babbie, 2016). For example, participants who are genuinely interested in being part of the study may engage more than those who are participating in research for other reasons, such as boredom or time compensation. This bias can result in the researcher erroneously concluding that differences observed on the dependent variable were caused by the intervention when indeed the pre-existing differences impacted the outcome. Also, if individuals with more severe symptoms or scores are selected to participate in a study, their symptoms might improve over time due to the regression toward the mean phenomenon instead of the intervention itself. Further, individuals willing to participate in an experiment might intrinsically differ on the study variables, also impacting the degree of internal validity. Multiple pre-assessments should be administered to determine whether individuals are more or less susceptible to respond to the treatment in a certain way (Thyer, 2012).

INSTRUMENTATION

As with any research study, measurement error is a potential threat to the internal validity and appropriate reliability and validity evidences should be evaluated *prior* to adopting an instrument for use. There are specific considerations for instrumentation in experimental designs in which an intervention is implemented by researchers or other trained professionals. For example, when collecting diagnostic type data from participants that involve interviewing or observation, the researcher *is* the instrument or data collection tool. The researcher or trained professional is, of course, invested in the treatment, service, or treatment being provided (Thyer, 2012). The involvement of the researcher in the treatment implementation might introduce a **researcher effect** or **therapist effect** not only on participants' response to treatment, but also on the measures. Further, if a different individual collects diagnostic data at the different time points in a pretest-posttest or longitudinal experimental design, differences observed on the dependent variable could be attributed to the change in diagnostician and not the treatment (Thyer, 2012).

To minimize researcher effects, a single- or double-blind study previously described in this chapter can be employed. In addition, professionals with the appropriate credentials and experience in administering the specific treatment and instruments should be selected for implementation. Multiple ratings or use of multiple raters in the case of evaluating diagnostic criteria can be employed to compute **intra-rater** (within rater agreement) and **inter-rater reliability** (between rater agreement). Finally, methods typically used in qualitative inquiry might be adopted to monitor one's subjectivity such as **peer-debriefing** and **bracketing** throughout the research process. At a minimum, researchers should disclose any conflict of interest if they are involved in the treatment implementation and collection of data.

An additional threat to internal validity related to instrumentation is the interaction between the measure and treatment, referred to as **assessment treatment interaction** (Thyer, 2012). This phenomenon occurs when engaging in completing the measures influences participants' responses instead of the treatment itself. For instance, baseline measures might prompt participants to self-reflect or increase their self-monitoring based on the questions or statements presented. If, say, participants complete a measure of stress at baseline, they might become more aware of their perceived stress levels (low or high) and, consequently, become more or less engaged in a tested intervention to lower stress. Indeed, it has been suggested that the very act of having participants engage with a survey instruments can increase participants' awareness of experiencing the construct being assessed (Koskey, 2016).

Treatment Fidelity

The extent to which the intervention is implemented as intended is referred to as **treatment fidelity** (Yeaton & Sechrest, 1981). If there is lack of treatment fidelity, the researcher is not able to conclude the causal effect was between the intervention and dependent variable. It might be that the treatment is effective but there was lack of treatment fidelity, resulting in lack of a causal effect. Methods for monitoring treatment fidelity should be systematically built into the design.

Dane and Schneider (1998) outlined a multi-dimensional framework for treatment fidelity consisting of five components to monitor. **Adherence** is the first dimension and is the degree the critical elements of the intervention are implemented as intended. **Quality of delivery** is the second dimension and refers to the accuracy of how the intervention is implemented, including the consistency of implementation. **Exposure** is the third dimension and consists of the amount of dosage (e.g., time in therapy). **Participant responsiveness** is the fourth dimension and is the extent the participant responds to the treatment. The fifth dimension is program differentiation, which is highly applicable to experimental research. **Program differentiation** is the extent to which the implementation differs across the groups so as to avoid overlap among the critical element(s) being tested.

If there is overlap in the elements being tested across the conditions, then **contamination of treatments** can occur where elements in one condition are diffused into the other conditions being compared (Thyer, 2012). This overlap makes it difficult to draw comparisons of the effect of each condition on the dependent variable. Dismantling studies are at high risk for this threat to internal validity where one group receives the full treatment and the other group(s) receive only elements of the treatment. To minimize the potential of this risk, experimental researchers need to clearly delineate the core elements of each condition.

Experimental laboratory studies increase treatment fidelity because the study is implemented under controlled conditions. However, when conducting laboratory or field experiments, methods for increasing treatment fidelity should be purposefully built into the research design. These methods include, but are not limited to: (a) adopting a procedure manual or protocol, (b) use of appropriate credentialed professionals with specific training in the intervention being implemented, (c) piloting implementation such as through practice sessions, (c) collecting data on activities participants are engaged in during the study outside of the intervention that might impact the causal effect, and (d) ongoing supervision of implementation.

Supervision of implementation might be through use of in-person observations or audio/video recordings of implementation (with proper informed consent). Existing tools to evaluate treatment fidelity might also adopted to monitor treatment fidelity. In cases where a tool does not exist, a tool should be developed and piloted prior to use. In their systematic review of tools used to monitor treatment fidelity, Sanderson et al. (2007) evaluated over 86 tools available for assessing components related to treatment fidelity such as biases that might occur during implementation of randomized and non-randomized studies. Although the review was in the context of studies in epidemiology, the tools identified transfer to the fields of counseling, counseling psychology, and sociology. If treatment fidelity varies across sites or conditions, it can be included as an additional variable in the statistical model when analyzing the data.

INFLUENCE OF CONFOUNDING VARIABLES

The influence of confounding variables will impact the degree of internal validity particularly in field experiments that are conducted in real-world settings. Although the influence of confounding variables cannot be completely eliminated, methods specific to experimental research can be employed to minimize their influence. Table 5.4 summarizes some of the leading confounding variables in experimental research and methods to incorporate in the research design or data analysis to address each.

PUBLISHED GUIDELINES FOR INCREASING RIGOR

We point the reader to two additional resources that provide guidelines for upholding rigor in experimental designs. The first resource is the What Works Clearinghouse Standards Handbook Version 4.0 (available at https://ies.ed.gov/ncee/wwc/Handbooks) that outlines standards for randomized controlled trials and quasi-experimental designs. Quality standards for sample selection and assignment, methods for analyzing data with special cases (attrition, missing baseline data, baseline differences), methods for addressing confounding variables, and outcome requirements are outlined in this handbook. The second resource is the Coalition for Evidence-Based Policy guidelines for comparison group research designs and randomized controlled trial

TABLE 5.4 **Examples of Confounding Variables and Methods for Minimizing in Experimental Research**

CONFOUNDING VARIABLE	PHENOMENON	METHODS FOR INCREASING RIGOR
Concurrent history	Events or experiences outside of the intervention impact the causal effect	Collect data on activities participants are engaging in during the experiment (e.g., additional outside individual therapy or support groups engaged in) and any significant events taking place during the experiment (e.g., change in marital status, traumatic event) that might impact the causal effect.
Maturation	Developmental changes in participants over time	In longitudinal studies, collaborate with a professional familiar with the developmental changes of the target population (e.g., children, adolescents, young adult, adult, elderly) to document any potential changes that might impact the causal effect being studied. This may also lead to adding covariates related to maturation to statistically control their potential effects.
Placebo effect	A change on the dependent variable due to the belief that one is receiving an impactful intervention	Build in a **withdraw phase** whereby the treatment is removed after a period of time to assess whether relapse occurs.
Differing treatment credibility	Participant perception of the credibility of the treatment impacts the response to treatment	Design placebo and control conditions that are reasonable alternatives.
Differential attrition	Participants drop out of the experiment at different rates across the conditions (between-subjects) or time points (within-subjects)	Offer an incentive for participating in the full study, including services offered to the control group at conclusion of the study. Increase the mininum sample size criterion for target populations with a history of high attrition rates. Engage in multiple attempts to follow-up with participants to gain insight into why they dropped out of the study to determine if the reasons were due to the intervention or otherwise. Test for systematic differences between those who dropped out of the study to those who were retained on data available for the groups (e.g., baseline measures).

designs for social programs (available at http://coalition4evidence.org/468-2/publications/). This set of guidelines focuses on elements to build into the research design to increase the validity of the results and replicability of the study. Grant funders might specify that these guidelines need to be adhered to when submitting a research proposal evaluating the impact of an intervention program.

MULTICULTURAL CONSIDERATIONS

In addition to considerations for increasing external and internal validity in experimental designs, experimental researchers need to reflect on multicultural considerations. The Council for Accreditation of Counseling and Related Education Programs (CACREP) emphasizes the need for students to learn "culturally relevant strategies for conducting ... research" in its 2016 standards of accreditation (CACREP, 2015, p. 14). Experimental designs can be effectively used to summarize data from diverse groups and provide cause-and-effect explanations for various outcomes (Fassinger & Morrow, 2013). However, there is "ambivalence toward quantitative methods" regarding its effectiveness for examining diverse groups compared with other research designs (Cokley & Award, 2013, p. 26). Some of the primary issues related to experimental designs include awareness of bias, care when selecting participants, and attention to measures selected.

Research on diverse groups and multiculturalism itself has increased in recent years (Heppner et al., 2016), and quantitative methods, including experimental designs, can be appropriately used to assess these constructs (Cokley & Awad, 2013). However, these designs are subject to bias that may draw inaccurate conclusions about diverse groups. For example, experimental designs often make use of comparisons across different groups of people, such as in quasi-experiments and counterbalanced crossover analyses. Historically, these designs have been used to compare those from a dominant group (e.g., White, male, heterosexual) to those from minority groups (e.g., Black, female, LGBTQ). Such comparisons often implicitly set up the dominant group as the "control condition" to which minority groups are compared (Awad et al., 2016; Cokley & Awad, 2013). Within-groups designs, which allow participants to serve as their own controls, might help to control this type of bias. Relatedly, demographic grouping variables, or **distal variables**, have then been used as explanations for why differences exist. However, group identity differences, or **proximal variables**, have been shown to provide more accurate explanations. For example, racial group differences (e.g., Black and White) are often less predictive of dependent variables than are racial identity differences. Consequently, proximal variables may be a better fit for experimental designs than are distal variables (see Cokley & Awad, 2013).

An additional consideration when using experimental designs is in gathering participants. It is important to first operationalize exactly what is being studied and who is being recruited, which can be inherently difficult due to the myriad definitions available for basic demographic differences (Heppner et al., 2016). For example, there are no agreed-upon definitions of race, ethnicity, and culture. Relatedly, some terms have been used interchangeably in the literature, such as sex and gender, although their definitions are quite different. These issues can create confusion in research, especially when researchers and participants conceptualize questions about these constructs differently. Consequently, it is necessary for researchers to carefully operationalize from whom data will be collected, including defining key demographic terms for participants.

Another consideration in data gathering of diverse populations is sample size (Awad et al., 2016). Larger sample sizes are related to increased levels of **power**, or the ability to detect a difference among conditions when one exists. Minority populations are often underrepresented when data are collected, especially if they make up a small proportion of the general population (e.g., transgender individuals). In some cases, gathering representative samples involves additional effort to recruit individuals from specific populations. This may be compounded by a lack of trust from members of minority groups. Such distrust can be based on historical harm from researchers (e.g., the unethical Tuskegee syphilis experiment in which African American men with and without syphilis were monitored to determine the course of the disease; they were not told the true nature of the experiment or given appropriate treatment) or the concern that researchers from dominant groups are merely "curious" about participants from minority groups and uninterested in using their findings to benefit these groups. As a result, it may be important for researchers to seek out and involve individuals from minority groups in different aspects of the research process in order to build trust (Awad et al., 2016).

A final issue relates to measurement. Experimental designs often make use of self-report measures to assess dependent variables. It is important that measures selected are appropriate for the population from which the sample is drawn (Heppner et al., 2016). There are many considerations, including how constructs and items are understood across groups, the **factor structure** of measures (how different items on a measure come together to form scales and subscales) for different populations, and other aspects of **reliability** (consistency across items and participants) and **validity** (if a measure assesses what it was developed to assess). These can vary across groups such that findings from one population do not generalize to other populations. This may be compounded by issues of language and acculturation when recruiting participants from countries outside of the one in which the measures were originally developed (Awad et al., 2016). As a result, it is important to select measures that have been developed or assessed using samples from the population of interest or, when this is not possible, engaging in appropriate practices to translate the measure as needed (Heppner et al., 2016).

Taken together, experimental designs can yield accurate and meaningful information about diverse groups. However, care must be taken to avoid their misuse.

Case Study

Shin, R. Q., Smith, L. C., Welch, J. C., & Ezeofor, I. (2016). Is Allison more likely than Lakisha to receive a callback from counseling professionals? A racism audit study. *The Counseling Psychologist, 44*, 1187–1211. https://doi.org/10.1177/0011000016668814

BACKGROUND

Shin et al. (2016) conducted a study related to racial disparities in mental health treatment between Black and White individuals. They were particularly interested in telephone callbacks to potential clients received from mental health professionals when attempting to access services. Citing research on multicultural competence, implicit racial bias, and racial disparities, they hypothesized that potential clients leaving voicemail messages regarding interest in services would be more likely to be called back by therapists if they had a White-sounding name compared to a Black-sounding name. They also hypothesized that therapists who did return the phone call would be more likely to promote their services for clients with White-sounding names compared to Black-sounding names. To conduct the study, the authors prerecorded two messages from a fictional potential female client interested in therapeutic services. The only difference between the messages was the name of the client, which was either White-sounding (Allison) or Black-sounding (Lakisha). Practicing counselors and psychologists with online listings were randomly assigned to receive a voicemail message from either "Allison" or "Lakisha." Shin and colleagues then analyzed the presence or absence of a returned phone call, and the content of the returned phone call if it occurred.

This study is an example of a "between-subjects field experiment design" (Shin et al., 2016, p. 1194). First, it is a true experiment, since it includes a manipulated independent variable with at least two conditions (the name of the fictional client) that is hypothesized to have an impact on at least one dependent variable (whether or not the phone call was returned and, if so, whether the therapist promoted their services). Second, it is a field study, as it took place in a real-world setting. The therapists received the voicemails as part of their typical workday and were unaware that the caller was a fictional client. Finally, this study is between-groups, as the therapists were randomly assigned to receive one of the two voicemail messages, and the two groups were independent of one another. This study is more suited to a between-groups design than a within-groups design. If all participants were to receive voicemails from both "Allison" and "Lakisha," the scripts would have needed to be altered in other ways than just the name (e.g., text, voice) in order to maintain their realism. This would have led to variables other than the name of the caller being manipulated, which would have introduced confounds.

RESEARCH PROCESS

Shin and colleagues' (2016) participants were practicing counselors and psychologists located in one state on the East Coast who advertised their services online. These participants were randomly assigned to two groups and called at the phone number provided online. Since the manipulation involved a voicemail message, if a therapist or answering service answered the call, they were told the caller had a wrong number. When a therapist's voicemail answered, a prerecorded message was left from a fictional female client asking to set up an appointment "for something I'm struggling with" (p. 1204) and leaving a callback number. All voicemail messages were identical, except for the client's name, which was either "Allison" or "Lakisha." The callback number went to a voicemail set up by the researchers. The researchers kept track of two dependent variables: (a) whether the therapists called back (yes or no), and (b) if therapists called back, whether they promoted their services or declined to see the client for any reason. Therapists who promoted their services received a return call stating that the client was no longer interested.

To examine if therapists were more likely to call back "Allison" or "Lakisha," Shin and colleagues (2016) ran a chi-square test, which assesses group differences for two categorical variables. As is typical, the independent variable (the name of the fictional client: Allison or Lakisha) was categorical and, in this case, so was the dependent variable (whether the therapists called back: yes or no). "Allison" left 198 voicemail messages for therapists, and "Lakisha" left 173. The majority of therapists in both conditions returned the phone call, with 131 for "Allison" and 99 for "Lakisha," which was not significantly different using the chi-square test. This suggested that therapists were not more likely to call back a client with a White-sounding name compared to a client with a Black-sounding name.

Shin et al. (2016) also used a chi-square test to examine if the 230 therapists who called back were more likely to promote their services to "Allison" compared with "Lakisha." The result was statistically significant, indicating that therapists were more likely to want to speak about services, rather than decline services, to a client with a White-sounding name compared to one with a Black-sounding name.

DISCUSSION

The study conducted by Shin and colleagues (2016) used an experimental design to assess callbacks for clients with White- and Black-sounding names. Due to the manipulation of an independent variable while holding other potential confounding variables constant, experimental designs have higher levels of internal validity (likelihood the differences in the groups was due to the independent variable) than other research designs. Consequently, the researchers can be fairly certain that the difference in promotion of services was due to the name of the client. Additionally, as this is a field study in which the participants were acting in their actual capacity as therapists, the study also has higher levels of external validity (generalizability to other mental health professionals) than it would have had it been conducted in a laboratory setting under contrived conditions.

Random assignment in this study was important to help ensure that those who received phone calls from "Allison" were similar to those who received phone calls from "Lakisha." Shin et al. (2016) detailed their procedures for randomizing therapists. However, they also acknowledged that they did not use therapists who answered their phones (and, therefore, did not receive a voicemail); whether therapists answered their phones may have been a confounding variable. Additionally, the voicemails left by the therapists were not further coded beyond whether therapists promoted or declined their services. Results may have been different if these reasons had been further delineated. For instance, the authors indicate therapists might be interested in speaking with clients (coded as promoting services) to refer them. Additionally, therapists in one condition may simply, by chance, have had somewhat more open caseloads.

Finally, Shin and colleagues (2016) thoroughly discussed the ethical reasoning behind using therapists who were unaware they were participating in the study. This included approval from an internal review board, which determines if and to what degree studies present harm to clients.

SUMMARY

Similar to other quantitative approaches, experimental research is guided by a post-positivistic lens. Experimental research is distinct from correlational research in that the purpose is to test for a causal effect between a manipulated independent variable and a dependent variable(s). To test for a causal effect, specifications must be met in the research design such as a nonspurious relationship between variables. True experimental and quasi-experimental research designs are two overarching types. Variations within these two types include laboratory and field experiments that might focus on between-groups comparisons or within-group comparisons of individuals over time. True experimental designs are the most robust type of designs for testing a causal effect due to the use of random assignment and a control group. Although experimental designs increase the degree of internal validity of study results compared to other quantitative designs, limitations to these designs exist as were outlined in this chapter. Researchers can employ multiple methods within the research design to minimize these threats, as well as to attend to multicultural considerations.

STUDENT ACTIVITIES

Exercise 1: Applying Understanding of Experimental Research as Compared to Other Quantitative Traditions

Directions: Consider the paradigmatic foundation, purpose, and basic design characteristics of experimental research compared to other quantitative traditions to:

1. Create a Venn diagram outlining the similarities and differences between experimental research and other quantitative research.

Next, reflect on the distinctions between experimental laboratory and field experiments to:

2. Search the scholarly literature for an example of a recent experimental laboratory study or field experiment related to your research interest. Identify the (a) experimental and

control group, (b) independent and dependent variable(s), (c) potential confounding variables, and (d) potential threats to internal and external validity.

Finally, apply your understanding of experimental research as it relates to your area of research to:

3. Generate an example of an experimental laboratory study or a field experiment. In your example (a) state the research purpose, (b) state the research question, (c) describe the basic design characteristics, and (d) discuss potential threats to internal and external validity.

Exercise 2: Applying Understanding of Between-Groups Designs

Directions: Apply your understanding of between-groups designs to:

1. Discuss the distinctions among the variations of between-groups designs including experimental designs (pretest-posttest control group designs and posttest only designs) and equivalent-groups and non-equivalent groups quasi-experimental designs. Identify which these impact the internal validity of the results?

2. Generate a research question and scenario calling for a true experimental or quasi-experimental research design aligned to your research interest by (a) illustrating the design using the notation system, (b) describing the procedure used to formulate the experimental and control groups, and (c) identifying what statistical analysis might be used to test the causal hypothesis.

Exercise 3: Applying Understanding of Within-Groups Experimental Designs

Directions: Apply your understanding of within-groups designs to:

1. For what type of research questions are crossover designs preferred to time-series designs and vice versa? Generate potential research questions for both designs and state how each design is appropriate to answer the question.

2. Choose one of the research questions generated in Part 1 of this exercise and further explain it by (a) illustrating the design using the notation system, (b) describing the procedure used to formulate the experimental and control groups, and (c) identifying what statistical analysis might be used to test the causal hypothesis.

Exercise 4: Applying Understanding of Multicultural Considerations

Directions: Consider the following scenario. Then, discuss the related questions.

A researcher is interested in examining the effectiveness of "matching" clients and therapists on different demographic variables. She is especially interested if there are differences in the therapeutic relationship for Asian, Black, Hispanic, and White clients paired with therapists from a similar or different racial/ethnic background.

1. What are multicultural considerations that the researcher should take into account when designing her study?

2. What would you recommend the therapist do in terms of multicultural considerations that would be most likely to lead to meaningful and accurate conclusions?

Exercise 5: Applying Understanding of the Experimental Research Case Study

Directions: Answer the related questions based on the case study you just read.

1. What are potential multicultural and ethical considerations that might be present in the case study that were not discussed? How might they be addressed?

2. Design a follow-up to this study using a *different* experimental design: quasi-experimental, crossover, or time series. How might your study complement the existing study? What would be the pros and cons of the study you designed? How might you design the study to increase the experimental validity?

ADDITIONAL RESOURCES

Software Recommendations

Arbuckjle, J. L. (2014). *Amos* (version 23.0) [Computer software]. IBM SPSS.

Hayes, A. F. (2019). *PROCESS* (version 3.4) [Computer software]. processmacro.org/download.html

Iacus, S. M., King G., & Porro, G. (2009). CEM: Software for Coarsened Exact Matching. *Journal of Statistical Software, 30.* http://j.mp/2oSW6ty

IBM Corp. (2016). *IBM SPSS Statistics for Windows* (version 24.0) [Computer software]. IBM Corp.

Jöreskog, K. G., & Sörbom, D. (2019). *LISREL* (version 10.1) [Computer software]. Scientifics Software, Inc.

Muthén, L. K., & Muthén, B. O. (2018). *MPLUS* (version 8.3) [Computer software]. Muthén & Muthén.

R Core Team (2017). *R: A language and environment for statistical computing* [Computer software]. Vienna, Austria: R Foundation for Statistical Computing. http://www.R-project.org

SAS Institute Inc. (2019). *SAS/STAT software* (version 8.0) [Computer software]. SAS Institute Inc.

Helpful Links

- https://ies.ed.gov/ncee/wwc/
- http://coalition4evidence.org/468-2/publications/
- https://about.citiprogram.org/en/homepage/
- https://www.hhs.gov/ohrp/
- https://osp.od.nih.gov/clinical-research/irb-review/

Helpful Videos

Designing studies consistent with What Works Clearinghouse Standards: https://www.youtube.com/playlist?list=PLVHqsnePfULrpYTWrOpiXGxUXUMzIuJD8

Coalition for Evidence-Based Policy on Which Comparison Group Studies ("Quasi-Experimental") Are Most Likely to Produce Valid Evidence of Effectiveness: http://coalition4evidence.org/video-comparison-group-studies/

Helpful Reading

Austin, P. C. (2011). An introduction to Propensity Score Methods for reducing the effects of confounding in observational studies. *Multivariate Behav Research, 46,* 399–424. https://doi.org/10.1080/00273171/2011.568786

Blake, D. D., Weathers, F. W., Nagy, L. M., Kaloeupek, D. G., Gunsman, F. D., Charney, D. S., & Keane, T. M. (1995). The development of a clinician-administered PTSD scale. *Journal of Traumatic Stress, 8,* 75–90. https://doi.org/10.1007/BF02105408

Bloom, H. S. (2012). Modern regression discontinuity analysis. *Journal of Research on Educational Effectiveness, 5*(1), 43–82.

Calonico, S., Cattaneo, M. D., & Titiunik, R. (2018). *rdrobust: Robust data-driven statistical inference in regression-discontinuity designs. R package version 0.99.4.* https://CRAN.R-project.org/package=rdrobust

Cappelleri, J. C., Darlington, R. B., & Trochim, W. M. K. (1994). Power analysis of cutoff-based randomized clinical trials. *Evaluation Review, 18*(2), 141–152.

Cook, T. D., Campbell, D. T., & Shadish, W. (2002). *Experimental and quasi-experimental designs for generalized causal inference.* Houghton Mifflin.

Field, A. (2017). *Discovering statistics using IBM SPSS Statistics* (5th ed.). Sage.

Lee, H., & Munk, T. (2008). Using regression discontinuity design for program evaluation. In *Proceedings of the 2008 Joint Statistical Meeting* (pp. 3–7). American Statistical Association.

National Center for Education Evaluation and Regional Assistance (2017). *What Works Clearinghouse™: Standards handbook* (Version 4.0). https://ies.ed.gov/ncee/wwc/handbooks

National Institute of Health. (2016). *Design requirements manual.* https://www.orf.od.nih.gov/PoliciesAndGuidelines/Pages/DesignRequirementsManual2016.aspx

Salkind, N. J. (2010). *Encyclopedia of research design.* SAGE.

Sheperis, C. J., Young, J. S., & Daniels, M. H. (2017). *Counseling research: Quantitative, qualitative, and mixed methods.* Pearson.

KEY REFERENCES

Only key references appear in the print edition. The full reference list appears in the digital product found on http://connect.springerpub.com/content/book/978-0-8261-4385-3/part/part02/chapter/ch05

Awad, G. H., Patall, E. A., Rackley, K. R., & Reilly, E. D. (2016). Recommendations for culturally sensitive research methods. *Journal of Educational and Psychological Consultation*, 26, 283–303. https://doi.org/10.1080/10474412.2015.1046600

Campbell, D. T. (1957). Factors relevant to the validity of experiments in social settings. *Psychological Bulletin*, 54, 297–312.

Campbell, D. T., & Stanley, J. C. (1963). *Experimental and quasi-experimental designs for research.* Rand McNally.

Campbell, D. T., & Stanley, J. C. (1979). *Quasi-experimentation: Design and analysis issues in field settings.* Houghton Mifflin.

Hayes, A. F. (2013). *Introduction to mediation, moderation, and conditional process analysis: A regression-based approach.* Guilford Press.

Heppner, P. P., Wampold, B. E., Owen, J., Thompson, M. N., & Wang, K. T. (2016). *Research design in counseling* (4th ed.). Cengage.

Kontopantelis, E., Doran, T., Springate, D. A., Buchan, I., & Reeves, D. (2015). Regression based quasi-experimental approach when randomization is not an option: Interrupted time series analysis. *The BMJ*, 350, h2750. https://doi.org/10.1136/bmj.h2750

Phan, H. P., & Ngu, B. H. (2017). Undertaking experiments in social sciences: Sequential, multiple time series designs for consideration. *Educational Psychology Review*, 29, 847–867. https://doi.org/10.1007/s10648-016-9368-0

Rausenbaum, P. R., & Rubin, D. B. (1985). Constructing a control group using multivariate matched sampling methods that incorporate the propensity score. *The American Statistician*, 39, 33–38.

Rubin, A., & Babbie, E. R. (2016). *Essential research methods for social work* (4th ed). Brooks/Cole.

St.Clair, T., Hallberg, K., & Cook, T. D. (2016). The validity and precision of the comparative interrupted time-series design: Three within-study comparisons. *Journal of Educational and Behavioral Statistics*, 41, 269–299. https://doi.org/10.3102/1076998616636854

CHAPTER 6

PREDICTION RESEARCH

Joshua J. Castleberry and Michael S. Leeman

LEARNING OBJECTIVES

After reading this chapter, you will be able to:

- Recognize the philosophical difference between explanatory and predictive research
- Comprehend and interpret various statistical models and analyses used in predictive research
- Understand basic research design for answering predictive research questions
- Recognize basic statistical analysis relevant to predictive research utilizing SPSS

INTRODUCTION TO PREDICTIVE AND EXPLANATORY RESEARCH

The goal of much scientific research is to understand causal underpinnings and/or to accurately forecast observed and non-observed outcomes. Explanatory research pertains to research focusing on testing hypotheses relating to causal inferences using previous theoretical constructs, whereas prediction research is aimed at identifying patterns that predict future outcomes within a set of variables. There are several important differences between the two; however, they are rarely explicitly distinguished. Explanatory research often facilitates prediction, and prediction research can offer an explanation of causality. We see this even without the identification of causal variables in predictive research. Likewise, explanatory research may serve as a means for prediction and predictive research a source of insight into theoretical formulations. These two forms of research are so deeply intertwined that it becomes a philosophical exercise to disentangle them (Table 6.1) (Pedhazur, 1997; Stevens, 2009).

PREDICTIVE METHODOLOGY

The term predictive research is used in a variety of research settings in which prediction is the goal of the methodology and design. Whether used in a non-experimental design, correlational

TABLE 6.1 **Statistical Terminology and Symbols**

STATISTIC SYMBOL	
x	Independent variables
y	Dependent variables
r	Correlation coefficient
R^2	R-square (coefficient of determination)
SS_{tot}	Total sum of squares (tells you how much variation there is in the dependent variable)
SS_{res}	Sum of squares of the residuals
SS_{reg}	The sum of squares of the regression, equivalently the explained sum of squares
$\bar{X}$	Sample means
$\bar{Y}$	Mean of the random variable
N	Population size
n	Sample size
	Sum
$SD\ \Sigma$	Standard deviation
$\check{Y}$	Predicted value of Y (the dependent variable) in a regression equation.
bX	Slope
a	Slope intercepts
Y'	Y' (read Y prime) is the predicted value of the Y variable
F_{obs}	Observed F statistic to be compared to the F critical
F_{crit}	F Critical value
MS_{reg}	The mean squared errors of the regression
MS_{res}	The mean squared errors of the residuals
p	p-value the level of significance
α	Symbol of p-value. The level of significance.
k	Number of predictors
Δ	Change in the variable it precedes
β	Beta coefficients or beta weights are the estimates resulting from a regression analysis
H_0	Null hypothesis

analysis, regression analysis, multiple regression analysis, or hierarchical regression methodology, prediction is concerned with the use of empirical data to forecast future outcomes. For example, a researcher might collect addiction treatment data, such as frequency of use, alliance scales, and self-efficacy measures, in order to predict such treatment success as recidivism, problematic substance use, well-being, and likelihood of abstinence. The research is using varying analyses to determine and measure the relationship between variables and predict the changes in one set of variables based on the value of another. Again, the main distinction is between prediction and explanation, however there is much overlap between varying methodologies and research designs.

Single subject design (sometimes referred to as single case design) focuses on a single subject or case ($N = 1$). This single subject is followed longitudinally through differing phases of baseline/nontreatment (A) and treatment (B). These phases are used strategically to determine the impact of a specified treatment or intervention. Overall, single subject design does not lend itself to predictive methodology as its primary focus is on the success of the intervention. The process of identifying desired changes, preintervention measurement, postintervention measures, and making decisions about the efficacy of your intervention better parallels an evaluating practice of client progress and clinical effectiveness. Similarly, the processes of quantitative content analysis have little overlap with predictive design. Though they can share similar statistical analysis, quantitative content analysis works to examination of symbols of communication in order to describe the communication, draw inferences about its meaning, or infer from the communication to its context, both of production and consumption (Riffe et al. 1998, p. 20).

Survey research and experimental research have many parallels to predictive methodology. For review, Hackett (1981) indicated that survey research process includes (a) identifying the research problem, (b) selecting a survey research design, (c) selecting a representative sample, (d) selecting surveys, (e) collecting data, and (f) analyzing the data and generating the results. Survey research uses subjective data collected from a sample of respondents to examine relationships among certain variables and describe some aspects of the population that they represent. Survey research can use quantitative research strategies such as questionnaires with numerically rated items, qualitative research strategies via interviews with open-ended questions, or both strategies as in the case of mixed methods. Experimental research is an approach where one or more independent variables are manipulated and applied to one or more dependent variables to measure their effect on the latter. Distinct experimental research, independent and dependent variables define the scope of a study but cannot be explicitly controlled by the researcher. Whereas in experimental research independent variables are manipulated to detect causal effects. The purpose of experimental research is to test for causal effects. A causal effect is when a change in one (or more) variables explains the change in another variable, with all other variables being equal (Heppner et al., 2016). The manipulated variable is the independent variable (x), and the affected variable is the outcome known as the dependent variable (y). In other words, the manipulated independent variable is the *cause*, and the dependent variable is the *effect* being studied. Predictive research can occur in the form of survey as well as experimental research.

JUSTIFIED TRUE BELIEF

To help us understand this difference we look at where prediction research is situated in a paradigmatic hierarchy (Crotty, 2003). This hierarchy encompasses five levels: ontology (i.e., form and nature of reality); epistemology (i.e., theory of knowledge acquisition); theoretical stance (i.e., philosophical stance); methodology (i.e., process for discovering what is knowable); and method (i.e., procedures to gather and analyze data). As mentioned in Chapter 1, prediction is situated in the quantitative traditions. Specifically, prediction research is based on the ontology of realism, or the belief that there is a true, universal reality existing outside of subjective understanding. Epistemologically speaking, prediction research is centered within objectivism, which takes the philosophical stance that there exists "Truth," and that this "Truth" can be known. The theoretical stance of predictive research is a subtype of positivism known as post-positivism. Post-positivists see knowledge and meaning as existing objectively, independently of human concern; however, post-positivists do not believe it is possible to comprehend a single unifying reality (Kivunja & Kuyini, 2017).

Our epistemology, or how do we know what we know, informs much on how we view and perceive knowledge. For quantitative traditions, let us refer to Plato's Theaetetus. In Plato's famous dialogue, Theaetetus and Socrates are discussing this question: What is knowledge? After many failed attempts to satisfy Socrates, Theaetetus offers the definition that knowledge is "true belief with an account" (Theaetetus, 201c–d). This line of dialogue later forms Plato's soliloquy that knowledge is "justified, true belief." To have an account or to justify "Truth," we look to our research methods, questions, and statistical models (e.g., the statistical analysis and assumptions relating to the data in response to your study questions). Positivism offers more specific direction in these goals and methods that aim at prediction; however, prediction exists as only one of these goals and uses a scientific approach that is founded in operationalization and observation. These methods of prediction research vary depending on the questions of research but are quantitative in nature. Confusion still arises because another goal in this tradition is explanation. To distinguish the two more, we look at our research designs. Prediction research often utilizes experimental, sample, and randomized controlled trial (RCT) factorial and longitudinal data in our designs, whereas in explanation, we often utilize convenience sampling, cross-sectional, and survey data.

Positivism offers a helpful framework for understanding this entanglement. Positivist research is directed at explaining relationships and identifying causes (Creswell, 2009, p. 7), and working to ultimately uncover laws and theories to lay foundations for prediction and generalization. The positivist researcher's epistemology is one of objectivism, believing they can impartially discover "Truth" or absolute knowledge about an objective reality, in which they separate themselves as the researchers from the researched. This gives meaning and truth solely to the objects of study, not in the subjectivism of the researcher. Crotty (1998, p. 8) elaborates, "A tree in the forest is a tree, regardless of whether anyone is aware of its existence or not. As an object of that kind, it carries the intrinsic meaning of treeness. When human beings recognize it as a tree, they are simply discovering a meaning that has been lying in wait for them all along." While this offers a secure position to conduct prediction research, positivism does have its limitations, specifically in the social sciences. As positivism attempts to explain and predict phenomena by controlling variables, some variables are not seen by researchers, and are not accounted for until their effects are obvious. Thus, a researcher may not reject many of their null hypotheses because they are unable to consider contextual variables (House, 1991).

We need to appreciate the tension in this entanglement, as it has significant implications on how research is conducted. Unfortunately, underappreciating this tension has led to wide variation in the methodologic quality of prediction research (Hagerty & Srinivasan, 1991; Shmueli, 2010; Wu, Harris & Mcauley, 2007). This distinction is particularly relevant to the valid use of specific statistical analysis (i.e., regression, multivariate analyses) and the interpretation of results. Ultimately, we need to distinguish between research design to answer questions of prediction and those primarily for explanatory purposes. Thus, the goal becomes clarifying the two not only for proper use of statical analysis, but also for better science as both are necessary for generating and testing theories, yet each play a different role in doing so.

We assume that many of our readers are already familiar with the value of explanatory research. Specifically, in the testing of causal theory, and the development of mechanistic models to better explain thoughts, feelings, and behaviors. In these designs statistical methods are used to test causal hypotheses, in which a set of factors (X), that are assumed to be the underlying cause of the measured variable (Y), are evaluated. The pursuit of such questions should not be confused with the ability to predict outcomes. In answering questions pertaining to causal relationships researchers rely heavily on theory itself to provide the justification for causality. In other words, the researcher interprets the data and statistical methods through the lens of a theoretical model. Due to the increased reliance on interpreting data through a theoretical model, research papers rarely take steps to verify that the models they propose are able to predict the measured outcome modeled (Yarkoni & Westfall, 2007). Thus, causal models found through explanatory research have been known to fail to accurately predict the same outcomes they reportedly model. Some argue that these kinds of papers have contributed to the mounting evidence supporting an ongoing replication crisis, arguments of increased "p-hacking" (e.g., the selective reporting or misreporting of true effect sizes in a study), and other questionable practices in behavioral research (Ebersole et al., 2015; Nosek & Lakens, 2014; Simmons et al., 2011). The purpose of prediction is to demonstrate simple links between two variables, testing hypotheses about clusters of variables that predict a phenomenon, or predicting the likelihood of an event happening. An example predictive research questions may be, "To what degree do attachment styles predict college adjustment among college student completing a STEM degree?"

SEMANTICS

As mentioned, predictive research is the pursuit of identifying variables that forecast future phenomena. Through the interpretations of explanatory research, predictive variables are identified and examined in the practical application of predicting a specific phenomenon. These predictive variables are often identified through their correlation with the desired outcome. Correlation and prediction are closely connected in that if two variables are correlated with each other, then the value of one variable should estimate, with some degree of accuracy, the value of the other variable (Hayes, 2017). Therefore, it becomes apparent that the choice of predictive variables does not strictly rely on explanatory research or theory but are also empirically determined. This is most commonly discussed in issues pertinent to criterion-related validation in measurement development.

To prevent confusion between the two types of research we will cover some important terminology that will be used as we describe different research designs. In the use of predictive research, independent variables (x) are frequently referred to as *predictors*, and the dependent variable (y) or specified outcome is called the *criterion*. When using regression analysis in the pursuit of predictive research questions, predictors are referred to as *regressors* and criterion variables are called *regressands* (Thus, Wold, & Jureen, 1953). In this case, predictor or regressor are both adequate nomenclature in identifying the independent and dependent variables. This nomenclature changes in explanatory research in which the independent variable is considered the *cause*, and the dependent variable is the *effect*. Again, these distinctions become important in interpreting research. Regression is a prime example of this. Researchers can use regression analysis in the pursuit of explanation or prediction. As we will cover later in this chapter, regression analysis specifically poses less risk for misinterpretation when used in predictive research, while less so when used in explanatory research. For the purposes of this chapter, we will refer to our independent and dependent variables as predictors and criterion.

ANALYSIS AND SELECTION
Variable Selection

As we have discussed, there is an important distinction between predictive and explanatory research. There is also much confusion in research practices when one or the other occurs. Often, we see that research aimed at prediction utilizes analytic approaches satisfactory only for explanation. We also see instances when predictive analytics are used for explanatory purposes. There are a few signs that help us see when these misuses occur. Chief among them is in the selection of the variables without a theoretical rationale to support them. Before developing the predictive design, it is necessary to choose the predictors and criterion, define them, and have valid reliable measures to assess them. This process is too complex for our purposes here. If you are interested in measurement and psychometrics, please review Cronbach,1971; Cronbach and Gieser, 1965; Cureton, 1951; Nunnally, 1978; Pedhazur and Schmelkin, 1991; and Thorndike, 1949. Suffice it to say that your variable selection is dependent on your intended purpose and follows your research questions. Assuming the researcher has valid and reliable measures for their criterion, and selected predictor variables on the basis of theoretical considerations, we need not be as concerned about the misuse of their predictive analytics.

The concerns around variable selection do not stop here. Many variables that are studied in counseling are often intercorrelate (e.g., meaning the independent variables have high correlations with each other). This makes the pool of possible predictors of a criterion rather large. The aim then becomes to select the minimum number of predictor variables possible to account for as much variance as possible in the criterion. The procedures used in selecting variables can vary widely depending on, for example, the aims of the research, costs, resources, and time. We cannot offer a systematic evaluation method that could account for all of a researcher's needs in this chapter. For more on variable selections methods read Daniel and Wood, 1980; Draper and Smith, 1981; and Hocking, 1976.

DATA COLLECTION

Data collection is a fundamental part of research that is easy to overlook. How you collect your data is very important. There are many different ways of collecting data on your sample/population. Taken even further, your sample greatly informs the interpretation of the data, as well as implications and limitations. Here we will cover a couple of different data collection methods as we develop the research design that best answers our research questions. Whether it be explanatory or predictive research, the manner in which data are collected makes it possible to establish predictors and causal factors. Specifically to causation, three criteria are often described as being necessary: covariation, temporal ordering, and the elimination of competing explanations. Temporal ordering is very relevant in our discussion of data collection. This perspective does not mean that causation is implied solely on longitudinal data, nor that statistical models are limited by the methods used in data collection. Rather, how a researcher goes about collecting data is as important as the research design or the statistical models used. For more on data collection and sampling methods there are a number of reviews and texts that go deeper in the subject (see Altmann, 1974; Cohen, 2013; Csikszentmihalyi & Larson, 2014; Tashakkori & Teddlie, 2009).

For our purposes and in the case of multiple regression, the question of data collection comes down to the research question and hypothesis. The best sampling method that most effectively meets the particular goals depends on many factors. A simple strategy to identify your best sampling methods is provided here.

1. List your research goals.
2. Identify potential sampling methods that might effectively achieve these goals (i.e., simple random sampling, stratified sampling, cluster sampling).

a. For example, if the research goals have a specific population in mind requiring high precision, we would know that SRS or One-Stage CS would best meet those goals.

3. Test the ability of each method to achieve identified goals.

4. Choose the method that does the best job achieving identified goals.

PROCEDURES

The procedures of a study are the methods or description of how the study was actually conducted. Detailed procedures take the reader or researcher through the steps the participants took to complete the study. Some steps are unique to a particular study, but in general, most procedures cover the following:

- How the participants were recruited for the study

- The kind of compensation (e.g., money, extra credit) given in exchange for participation

- How the participants gave informed consent for the study

- How the participants completed the study (e.g., online, came to the lab to complete questionnaires)

- What the participants actually did (e.g., complete questionnaires, completed a discussion)

- How the participants were debriefed

PROCEDURE SELECTION: EXAMPLE

Participants were recruited from undergraduate courses and participated in exchange for a small amount of course credit. Participants completed the study online. Participants first gave consent to participate and then completed the questionnaires. Participants completed the questionnaires in relation to a religious/spiritual leader who had committed an actual transgression in a church. Participants were asked to describe the offense and fill out a series of questionnaires in relation to the offense and the religious/spiritual leader. Participants were debriefed and given the contact information of the researcher should they have questions.

STATISTICAL MODELS AND ANALYSIS

Correlation

In this section, we examine correlational research methods, procedures, and data analysis. Correlational research is a type of non-experimental research method in which researchers determine the nature of the relationship between two naturally occurring variables without trying to control other extraneous variables. In non-experimental or correlational research, we simply determine whether a relationship exists between two variables. For example, in a correlational study, we may find that people who suffer from insomnia tend to struggle with anxiety. But do people suffer from insomnia because they struggle with anxiety, or do people struggle with anxiety because they suffer from insomnia? Until further investigation is conducted, we cannot conclude which possibility is true by way of a simple correlation. However, in experimental research, we actually manipulate some variable and then measure the effects of this manipulation on other variables. For instance, in an experimental study, we might introduce a sleep aid to increase sleep and then measure anxiety levels.

Therefore, correlational studies do not determine causation, but rather, they allow us to effectively describe the strength and direction of the relationship between two measured variables. Additionally, once a relationship has been established, we can make sound statistical predictions about the measured variable scores. Correlational studies are preferred to experimental studies for two reasons. First, correlations are conducted when researchers do not expect that the statistical relationships between variables are causal in nature. Second, correlations are conducted when researchers postulate that the statistical relationship of interest is causal in nature but cannot manipulate the independent variable because it is impractical or unethical. For example, if researchers wished to explore memory and prolonged alcohol use, it would be both impractical and unethical to randomly assign participants to a condition of prolonged alcohol use.

Remember that correlations are important to predictive design. Not only in checking regression assumptions (something we'll talk about later), and detecting multicollinearity, but a correlation matrix (e.g., the matrix of the correlations between variables) is the foundation of regression analyses. Correlations can differ in strength or the degree to which two variables are related, and is measured by the correlation coefficient, which can range between -1.00 and $+1.00$. The absolute value of the correlation coefficient indicates the relationship strength. The closer the coefficient is to -1.00 or $+1.00$, the stronger the relationship between the measured variables. As the correlation coefficient value moves closer to 0, the relationship between the two variables gets weaker. Zero indicates no relationship between the two measured variables. Additionally, a correlation has direction and can be either positive or negative. A positive correlation indicates that as one variable increases, the other also increases. A negative correlation, or inverse relationship, indicates that as one variable increases, the other variable decreases. For example, a study by Osborn and Stein (2018) using a sample of 60 adults with serious mental illness at an inpatient treatment facility found that the working alliance between client and counselor was significantly positively correlated with the client's well-being ($r = .59$). Inferring from this statistic, this sample showed that the higher clients reported their working alliance with their counselor, the higher they reported their well-being. Within the same sample working alliance was significantly negatively correlated with psychiatric symptoms ($r = -.26$). Meaning that as the working alliance increased, psychiatric symptoms decreased.

Before discussing the usual players in correlations, it may be helpful to have a brief reminder of the difference between parametric and non-parametric tests. The short answer is that parametric tests require several conditions of validity so that the results may be considered reliable. Ultimately this comes down to the distribution of the data being used. For example, t-tests are reliable only if each sample follows a normal distribution and homoscedastic (e.g., the error between your independent and dependent variables is the same). In this instance t-tests are parametric tests. Whereas non-parametric tests have no such conditions. Often, we find that parametric tests have non-parametric equivalents, and in some situations only non-parametric tests exists (e.g., Kolmogorov-Smirnov's test)

Typically, four types of correlations are measured: Pearson correlation, Spearman correlation, Kendall rank correlation, and the Point-Biserial correlation. The two most-often used correlational measures are Pearson and Spearmen (Coladarci & Cobb, 2014). Pearson correlation is the most widely used approach to measure the degree of a relationship between measured variables. Though the Pearson correlation coefficient itself is neither parametric nor non-parametric, some basic assumptions must be met when conducting a Pearson correlation. Both measured variables should be approximately normally distributed (illustrated by a bell-shaped curve), the variance of the two measured variables is similar (homoscedasticity), the relationship between the two measured variables is linear (linearity), and both measured variables must be continuous.

Spearman correlation is a non-parametric test (e.g., a test that does not rely on any distribution) that is used to measure the degree of the relationship between two variables and does not hold any assumptions about the distribution of data. Spearman correlation is the preferred correlation analysis when the variables are measured on an ordinal scale. Typically, ordinal scales measure non-numeric constructs such as satisfaction, attitudes, and beliefs. For example, researchers can rate student satisfaction of their educational experience via a Likert scale (i.e., completely dissatisfied, somewhat dissatisfied, dissatisfied, somewhat satisfied, satisfied, completely satisfied). Satisfaction can be logically ordered or ranked, but a numeric difference between each category cannot necessarily be established.

PARTIAL AND SEMIPARTIAL CORRELATION

Further discussing correlations, let's look at partial and semipartial correlation. If you only have two variables (X and Y) you can look at bivariate correlation Pearson's r. When you start to have three or more correlations (X, Y, and Z), you can look at partial and semipartial correlation. Remember your equations for correlation and multiple correlation (Table 6.2).

We will go more in depth on the meaning of these equations when we get to multiple regression. Consider now the definition of partial correlation: a measure of the strength of the linear relationship between two variables after controlling for the effects of other variables (Coladarci & Cobb, 2014). If we refer to multiple correlation, we are looking at the relationship between Y and multiple Xs all at the same time, whereas in partial correlation, we pick one variable ($X1$) and use the second variable ($X2$) as a control variable. So, when would you want to use partial correlation? Take, for example, wanting to look at choice and its relationship to treatment outcomes in recovery centers. Self-determination theory tells us that we would observe that individuals who have more choice will have better treatment outcomes because it's confounded with socioeconomic status. We know from previous research that socioeconomic status would affect treatment outcomes. If we define socioeconomic status as private insurance, then it would make sense to correlate choice and treatment outcomes, after we've controlled for socioeconomic status. We can then see if choice has any relationship with treatment outcomes after controlling for the SES variable. Often in predictive research situations, you will be interested in looking at the relationship between two constructs

TABLE 6.2 Equations for Correlation and Multiple Correlation

R-square	$R^2 = \dfrac{SS_{reg}}{SS_{tot}} = r^2_{y\hat{y}}$
Multiple R	$\sqrt{R^2} = r_{y\hat{y}}$
Partial correlation	$r^2_{y1\cdot2} = \dfrac{2}{1+2}$

after controlling for other variable(s). For example, a researcher may be interested in academic variables that predict college success in a sample of students from various high schools. In this situation the researcher may need to control for the specific high school the student attends, or even economic status as this may influence the statistical results.

Semipartial correlation, also known as part correlation, is very different from partial correlation. Semipartial correlation is defined as the correlation between all of Y and the part of X1 that is independent of X2. The best way to understand how it differs is to take a look at the equation (Table 6.3) and the Venn diagram in Figure 6.1.

Looking at our Venn diagram, each circle is the variation in the variable. You may want to know how much of the variation in Y (1, 2, 4, 5) is coming from X1 (2, 5) and X2 (4, 5). Partial correlation would be centered on the variation of 1 and 2 because 4 and 5 comprise X2. We see this reflected in the equation in Figure 6.2. Continuing to look at the Venn diagram, we can see that semipartial correlation is accounting for both X1 and X2 (1, 2, 4, 5) (Figure 6.2). The reader is encouraged to see the following review for a more indepth look at partial and semipartial correlation and their residuals (Cohen, West, & Aiken, 2014).

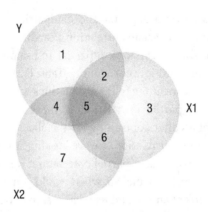

FIGURE 6.1 Venn Diagram.

$$\Sigma(Y - \bar{Y})^2 = \Sigma(Y' - \bar{Y})^2 + \Sigma(Y - Y')^2$$
$$SS_{tot} = SS_{reg} + SS_{res}$$

FIGURE 6.2 Total Variation, Regression, and the Residual.

TABLE 6.3 **Correlation Equations**

Partial correlation	$r^2_{y1\cdot2} = \dfrac{2}{1+2}$
Semiartial correlation	$r^2_{y12(s)} = \dfrac{2}{1+2+4+5}$

CORRELATION IN PREDICTIVE RESEARCH

In most research, the first thing you will report on your data is the correlations between all variables. This refers to the relationships between variables. In other words, are higher scores on one variable associated with higher or lower scores on another variable? Remember the points discussed about correlation:

1. Correlations can range from −1 to 1.

2. A positive correlation between two variables (i.e., above 0) means that high scores on one variable are associated with high scores on the second variables. A negative correlation between two variables (i.e., below 0) means that high scores on one variable are associated with low scores on the second variable. A correlation of 0 means there is no relationship between the two.

3. The number represents the strength of the relationship. Correlations closer to 0 represent weaker relationships. Correlations closer to −1 or 1 represent stronger relationships. One rule of thumb is that correlations of around .10 (or −.10) are considered small, correlations of around .30 (or −.30) are considered medium, and correlations of around .50 (or −.50) are considered strong.

SPSS: Descriptive Information (Correlation)

Correlation Table:

- Analyze
- Correlate
- Bivariate
  - Send over your main variables to the box on the right
  - OK (or Paste)

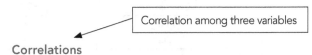

Correlation among three variables

Correlations

		PTG	CTQ	RUMINATION
PTG	Pearson correlation	1	.042	.161**
	Sig. (2-tailed)		.331	.000
	N	542	542	542
CTQ	Pearson correlation	.042	1	.122**
	Sig. (2-tailed)	.331		.005
	N	542	542	542
Rumination	Pearson correlation	.161*	.122*	1
	Sig. (2-tailed)	.000	.005	
	N	542	542	542

*Correlation is significant at the 0.01 level (2-tailed).

Hopefully this gives you a sense of how you would address correlation in the descriptive statistics in your results section. Now, let's look at partial and semipartial correlation in SPSS.

SPSS: Partial Correlation

- ▨ Analyze
- ▨ Correlate
- ▨ Partial
  - ◉ Send over your main variables to correlated to the box on the right (Variables:) and your variables to control for in the box below (Controlling for:)
  - ◉ Options
    - ○ Check: Means and standard deviations
    - ○ Check: Zero-order correlations
    - ○ Continue
  - ◉ OK (or Paste)

*Note: You can also use regression to get these results. More on that later in the chapter.

Correlations

CONTROL VARIABLES			PTG	RUMINATION	CTQ	
-none-[a]	PTG	Correlation	1.000	.883	-.017	
		Significance (2-tailed)	.	.000	.01	
		df	0	540	540	
	Rumination	Correlation	.161	1.000	.324	Both are significant
		Significance (2-tailed)	.000	.	.000	
		df	540	0	540	
	CTQ	Correlation	-.017	.883	1.000	
		Significance (2-tailed)	.701	.000	.	
		df	540	540	0	
CTQ	PTG	Correlation	1.000	.492		
		Significance (2-tailed)	.	.000		After controlling for CTQ. *Partial.*
		df	0	539		
	Rumination	Correlation	.176	1.000		
		Significance (2-tailed)	.000	.		
		df	539	0		

[a] Cells contain zero-order (Pearson) correlations.

REGRESSION

Up to this point we have discussed correlation and touched on univariate analysis. Univariate analysis investigates only one variable. It does not determine causal relationships and the primary

TABLE 6.4 **Equation for Variance**

z	$Sx^2 = \dfrac{\sum(X-\bar{X})^2}{N-1} = \dfrac{\sum(X-\bar{X})(X-\bar{X})}{N-1}$
Covariance	$S_{xy} = \dfrac{\sum(X-\bar{X})(Y-\bar{Y})}{N-1}$
Correlation	$r_{xy} = \dfrac{S_{xy}}{S_x S_y}$

purpose of the analysis is to describe the data and find patterns that may exist within them. For example, investigators can measure the weight of each member of a yoga class to describe patterns found in the accumulated data and draw conclusions via central tendency measures (mean, median, and mode), dispersion of data (range, variance, and standard deviation) and by using frequency distribution tables, histograms, and different types of charts.

While univariate analyses can be useful, they are limited to only examining one variable at a time. Procedures that attempt to measure relationships between just two variables at a time are bivariate. When conducting bivariate studies, researchers explore measures on two variables and determine the degree to which they are related and whether the direction of the relationship is positive or negative. For instance, researchers can investigate the relationship between student test scores and daily hours of sleep. In this example, researchers may discover a strong positive relationship between the two measured variables—that is to say, higher student test scores are linked to increased daily hours of sleep; however, no causal inferences can be concluded because the researchers have not accounted for other variables that may have contributed to increased test scores, such as number of study hours, attitude about the course material, classroom environment, and so on.

Before we move on to the topic of multiple regression, we will review simple regression, variance, covariance, and correlation. Remember your equation for variance (Table 6.4).

With variance, we are summing up the deviation score squared. Remember $X - \bar{X}$ is the deviation score. We then divide by $N - 1$. We could divide by N if we were talking about descriptive statistics; however, in the context of regression statistics we use $N - 1$. Let us then compare variance and covariance. If you look at part of the variance equation $\sum(X-\bar{X})(X-\bar{X})$ and the covariance equation $\sum(X-\bar{X})(Y-\bar{Y})$ you see the only difference is that our variance equation only deals with one variable (X). While the covariance equation, as the name suggests, has two variables (X and Y).

Correlation equation in the context of covariance and variance is $Correlation = \frac{Covatiance}{SD\ of\ x \times SD\ of\ y}$. Thus, we see that covariance and correlation measure the same thing on a different scale. Covariance keeps its original scale of your measurement ($N - 1$), while correlation has been standardized. Correlation is standardized because it has been divided by the standard deviation ($SD\ of\ x \times SD\ of\ y$). If you recall, this is similar to how we calculate the Z score $\left(Z = (X-\bar{X})/SD\right)$. Therefore, in the case of correlation we are standardizing the covariance. This limits the value we get for correlation resulting in the correlation being somewhere between -1 and 1, whereas, covariance, not being standardized, can be any value. Understanding these basic equations will allow you to extend that knowledge to the formation of predictive regression equations and multiple regression analysis.

Building on these formulas, we will now look at linear regression. The regression equation is $\hat{Y} = b_0 + b_1 X$. This equation can also be written as $\hat{Y} = a + bX$. No matter the notation, we are most interested in the slope (bX or b_1X) and the intercept (a or b_0). To calculate the slope, we expand the equation so that $= \frac{\Sigma xy}{\Sigma x^2}$, and the intercept so we see that $a = \bar{Y} - b\bar{X}$.

$$\hat{Y} = (\bar{Y} - b\bar{X}) + \left(\frac{\Sigma xy}{\Sigma x^2}\right)$$

To uncover how these formulas came about would require a deeper dive into calculus. (Note: Calculus was discovered by the mathematicians Newton and Leibntz in the 1600s.) We can now calculate our best line of fit given the observed data and produce our regression (prediction) equation.

We are now ready for our regression analysis. We begin by taking our regression equation $\hat{Y} = a + bX$. We can then calculate a predicted value (Y'), or any observed datum, and use this to determine how much of the variation in our predicted values is accounted for from regression or residual. We start by calculating the total variation $(Y - \bar{Y})^2$, the regression $(Y' - \bar{Y})^2$ and the residual $(Y - \bar{Y}')^2$. As we will see, the sum of the squared values for regression in addition the sum of the squared vales for the residual, equal the total variation (see Figure 6.2).

We can take this equation and put it in the context of the analysis of variance (ANOVA). Similar to a one-way ANOVA (univariate analysis), regression is similar to between variance and residual is akin to within variance. With these equations, we can test the null hypothesis H_0: X (or Xs) does (do) not explain a significant amount of variation in Y. We could apply this to a set of data and evaluate the $F_{obs} = MS_{reg}/MS_{res}$, and the $F_{crit} = F_{(alpha)'k,N-k-1}$. Rarely would one do this by hand today as programs such as SPSS will calculate the p-value (ANOVA table, Table 6.5). If we were to evaluate the F_{obs} and the F_{crit} the decision rule would be to reject H_0 if $F_{obs} \geq F_{crit}$.

One way to test the significance of individual variables is to use ANOVA. One would use this approach when the goal is to predict a continuous criterion (e.g., GPA, symptom severity, income) on the basis of one or more categorical predictor variables (gender, race, employment). We expand this statistical model to use in multiple regression, whereas in simple regression we have $k = 1$ (predictors) and with multiple regression we have $k > 1$.

In addition to the F statistic and Sum of Squares to test significance, we can also use the slope of a regression line. The slope is also referred to as the regression coefficient (b). The null hypothesis for testing the regression coefficient is as follows: H_0: $B = 0$. In other words, the null hypothesis is testing if the slope is 0 in a population ($Y' = a + \mathbf{bX}$). In this analysis, we will use a t as the test statistic. As a reminder, t follows the following formula (Table 6.6).

To test the t statistic, we need to know the standard error of b. We will also need to know the mean square residual (MS_{res}). So far, we have noted this as MS_{res}, however, the notation changes

TABLE 6.5 **Test of Significance**

SOURCE	SS	DF	MS	F
Regression	$\Sigma(Y' - \bar{Y})^2$	k	SS_{reg}/k	MS_{reg}/MS_{res}
Residual	$\Sigma(Y - Y')^2$	N-k-l	$SS_{res}/N-k-l$	
Total	$\Sigma(Y - \bar{Y})^2$	N-l	$SS_{tot}/N-l$	

NOTE: where N = number of observation, k = number of predictors.

TABLE 6.6 *t* as a Test Statistic

t statistic	$\dfrac{statistic - parameter}{SE} = t_{obs} = \dfrac{b}{S_b}$
Standard error of b	$\sqrt{\dfrac{MS_{res}}{\Sigma x^2}} = \sqrt{\dfrac{MS_{res}}{S_x \cdot \sqrt{N-1}}} = S_b$
Mean square residual	$MS_{res} = S^2_{y \cdot x}$

TABLE 6.7 *t* Critical Value

t critical	$t_{\alpha/2}, N-k-1$
Decision rule	Reject if $|t_{obs}| \geq t_{crit}$

when using regression to $S^2_{y.x}$. In the preceding equations, we see that the square root of MS_{res} gives us the standard error of estimate notated as $S_{y.x}$. Once we get the standard error of b, we can calculate the test statistic t (Table 6.6) where b is the slope and S_b the SE of b. To test whether to reject or accept our null hypothesis we compare the t statistic with the t critical value (Table 6.7).

Like the F test completed earlier, statistical programs will calculate the p-value (significant value). In the event of multiple b's (slopes), we will need to test the slope. In the case of simple regression, our decisions regarding the null hypothesis would be identical to that of the ANOVA. Not so with multiple regression, as we have multiple slopes (b). So far, we have used statistical models for hypothesis testing. To better understand regression, we will now take a quick look at the relationship between correlation and regression.

Correlation and prediction are closely connected, in that if two variables are correlated with each other, then the value of one variable should estimate with some degree of accuracy the value of the other variable (Hayes, 2013). Correlation and slope are, in fact, related. We see this in the equation (Figure 6.3).

Here r_{xy} is the correlation and b is the slope. Thus, we can see that if the correlation is 0, the slope would also be 0, or if the correlation is positive/negative the slope is also positive/negative. It also may be helpful to know that correlation is symmetric, meaning that the correlation of X, Y is the same as Y, X. However, for regression, it does not matter which is the predictor (X) and which is the criterion (Y). Our b (slope) is calculated given that X is the predictor and Y is the criterion. If you were to reverse their placement you would result in a different slope. We can take our calculations further by squaring our correlation and resulting in a statistic known as the coefficient of determination (r^2_{xy}). This is the variation in Y knowing X. In the context of regression, we use the notation R^2. This can be calculated using the sum of squares discussed earlier ($R^2 = SS_{reg}/SS_{tot}$). While correlation (r^2_{xy}) is limited to one set of variables, regression (R^2) allows for multiple predictors.

$$b = r_{xy} \frac{S_y}{S_x}$$

FIGURE 6.3 Correlation and Scope.

$$F = \frac{R^2 / k}{(1 - R^2)/(N - k - 1)}$$

FIGURE 6.4 F Statistic Formula.

TABLE 6.8 Simple and Multiple Regression

Simple regression (k = 1)	$\hat{Y} = b_0 + b_1 X$
Multiple regression (k =2)	$\hat{Y} = b_0 + b_1 X_1 + b_2 X_2$
Multiple regression (k >2)	$\hat{Y} = b_0 + b_1 X_1 + b_2 X_2 + \ldots + b_k X_k$

Similar to sum of squares and slope, we can also use our R^2 to test for significance. Again, we calculate an F statistic (Figure 6.4) and apply the same decision rules previously mentioned.

To review, we've covered three approaches to hypothesis testing: (a) test for regression; (b) test for slope; and (c) test for R^2. We will now take these three tests and expand them into multiple regression (k > 1; multiple independent variables or predictors). We first need to consider the factors that affect the precision of our regression equations, specifically the effect of our sample size on our test statistics. In the case of hypothesis testing, the larger the F the more likely we are to reject a null hypothesis. Sample size specifically effects the size of our F statistic. The larger the sample size the larger the F. In addition to sample size, we must pay close attention to the standard error of estimate. Inversely to sample size, the larger the SE the smaller the F statistic. Last, is the range of X in your data. The larger the range of X, the larger the F statistic. Recall the SE formula (Table 6.4). S_b needs to be small because, as we see in our t statistic formula $\frac{b}{S_b}$, the smaller the S_b the larger the t statistic, thus the more likely you will reject the null hypothesis. All these factors are to be considered as we conduct our prediction research.

As we have a better understanding of simple regression, we can apply these concepts to multiple regression. The main change from regression to multiple regression is the increase in the number of independent variables (predictors) from one to two or more. Recall our simple regression equation and see the difference in our new multiple regression equation (Table 6.6). Of course, multiple regression is not limited to just two predictors, so there is a more general equation that fits having predictors (k) >1 (Table 6.8). To better understand our move from simple regression to multiple regression we will look at the following fictional data set (Example 6.1).

Y (ACHIEVE)	X1 (HOURS)	X2 (MOTIVATION)	Y
16	2	15	16.67
14	3	12	16.29
20	4	17	19.18
19	4	14	17.95
23	5	18	20.44
20	6	20	22.10
22	6	16	20.46
25	8	24	25.43
26	8	23	25.02
24	9	22	25.46

	Y (ACHIEVE)	X1 (HOURS)	X2 (MOTIVATION)	Y
mean	20.90	5.50	18.10	
var	14.99	5.39	16.30	
SD	3.87	2.32	4.04	

CORRELATION MATRIX				
	Y	X1	X2	
Y	1	0.8840	0.8745	
X1		1	0.8826	
X2			1	

First, we calculate the descriptive stats and correlation matrix. We would expect the correlation between motivation, study, and test scores to be high. As it tracks, the more motivated you are the longer you study, and the greater the achievement. Remember this is just a hypothetical data set. We will want to calculate slopes for our regression lines. From our review we could find the simple regression line from the equation (Table 6.9). Here we are going to expand this to multiple regression (Table 6.9). For the purposes of this chapter we are not going to derive the formulas, but rather take a look at them to get a sense of what we have.

Since we have two predictors, we will have two slopes. Notice in the simple regression equation you only have one r. In the case of multiple regression, we first expand the equation to include the multiple correlations between the predictors. In our example, we are including three additional correlations. The correlation between Y and X_1, Y and X_2, and X_1 and X_2. All these take the place of the single r from before. We can calculate our correlations from the descriptive and correlation matrix and calculate the slopes of X_1 and X_2 (Table 6.9).

Now what we have our slopes, let's look at the intercepts (a, where the slope crosses the y-axis). Before our simple regression intercept formula was b_0 (a). Similar to what we did with our slope formulas, we can expand it to include our multiple predictors (Table 6.10). This is a much simpler expansion and again, we can get all of this information from our descriptive stats.

TABLE 6.9 Finding the Regression Line

$$b = r \frac{S_y}{S_x}$$

$$b_1 = \frac{(r_{y1} - r_{y2} \cdot r_{y12})}{1 - r_{12}^2} \cdot \frac{S_y}{S_{x1}} = \frac{.8840 - (.8745)(.8826)}{1 - (.8826)^2} \cdot \frac{3.872}{2.321} = .846$$

$$b_2 = \frac{(r_{y2} - r_{y2} \cdot r_{y12})}{1 - r_{12}^2} \cdot \frac{S_y}{S_{x2}} = \frac{.8745 - (.8840)(.8826)}{1 - (.8826)^2} \cdot \frac{3.872}{4.040} = .409$$

TABLE 6.10 Expanding for Multiple Predictors

$$b_0 = \bar{Y} - b_1 \bar{X}$$

$$b_0 = \bar{Y} - b_1 \bar{X}_1 - b_2 \bar{X}_2 = 20.9 - (.846)(5.5) - (.409)(18.1) \approx 8.85$$

$$\hat{Y} = b_0 + b_1 X_1 + b_2 X_2 + b_3 X_1 X_2$$

FIGURE 6.5 Including Interaction.

Since we have two predictors it is possible to run two simple regressions: one for $X_1 (\hat{Y} = 12.8 + 1.47X_1)$ and one for $X_2 (\hat{Y} = 5.79 + .84X_2)$. Since we are no longer interested in the single lines, but rather two variables simultaneously, we calculated the following equation $\hat{Y} = 8.85 + .846X_1 + .409X_2$. Notice, that if we do two simple regressions, we get different slopes and intercepts. Focusing on our regression equations, we interpret our slope of .846 as the rate of change if X_1 is 1 and keeping $.408X_2$ constant. Stated differently, given the same motivation level if you study one more hour, you are expected to increase your test score (achievement) by .846. It is the same concept for .409. Again, holding motivation $(.846X_1)$ constant, for every 1 increase in motivation you increase your test score (achievement) by .409. Finally, how would you interpret the 8.85 of the equation? This 8.85 is the score you would obtain if X_1 and X_2 where 0. In other words, 8.85 is the score you would get if you studied 0 hours and had 0 motivation.

Now, what if your theory or question supposes interaction? Note that we have assumed that our model has no interaction. We can easily incorporate that interaction into the model. Your regression equation changes to include $b_3 X_1 X_2$ (Figure 6.5). We call this our interaction term. In our example, if we think that the relationship between achievement and study hours is dependent on motivation level, we have an interaction. You can test whether the inclusion of this term is significant or not. We refer to this as testing full and reduced models.

Now that we better understand our slope equations, we can look at multiple regression analysis. Our main difference is how we calculate $\hat{Y}$. In the case of multiple predictors, we still only get one predicted score $(\hat{Y} = b_0 + b_1 X_1 + b_2 X_2 + b_3 X_1 X_2)$. Then, the relationship we saw earlier stays the same (Figure 6.5).

Take a look at the ANOVA table (Example 6.2).

ANOVA TABLE				
SOURCE	SS	DF	MS	F
Reg	110.382	k = 2	55.42	16.12
Res	24.068	N - k - 1 = 7	3.43	
Tot	134.900	N - 1 = 9		
$F^*_{(\alpha,k,N-k-1)} = F^*_{(.05,2,7)} = 4.74$				
$H_0 : \beta_1 = \beta_2 = 0$	(or equivalent to H_0: $R^2 = 0$)			

EXAMPLE 6.2

As with our simple regression we can compare our F_{obs} to our F_{crit}. When running this in a statistical program you can look at your provided p-value to see significance. In this case, we can see that our F_{obs} is larger, so this time we reject our null hypothesis. In this test we have found that the regression was significant. We are also testing the null hypothesis that the slope will be different from 0. We can conclude that taken together X_1 and X_2 explain a statistically significant amount of variation in Y.

$$F = \frac{(R_{FM}^2 - R_{RM}^2)/(k_{FM} - k_{RM})}{(1 - R_{FM}^2)/N - k_{FM} - 1}$$

FIGURE 6.6 Testing for Project Contribution.

Suppose, as in our case, that our null hypothesis is rejected, and you want to know if one of the predictors explains more or less of the variation than the other or if each variable explains a significant amount of variation. Think about a group project. Let's say that your group got an A. Did each person in the group contribute a significant amount, or did one person do most of the work? We can test this with the following formula (Figure 6.6).

FM refers to the full model, which is a model containing all the predictors, while *RM* refers to a reduced model, which is a model absent of one or more predictors. This is a very convenient formula to know. In our case, let's see if we should have X_2 in the model when the models already have X_1. Our null hypothesis would be $H_0 : \beta = 0$. As you can see, the full model (*FM*) has both predictors, and the reduced model (*RM*) has X_1. Taken the difference, we are really testing the addition of the $b_2 X_2$ term. We calculate our R^2 and plug in our remaining numbers to get the following (Figure 6.7).

Our critical value is $F^*_{\alpha, k_{FM} - k_{RM}, N - k_{FM} - 1} = F^*_{.05,1,7} = 5.59$. Here we see that the difference is non-significant. We thus conclude that X_2 does not appear to explain a significant amount of variance in test scores beyond what is already explained by X_1. We could do the same for our variable X_1; *that is, to test if we should have X_1 in the model when the model already has X_2*. We plug in our numbers and see that this is also non-significant. Thus, again we conclude that X_1 does not appear to explain a significant amount of variance in test scores beyond what is already explained by X_2. We could come to similar results by testing the regression coefficients; however, by comparing regression models, we have more flexibility. Take a look at the following equations:

FM: $\quad\quad \hat{Y} = b_0 + b_1 X_1 + b_2 X_2 + b_3 X_3 + b_4 X_4 + b_5 X_5$

RM: $\quad\quad \hat{Y} = b_0 + b_1 X_1 + b_2 X_2$

With this approach we can compare any combination of competing models. In the preceding example we are testing if three additional predictors explain a significant amount of variance when added. This is very helpful because often variables can be bundled. For example, X_1 and X_2 may be constructs related to internal behavior and X_{3-5} may be constructs related to external behavior. We can test how the addition of a concept/theory changes a regression model. When testing the regression coefficients like a slope we are only looking at one variable at a time. Therefore, comparing models allows for more flexibility.

$$F = \frac{(.822 - .78)/(2-1)}{1 - .822)/10 - 2 - 1} = 1.578$$

FIGURE 6.7 Calculation R².

So, what can we say about study hours and motivation in terms of test scores? We can say that each contributes a significant amount of variation to test scores, but you don't need both. If you have one, the addition of the second is not significant. So, which one should you drop? We will have to consider practical implications as well. In this case study, hours would be much easier to measure than motivation. You would want to consider dropping motivation and keeping study hours, because that will be an easier variable to measure and will be a significant predictor of test scores.

MULTICOLLINEARITY

Before we move on to examples, let's take a look at multicollinearity. Multicollinearity happens when two or more predictors are highly correlated with one another. This can cause problems in conducting a regression analysis. When this occurs, the standard errors associated with the slopes may become highly inflated. This leads to incorrect conclusions from the significance tests of the slopes. Usually, predictors can be correlated with one another to about .8 before it becomes a problem. Basically, when there is a high correlation between the variables, the size of R is limited. This in turn makes determining the importance of a given predictor difficult because the effect of the predictors is confounded due to the correlation among them. Additionally, it increases the variance of the regression coefficients. The greater the variances, the more unstable the prediction equation will be. This happens because the standard errors have become large. So, from sample to sample, the regression coefficients can vary quite a bit.

There are a number of diagnostic tools to use to determine if there is multicollinearity. First, we can examine the correlation matrix for high correlation among the predictor variables; however, this does not always indicate multicollinearity. Second, we can examine the b and Sb. If multicollinearity is an issue, we will see large changes in b when a variable is added or deleted. We can also use common sense: When we see non-significant b for IVs, we know this to be important. If we see an unexpected sign of b or a wide confidence interval, we can suspect multicollinearity. We can also use the statistical analysis VIF (Variance Inflation Factors) and Tolerance. These two things measure the same thing but are calculated differently. SPSS provides the option of running these analyses while conducting regression analysis. The common rule is that if VIF > 10 or Tolerance <.10, you may have a problem in your data (Myers, 1990).

If you discover that there is a problem of multicollinearity, you have a few options. First, you can combine predictors that are highly correlated (add them to form a single measure). A less simple solution would be to conduct a principle comparison analysis to reduce the number of predictors, however, that involves factor analysis, and is not addressed in this chapter. For more information on this, please read Myers (1990).

POWER

Finally, we will discuss sample size. This is probably one of the most frequently asked questions when using regression as a statistical model. There are some recommendations you may have heard of. The roughest of all is "at least 100 subjects." Another, one-size-fits-all recommendation you may have heard is 30 subjects per one IV. This is a little better, only in that it communicates a truth that the more IVs, you have the more subjects you need. In this author's opinion, the best way to come up with the sample size is to use Cohen's Table. Cohen (1988) provides sample size charts in "statistical power analysis for the behavioral sciences." It can, however, be cumbersome

$N \geq \dfrac{L}{f^2}$	$N \geq \dfrac{9.5}{.15} \geq 64$
$f^2 = \dfrac{R^2}{(1-R^2)}$	$f^2 = \dfrac{.13}{(1-.13)} = .15$
$L = 6.4 + 1.65k - .05k^2$	$L = 6.4 + 1.65(2) - .05(2)^2 = 9.5$

FIGURE 6.8 Sam Green's Formula.

TABLE 6.11

	R²	F²
Small	.02	.02
Medium	.13	.15
Large	.26	.35

to look up the charts and so forth, so there are a few alternatives. Sam Green's formulas (found in Green, S. [1991]. "How many subjects does it take to do a regression analysis?") provides an easy path. You can also refer to the software G*Power (http://www.psychologie.hhu.de/arbeitsgruppen/ allgemeine-psychologie-und-arbeitspsychologie/gpower.html). This author highly recommends using this free software in computing your statistical power.

Let's look at Sam Green's formula (Figure 6.8; Table 6.11). Like any other sample size requirement, you will need to know the effect size, alpha level, and desired power. Suppose you want to use an alpha of .05 and your desired power is .8. Given that, all you need to know is your effect size estimate. R^2 is an example of an estimate of effect size.

To use Sam Green's formula, you will need to convert your R^2 to the effect size estimate of f^2. It is the same for G*Power as well. We can use the following formula (Figure 6.9) to convert R^2 to f^2. Next, we can use Sam Green's formula where he provides the equation for L. This gives us our sample size requirement of $N \geq 64$. To achieve the power .8, we need at least 64 subjects given our example. There are a number of papers that can be read on power and sample size (Faul, Erdfelder, Buchner, & Lang, 2009).

So far, we have discussed simple linear regression, as well as multiple regression. We will now spend some time better understanding the regression equation in terms of prediction. Recall we discussed the regression equation, and given data, we were able to come up with said equation $\hat{Y} = 12.8 + 1.47X$. This was the regression equation we used for study hours and achievement. We had a second variable (motivation), but for illustrative purposes here we are not going to use the second variable. We would now like to use this equation to predict outcomes with a new sample. Suppose you have the X for a new sample $\left(X = 4, \hat{Y} = 12.8 + 1.47(4) = 18.67\right)$. Of course, this predicted $\hat{Y}$ is just a point estimate, so there must be some error associated with it. We cannot expect that this subject will get exactly 18.67. There must be a range of values. There are two ways to look at this predicted $\hat{Y}$. We can view $\hat{Y}$ as an estimate of the mean of Y at the X value in question, or view it as an estimate of Y for any given individual with such an X. To put it in context, suppose an instructor said that the average grade in this class is a B, but some students do better and other students do worse. They

$$Y' \pm t_{\alpha/2,\, N-k-1} \cdot (SE)$$

FIGURE 6.9 Confidence Interval Equation.

TABLE 6.12

Question 1	$S_{(\mu_y/x_0)} = S_{Y \cdot X} \sqrt{\dfrac{1}{N} + \dfrac{(X_0 - \bar{X})^2}{(N-1)S_x^2}}$
Question 2	$S_{Y'} = S_{Y \cdot X} \sqrt{1 + \dfrac{1}{N} + \dfrac{(X_0 - \bar{X})^2}{(N-1)S_x^2}}$

also indicated that how much time a student spends studying is related to their test performance. This produces two types of questions: (a) How well do students who study X hours for the exam do? and (b) If one student studies for X hours, how well can the student expect to do? These are two very different questions. Stated differently, question 1 relates to how much variation can you expect in $\hat{Y}$, when a population is the subject of study, for X hours (let's say 4 hours). If you are interested in question 2, then your margin of error gets bigger, but you have to take individual difference into account. Let's move through these two questions. First, your predicted value for $\hat{Y}$ will be the same for both questions (18.86), however, your SE will differ; because question two must account for individual difference (Table 6.12).

Given the difference in the formulas we can see that question a will be larger, again, as it must account for individual difference, and question b will be smaller. In accounting for individual difference, the X moves further from the mean. This is known as leverage. As the X moves further from the mean the standard error increases. Let's calculate the confidence interval (CI). Suppose we are interested in $X_0 = 4$. Recall that whenever we want to know our confidence interval, we use the equation in Figure 6.9.

For our example we will use a 95% CI denoted by using an "alpha" of .05 in the CI equation. So, for question a, we use our question to get our SE (.735). We then use the SE in the CI equation $18.7 \pm 2.307(.735) = (17.01, 20.39)$. Remember that given X = 4, we get a Y' of 18.7, but we can say that if a subject studies for 4 hours they will get a test score anywhere from 17.01-20.39. If we look at question b and apply the same formula, we get a different range: $S_{Y'} = 2.055$; $18.7 \pm 2.307(2.055) = (13.096, 23.44)$. So, to answer the question, how would one do if they studied for 4 hours? We can expect a score between 13.96 and 23.44. This is a very simple run at how regression equations can be used for prediction. This differs from regression analysis in prediction research but is one of the many uses of regression lines and regression as a statistical model.

EXAMPLE: MULTIPLE AND HIERARCHICAL REGRESSION

Recall that regression is used when we want to predict a dependent variable from two or more independent variables. It is similar to correlation in that we are looking at the relationship between variables. However, correlation can only look at two variables. Regression can look at two or more. There are two main types of multiple regression:

1. Multiple Regression (sometimes referred to as Simultaneous Regression): All the IVs are entered at once.
2. Hierarchical Regression: IVs are entered in different steps. This allows the researcher to test more nuanced hypotheses. For example, you could test the question: Controlling for trauma (IV entered in Step 1), is rumination (IV entered in Step 2) a significant predictor of posttraumatic growth?

REGRESSION: SPSS

- Analyze
- Regression
- Linear
  - Send your DV to the "Dependent" box on the right.
  - Send your IV(s) to the "Independent" box on the right.
    - If you are doing a multiple regression, send all IVs into the box at once.
    - If you are doing a hierarchical regression:
      - Send the IV(s) for Step 1 into the box.
      - Click Next. (Notice above it says, "Block 2 of 2" This indicates you are now at Step 2.).
      - Send the IV(s) for Step 2 into the box. (Notice you can toggle back and forth between Step 1 and Step 2. Also, notice you can have more than two steps if desired.).
  - Statistics
    - In addition to the default selections, select:
      - R squared change
      - Descriptive
      - Part and partial correlations
      - Collinearity diagnostics
- Ok (or Paste)

HYPOTHESIS

This is the main part of your results section. In this part, you will walk through each of your hypotheses and present the results of your analyses. In this section of the guide, the first thing we will do is walk through a general progression for how to write up this section. We will then walk through how to conduct some of the most common analyses used. Writing up this section in your paper will likely be a collaborative effort between you and a collaborator or advisor, because we will need to discuss what our hypotheses are, and what the best analysis to use would be. But this should give you a starting point.

GENERAL WRITE-UP

For each hypothesis, you will have a few main parts: We will use these hypotheses in the following regression models.

- Restate the hypothesis (e.g., our first hypothesis was that childhood emotional abuse would be negatively associated with Posttraumatic Growth (PTG) and rumination would be positively associated with posttraumatic growth, controlling for trauma.)
- Describe the analysis used to test the hypothesis (e.g., we tested this hypothesis using a hierarchical regression analysis with posttraumatic growth as the dependent variable, childhood trauma entered in Step 1, and rumination entered in Step 2.)
- State whether the hypothesis was supported (e.g., this hypothesis was supported.)
- Then give the numbers (e.g., Step 1 and Rumination entered in Step 2. This hypothesis was supported. In Step 1, Childhood Trauma (CTQ) predicted <1% of the variance in forgiveness ($R^2 = .00$, $F(1, 540) = .128$, $p = .721$). In Step 2, controlling for CTQ, Rumination predicted an additional 3% of the variance in PTG ($\Delta R^2 = .03$, $\Delta F(1, 539) = 15.42$, $p < .001$). In the final model, CTQ was not a significant predictor of PTG ($\beta = -.05$, $p = .296$). Rumination was a significant positive predictor of PTG ($\beta = .18$, $p < .001$.)

EXAMPLE: MULTIPLE REGRESSION

Hypothesis for Examples:

- Hypothesis 1: Childhood Trauma (CTQ) and Rumination would predict a significant amount of variance in Posttraumatic Growth (PTG).
- Hypothesis 2: CTQ would be significant negative predictor and Rumination would be a significant positive predictor of PTG

Descriptive Statistics ←

	MEAN	STD DEVIATION	N
PTG	78.9889	26.66092	542
CTQ ←	10.3958	5.39765	542
Rumination	23.9207	9.11327	542

Means and standard deviations for your variables

DV: Posttraumatic Growth (PTG) IVs: Childhood Trauma (CTQ), Rumination

Correlation table for your variables

Correlations ←

		PTG	CTQ	RUMINATION
Pearson Correlation	PTG	1.000	.015	.161
	CTQ	.015	1.000	.353
	Rumination	.161	.353	1.000
Sig. (1-tailed)	PTG	.	.360	.000
	CTQ	.360	.	.000
	Rumination	.000	.000	.

(continued)

Correlations (continued)

		PTG	CTQ	RUMINATION
N	PTG	542	542	542
	CTQ	542	542	542
	Rumination	542	542	542

Variables Entered/Removed[a]

Just tells you which variables are

MODEL	VARIABLES ENTERED	VARIABLES REMOVED	METHOD
1	Rumination, CTQ[b]	.	Enter

Only one model since this is simultaneous regression — IVs entered at once.in the model

a. Dependent Variable: PTG
b. All requested variables entered

Gives an indication of the overall relationship between your IVs and DV

Overall statistics for the model

Model Summary

CHANGE STATISTICS									
MODEL	R	R SQUARE	ADJUSTED R SQUARE	STD. ERROR OF THE ESTIMATE	R SQUARE CHANGE	F CHANGE	DF1	DF2	SIG. F CHANGE
1	.167[a]	.028	.024	26.33318	.028	7.775	2	539	.000

a. Predictors: (Constant), Rumination, CTQ

Gives the percent of variance in your DV that is accounted for by the variables in your model

3% of the variance in PTG is accounted for by CTQ and Rumination

For the model as a whole, do the IVs predict a significant amount of variance in the DV?

p-value is less than .05, so yes, they do

Basically, gives the same information as the table above it, in a slightly different way

ANOVA[A]

MODEL		SUM OF SQUARES	DF	MEAN SQUARE	F	SIG.
1	Regression	10783.235	2	5391.617	7.775	.000[b]
	Residual	373762.199	539	693.436		
	Total	384545.434	541			

a. Dependent Variable: PTG
b. Predictors: (Constant), Rumination, CTQ

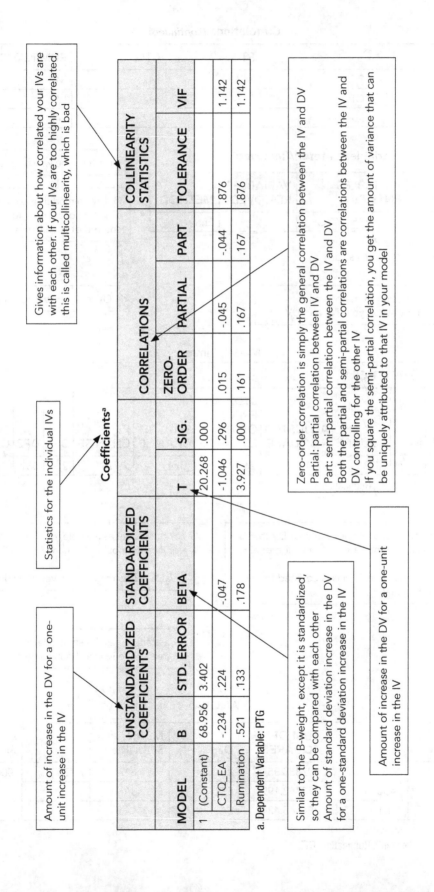

Gives information about how correlated your IVs are with each other. If your IVs are too highly correlated, this is called multicollinearity, which is bad

Statistics for the individual IVs

Amount of increase in the DV for a one-unit increase in the IV

Coefficients[a]

| MODEL | UNSTANDARDIZED COEFFICIENTS | | STANDARDIZED COEFFICIENTS | | | CORRELATIONS | | | COLLINEARITY STATISTICS | |
	B	STD. ERROR	BETA	T	SIG.	ZERO-ORDER	PARTIAL	PART	TOLERANCE	VIF
1 (Constant)	68.956	3.402		20.268	.000					
CTQ_EA	-.234	.224	-.047	-1.046	.296	.015	-.045	-.044	.876	1.142
Rumination	.521	.133	.178	3.927	.000	.161	.167	.167	.876	1.142

a. Dependent Variable: PTG

Zero-order correlation is simply the general correlation between the IV and DV
Partial: partial correlation between IV and DV
Part: semi-partial correlation between the IV and DV
Both the partial and semi-partial correlations are correlations between the IV and DV controlling for the other IV
If you square the semi-partial correlation, you get the amount of variance that can be uniquely attributed to that IV in your model

Amount of increase in the DV for a one-unit increase in the IV

Similar to the B-weight, except it is standardized, so they can be compared with each other
Amount of standard deviation increase in the DV for a one-standard deviation increase in the IV

Amount of increase in the DV for a one-unit increase in the IV

Example Write Up From Analysis

Our first hypothesis was that CTQ and rumination would predict a significant amount of variance in PTG. Specifically, we hypothesized that CTQ would be a significant negative predictor and rumination would be a significant positive predictor of PTG. We tested this hypothesis using a simultaneous multiple regression analysis with PTG as the dependent variable and CTQ and Rumination as independent variables. This hypothesis was partially supported. The overall model was significant. CTQ and Rumination predicted about 3% of the variance in PTG (R^2 = 2.8, $F(2, 539)$ = 7.77, $p < .001$). CTQ was not a significant predictor of PTG (β = -.05, p = .296). Rumination was a significant positive predictor of PTG (β = .18, $p < .001$).

EXAMPLE: HIERARCHICAL REGRESSION

Descriptive Statistics

	MEAN	STD DEVIATION	N
PTG	78.9889	26.66092	542
CTQ	10.3958	5.39765	542
Rumination	23.9207	9.11327	542

Most of the interpretations are similar to simultaneous regression. I noted the differences.

DV: PTG
IV Step 1: Childhood Trauma (CTQ)
IV Step 2: Rumination

Correlations

		PTG	CTQ	RUMINATION
Pearson correlation	PTG	1.000	.015	.161
	CTQ	.015	1.000	.353
	Rumination	.161	.353	1.000
Sig. (1-tailed)	PTG	.	.360	.000
	CTQ	.360	.	.000
	Rumination	.000	.000	.
N	PTG	542	542	542
	CTQ	542	542	542
	Rumination	542	542	542

Notice that for all the tables you have two models. Model 1 is just with the first IV that was entered in Step 1 (e.g., CTQ). Model 2 is with both CTQ as well as the IV that was entered in Step 2 (e.g., Rumination).

Variables Entered/Removed[a]

MODEL	VARIABLES ENTERED	VARIABLES REMOVED	METHOD
1	CTQ[b]	.	Enter
2	Rumination[b]	.	Enter

a. Dependent Variable: PTG
b. All requested variables entered

Model Summary

Model 1 with CTQ predicts less than 1% of the variance in PTG

R2 change indicates the amount of variance in PTG accounted for by Ruination over and above the amount of variance accounted for by CTQ

Not significant

Is this additional variance (by Rumination) significant?

Yes, it is

Model 2 with both predicts about 3% of the variance in PTG (notice this is identical to the simultaneous regression we did earlier—same variables, so it should be the same)

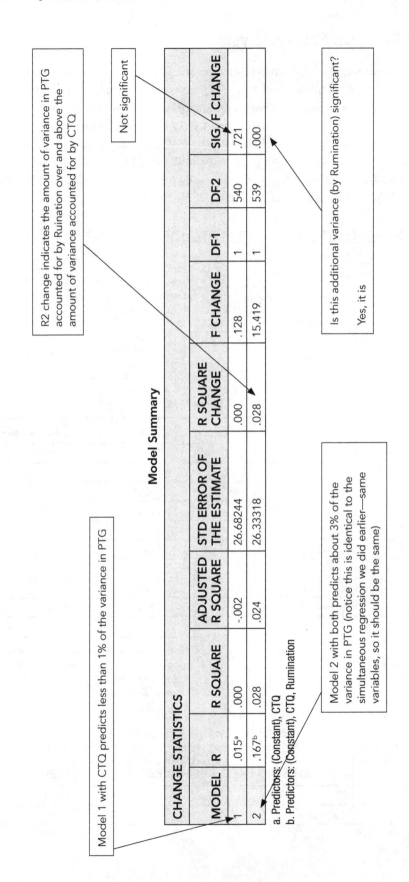

CHANGE STATISTICS										
MODEL	R	R SQUARE	ADJUSTED R SQUARE	STD ERROR OF THE ESTIMATE	R SQUARE CHANGE	F CHANGE	DF1	DF2	SIG. F CHANGE
1	.015[a]	.000	-.002	26.68244	.000	.128	1	540	.721
2	.167[b]	.028	.024	26.33318	.028	15.419	1	539	.000

a. Predictors: (Constant), CTQ
b. Predictors: (Constant), CTQ, Rumination

ANOVA[A]						
MODEL		**SUM OF SQUARES**	**DF**	**MEAN SQUARE**	**F**	**SIG.**
1	Regression	91.036	1	91.036	.128	.721[b]
	Residual	384454.397	540	711.953		
	Total	384545.434	541			
2	Regression	10783.235	2	5391.617	7.775	.000[c]
	Residual	373762.199	539	693.436		
	Total	384545.434	541			

a. Dependent Variable: PTG
b. Predictors: (Constant), CTQ
c. Predictors: (Constant), CTQ, Rumination

Example Write Up

Our first hypothesis was that Rumination would be a significant positive predictor of PTG, controlling for CTQ. We tested this hypothesis using a hierarchical regression analysis with PTG as the dependent variable, CTQ entered in Step 1, and Rumination entered in Step 2. This hypothesis was supported. In Step 1, CTQ predicted <1% of the variance in forgiveness (R^2 = .00, $F(1, 540)$ = .128, p = .721). In Step 2, controlling for CTQ, Rumination predicted an additional 3% of the variance in PTG (ΔR^2 = .03, $\Delta F(1, 539)$ = 15.42, p < .001). In the final model, CTQ was not a significant predictor of PTG (β = -.05, p = .296). Rumination was a significant positive predictor of PTG (β = .18, p < .001).

FACTORIAL DESIGNS

Like multiple regression, factorial designs involve a research design that includes two or more independent variables entered simultaneously (sound familiar?). This starts to get more complicated as factorial designs also allow us to evaluate multiple categorical variables as well as continuous variables. For the purposes of this section there is some terminology that we need to cover to make sure we are on the same page semantically. First, in factorial design we refer to independent variables or our predictors as *Factors*. So, a study investigating the impact of hours spent meditating on different ages and its effect on productivity would be a two-factor study as both age and hours spent meditating are independent variables. So, a study looking solely at the effect of hours spent meditating would be one factor design, whereas study looking at age and hours is a two-factor design. If we added a third independent variable, say for example a mindfulness intervention, we would have a three-factor design as our study would have three independent variables. Another important term to know is *levels*. Levels denote the number of groups or conditions for each factor. If we were doing a *t*-test with two groups, we would have two levels, or an ANOVA with three conditions we would have three levels. Again, this is for each factor. So, for our fictitious study with age and meditation, let's say that we define age as child, adolescent, and adult. This is three levels for age. Also, for hours meditation we say less than 1 hour a week and more than 1 hour a week. This would give us two levels. Thus, in this example, we have a 3x2 factorial design. Three is the number of levels for age and two is the number of levels for mediation.

Gives the statistics for the individual predictors, but for both Model 1 and 2

Gives the significance of Model 1 (as a whole) and Model 2 (as a whole)

Coefficients[a]

| MODEL | | UNSTANDARDIZED COEFFICIENTS | | STANDARDIZED COEFFICIENTS | T | SIG. | CORRELATIONS | | | COLLINEARITY STATISTICS | |
		B	STD ERROR	BETA			ZERO-ORDER	PARTIAL	PART	TOLERANCE	VIF
1	(Constant)	78.199	2.489		31.418	.000					
	CTQ	.076	.213	.015	.358	.721	.015	.015	.015	1.000	1.000
2	(Constant)	68.956	3.402		20.268	.000					
	CTQ	-.234	.224	-.047	-1.046	.296	.015	-.045	-.044	.876	1.142
	Rumination	.521	.133	.178	3.927	.000	.161	.167	.167	.876	1.142

a. Dependent Variable: PTG

In Model 1 (with just CTQ), CTQ is not a significant predictor of PTG

However, when Rumination is added in, CTQ moves closer to be a significant predictor

	B_1	B_2	B_3
A_1	A_1B_1	A_1B_2	A_1B_3
A_2	A_2B_1	A_2B_2	A_2B_3

FIGURE 6.10 2x3 Design.

What you need to know is that the number of numbers indicated the number of factors, and the actual number indicated the levels for the specific factor. Another example would be a 3x3. In this case, you have a three-factor design where each of your factors has three levels. With the factorial design we are looking at the effect of each individual factor, and its effect at each level. The x in between the numbers indicates that we are not only looking at the effect of each level, but also the interaction of factors as well. Factorial designs are most commonly displayed as in Figure 6.10, which is representative of a 2x3 design, or comprises two independent variables A and B, with two levels of A: A1 and A2, and three levels of B: B1, B2, and B3. The cells indicate the interactions are indicated by A1B1, A1B2, and so on.

As we saw with regression analysis, statistical modeling is not limited to a single independent variable or predictor. Explaining and predicting psychological phenomena are complex, and rarely is one variable adequate to answer our research questions. As in our explanation of regression, we see that it is not only the predictors that account for the variance in our criterion, but potentially the interaction between variables as well. From our discussion of prediction and regression we will see that factorial designs provide a significant advantage in understanding the effects of our predictors and their interactions. Additionally, we will see that factorial designs offer us greater control in our models. As we saw with our review of simple linear regression, all the variance not explained by our single predictor is accounted for in the error term. We also learned in multiple regression that the larger the error, the less sensitive the statistical model. Factorial design opens our ability to identify more sources of the variance in the dependent variable. In addition, and most importantly, factorial design also allows us to evaluate the interaction between our independent variables and their effect on our dependent variable. There are two other advantages we see in the use of factorial design. First, they are efficient. Second, in the case of experimental designs, they allow for broader generalizations. Let us use the example of meditation and productivity. Here we assume a design in which hours meditating is the independent variable, or factor, and productivity is the dependent variable. We would assume that all the variance not explained by meditation would be accounted for in the error term. But suppose our sample consists of an equal number of men and women, and that there is a relationship between age and productivity. Here some of the variance of productivity is accounted for by age. Thus, the introduction of age as another independent variable reduces the error estimate, and, while doing so, the proportion of variance due to mediation remains unchanged. Again, as we learned with regression, as the error term decreases the test for significance of the effect becomes more sensitive.

During our review of regression, we discussed that when an independent variable is categorical, regression or analysis of variance can be used. From there we went into the advantages of using multiple regression in place of ANOVA. While multiple regression is an advantageous statistical model, for our purposes we will continue our discussion and subsequent examples of factorial design with two-way ANOVA; which is a special case of factorial ANOVA. We will occasionally

	NO MEDITATION (X)	MEDITATE <1HPW (Y)	MEDITATE < 1HPW (X)
Men	Productivity levels for a group of men who do not meditated	Productivity levels for a group of men who meditated less than an hour per week	Productivity levels for a group of men who meditated more than an hour per week
Women	Productivity levels for a group of women who do not meditated	Productivity levels for a group of women who meditated less than an hour per week	Productivity levels for a group of women who meditated more than an hour per week

FIGURE 6.11 One Manipulated Variable and One Classificatory Variable.

reference multiple regression to illustrate specific points. We will also keep our focus on making inferences about the categories included in the design being analyzed. In other words, we will mainly focus on the main effects and the interactions in our model (see Hayes, 2013; Keppel, 1991; Winer, 1971, for discussions of fixed and random effects models). As much of our analysis will be a review of the previous section (Multiple Regression) we begin with a smaller factorial design: a 2x3.

In Figure 6.11, we see an illustration for two factors (Meditation and Gender), with Meditation consisting of three levels, and Gender consisting of two levels. You may also think of this design as consisting of one manipulated variable (meditation) and one classificatory variable (gender).

The Structure of a 2x3 factor design in which meditation (Factor A) is manipulated and Gender (Factor B) is classificatory.

Since we are manipulating Factor A (Meditation) and Factor B (Gender) is classificatory, we must first randomly assign participants from our three age classifications to the meditation dosage (more or less than 1 hour per week). Having done this, we may proceed as though both factors are manipulated. While this may no longer have an effect on the analysis, it will influence how we interpret the results. This is a complex issue. The more the researcher knows about the area under study, the greater the potential for an accurate interpretation. If you wish to learn more about factorial designs consisting of manipulated and classificatory variables you can read the following text (McAlister, Straus, Sackett, Altman, 2003; Sharpe, 2004). For the purposes of this section, we focus on demonstrating how to analyze data from factorial designs by using multiple regression.

ANALYSIS

Before we review the analysis, we need to have a brief discussion about coding. Coding is an important topic of discussion, and most relevant in the case of Multiple Regression. Recall that factorial designs (like factorial ANOVA, and Multiple Regression) allow us to examine both the main effects a factor has on a dependent variable, but also the interaction effect of the factors as well. Since regression equations are best used with dichotomous or continuous variables, categorical variables require some special attention in the analyses. They must first be recoded into a variable that can then be entered into the analysis. There are many coding systems that can be used, as well as many arguments in supporting them. If the reader wishes to know more about coding systems for categorical variables in regression analysis please review Pedhazur and Kerlinger (1982, Chapter 11.

As we walk through factorial design and the use of Factorial ANOVA, we assume that the readers have some basic understanding of analysis of variance.

SPSS: Two-Way ANOVA Analyze

- ▥ General Linear Model
- ▥ Univariate
  - ● Send your DV to the "Dependent" box on the right.
  - ● Send your IV(s) to the "Fixed Factors" box on the right.
  - ● Options
    - ○ Check: "Descriptive Statistics", "Estimates of Effect Size", "Observed Power", and "Homogeneity Tests".
    - ○ Click Continue.
  - ● Plots
    - ○ Move your first factor to the "Horizontal Axis" box and click add.
    - ○ Move your Second Factor to the "Horizontal Axis" box and click add
    - ○ Next you will plot the interaction. Depending on the factors chosen, you will have to decide on your interactions. In the case of our data, we will plot the interaction Treatment Group*Gender. We do this by moving the factor Treatment group to the "Horizontal Axis" box and Gender to the "Separate Lines" box and click add.
    - ○ Click Continue
  - ● Post Hoc
    - ○ Move the factors that over that have more than two levels.
    - ○ Select "Tukey"
    - ○ Continue
  - ● Ok (Paste)

FACTORIAL ANOVA (TWO-WAY ANOVA)

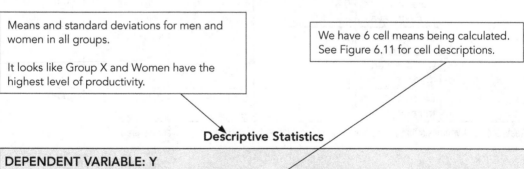

Means and standard deviations for men and women in all groups.

It looks like Group X and Women have the highest level of productivity.

We have 6 cell means being calculated. See Figure 6.11 for cell descriptions.

Descriptive Statistics

DEPENDENT VARIABLE: Y				
A1	B1	MEAN	STD DEVIATION	N
X	Male	39.6624	1.32811	39
	Female	54.9231	2.98094	39
	Total	47.2927	4.49073	78

(continued)

Descriptive Statistics *(continued)*

DEPENDENT VARIABLE: Y				
A1	B1	MEAN	STD. DEVIATION	N
Y	Male	35.2393	1.63111	39
	Female	47.1838	0.95574	39
	Total	41.2115	2.15584	78
Z	Male	22.9487	2.98758	39
	Female	43.5214	1.13373	39
	Total	33.2350	1.48534	78
Total	Male	32.6168	1.23843	117
	Female	48.5427	2.62426	117
	Total	40.5798	0.64046	234

This addresses the question of whether there are homogeneous variances in relation to productivity (Y)

Notice in the descriptives you don't want a wide difference between SDs

Here our p-value is .999. We want $p > .05$
Suggesting that our assumption of homogeneity is correct

Levene's Test of Equality of Error Variances[a,b]

		LEVENE STATISTIC	DF1	DF2	SIG.
Y	Based on mean	1.546	5	228	.999
	Based on trimmed mean	0.819	5	228	.999
	Based on median and with adjusted df	2.189	5	91.740	.999
	Based on trimmed mean	0.819	5	228	.999

Tests the null hypothesis that the error variance of the dependent variable is equal across groups

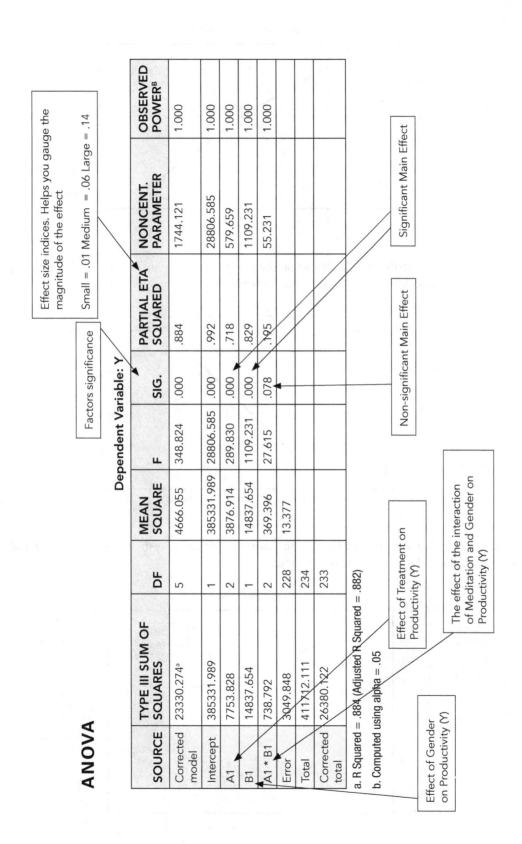

ANOVA

Dependent Variable: Y

SOURCE	TYPE III SUM OF SQUARES	DF	MEAN SQUARE	F	SIG.	PARTIAL ETA SQUARED	NONCENT. PARAMETER	OBSERVED POWER[b]
Corrected model	23330.274[a]	5	4666.055	348.824	.000	.884	1744.121	1.000
Intercept	385331.989	1	385331.989	28806.585	.000	.992	28806.585	1.000
A1	7753.828	2	3876.914	289.830	.000	.718	579.659	1.000
B1	14837.654	1	14837.654	1109.231	.000	.829	1109.231	1.000
A1 * B1	738.792	2	369.396	27.615	.078	.195	55.231	1.000
Error	3049.848	228	13.377					
Total	411712.111	234						
Corrected total	26380.122	233						

a. R Squared = .884 (Adjusted R Squared = .882)

b. Computed using alpha = .05

Effect size indices. Helps you gauge the magnitude of the effect

Small = .01 Medium = .06 Large = .14

Factors significance

Significant Main Effect

Non-significant Main Effect

Effect of Treatment on Productivity (Y)

The effect of the interaction of Meditation and Gender on Productivity (Y)

Effect of Gender on Productivity (Y)

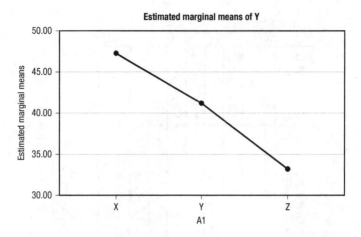

This is the plot of Meditation. It shows that the group that has no meditation (Z) has the lowest productivity, while Group X, Y had higher productivity with increased meditation.

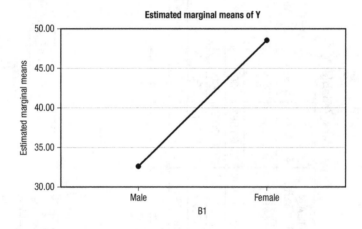

Plot shows us that women scored higher on average on productivity than men. This is graphically showing what was shown in the ANOVA Table.

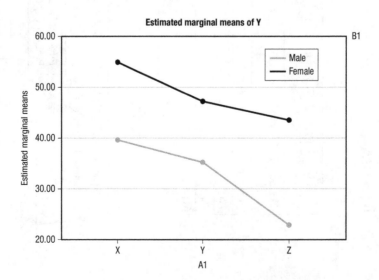

This graph shows us our interactive effect. Interestingly, this shows that there is not a significant interaction effect. Given that the lines run parallel, we see that the relationship between meditation and productivity does not vary if you are a man or woman.

Example Results

Our first hypothesis was that there would be productivity differences between groups that meditated for >1 hpw, meditated for <1 hpw, and the groups that did no meditation. Specifically, we hypothesized that the group that meditated for >1 hpw would have higher levels of productivity than participants from other groups. We also hypothesized that women and men would differ significantly from each other in their levels of productivity. We tested this hypothesis using a two-way analysis of variance (ANOVA) with productivity as the dependent variable and meditation groups and gender as the independent variables. This hypothesis was supported. There was a significant difference in productivity based on meditation group, $F(2, 233) = 3876.914$, $p < .001$, while the interaction of Gender and Meditation did not have a significant effect on productivity $F(2, 233) = 369.396$, $p < .078$.

MULTICULTURAL ISSUES

Cultural competence in the area of research requires that researchers understand the potential role of racial, ethnic, and cultural differences among population groups; how such differences may impact their research study design, analysis, and interpretation; and correspondingly how to effectively include diverse populations in research. Cultural competence can play a critical role in research study design, including the development of research questions and hypotheses, recruitment strategies, data collection procedures, analyzing and interpreting data, and drawing conclusions about results. Ultimately, whether or not research is relatable to diverse populations or can be suitably applied to meet the social and cultural needs of the sample population depends on the cultural competence of the research process.

According to Sue (2001), multicultural competence is acquiring the awareness, knowledge, and skills to engage with people of diverse backgrounds in an effective and sensitive manner. Sue et al. (1982) developed the tripartite model of multicultural competencies that includes attitudes and beliefs, knowledge, and skills acquisition and practice. As such, culturally competent mental health practitioners are self-aware and attuned to their beliefs, attitudes, values, and worldviews that might influence their interaction with their clients. Additionally, they have knowledge of the essential beliefs, attitudes, values, and worldviews of the specific populations with which they work. Moreover, they possess the necessary skills to work with diverse populations (Sue et al., 1982).

Findings from a study on the willingness to participate in biomedical research (Katz, 2015) revealed that African Americans self-reported greater apprehension to participate in biomedical studies as compared to non-Hispanic Whites, and that African American participants were affected more by the investigator who was conducting the study than by what they were required to do as research participants.

Cultural competence can be crucial to successfully and safely recruiting and retaining diverse individuals as participants and can help to improve participation of minority populations in research studies by ensuring that different subgroups in the population are represented proportionally (O'Brien, Kosoko-Lasaki, Cook, Kissell, Peak, & Williams, 2006). Studies reveal that many researchers have not received training and are not familiar with multicultural competencies that include awareness (e.g., familiarity with one's own cultural values and biases), knowledge (e.g., acknowledge people in their cultural context), and skills (e.g., obtaining valid consent from isolated minorities; Rabionet, Santiago, & Zorilla, 2009). Thus, researchers are not properly equipped to integrate the perspective of minority populations, such as historically socially and culturally marginalized groups, into their research to effectively conceptualize, design, conduct, and interpret outcomes without imposing the majority cultural perspective upon the study. Consistent with Multicultural and Social Justice Counseling Competencies (MSJCC, 2015), researchers, both privileged and marginalized, should be aware of and possess knowledge of self and other social identities, social group statuses, power, privilege, oppression, strengths, limitations, assumptions, attitudes, values, beliefs, and biases. Furthermore, they should possess skills that enhance and enrich their awareness and knowledge of self and others.

Case Study

Castleberry, J., Rice, K. (Under Review). Attachment, gender, and college adjustment in STEM students: Psychometric properties and predictive validity of the Experiences in Close Relationship Scale-Short Version.

This quantitative example is from a study under review by Castleberry and Rice. The study examined the concurrent and longitudinal relations between attachment and personal problems in a sample of freshman college students completing a STEM degree. Students pursuing a STEM degree face unique difficulty within their academic environment, finding themselves in courses designed to "weed-out" weaker students. Underrepresented students may face stereotype threat, hostile, or "chilly" climates in the classes that create additional pressures. Based on this, Castleberry and Rice wanted to know if attachment predicted a distal academic outcome, for which predictive methods are better suited. An argument for descriptive survey could be made. Descriptive survey seeks to understand and meet program and policy needs (e.g., needs assessment, evaluating programs throughout outcome and satisfactory surveys, or understanding characteristics of a group of interest); however, Castleberry and Rice's research question was not asking about the degree to which students experience distress or report satisfaction with their program of study. Specifically, they wanted to know if attachment predicted distal outcomes.

Castleberry and Rice collected data on five variables or indicators of variables from 209 freshman pursuing STEM-related majors recruited from two public universities located in the same metropolitan area in the southeastern United States. Participants were recruited through randomized lists of emails of first-time freshman students. To balance participation, the sample was stratified with caps placed on the number of the participants specified groups and were offered $5 to complete the survey at Time 1 and $10 for Time 2. The researchers used the following assessments: The Experience in Close Relationships scale (ECR; Brennan et al., 1998); the Personal Problems Inventory (PPI) (Cash et al., 1975; Ponce & Atkinson, 1989); and collected student GPAs. Analyses for their study were conducted with IBM SPSS Version 24 (2016) and Mplus Version 8.2 (Muthén & Muthén, 1998-2018), using the robust MLR estimator. The research assessed the adequacy of the measures by using confirmatory factor analyses (CFAs) to evaluate their goodness of fit. Having provided support for a reasonable measurement model, Castleberry and Rice utilized Structured Equation Modeling (SEM; Path analysis) to test significance of regression coefficients. SEM was used due to its ability to account for missing data with full-information maximum likelihood (Yuan & Bentler, 2000), and to better account for error variance when testing a theoretical model.

The researchers found that their hypothesis was only partially supported. Their results indicated that while anxious attachment was a significant predictor of college adjustment, avoidant attachment was not. Additionally, their data showed that attachment, neither anxious nor avoidance, predicted GPA with their sample of STEM students. Notice in the table that follows that ECR-Anxiety had a significant p-value ($p = .001$), while ECR-Avoidance ($p = .057$) did not.

There were a number of strengths and weaknesses to this study. The researchers are clear in their question and hypotheses that their interest is in the predictiveness of attachment. This led them to intentionally collect data and utilize regression-based analysis. One unique strength of this study was that the researchers take an extra step to check their measurement models. The researchers of this study looked closely at how their measures functioned, reporting that the intended factor structure of their measures was replicated with their participants. By reporting such psychometrics, future researchers are better able to evaluate the effectiveness of measures within varying samples. This study also demonstrates a number of weaknesses, principal among these was that this study used the ECR subscales for anxious attachment and avoidant attachment. While using subscales and latent factors as predictors can create more precise results, it makes generalizing the results difficult as they focus on specific areas of attachment and may not be representative of broader definitions.

RIGOR

Research communities, particularly those that utilize predictive research, rely on null hypothesis significance testing for claims and new discoveries. This reliance on the P value threshold requires rigor methods to ensure the trustworthiness of claims made by researchers. There are many recommendations for increasing rigor, but rigor does not necessarily mean complicated. Most importantly, rigor is determined by quality and transparency. While we can do much to increase our methods (e.g., random assignment, enhancing internal validity, enhancing external validity, reducing measurement error, enhancing treatment fidelity), there is no substitute for researcher judgment and clear communication of methods, materials, procedures, and outcomes, without which science risks increasing power and significance over quality and transparency.

When we think about enhancing rigor to predictive research, we need to consider internal validity, external validity, and construct validity. Said simply, internal validity is concerned with the trustworthiness that the independent variable (predictor) causes the effect in the outcome. To enhance internal validity, it helps to understand the threats to it. In predictive design, temporal ambiguity (when the variables being examined occurred in time) threatens the internal validity of a study's findings. If a researcher is hypothesizing that X predicts Y, then X needs to have occurred first. This concern is mainly with correlation or cross-sectional studies (where data are collected at one point in time). Two ways to account for this is first by collecting longitudinal data. This is when a study is collecting data over multiple points in time, thus establishing the temporal order of the variables investigated.

Where internal validity is concerned with an independent variable's effect on an outcome construct, validity is concerned with inferences made on the measures of a study. Said differently, construct validity is the trustworthiness that a measure is measuring what it is supposed to measure—a common concern in the social sciences, which tend to measure more intangible variables (e.g., happiness, well-being, humility). Intentional choice of measures, review of measurement performance (Cronbach alpha's) help in guarding against threats to construct validity.

TABLE 6.13 **Predictive Definitions and Terms**

TERMS	DEFINITIONS
Absolute value	The absolute value of a number is its distance from zero on the number line.
Bivariate statistics	A type of inferential statistics that deals with the relationship between two variables; examines how one variable compares with or influences another variable.
Causal effect	Dichotomous variables and assumes that no random error attributable to sampling variability exists.
Convenience sampling	A type of nonprobability sampling in which people are sampled merely because they are "convenient" sources of data for researchers.
Correlation	A bivariate analysis that measures the strength of association between two variables and the direction of the relationship.
Covariation	A measure of the joint variability of two random variables.
Cross-sectional data	The result of a data collection, carried out at a single point in time on a statistical unit.
Dependent variable	A variable (Y), the value of which depends on another variable.
Experimental research	Experimental research is a study that includes a variable that can be manipulated by the researcher, and variables that can be measured, calculated, and compared.
Factorial design	A type of research methodology that allows for the examination of effects between two or more independent variables and on one or more outcome variable(s).
Hierarchical regression methodology	Hierarchical regression is a way to show if variables you have identified explain a statistically significant amount of variance in your Dependent Variable (DV) after accounting for all other variables.
Homoscedasticity	Occurs when the variance in scores on one variable is somewhat similar at all the values of the other variable.
Independent variable	An experimental or predictor variable; a variable that is being manipulated in an experiment in order to observe the effect on a dependent variable, or outcome variable.
Intercorrelate	When two or more variables in a research study have a mutual relationship or connection.
Longitudinal design	Measuring identified variables in a research study on two or more occasions over time.
Multicollinearity	A state of very high intercorrelations or inter-associations among the independent variables.
Multiple regression analysis	An extension of simple linear regression used to predict the value of a variable based on the value of two or more other variables.
Multivariate	A study with more variables than are contained in either a univariate or bivariate design.
Non-parametric	A statistical test that does not involve any assumptions as to the form or parameters of a frequency distribution.
Null hypothesis	A statistical hypothesis that assumes that the observation is due to a chance factor; denoted by H0: $\mu1 = \mu2$, which shows that there is no difference between the two population means.
Ordinal scale	A scale where data are shown in order of magnitude with no standard of measurement of differences.
Parametric	A statistical test assuming the value of a parameter for the purpose of analysis.

TABLE 6.13 **(continued)**

TERMS	DEFINITIONS
Partial correlation	The measure of association between two variables, while controlling or adjusting the effect of one or more additional variables.
Power	Sometimes called sensitivity. Power is how likely the study is to distinguish an actual effect from one of chance.
p-value	The value given to the level of significance in a statistical test.
Regression analysis	A predictive analysis, in which variables are mathematically identified as having effect on a dependent variable.
Semipartial correlation	Semipartial correlation measures the strength of linear relationship between variables $X1$ and $X2$ holding $X3$ constant for just $X1$ or just $X2$.
Standard deviation	A statistic that measures the dispersion of a dataset relative to its mean and is calculated as the square root of the variance.
Univariate analysis	Statistical analyses that involve only one dependent variable and which are used to test hypotheses and draw inferences about populations based on samples.
Variables	Numerical value or a characteristic that can measured or counted that can vary between data units in a population and may change in value over time.
Variance	The expectation of the squared deviation of a random variable from its mean; how far a set of numbers are spread out from their average value.

Lastly, we need to be concerned with external validity, as it relates to increasing the rigor of our studies. External validity is mainly an issue of the generalizability of the findings from a study. Often results can be affected by inadequate sampling, interactions between people within the study, or even unknown effects that occur independent of the study's predictors and outcomes. To help guard against these threats, the use of randomization in sampling is often employed. We briefly discussed the importance of randomization of a sample population in covering regression assumptions. The more random our data appear, the stronger their generalizability becomes. Additionally, through a process of random assignment, also known as blocking, we can not only control extraneous variables, but also include them as independent variables themselves. For example, if a researcher wanted to know if motivation predicted a specific outcome to a novel treatment, they would benefit from randomly assigning men and women to different treatment groups. This would control for the effect of gender and offer the opportunity to explore if gender moderated the effect.

Again, it is important to remember that enhancing rigor is not following recommendations to methods alone, but also clearly documenting and communicating the decisions you make as you investigate your data. During the documentation and communication process, Table 6.13 can assist you in using the appropriate nomenclature.

SUMMARY

Meaningful research is found in epistemological honesty, and the application of thoughtful analyses. Unfortunately, behavioral science research is replete with examples of misapplications and misinterpretations of predictive methods and statistical models. We must remember that analyses are not routine, and the researcher should be mindful that the research questions inform the analytic methods. Sadly, due to a lack of attention and appreciation to the tension between explanatory and predictive methods, there is a lack of understanding of the properties the two contain ranging from variable selection to statistical models. Sound predictive research is not in feeding your variables into a computer and hoping for the best. Nor is it rushing to results, or inflating methods with too many variables and too small of a sample. Rather it is an intentional decision-making process by which your methods and analysis are guided by research questions and hypotheses. Ultimately, it is the responsibility of the researcher to take time to consider their methods and analysis, and to do so discerningly.

STUDENT ACTIVITIES

Exercise 1: Prediction and Explanation

Directions: Research questions guide the scientific process. Consider what we have discussed so far and take a moment to reflect on research problems/topics that are of interest to you. Practice writing two different research questions to address the problem/topic you're thinking about. First, write a research question as if you were to address your chosen problem from an explanatory position. Then write a second a research question as if you were pursuing predictive research. Be mindful of language and the types of variables you would use in your research questions.

Exercise 2: Partial and Semipartial Correlation

Directions: Connecting correlation to your predictive designs is central to the research process. Consider the research questions you developed in Exercise 1, and respond to the following prompts: How might the variables in your research question be correlated? Are there any confounding variables that you had not yet considered that may effect the relationship between your variables? Rewrite your questions to include the need to control for said variables.

Exercise 3: Multiple Regression Interpretation

Directions: A researcher is interested in the extent to which a final test grade (Final) can be predicted by a set of five academic variables: GPA; College Boards (boards); a pretest for the course (Pretest); and two midterm grades (Midterm 1 and Midterm 2). Data from 40 students were collected for each of these variables. Multiple regression analysis was conducted, and the outputs are listed in the following. Use the following outputs to answer these questions:

a. Write the full prediction equation, based on the outputs
    Answer: $Y' = 12.731 \cdot GPA + .015 \cdot Boards + -.460 \cdot Pretest + .785 \cdot M1 + .298 \cdot M2$

b. Is the overall model statistically significant? What information from the output did you use in your conclusion?
    Answer: Yes: $F(5,34) = 6.389\ p < .001$

c. Which, if any of the predictors significantly contributes to the prediction equation? What information did you use to come to your conclusion?
    Answer: None of the individual predictors significantly contribute to the prediction equation given the lack of significance indicated on the Coefficients output for the t-test.

This could be the case due to predictors being highly correlated. GPA and Midterm 1 were highly correlated at $r = .721$. Consequently, the F-test has a low p-value indicating that the predictors together are highly significant in explaining the variation in the DV: Final. The t-tests for each predictor have high p-values because, after allowing for the effect of the other predictors, there is not much left to explain.

Descriptive Statistics

	MEAN	STD DEVIATION	N
Final	99.48	30.323	40
GPA	3.3758	.35316	40
Boards	524.25	114.665	40
Pretest	18.13	7.425	40
Midterm1	46.05	15.396	40
Midterm2	62.88	20.087	40

Correlations

		FINAL	GPA	BOARDS	PRETEST	MIDTERM1	MIDTERM2
Pearson Correlation	final	1.000	.596	.463	.296	.644	.585
	gpa	.596	1.000	.465	.469	.721	.682
	boards	.463	.465	1.000	.147	.546	.569
	pretest	.296	.469	.147	1.000	.553	.433
	midterm1	.644	.721	.546	.553	1.000	.671
	midterm2	.585	.682	.569	.433	.671	1.000
Sig. (1-tailed)	final	.	.000	.001	.032	.000	.000
	gpa	.000	.	.001	.001	.000	.000
	boards	.001	.001	.	.182	.000	.000
	pretest	.032	.001	.182	.	.000	.003
	midterm1	.000	.000	.000	.000	.	.000
	midterm2	.000	.000	.000	.003	.000	.
N	final	40	40	40	40	40	40
	gpa	40	40	40	40	40	40
	boards	40	40	40	40	40	40
	pretest	40	40	40	40	40	40
	midterm1	40	40	40	40	40	40
	midterm2	40	40	40	40	40	40

ANOVA[a]

MODEL		SUM OF SQUARES	DF	MEAN SQUARE	F	SIG.
1	Regression	17371.332	5	3474.266	6.389	.000[b]
	Residual	18488.643	34	543.784		
	Total	35859.975	39			

a. Dependent Variable: final
b. Predictors: (Constant), midterm2, pretest, boards, gpa, midterm1

Coefficients[a]

MODEL		UNSTANDARDIZED COEFFICIENTS		STANDARDIZED COEFFICIENTS	t	SIG.	95.0% CONFIDENCE INTERVAL FOR B		COLLINEARITY STATISTICS	
		B	STD. ERROR	BETA			LOWER BOUND	UPPER BOUND	TOLERANCE	VIF
1	(Constant)	-12.731	44.628		-.285	.777	-103.426	77.965		
	GPA	17.122	16.610	.199	1.031	.310	-16.635	50.878	.405	2.468
	Boards	.015	.043	.056	.345	.732	-.072	.102	.581	1.722
	Pretest	-.460	.633	-.113	-.727	.472	-1.747	.826	.631	1.584
	Midterm1	.788	.415	.400	1.897	.066	-.056	1.632	.341	2.932
	Midterm2	.298	.288	.198	1.035	.308	-.287	.884	.416	2.403

a. Dependent Variable: final

Exercise 4: Factorial Design

Directions: In the following factorial experimental design, indicate the factor design and illustrate the interaction term.

Factors X, Y have three and four categories, respectively.

Answer: 3x4 design

	Y_1	Y_2	Y_3	Y_4
X_1	X_1Y_1	X_1Y_2	X_1Y_3	X_1Y_4
X_2	X_2Y_1	X_2Y_2	X_2Y_3	X_2Y_4
X_3	X_3Y_1	X_3Y_2	X_3Y_3	X_3Y_4

ADDITIONAL RESOURCES

Software Recommendations

- SPSS
  - SPSS, I. I. B. M. (2011). IBM SPSS statistics for Windows, version 20.0. *New York: IBM Corp, 440.*
- SAS
  - SAS Institute. (1990). *SAS/STAT user's guide: version 6* (Vol. 2). Sas Inst.
- R
  - Team, R. C. (2013). R: A language and environment for statistical computing.

Helpful Links

- https://www.statisticssolutions.com/what-is-linear-regression/
- https://www.statisticshowto.com/probability-and-statistics/regression-analysis/
- https://www.youtube.com/watch?v=zPG4NjIkCjc

Helpful Books

Cohen, J., Cohen, P., West, S. G., & Aiken, L. S. (2003). *Applied multiple regression/correlation analysis for the behavioral sciences, 3rd ed.* Lawrence Erlbaum Associates Publishers.

Cureton, E. E., Cronbach, L. J., Meehl, P. E., & Ebel, R. L. (1996). Validity. In A. W. Ward, H. W. Stoker, & M. Murray-Ward (Eds.), *Educational measurement: Origins, theories, and explications, Vol. 1: Basic concepts and theories* (pp. 125–243). University Press of America.

Draper, N. R., & Smith, H. (1981). *Applied regression analysis.* John Wiley and Sons. *407.*

Myers, R. H., & Myers, R. H. (1990). *Classical and modern regression with applications* (Vol. 2). Duxbury press Belmont.

Winer, B. J., Brown, D. R., & Michels, K. M. (1971). *Statistical principles in experimental design* (Vol. 2). McGraw-Hill New York.

Helpful Videos

- https://www.youtube.com/watch?v=LF0WAVBIhNA

- https://www.youtube.com/watch?v=OpAf4N582bA

- https://www.youtube.com/watch?v=zPG4NjIkCjc

KEY REFERENCES

Only key references appear in the print edition. The full reference list appears in the digital product found on http://connect.springerpub.com/content/book/978-0-8261-4385-3/part/part02/chapter/ch06

Altmann, J. (1996). Observational study of behavior: Sampling methods. In L. D. Houck & L. C. Drickamer (Eds.), *Foundations of animal behavior: Classic papers with commentaries* (pp. 177–217). University of Chicago Press.

Cohen, J. (1977). *Statistical power analysis for the behavioral sciences, Rev ed.* Lawrence Erlbaum Associates, Inc.

Cohen, J., Cohen, P., West, S. G. & Aiken, L. S. (2003). *Applied multiple regression/correlation analysis for the behavioral sciences,* 3rd ed. Lawrence Erlbaum.

Cohen, P., West, S. G., & Aiken, L. S. (2014). *Applied multiple regression/correlation analysis for the behavioral sciences.* Psychology Press.

Council for Accreditation of Counseling and Related Educational Programs (CACREP). (2016). *2016 CACREP standards.* Retrieved from http://www.cacrep.org/wp-content/uploads/2016/06/2016-Standards-with-Glossary-rev-2.2016.pdf

Cronbach, L. J. (1971). Test validation. In R. Thorndike (Ed.) *Educational measurement* (2nd ed., p. 443). Washington DC: American Council on Education.

Crotty, M. (1998). *The foundations of social research: Meaning and perspective in the research process.* SAGE.

Cureton, E. E., Cronbach, L. J., Meehl, P. E., & Ebel, R. L. (1996). Validity. In A. W. Ward, H. W. Stoker, & M. Murray-Ward (Eds.), *Educational measurement: Origins, theories, and explications, Vol. 1: Basic concepts and theories.* (pp. 125–243). University Press of America.

Green, S. B. (1991). How many subjects does it take to do a regression analysis? *Multivariate Behavioral Research, 26*(3), 499–510. https://doi.org/10.1207/s15327906mbr2603_7

Hayes, A. F. (2013). *Introduction to mediation, moderation, and conditional process analysis: A regression-based approach.* Guilford Press.

Myers, R. H., & Myers, R. H. (1990). *Classical and modern regression with applications* (Vol. 2). Duxbury Press Belmont.

Pedhazur, E., & Pedhazur Schmelkin, L. (1991). Exploratory factor analysis. *Measurement, design and analysis: An Integrated Approach.* Lawrence Erlbaum, 590, 627.

Ratts, M. J., Singh, A. A., Nassar-McMillan, S., Butler, S. K., & McCullough, J. R. (2016). Multicultural and social justice counseling competencies: Guidelines for the counseling profession. *Journal of Multicultural Counseling and Development, 44*(1), 28–48.

Sharpe, D. (2004). Beyond Significance testing: reforming data analysis methods in behavioral research. *Canadian Psychology/Psychologie canadienne, 45*(4), 317–319. https://doi.org/10.1037/h0087004

Sue, D. W., Bernier, J. E., Durran, A., Feinberg, L., Pedersen, P., Smith, E. J., & Vasquez-Nuttall, E. (1982). Position paper: Cross-cultural counseling competencies. *The Counseling Psychologist, 10*(2), 45–52.

Winer, B. J., Brown, D. R., & Michels, K. M. (1971). *Statistical principles in experimental design* (Vol. 2, pp. 143–160). McGraw-Hill New York.

CHAPTER 7

SINGLE CASE DESIGN RESEARCH

Tiffany Nielson, Hailey Martinez, and Ann McCaughan

LEARNING OBJECTIVES

After reading this chapter, you will be able to:

- Describe the distinguishing features of single case design research
- Understand basic designs within the single case methodology
- Interpret visual and statistical analyses from single case design research
- Design hypothetical methods and visual analyses for clinical settings

INTRODUCTION TO SINGLE CASE RESEARCH

Single Case Design (SCD) offers an intuitive, pragmatic, and flexible methodology for the practicing clinician to demonstrate effectiveness and establish evidence-based practice (Hott et al., 2015; Lenz, 2015; Nielson, 2015; Ray, 2015). SCD is an exciting realm of research that is untapped in its potential as a quantitative research design within counseling research. In contrast to its cousins in quantitative design (the between-group designs), SCD is seemingly new to the scene of experimental methods yet is gaining momentum in the literature (Kazdin, 2011). The term "new"is used loosely, as historical uses of similar methods to the SCD have been foundational in the scientific method (Kazdin, 2011). For example, Pavlov's behavioral methods on dogs is an early example of a single subject being used in scientific analysis. Amid its early use, SCD is resurfacing as a viable methodology for the applied sciences. With its frequent use in behavior modification research in education, it is a natural fit within clinical settings for counselors, social workers, marriage and family therapists, and psychologists.

There has been a recent push for increased use of SCD in the counseling literature; for example, the *Journal of Counseling and Development* published an entire issue specifically devoted to SCD to increase its use in counseling at both the master's and doctoral levels (see Lenz, 2015). Heppner et al. (2016) recommend increased use of this methodology specific with group and family counseling due to the ability to design the research specific to those populations. Peterson et al. (2016) highlight the importance of clinicians learning SCD methodology to track and monitor client outcomes. This push for an increase in research is coupled with training focused on program evaluation at the clinical level. Training in research and program evaluation at both the master's and doctoral levels are highlighted in current accreditation standards. For example, the 2016 standards by the Council for Accreditation of Counseling and Related Educational Programs (CACREP) describe both the ability to consume and produce outcome research to contribute evidence-based practice (CACREP, 2016). Amid the focus on research training, current counselors report a need for specific training in single-case research designs (Peterson et al., 2016). The doctoral accreditation standards more explicitly describe researcher identity as core to the counselor education curriculum (CACREP, 2016), which further highlights the need for counselors and counselor educators to be producers and not just consumers of outcome research (Guiffrida & Douthit, 2010; Nielson, 2015; Peterson et al., 2016). The Commission on Accreditation for Marriage and Family Therapy Education (COAMFTE, 2017) reiterates the multiple roles that marriage and family therapists may engage in, including researcher. The accreditation standards echo this role by explicitly stating the need for a "culture of research" and contributing to the literature for the advancement of the profession (COAMFTE, 2017). Similar emphasis is placed at the doctoral level for increased rigor of research preparation in their training.

To understand what SCD is, it is also important to know what SCD is not. The terms single-case design is synonymously referred in the literature as single-subject research design. The primary distinguishing feature of SCD is the use of a single subject or case longitudinally as both the control and treatment group through differing phases of baseline/nontreatment (A) and treatment (B). These phases are used strategically to determine the impact of a specified treatment or intervention. This is a vast deviation from other quantitative experimental designs that rely on the use of a control or comparison group to establish causality. Rather than using a control group for comparison to establish causality, the use of a single subject (individual or group) serves the role as both treatment and control group for SCD. Without the need for a control group and large sample sizes, the feasibility of SCD rises to meet the needs of the practicing clinician (Lenz 2015; Nielson, 2015; Ray, 2015). This method additionally eliminates the ethical dilemma of withholding treatment as, typically, randomization is not requisite (although can certainly be used) and all participants in SCD undergo the treatment phase. The ethical implications on treatment and research protocol and implications in applied settings are discussed throughout the chapter.

It is important to differentiate SCD, which can be confused with the use of qualitative case study research. The two are vastly different with SCD/single-subject design being an experimental or quasi-experimental method and case study research being a qualitative and descriptive method. Further description of the differing theoretical paradigm (see the section The Paradigmatic Hierarchy) highlights the objective quantitative perspective of SCD in contrast to the subjective or constructionist perspective that may be found in qualitative case research. While their differences are highlighted to provide clarity in the methodological identity of SCD, overlap between the two methodologies certainly exists. First is the use of small groups or individual cases as the focus of the research. This idiographic perspective is central to SCD and is similarly shared in case study research. To draw information from a singular case using a quantitative methodology is the foundation of the SCD research.

SCD most often occurs in applied settings, that is, where the treatment is naturally occurring. As with all research, the balance of applied versus laboratory or highly controlled settings creates implications for validity, reliability, and generalizability. SCD is not concerned with removing confounding variables; rather, through the method itself, the research is identifying that the treatment provided caused the change in the dependent variable (Kennedy, 2005). While some approaches to SCD encourage higher controls through regimented treatment protocols and strict observance to treatment manuals (e.g., Hott et al., 2015), others argue for a more flexible approach where the treatment provided, including length of treatment, is guided by the response of the client/participant simultaneous to the research process (Kazdin, 1978; Lenz, 2015). Both methods require a thorough description of the treatment when describing the methods to inform the consumer of the treatment provided. The flexibility of the latter choice deviates from traditional quantitative methods and exemplifies yet another difference from other quantitative methods. Additionally, one can find variations of either experimental or quasi-experimental designs within this methodology. While most SCDs are quasi-experimental, in that they do not utilize randomization for the participant sampling, there are certainly variations and some uses of this design that incorporate random sampling (e.g., Fluckiger et al., 2018).

The second primary deviation from other quantitative methods is the type of analyses utilized in SCD. Visual analysis is the foundational method of analysis typically used in SCD research (Hott et al., 2015; Kazdin, 2011; Kennedy, 2005; Lane & Gast, 2014; Ledford et al., 2017). While some have encouraged applications of traditional quantitative statistical analyses such as ANOVA and *t*-tests, the analyses used in SCD often rely on the visual graphing of data and varying forms of calculating effect sizes. There is a need for increased rigor and consistency in analyses in addition to the consistent use of effect sizes (Manolov & Moeyaert, 2017; Vannest & Ninci, 2015). The use of an effect size, in addition to the traditional visual analysis in SCD, is encouraged to provide an objective measure and point for comparison across research and in metanalytic studies (Moeyaert et al., 2015; Parker & Brossart, 2003; Vannest & Ninci, 2014). An effect size provides a statistical measure to describe the strength of the relationship between the independent and dependent variable. In other words, the greater the strength in the relationship, the more confident researchers can be that the treatment had an influence on the outcome. Common analyses to measure a form of effect size include the percent of nonoverlapping data (Scrugg et al., 1987), the percent of data exceeding the median (Ma, 2006), improvement rate difference (Parker et al., 2009), nonoverlap of all pairs (Parker & Vannest, 2009), and Tau-U (Parker et al., 2011). It is also noted that the simplicity of the analyses used generally eliminates the need for expensive statistical software or an extensive statistical knowledge (Kazdin, 2011), which creates accessibility for use among the everyday clinician.

With its distinctive features of small groups or individuals, applied research settings, and simple analyses, SCD is well-positioned for use by clinicians (Lenz, 2015; Nielson, 2015; Ray, 2015). Having a feasible method for demonstrating both effectiveness and creating a larger pool of evidence to support clinical treatments will be essential for surviving in the current trends of medically managed care and rigorous insurance oversight. As you move through the chapter, continue to consider the invaluable role that SCD offers in applied clinical settings to demonstrate the effectiveness of clinical practice.

BASIC DESIGN CONCEPTS OF SINGLE CASE DESIGN

To understand the varying SCDs, it is necessary to clarify terminology and language that describes each design. The capital letters A, B, and C are used to denote the presence or absence of the independent variable across the research protocol. The baseline or no-treatment phase is referred to as "A" and the independent variable is absent at this time. The treatment phase is referred to as "B" and denotes the introduction of the independent variable. When a second independent variable or treatment condition is introduced, it is referred to as "C." Note that the use of the term treatment can include a specific intervention or condition as specified by the researcher. The letters are then combined to briefly describe the structure and introduction of the independent variable(s). For example, if a researcher used an ABA design, the reader would know that there was a baseline phase (A), followed by a treatment phase (B), with a subsequent no-treatment or post-treatment phase (A). Depending on the methodology, one can repeat baseline and treatment phase and/or change the treatment (C). Some of the more frequently used methodological structures for SCD are described in this chapter, namely ABA, ABAB, ABAC, multiple baseline, and alternating treatment design.

As described previously (see the section Distinguishing Single Case Research), SCD does not use a control group to determine the effect of a treatment. Rather, the individual and/or group become their own control through the use of the baseline and post-treatment measures. The replication of the baseline or other phases of treatment become essential in distinguishing any changes that happen in the treatment phase from other confounding variables. A common confounding variable in SCD is time or the natural development of the subject, due to the longitudinal nature of the research. For example, if a counselor wanted to determine that a grief and loss group was effective at reducing distress for participants that recently lost a loved one, one may conclude that improvements may be due to the time that has elapsed since the loss and not merely the treatment offered. There are unique design options with SCD to address the issue of time and the endless array of confounding variables that belie applied research. Variations and options within this quantitative method based on the client population and research question will be briefly described later in this chapter. Based on the design selected, there are varying amounts of flexibility. For example, some designs allow the researcher to determine the length of each phase of the design based on the responsivity of the research participant(s) either before or during the research. Implications of this variability in phase length are further discussed when addressing ways to increase rigor within this methodology (see the section Increasing Rigor).

Establishing Baseline

Baseline logic serves as a foundational assumption in SCD, namely that through an established baseline we can determine causality through prediction, verification, and replication (Kazdin, 2011). Within this logic, we are looking at the ability to *predict* future behavior based on performance as reported at the baseline. We *verify* this prediction through the introduction of the treatment and further *replication* of the baseline through withdrawal of treatment solidifies the findings.

With all SCD methods, it is recommended to have multiple points of pre-treatment/baseline measures. It is common practice to obtain a minimum of three or more baseline measures to establish a pattern. If the baseline measure appears to fluctuate greatly, further baseline measures may be indicated until a clear level of **trend** can be identified. Sidman (1960) proposed the use of the **steady state strategy** to determine the length of each phase. Using this strategy, the researcher would keep the participant in each phase until a consistent and stable trend is observed. Establishing **steady state** at each phase will assist the researcher in analyzing the results and is a necessary step in **baseline logic**. If there is great variability at baseline, it becomes difficult to predict future behavior. This then creates a challenge in determining the degree of change once the treatment (B) is introduced with limited ability to deduce that any improvement or change in the dependent variable was due to the effect of the treatment. To strengthen the ability to conclude causality from a treatment or intervention, a consistent and stable pattern at baseline (A) is recommended.

Varying types of trend may exist, and the ability to predict future behavior is strengthened based on the observation of a stable trend. The exercise following provides examples of different types of trends or lack of trend that may be observed in a baseline phase. While a flat trend is preferred, in applied research there may be other variations that can be deemed a consistent pattern or trend at baseline. It is also noted that most of statistical analysis relies on a flat trend or **steady state**. Kennedy (2005) highlights the ethical dilemma associated with establishing baseline. The researcher/clinician is faced with the decision regarding the degree to which they withhold treatment to establish a consistent baseline, which may have implications for the needs of the participants.

Data Collection

SCD research requires consideration on the types of data collected. Data collected for analysis will be numerical and can range from observations to formalized assessment measures that are measured repeatedly across the duration of the research. Due to the frequency of gathering data, an assessment measure needs to be replicable and easily administered. Nielson (2015) described the use of feedback informed treatment (FIT) measures within SCD. These measures are a natural fit with SCD as they can be administered frequently, are brief in nature, and lend themselves to graphical analysis consistent with SCD. Examples of FIT assessments include the Outcome Rating Scale (Miller & Duncan, 2000) and PCOMS (PCOMS International, 2014). Heppner et al. (2016) describe the limitation of researcher bias when collecting data, particularly when using self-report or the clinician is simultaneously observing targeted behavior. The use of an identified observer and interrater reliability strengthen the methodological rigor with the data collection (Hott et al., 2015). The numerical data collected are used for both visual and statistical analysis.

THE PARADIGMATIC HIERARCHY OF SINGLE CASE RESEARCH

In considering the hierarchical process outlined by Crotty (1998) as an idiographic (meaning the study of individual cases or events) quantitative method focused on studying the behavior of an individual or a small number of people, single-case research takes an objective stance on the acquisition of knowledge. This objectivist epistemological perspective further informs the post-positivist theoretical perspective (aligned with a realist ontological stance; Crotty, 2003) of the research design (Creswell, 2008). As an experimental methodology, this idiographic approach is searching for causality and striving to identify the impact of specific treatment with individual clients, utilizing measurement, observation, and statistical analysis to make inferences about observed behaviors.

While deviating from the between-group experimental approaches, this SCD is uniquely positioned to examine causality in applied settings, where the subject serves as both the experimental and control "group." It is important to distinguish the quantitative single-case/single-subject design approach to research from the qualitative case-study approach, which focuses on subjective reality to understand the experiences of single research subjects/clients, utilizing non-experimental methodology. Figure 7.1 displays the paradigmatic hierarchy for SCD research.

ABA DESIGN

The ABA design, also referred to as a withdrawal design, is one of the basic structures for experimental use of SCDs. This three-phase design uses a baseline phase, treatment/intervention phase, with a return to baseline. Potential uses of the ABA design can include basic behavior modification or

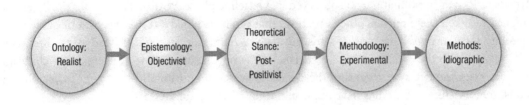

FIGURE 7.1 Paradigmatic Hierarchy for Single Case Design Research.

use of a single treatment in which the dependent variable will return to baseline functioning upon withdrawal of treatment. Within this basic structure, examples of current research highlight its applicability and use for clinical and educational settings.

DATA COLLECTION METHODS AND EXAMPLES

Data collection, as described previously, will be a repeated measure of the dependent variable across the three phases of the ABA design. A clear outline and description of the dependent variable is needed, whether using observational or assessment data. The research of Meany-Walen (2015) and Swank et al. (2015) both provide examples of observational data in an ABA design through the use of the Direct Observation Form (McOnaughy & Achenbach, 2009). This observational measure is especially applicable to school settings to measure problematic classroom behaviors and requires reaching interrater reliability. Interrater reliability applies, in particular, to observational data used in SCD. Through establishing interrater reliability, the researcher ensures consistency of the data collected and increases the fidelity of the results. Swank et al. (2015) provided training for the teachers that included practice observations and measured interrater reliability through the intraclass correlation. Additionally, the use of multiple scorers or observers can be used either selectively or consistently throughout the research to establish interrater reliability. Weeden et al. (2016) used a second trained observer at select points across the study and compared the difference between the two raters using percent agreement. Cohen's kappa coefficient can be used to measure interrater reliability and provides a stronger statistical measure of interrater reliability by taking into consideration the possibility of chance agreement (McHugh, 2012). In the research of Miller et al. (2015), multiple raters are used as each student in the study had two or three teachers consistently providing behavior ratings. A moderate level of interrater reliability was found in their research using a kappa rating. Depending on the research design, there are numerous ways to approach and attain interrater reliability within SCD.

To establish baseline, Swank et al. (2015) observed child behaviors in a classroom setting prior to providing nature-based child-centered play therapy. The classroom observations at baseline were conducted three times a week for a 3-week period to establish baseline. The three observations from each week were averaged to determine the data point for the week. During the subsequent phases of the research, observations occurred weekly until the conclusion of the research. This research is one example of observational data for an ABA design.

Ikonomopolous, Smith, and Schmidt (2015) used self-report assessment data in the AB and ABA research designs on the effects of narrative therapy for incarcerated adolescents. The Brief Symptom Inventory (BSI; Derogatis, 1993) was used to measure varying levels of symptomology such as obsessive-compulsive behaviors, hostility, and interpersonal sensitivity. Uniquely, the goals of treatment for each participant ($N = 8$) were individualized from their reports on the BSI, while the overall score was also used in analysis. The questions on the assessment were randomized to maintain validity of the repeated measure each week. Five weeks of baseline data were collected on a weekly basis before the specified treatment phase began. The researchers continued to gather data weekly through treatment and post-treatment phases as available. There were limitations in gathering post-treatment data due to some participants leaving the residential facility, resulting in a mix of AB and ABA design.

The research examples of Meany-Walen (2015), Swank et al. (2015), and Ikonopolous et al. (2015) each display how either observational or assessment data can be used across each phase of an ABA design. Some of the challenges and unique features of applied settings are evident in the research examples provided, such as client withdrawal and working with other stakeholders or in systems such as schools or residential facilities to obtain the necessary data.

PROCEDURES AND EXAMPLES

The procedure involves a description of the research protocol including length of each phase of the design, participants, and the treatment protocol. A clear identification of the dependent variable for the research procedure includes how, when, and what is being measured. The dependent variable needs to be regularly monitored as described regarding data collection. In addition to the data collection details, the frequency and length of each phase is to be specified and clearly identified. Prior to beginning the research, the participants are to be selected, typically through purposive sampling. Participants can be either a group or individual or a small selection of individuals. Ikonopolous (2015) used a screening tool to identify adolescents at risk with high, clinically significant need. To further enrich the research, a rich description of each participant gave clarity and a strong foundation to the research findings of Ikonopolous (2015). In educational settings, teachers or other stakeholders may often identify students in need and be highly involved throughout the research.

Another essential component of the procedure is a clear description of the treatment. A thorough description and adherence to the treatment protocol establishes and maintains fidelity of the research (Hott et al., 2015; Lenz, 2015). Swank et al. (2015) used a treatment description from the literature while Ikonopolous used symptom-specific treatment goals grounded in narrative therapy. These are two examples of variability of the independent variable for counseling settings. There are a myriad of treatments/interventions that can be the independent measure within this research design. Examples throughout the chapter give a brief window into the adaptations and applications of this method for numerous educational and clinical settings.

DATA ANALYSIS AND EXAMPLES

When interpreting data, there are a number of statistical and visual methods to employ. Visual analysis has long been one of the distinguishing features of the analysis used across SCDs. Typically, time is graphed along the x-axis with the dependent variable on the y-axis. Figure 7.2 shows how a simple line graph can be used to display the trend of data across the three phases of the research protocol: baseline (A), treatment (B), and post-treatment (A). Points are plotted on the graph with a line drawn to each point of data for each phase. In this example, a clear difference in the dependent variable occurred with a stable baseline (A) followed by a downward trend during

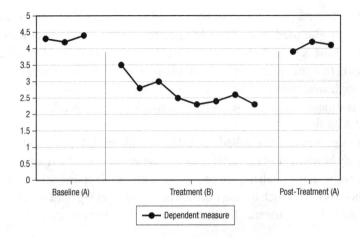

FIGURE 7.2 Visual Analysis: Example of ABA Design.

NOTE: The line graph delineates the three phases of the ABA design across time. The dependent measure is plotted with a line graph drawn for each phase of the treatment. A vertical line is drawn between each phase to further distinguish the differing conditions of the research.

treatment (B) with subsequent change directly following withdrawal of treatment (post-treatment, A). In this visual analysis example, the dependent variable decreased throughout the treatment and upon withdrawal returned to pre-treatment functioning.

The visual analysis can be used to demonstrate change for individuals or groups. Typically, when there are multiple participants, each participant's data will be plotted on a separate line graph and individually analyzed. When analyzing these data, researchers are looking for a change in trend once the independent variable is changed or introduced (phase B) and then withdrawn (second phase A) as it pertains to the prediction of the research hypothesis. Looking again at Figure 7.2, one would predict (null hypothesis) that behavior would continue to maintain a **steady state** between the 4–4.5 range as there are three consistent points in that range prior to treatment. Once the treatment is introduced, the behavior does not follow that prediction, and instead consistently ranges between 3.5 and 2.3. The relationship between the independent and dependent variable is further strengthened as the behavior changes as a direct result of the withdrawal of treatment. One would then conclude that the change in behavior was due to the treatment.

When withdrawing treatment, there are generally two types of trend in the post-treatment phase depending on the type of dependent variable. Often, a return to baseline functioning is anticipated for dependent behavior once the treatment is no longer present. This strengthens the ability to claim that the change in behavior is a result of the treatment. In contrast, Meany-Walen et al. (2015) note that within counseling, it is hoped that the positive effect of the treatment (B) is maintained post-treatment (A) and has created lasting change. Other reasons that the dependent variable maintains post-treatment can include a skill-based dependent variable, or the treatment is still being provided unintentionally (e.g., teachers continue to interact with student-participants following the intervention phase), or other confounding variables (e.g., natural maturation) have an influence on the variable (Kazdin, 2011). The varying reasons for the dependent variable maintaining post-treatment poses potential limitations in claiming causality; however, within clinical treatment the lasting impact of treatment provides further evidence of its effectiveness. For instances in which the change is intended to last post-treatment, a withdrawal design is contraindicated and other research designs such as the multiple baseline design described later provide other ways to creatively design the research protocol to isolate the impact of the independent variable. Further replication of phases, such as an ABAB design, with intentional investigation of confounding variables, can enhance the ability to identify the relationship between the dependent and independent variable (Kratochwill et al., 2010). While replication is typically referring to additional phase changes within a case, it can also include replication among different cases as in the multiple baseline design.

Two examples of statistical analysis which can be used to describe the effect of the treatment based on the overlap of data from the baseline to the treatment phase are described. The first is the **percentage of non-overlapping data (PND**; Scruggs et al., 1987). To calculate the **PND** the researcher determines the number of treatment measures that exceed the baseline measure based on the intended directionality of the data. This number is then divided by the total number of treatment data points for the score (Scruggs et al., 1987). For example, when looking at Figure 7.2, if it was intended that the dependent variable would decrease upon introduction of the treatment, then all the eight data measures during the treatment phase exceed (are below) each of the baseline data measures. This would result in a 100% score. A score greater than 90% indicates a strong treatment effect; 70% to 90% moderate treatment effect; 50% to 69% uncertain effect; and below 50% is considered no treatment effect (Scruggs & Mastropieri, 1998). Scruggs et al. (1987) encourage the use of this simple analysis to provide a statistical way to compare the results of SCD rather than relying on subjective analysis of visual graphs of data. They do, however, give parameters and limitations for application, and caution against overestimating effect when baseline measure is trending toward desired change, underestimating effect in ABAB designs, and limitations with more complicated designs in which a simple PND does not capture the nuance of the change.

Meany-Walen et al. (2015) acknowledged the challenge they encountered in analysis due to having outlier data (one unusually high data point) at the baseline. In their research on behavioral problems and on-task behavior of three elementary aged children, two of the three children had an outlier at baseline for on-task behavior that made it difficult to use PND for their analysis. They discuss the implications of this outlier and the challenges in describing the effect of the treatment. However, the decision to extend the baseline measure and prolong treatment is not always clear-cut. Meany-Walen et al. (2015) were faced with the ethical dilemma of whether to delay treatment to establish a trend at baseline or to continue to the treatment phase. They described the anticipation of the teachers to begin treatment to remedy the severity of the behavioral issues in the classroom and therefore decided to move to the treatment phase. This research is one example that highlights the responsibility of the researcher to balance the length of the baseline and treatment phase based on the individual needs of the participants and stakeholders.

Another measure for establishing overlap between baseline and treatment phase is the **percentage of data exceeding the median (PEM**; Ma, 2006). In this statistical analysis, the treatment data are compared to the median score of the baseline. The percentage of points that exceed this median become the **PEM** effect size. In Figure 7.2 the three baseline data points of 4.2, 4.3, and 4.4 are averaged to a median score of 4.3. All of the treatment data points exceed this median score, resulting in a 1.0 PEM score. The **PEM** effect size is rated between a 0 and 1.0 with 1.0 meaning high effect and 0 to .5 meaning no effect (Ma, 2006). Both Swank et al. and Ikonopolous (2015) used this statistical analysis in their ABA design. It is not recommended to use PEM when a trend in baseline is observed, as the median score does not take into consideration the upward or downward slope; this analysis is best applied with steady/flat data.

Vannest and Ninci (2015) also discuss the potential use of the improvement rate difference (IRD; Parker et al., 2011) for analysis. The IRD (Parker et al., 2011) is also known as the risk-reduction ratio and is viewed as more robust and frequently accepted within medical research (Vannest & Ninci, 2015). This uses basic division to remove any overlapping data points between baseline and treatment, and then determines the ratio of change at both baseline and treatment phases. Any change from baseline is then subtracted from change at treatment to result in an IRD effect score. Vannest and Ninci propose this statistical analysis as "superior" to PND and PEM. Vannest and Ninci give further descriptions on the use of the IRD statistical analysis (Parker et al., 2009), nonoverlap of all pairs (Parker & Vannest, 2009), and the Tau-U (Parker et al., 2011).

ABAB OR WITHDRAWAL-REVERSAL DESIGN

The ABAB or withdrawal-reversal design adds a second baseline measure to the previously described ABA design to further isolate the effect of the independent variable across time. Further baseline and treatment phases can be added as part of the withdrawal-reversal design. The replication of the baseline and treatment phases is often seen as increasing experimental rigor and improving the ability to claim causality (Kazdin, 2011). However, recent literature debates the necessity of the withdrawal-reversal design, particularly in clinical arenas in which removal of treatment or intervention would be unethical or harmful for client welfare (Lanovaz, Turgeon, Cardinal, & Wheatley, 2019). Clinical examples in which removal of treatment may be considered unethical include vulnerable or high-risk clients such as chronic or high suicidality, ongoing trauma treatment, and severe psychosis. Additionally, the ethical duty of counselors to do no harm and also promote the welfare of clients demands that the researchers closely monitor research results. If a treatment modality is working effectively, and once withdrawn the client demonstrates significant decomposition of functioning, the clinician needs to have a protocol for intervening or monitoring to ensure client safety. Likewise, if a treatment provided does not result in the desired outcome, this creates a unique opportunity for the clinician to adapt and adjust treatment modality to best help clients. Through intentional foresight and planning, the flexibility of SCD can support transition to a secondary treatment such as an ABC or ABAC model in such instances in which the client is not improving or treatment may be causing harm. Implementation of the ABAB design can include and is not limited to research focused on behavior modification, ongoing clinical treatment with removal and reintroduction of treatment, and long/frequent gaps between treatment (e.g., couples counseling once a month). Examples from clinical and applied research of the ABAB design will be described to highlight the unique data collection methods, procedures, and analyses in applied settings.

DATA COLLECTION METHODS AND EXAMPLES

The methods for the ABAB design generally mirror the ABA design, with the addition a second treatment or intervention phase (B). A behavioral study in a school setting exemplifies the use of the withdrawal-reversal design. Weeden, Wills, Kottwitz, and Kamps (2016) used observational data of on-task behavior of an entire classroom and teacher interventions for specified intervals in the school day across multiple phases of baseline and intervention. The data were collected in a similar fashion across baseline, intervention and was repeated for multiple data points. To increase their reliability, Weeden et al. also used a second observer throughout some of the observations and compared the consistency of each observer's results. High reliability across the data collected was found in their analysis. In addition to the observer data, Weeden et al. also gathered customer satisfaction scores of both the students and teachers to gain their perspective on the intervention utilized. These survey data were used to supplement the experimental data from the observers.

PROCEDURES AND EXAMPLES

Procedure includes identification and specification of the participants and treatment protocol. In the behavioral research of Weeden et al. (2016), a teacher was trained for the specific intervention protocol that was to be used for the independent variable, namely, a specific classroom management technique for increasing on-task behaviors. To maintain fidelity, the teacher was observed and monitored for 90% compliance with the intervention protocol as trained. This is an example of the type of research design and protocol that increases and maintains rigor of SCD. As with all SCDs, the implementation will be based on the unique design of the study. Examples of variations of the ABAB design include the use of more than one dependent variable (Miller et al., 2015) and the use of randomization or a control group (Fluckiger et al., 2018). This section briefly describes a repeated withdrawal-reversal design; however, researchers are encouraged to create a design that fits their specified population and intervention as guided by the research question.

In considering the withdrawal-reversal or ABAB design, the treatment or intervention selected needs to be replicable across time, with an ability to withdraw or withhold intervention at varying intervals. In contrast to the behavioral classroom example of Weeden et al. (2016), there are two methodological considerations for clinical applications of this design. First, this design may not fit for some clinical settings in which withdrawal of treatment may have ethical concerns regarding client welfare. Second, a withdrawal-reversal design may not accurately display a change in the dependent variable for some clinical measures. As discussed previously, it is anticipated in counseling settings that the client is able to maintain positive growth across time, therefore the withdrawal of treatment may not show the immediate decline in the dependent variable as behavioral-based studies may demonstrate. The researcher needs to determine the design that is most appropriate for their identified treatment, participants, and the outcome measures.

DATA ANALYSIS AND EXAMPLES

Analysis follows similar methods of the ABA design, namely visual analysis with options for statistical analysis. Weeden et al. (2016) relied on visual analysis to display the increase in student on-task behavior coupled with the teacher improvement in classroom management techniques and compliance with the treatment protocol. In their visual analysis, they were able to demonstrate the withdrawal-reversal design across time. Their analysis shows an increase in on-task behaviors each time the intervention was reintroduced coupled with an increase in teacher praises and decrease in teacher reprimands. Likewise, on-task behaviors decrease when teacher praises decrease. Lastly, this improvement was observed at both a 4- and 8-week follow-up (see figure in Weeden et al., 2016, p. 290).

A hypothetical example of a visual analysis of an ABAB design is shown in Figure 7.3. In this example, a school counselor is monitoring the impact of group counseling curriculum on prosocial behaviors on improving appropriate behaviors in school for select students. To establish baseline, they gather data from the teachers on the daily behavior performance of four identified students for 3 weeks. Following baseline, students are enrolled in weekly group counseling on prosocial behavior. Throughout the day the teachers rate student performance on the student behavior scale

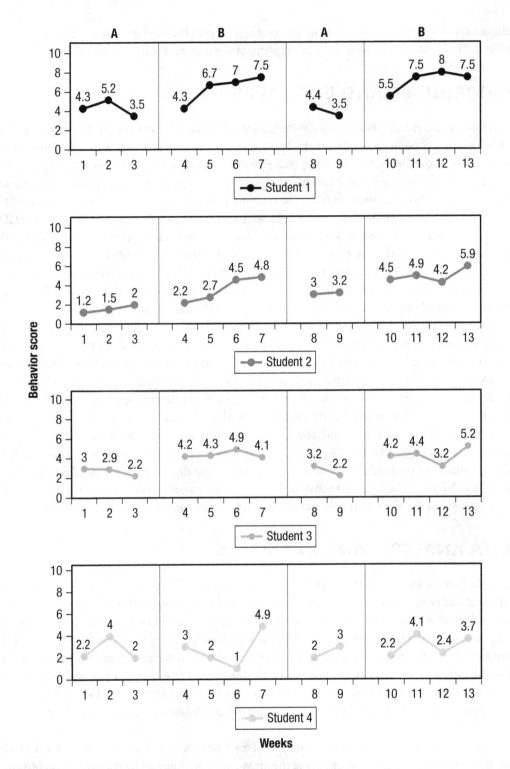

FIGURE 7.3 Visual Analysis of ABAB Design on Group Counseling in a School.

NOTE: A withdrawal-reversal design was used in a SCD of classroom behavior. Average weekly behavior was reported across a 13-week period. A change in weekly average behavior is noted each time the group counseling was implemented (B) with a decrease when withdrawn (A) for students 1 to 3.

and at the end of the week their behavior score is averaged. In the group counseling experience, students receive praise and rewards for positive behavior reports. They continue the group counseling for 4 weeks. Following the group counseling, the teachers continue to monitor and rate students for 2 weeks (withdrawal; phase A). Then, they resume the group counseling with the school counselor for 4 more weeks. Note that this phase could be continued until a trend is visible in the data. Another variation to the design would be the addition of further AB phases.

Visual analysis of hypothetical data in Figure 7.3 shows how the removal of the treatment through re-establishing baseline localizes the impact of the treatment provided. The low scores of student behavior at baseline and withdrawal of treatment are evident in the graphical analysis of the behavior performance of students enrolled in the program (Figure 7.3). The increase in positive behaviors when the treatment is provided demonstrates the effect of weekly group counseling on prosocial behaviors for students 1, 2, and 3. The effect of the group counseling is inconsistent for student 4. Note that it was unclear after the initial AB phase whether student 2 was increasing simply due to the monitoring of the teacher, as the behavior scores were increasing each week prior to intervention. The subsequent AB phases help establish that the group counseling was influential on student 2 behavior changes. Ultimately, the value of the use of graphical displays demonstrates how the repeated use of baseline and intervention create a clear trend in the data to support that the intervention had an effect on the desired behavior. The use of the ABAB design is supported as an experimental design and has implications in clinical settings to demonstrate clinical effectiveness.

ABAC OR COMBINED SIMPLE PHASE CHANGE DESIGN

The ABAC design is one of many multiple treatment designs and can also be referred to as a combined simple phase change design. This design shares similarities to the withdrawal-reversal design in which the treatment is given (B) and withdrawn (A) however the subsequent treatment (C) is different from the original treatment provided in phase B. Similar considerations need to be made regarding client welfare and withdrawal of treatment. In general, for this design to be effective at demonstrating impact of treatment, the dependent variable needs to be something that would return to or change at baseline (A) following withdrawal of the treatment (B) to allow for subsequent introduction of a secondary treatment (C) to observe change. Uses of the ABAC design can include, but are not limited to, showing the difference in treatment responses, identifying the impact of compounding or providing two forms of treatment (e.g., group and individual) across time, or when the initial treatment (B) has little or no impact, a secondary treatment (C) may be offered (Kennedy, 2005). A literature review of current applied settings returns limited use of this methodology amid its potential within counseling and related fields.

DATA COLLECTION METHODS AND EXAMPLES

Within the basic form of the ABAC design, the two treatments are not offered simultaneously, therefore data are gathered across an initial baseline (A) and treatment (B) phase with a subsequent baseline (A) and change in treatment phase (C). Methods for collecting data again range from observational to assessment data that provide a numerical value. A hypothetical research scenario will demonstrate the application of this design. A family counselor wants to know the impact of providing Gestalt-based individual counseling followed by family counseling with the child and parents to improve or maintain overall functioning for both the child and the parents of children with oppositional defiant disorder. To collect the data, the counselor would identify potential measures for the dependent variable. For this example, the counselor uses the Outcome Rating Scale (ORS; Miller & Duncan, 2000) or the Child Outcome Rating Scale (CORS; Duncan et al., 2003) for both the parents and child each week across the duration of the research study. The cut-off score on the ORS/CORS indicates clinically significant distress across the combine scores for the domains of individual, personal, social, and overall well-being (score of 25 or below for adults; 28 or below for ages 13–18; 32 or below for ages 6–12). This measure can be used weekly for each member of the treatment unit to monitor the progress across time.

PROCEDURES AND EXAMPLES

The counselor specifies the use of Gestalt-based therapy and provides a description of the treatment provided. Namely, the counselor specifies the interventions utilized in the individual and subsequent family counseling sessions. This specificity provides clarity for the independent variable and replicability for future research. The participants selected in this research example may have been chosen using purposive sampling based on the child scores on the Child and Adolescent Disruptive Behavior Inventory (Burns, Taylor, & Rusby, 2001) and a child's ORS/CORS scores below the cut-off. To gather baseline data, the counselor may collect the ORS/CORS scores for the child and parents at the initial request for services, intake interview, and 1 more week prior to beginning services. The counselor would then provide weekly, outpatient individual services using Gestalt-based therapy to the child for an identified period. For this example, the counselor may meet with the child for 12 weeks. Following the individual counseling, they would take a 3-week break for a baseline phase, while continuing to obtain ORS/CORS scores. They would then provide weekly family counseling for another 12-week period. The total research protocol would span across a 30-week period.

DATA ANALYSIS AND EXAMPLES

To analyze the results, the counselor may use both visual and statistical analysis of the ORS/CORS scores across each phase of treatment. An example of a visual analysis may be seen in Figure 7.4. This figure shows how to graph multiple participants in a treatment unit in one figure for their change across two forms of treatment (B and C). The scores of each could also be separated into their own graph. A simple line graph is used to plot their ORS/CORS scores across a 3-week baseline (A), 12-week individual treatment for the child (B), 3-week baseline (A), and 12-week family treatment for parents and child. In viewing each phase, we can see that both treatments appeared to improve ORS/CORS scores which indicates an increase in well-being. Note that the second baseline showed a downward trend for the child and both treatment phases showed an upward trend in functioning. The family counseling treatment maintained and increased well-being scores on the ORS/CORS.

Statistical analysis using PND (Scruggs et al., 1987) results in a PND score for individual counseling of 75% for both the mother and child and only a 33% for the father. The family counseling PND score can either be calculated against original baseline which results in 100% effect size for child, mother, and father. Or it can be compared against the second baseline (Scruggs et al., 1987), in which it continues to show an effect size for mother (75%) and father (83%) with uncertain effect size for the child (67%). Overall, both the visual and statistical analyses of PND

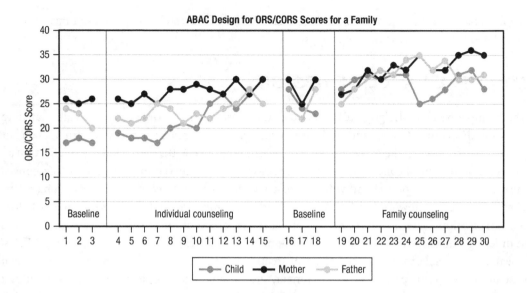

FIGURE 7.4 Visual Analysis of ABAC Design: Example of Two Treatments.

NOTE: A cut-off score of 25 or below for adults; 28 or below for ages 13 to 18; 32 or below for ages 6 to 12 indicates potentially clinically significant distress. The scores were gathered weekly across baseline, individual counseling, and family counseling. The visual trend displays increased well-being scores as rated on the ORS/CORS.

show an effect across treatment with an average PND effect size across the two treatments (when comparing family counseling against second baseline) of 71% for the child, 75% for the mother, and 58% for the father. When comparing their improvement across all treatments to the original baseline, the effect size increases to 87.5% for mother and child and 66.5% for the father.

In this example of a simple form of ABAC analysis, it is somewhat difficult to isolate the impact of the treatment effects; namely, would the family counseling treatment (C) be as effective without the prior individual counseling treatment phase (B). The PND score does indicate that there was an effect of the family treatment for the mother and father for improving their well-being, with uncertain effect for the child when compared to the second baseline measure. This indicates that there was improvement in well-being for the mother and father even after the original individual counseling. The greatest treatment effect for the child occurred during individual counseling with an uncertain effect in family counseling. However, the child continued to improve and maintain change with the introduction of the family counseling phase. If there had been no change in client well-being prior to the introduction of family counseling (as occurred with the father in this scenario), the impact of family counseling may be more conclusive. Within this hypothetical example, the researcher could state that individual counseling and subsequent family counseling combined improved the well-being for the child and parents of a child with oppositional defiant disorder.

A number of variations exist within this design. Within applied settings, it may not be feasible or ethical to withdraw treatment or intervention, therefore an ABC design may be indicated to incorporate the use of two intervention phases. McCaughan, Binkley, Wilde, Parmanand, and Allen (2013) used an ABC design to investigate the use of constructivist teaching for counselor education doctoral students in a pedagogy course. They observed the use of constructivist pedagogy prior to being taught constructivism (A), following instruction (B), and when utilizing a pedagogy of choice (C). In their design, it was not possible to withdraw the instruction (B), therefore the ABC design met their needs (see the Case Study for further description of this research). This exemplifies the flexibility and the innumerable designs available in SCD research for applied settings, as it can be tailored to client and setting circumstances.

MULTIPLE BASELINE DESIGN

The multiple baseline design (MBD) is one of the most widely used designs as an alternative to withdrawal/reversal designs and addresses what some researchers identify as problematic or perceived threat within the ABAB design. Ray (2015) notes that MBD is selected when "effects of an intervention or ethical concerns prohibit the removal of the intervention" (p. 396). MBDs consist of repeated measures for each individual during a baseline (A) and treatment (B) within phase. The effect of the treatment within MBD is assessed with the comparison of trajectory of outcome before the intervention (baseline) and after (treatment) the intervention across the multiple baselines at differing points in time (Kazdin, 2011). Hembry et al. (2015) points out that by using MBDs, researchers are able to predict the effect of treatment based on the outcome trajectory in each baseline for the participant receiving treatment, and the outcome trajectory for the participant not receiving treatment will remain unchanged. MBD utilizes a varying time schedule thus allowing time to determine the influence of the change in behavior as a result of the treatment. Multiple baselines of data collection can be used on different dependent measures (Heppner et al., 2016). It is assumed that with one or more variables, one of these serves as a control simultaneously as intervention is given to dependent measure. It is important to highlight that the application of the intervention is to be applied at different times to the dependent measures. The MBD consists of three tiers, including across settings/conditions, behaviors, and participant (individual)/group. Intervention occurs on the first tier when baseline data are stable across all tiers. It is important to look for immediacy of effect, while also looking to see if the independent variable is introduced on a tier and is associated with changes in the baseline of the remaining tiers. Setting a criterion level will inform when to implement the independent variable in the next tier.

DATA COLLECTION METHODS AND EXAMPLES

In SCD, such as MBD, data collection methods differ from other group designs. Focus is given to what is observable behavioral change, while psychological research will look at survey response and self-report data are utilized in combination to direct observation to measure behavior. Behaviors have to be given an operational definition, followed by defining the data collection procedures. In data collection, it must be specified when the data will be collected, how often the data will be collected, who will collect the data, and who will analyze the data. The measure of behavior has to be repeated across time. The control component of group designs looks different in SCD, where the participant(s) serve(s) as their own control. The treatment is applied to all phases of the study and the control condition is the baseline with no treatment provided, while behavior is still observed and recorded. The visual analysis of data consists of a minimum of three observations throughout the baseline phase (Barlow & Hersen, 1984; Lundervold & Belwood, 2000).

DATA ANALYSIS AND EXAMPLES

The visual analysis of data consists of the following plotted data points: latency of change, trend, level, slope, stability, and lack of overlap in data points from baseline to intervention phase. Graphs are used to represent data for visual and statistical analysis to support evidence-based decisions. Each intervention has to be determined for an effect in order for interpretation to be made. Specific to MBD, after a stable baseline is established, change is expected to be observable as the intervention is introduced to each participant, with participants not yet in the intervention phase not displaying treatment effects in baseline (Lundervold & Belwood, 2000).

MBD requires change to be shown in one assessed behavior while the other assessed behaviors remain constant. A concern for this design is due to this independence of the dependent variable. When there is a relationship between two or more of the behaviors, there will be a change in another behavior as a result of the initial behavior change. When two behaviors show simultaneous change, however only one received the independent variable, the rule out of threats to internal validity (i.e., history and mutation) is much greater. Unintended changes to the baseline present a threat to the strength of the design and result in uninterpretable results (Heppner et al., 2016).

MBD present unique challenges to utilize across behaviors, specifically with disciplines that consist of more holistic interventions and humanistic approaches, such as the counseling profession, because of the behavioral focus (Ray, 2015). MBD baseline across subjects is a more popular option for across subjects. Across participants design consists of the researcher selecting three or more similar individuals in presentation followed by a staggering of these participants at the introduction of the intervention (B) phase. Baseline interval will vary by each participant. The conclusions made from this design are a result of the replication across the individuals where the behavior identified had no improvement over numerous intervals of the baseline, while the intervention phase resulted in improvement with each participant (Ray, 2015).

The use of the multiple baseline across subjects can attend to unique confounding variables such as natural maturation, as the timing of the intervention differs with each participant, which further isolates the influence of the independent variable on the dependent variable. For example, a treatment facility may differ the timing in which they offer a specified treatment for three different participants. For participant A, they receive a mindfulness-based treatment after three baseline measures. Participant B begins mindfulness-based treatment after five baseline measures, and participant C after seven baseline measures. Additional participants can also be used. With this design, stability of the baseline is important for all three participants in addition to the immediacy of the effect of treatment (e.g., how quickly does the dependent variable change in response to treatment). If all three participants had a stable baseline and did not show improvement prior to treatment, it is easier to rule out natural maturation or other confounding variables. Likewise, an improvement in functioning quickly following the introduction of the mindfulness-based treatment strengthens the conclusions of the results, without needing to withdraw the treatment. Overall, the unique features of MBD and multiple baseline across subjects can be applied in clinical research in which the removal or withdrawal of treatment is not feasible, ethical, or would not result in a reversal of the dependent measure.

ALTERNATING TREATMENT DESIGN

Alternating Treatment Designs (ATD) differ from the phase designs discussed earlier in this chapter on SCD, as ATDs allow the varying levels of independent variable (IV) to be present at each measurement and is applicable in situations of rapid and frequent alternation of treatments (Manolov & Onghena, 2018). ATD consists of an alteration at random of two or more conditions that present as having equal opportunity to be measured (Hays & Blackledge, 1998). Wolery et al. (2010) refer to ATDs as comparative single subject designs, allowing for fast comparison of immediate reversible behavior. The rapid and frequent alternation means that few measurements are recorded for a specific condition after changing to another condition (Manolov & Onghena, 2018; Heyvaert & Onghena, 2014; Kratochwill et al., 2013; Wolery et al., 2010). ATDs are especially useful in studying the effect of more than one intervention.

Hays and Blackledge (1998) provided a research example of utilizing ATD in a study observing a counselor-in-training (CIT) across multiple sessions, with the CIT alternating between two conditions: remaining distant and cold while leaning away from a client in session, and another with the CIT becoming warm and empathetic with the client and leaning forward. It was predicted that the client would respond by self-disclosing more in session when the CIT is leaning toward the client and share less when the CIT is leaning away from the client. In their research, they found that the client had increased self-disclosures during the warm and empathic condition in comparison to being distant and cold. An example of a visual analysis of this research design is represented using hypothetical data based off the research design of Hays and Blackledge (1998; see Figure 7.5).

Another example of ATD is a study conducted by Van Houten (1993) in which procedures were interspersed with rote-learning trials (i.e., different treatment conditions). One group of children were taught subtraction in a group that used a general rule, while the other utilized rote learning. Procedures were randomly alternated every 15 min over the length of 15 or more sessions, while subtraction problems were used in each session to counterbalance across subjects in order for effects to be attributed to teaching methods and not the problem sets. A benefit of ATD is its simplicity in comparing three or more treatment conditions. One additional advantage of ATD is that treatment does not need to be withdrawn. Moreover, comparisons between components can be made more quickly. ATD requires a minimum of two alterations per data series. A limitation to ATD is that effects observed could be a result of the way in which conditions are presented and combined. Areas of concern for multiple treatment interference are sequential confounding, carry-over effects, and alternation effects (Van Houten, 1993; Barlow & Hayes, 1979; Ulman & Sulzer-Azaroff, 1975).

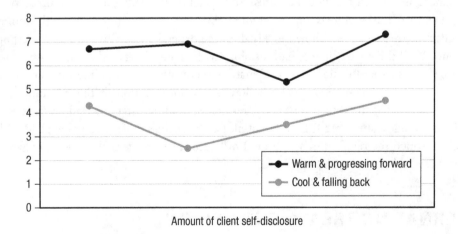

Amount of client self-disclosure

FIGURE 7.5 Visual Analysis of Alternating Treatment Design.

NOTE: This figure shows a hypothetical analysis of alternating treatment design looking at the implementation of a counselor-in-training (CIT) remaining cool and falling back (light gray) in session with a client and how this impacts the amount of client self-disclosure and the CIT remaining warm and leaning forward (black) with the client's self-disclosure and progress in session (Hays & Blackledge, 1998).

INCREASING THE RIGOR OF SINGLE CASE DESIGN

To address current limitations in SCD, increasing rigor entails consideration of both the design and analysis for this methodology. In regard to design, repetition and replication can be applied to enhance reliability over time and generalizability in different populations (Kazdin, 2011; Hitchcock, Kratochwill, & Chezan, 2015). Increased repetition of baseline and treatment phases in the same research study can provide greater evidence of a relationship between the treatment and the changes that occur (Kratochwill et al., 2013). Similarly, replication of the same study with different populations with either the same or a different counselor serves to bolster the findings and create a mechanism to establish generalizability (Hithcock et al., 2015). Heppner et al. (2016) recommend increased use of randomization in AB designs. They describe the implications and application for counseling settings to increase the identification of causality due to random assignment to different treatment groups. To meet the highest standard of SCD design, Chambless et al. (1998) recommend ABAB or multiple baseline designs coupled with stable baseline data. While the highest standard is encouraged in methodological designs, Lenz (2015) acknowledges the ethical imperative of counselors to adapt the design to the needs of their clients.

The use of external or additional observers/assessors to verify data increases the internal validity of the research results in SCD (Hott et al., 2015; Kratochwill et al., 2013). Hott et al. (2015) recommend the use of interobserver agreements in which an outsider observes both the dependent and independent variable for 20% to 30% of the data. In counseling research, the independent variable is typically a treatment, in which case, Hott et al. emphasize a rich and clear treatment protocol with adherence to said protocol, which can be confirmed through the interobserver at varying times throughout the research process. A detailed description of the treatment also includes unique events and changes that would be important for the audience to contextualize the research findings. While some settings allow for strict adherence to phase length, other clinical settings and populations may require adaptation of phase length during the research process. To maintain fidelity of the research with this high level of fluidity in protocol, a detailed description of both baseline and treatment phases are imperative. These design recommendations increase the integrity of SCD research.

Establishing standards for SCD in visual and statistical analysis will also attend to the need for greater rigor in SCD research. There continues to be great variability within the analyses used within this methodology. While this provides flexibility and accessibility for the researcher based on their individualized method and client case(s), it creates challenges in consistency and the ability to compare varying SCD research methods (Vannest & Ninci, 2015; Hitchcock, et al., 2015; Hott et al., 2015). To increase rigor in analysis, the SCD researcher can use more than one statistical analysis to report their results, in addition to any use of visual graphing. It is hoped that, with establishing standards and guidelines for analyses, SCD will be further established as a quantitative method to compete with traditional between-group research designs.

MULTICULTURAL ISSUES

The United States is an ethnically diverse country with a constant changing of demographics (Awad et al., 2016). What is considered a minority population will see a shift where those who identify as racially White will become a minority with those who come from non-White backgrounds. As diversity increases in representation, it is imperative for institutions to address this shift in the research methods to make for more culturally sensitive research methodology. How research is addressing the creation of research questions, recruitment of participants, data analysis, validity, and interpretation will need to be outlined and discussed (Awad et al., 2016). Psychology and the healthcare field adhere to a traditional research paradigm, operating from a Western belief system in adherence to claims of truth, neutrality, and objectivity that follow the self-contained individual and narrative of progress as a universal standard to scientific investigation. Psychological and health-related fields operate from a Western bias, which provides inadequate measurement of the context, and emphasis is placed on significant test results, thus overlooking effect size and pattern differences. Social science often will place emphasis on decisions based on desired value over others, favoring values, social groups, and social activities of a specific culture (Awad et al., 2016).

Examining causal relationships is established through research conducted with internal and external validity. External validity is seen as less significant in the research community. The test for generality requires use of diverse populations and settings. Emphasis is placed on exploring and understanding the internal validity while dismissing the significance of external validity. In psychological research, it is common to find descriptive and elaborate findings on internal validity, while discussion surrounding external validity is condensed into a couple of sentences with future implications.

Practices of psychological science show the lack of attendance on external validity and non-acknowledgment of multicultural research (Constantine & Sue, 2005). Constantine and Sue (2005) discuss how research in the psychology field on college students and the theories derived as a result, only include research findings that are derived from a compliant and impressionable population. The reliance on college student populations shows the failure and inability to apply the findings to other populations outside of college and differing cultural groups. These studies focused on college students have shown individuals to be compliant and sensitive to social influences, and they indicated that attitudes are poor predictors of actual behavior. Research has demonstrated that self-perceptions are based on external cues compared to introspection. Moreover, these findings have influenced the view of individuals as being egocentric and having a weak sense of self (Constantine & Sue, 2005).

The college population is a false representation of the U.S. population as it pertains to attainments in education, age, ethnicity, social class, attitudes, values, and other critical variables. This comparison of the normal population with the college population is an example of the limitations of the generalizability of these findings to a non-representative sample (Constantine & Sue, 2005). These findings pertain to SCD as studies are being conducted on various individuals. Cultural influences of each research participant in SCD is attended to in knowing how these influences impact the data and outcomes. Because of the individualized nature of SCD, it is naturally poised to explore and attend to unique cultural dimensions, while being cautious of generalizability to entire cultural groups. Rich descriptions of each participant or case used in SCD allow the reader to accurately interpret and apply the findings (e.g., Meany-Walen et al., 2015). Additionally, populations for which it may be difficult to obtain a large sample size for other research designs, such as small ethnic or cultural groups, may be particularly suited for SCD. Inclusion and attention to applications of diversity with this research design can increase adequate representation of diversity within clinical research.

LIMITATIONS TO SINGLE CASE DESIGN RESEARCH

The SCD and the single-case experimental design involve more systematic observations and experimental control resulting in less limitations than, say, a traditional case study design. According to Alnahdi (2013), external validity continues to be the greatest limitation of the SCD. The generalizability of the findings to other individuals or situations presents as a limitation to SCD. Heppner et al. (2016) point out that although "one isolates specific relationships among variables, it is unclear whether the results would generalize to other clients with similar concerns or diagnoses (client generalizability) or whether a particular technique would work in a different setting (setting generality)" (p. 353). More so, it is important to use caution when using SCD findings for exemplars or counterinstances. For example, early research consisted of uncontrolled case studies which were overused as the primary database for the construction of personality theories and broad generalizations for describing human behavior. Thus, the results of SCD can be to highlight a significant point or produce doubt on previously held beliefs, which presents the notion that there are exceptions to the rule (Heppner, 2016), while being cautious of generalizability.

One additional disadvantage of SCD would be that the experimenters may find what they had initially expected to find while overlooking pertinent information contrary to their expectations. Having the duality of clinician and researcher can muddy the internal validity, as researcher bias may limit or skew the observations of participants. To remedy this threat to internal validity, the use of interrater observer can minimize the likelihood of researcher bias while also increasing the fidelity of the research (Hott et al., 2015).

The validity and reliability of the visual analysis for this methodology is questioned. Dart and Radley (2017) found the interpretation of visual analysis could be manipulated through the scaling of the analysis for SCDs. In their research, they had raters determine the effect of various SCD based on visual analysis. Participants were knowledgeable in SCD and were given three different iterations of the same data for 32 sets of ABAB data. It was found that the design and scaling of the visual analysis influenced the accuracy of the results, in which smaller scaling resulted in overestimation of effect. This has vast implications for the heavy reliance on visual analysis and a need for establishing standards for visual analyses. Amid differing standards, Ledford et al. (2017) emphasize the value and use of visual analysis for demonstrating effect over time and offer clear descriptions on how to utilize visual analysis.

Case Study: Single Case Design Research

McCaughan, A. M., Binkley, E. E., Wilde, B. J., Parmanand, S. P., Allen, V. B. (2013). Observing the development of constructivist pedagogy in one counselor education doctoral cohort: A single case design. *The Practitioner Scholar: Journal of Counseling and Professional Psychology, 2*(1), 95–107. Retrieved from http://www.thepractitionerscholar.com/article/view/10980

BACKGROUND RESEARCH

One four-member research-participant team, comprised of a counselor education doctoral cohort, served as the single case design population (McCaughan, Binkley, Wilde, et al., 2013). This study took place in 2009 in a counselor education doctoral program at a public university. The goal of this study was to observe the development of constructivist pedagogy, as measured by constructivist teaching interventions. Single-case design was identified as the methodology for this study due to the design's emphasis on observing phenomena in their natural habitat as opposed to measuring experimental conditions, or comparing to control groups or expected behaviors.

The research-participant team was comprised of two women and two men, all of whom were members of a four-person counselor education doctoral cohort. This study was designed in conjunction with an undergraduate course that researchers were co-teaching as part of their enrollment in a doctoral level instructional design course, and participants self-selected for the study, which was borne from a goal of observing pedagogical development as measured by number of teaching interventions during each 50-minute class session (McCaughan et al., 2013).

RESEARCH PROCESS

Participants took turns instructing an undergraduate introduction to counseling course over a 12-week term. Each participant taught 3 weeks of the course. The cohort system was treated as an $N = 1$ population. Class sessions were video-recorded, and later analyzed using the Landro Play Analyzer (LPA) software.

> *The treatment was divided into three separate phases, or an ABC design. The first phase, (Phase A, or the baseline phase) was a 4-week duration in which each doctoral student member of the cohort taught one class period of the Introduction to Counseling course. The second phase (Phase B) occurred when the cohort was introduced to constructivist teaching pedagogy and specific constructivist teaching interventions during their Instructional Theory course. The third phase (Phase C) consisted of the cohort continuing to solidify their constructivist pedagogical theory and attempting to teach the Introduction to Counseling course using constructivist teaching interventions. (McCaughan et al., 2013, p. 99)*

Analysis consisted of counting constructivist interventions within Brooks and Brooks's (1993) 12-intervention framework using the LPA. Researcher-participants were randomly assigned to code one another's teaching sessions, so that no one researcher-participant was coding their own teaching session. One of the 12 class sessions recordings was compromised, resulting in a total of 11 class sessions being coded. After coding with the LPA, data were exported to Excel for calculation of descriptive statistics (McCaughan et al., 2013).

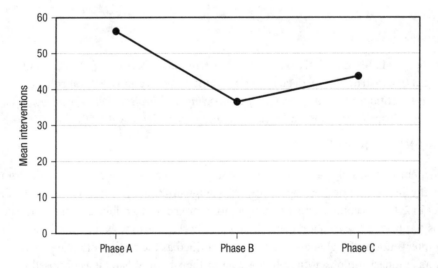

FIGURE 7.6. Mean number of teaching interventions for each phase, across the duration of the semester. Phase A (Baseline) had a mean number of teaching interventions of $M = 56.25$. Phase B (Theory Training) had a mean number of teaching interventions of $M = 36.50$. Phase C (Theory Choice) had a mean number of teaching interventions of $M = 46.37$.

SOURCE: Figure 7.6 originally published in The Practitioner Scholar. *Journal of Counseling and Professional Psychology.* volume 2 edition 1 as Table 2, p.103.

DISCUSSION

Constructivist theory relies heavily on learner participation, and researchers anticipated that as the semester progressed and application of constructivist theory became more solidified, there would be a resulting decrease in the number of teaching interventions. Contrary to this expectation, results showed the lowest number of constructivist teaching interventions occurring in Phase B, with a slight increase in Phase C (see Figure 7.6 Mean Number of Teaching Interventions, from Table 2 in McCaughan et al., 2013, p. 103).

While single-case design was appropriate for counting observed teaching interventions in this case, there were limitations to its application. Specifically, concerning constructivist interventions, this methodology did not allow for the observation of internal, or more covert teaching interventions, and instead only accounted for overt instructional behaviors. In addition, as the four-member cohort system was treated as an $N = 1$ in this study, analysis did not account for individual differences in observed teaching behaviors. Replicating this study utilizing an individual instructor's pedagogical development over the course of one term would eliminate individual differences (McCaughan et al., 2013), and ultimately seems an effective method of measuring overt teaching behaviors.

SUMMARY

This chapter reviews the distinguishing features of the single case research design. The use of individuals or small groups as both the control and treatment group create a unique quantitative method to explore causality in applied settings. Clinicians of varying backgrounds are encouraged to use this design to contribute to evidence-based research while simultaneously evaluating their effectiveness. This quantitative method relies heavily on visual analysis with increased use of statistical analyses to determine effect size. To increase in rigor, standardization of statistical analyses and consistency in visual analyses are essential to continue to establish this research design as valid and reliable among other quantitative methods. Consideration as to the myriad of design options are required to simultaneously meet the needs of client populations and design a single-case methodology that allows for the deduction of causality to contribute to evidence-based literature.

STUDENT ACTIVITIES

Exercise 1: Questions for Consideration

Directions: Critically respond to the following questions about the use of single-subject design for your specific discipline:

- Describe the unique features of SCD?
- Describe the strengths of SCD for use in clinical and applied settings.
- How does the flexibility and feasibility of SCD help and also hinder its place among other quantitative methods?
- What ideas do you have in combating the perspective that a large sample size and the use of a control group are necessary to establish causality?

Exercise 2: Establishing Baseline Trend: Example of Clients With Depression

Directions: Review the following clinical example and graph demonstrating various types of trend that may be found at baseline.

A clinician/researcher is doing a SCD and obtained measurements for three clients, Anna, Byron, and Chauntell. They measure depression utilizing the Beck Depression Inventory (BDI) across a 3-week period. Applying the **steady state** concept, look for a clear trend in the baseline data. Figure 7.7 parts A to C show how each participant in this study varied in their responses to the baseline measure.

  ▧ Based on their results, which participant(s) demonstrate(d) a trend as reported at baseline?
  ▧ How would you recommend the researcher proceed?

In reviewing the visual display, Anna demonstrates an upward trend with Chauntell having a flat trend. Downward trends are also observed in SCD data. If the researcher had the ability to continue

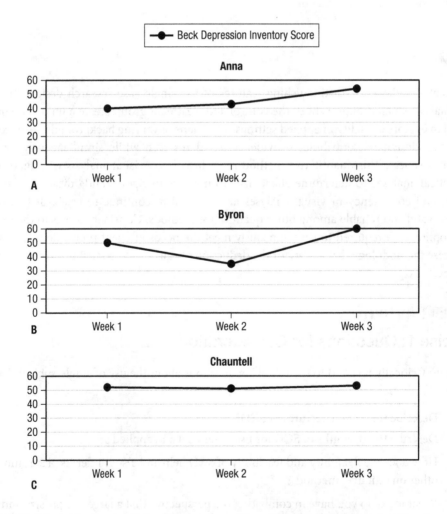

FIGURE 7.7 Graph demonstrating various types of trend that may be found at baseline.

to gather baseline data for Byron, they may then be able to deduce a trend. With further baseline measures with Byron, the data may stabilize. When establishing a steady state, look for stability and consistency in the baseline data. While a steady state prefers flat maintenance of data, a trend may also include an upward or downward trend. Kennedy (2005) emphasizes the preference for steady state data, however in behavioral and applied settings, varying forms of consistency may be identified. Generally statistical analyses involve comparisons to the mean, therefore highly variable or sloped data may pose limitations in analysis. Note that the BDI is much more robust across measures and great fluctuations in scores across a short period of time may indicate clinical concern.

Exercise 3: Designing an SCD Protocol

Directions: Create a research protocol for the following scenarios using a single case research design. Specify what design you would use within SCD. Describe the following: research question, population, dependent variable including potential observational or assessment measures, independent variable, and analysis to be utilized.

- A family counselor working with adoptive foster families wants to track the efficacy of using theraplay to reduce behavioral outbursts and increase the bond between caregivers and children.

- A program director wants to know whether the mindfulness-based treatment is more effective than the psychoeducation treatment at reducing obsessive-compulsive behaviors for clients with eating disorders in their in-patient treatment facility.

- A social worker would like to provide information for their stakeholders to demonstrate that their clients at a homeless shelter are improving with a decrease in substance use, increase in job seeking behavior, and improvement in medication management.

- A school counselor wants to confirm that the improvements in behavior from a social skills group are not due to natural maturation.

Exercise 4: Practice in Visual Analysis

Directions: Use hypothetical data to create a visual analysis for one of the research scenarios in Exercise 3: Designing an SCD Protocol.

Exercise 5: Questions for Consideration: Evidence-Based Practice

Directions: Respond to the following questions regarding the implications of SCD for practitioner led research.

- What role do you see SCD play in expanding and establishing evidence-based practice in counseling?

- How might you encourage practicing clinicians to use this methodology to both enhance their effectiveness and contribute to the research?

- What inhibits your use of this design in applied settings?

- How can SCD attend to unique cases while addressing the need for greater diversity in clinical research?

ADDITIONAL RESOURCES

Software Recommendations

- Time-Series Analysis in the following Software
  - SPSS, SAS, Systat, Statistica, Stata (Kazdin, 2011)
- Microsoft Excel

Helpful Links

- https://academy.pubs.asha.org/2014/12/single-subject-experimental-design-an-overview/
- https://opentextbc.ca/researchmethods/chapter/single-subject-research-designs/

Helpful Books

Kazdin, A. E. (2011). *Single-case research designs: Methods for clinical and applied settings* (2nd ed.). Oxford University Press.
Kennedy, C. H. (2005). *Single-case designs for educational research.* Pearson Education, Inc.

Helpful Videos

- Single case design video series from Psycho Core:
  - https://youtu.be/o5_p1PhZzSE
  - https://www.youtube.com/watch?v=LaV7Dif9Nag
  - https://www.youtube.com/watch?v=lySgsuSYVPY
  - https://www.youtube.com/watch?v=DHkGTMZW3nY
  - https://www.youtube.com/watch?v=RhNY5Nur0SU
- Single case experimental design overview:
  - https://academy.pubs.asha.org/2014/12/single-subject-experimental-design-an-overview/

KEY REFERENCES

Only key references appear in the print edition. The full reference list appears in the digital product found on http://connect.springerpub.com/content/book/978-0-8261-4385-3/part/part02/chapter/ch07

Kazdin, A. E. (2011). *Single-case research designs: Methods for clinical and applied settings* (2nd ed.). Oxford University Press.
Kennedy, C. H. (2005). *Single-case designs for educational research.* Pearson Education, Inc.
Lenz, S. (2015). Using single-case research designs to demonstrate evidence of counseling practices. *Journal of Counseling and Development, 93,* 387–393. https://doi.org/10.1002/jcad.12036
Morgan, D. L., & Morgan, R. K. (2008). *Single-case research methods for the behavioral and health sciences.* SAGE.
Ray, D. C. (2015). Single-case research design and analysis: Counseling applications. *Journal of Counseling and Development, 93*(4), 394–402. https://doi.org/10.1002/jcad.12037

CHAPTER 8

SURVEY RESEARCH

Yue Dang and Varunee Faii Sangganjanavanich

LEARNING OBJECTIVES

After reading this chapter, you will be able to:

- Identify the purposes of survey research
- Describe survey research designs
- Discuss ethical and multicultural considerations when implementing survey research
- Evaluate the use and limitations of survey research

INTRODUCTION TO SURVEY RESEARCH

The use of surveys to collect data pertaining to public opinion is not a new phenomenon. Many of us may have had some sort of experience with surveys in our daily lives. For instance, you may have been invited to complete a customer satisfaction survey at a department store regarding your purchasing experience. You may have found yourself being approached by surveyors for intercept surveys in a shopping mall. Or you may have seen your colleagues poll your availability to schedule meetings with you. The use of surveys can be seen on a daily basis.

Survey research involves using a survey research design to guide data collection from a sample in order to make an estimation about the research population in terms of their characteristics and/or the relationship among the characteristics. Generally speaking, survey research serves three purposes: *description, explanation,* and *exploration* (Babbie, 1973, p. 57). The description purpose allows researchers to estimate the characteristics of the population they intend to study (e.g., preferences, attitudes, beliefs). The explanation purpose helps researchers identify the reasons that may explain the characteristics of the research population (e.g., relationships among the preferences, attitudes, and/or beliefs that people have). The exploration purpose helps researchers explore possible factors that may contribute to the characteristics of their research population (e.g., contributing factors of the preferences, attitudes, and/or beliefs that people have). It is based on the description, explanation, and exploration of the characteristics obtained from the research sample that the researchers seek to generalize their survey results to their research population (Babbie, 1973). You can think about survey research as a way to collect data or information from a group of people in order to make a judgment about them and to extend that judgment to a broader group of people. For example, by collecting data pertaining to their wellness from a group of counselors across the country, you may be able to not only understand the group of counselors' overall wellness but also estimate counselors' overall wellness by extending the results you found within the sample to counselors in general.

Since the 1930s, scholars in different disciplines have utilized survey research in their studies. Examples of the utilization of survey research designs can be found in various disciplines such as sociology, marketing, public health, and education. Specific to the counseling profession, in 1960, C. H. Patterson clearly identified the significance of survey research in the social sciences and called for more survey research in his writing published in the *Personnel and Guidance Journal*, now known as *Journal of Counseling and Development (JCD)*, which is the leading academic journal in the counseling profession published by the American Counseling Association (ACA). By surveying a national sample of 911 counselors, Peterson et al. (2016) highlighted the essentiality of survey research in counseling and noted that survey design was one of the top three research areas in which counselors reported a high training need. You may wonder why that is. This is because counseling researchers have been engaging in scholarly activities to further and refine research skills. Many counseling research studies are conducted with survey research due to its ease of use, convenience, and resource limitations.

It is vital that counseling professionals possess research knowledge. Although you may not envision yourself conducting research studies, you are a consumer of counseling research. You may find yourself interested in a new counseling technique and want to know more about its efficacy and effectiveness. You can obtain such information from research studies. In other words, research findings advance counseling knowledge and inform counseling practice. This means it is critical that you have a basic understanding of research designs used in counseling research. The Council for Accreditation of Counseling and Related Educational Programs (CACREP) has outlined research knowledge that entry-level and doctoral level counseling students need to possess respectively (CACREP, 2015). In addition, the ACA has dedicated an entire section (Section G) to addressing ethical issues pertaining to research in its *Code of Ethics* (ACA, 2014). These standards are meant to guide you and fellow counselors as producers and consumers of research.

This chapter focuses on survey research. In this chapter, you will learn about a conceptual framework and the philosophical foundations of survey research and its relationship to other quantitative traditions. You will also have the opportunity to learn about different survey research designs and data collection methods through research examples. Importantly, as you go through this chapter, you will learn strategies used to enhance the rigor of survey research. In addition, you will get to know essential ethical and multicultural considerations pertaining to survey research and its limitations. Last but not least, you will be introduced to a case study that illustrates the use of survey research in the counseling profession.

THE PARADIGMATIC HIERARCHY OF SURVEY RESEARCH

Despite the long history and popularity of surveys, it is important that researchers pay close attention to methodological issues when conducting survey research. Utilizing surveys to collect information does not automatically make a study survey research (Fong, 1992). Before moving further in this discussion, perhaps it is helpful if we first discuss the paradigmatic hierarchy (Crotty, 1998) of survey research, which includes five interrelated levels: ontology, epistemology, theoretical stance, methodology, and methods. By identifying the implications of this hierarchy to survey research, we hope to assist you in building a conceptual framework to understand the philosophy that guides survey research.

ONTOLOGY

Ontology explains the nature of reality (Crotty, 1998). Different scholars may find themselves leaning toward different ways to approach reality/realities. Counseling survey researchers often survey their research participants' attitudes, perceptions, or beliefs which constitute their research constructs. While attitudes, perceptions, or beliefs may be subjective and constructed differently by different individuals, survey researchers tend to hold the belief that the measurements of their research constructs are objective and can be justified (Babbie, 1973). In other words, objectivity resides in the measurements and, therefore, survey results. As they describe, explain, and/or explore their research constructs that are often quantified in survey research, survey researchers tend to assume a position as an objective investigator.

EPISTEMOLOGY

Epistemology describes a way of knowing. That is, *how we know what we know* (Crotty, 1998, p. 8). One common epistemology that survey research reflects is objectivism, which claims that reality and its meaning remain independent of individual awareness (Crotty, 1998). The core of objectivism is that researchers and their participants remain independent without influencing one another in the research process (Ponterotto, 2005). This perspective may seem paradoxical for some social science researchers, because there are interactions between researchers and participants in survey research. As a result, it may be difficult for survey researchers to claim objectivism. In addition to objectivism from an absolute sense, Ponterotto (2005) also noted a modified objectivistic perspective, in which the researchers recognize the influence that researchers and their participants may have on one another but strive to remain objective and independent of their participants in the research process.

THEORETICAL STANCE

The theoretical stance is the philosophical stance including assumptions that inform research methodology (Crotty, 1998). Like other research designs, survey research reflects certain philosophical perspectives and assumptions. For example, by surveying the therapeutic alliance between counselors and clients based on the counselors' perspective, survey researchers attempt to quantify the construct of therapeutic alliance to understand this construct and generalize the results from the survey participants to the broader population of counselors. This practice reflects the post-positivistic stance, which strives to explain the reality by focusing on universally existing characteristics that can be applied to a general population, while acknowledging that such reality may not be fully known (Crotty, 1998; Ponterotto, 2005). When survey researchers attempt to maximize their control over the research process (e.g., random selection, random assignment), their practice is likely to reflect the positivistic stance, which seeks truth, objectivity, and certainty.

METHODOLOGY

Methodology is the plan of action for knowledge acquisition that guides research methods (Crotty, 1998). When describing their methodology, it is important that researchers not only describe their research design but also provide sufficient information to justify their research design based on their research purpose (Crotty, 1998). This said, when selecting a survey research design, researchers need to articulate a sound rationale as to why and how such design enables them to describe, explain, and/or explore the phenomenon they intend to study. For instance, a researcher is interested in studying professional identity development among counseling students over time, from the start to the end of their program. When using survey research, the researcher would need to select a design that is suitable for the type of the study in which data would need to be collected over a period of time (longitudinal survey in this case, which we will discuss later in this chapter). This idea is similar to clinical functions (e.g., diagnosis, treatment planning) of counselors. For example, counselors need to be able to provide a rationale as to why certain decisions are being made on client treatment. There should be a reason behind the decision to ensure that the decision is well-thought out and sound.

METHODS

Methods are specific procedures for data gathering and analysis (Crotty, 1998). In survey research, the description of methods is a comprehensive guide of (a) what concrete steps survey researchers would take, and (b) how survey researchers would take these concrete steps to gather and analyze data. Let's think of a research method as a recipe. The purpose of thorough description and step-by-step process is to allow others to be able to perform and follow the very same method if they would like to replicate the research procedures. For example, in our aforementioned professional identity development study example, the researcher needs to clearly and thoroughly describe each step of the research process such as obtaining institutional review board (IRB) approval for research involving human subjects, sampling, data collection, and data analysis. Survey research designs rely on several data collection methods, which are introduced in this chapter. In terms of data analysis, survey researchers often utilize quantitative data analysis methods including descriptive statistics and inferential statistics. Again, this is similar to other things counselors do. For instance, counselors need to be able to obtain informed consent from clients prior to the start of treatment and accurately document the informed consent process. In addition, depending on their clients' presenting concerns, treatment goals, and treatment modalities, counselors need to be able to work with their clients to address their presenting concerns and accomplish treatment goals. Important to note, counselors need to document each step they take with clients clearly and accurately during the entire treatment process.

DISTINGUISHING SURVEY RESEARCH FROM OTHER QUANTITATIVE TRADITIONS

From a philosophical perspective, survey research shares similarities with many other quantitative traditions because of the influence of positivism and post-positivism. Consequently, survey researchers take an objective position (or at least a relatively objective position) in the research process to investigate their research constructs and/or their relationships. In addition, the process of survey research appears to be similar to other quantitative traditions. Hackett (1981) indicated that survey research process includes (a) identifying the research problem, (b) selecting a survey research design, (c) selecting a representative sample, (d) selecting surveys, (e) collecting data, and (f) analyzing the data and generating the results. Many quantitative traditions follow a similar research process that usually involves describing the research problem, determining the research design, drawing the sample, collecting and analyzing data, and reporting the results.

DIFFERENCES BETWEEN SURVEY RESEARCH AND OTHER QUANTITATIVE TRADITIONS

Despite the similarities that survey research shares with other quantitative traditions, there are salient differences between survey research and other quantitative traditions. Hackett (1981) suggested that the distinctive components of survey research include "(a) the choice of a survey design, (b) the selection of a representative sample, and (c) interview and questionnaire design and administration" (p. 600). Accordingly, research that does not employ a survey research design to collect survey data from a representative sample is not survey research.

When conducting survey research, it is important that researchers use quality instruments (e.g., questionnaires, interview schedules) to collect proper and useful survey data. The process by which survey instruments are designed and developed are often known as scale construction or scale development. While scale construction is a complex and time-consuming process, we will briefly describe the scale construction process here so you can develop a general understanding of including the steps that may need to take place even prior to the actual survey research.

Generally speaking, in order to develop an instrument to measure a construct, for example, therapeutic alliance, researchers need to first comprehensively conceptualize the construct of the therapeutic alliance based on the existing literature. Then the researchers may determine the scope of the instrument (e.g., therapeutic alliance based on counselor self-report) and draft questions/items including their response format (e.g., rating scales, true/false questions) to be included in the instrument under development. Once the researchers have finished drafting the instrument questions/items, they may solicit experts on therapeutic alliance–related research to review the questions/items for improvement, which also strengthens the content validity of the instrument. The researchers may also conduct a pilot study to administer the instrument to a small group of individuals to test the instrument and collect feedback regarding the group's experience with the instrument (e.g., readability, format). Then the researchers can administer the instrument to a sample representing its intended population to establish the initial reliability and validity evidence to support the use of the instrument. In addition, the researchers may validate their instruments through further scale validation studies. Throughout the scale construction and validation process, researchers typically use advanced statistical analysis methods (e.g., exploratory factor analysis, confirmatory factor analysis) to understand the underlying structure of therapeutic alliance as a construct. As you can imagine, the instrument developed following these steps is more likely to accurately capture the construct of therapeutic alliance compared to an instrument with only one question asking counselors to rate the strength of their therapeutic alliance with clients on a Likert scale from 1 (very weak) to 5 (very strong). Although the one Likert scale question instrument may appear to be valid based on its face value, such a measure lacks psychometric evidence to support its utility to measure the construct of therapeutic alliance.

TABLE 8.1 **Key Aspects of Survey Designs**

SURVEY RESEARCH DESIGN	PRINCIPAL DESIGN	SAMPLE	PURPOSE	DATA COLLECTION	DATA ANALYSIS
Longitudinal survey designs	Trend studies	Samples representing a general population (Babbie, 1973)	Identifying stability or development over time (Babbie, 1973; Farrington, 1991)	Data are collected over time using one or more methods such as questionnaires and interviews	Various data analysis methods may be used
	Cohort studies	Samples representing a specific population with shared characteristics (Babbie, 1973)			
	Panel studies	The same sample (Babbie, 1973)			
Cross-sectional survey design	n/a	Representative samples of a general population or a specific population	Investigating differences within variables across research participants (Farrington, 1991)	Data are collected one time using one or more methods such as questionnaires and interviews	Various data analysis methods may be used

Depending on the construct(s) that researchers' study and the existing measures of the construct(s), researchers may need to develop instruments to use in their survey research. The steps of developing instruments for survey research, when needed, typically take place before the actual survey research in order to produce reliable and valid survey research results. In the following sections, we take a look at survey research designs, survey data collection methods, multicultural and ethical considerations pertaining to survey research, and limitations to survey research.

SURVEY RESEARCH DESIGNS

There are two common survey research designs: longitudinal survey designs and cross-sectional survey design (Babbie, 1973). The key difference between these two types of survey research designs is about how the data are collected based on the research purpose. Researchers often take several factors such as research purpose, research question, population and sample, and practicality into consideration as they select survey research designs. Table 8.1 summarizes the key aspects of each survey design.

LONGITUDINAL SURVEY DESIGNS

Longitudinal survey designs entail collecting data at multiple points in time to reveal stability or development over time (Babbie, 1973; Farrington, 1991). Such practice allows researchers to examine changes (or lack thereof) including the order in which the changes have occurred within the research variables over time (Farrington, 1991). Accordingly, longitudinal survey researchers can (a) make comparisons within or across their research participants and (b) make predictions using the data that are collected at multiple points in time (Farrington, 1991). Three principal longitudinal survey designs include trend studies, cohort studies, and panel studies (Babbie, 1973), which are explained in the following subsection.

Procedures and Examples

While the universal feature of longitudinal survey designs is that data are collected over time, there are variations in the research procedures for conducting trend studies, cohort studies, and panel studies.

Trend studies involve surveying samples that represent a general population at multiple points in time (Babbie, 1973). For example, if a researcher is interested in understanding graduate counseling students' multicultural counseling competence over time, the researcher may survey a sample of graduate counseling students every academic year and examine the trend or changes, if any, of multicultural counseling competence in the population over several academic years.

Cohort studies draw samples from a specific population based on shared characteristics at multiple points in time and examine any changes that occur over time (Babbie, 1973). For instance, if a counselor educator in a counseling program is interested in examining the program's newly admitted graduate counseling students' multicultural counseling competence development using a cohort study, the counselor educator may survey a sample of students from this particular cohort each semester throughout the course of their graduate training. This way, the counselor educator can track the development of multicultural counseling competence within this particular group.

Panel studies survey the same sample over time to draw conclusions about the population (Babbie, 1973). Going back to our multicultural counseling competence study as an example, if a researcher would like to investigate graduate counseling students' multicultural counseling competence over time using a panel study, the researcher would need to select a sample that represents the research population and survey the same sample at multiple points in time concerning their multicultural counseling competence. This way, the researcher may be able to not only reveal what and how the changes occur but also explain why the changes occur.

Data Collection Methods and Examples

We now present two longitudinal studies in counseling to show examples of the data collection methods used in longitudinal survey designs.

Fong et al. (1997) conducted a longitudinal study, which spanned 5 years from 1989 to 1994, on counseling students' cognitive development in a CACREP-accredited counseling program. A total of 43 graduate counseling students participated in the study upon the start of their graduate training in the program. Data were collected from these students at four points in time—the beginning of their training program, the end of their first semester counseling skills training, the end of their counseling practicum, and the end of their internship to capture the cognitive changes that occurred across the course of the training program within these students. Data collection methods used in this study included (a) role play audio recordings (collected at the beginning of the training program and the end of the first semester counseling skills training) to measure the students' counseling performance and (b) several questionnaires, including objective (e.g., Likert-type scale) and semiprojective (e.g., sentence-completion) questionnaires, to measure the students' cognitive functioning.

Another longitudinal study example is Helwig's (2004) study that that spanned for 10 years starting in 1987, which examined students' career development, particularly career aspirations and occupational expectations. A total of 208 second graders participated in the study as a representative sample of students in a suburban area in Colorado. Data collection methods in this study primarily included questionnaires and interviews. The participants' parents were invited to complete a questionnaire to provide basic demographic information (e.g., parent age, education, marital status, employment). In addition, each participant was interviewed individually in the second grade, fourth grade, sixth grade, eighth grade, tenth grade, and twelfth grade, using the Survey of Interests and Plans (SIP) that was developed by the author. While the primary focus of the study was to examine students' career development, the SIP consisted of questions inquiring about various aspects relating to students' career development, such as out-of-school activities and favorite and least favorite school subjects, in addition to career aspirations and occupational expectations.

Data Analysis and Examples

Longitudinal survey designs may require various data analysis methods ranging from basic descriptive statistics to inferential statistics that involve multiple variables. In the aforementioned study, conducted by Fong et al. (1997), the authors used a variety of different statistical methods including descriptive statistics (frequency, mean, standard deviation) and inferential statistics (e.g., chi-square, analysis of variance [ANOVA], t-test) to detect and present changes that occurred over time. The results showed counseling students' cognitive development from initial thought changes to cognitive self-appraisal changes based on the data collected at different points in their training programs. Specifically, Fong et al. (1997) noted an increasing focus on clients' psychological functioning with a higher level of complexity of counseling responses and effectiveness at the end of the first semester of counseling skills training among the research participants. As the students moved through practicum and internship, they perceived themselves as more confident in providing counseling. At the end of their internship experience, the students started to consider providing counseling as less difficult. Yet, the authors stated that they did not find any significant changes in the participants' cognitive complexity over time.

Similarly, in the second longitudinal study example described previously, Helwig (2004) used both descriptive statistics (e.g., mean, standard deviation) and inferential statistics (e.g., paired t-test) to analyze the data he collected over 10 years. Based on the data analysis, Helwig (2004) found that students, about 7 to 9 years old, tended to select occupations based on gender. When they turned 12 to 14 years old, these students tended to select occupations based on social status and values. As they continued to develop, the students later reported choosing occupations based on their interests and needs. Helwig (2004) noted that such results also supported previous theoretical perspectives on career aspirations and expectations.

CROSS-SECTIONAL SURVEY DESIGN

Let's turn to the other design used in survey research: cross-sectional survey design. While longitudinal survey designs involve data collection over time, cross-sectional survey design requires data collection at one point in time (Babbie, 1973). Such design allows researchers to examine any differences within research variables across research participants at a given point in time (Farrington, 1991).

Procedures and Examples

We now present two cross-sectional studies in counseling as examples of the research procedures using this design. In an exploratory study investigating counseling trainees' emotional intelligence, Gutierrez et al. (2017) utilized a cross-sectional correlational research design to examine the relationship between emotional intelligence and several constructs including empathy, stress, distress, and demographic characteristics. Specifically, using a convenience sampling method, the authors recruited 305 entry-level counseling trainees from four CACREP accredited counseling programs. Unlike the research procedures in the aforementioned longitudinal studies, participants in this cross-sectional study were surveyed only once for the purpose of the study.

In a different study using cross-sectional design, Cheng et al. (2018) examined the contribution of self-stigma of psychological help-seeking and mental health literacy to attitudes toward psychological help-seeking among college students. The authors recruited research participants in a higher education institution in the Midwest via email. Prospective participants were invited to complete an electronic survey. The final sample in this study included 1,535 college students. Participants in this study were also surveyed once given the cross-sectional nature of this study.

Data Collection Methods and Examples

In the study conducted by Gutierrez et al. (2017), the authors employed four questionnaires including a demographic questionnaire to measure the participants' emotional intelligence, stress, cognitive empathy, affective empathy, personal distress, and demographic characteristics. All of these measures except the demographic questionnaire were Likert-type scales. The authors administered these questionnaires to the research participants in person in a paper-and-pencil format.

The survey instruments in the study conducted by Cheng et al. (2018) consisted of six measures. Specifically, the authors utilized four Likert-type questionnaires to measure the participants' depression symptoms, anxiety symptoms, self-stigma of psychological help-seeking, and attitudes toward psychological help-seeking. The participants' mental health literacy was measured using vignettes. Their responses to the vignette questions were then coded dichotomously. The authors also used a demographic survey to collect demographic information from their research participants.

Data Analysis and Examples

Similar to longitudinal research, researchers who conduct cross-sectional survey research also use various data analysis methods to help them achieve their research purpose. For example, Gutierrez et al. (2017) used multiple data analysis methods including descriptive statistics, Pearson product moment correlation, t-tests, one-way ANOVA, Spearman's rank correlations, and multiple regression analysis. Based on the data analysis, Gutierrez et al. (2017) indicated that the main result of the study was that counseling trainees' emotional intelligence was positively associated with their empathy, whereas their emotional intelligence was negatively associated with their stress and personal distress. From this study, you can see that the researchers investigated how emotional intelligence related to empathy, stress, distress, and demographic characteristics during a brief period of time and there was no comparison between or among data collection points, since there was only one time that data collection occurred during the study.

In the second cross-sectional study example described previously, Cheng et al. (2018) utilized both descriptive statistics and hierarchical regression analysis for data analysis. To address the main research results, the authors noted that self-stigma of psychological help-seeking and mental health literacy predicted attitudes toward psychological help-seeking among college students after controlling covariates (e.g., psychological help-seeking experience, depression symptoms, anxiety symptoms, gender, race/ethnicity) in the study. Yet the authors indicated that there was no statistically significant interaction between the participants' self-stigma of psychological help-seeking and mental health literacy in predicting their attitudes toward psychological help-seeking.

APPROACHES TO COLLECTING SURVEY DATA

As you may see in the previous longitudinal and cross-sectional survey research examples, survey researchers often use a few different data collection approaches to gather information from their research participants. The primary data collection methods in survey research include questionnaires and interviews. Survey researchers often select data collection methods based on their research purpose, the information needed, and available resources (Alreck & Settle, 1995).

Questionnaires can be delivered and returned in a few different ways. Traditionally, questionnaires, along with informed consent forms, are delivered through post mails. Prospective research participants receiving the questionnaires, typically read and sign the informed consent form, and complete the questionnaires if they decide to participate in the study. Home delivery has also been documented as a way of survey delivery in which the surveyors recruit survey participants by visiting their homes (Babbie, 1973). Given the development of technology, electronic survey delivery (email surveys, web-based surveys) has been widely used by survey researchers in various disciplines, including counseling. In terms of survey returning, researchers who choose mail survey delivery often provide their participants with return envelopes and stamps for survey returning (Alreck & Settle, 1995; Babbie, 1973). Participants are typically instructed to return their signed informed consent and the completed questionnaires using the return envelopes being provided. Home delivery requires the surveyors to either pick up the completed surveys including signed informed consent at a later time or provide the participants with return envelopes and stamps along with instructions for postal survey returning (Babbie, 1973). Electronic surveys often require survey participants to provide their informed consent electronically, typically through clicking the "I agree" button toward the bottom of the informed consent page and prior to the start of the survey. In addition, electronic surveys allow participants to submit their survey results electronically, usually through clicking the "submission" or "proceed" button on the survey web page upon completion of the survey. You may have seen this in your everyday life. Regarding survey administration, questionnaires are commonly self-administered, which means that the survey participants read the survey instructions and administer the surveys to themselves if they agree to participate in the research. By using questionnaires, survey researchers usually have a relatively low level of direct contact or no interaction with their research participants (Alreck & Settle, 1995), which at times, may appear impersonal.

There are also times when the survey researchers administer surveys to their survey participants. Survey interviewing is an example of such a situation. During survey interviews, survey researchers ask their participants questions based on the research instruments and record the participants' responses accordingly. Survey interviews can take place in a face-to-face format, in which survey researchers and their participants meet in person for data collection. Depending on the research purpose, population, sample, and practicality, survey researchers may not always be able to meet their participants in person. As a result, survey researchers may interview their participants via phone calls or virtual meetings. For example, when conducting a survey interview, instead of traveling to San Francisco to meet a participant in person, a survey researcher in Boston can set up a virtual meeting with the participant (or multiple participants in some circumstances) so they can remain in their own geographic locations while interacting synchronically. Interviews generally allow a relatively higher level of contact and interpersonal interaction between the survey researchers and participants (Alreck & Settle, 1995). As they conduct survey interviews, a critical point survey researchers need to keep in mind is to ensure that they follow the wording of the questions on their survey questionnaires and record their participants' responses accordingly during the interviews (Babbie, 1973). This is to ensure consistency of survey interviews.

You may wonder if researchers use both data collection methods (e.g., inviting the research participants to fill out questionnaires and interviewing them in the same study). The answer is they do. Some survey research studies are designed to gather information through questionnaires and interviews. For instance, in the aforementioned longitudinal study examining students' career development, Helwig (2004) utilized survey interviews to gather data from the students who participated in the study. Interestingly, the author also employed a questionnaire to gather data from the students' parents.

In addition to the aforementioned data collection methods for survey research, researchers have also noted other survey data collection methods. For example, Stanton et al. (1956) proposed that role-playing may be used in survey research to examine the participants' behaviors and perceptions, or even personality. Alexander and Becker (1978) suggested using vignettes in survey research to enhance clarity, objectivity, and uniformity, while allowing concreteness and insight regarding the research constructs under investigation. In the aforementioned cross-sectional study example conducted by Cheng et al. (2018), the authors used vignettes to measure their research participants' mental health literacy.

PRACTICAL CONSIDERATIONS

When conducting survey research, researchers need to attend to its practicality. In this section, we discuss three major practical considerations relating to survey research including survey sampling, instrumentation, and response rates.

Sampling

A primary goal of survey research is to make an estimation of a population based on its sample. Given this consideration, one of the most important practical considerations of survey research is to ensure that the sample represents the population one intends to study (Babbie, 1973; Patterson, 1960). Sample representation in survey research is achieved through probability sampling, which provides every individual in the population an equal and independent chance to be selected for the study (Babbie, 1973). However, probability sampling may not always be feasible in counseling survey research due to sampling criteria. For example, many counseling survey researchers seek participants who meet specific inclusion criteria (e.g., education, licensure type, clinical experience). There may be times when such inclusion criteria become too specific to utilize probability sampling. It is important that counseling survey researchers comprehensively understand the population they intend to study and select a sampling method that would yield a highly representative sample (Hackett, 1981). Meanwhile, survey researchers need to be cognizant when discussing and applying their survey results and avoid overgeneralizing their results. For example, through a survey research project centered on substance use among clients receiving individual counseling in one particular county in one particular state, a researcher may find that substance use is prevalent among the research participants. While the research result can reveal informative clinical implications for helping professionals in that particular area, the researcher should be cautious not to generalize such results to all clients receiving individual counseling across different states, because it is unknown how well the sample from one county in one state can represent the entire client population across different states.

Instrumentation

Survey instrumentation is essential in determining the validity and reliability of the survey research results (Alreck & Settle, 1995). Considering that it can be difficult for survey researchers to collect quality data using poorly designed questionnaires, Hackett (1981) suggested researchers to attend to survey construction (e.g., question wording, sequencing, pretesting). While scale construction (e.g., writing questions/items, validation) is beyond the scope of this chapter (see DeVellis, 2017, for a review of scale development), when selecting survey research instruments, it is extremely critical that researchers use instruments with sound psychometric properties. This is because, as mentioned earlier in this chapter, instruments with sound psychometric properties are constructed through a rigorous scale development process to ensure their utility. In addition, survey researchers need to select instruments that align with their research purpose and population. Moreover, it is important that survey researchers routinely examine and report the psychometric properties of the instruments they use in their studies based on their research samples. This reporting process helps their readers comprehensively evaluate the utility of the survey instruments.

Response Rates

Survey response rates warrant thoughtful consideration in survey research, although many researchers do not routinely report response rates in their studies (Poynton et al., 2019). Babbie (1973) claimed that a survey response rate of 50% or more is adequate. A response rate of 60% or more is good. A response rate of 70% or more should be considered very good. However, it can be difficult for counseling survey researchers to apply such guidelines, especially considering the decline in survey response rates in the field (Van Horn et al., 2009).

When survey researchers report response rates, it is documented that survey response rates vary based on the data collection methods. For example, Sax et al. (2003) found a lower response rate for electronic surveys compared to paper-and-pencil surveys among college students. By examining mail survey response rates in counseling and clinical psychology through a meta-analysis of research published between 1985 and 2005, Van Horn et al. (2009) found an average survey response rate of 49.6%. In a meta-analysis of survey response rates in electronic surveys, Cook et al. (2000) noted that the average response rate of electronic surveys was 39.6%. Recently, Poynton et al. (2019) reviewed response rates of empirical research articles published in four counseling journals including *Counselor Education and Supervision*, *Journal of Counseling & Development*, *Journal of School Counseling*, and *Professional School Counseling* that used online recruitment from 2007 to 2015. It was noted that while the average response rate of studies using online recruitment was 34.2%, the average response rate of quantitative research using online recruitment was 31.6% (Poynton et al., 2019).

Researchers have also noted that survey response rates vary across different populations. For example, Van Horn et al. (2009) found relatively low mail survey response rates among practitioners, psychologists, and students compared to relatively high response rates among faculty and program directors in counseling and clinical psychology. Poynton et al. (2019) noted that response rates to online recruitment varied across different populations, with the lowest response rate (15.7%) found among certain counseling professional association members (e.g., state and regional counseling associations).

INCREASING THE RIGOR OF SURVEY RESEARCH

You may wonder what distinguishes well versus poorly conducted survey research. There is a thing called the "rigor" of survey research. The rigor of survey research is critical because it determines the research quality. To promote the rigor of survey research, survey researchers need to attend to issues pertaining to survey research design, research procedures, and data analysis. In this section, we discuss these issues.

INCREASING SURVEY RIGOR THROUGH RESEARCH DESIGN

To increase the rigor of survey research it is critical that researchers articulate their research purpose and provide justification for the use of survey research design to achieve their research purpose. Second, instead of alluding to survey research design, survey researchers should consider clearly identifying the survey research design used and demonstrate how the design was implemented. Such practice may enhance the validity of the survey research. Third, when designing survey research, researchers need to identify their research population so they can draw the connection between the target population and sample. Last, but not least, it is necessary that survey researchers comprehensively conceptualize the constructs they intend to study and provide well-rounded operational definitions of the constructs (Babbie, 1973). This way, survey researchers can guide their readers in understanding the research decisions (e.g., instrument selection, data collection, data analysis) that are made in the research process, which ultimately helps readers understand the survey results and the scope in which the results may be applied.

INCREASING SURVEY RIGOR THROUGH RESEARCH PROCEDURES

To increase the rigor of survey research through research procedures, first, survey researchers need to clearly identify their research sample and their rationale for sampling. Second, it is important that survey researchers select quality instruments that align with the scope of their research for data collection. Fong (1992) indicated that the two vital issues that researchers need to take into consideration in descriptive design include: (a) generalizability of the results and (b) that reliable and valid results were derived from the measures. By attending to sampling and instrumentation, survey researchers attend to these two vital issues. As previously stated, an important aspect of creating a rigorous survey research study is the utilization of validated instruments that are developed based on rigorous scale construction procedures. Without a rigorously created survey instrument, researchers may not be able to study the construct they intend to study. Third, survey researchers need to have a concrete plan to promote their survey response rates, especially when nonprobability sampling methods (e.g., convenience sampling) are used. Several strategies to increase survey response rates such as prenotification, personalization, and use of incentives have been documented by previous researchers (Helgeson et al., 2002; Weathers et al., 1993). In addition, Babbie (1973) suggested that in order to increase survey data using questionnaires, researchers should place the most interesting and important survey questions first and demographic questions last. Babbie (1973) also suggested that when conducting interviews, researchers should ask demographic questions first to build trust with the survey participants prior to collecting other information. Survey researchers may also consider piloting their research to promote quality survey research (Fan & Yan, 2010; Granello & Wheaton, 2004). When possible and appropriate, survey researchers may consider using replication to verify survey research data (La Sorte, 1972).

INCREASING SURVEY RIGOR THROUGH DATA ANALYSIS

To increase the rigor of survey research through data analysis, in addition to selecting appropriate data analysis methods to answer survey research questions, it is important that survey researchers pay close attention to patterns existing in the survey data. For example, it is important that survey researchers properly handle and report missing data in survey research, because missing data, although seemingly trivial at times, may drastically impact the survey results (Sterner, 2011). By outlining the steps they take to address missing data, survey researchers provide their readers with guidance in understanding the research results.

CONSIDERATIONS

Ethical Considerations

When engaging in survey research with human participants, it is critical that counseling survey researchers attend to their academic and professional ethical responsibilities to produce quality research. While detailed information and relevant guidelines pertaining to research ethics can be obtained from the IRB through the researchers' institution in most cases, this section addresses several pertinent ethical considerations specifically related to counseling survey research. Survey researchers need to consider their academic and professional ethical responsibilities during the research process.

One of the most important ethical considerations pertaining to survey research is informed consent (ACA, 2014, Standard G.2.a.). It is extremely important that survey researchers provide prospective participants with comprehensive information about the study and ask for their consent to participate in the study prior to collecting any survey data. Information pertaining to the research such as purpose, researcher information, conditionality, anonymity, data collection and storage, and risks and benefits for participation should be clearly presented to prospective participants so they can make an informed decision. It is also the researchers' ethical responsibility to protect the identity of their participants (ACA, 2014, Standard G.4.d.) and to ensure the confidentiality of their participants' data (ACA, 2014, Standard G.1.b.). This is often done through using password-protected programs for data collection and encrypted drives for data storage. Important to note is that protecting participants' identity and confidentiality does not merely happen during the research process. Researchers are typically required to retain their research data for a certain period of time following pertinent policies and guidelines at the institutional, state, and federal levels. Last but not least, survey researchers should not force participants to answer any survey questions they do not wish to answer once they provide consent to participate in the survey. That is, there shall be no restrictions preventing the participants from moving forward in the survey after they consent to take the survey. In the event that there are missing data due to the participants' partial incompletion of the survey, researchers need to address missing data properly. When navigating ethical dilemmas in survey research, survey researchers may consider seeking research consultation from members on their research teams, experienced colleagues, or research support within their institutions or professional organizations.

MULTICULTURAL CONSIDERATIONS

In addition to ethical considerations, survey researchers should also attend to multicultural considerations relating to survey research. First, survey researchers need to be mindful that not every culture is equally familiar with survey research (Bulmer, 1998). It is important that survey researchers design and conduct their research (e.g., designs, sampling) while taking the research cultural context into account (Bulmer, 1998). Second, it is critical that survey researchers understand that individuals from different cultural backgrounds may conceptualize their research constructs differently (Bulmer, 1998). This is particularly the case in counseling survey research, because many research constructs that counseling survey researchers are interested in examining are culturally informed constructs (e.g., mental disorders, mental health literacy, psychological help-seeking; Cheng et al., 2018). Third, when selecting survey instruments, survey researchers need to understand the utility of each instrument and its intended population. Reliability and validity of the survey results may vary drastically across different populations even based on the same instrument. Last, but not least, there may be times survey researchers decide to translate their survey instruments into a different language for the purpose of their research. If this is the case, survey researcher should follow relevant guidelines (see Brislin [1970] for an example) to ensure quality translation, which impacts the validity of the survey results.

LIMITATIONS TO SURVEY RESEARCH

You have now learned all of the important aspects of survey research, except its limitations. Like any other research design, there are limitations to survey research that researchers need to take into consideration. We now discuss three main limitations to survey research including its application, response rates, and cost.

First, survey research may be easily misused (Hackett, 1981). It is important that counseling researchers understand the scope of survey research. For example, survey research does not imply cause-and-effect relationships (Alreck & Settle, 1995). Meanwhile, possible biases, such as nonresponse bias (differences between individuals who respond to the survey and those who do not) and response bias (e.g., social desirability), may impact the survey results (Sax et al., 2003). Second, it can be problematic when survey research yields a low response rate (Hackett, 1981). Low survey response rates limit the power of the survey research. In addition, depending on the sampling procedure, low response rates may potentially limit the representativeness of the samples (Krosnick, 1999). Third, survey research, especially longitudinal survey research, can be pricey in terms of its required time, effort, and resources (Alreck & Settle, 1995; Hackett, 1981). When conducting a longitudinal survey that spans a long time period, the results may be delayed (Farrington, 1991) and attrition may become an issue (Babbie, 1973).

Case Study

Lam, S., Tracz, S., & Lucey, C. (2013). Age, gender, and ethnicity of counsellor trainees and corresponding counselling self-efficacy: Research findings and implications for counsellor educators. *International Journal for the Advancement of Counselling*, 35(3), 172–187. https://doi.org/10.1007/s10447-012-9175-3

BACKGROUND

With the increasing focus on multiculturalism and diversity in counseling, Lam et al. (2013) highlighted the importance for counseling professionals to understand the contribution of diversity factors to professional development among counselors. Given this notion, in their research study published in 2013, the authors investigated the relationship between counseling self-efficacy and age, gender, and ethnicity among counseling trainees. Specifically, the authors asked one research question: "Are there significant differences in counseling self-efficacy among counselor education students of different age groups, genders, and ethnic backgrounds?" (Lam et al., 2013, p. 175).

To answer the research question, the authors conducted a cross-sectional study to compare self-reported counseling self-efficacy across their participants based on different demographic characteristics including age, gender, and ethnicity.

RESEARCH PROCESS

Given the focus of this study on counseling trainees, the research participants consisted of graduate counseling students. The authors selected one higher education institution that is ethnically diverse in the western region of the United States. To draw counseling trainees at different stages in their training program, the authors recruited research participants in different didactic and clinical courses in the counseling program. Specifically, Lam first contacted the instructors of several didactic and clinical courses (e.g., counseling theories, practicum, internship) to request a class visit regarding the research. Once the request was approved by the instructors, Lam visited each class to recruit participants. A total of 233 counseling trainees participated in this study.

To measure the participants' counseling self-efficacy, Lam et al. (2013) selected the *Counseling Self-Estimate Inventory* (COSE; Larson et al., 1992), a Likert-type scale consisting of 37 items. There are five subscales within the COSE measuring one's confidence concerning Micro Skills, Counseling Process, Difficult Client Behaviors, Cultural Competence, and Awareness of Values. In this study, Lam et al. (2013) used both composite score (full scale score) and subscale scores in their data analysis, which includes three series of one-way ANOVAs. The COSE composite and subscale scores were treated as dependent variables, whereas the participants' age, gender, and ethnicity were treated as independent variables for each of the three series of one-way ANOVAs. It is important to note, in addition to gender and ethnicity, the authors treated age as a categorical variable that included four age groups (19–22, 23–29, 30–39, and >40).

DISCUSSION

Based on the data analysis, Lam et al. (2013) did not find any statistically significant differences in the participants' counseling self-efficacy scores (full scale and subscale scores) by age. Similarly, the authors did not find any statistically significant differences in the participants' counseling self-efficacy scores (full scale and subscale scores) by gender. However, the results revealed statistically significant differences in the participants' composite counseling self-efficacy score and two subscale (Difficult Client Behaviors and Cultural Competence) scores by ethnicity.

Specifically, given the composite counseling self-efficacy score, Lam et al. (2013) noted that biracial and African American counseling trainees reported the highest counseling self-efficacy, whereas Caucasian and Asian counseling trainees endorsed the lowest counseling self-efficacy. Post hoc analysis results showed that African American counseling trainees had a higher level of counseling self-efficacy than did Caucasian counseling trainees. Latinx counseling trainees had a higher level of counseling self-efficacy than did Asian and Caucasian counseling trainees. Meanwhile, biracial counseling trainees had a higher level of counseling self-efficacy than did Asian and Caucasian counseling trainees. In terms of the Difficult Client Behavior subscale score, the authors stated that African American counseling trainees reported the highest self-efficacy, whereas Caucasian counseling trainees reported the lowest self-efficacy. Concerning the Cultural Competency subscale score, the authors indicated that African American counseling trainees reported the highest self-efficacy, whereas Caucasian counseling trainees reported the lowest self-efficacy (Lam et al., 2013). Given such results, Lam et al. (2013) called counselor educators to attend to counseling students' backgrounds and the impact of their backgrounds on their professional development.

SUMMARY

In this chapter, we discussed various aspects pertaining to survey research. Specifically, we discussed the context of survey research and survey research designs including longitudinal and cross-sectional survey designs. Although longitudinal and cross-sectional designs have different purposes, both are used to collect data to inform the population based on the sample. We also presented strategies to promote the rigor of survey research. Ethical and multicultural considerations, along with limitations to survey research, were also discussed.

STUDENT ACTIVITIES

Exercise 1: Longitudinal Survey Design

Directions: Given the information presented on longitudinal survey designs and the brief description of Fong and colleagues' (1997) study and Helwig's (2004) study, please answer the following questions:

1. Which longitudinal survey design (trend studies, cohort studies, or panel studies) do you believe Fong and colleagues used in their study? Please explain your rationale.
2. Which longitudinal survey design (trend studies, cohort studies, or panel studies) do you believe Helwig used in his study? Please explain your rationale.

Exercise 2: Cross-Sectional Survey Design Versus Longitudinal Survey Design

Directions: Describe the advantages of cross-sectional survey design compared to longitudinal survey designs. How about limitations?

Exercise 3: Advantages and Limitations of Questionnaires and Interviews

Directions: Identify the advantages and limitations of using questionnaires and interviews for data collection in survey research.

Exercise 4: Survey Strategies

Directions: What are the strategies that you have seen researchers use to address the practical considerations relating to survey sampling, instrumentation, and response rates? Do you believe they are effective? Why or why not?

Exercise 5: Ethical and Multicultural Considerations

Directions: Review one counseling survey research paper presented in this chapter (Cheng et al., 2018; Fong et al., 1997; Gutierrez et al., 2017; Helwig, 2004; Lam et al., 2013) and discuss how the authors(s) addressed ethical and multicultural considerations in the study.

Exercise 6: Designing a Longitudinal Survey Related to Diversity

Directions: In the case study provided earlier, Lam et al. (2013) conducted a cross-sectional study to examine the contribution of diversity factors to professional development among counselors. Based on the information discussed in this chapter, design a longitudinal study examining the contribution of diversity factors to professional development among counselors. Describe the design, research process, data collection, and data analysis you would use.

ADDITIONAL RESOURCES

Software Recommendations

When it comes to data collection, survey researchers may encounter many different options such as Google Forms, Microsoft Forms, Qualtrics, and SurveyMonkey to collect questionnaire data and GoToMeeting, Microsoft Teams, Skype, WebEx, and Zoom to collect interview data. By surveying a national sample of counselors, Peterson et al. (2016) noted that SurveyMonkey was the most widely used survey software by counselors. Considering issues relating to electronic surveys (e.g., response rates, credibility), Cho and LaRose (1999) suggested to include institution information (e.g., university name) in the electronic survey domains to enhance the survey credibility and to promote response rates. Given this notion, survey software such as Qualtrics, WebEx, and Zoom have embedded institution names in the electronic survey domains for their customers. Survey researchers are highly encouraged to examine the data collection software options that are available to them and select the ones that can promote the credibility and response rates of their surveys.

There are various kinds of software such as Microsoft Excel, R, Statistical Analysis System (SAS), and Statistical Package for the Social Sciences (SPSS) that researchers use for data analysis in different professions. Specific to the counseling profession, SPSS is commonly used in academics, while Microsoft Excel is mostly used by counselors (Peterson et al., 2016). Microsoft Excel can help researchers perform some descriptive statistics (e.g., mean, standard deviation). As a widely used statistical software in social sciences, SPSS allows counseling survey researchers to conduct not only descriptive statistics but also inferential analyses. Survey researchers are encouraged to evaluate their research purpose and select the software that would allow them to achieve their research purpose.

Often, counseling research involves collecting protected health information (PHI). PHI is defined in the Health Insurance Portability and Accountability Act of 1996 (HIPAA) as *individually identifiable health information* (U.S. Department of Health & Human Services, n.d.). As you think about collecting PHI of individuals for survey research, it is critical that you utilize a HIPAA compliant platform where there are added security and protections of data during electronic transfers.

Helpful Links

- https://writing.colostate.edu/guides/guide.cfm?guideid=68
- https://www.scribbr.com/methodology/survey-research/
- https://blog.hubspot.com/service/survey-questions

Helpful Reading

Bryan, J. A., Day-Vines, N. L., Holcomb-McCoy, C., & Moore-Thomas, C. (2010). Using national education longitudinal data sets in school counseling research. *Counselor Education & Supervision*, *49*(4), 266–279. https://doi.org/10.1002/j.1556-6978.2010.tb00102.x

Granello, D. H., & Wheaton, J. E. (2004). Online data collection: Strategies for research. *Journal of Counseling & Development*, *82*(4), 387–393. https://doi.org/10.1002/j.1556-6678.2004.tb00325.x

Sterner, W. R. (2011). What is missing in counseling research? Reporting missing data. *Journal of Counseling & Development*, *89*(1), 56–62. https://doi.org/10.1002/j.1556-6678.2011.tb00060.x

Helpful Videos

- https://www.youtube.com/watch?v=mdVWbuffdNY
- https://www.youtube.com/watch?v=FkX-t0Pgzzs
- https://www.youtube.com/watch?v=IarEwuUP1oQ

KEY REFERENCES

Only key references appear in the print edition. The full reference list appears in the digital product found on http://connect.springerpub.com/content/book/978-0-8261-4385-3/part/part02/chapter/ch08

American Counseling Association. (2014). *Code of ethics*. Author.

Babbie, E. R. (1973). *Survey research methods*. Wadsworth Publishing Company, Inc.

Council for Accreditation of Counseling and Related Educational Programs. (2015). 2016 standards. http://www.cacrep.org/wp-content/uploads/2017/08/2016-Standards-with-citations.pdf

Crotty, M. (1998). *The foundations of social research: Meaning and perspective in the research process.* SAGE.

Hackett, G. (1981). Survey research methods. *Personnel & Guidance Journal*, 59(9), 599–604. https://doi.org/10.1002/j.2164-4918.1981.tb00626.x

CHAPTER 9

CONTENT ANALYSIS RESEARCH

Cassandra A. Storlie and Hongryun Woo

LEARNING OBJECTIVES

After reading this chapter, you will be able to:

- Explain the origin, history, and ongoing development of content analysis
- Compare and contrast various approaches of content analysis
- Synthesize the various approaches of content analysis and apply to the case studies provided
- Explain the significance of enhancing the rigor of qualitative and quantitative content analysis approaches

INTRODUCTION TO CONTENT ANALYSIS IN THE HELPING PROFESSIONS

This chapter provides you with an introduction to content analysis research in the helping professions. Various helping professions such as nursing, social work, and counseling have used content analysis methodology because of its flexible methods and inclusion of a range of analytic approaches. In the helping professions, professionals regularly use verbal and written communication to better support individuals, groups, and programs to work on goals that align with improving outcomes. Goals are often generated from a thorough understanding of the meaning of past experiences or trends that have encompassed one's background. Similarly, content analysis provides social science researchers a framework to better understand and make sense and meaning of large amounts of material (data), much of which is narrative in nature.

Trying to analyze and better understand meaning from textual information has been of interest to individuals well before content analysis research came to fruition. The ways in which we understand meaning from the use of words, language, and symbols also have roots since the beginning of time. Although we will present various approaches to content analysis within this chapter, we encourage early researchers to build on their knowledge of this methodology by carefully reading the primary sources listed at the end of this chapter. As with all studies in the counseling/helping professions, it is essential for researchers to have a thorough understanding of content analysis in order to complete a study in an ethical and multiculturally responsive way.

In its most concise form, those that use content analysis for research "examine data, printed matter, images, or sounds/texts in order to understand what they mean for people, what they enable or prevent, and what the information conveyed by them does" (Krippendorff, 2004, p. xviii). Our aim for this chapter is to provide researchers detailed information that will increase their knowledge, understanding and application of content analysis by grasping the meaning of content in a rigorous and systematic fashion. In doing so, we hope that researchers will gain better utility in sorting through the vast methodological choices they have to best answer their research questions.

ORIGIN, HISTORY, AND ONGOING DEVELOPMENT OF CONTENT ANALYSIS

To begin, we explore how the origin and history of content analysis has influenced our current understanding of this methodological approach. Next, we discuss the ongoing transformation of content analysis. Then we share the contemporary understanding of content analysis while also providing specific uses for this approach. We end this section with examples of data that are commonly used in content analysis, considerations for the helping professions (specifically counseling), philosophical and paradigmatic hierarchy, and a glossary of terms that will help you in your conceptualization of the various approaches of content analysis.

EARLY ORIGINS

Investigation into the meaning of communications were first recording in the late 1600s (Krippendorff, 2004) with early origins of content analysis becoming more evident during the mid 1700s (Krippendorff & Bock, 2008). It was during this time that the Swedish State Church began investigating if the content of their hymns were developed by sources that were unsanctioned by the church. The Swedish State Church was concerned about individuals reading the written word after the development of the printing press and moralized textual information that was nonreligious in nature (Krippendorff, 2004). As time progressed and the collection of hymns were more closely examined by scholars through the counting of words (Drisko & Maschi, 2016), it was noted that symbols and text generated different meanings depending on the context in which it was read. Controversy emerged among scholars and elders in the church surrounding the accurate interpretation of meaning versus symbolic interpretation (Krippendorff, 2004).

TRANSFORMATION OF CONTENT ANALYSIS

In the late 1700s, an early form of content analysis was discovered within the political commentary of a newspaper. This commentary appeared to convey a humorous and sarcastic tone, exemplifying different meanings of words to readers (Drisko & Maschi, 2016). As newspapers and print continued to have increased visibility over decades and across the world, additional inquiry was being made into how the content had evolved from "religious, scientific, and literary matters" to "gossip, sports and scandals" in the late 1800s/early 1900s (Krippendorff, 2004, p. 5). The development of a quantitative newspaper analysis emerged, centered within the discipline of journalism

(Drisko & Maschi, 2016; Krippendorff, 2004), which incorporated measuring the frequency of certain words and the length of specific newspaper columns. Yet, further transformation of how we understand the meaning of the written and spoken word was yet to evolve.

Krippendorff (2004) described four salient factors that influenced the transformation of content analysis: (a) Mass media was being partially blamed for rising crime rates and the breakdown of cultural values after the U.S. economic crisis; (b) the development of television and radio powered communication and challenged the power of newspapers; (c) radio was thought to, in part, influence political change (e.g., Facism); and (d) social and behavioral sciences were more accepted, as were their theories and ways in which research was investigated. In combination with these factors, the first textbook on content analysis was published in 1952 (*Content Analysis in Communication Research*) by Berelson and was "born as a quantitative technique" (Franzosi, 2008, p. xxi). Content analysis was primarily used as a quantitative method with "text data coded into explicit categories and then described using statistics" (Hseih & Shannon, 2012, p. 1278). However, as content analysis moved outside journalism and expanded beyond frequency counts, the development of Qualitative Content Analysis (Kracauer, 1952) originated. Although it was not as well-known as quantitative content analysis, qualitative content analysis was developed in reaction to Berelson to establish that meaning is not always understood based on frequency counts and that "latent meaning" (Schreier, 2012, p. 15) was also essential for our understanding.

CONTEMPORARY UNDERSTANDING OF CONTENT ANALYSIS

The current understanding and ontology of content analysis is best described by Krippendorf (2019). Krippendorf states that there are three distinguishing characteristics of how we understand contemporary content analysis. The first characteristic embodies content analysis as "an *empirically grounded method*, exploratory in process, and predictive or inferential in intent" (Krippendorf, 2019, p.1). This characteristic further includes social science researchers' inquiry into gathering and generating new knowledge by better understanding the meaning of information.

The second distinguishing characteristic describes our contemporary understanding of content analysis as transcending "traditional notions of symbols, contents, and intents" (Krippendorff, 2019, p.1). This second characteristic exemplifies the expansion of the modality with which we communicate (e.g., social media, messages, symbols), the systems from which we communicate (e.g., networks, mass media systems), and the modality of co-constructed realities (Krippendorff, 2019). The concept of co-construction embraces collaboration and how we "live together in language" (Krippendorff, 2019, p. 2). From an epistemological point of view, the emphasis on constructionism/constructivism has a strong hold on how we best understand meaning.

The third distinguishing characteristic includes how content analysis has developed its own methodology that "enables researchers to plan, execute, communicate, reproduce, and critically evaluate their analyses" (Krippendorff, 2019, p. 4). Krippendorff discussed how context changes over time to more fully embrace complex worlds in which researchers collaborate and respond to larger scale content being readily available electronically (Krippendorff, 2019, p. 4). While our contemporary understanding of content analysis has been established by key figures within the origin and history of this methodology, it is essential for researchers to also be familiar with the ontology, epistemology, theoretical stance, methodology and methods (Crotty, 2003) within content analysis.

COMPARABLE TRADITIONS IN QUALITATIVE AND QUANTITATIVE METHODOLOGIES

Predictive Design: Predictive research is the pursuit of identifying variables that forecast future phenomena. Through the interpretations of explanatory research, predictive variables are identified and examined in the practical application of predicting a specific phenomenon. These predictive variables are often identified through their correlation with the desired outcome. Correlation and prediction are closely connected in that if two variables are correlated with each other, then the value of one variable should estimate, with some degree of accuracy, the value in the other variable (Hayes, 2017).

Single Subject Design (SSD): The primary distinguishing feature of the SSD is the use of a single subject longitudinally as both the control and treatment group through differing phases of baseline/non-treatment (A) and treatment (B). These phases are used strategically to determine the impact of a specified treatment or intervention.

Grounded Theory: According to Houser (2020), "the primary approach in grounded theory is the dynamic interaction of identifying categories, which are analyzed and reconstituted into more complex ones with each continuous level of analysis" (p. 73).

Phenomenology: Phenomenology attempts to gather a deeper meaning of the lived experiences of individuals and groups. It does not offer a theory grounded in the data, but "the possibility of plausible insights that bring us in more direct contact with the world" (VanManen, 1990, p. 9).

PHILOSOPHY AND PARADIGMATIC HIERARCHY IN CONTENT ANALYSIS

Content analysis research is situated in the quantitative and qualitative traditions. Qualitative content analysis has the ontological positions of relativism, while quantitative content analysis takes the realism position. Constructionism and subjectivism are the epistemological positions informing the qualitative content analysis, while objectivism informs quantitative content analysis. The theoretical stance of quantitative content analysis is a subtype of positivism known as post-positivism. Depending on the theoretical perspective of the investigation, qualitative content analysis can take a variety of theoretical stances including symbolic interactionism, phenomenology, feminism, postmodernism, and critical inquiry. Additional details about the paradigmatic hierarchy of content analysis are given in the following paragraphs.

The current ontology of content analysis has advanced since its early inception and can incorporate both relativism and realism depending on the type of content analysis utilized. Relativism is embedded in the understanding that we have "interdependent realities through what we say to and do with each other" (Krippendorff, 2019, p. 3). In addition, realism is also rooted in content analysis while one may utilize methods of interrater reliability (e.g., Cronbach's alpha) to support the rigor and authenticity of results. As we consider our conceptualization of content analysis and its various forms, we find that relativism tends to situate itself more strongly in qualitative content analysis and realism tends to position itself in quantitative content analysis.

Within content analysis, authors have suggested that researchers distinguish the significance of a study by discussing the epistemology that was used to orient the study (Drisko & Maschi, 2016). Epistemology helps us conceptualize the way in which the researchers believe the nature of knowledge is constructed. Although it is common for researchers using content analysis to hold a constructivist epistemology (Krippendorff, 2004; 2019), particularly within the counseling profession/helping professions, it is not a complete or unanimous way in which researchers conceptualize knowledge acquisition. As such, epistemological choice helps to outline the ways in which researchers engage in reliability, validity, credibility, and transferability (Drisko & Maschi, 2016; Patton, 2015), which are essential in enhancing the rigor of content analysis research.

Within content analysis, one's theoretical stance is informed by epistemology and is considered the philosophical position or lens of the research aim. Researchers using content analysis may aim to extend, support, or negate a variety of different theoretical stances based on qualitative content analysis approaches utilized. As such, researchers may use a theoretical stance to best frame the way in which they will engage with the data they have collected.

According to Krippendorff (2004), "methodology provides a language for talking about the process of research, not about the subject matter" (xxiii). Within content analysis, the examination of data helps the research gain meaning of written, spoken, and textual data through the methodology. The methods of content analysis methodology include the procedures in which data are both guided and analyzed. Several approaches will be reviewed under the umbrella of content analysis, but specifically in terms of what is commonly considered qualitative and quantitative content analysis. For more detailed information encompassing the procedures, readers are asked to go to primary sources and content analysis guidebooks (e.g., Krippendorff, 2019; Neuendorf, 2017) for specific methods.

EXAMPLES OF SPECIFIC USES OF CONTENT ANALYSIS

- Analyze qualitative focus group interviews and/or individual interviews with open-ended questions to complement quantitative data in order to provide readers with a holistic understanding of research
- Use as a pre-test and improve an intervention/survey prior to launch
- Identify the intentions, focus or communication trends/patterns of an individual, group, or institution
- Describe attitudinal and behavioral responses to communications

EXAMPLES OF DATA USED FOR CONTENT ANALYSIS

Content analysis can be applied to all kinds of written text such as:

- Speeches
- Letters or articles whether digital or in print
- Text in the form of pictures, video, film, or other visual media

Content analysis is used to examine both the manifest and the latent content of a text. Manifest content refers to "what is overtly, literally present in a communication" (Drisko & Maschi, 2016, p. 2). Latent content refers to the meaning that is not apparent in a communication and that lies behind the manifest content. Manifest content in the form of images of women in commercials engaged in domestic work or childcare, for example, might be interpreted to demonstrate gender stereotyping, a latent concept.

CONSIDERATIONS FOR THE HELPING PROFESSIONS

Within the counseling profession specifically, it is important to note that content analysis methodology has most recently been used with the exploration of trends within the field such as an exploration of the research trends in counseling journals (e.g., Flynn, Korkuska, Brady, & Hays, 2019) and the prevalence of competencies (e.g., Worthington, Soth-McNett, & Moreno, Matthew, 2007). This flexible methodology allows for researchers to examine data and use interpretation to help convey meaning and answer salient research questions within the helping professions about current issues and trends.

Counselor Education and Supervision: In alignment with the 2016 doctoral standards in Counselor Education and Supervision from the Council for Accreditation of Counseling and Related Educational Programs (CACREP), content analysis is a methodological approach that can help to answer both qualitative and quantitative research questions (4.a.), approaches to quantitative and qualitative data analysis (4.b. and c.), and is an emergent research practice (4.d.) that can assist students to present scholarly work in journal publications (4.h.) and conference proposals (4.i.). In addition, content analysis may also serve as an appropriate methodology to support grant proposals and other sources of funding (4.k.) while also serving as an ethical and culturally relevant strategy in conducting research (4.l.)

Before we present the various approaches used in content analysis, it is important for readers to have a solid understanding of core terms that are used within this methodology. Having a solid understanding will help you conceptualize terms that we will use in presenting our quantitative and qualitative content analysis overviews and examples.

GLOSSARY OF TERMS COMMON TO CONTENT ANALYSIS METHODOLOGY

Categorizing: "The process of grouping ideas, objects, and data into mutually exclusive sets. Categorizing reduces a diversity of recording/coding units into convenient kinds" (Krippendorf, 2019, p. 407).

Coding: "The process of categorizing, describing, evaluating, judging or measuring descriptively undifferentiated units of analysis, thereby rendering them analyzable in well-defined terms" (Krippendorff, 2019, p. 407).

Category and Subcategory: A category is formed by grouping together those codes that are related to each other through their content or context. In other words, codes are organized into a category when they are describing different aspects, similarities or differences, of the text's content that belong together. A category answers questions about who, what, when, or where. In other words, categories are an expression of manifest content, that is, what is visible and obvious in the data. When analysis has led to a plethora of codes, it can be helpful to first assimilate smaller groups of closely related codes in sub-categories. Sub-categories are narrower categories and can be reviewed for possibilities of further aggregation into categories (Erlingsson & Brysiewicz, 2017).

Theme: A theme can be seen as expressing an underlying meaning, that is, latent content, found in two or more categories. Themes are expressing data on an interpretative (latent) level. A theme answers questions such as why, how, in what way, or by what means (Erlingsson & Brysiewicz, 2017).

Inductive Inference: "The process of proceeding from particular propositions, such as a sample of observations, to general propositions, such as to statistical generalizations of that sample, accounting for these observations in most if not all respects" (Krippendorf, 2019, p. 409).

Deductive Inference: "The process of proceeding from a general proposition, considered true, to particular propositions that are logically implied and are therefore considered true as well" (Krippendorff, 2019, p. 408).

Researcher as Human Instrument: It is this term that stresses the uniqueness of the researcher's role in the process of scientific inquiry. Researcher as "human instrument has the unique capability of summarizing data on the spot and feeding it back to an informant for clarification, correction, and amplification" (Lincoln & Guba, 1985, p. 194).

Data Immersion: Inductive analysis immersing in the details and specifics of the data to discover important patterns, themes, and inter-relationships. It begins by exploring, then confirming findings, guided by analytical principles rather than rules (Merriam, 2009).

Phenomenon: "A phenomenon (plural, phenomena) is a general result that has been observed reliably in systematic empirical research. In essence, it is an established answer to a research question" (Price, Jhangiani, & Chiang, 2015).

Theoretical Framework: The structure that can hold or support a theory of a research study. The theoretical framework introduces and describes the theory that explains why the research problem under study exists (Ravitch & Riggan, 2012).

Semi-Structured Interviews: "A qualitative data collection strategy in which the researcher asks informants a series of predetermined but open-ended questions" (Given, 2008).

CONTENT ANALYSIS APPROACHES IN THE HELPING PROFESSIONS

Understanding the various approaches to content analysis can provide researchers in the helping professions additional choices as they consider how to best answer their research questions. There are significant differences in the approaches and philosophy of qualitative and quantitative content analysis in contemporary research within the social sciences. We will provide you an overview about the basic approach to quantitative content analysis and further include common qualitative content analysis approaches in our discussion, including conventional, directive, and summative approaches. In the following we will describe the salient differences among these approaches and provide examples of when/how to use these methods in alignment with your research questions.

QUANTITATIVE CONTENT ANALYSIS

Content analysis can be conducted in a quantitative as well as qualitative manner, although this distinction is not always that easy to draw. In fact, some content analysis scholars do not engage in the distinction between qualitative and quantitative content analysis, making a case that all textual information is qualitative in nature (Krippendorff, 2004). Nonetheless, the appropriate approach in using a form of content analysis should depend on a researcher's research questions. According to Riffe and colleagues:

*Quantitative content analysis is the systematic and replicable examination of symbols of communica-
tion, which have been assigned numeric values according to valid measurement rules, and the analysis
of relationships involving those values using statistical methods, in order to describe the communication,
draw inferences about its meaning, or infer from the communication to its context, both of production and
consumption. (Riffe et al. 1998, p. 20)*

Quantitative content analysis has the power to address these downsides by the following points:

- As it analyzes secondary data, hence data that have not been collected for the study's
  purpose, quantitative content analysis reduces the respondent's bias. It is considered an
  unobtrusive method (Krippendorff, 2013).

- Validity and reliability checks (for instance, inter-coder tests) are usually easy to produce
  and therewith the reliability of the data collection can be controlled.

- Quantitative content analysis opens the door to triangulation, thus the use of multiple
  methods using one set of data (Harris, 2001).

- The biggest advantage of the method is the vast scope of application that content analysis
  offers.

BASIC CONTENT ANALYSIS

Basic content analysis is one of the most common approaches in the scholarly literature (Drisko
& Maschi, 2016). Scholars (e.g., Berelson, 1952; Neuendorf, 2017) of basic content analysis
describe it as an approach that uses quantitative analytic techniques predominantly addressing
manifest content. The key research purposes of basic content analyses are description and
data organization. This approach typically samples existing texts initially generated by others
for their own purposes other than the content analysis. Basic content analysts code mainly
manifest content utilizing deductively or inductively established preliminary codes and have
little interpretation. Basic content analysis uses descriptive statistics such as word counts and
other quantitative analytic methods to analyze data and to determine the relative importance of
specific content. To determine the reliability and validity of the analytic processes, quantitative
criteria are employed.

Figure 9.1 outlines major steps in quantitative content analysis (Rose, Spinks, & Canhoto, 2014).
The design begins with the identification of relevant ideas and, where appropriate, the formulation of
hypotheses aligned with the research question. This is where you provide the rationale behind your
proposed project and avoid the risk of engaging in pointless "word crunching" rather than purposeful
analysis (Insch et al., 1997). Existing literature and prior research play a significant role in helping you
develop the conceptual foundation for your research. This is a very important stage of the research
as the ideas and concepts will form the basis of your coding scheme and your final analysis as well.

Sampling includes identifying and selecting the material that you plan to analyze. Suppose, for
example, that your interest was in magazine advertisements. The sampling process would require
decisions about what type of advertisements are of interest, in which magazines they appeared,
over what time frame, and so on. You would also need to choose between including all eligible
advertisements or selecting a sample.

Similar to developing a sampling plan, you will then need to decide on the unit of text that you
will classify during the coding process. We will refer to this as the coding unit, although terminology
varies. Examples of coding units include words, phrases, sentences, images, paragraphs, or whole

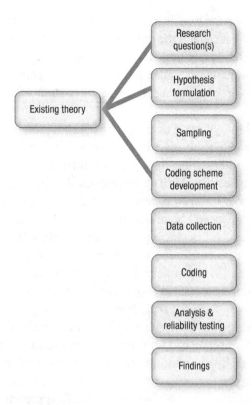

FIGURE 9.1 Major Steps in Quantitative Content Analysis.

documents. You should choose your coding unit taking into account your research question and the concepts that you wish to identify in your analysis.

The next step is to develop a coding scheme. This is the process of developing classification rules to assign coding units to particular categories or concepts, for example, assigning the numerical code 0 to an advertisement if the central figure is an image of a male and 1 if it contains a female. The code book helps to ensure systematic and replicable coding of the data. In preparing your code book (i.e., category, description, examples, and coding rules) you should make sure that each category is exhaustive and mutually exclusive and that the instructions for coding are clear. Your coding scheme may draw on existing schemes developed by other researchers. In addition, there are a number of existing content analysis dictionaries which are available to support the analysis of written text (see Krippendorff, 2019; Neuendorf, 2017). These dictionaries specify a range of concepts and the words or phrases that are indicators of the concepts. Alternatively, your coding scheme can be developed inductively from the data using techniques similar to those used when analyzing qualitative data. In addition to a code book, you will also need to prepare a coding form (see Neuendorf, 2017). This form can be used to record details of the codes applied to the data during the coding process. That information can then be transferred from the coding form into a software program for further analysis.

Once your initial coding scheme has been developed it needs to be piloted, which further enhances the rigor. This can be done on a randomly selected sample of the data. Piloting is essential to identify problems with the coding scheme or the coders' ability to apply it. Any such problems need to be addressed before the study proceeds (Neuendorf, 2017).

When the coding scheme is finalized, coding can begin. While coding can be done by a single person the use of multiple coders allows the principal researcher to see whether the coding scheme can be applied in a reliable way. In addition, if there is a large amount of data, more than one coder is likely to be needed. An alternative to human coding is to use a computer; a number of specialized computer software programs exist to support quantitative content analysis, particularly of written text.

Final analysis involves the application of quantitative techniques. Descriptive statistics, such as frequency counts, can be used to summarize findings from the sample and appropriate inferential statistics used to test any hypotheses that have been formulated. An important additional step for content analysis is reliability testing. Particularly relevant if more than one coder is used, is the examination of the consistency between coders. Unless the coding scheme has been applied in a consistent way, the resulting data will be unreliable. This can be tested by getting coders to code the same set of material and then measuring interrater reliability (Rose et al., 2014). Interrater reliability or agreement determines the extent to which two or more independent coders or raters obtain the same result when using the same instrument. The concept addresses the consistency of the implementation of a rating system. There are a number of statistics that can be used to estimate agreement between two coders (Sicanore et al., 1999).

Percent agreement is the simplest interrater agreement measure. Considering the design of two raters each rating n subjects once, we can summarize the results in a 2x2 table by considering the four possible pairs of ratings. The percent agreement is the proportion of all subjects for whom both raters agree about the presence or absence of the code as judged by both raters. Miles and Huberman (1994) suggested that interrater agreement should approach or exceed 90%. However, proportion of agreement has been criticized since it fails to account for any agreement due to chance alone. Consequently, it can lead to inflated true levels of reliability.

Cohen proposed a method, the Cohen's kappa statistic (κ), to counteract this problem of agreement caused by chance. The computation subtracts the proportion of agreement that could be expected by chance alone from the observed proportion of agreement (Fleiss, 1981). The maximum possible value of kappa is 1, indicating perfect agreement. Inversely, values of kappa between 0 and −1 signify that agreement is less than what can be attributed to chance. According to the classification interpretative guidelines suggested by Landis and Koch (1977), kappa values of 0.40 to 0.60 represent moderate agreement, 0.60 to 0.80 substantial agreement, and 0.80 to 1.00 almost perfect agreement. However, although kappa is widely accepted as an appropriate statistic, there are two situations that adversely influence the magnitude of the values and may confound their interpretation: the prevalence of the trait (e.g., infrequently found codes) and the pattern of disagreement between raters (e.g., unbalanced marginal totals in contingency tables; Gwet, 2002; Hoehler, 2000).

Coefficients based on the theory of generalizability is an alternative approach for measuring agreement that does not present as many weaknesses as the crude and chance-corrected agreement indices. It represents the most comprehensive and complex way of assessing reliability. The ideas of the generalizability theory have been addressed extensively in the statistical literature and have become increasingly popular in various fields of science (Donnon & Paolucci, 2008; Kan, 2007; Lakes & Hoyt, 2009; O'Brian et al., 2003; Wasserman et al., 2009). The coefficients of generalizability, also called intraclass correlation coefficients, are a generic class of reliability coefficients. They might be derived from a specific formula depending on the experimental plan and calculated from an analysis of variance approach (Crocker & Algina, 2008). The values of generalizability coefficients range from 0, which indicates no agreement, to 1, indicating perfect agreement among raters. Values are regarded as acceptable if they equal or surpass 0.8 (Landis & Koch, 1977; Nunnally, 1978).

An example demonstrates a quantitative content analysis study of the portrayal of women in James Bond films:

Neuendorf, K. A., Gore, T. D., Dalessandro, A., Janstova, P., & Snyder-Suhy, S. (2010). Shaken and stirred: A content analysis of women's portrayals in James Bond films. *Sex Roles, 62*(11–12), 747–761.

How women are portrayed in the media has long been a subject of interest to researchers. The Neuendorf et al. (2010) study uses quantitative content analysis to investigate how women are depicted in the long-running and very popular series of James Bond films. Three research questions are linked to how the portrayal of women has changed over time with respect to (a) their physical characteristics, (b) their level of sexual activity, and (c) the amount and level of violence directed against them. Three further questions analyze whether the way that a female character is portrayed (in terms, for instance, of her physical characteristics) predicts (a) the amount of sexual activity in which she is involved, (b) the amount of aggression directed at her, and (c) whether the character survives the film. The coding unit is female characters who meet certain criteria (e.g., they speak or are spoken to). The code book defines a range of variables to be measured for each character, such as race, hair color, body size, physical attractiveness, along with variables measuring aspects of sexual activity and violence by and against the character. Eight coders were used to code the 20 films. Inter-coder reliability was tested using one of the 20 films and the results are reported in the study. Research findings showed some minor changes over time in terms of more female roles, more sexual activity, and greater likelihood of being recipients of physical violence but found much consistency in terms of age, body type and attractiveness. The findings on prediction showed clear links between sex and violence in the way women are portrayed in Bond films. According to the authors "the collective body of Bond films ... stands to serve as an important source of social cognitive outcomes regarding appropriate role behavior for women – still stereotyped, with persistent allusions to violence and sex (and their linkage), and with unrealistic standards of female beauty" (Neuendorf *et al.*, 2010, p.758–759).

As mentioned, quantitative content analysis is one of the most common types of content analysis used in the helping professions. There are similarities between quantitative and qualitative content analysis as you will see in the following which centers on qualitative content analysis approaches.

QUALITATIVE CONTENT ANALYSIS

Like quantitative content analysis, qualitative content analysis is a research methodology in which one can describe the meaning of qualitative data in a systematic way (Schreier, 2012). According to Schreier (2012), qualitative content analysis is completed by "classifying material as instances of the categories of a coding frame" (p. 1). Qualitative material may include textual data (such as transcribed interviews, documents, or written text), visual data (such as artifacts and observations), or other rich data that may require interpretation in order to answer your research question. However, qualitative content analysis is most often applied to verbal data such as transcripts and emails (Schreier, 2012). Meaning is constructed from qualitative material via the researcher in their role as a human instrument (Patton, 2015). This role is a complex process in which the researcher brings in their own worldview and background to help interpret data. Most importantly, qualitative content analysis is systematic in that steps are taken in sequence (from deciding on a research question to interpreting and presenting findings) but also flexible so that analysis and coding is tailored and adjusted to be data driven (Schreier, 2012). Drisko and Maschi (2016) identified that qualitative content analysis includes both inductive and deductive approaches in coding.

Qualitative content analysis is used when interpretation is needed to better understand data. If little interpretation is necessary, one should consider a quantitative content analysis approach instead. There are three common approaches to qualitative content analysis that are commonly used within the helping professions when conducting research: conventional content analysis, directive content analysis, and summative content analysis (Hseih & Shannon, 2005).

CONVENTIONAL CONTENT ANALYSIS

Conventional content analysis is often used when the research question is designed to describe a phenomenon and is "usually appropriate when existing theory or research literature on a phenomenon is limited" (Hseih & Shannon, 2005). After establishing a research question, researchers are often gathering data directly from participants, commonly through the use of semi-structured interviews without imposing any prearranged categories or theories on the qualitative data collected. Semi structured interviews generally use open-ended questions in order to allow participants to provide their unique perspective to the interview questions. Prompts (or probes) are then used so participants can elaborate more on their answers in lieu of the researcher returning to the theoretical framework (Hseih & Shannon, 2005). Researchers can then use an inductive process in their coding in which they deeply engage in the qualitative data and allow categories to emerge, instead of having a predetermined coding framework. As such, conventional content analysis centers in on the ways in which codes relate to one another and the way in which categories relate to one another in a descriptive way. In using a research team to code data, methods of interrater reliability may enhance the trustworthiness of the results.

DIRECTIVE CONTENT ANALYSIS

Directive content analysis differs from conventional content analysis in that in this approach there is the use of an existing theory stance or framework in which the methodology is used to validate or extend that theory (Hseih & Shannon, 2005). Directeive approaches apply more structure to the process of coding and analysis because there are existing categories that can be used that are representative of the chosen theoretical framework. That is to say, directive approaches do not allow for the emergence of categories but use pre-existing categories instead. Directive content analysis often uses a deductive approach and may integrate the use of a codebook (MacQueen et al., 1998) to help the research team have a uniform understanding of the definitions, descriptions, and examples in relation to the theoretical framework. Codebooks are a benefit to the research team and assist with clarity when teams engage in large amounts of data. Data are mainly collected through the use of semi-structured interviews (Given, 2008) which include specific questions that center on the existing categories.

Below, we provide an example of a directed content analysis. The full study is cited here:

Storlie, C.A., Chan, C., & Vess, L. (2019). Examining Positive Youth Development in diverse youth using the Future Career Autobiography. *Journal of Child and Adolescent Counseling, 5*(2), 183–203. https://doi.org/10.1080/23727810.2019.1609837

In this example, the research question was: "How does the existing Positive Youth Development framework align with the narrative responses of a diverse group of students completing the Future Career Autobiography?" (Storlie et al., 2019, p. 187). Here, authors used the Positive Youth Development (PYD; Lerner et al., 2003) framework as their existing framework in which to develop their codebook. The codebook, developed by the first author, included essential definitions related to PYD and allowed the coding team to have uniformity when engaging with the data in multiple consensus building meetings. The data collected for this study were the narrative responsive from a diverse school district who had completed the Future Career Autobiography (FCA; Rehfuss, 2009). Authors coded the data in relation to the pre-existing categories defined by the codebook and took additional steps to ensure credibility and dependability by using inter-coder agreement (Creswell, 2017) and the use of a peer auditor (Patton, 2015). Here, the structure in the use of the pre-existing framework on PYD assisted both the development of the codebook and helped to keep the research team connected to their agreed upon definitions.

SUMMATIVE CONTENT ANALYSIS

Summative content analysis, according to Hseih and Shannon (2005), incorporates quantification of qualitative data while also engaging in interpretation later in the analysis. For instance, the approach begins with first detecting and providing frequency counts of specific words within the context of the data. As with basic quantitative content analysis (Drisko & Maschi, 2016), interpretation and meaning making is not the goal of quantifying words but instead is a way in which researchers can get the sense of how frequently certain words are used. As such, qualitative interpretation does not happen at the beginning stages of summative content analysis (Hseih & Shannon, 2005). Interpretation begins after the frequencies are established and subsequently a "latent content analysis" results where "underlying meaning" (Hseih & Shannon, 2005, p. 1284) is revealed within the data. Summative content analysis is often used when researchers are examining the content (trends) of a journal or perhaps the types of research methods (e.g., qualitative, quantitative, mixed methods) used within volumes of a journal (Hseih & Shannon, 2005). The use of member checking (Lincoln & Guba, 1985) and content consultants may assist with establishing trustworthiness of results.

ADDITIONAL QUALITATIVE APPROACHES TO CONTENT ANALYSIS

Krippendorff (2004) has elaborated that there are various approaches that have been deemed qualitative in nature that do not fully capture the essence of our contemporary understanding of content analysis. For example, discourse analysis can "focus on how different phenomenon are represented" in textual information within a variety of contexts (Krippendorff, 2004, p. 16). Rhetorical analysis "focuses on how messages are delivered and their intended or actual effects" (Krippendorff, 2004, p. 16). Lastly, ethnographic analysis centers its approach on categories that emerge from textual data but tends to limit its engagement with quantifying or frequency counts (Krippendorff, 2004). Although there are other analyses that may be considered qualitative in nature, it is important to note that some approaches may use both elements of qualitative and quantitative analysis.

INTERPRETIVE CONTENT ANALYSIS

Interpretive content analysis is considered a blend of both quantitative and qualitative content analysis approaches. Authors (e.g., Holsti, 1969; Osgood, 1959) of interpretive content analysis define it as an approach that aims to make interferences about the texts and receivers of communication; thus, not only manifest content but also latent content. Ginger (2006) described interpretive content analysis as a flexible approach that "may explore key story lines, subjects and objects of texts, normative positions, and the methods used to claim these positions" (Drisko & Maschi, 2016, p. 5). Interpretive content analyses examine mostly newly generated texts but use existing data sets as well. Interpretive content analyses use inductively established codes (i.e., researcher-created summaries and explanations) rather than the frequency of word or other quantitative analytic methods. Qualitative criteria are used to determine the reliability and validity of the coding processes. For further information on the various coding frames and analytical recommendations that can be utilized in qualitative content analysis, the authors recommend accessing additional information from:

Saldaña, J. (2013). *The coding manual for qualitative researchers* (2nd ed.). Sage.

DISTINGUISHING CONTENT ANALYSIS FROM OTHER METHODOLOGICAL APPROACHES

Most research methods in the social sciences have structured and systematic steps as a part of their implementation. To be put simply, content analysis can be used as a both a qualitative and quantitative approach to answer important research questions for researchers. This differs from some purely qualitative approaches, such as phenomenology, in which the meaning making of the lived experience is the core of the methodology. Similarly, due to the interpretative nature of qualitative content analysis approaches, it would not be fitting to use one of them with a purely quantitative research question that wants to address correlates or perhaps prediction, as in a regression analysis. As with all research, the research question is what should direct the methodology chosen.

STRENGTHS AND LIMITATIONS OF CONTENT ANALYSIS

Content analysis is a flexible research approach that can be applied to a wide variety of text sources. Helped by the availability of computer software programs, content analysis can manage large amounts of data. It can be used to investigate a topic longitudinally through the examination of contemporary texts. Content analysis can also be seen as an unobtrusive research approach in that it can be used to analyze naturally occurring data. As a result, content analysis may be helpful in reducing the problem of social desirability bias among respondents when researching sensitive topics (Harris, 2001).

Potential weaknesses of content analysis arise in connection with the process of sampling and coding. Document availability and the sampling process can introduce bias. Developing the coding scheme and coding always involve interpretation, even of manifest content, and thus risk similar biases to those faced by other measurement techniques (Insch et al., 1997). Interpretation of abstract content situated within various contexts can also create problems. Taking a word or phrase in isolation of other parts of the text, for instance, may result in loss of meaning. In addition, content analysis risks overlooking what is not said in a particular text. In some situations, what is omitted may be as significant as what is included.

SYNTHESIS AND APPLICATION TO CASE STUDIES

Understanding content analysis can be challenging. The following is an example for you to expand on your understanding of content analysis.

Upon reading the case study that follows later, consider the following questions:

1. How does content analysis research provide us with information about the utility of frameworks?
2. What could have been included within the data analyzed that was not? How would have including this additional data enhanced the study?
3. How would you enhance the rigor of this study?
4. Would there have been a better methodology to explore the same research question? Why/Why not?

INCREASING THE RIGOR OF CONTENT ANALYSIS

Enhancing the rigor of content analysis within the counseling and other helping professions is essential to strive for to increase the quality and consistency of the use of this methodology. Drisko and Maschi (2016) identify salient areas in which researchers can improve the rigor of their content analysis study. To begin, Drisko and Maschi remind researchers that they need to start with a clear research aim and question with a substantial rationale that supports content analysis methodology. Rigor can also be improved within content analysis methodology, depending on the type of content analysis approach.

ENHANCING RIGOR IN QUANTITATIVE CONTENT ANALYSIS

In order to enhance the rigor in quantitative analysis, the nature of the sample should be clearly explicated. Researchers undertaking content analyses employ many different sampling techniques. How the chosen sampling plan provides appropriate evidence for answering the study question(s) should be explained to the reader. The nature of the sample will also shape the appropriate use of some analytic methods. Researchers should also explain if and how the chosen sample size supports generalizations or transferability across people and settings. Transparent statements of the characteristics of the sample are crucial to establishing the potential replication of any content analysis.

To strengthen sampling in basic content analysis, researchers should give careful thought to the connection between the sample of a basic content analysis and its later impact on the appropriate use of statistics. The use of parametric statistics will often require use of a probability sample, giving each case in the population equal chance of selection. Such statistics are not appropriate to apply to nonprobability samples. Krippendorff (2013) also reminds researchers that the independence of the elements within a sample in basic content analysis is often compromised. Establishing the independence of elements to be compared with each other or that will be used as grouping variables is important in order to meet the assumptions of some inferential statistics. Further, specific sample sizes may also be required to ensure the statistical power of the researcher's selected analysis (Dattalo, 2008).

ENHANCING RIGOR IN QUALITATIVE CONTENT ANALYSIS

Much of the support in enhancing the rigor in qualitative content analysis includes encompassing quantitative components. For example, Drisko and Mashi (2016) support various ways to enhance validity and reliability with coding, particularly when there are multiple coders on a research team. Validity and reliability are significant in the coding process so readers have a sense of how coders stay consistent in their engagement with the data. As such, Cohen's kappa statistic is often used to validate the inter-rater reliability in qualitative content analysis (Drisko & Mashi). This quantitative approach can be viewed as contrary to the very nature of a qualitative approach in content analysis. However, codes and categories must be credible and trustworthy so at the very minimum, we encourage teams of coders to increase interrater reliability, utilization of a codebook (when appropriate), and sound documentation of the coding process and category development. One way in which to demonstrate documentation of the coding process could be the utilization of a flow chart or conceptual diagram (Drisko & Mashi). The transparency of a flow chart/conceptual diagram can further demonstrate the inductive and deductive reasoning that occurred throughout the research process. Finally, we further agree with the call from Storlie et al. (2017) that researchers "consider qualitative content analyses as a rigorous and robust methodology to expand the depth of understanding of salient and contemporary issues in counselor education in supervision" (p. 239).

MULTICULTURAL CONSIDERATIONS IN CONTENT ANALYSIS RESEARCH

Multicultural considerations are essential in every research study published in the helping professions. As helpers, our training has made us aware of the need to be not only sensitive to culturally diverse populations but to also be responsive to those populations. This also holds true in the research that we conduct with multicultural populations. Throughout the origins and transformational development of content analysis, we have understood the importance and significance of context—and without a doubt, various dimensions of identity will indeed influence the context of written and spoken words.

Fassinger and Morrow (2013) recommend best practices for conducting qualitative, quantitative and mixed methods research with diverse populations that can also serve social justice objectives. Through multicultural and feminist perspectives, Fassinger and Morrow recommend that researchers maintain cultural competence as a researcher and understand and respect the values of their participants. This cultural competence includes researchers having self-awareness of their different identities and demonstrate transparency so that power differentials are addressed. Furthermore, Fassinger and Morrow encourage the "framing of research in ways that legitimize cultural knowledge and social change goals" (p. 74). All of these tenets assist in allowing for best practices to emerge when working with culturally diverse populations.

We also agree that one way in which to conduct best practice research with cultural sensitivity and responsiveness in the forefront, is to ensure that research teams (coders and analyzers) also represent diversity. An "inclusionary approach" (Fassigner & Morrow, 2013, p. 77) will assist in a deeper understanding of the context in which data are situated. For example, if a team of researchers wanted to complete a qualitative content analysis by exploring the narratives of African American female college students' first year experiences in their residence halls, it would be remiss to not ensure that someone on the research team (specifically the coding team) be an African American female who had lived in a residence hall during their first year on a college campus. Ultimately, multicultural considerations in all content analysis should ensure inclusion of diversity within the research team, diversity of literature explored that is providing the rationale for the inquiry, and when possible, the inclusion of participants in the analysis (Fassinger & Morrow, 2013). We know that the latter is not always possible. However, with adequate planning and the use of best practices prior to starting a research study, steps can be taken to advocate for and with communities that have traditionally experienced marginalization and discrimination.

Case Study

Storlie, C.A., Woo, H., Fink, M., & Fowler, A. (2019). A content analysis of the domains of Advocacy Competencies in select counseling journals: 2004-2016. *Journal of Counselor Leadership and Advocacy, 6*(1), 42–54. https://doi.org/10.1080/2326716X.2018.1545613

BACKGROUND

The 2003 American Counseling Association (ACA) Advocacy Competencies include domains in which counselors can act with or act on behalf of clients, students, schools, communities, and the public. The four authors of the study completed a content analysis on 23 counseling journals (2004–2016) to explore how counseling literature infused dimensions of ACA Advocacy Competencies. The first member of the research team identified as a Latina counselor educator and published multiple articles using various content analyses methodologies. The second member, an Asian counselor educator, also conducted multiple qualitative research studies and content analyses. The third member was a doctoral student and graduate assistant in counselor education and supervision. The fourth member was a doctoral student and graduate assistant in the same department with the second author.

The research question guiding the content analysis study was: How have ACA professional counseling journals integrated the domains of the 2003 Advocacy Competencies? To answer this question, the research team implemented the use of directed content analysis (DCA; Hsieh & Shannon, 2005; Krippendorff, 2013) in which they analyzed data from a deductive approach with the framework of 2003 Advocacy Competencies. Directed content analysis (Hsieh & Shannon, 2005; Krippendorff, 2013) was an appropriate methodology for the study because the 2003 Advocacy Competencies had an existing framework (Lewis et al., 2003) that would benefit from confirming how this framework had been integrated in counseling literature.

RESEARCH PROCESS

In terms of data, the authors sought to collect all articles related to the topic of advocacy in the field of counseling published within 23 ACA-affiliated counseling journals. Each of the ACA sponsored journals were searched in their entirety within the target time frame (2004–2016). In addition, they added in the *Journal of Counselor Leadership and Advocacy* and *The Professional Counselor* because they were counseling journals representing a strong counselor identity related to their affiliation with CSI and National Board of Certified Counselors, respectively. The time frame of publication for these articles was between 2004 and 2016. This time period was intentionally chosen to explore advocacy-specific publications in counseling journals related to an increased interest in advocacy in the counseling field (e.g., Adelman & Taylor, 2012; Paternite & Johnston, 2005) in addition to being approximately 1 year after the Advocacy Competencies were published and endorsed by the ACA governing council.

To start, all abstracts were read and examined for certain key words such as *advocacy, social justice, professional competencies,* and so forth. After all relevant abstracts were collected, each full article was then examined to make sure that the article was pertinent to the analysis. One criterion for inclusion was that the article must address one or more of the six domains of the 2003 Advocacy Competencies. The analysis included both research-oriented articles that involved the data collection and analyses processes and non-research–oriented articles such as literature reviews, introduction of theory and/or models, and case studies. This process led the team to identify 280 out of 6,945 articles published in 23 counseling journals over the 13-year period to be relevant for the study.

Prior to conducting data analysis, the research team thoroughly reviewed and discussed the ACA-endorsed 2003 Advocacy Competencies developed by Lewis, Arnold, House, and Toporek. They also reviewed a large amount of literature on content analyses of diverse topics (e.g., Loveland et al., 2006; Smith et al., 2008; Woo et al., 2016) to guide them in content development and data coding and analysis. The first author created a codebook that evolved to include six basic components: the code, a brief definition, a full definition, guidelines for when to use the code, guidelines for when not to use the code, and examples (MacQueen et al., 1998). The codes specifically included the six content areas directly derived from the Lewis et al. (2003) Advocacy Competencies.

Next, the research team discussed the content areas developed and noted any disagreement. Inter-rater agreement among research team members was influenced by the consensual qualitative research (CQR; Hill et al., 2005) approach guided by the notion that each member of the research team has different but important sets of skills, background, knowledge, and point of view to contribute to decisions regarding the categorization and interpretation of data. Consensus for the content analysis was achieved through collaborative discussions during which the authors contributed uniquely and respectfully via online meetings. Specifically, during the consensus building process, the authors discussed the differences between advocacy and empowerment, and added specific examples into the codebook for clarification. They also added one content area (i.e., frequency of articles) as they believed it is an important piece of information in helping us understand trends of advocacy research in the field. The finalized content areas were: (a) frequency of articles, (b) client/student empowerment, (c) client/student advocacy, (d) community collaboration, (e) systems advocacy, (f) public information, and (g) social political advocacy.

Prior to coding the data, the authors performed a pilot analysis using the articles published in a journal (i.e., *Journal of Counseling and Development* [JCD]), which were randomly selected to see if they could reach consensus on the categories developed in the codebook. They independently analyzed the articles and organized the article content supporting the six content areas identified in the 2003 Advocacy Competencies. During this process, the authors used the summative content analysis approach; they examined each article for evidence of the competencies and critically looked for specific words, expressions, and phrases relevant to the competencies and subcompetencies

(Hsieh & Shannon, 2005). In order to strengthen the findings, they cross-checked each other's analysis (Schreier, 2012) and discussed discrepancies in the categorization. In the final step, the authors independently coded and analyzed the remaining articles and once again cross-checked the analyses and examined any discrepancies.

DISCUSSION

Based on the results of the content analysis, the authors found that the first two domains, client/student empowerment and client/student advocacy, were found to be the most prevalent within the 280 articles analyzed. Community collaboration was also frequently found in the articles analyzed, and heavily apparent when there was a connection with allies. The systems advocacy and public information domains were also apparent, although found less frequently, in the analyzed articles. Intentionality with populations that are being served, in addition to educating the public about important issues related to mental health and well-being continue to be essential to our roles as counselors (Newsome & Gladding, 2014). In addition, social political advocacy was also noted in the articles analyzed. Social political advocacy is not only evident in the counseling literature since the endorsement of the 2003 Advocacy Competencies (Lewis et al., 2003) but has also grown in its role within multiple counseling organizations.

Although there are six separate domains within the 2003 Advocacy Competencies, there was a complex intersection noted in the analysis based on the various levels and types of advocacy (e.g., client advocacy, social-political advocacy). This intersection of advocacy on behalf of the client and of the profession supports scholarship generated from Myers et al. (2002) and Sweeney (2012) in recognizing that client and professional advocacy efforts are both essential for the livelihood of the profession and in our ability to serve clients. The authors recognized that 4.03% of the total 6,945 articles from 23 counseling journals met criteria for the content analysis centered on the domains of the 2003 Advocacy Competencies. They also noted the lower numbers of research-oriented articles versus conceptual articles centered on advocacy.

As noted, one limitation in conducting a content analysis was related to the data collection process. The authors limited their search exclusively to the 23 ACA-affiliated counseling journals. Thus, findings should not be generalized to other journals associated with the helping professions (e.g., *Journal of Social Work*; *Human Development*). More comprehensive searches including American Psychological Association-affiliated, international counseling journals, and advocacy specific journals (e.g., *Journal of Counselor Leadership and Advocacy*) could have impacted the total number of articles selected for the analysis. Additionally, content analysis is non-experimental in nature; thus, one should not draw definite conclusions about reasons for the trends and themes of advocacy-specific articles. Next, in the coding and analysis process, the authors noticed that some advocacy strategies mentioned in the articles belonged to more than one advocacy competency category because they are oftentimes intertwined and cannot be separated from each other. This may have increased the percentages they reported for each category of advocacy competencies. Finally, the authors focused on the six domains of the 2003 Advocacy Competencies as the framework in our analysis. They recognized that domains of advocacy might be different from those of the 2003 Advocacy Competencies, hence, a content analysis based on the different.

SUMMARY

Content analysis research encompasses a variety of approaches to assist researchers in answering salient research questions within the helping profession. After reviewing the historical progression and development of content analysis, we provided a strong overview of basic quantitative content analysis, and three common qualitative content analysis approaches—conventional, directive, and summative. Within each of the approaches outlined, we encourage researchers to be culturally competent and use ethically sound judgment when working with all participants, but particularly among participants with under-represented identities. We further recommend researchers read and use primary sources when considering content analysis and to take steps to enhance the rigor of both qualitative and quantitative content analysis approaches.

STUDENT ACTIVITIES

- Exercise 1: Compare and contrast how realism and relativism is embedded within the different approaches in content analysis

- Exercise 2: Develop two research questions, one with the aim of using basic quantitative content analysis and the other with the aim of using one of the three qualitative approaches discussed in this chapter. How do these research questions differ? What is similar about them? Why would a content analysis approach be the best method for your research question(s)?

- Exercise 3: Obtain the research and conceptual articles from the last 3 years in the flagship journal for your discipline. Develop an outline on how you would use steps within content analysis to inquire about the following:

  - Types of methodologies used in each study
  - Trends of content
  - Author's discipline
  - Frameworks used

- Exercise 4: Write a research question for each of the aforementioned inquiries.

- Exercise 5: List the pros and cons of each of the qualitative and quantitative content analysis approaches in this chapter. In which ways do you see their utility in your philosophy of research? In which ways do you see yourself gravitating toward other methods in order to answer your research questions?

ADDITIONAL RESOURCES

Software Recommendations

- Nvivo
- Atlas Ti
- Microsoft Excel
- R- RQDA package – assists with both textual and numerical information.

▦ We recommend that students and emerging researchers understand that software in relation to content analysis assists in the organization of lots of data. It should be noted that software does not assist in the coding or analysis of data; that is the job of the researcher

Helpful Links

▦ https://www.terry.uga.edu/management/contentanalysis/research/

▦ https://www.mailman.columbia.edu/research/population-health-methods/content-analysis

▦ https://www.tandfonline.com/doi/pdf/10.1080/07399339209516006

Helpful Books

Drisko, J. W., & Maschi, T. (2016). *Content analysis*. Oxford University Press.
Krippendorff, K. (2019). *Content analysis: An introduction to its methodology* (4th ed.). SAGE.
Neuendorf, K. A. (2017). *The content analysis guidebook* (2nd ed.). SAGE.

Helpful Videos

▦ https://www.youtube.com/watch?v=iZZABFd8cSA

▦ https://www.youtube.com/watch?v=tBbGCQnxqys

▦ https://www.youtube.com/watch?v=Y0__d1QsR04

KEY REFERENCES

Only key references appear in the print edition. The full reference list appears in the digital product found on http://connect.springerpub.com/content/book/978-0-8261-4385-3/part/part02/chapter/ch09

Berelson, B. (1952). *Content analysis in communication research*. Free Press.
Drisko, J. W., & Maschi, T. (2016). *Content analysis*. Oxford University Press.
Franzosi, R. (2008). *Content analysis: Volume 1*. SAGE.
Hsieh, H. F., & Shannon, S. E. (2005). Three approaches to qualitative content analysis. *Qualitative Health Research*, 15(9), 1277–1288. https://doi.org/10.1177/1049732305276687
Krippendorff, K. (2004). *Content analysis: An introduction to its methodology*. SAGE.
Krippendorff, K. (2013). *Content analysis: An introduction to its methodology* (3rd Ed.). Sage.
Krippendorff, K. (2019). *Content analysis: An introduction to its methodology* (4th ed.). SAGE.
MacQueen, K., McLellan, E., Kay, K., & Milstein, B. (1998). Codebook development for team-based qualitative analysis. *Cultural Anthropology Methods*, 10(2), 31–36.
Neuendorf, K. A. (2017). *The content analysis guidebook* (2nd ed.). SAGE.
Rose, S., Spinks, N., & Canhoto, A. I. (2014). *Management research: Applying the principles*. London, Routledge.
Sicanore, J. M., Connell, K. J., Olthoff, A. J., Friedman, M. H., & Geght, M. R. (1999). A method for measuring interrater agreement on checklists. *Evaluation and the Health Professions*, 22(2), 221–234.

PART III

QUALITATIVE RESEARCH

CHAPTER 10

CASE STUDY RESEARCH

Dalena Dillman Taylor and Ashley J. Blount

LEARNING OBJECTIVES

After reading this chapter, you will be able to:

- Understand the etiology and learn the basic components of case study research
- Comprehend the different types of case study research
- Recognize the sequential procedures in case study methodology
- Comprehend specialized areas in case study research (i.e., counseling applications, publishing research in academic venues, multicultural considerations, limitations to research)

INTRODUCTION TO CASE STUDY RESEARCH

Some researchers tend to rule out case studies as a desirable method due to concerns such as rigor, confusion with non-research-based studies, generalizability, intensity of effort, and ability to compare across studies. Many of these concerns (addressed later) relate to the research design and diligence of the researcher in conducting a strong study. When researchers conduct case studies with intent and follow the appropriate steps, case studies can provide invaluable information answering a specific inquiry and offer some of the most robust, thorough analysis of a particular "case." Therefore, we propose that case study research offers an in-depth analysis of a concept/case and provides some of the most holistic analyses of all available research methods. In the following areas, we discuss: (a) case study research and its etiology, (b) when to use case study research, (c) the types of case study methodologies, (d) special issues in case study research, and (e) limitations to conducting case study research.

CASE STUDY RESEARCH

The research paradigm that informs case study research is idiographic, descriptive, and qualitative in nature. From an ontological position, relativism informs the case study approach.

Constructionism and subjectivism are the epistemological positions informing the case study approach; depending on the theoretical perspective of the investigation, qualitative case study research can take a variety of theoretical stances including symbolic interactionism, phenomenology, feminism, postmodernism, and critical inquiry. It is important to differentiate case study research from single study design, which is an experimental or quasi-experimental method that is objective and post-positivistic in nature (Crotty, 1998). Even within qualitative case study design, several authors defined case study research in various ways. The differences in many of the definitions are nuanced. Highlighted in the following are a few of the definitions/explanations of case study research:

- "Case study research involves the study of an issue explored through one or more cases within a bounded system" (Creswell, 2007, p. 73)

- Case study research is often viewed as a methodology or type of qualitative research design (Denzin & Lincoln, 2005; Merriam, 1998).

- Case study research is less of a methodology and more of a researcher choice as to what is being studied (i.e., specific event at a certain point in time; Stake, 2005).

- "A case study investigates a contemporary phenomenon (the 'case') in its real-world context, especially when boundaries between phenomenon and context may not be clearly evident" (Yin, 2018, p. 15).

- Properly conducting case study research means addressing five traditional concerns about case studies: (a) conducting rigorous research; (b) avoiding confusion with teaching cases; (c) knowing how to arrive at generalized conclusions is desired; (d) carefully managing the level of effort; and (e) understanding comparative advantage of case study research (adapted from Yin, 2018).

For the purposes of this chapter, we utilize Creswell's (2007) conceptions that case studies are a type of qualitative research in which the investigator explores a bounded case or cases over time, through "detailed, in-depth data collection involving multiple sources of information...and reports a case description and case-based themes" (p. 73). Further, we include Yin's (2018) analysis that case studies should: "(a) investigate a current phenomenon/variable in a real-world context, (b) realize the case may have unclear boundaries, (c) cope with the situation and realize there may be many more variables of interest than data points, (d) utilize prior development of theoretical propositions to guide design, data collection, analysis, results, and (e) rely on many sources of evidence" (p. 15). Thus, whether utilizing a single case or multiple, bounded cases, your case study research should investigate contemporary phenomena in a real-world context and ultimately aim at answering "how" or "why" questions related to the phenomena in question.

WHERE CASE STUDY RESEARCH STARTED

According to Tellis (1997), case study research originated in Europe, and it was here in the mid-nineteenth century where Frederic Le Play began investigating families in his "The Workers of Europe" case investigation. This case study was "one of the most monumental and successful studies ever conducted in the social sciences" (Thorton, 2005, p. 2) and one of Le Play's main contributions was a system for categorizing family types, which is still used today (Thorton, 2005). Furthermore, Le Play described the "the geographical distribution of family types in mid-nineteenth century Europe" (Thorton, 2005, p. 2), which has since been verified by numerous family researchers in the second half of the twentieth century. In addition to the aforementioned contributions, Le Play was one of the first case researchers to utilize purposive sampling in that he specifically selected certain families that he believed represented a larger group of families (e.g., beginning workings of attempting to generalize results to the larger population). Thus, Le Play is an integral force in case study research.

Following Le Play, another European scientist, Dr. B. Malinowski, embarked on a seminal case study research project where he studied a native tribe in the Trobriand Islands. During this time (i.e., 1914 to 1920), he gained valuable information on the social, economic, industrial, and religious life of the Trobriand Islanders (Malinowski, n.d.) and in doing so, created one of the first and most thorough and methodologically sound case investigations. Malinowski stated that individuals with academic training are far more suited for conducting research as he claimed "…scientific, methodic inquiry can give us results far more abundant and of better quality than those of even the best amateur's work" (Malinowski, p. 5, n.d.). Malinowski (n.d.) contributed three (among many) ideas about conducting case study work: (a) have real scientific aims (e.g., know what questions you want to investigate); (b) place yourself in proper conditions of work (e.g., immerse yourself in the case without disturbing the population/case); and (c) apply a number of methods of collecting, manipulating, and analyzing data (i.e., learning what data matter and how to analyze the results so you collect concrete, factual data, and find sound results).

The earliest case study research in the United States, however, can be traced to the Chicago School of Sociology (1900s to 1930s). Here, a wealth of information was gathered during this time in areas such as poverty, unemployment, and other conditions due to the immigration influx in Chicago (Platt, 1992). This type of case study methodology did not begin to emerge in research textbooks until the 1980s, when in 1984, Yin was the first individual to separate case study research from fieldwork and describe applications of case study research in textbook form. Two years later, Bromley (1986) conducted a landmark investigation on case study research and published a text on case study methodology and its applications in psychology and other fields. Due to the infancy of this type of research, there appears to be misconceptions (discussed later) and lack of understanding of the complexity of case study research. Since the 1980s, researchers have sought to increase the rigor through detailed procedures and clear guidelines of design, analysis, and interpretation (Tellis, 1997). It is important to understand when case study is more applicable, throwing out the notion of a hierarchy of research and embracing matching research questions to research design more effectively. Therefore, the next section outlines when to utilize case study research.

WHEN TO USE CASE STUDY RESEARCH

Researchers argue the significance of case study research (Merriam, 1998; Stake, 2005; Yin, 2018); however, when it comes to human development and behavior, it can be difficult to paint a thorough picture of a subjective experience (Rolls, 2015). Case studies afford researchers the opportunity to investigate real-life situations, without breaking moral or ethical boundaries. One way to apprehend what type of methodology is appropriate for the specific population of interest is to look at what types of studies might fit that specific sample. For example, the researcher can start by asking: (a) can I gather detailed information about the individual or sample with _____ (insert specific methodology here)?; and (b) is it ethically and/or morally acceptable to gather information about this individual/sample this way? Once these questions have been answered, the researcher will have a greater knowledge of the type of research one is interested in conducting and the type of methodology that may be acceptable with that population.

TABLE 10.1 Comparison of Different Research Methods

METHOD	WHAT IS THE RESEARCH QUESTION FORM?	DOES THE STUDY REQUIRE CONTROL OVER BEHAVIORAL EVENTS?	DOES THE STUDY FOCUS ON CONTEMPORARY EVENTS?	EXAMPLE RESEARCH QUESTION
Experiment	How, why?	Yes	Yes	Does Adlerian Play Therapy decrease problematic behaviors?
Survey	Who, what, where, how many, how much?	No	Yes	What percentage of school counselors implement evidence-based approaches?
Archival Analysis	Who, what, where, how many, how much?	No	Yes/No	Who first developed play therapy?
History	How, why?	No	No	Why is the theoretical relationship deemed the crux of therapy?
Case Study	How, why?	No	Yes	How does play therapy work during and across sessions?

NOTE: Data from Yin, R. K. (2018). *Case study research and applications: Design and methods* (6th ed.). SAGE.

When deciding upon your research methodology, you must be aware that in all instances, your research question(s) will drive the design. Although Hancock and Algozzine (2017) and Yin (2018) varied in the number of steps for conducting case study research, all determined that the first step was to compare other possible research methods prior to selecting the most appropriate one (see Table 10.1). Thus, the researcher is encouraged to consider three important criteria when making the decision as to what method to select: (a) the form of the research question, (b) level of control the researcher holds over the behavioral events, and (c) focus of contemporary versus historical events. According to Yin (2018), the top five social science research methods are experiments, surveys, archival analyses, histories, and case studies. We compare these methods across the three criteria, narrowing down the approaches until the researcher ends up with case study as their selected methodology (Table 10.1).

Research Question

Typical questions strive to answer "who," "what," "where," "how," and "why." The methodology is dependent upon which question the researcher aims to answer; and therefore, we examine each of these types of questions. If the focus of the study is to answer a "what" question, the researcher can choose one of two possibilities for their research methodology, either a "what" question that is exploratory in nature or a "what" question that works to answer "how many, "how much," or "to what extent." Exploratory studies can answer any of the possible five questions depending on what is being asked and how it is being studied. For example, "What can be learned from a study of the different theoretical approaches to counseling?" The researcher could use an exploratory survey (i.e., exploring the potential benefits based on perception of those answering the survey of different theoretical approaches to determine which approach might be more worthy of a definitive experiment) or case study (i.e., testing the differences between humanistic and behavioral approaches to counseling as a prelude for selecting case(s) for a subsequent case study). For the second type of "what" question, researchers may select studies to answer "to what extent" the question can be answered. For example, counselors may elect to examine "what have been the ways in which counselors have integrated research findings of particular approaches into their work?" Researchers that strive to identify such ways are likely to design a survey or archival approach.

Similarly, "who" and "where" questions are likely to favor survey methods or analysis of archival data. When the research goal is to describe the prevalence or incidence of a phenomenon or to track certain outcomes, these methods are more advantageous. For example, Lambert et al. (2007) polled registered play therapists (RPTs) from the Association for Play Therapy's database to determine what theoretical approach was most used by current, in good-standing RPTs. The goal was to determine which methods are most widely used to determine the focus of future research and training. Another example is that of clinical mental health counselors (CMHC) conducting a needs assessment as to where in a city might clients most under-utilize mental health services. In both areas, the researcher is asking either "who" is using what theoretical orientation (Play Therapy example) or "where" (in the CMHC example).

In opposition, "how" and "why" questions tend to be more exploratory in nature and likely lead to the use of case study, history, or experimental designs. These questions are more inclined to trace operational processes over time as opposed to frequency of occurrences. Researchers would likely select a case study if they wanted to understand the process of a counseling session or sessions over time. For example, several studies point to the importance of the counseling relationship for change to occur; however, counselors have yet to understand why the relationship is the most influential component of the counseling process. Therefore, the use of case study research could help answer this question by the study of the operational process of what occurs within a single counseling session or multiple sessions over time.

To sum, it is critical for researchers to understand the form of their research questions prior to designing a study. The type of question fuels the development of the research study. There are incidents in which more than one method is appropriate for the specific question. Researchers are encouraged to also consider: (a) which method is more acceptable in their field of study, and (b) can the question be formed to match the method the researcher favors while still answering the goal of the question. Defining the research question is step one of conducting a case study. Additional steps are outlined in subsequent sections.

Researcher Control

At this point, the researcher has narrowed the question to answer the "how" or "why," leaving only three possibilities for research design: history, case study, and experimental. Researchers have no control over behaviors in history and case study methods whereas researchers use experimental designs to manipulate behaviors or variables. To answer the question of "why the therapeutic relationship is the most influential component of client change," experimental designs would not suffice given that the researchers aims to study what is currently happening within the session and not manipulate the process. A history method examines events that occurred in the past, relying on primary documents, secondary documents, and cultural and physical artifacts as main sources of evidence; whereas a case study method relies on direct observations of events and/or interviews with participants (more present focused), providing more options for data. Additional sources include documents, artifacts, and participant observations and thus, case study research would be a solid fit for the research question. For example, researchers could review videotaped sessions of a client and counselor from a variety of theoretical approaches, interview the clients and counselors separately, collect assessment data, and so forth to explain the phenomenon of why the relationship tends to be the key in client progress—resulting in a thorough case analysis.

Contemporary Versus Historical

As stated previously, historians rely on past documents and artifacts. However, a more contemporary history method could include oral histories. Oral histories are a type of interview and begin to blur the lines between history and case study methods. In large part, history methods are considered historical. Whereas case study methods are considered contemporary⊠meaning a fluid interpretation of both recent past and present events. Returning to our primary question in this example, a case study is the most relevant method to answer the "why" of the therapeutic relationship. In the next section, we discuss types of case study designs prior to outlining additional steps in conducting case study research.

TYPES OF CASE STUDY DESIGN
Context-Oriented Case Study Designs
INTRINSIC

This type of design focuses on a specific individual, group, event, or organization—case specific. Researchers who use this method are less interested in creating new theories or generalizing research findings beyond a single case. Therefore, the case is selected based on its own merit, for its uniqueness rather than for its potential to be generalized (Stake, 1995). For example, a counselor may explore the daily schedule of their client, looking for triggers for the onset of behavioral outbursts.

INSTRUMENTAL

The purpose of instrumental case study designs is to gain a better understanding of a theoretical question or problem that strengthens the answer. Researchers select a case to aid in greater understanding of a theory or phenomenon. Sometimes the researcher opts to select an "atypical" case, which can provide information regarding potential causes, processes, and/or competing theories for a phenomenon. For example, counselor educators want to understand how counselors-in-training acquire multicultural awareness and knowledge or educators want to examine student outcomes in a single play therapy course (see Dillman Taylor et al., 2017 for a full example).

COLLECTIVE

This design—multiple case studies⊠combines the first two: addressing an issue *and* attempting to conceptualize a theory supporting the issue to add to the literature base. This method includes conducting several instrumental case studies. The researcher selects multiple cases for inquiry. Some advantages of utilizing a collective design include comparing cases and replication of findings from one case. Yin (2009) suggested using three cases for replication if the theory is relevantly simple or five cases if the theory is more complex. For instance, a counseling researcher exploring each of the foundational counseling skills as it relates to the theory of therapeutic alliance in a series of studies, would fall under a collective replication design.

PURPOSE-ORIENTED CASE STUDY DESIGNS

Exploratory

In exploratory case studies, fieldwork and data collection may be undertaken prior to defining the research questions and hypotheses. This type of study has been considered a prelude to some social science research. However, the framework of the study must be created ahead of time. For example, researchers may opt to conduct pilot projects to determine final protocols that will be used prior to implementing a larger study. Through the pilot project, researchers may find that some questions need to be dropped, added, or reworded to capture more relevant data. Further, selecting cases can be a difficult process, but the literature provides guidance in this area (Yin, 1989a). Stake (1995) recommended that selection of cases offers the opportunity to maximize what can be learned, knowing that time is limited. Hence, the cases that are selected should be easy and utilize willing subjects that can provide preliminary data in this exploratory design.

Descriptive

Descriptive cases require that the investigator begin with a descriptive theory or face the possibility that problems will occur during the project. Pyecha (1988) used this methodology to study special education, using a pattern-matching procedure. Researchers studied several states and compared the data about each state's activities to another, with idealized theoretic patterns. Thus, what is implied in this type of study is the formation of hypotheses of cause–effect relationships. Descriptive theory, therefore, must cover the depth and scope of the case under investigation. The selection of cases and the unit of analysis develops in the same manner as the other types of case studies.

Explanatory

Explanatory cases are suitable for doing causal studies. In complex and multivariate cases, the analysis can make use of pattern-matching techniques. Yin and Moore (1988) conducted a study to examine the reason why some research findings get into practical use. They used a funded research project as the unit of analysis, where the topic was constant but the project varied. They explained the utilization outcomes by three rival theories: a knowledge-driven theory, a problem-solving theory, and a social-interaction theory.

Knowledge-driven theory means that ideas and discoveries from basic research eventually become commercial products. For example, a knowledge-driven theory might include a new version of a vehicle that takes into account crash-tests, safety ratings, comfortability, and a variety of other basic research variables. Problem-solving theory follows the same path, but originates not with a researcher, but with an external source identifying a problem. A problem-solving theory might also result in a new version of a vehicle, but the change/upgrade would be based on an external issue (like poor performance ratings) which would lead a researcher to find a better option to increase the vehicle's performance. The social-interaction theory claims that researchers and users belong to overlapping professional networks and are in frequent communication. Finally, a social-interaction theory example would include counseling researchers and counselors in the field working together to provide feedback to one another to improve counseling skills and counseling progress for clients. Researchers can conduct a case study that provides information about the counseling process as discussed earlier and provide this information to counselors. In turn, counselors implement research findings and provide feedback about what aspects work for which clientele best.

SEQUENTIAL PROCEDURES IN CASE STUDY RESEARCH

We adapted the steps for sequential procedures for case study research from Hancock and Algozzine's (2017) nine activities and Yin's (2018) six-step process. Our final model includes eight steps to guide the researcher in conducting quality case study research. By following these steps, researchers are less likely to commit common errors that reduce the credibility of their work in case study research. We outlined each of the steps previously in Table 10.1.

STEP 1. SETTING THE STAGE

Within the planning process, there are two steps: setting the stage and determining what we know. We discuss the process of setting the stage here. A quality case study research project consists of thorough planning prior to implementation. Setting the stage requires the researcher to examine: (a) What is to be studied? and (b) why is case study research most appropriate for this study? Refer to Table 10.1 for a refresher on how to determine the best method of research design for the study. Sometimes case study research is used among researchers as a catchall category. However, true case study research is defined as "conducting an empirical investigation of contemporary phenomenon within its natural context using multiple sources of evidence (Hancock & Algozzine, 2017, p. 15). Therefore, within this step, the researcher is encouraged to examine their study to ensure that it aligns with the definition of case study research prior to moving forward. Hancock and Algozzine (2017) created a checklist to help with this step. The researcher is highly encouraged to reflect through these planning questions prior to deciding on moving forward with case study research:

1. **Does the research topic address a question(s) that focuses on describing, documenting, or discovering characteristics of an individual, group, organization, or phenomenon?**

2. Does previous research literature support using case study methods to address similar questions?

3. Do the context and time frame for the research support case study methods?

4. Are data available to answer questions that focus on describing, documenting, or discovering characteristics of an individual, group, organization, or phenomenon under investigation?

5. Are data collection procedures feasible and clearly described in a research plan?

6. Is the potential for research bias controllable?

7. Are case study data collection strategies (e.g., participant observations, interviews, field notes, ongoing reanalysis) appropriate for and consistent with the purpose of the research?

8. Are technical adequacy expectations related to validity, reliability, and generalizability manageable?

9. Are case study data analysis strategies (e.g., categorizing, recombining, cross-checking) appropriate for and consistent with the purpose of the research?

10. Will answers to research questions and conclusions derived from the data support theory expansion and improved practice? (Hancock & Algozzine, 2017, p. 6).

If the majority of the answers to these questions is yes, then the researcher is most likely to use case study methodology.

Before diving into the case study process, it is also important for researchers to weigh the pros/cons of this type of methodology. Common concerns include rigor, confusion with the inclusion of "nonresearch" case studies, generalizability, effort, and comparative advantage (in other words, experimental designs are often considered stronger). Researchers can acknowledge these concerns and address those in their rigorous design through deliberate planning and following systematic procedures (see the limitations section at the end of this chapter for more information).

STEP 2. DETERMINING WHAT WE KNOW

Part two of the planning phase consists of determining what we know. Literature reviews come in handy to provide the background information regarding the topic to be explored. By asking the questions outlined in Table 10.1, researchers can determine if case study research is the necessary next step in understanding the phenomenon to be studied. If previous case studies were found in the literature, what questions are needed to expand those findings? Likely, the researcher will opt for other methods. However, if no previous case studies were found, the logical next step in exploration could be case study research. Therefore, the researcher should allow the previous research to guide the methodology to be used.

STEP 3. SELECTING A DESIGN

This step consists of designing the case study. First, the researcher defines the research design, which consists of five components: case study's questions, propositions, cases, logic linking the data to the propositions, and criteria for interpreting the findings. See Yin (2018) for a detailed explanation of each of these components. The researcher also identifies that theory to support this design, grounding all data collection and analysis. The final decision in this step consists of selecting the design for the case study research. The researcher can select from single- or multiple-case designs and holistic or embedded designs.

STEP 4. SOLIDIFYING THE PROCESS

Any good research starts with clear protocols and preparation. The same is true for case study research. In this step, the researcher must consider their own skills as a case study researcher or decide to expand the team to include an individual more versed in this methodology, train in this methodology and procedures for quality research, develop a protocol, and receive approval from human subjects research (generally known as the Institutional Review Board [IRB] in university settings). Based on the protocol, the researcher needs to finalize the cases selected through a comprehensive screening process and conduct a pilot study (if needed). In revisiting step 2, what we know, the researcher may determine that a pilot study already exists and therefore, one is not needed to continue with their research.

STEP 5. DATA COLLECTION

After preparing and planning for the collection of case study evidence, this step outlines the necessary considerations when collecting evidence. There are six sources of evidence that can be collected: documentation, archival records, interviews, direct observations, participant observation, and physical artifacts. Similar to other qualitative methodologies, it is critical to triangulate evidence from different sources that helps minimize the amount of research bias in the data collected. Triangulation involves gathering evidence from at least three sources to minimize bias in qualitative research. As the researcher collects data, development of a case study data base is required. This data base will enable the researcher to keep data organized and in order. Within this data base, it would also behoove the researcher to keep track of the chain of evidence. This process helps to increase construct validity of the information gathered. Caution is needed when using data from electronic sources (e.g., social media platforms). All sources of evidence could be collected or gathered via social media. Therefore, it is important for the researcher to understand those limitations and cross-check sources with other information.

STEP 6. SUMMARIZING AND INTERPRETING INFORMATION

Interpretation of data is critical; however, visualization is key. Many researchers display data in ways that they find helpful but leave the reader questioning the results or misinterpreting the findings (Hancock & Algozzine, 2017; Yin, 2018). Researchers are encouraged to reflect on what data they would like the reader to comprehend and what is the best way to display those data. Data can be presented as themes/sub-themes, matrices, flowcharts, graphics, sequences, or other methods. There is no right way to display data, yet there are better ways to display certain data. Therefore, in this step, the researcher is considering all options and deciding which visual is best.

Analytic Strategies

You might be wondering; how do I start analyzing my data once it's collected? In general, there are four overarching strategies to consider: (a) following theoretical propositions (e.g., your initial case study presumptions and guiding research questions); (b) working from the ground up (e.g., ignoring theoretical propositions and following your data); (c) developing a case description (e.g., organizing your study around a theoretical framework); and (d) defining and testing alternative explanations (e.g., assessing rival explanations; Yin, 2018). Following your selection, you then move into analytic techniques to guide your data analysis. According to Yin (2018), case study analysis involves five main techniques: (a) pattern matching, (b) explanation building, (c) time-series analysis, (d) logic models, and (e) cross-case synthesis.

In order to highlight the techniques, we will utilize the example of an athlete training for the Olympics. In pattern matching, you are comparing your data with other alternative predictions (both similar and different, if possible). In this area, it might help to think of the "discussion" portion of a general research manuscript, where authors compare their findings with existing literature. If your case study findings are similar to other results (e.g., if your patterns are similar), your argument is strengthened. Regarding the Olympic athlete, a pattern-matching technique might allow you to analyze the current workouts and compare the workouts to other, alternative training to gauge if your results are on pace with others. In the explanation building technique, you are using an advanced form of pattern matching by building an explanation for your case (Yin, 2018). To develop a sound explanation, you will be editing your explanation numerous times and making revisions based upon the results of your case study. With an Olympic athlete's training, the explanation building technique would be similar to adjusting training sessions (based on your results and current research) in order to find the best-fitting workout for the athlete. In time-series analysis, you are tracking a variable over time with the goal of measuring changes over that time period. Ultimately, the time analysis allows you to take an in-depth look at relationships between events over time (Yin, 2018). With the athlete example, you might begin measuring training progress at numerous times, and assess relationships between certain progress and other variables. When utilizing logic models, you are operationalizing several events or data points and attempting to show how they influence an overall event. For example, you might consider how an athlete who incorporates extra training could increase a certain skill and apply logic to make necessary changes. By using a logic model, you are evaluating all the events (e.g., extra training sessions) and determining their influence on the athlete's progress (overall event). Finally, cross-case synthesis is a sound analytic technique when analyzing multiple-case studies (Yin, 2018). In this technique, you attempt to maintain a holistic view of your cases, and analyze data based on entire case-by-case comparisons, rather than breaking the data down into variables (Yin, 2018). In a cross-case technique, you might consider comparing your athlete's Olympic training profile to that of another individual who is training in the same sport. By assessing two entire (e.g., whole) cases, you might obtain a holistic view on a training procedure that could benefit other athletes in the same sport.

Conducting Case Study Data Analysis

Though you have learned about the flow of a case investigation and specifically about analytic strategies for examining case study results, it is important to know how to begin and continue analyzing your data. Case study data collection is emerging, in that you are continuously learning from your data and determining appropriate data collection activities (Gall et al., 2007). The process is generally ongoing, so as the researcher, you will need to attempt to plan with the "end result" in mind (Gall et al., 2007). In general, there are three ways of analyzing case study data: (a) interpretational analysis, (b) structural analysis, and (c) reflective analysis. Interpretational analysis allows you to examine data and find the constructs, themes, and patterns allowing you to offer explanations for the phenomenon being investigated (Gall et al., 2007). Structural analysis is utilized in identifying patterns in "discourse, text, events, or other phenomena (Gall et al., 2007; p. 471). Finally, reflective analysis relies primarily on your intuition as a researcher and allows for judgments to be made based on personal evaluation (Gall et al., 2007). For an in-depth explanation on these three forms of data analysis, see Gall et al. (2007).

Once the researcher decides how to visualize the data for interpretation, Yin (2018) suggested developing a general analytic strategy then selecting one of the five analytic techniques: (a) pattern matching, (b) explanation building, (c) time-series analysis, (d) logic models, and (e) cross-case synthesis. Each of these is explained in depth in Yin (2018). Throughout the process of analyzation, the researcher compares findings to rival interpretations, meaning they look at plausible other explanations of their findings. Plausible rivals are those that are the most threatening to the original propositions. It is not important to consider *all* rivals.

Researchers use this step to demonstrate the quality of their research design and findings. In the analytic interpretation, researchers should attend to all evidence, investigate all plausible rival interpretations, address the most significant component of the case study, and demonstrate a familiarity with the prevailing thinking and discourse about the case study topic. By following these considerations as well as developing a thorough analytic strategy, researchers can counteract the biases of case study research, bringing quality and credibility to their findings.

STEP 7. REPORTING FINDINGS

Researchers need to decide who the audience is for the case study research and structure their findings to meet those needs. Example audiences could be academics, policy makers, practitioners, community leaders, other professionals who are not specialized in case study or social science research, dissertation committees, and/or funders. Each of these groups may have different needs of the type of information they deem valuable. Therefore, it is important for the researcher to understand these values and present findings in the most meaningful manner whether orally or visually. The researcher composes textual and visual materials early on in the process to best capture the data. Yin (2018) outlined six types of compositional structure based on the purpose of the case study (e.g., explanatory, descriptive, exploratory). See Yin (2018) for details about these six approaches. To be exemplar, case studies must be (a) significant, (b) complete, (c) consider alternative perspectives, (d) display sufficient evidence, and (e) composed in an engaging manner. By taking these points into consideration, the researcher is capable of displaying information in a thorough context that the reader or audience can comprehend and draw conclusions.

STEP 8. CONFIRMING FINDINGS

Prior to disseminating final reports to specified audience, the researcher must confirm the results of the case study analyses. Several strategies exist for confirming findings: (a) sharing findings with participants, (b) reviewing final reports by other case study researchers, (c) soliciting feedback from experts on the topic studied, (d) acknowledging researcher biases and how biases were mitigated during the study, and (e) triangulating findings from multiple sources. By participating in these strategies, the researchers increase credibility of their work. Once the researchers confirms the finding, the final report can be submitted.

COUNSELING APPLICATIONS

Case study research has a vivid history throughout disciplines like medicine, business, and law (Rolls, 2015; Yin, 2018), however this form of research is generally less common and less revered throughout the helping professions (e.g., psychology, counseling). Even so, helping fields benefit from a methodology affording researchers opportunities to gather in-depth information about an individual or population. In addition, case study research allows for a deep analysis of unique behaviors, actions, or experiences that might be impossible to study with any other research methodology. One reason case studies are particularly fitting for counseling and related helping fields, is that we often have a desire to develop a deep understanding of a phenomenon. Furthermore, we have a developmental responsibility to thoroughly understand people through the context of their behaviors, actions, and thoughts across bio-psycho-social contexts (American Counseling Association [ACA], 2014). As such, case study research can support a "whole view" approach of determining how and why things are happening in a real-world context, aligning with the holistic view of the ACA's 20/20 vision that "Counseling is a professional relationship that empowers diverse individuals, families, and groups to accomplish mental health, wellness, education, and career goals" (Kaplan et al., 2013, p. 92). In summary, an essential characteristic of case study research is the idea of gaining an understanding of cultural systems of action (Feagin et al., 1990) that allows us to operate under guidelines and recommendations for practice within the helping professions.

Within the counseling profession specifically, the Council for Accreditation of Counseling and Related Educational Programs (CACREP, 2015) has standards supporting the use of sound research methodologies and strategies for conducting research and appropriately analyzing results. Though the most recent version of the standards (i.e., CACREP 2016 Standards) includes no mention of case study research specifically, a case can be made for incorporating and conducting sound research into counseling. For example, Standard 2.E states that "Current counseling-related research is infused in the curriculum" (p. 9). Section 2.8 of the CACREP Standards (2015) includes an entire section devoted to research and program evaluation (see p. 13) and Section 6.B highlights the importance of research and scholarship for counselor education and supervision. Because of the explicit importance of engaging in research and scholarship outlined in counseling codes of ethics and competencies, how to publish rigorous case investigations is highlighted in the following.

PUBLISHING CASE STUDIES IN ACADEMIC JOURNALS

So far, we highlighted the historical significance (and importance) of case study research and how to conduct a thorough case investigation ripe with appropriate methodology, data analysis, and result formatting—now it is time to learn about writing up your case study, specifically for academic audiences. As is common when writing up and publishing other research articles, we suggest the following format: (a) Literature Review/Investigative Background, (b) Description of Cases, (c) Research Methodology, (d) Results/Findings, (e) Discussion of Results/Findings, and (f) Limitations, Conclusions, Take-Aways. See Figure 10.1 as an example.

Literature Review/Investigative Background

In this portion of your manuscript/paper, the author will want to consider any relevant information and *set the stage* for the audience. This introductory portion should highlight the issues/concerns being investigated and make a case for conducting this case study. The introduction section creates the rationale for this investigation and, by including a sound review of the literature, will ensure the reasoning is supported theoretically (Yin, 2017). Another area the author will want to address here, is the purpose for this particular case study investigation. The author may ask questions such as "why am I doing this study," "why am I using the case study methodology?," and "what do I hope to take away from this investigation?" Once these questions have been answered, attempt to make a convincing argument in the form of a purpose statement. For example, the

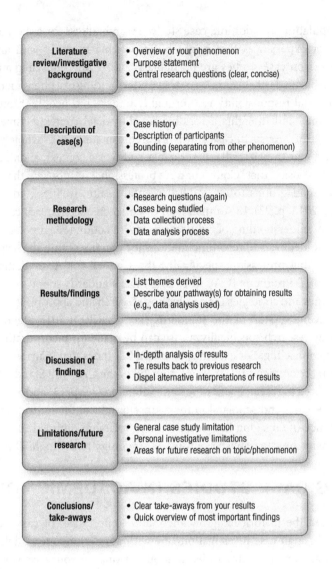

FIGURE 10.1 Case Study Publication Flow Chart.

author might write something like "the purpose of this exploratory case study investigation was to examine_____" or "the objective of this collective case study was to discover _____." Other useful information to incorporate in the purpose statement include referring to the participants in the study (e.g., individual, group); identifying the setting of the cases (e.g., schools, homes, corporations); and finish with an operational definition of your central idea. See Figure 10.2 for an example of a case study purpose statement.

Description of Cases

When offering a sound description of cases, it is important to clearly identify the participants (e.g., individual, group, entity). In this area, the author will need to define the case(s) so that the readers can easily understand who/what is being investigated. One way of defining the case involves developing research questions, identifying the purpose, and establishing boundaries coincidently,

> "The purpose of this case study investigation was to _____
> (insert action verb here such as understand, discover, learn more
> about) the _____ (case being studied) for _____ (the
> participants, such as the individual, groups) at _____
> (research site, such as schools, homes). For the purposes of this
> case study investigation, we define the _____ (case being
> studied) as _____ (provide a general definition)."

FIGURE 10.2 Case Study Purpose Statement Fill-In.

so that the author is able to *bound* the case (Merriam, 2009; Stake, 2006; Yin, 2018). Bounding or separating the case from other cases/participants is essential in clarifying what is being studied versus the "other" things (e.g., the plethora of other variables/phenomenon available for study; Yin, 2018). Finally, the case definition should be idiosyncratic, so that the author has the ability to relate the results to previous literature in the field of study (Yin, 2018).

Research Methodology

Even when considering publication in an academic journal, the audience might not be familiar with the methodological pathways involved in case study research. It is therefore the author's responsibility to enlighten the audience by describing exactly how the research was conducted, in a clear and concise manner. Furthermore, it is critical to emphasize the methodological rigor as well as clearly depicting (a) the research question(s), (b) the case(s), (c) the process for data collection, and (d) the process for data analysis (adapted from Yin, 2018).

Results/Findings

After the author outlines the research methodology, the results section will include the prominent themes derived from the selected analysis. In order to accurately report the case study findings, the author must offer a complete depiction of the results for the proposed audience. The results/themes section will include details about how the author arrived at the results and offer a clear path toward the outcomes (Darke, Shanks, & Broadbent, 1998). Furthermore, the appropriate methodological steps taken in the previous section will allow the author to determine sound research outcomes and counteract the biases of case study research, bringing quality and credibility to the findings.

Discussion of Results/Themes

The discussion will not only include analysis of the results and relate the results to previous literature/research but will contain an analysis of alternative interpretations and the author's reasoning as to why these options are being rejected (Darke et al., 1998). By dispelling alternative interpretations of the results, the author will further support the rigor and reliability of the findings (Darke et al., 1998) and provide sound argument as to why these derived themes are sufficient. One way to ensure the author is following an appropriate format for writing up the results and discussion sections is to find a theoretically sound, published case study and use it as a template for reporting the current results. Additionally, making a table or clear outline of the results will help to clearly identify which areas need to include sufficient evidence to support the conclusions.

Limitations, Future Research, Conclusions, Take-Aways

In the final areas of this manuscript, the author will want to address any limitations, areas for future research, and the conclusions of the current research. Basically, the author is providing the readers with valuable information for continuing this line of research (or similar work), offering a platform for others to build off of the results obtained, and offering readers key take-aways from this case study investigation. In the limitations section, it is important to list not only general limitations to case study research (see the later section on case study limitations), but also personal limitations of conducting the investigation. As examples, if the author made any researcher errors, allowed any biases to guide the decision-making, or had natural events influence the findings, the author should report them as such for the readers.

Following the limitations area, the author will want to provide a few (we suggest three) areas of future research tailored for the audience. Should this study be replicated? Should a different case or number of cases be examined? Take this opportunity to provide suggestions based on gained expertise in the area. Finally, the conclusion should provide a concise overview of the study and list the major contributions of the results. It is here in the conclusion that the author can offer quick "take-aways" for the audience so that anyone doing a swift skim of the article could look here and get a glimpse of the most important results from this case study analysis.

METHODOLOGICAL RIGOR

When conducting case study research (or any form of research for that matter), you will want to take steps to increase your methodological rigor. Specific to case study research, authors can partake in several steps to increase rigor, including using multiple in-depth interviews with the same individual(s); using multiple data collection points (e.g., interview, focus group, document analysis, journal analysis, artifact analysis); employing multiple rounds of data collection over time with the same case (i.e., longitudinal investigations); and using multiple qualitative trustworthiness procedures. Creswell (2003) recommends all qualitative researchers engage in eight strategies (if possible): (a) triangulating the data (gaining data from multiple sources of evidence); (b) using member-checking (get confirmation from participants that you are accurately representing what they said); (c) using rich, thick description to state findings (providing context to describe your results); (d) attempt to remove or clarify any bias (check your personal bias); (e) present counter information (include information that is different or discrepant from your own themes); (f) spend time in the field (engross yourself in the phenomenon under study); (g) use peer debriefing (have an external reviewer who is separate from the research team evaluate your themes); and (h) use an external auditor (have an auditor who is separate from the research team evaluate your entire project). In all, there are numerous ways you can increase the credibility and rigor of your case study research. For many of the suggestions noted, however, you will need to plan and have strategies in place prior to data collection and analysis.

MULTICULTURAL ISSUES

Case study research has the advantage of "celebrating human diversity" (Rolls, 2015, p. 3) in that it allows for deep analysis of individual and/or group experiences. The ability to take into account unique human situations or interactions can come in handy, especially when working within a counseling profession or other helping paradigm. The opportunity to account for multicultural concerns and exceptional issues working with human subjects is beneficial to a field that primarily focuses on supporting human growth and development (ACA, 2014), such as in counseling. When conducting case study research, however, there are a number of multicultural issues that need to be accounted for. Specifically, case study researchers need to: (a) process internal reactions and multicultural awareness, (b) educate themselves on the individual and systemic multicultural concerns relating to their case study, and (c) take the most ethical/most appropriate course of action regarding their specific case(s). See Figure 10.3 for a "quick" multicultural processing model.

In regard to processing reactions to multicultural concerns, case study researchers must be aware of both internal and external reactions to culture, as well as take into account individual, group, and systemic multicultural components. First and foremost, we suggest case study researchers be aware of and acknowledge personal bias related to different cultures and multicultural components. As such, case study researchers need to process any personal and societal microaggressions (statement or action that indirectly, unintentionally, or subtly discriminates against a marginalized group of

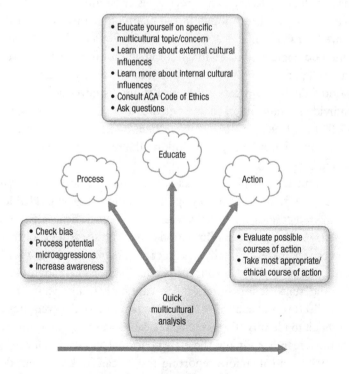

FIGURE 10.3 Quick Multicultural Analysis.

people) related to their participant(s) and work toward minimizing the effect of such bias. In addition, case study researchers need to be aware of common versus specific cultural participant differences (Nevid & Sta. Maria, 1999). For example, case study researchers should avoid grouping cases or individuals based on cultural cues and recognize the specific uniqueness to each case/individual participant. Further, education is a key component in working with unique multicultural cases and it would behoove case study researchers to learn about and acknowledge barriers to working with participants such as mistrust (Nevid & Sta. Maria, 1999), power distance (Robinson, 1996), and primary language (Flaskerud, 1990), to name a few. Finally, when faced with unique multicultural situations, after processing and increasing knowledge, case study researchers can move forward with the most appropriate and most ethical course of action. A positive course of action for the case study researcher includes the ability to provide detailed and rich information, often permitting investigation of otherwise impractical or unethical situations (Rolls, 2015) that would ultimately be difficult to assess using another research methodology. Therefore, case study research is an integral methodology for exploring multicultural issues in counseling, and other helping fields.

LIMITATIONS TO CASE STUDY RESEARCH

So far, we have primarily discussed the advantages of using case study research as the methodology of choice. The results of a case study can offer a robust description of phenomena nestled within a larger context; and at the same time, aspects of the case study that make it appealing for complex problems can also cause significant time and monetary hardship for the researcher. Furthermore, as with any methodology, there are a number of limitations to conducting case study research. An initial concern with the overall product of case results is methodological rigor. For example, if the researcher has not followed systematic procedures or is simply a poor case study researcher (Creswell, 2007; Yin, 2018), has been sloppy in the planning or instituting of the research (Yin, 2018), or has allowed bias or influence (e.g., societal) to affect the outcome or conclusions (Yin, 2018), the methodological rigor is in question. Also, in regard to case study results, a commonly viewed limitation is that of generalization, or the ability to apply research findings to other populations/individuals. With case study results, one is never generalizing to a sample or a population of individuals, but rather, making claims to a theory or theoretical underpinning (Creswell, 2007; Gall et al., 1996; Yin, 2018). Even then, case study results may be difficult to tie to theory or literature, and therefore explicitly linking the resultant "story" to a body of research findings may prove challenging.

Another potential limitation involves confusion with non-research case studies. Specifically, non-research case studies often do not follow specific methodological guidelines, and therefore, it behooves research-based case study investigators to distinguish their work from other kinds of case explanations (Yin, 2018). Yet another limitation comes in the form of contrasting case studies to the nomothetic approach; case studies by design cannot be replicated, as they involve in-depth analysis of a variable (an individual, a group of people). However, though this design can be a limitation in a "scientific" sense, it does not invalidate case study results. Case study research can be time consuming, as collecting and analyzing a sufficient amount of data requires time and energy. Cases can also be difficult to identify (Creswell, 2007), causing even greater time requirements and effort on the part of the researcher. Finally, there are no formal approaches for reporting case study research (Merriam, 1988), and therefore reporting results can look different depending on the researcher and publication audience.

Now that we have discussed the ins and outs of case study research, we would like to walk you through a contemporary case study example to provide an in-depth look. We describe the overview, methodology, data analysis, findings, and discussion within this example.

Dillman Taylor, D., Blount, A. J., & Bloom, Z. (2017). Examination of student outcomes in play therapy: A qualitative case study design. *International Journal for the Scholarship of Teaching and Learning, 11*(1), 1–6.

Dillman Taylor et al. (2017) conducted an instrumental case study investigation "to examine the influence of a constructivist-developmental format on a play therapy counseling course in a large CACREP accredited university in the southeastern United States" (p. 1). The case consisted of a single classroom of 19 students. The instructor of the course approached teaching and learning through a developmental-constructivist lens in which she implemented a collaborative teaching approach. Dillman Taylor el al (2016) investigated the impact of this approach on the overall learning of students engaged in the play therapy introduction course.

METHODOLOGY

The researchers implemented an instrumental case study investigation and followed the steps outlined in previous sections. In particular, the researchers indicated the following steps were followed: "(a) determine if case study methodology is the appropriate approach, (b) identify a specific case or cases, (c) collect participant information, (d) decide upon appropriate data analysis, and (e) interpret the meaning derived from the case or cases" (p. 3). Although these appear different than the steps outlined in previous sections, several are collapsed within this study. See Table 10.1 for comparison.

DATA ANALYSIS

The researchers coded the participant demographics, pre- and post-assessment data. Assessment data were open-ended questions to examine the knowledge gained in this type of course. The researchers then conducted descriptive statistics and content analysis, which consisted of developing overarching themes based on participant answers per question and a coding manual. According to Dillman Taylor et al. (2017), the "complete coding manual consisted of answers for 29 questions for 58 total possible points and allowed for an objective format for critiquing student answers" (p. 3). If discrepancies existed, the researchers met to discuss differences until they reached agreement.

RESULTS

Findings indicated increase in knowledge over the course. Researchers noted that 100% of the participants completed both pre- and post-assessments, with a marked increase of knowledge ($M = 24.57$ points from pre- to post-assessment). The researchers also examined the number of students that indicated zero knowledge on *any* of the pre-assessment ($M = 11.72$) versus on the post-assessment ($M = 2.34$) as well as mastery of content across the assessments (pre, $M = 1.14$; post, $M = 9.52$). In comparing results across the course objectives, Dillman Taylor et al. (2017) found that the students improved in assessment scores for five of the seven measured objectives.

DISCUSSION

Overall, Dillman Taylor et al. (2017) noted a 43% increase in the knowledge gained across the course. They highlighted the use of classroom instruction and course assignments as mechanisms in which to challenge student learning and engagement. They coupled the findings with reflective judgment, in which students enter the classroom with prior knowledge. Therefore, it is useful for the instructor to gauge this knowledge and adapt the learning atmosphere to build upon existing knowledge and meet the developmental needs of the students versus treating each class the same.

This case is one example of a possible instrumental design. In the knowledge that you have gained in this chapter, what are some strengths of the example? What are some limitations based on the best practices of case studies outlined in previous section? What additional information would you need to assess the accuracy of this example? Our hope is not to provide a perfect example but one that provides the opportunity to reflect on the steps in Table 10.1 and critique this example to enhance your learning regarding case study research.

SUMMARY

In this chapter, we highlighted the history of case study research, what it is, when to use it, and how to use it. Although some researchers minimize the value of case study research, we argue and support throughout this chapter that case studies can provide invaluable information answering a specific inquiry and offer some of the most robust, thorough analysis of a particular "case" when stringent guidelines are followed and well-documented through dissemination. Further, we explored the types of case study research (e.g., context-oriented and purpose-oriented designs) as well as counseling applications, multicultural considerations, and case study examples. We embedded student exercises throughout the chapter and concluded with limitations and a contemporary case example.

STUDENT ACTIVITIES

Exercise 1: Deciding on Case Study Research

Directions: We will revisit the checklist for planning for conducting case study research (Hancock & Algozzine, 2017). Consider a potential topic for case study research. For example, you may want to study how the therapeutic relationship affects the client's success in treatment. Or, take a look at the *Classical Case Studies* that follow, and consider how you might develop a case analysis from the information provided. Then, walk through the following 10 questions to determine if case study is the most appropriate:

a. What is the focus of the research question? Does it describe, document, or discover characteristics of an individual, group, organization, or phenomenon?

b. What evidence from previous research literature supports using case study methods to address related questions?

c. In considering the context and time frame, is case study methods the best approach?

d. Within this investigation, is it possible to collect data that focus on describing, documenting, or discovering characteristics of an individual, group, organization, or phenomenon to answer the research question(s)?

e. Does the researcher outline clear procedures that are feasible for data collection?

f. Can the researcher control or attempt to control the potential for research bias?

g. In considering the purpose of the research, are case study data collection strategies (e.g., participant observations, interviews, field notes, ongoing reanalysis) appropriate?

h. Are expectations related to validity, reliability, and generalizability controllable?

i. In considering the purpose of this research, are case study data analysis strategies (e.g., categorizing, recombining, cross-checking) appropriate and consistent?

j. Will the researcher be able to draw reasonable explanations, expand theory, and improve practice from the data derived from this study?

Therefore, as stated at the beginning of the chapter, if the majority of the answers to these questions is yes, then the researcher is most likely to use case study methodology. For your particular example, will you move forward with case study research? If so, what approach is most relevant? If not, what additional chapters do you plan to explore?

Exercise 2: Counseling Completion Success Rate

Directions: Consider the example of a counselor wanting to show their success rate for client completion of therapeutic goals. The counselor has three clients that recently completed therapy. The therapist is wanting to explore why their treatment was successful and led to completion of treatment. The counselor has the following information that can be displayed: length of treatment, treatment goals, and client feedback. What are some ways in which these data could be displayed that provides the "answer" to the counselor regarding client success? Is one approach more compelling than another? Why?

Exercise 3: Developing Your Purpose

Directions: Based on the example in Exercise 2, develop your own purpose statement for a counselor seeking to understand why some clients successfully complete therapy and others do not using Figure 10.1 as a guide.

Exercises 4 and 5: Classic Case Studies

Directions: We outline a few "classical" case studies within the helping professions (primarily psychology) to help illustrate early works. The first story is that of Victor, a young child who was found living in the wild in the south of France (Itard, 1962). The second analysis is that of Little Albert and assessing fear responses in children (Watson & Rayner, 1920). Each case is viewed as a classical case study and the individuals in each story achieved fame to some extent, whether in the developmental psychology field, or as curious anomalies in human functioning. Following each case, we ask a few critical questions for reflection about the analysis.

Case 1: Victor

Victor's case is a curious one, and is generally filed under developmental psychology, because of the in-depth focus on his development when he was "captured" as well as his progress toward acceptable human behavior of the time (e.g., think 1800 France). Though not specified, this type of case investigation could be labeled as *descriptive*, in that the researchers eventually based Victor's training on the "blank slate" concept of human development and attempted to offer changes to his environment to produce changes in overall behavior. In order to gauge the immense behavioral changes Victor achieved, we must start at the beginning (e.g., the "capturing" of the *Wild Boy of Aveyron*).

BACKGROUND

Victor was roughly 4 and a ½ feet tall and his body was covered in small scrapes and scabs. He also had a large, healed scar on his neck, which appeared as though someone had attempted to slit his throat at some point during his mysterious past. Victor was found in a tattered shirt and cared little about nakedness and defecating outside. He couldn't (or wouldn't speak) and would only eat hot potatoes directly from a fire. Victor was taken to a local orphanage and eventually transferred to a place meant for children who were deaf and/or mute to learn sign language— where he would remain for most of his re-integration training. During his training (which consisted primarily of re-education to human-like behaviors) he learned basic functions like bathing, using the bathroom, eating a variety of foods, completing commands/chores, and caring about other human beings. This re-education training was based on the "tabla rasa" theory, that individuals are products of their environments and therefore, behavior could change as a result of environmental influences. Victor was able to connect with at least two adults, a man named Jean-Marc Gaspard Itard and woman named Madame Guerin, who led his rehabilitation and cared for his well-being. Victor was reported to enjoy daily walks in the garden, taking baths, being warm (as indicated by dressing in comfortable, warm clothing when the temperatures got lower), and being around Madame Guerin. In summary, it appeared as though Victor had survived in the wilderness alone for 5 to 6 years and until his death around the age of 40, remained in Paris living with Madame Guerin, who helped with his training and was said to genuinely care for Victor. Upon re-integration to society, Victor was able to learn empathy, practice commands or "appropriate" behaviors, communicate with hand signals and flash cards, communicate limited words, and realize right versus wrong. For more information on this case, see the *Wild Boy of Aveyron* in Rolls's (2015) text.

When analyzing Victor's case, individuals generally attempt to split his rehabilitation into success or failure/civilized or wild arenas. With the information provided, what might you say? Do you feel you have enough information to make a case one way or another? What additional information would you like to have in order to make a sound assessment from this classical case study? Finally, if a "Victor" walked into your counseling office today, how might you help this child?

Case 2: Little Albert

Early attempts at quantifying theories often utilized humans as test subjects; however, this has become more difficult due to the increase safeguards included with the establishment of Institutional Review Boards in university settings. In the early 1900s however, such safety nets were not in place and an individual by the name of John Broadus (JB) Watson decided that he would steer his research toward human infants. It is here that the cases of Little Albert and Little Peter began, and an interest in assessing what conditions fear in children. Though this specific investigation was based on classical conditioning, a case can be made that the entirety of the data aligns within an *explanatory* conceptualization, as Watson used the results to answer "how" and "why" questions relating to Littler Albert's responses.

BACKGROUND

Albert was an 11-month-old infant who was termed a "normal" child in that he exhibited age-appropriate behaviors and reactions to stimuli. Watson and his assistant, Rosalie Rayner (see Watson and Rayner, 1920) put Albert through a number of experiments where they attempted to test his fear response. In one early instance, Watson and Rayner presented a white rat in a basket to Albert and when the young boy reached out to touch the rat, they banged a hammer and created a loud sound. They continued this behavior until Albert was afraid of the sound and eventually of the rat's presence without the sound, therefore conditioning a fear response in the boy. The response was also present with other animals and objects that were similar to the rat, as Albert appeared fearful and generalized the fear to other objects. Watson and Rayner reported the fear responses continued a month after the original period and that they would have liked to try to reverse the conditioned fear, however Albert was removed from the setting prior to any treatment.

In summary, Little Albert was conditioned to be afraid (if not terrified) of white rats and similar animals/objects (e.g., rabbits, dogs, Santa mask). Watson and Rayner have since been criticized for fabricating portions of the "case" and results, such as the fact that they knew Albert would not be available to go through the reconditioning process, a seemingly cruel bit of added information. Academics also question if this was a true experiment, as conditions were often changed in order to "freshen up" the fear response by re-scaring Little Albert if he did not initially react in fear—therefore resulting in inconsistencies in reporting (Rolls, 2015).

Regarding Little Albert's case, what are some of the ethical issues present? Do you think this type of case could be conducted with today's standards of human research? Do you feel as though Watson and Rayner's investigation caused Little Albert harm and if so, in what ways?

As you can see by reading through an overview of two classical case studies, there are a number of themes and pieces of information that can be derived by doing a thorough analysis of the story at hand. The more information you have the better, with the caveat that you need to follow a sound research methodology and learn how to appropriately organize the information that you acquire in order to sift out the important/crucial aspects. Based on what has been discussed in this chapter, would either case study meet the requirements for case study research today? Why or why not?

ADDITIONAL RESOURCES

Software Recommendations

a. Computer Assisted Qualitative Data Analysis

 i.   MAXQDA – Student license $47; https://www.maxqda.com/student-license

 ii. MAXQDA Standard Single-User License Educational $520 https://www.maxqda.com/shop/order

 iii. NVivo- Single User $650 - https://www.qsrinternational.com/nvivo-qualitative-data-analysis-software/buy-now

Helpful Links

▨   http://www.qualres.org/HomeCase-3591.html

▨   https://www.tesol.org/read-and-publish/journals/tesol-quarterly/tesol-quarterly-research-guidelines/qualitative-research-case-study-guidelines

Helpful Books

Creswell, J. W. (2007). *Qualitative inquiry and research design: Choosing among five approaches* (2nd ed.). SAGE.

Gall, M. D., Gall, J. P., & Borg, W. R. (2007). *Educational research: An introduction* (8th ed.). Pearson Education, Inc.

Hancock, D. R. & Algozzine, B. (2017). *Doing case study research: A practical guide for beginning researchers.* Teachers College Press.

Yin, R. K. (2018). *Case study research and applications: Design and methods* (6th ed.). SAGE.

Helpful Videos

▨   https://www.youtube.com/watch?v=ey4D5kKa4VY

▨   https://www.youtube.com/watch?v=kynoEFQNEq8

▨   https://www.youtube.com/watch?v=ectS1ote8uA

KEY REFERENCES

Only key references appear in the print edition. The full reference list appears in the digital product found on http://connect.springerpub.com/content/book/978-0-8261-4385-3/part/part03/chapter/ch10.

Crotty, M. (1998). *The foundations of social research: Meaning and perspective in the research process.* SAGE.

Denzin, N. K. & Lincoln, Y. S. (2005). *The SAGE handbook of qualitative research.* SAGE.

Nevid, J. S., & Sta. Maria, N. L. (1999). Multicultural issues in qualitative research. *Psychology & Marketing,* 16(4), 305–325.

Robinson, S. L. (1996). Trust and breach of the psychological contract. *Administrative Science Quarterly,* 41, 574–599.

Stake, R. E. (1995). *The art of case study research.* SAGE.

Tellis, W. M. (1997). Introduction to case study. *The Qualitative Report,* 3(2), 1–14. Retrieved from https://nsuworks.nova.edu/tqr/vol3/iss2/4

CHAPTER 11

PHENOMENOLOGICAL RESEARCH

Natoya Hill Haskins, Janise Parker, Kim Lee Hughes, and Unity Walker

LEARNING OBJECTIVES

After reading this chapter, you will be able to:

- Identify the paradigmatic hierarchy
- Describe the five types of phenomenological research
- Understand how to increase rigor of phenomenological research
- Recognize multicultural issues associated with phenomenological research

INTRODUCTION TO PHENOMENOLOGICAL RESEARCH

The phenomenological approach to qualitative research is rooted in philosophy and amplified in social justice and creativity. The general purpose of phenomenology is to seek the essence of its subject, and that may take the form of meaning making with a social justice context. Phenomenologist are interested in what lies at the heart of the matter. They stay in deep engagement with the participants of their inquiry and engage meaningfully to understand not only the actions and stories of their participants, but how those actions and stories fortify meaning in their participants lived experiences. As such, phenomenology is a peek into the soul of a community with the idea that soulful exchange engenders curiosity which transforms societies.

Phenomenology differs from other qualitative traditions in its unique quest for meaning making through essentialism. While all qualitative inquiry is an attempt to preserve a unique perspective, phenomenologists highlight the uniqueness as a community value, allowing the reader to engage in transference of a common purpose. Mark Vagle (2018) described phenomenological research as an ongoing dialogue, a way of living, and an encounter. Vagle's post-intentional approach is a bloom on an approach deeply rooted in philosophy, science, and art.

Other qualitative traditions contribute rich yet variant values. Narrative, grounded theory, and ethnographic researchers all value deep engagement with close attention to the particulars of their participants but each approach has its specificity (Hays & Singh, 2012; Yeh & Inman, 2007). The narrative researcher is a story collector. The grounded theory researcher is not seeking but building theory to offer insight toward a plan of action (Yeh & Inman, 2007). Likewise, ethnographers are engaged in prolonged observation of behaviors, customs, and values to describe and interpret meaning (Yeh & Inman, 2007, Vagle 2019)

Qualitative researchers using alternative approaches pursue a cumulative approach to or for a specific phenomenon, like case studies, consensual qualitative research (CQR), and participatory action research (PAR). A case study approach is a detailed and in-depth analysis of a bounded case from a myriad of angles developing a prism of perspective (Singh & Hayes, 2012; Yeh & Inman, 2007). In a closely related vein pushed by post-positivist notions and utilizing a quasi-statistical approach, CQR invites and highlights the idea of consensus among multiple researchers and an external auditor (Hill et al., 2005; Yeh & Inman, 2007). PAR also emphasizes the integration of multiple stakeholder in the research process with the participants being integral research collaborators beyond member-checking (Kidd & Kral, 2005; Yeh & Inman, 2007).

THE PARADIGMATIC HIERARCHY OF PHENOMENOLOGICAL RESEARCH

Ontologically (i.e., the nature of reality), researchers utilizing the phenomenological tradition are focused on the nature of reality and have the perspective that subjective reality depends on how participants and researchers perceive the real world experience (Creswell, 2007; Guba & Lincoln, 1994). Epistemologically (i.e., the nature of knowing), phenomenology is based on how knowledge is constructed with the relationship with the research, the world, and the phenomenon being studied (Creswell, 2007). In terms of the theoretical paradigm, phenomenological research is primarily based in the interpretivism paradigm (i.e., understanding and explaining reality). However, it is also used in the social constructivism paradigm, and recently researchers have used contemporary phenomenology traditions within the critical paradigm. Methodologically, phenomenology research encompasses the logic and flow of conducting a phenomenology study, to include the data collection, instrumentation, and data analysis processes within the various types of phenomenology.

PHENOMENOLOGICAL PHILOSOPHERS

Rene Descartes

Rene Descartes (1596–1650) was influenced by Aristotle and Thomas Aquinas, men of philosophy and religion. He reasoned that all that can be known with certainty is that one exists because one conceives that one does. Therefore, thoughts must exist because awareness of one's thoughts is what leads one to know that they do exist (Ruddle-Miyamoto, 2017). In short, the idea can only exist if you can think it.

Additionally, thoughts and ideas make new ideas manifest, which must have a point of origin. There must be some first idea that fuels the generation of new ideas. As such, Descartes is responsible for setting the tone for the Age of the World Picture (e.g., the starting point for thinking about the human), thus turning the human being into a self-affirming subject. Self-affirmation is not synonymous with all-knowing because one can be misguided or delusional (Ruddle-Miyamoto, 2017). This early philosophy toward qualitative research may have introduced the seeds of strategies for trustworthiness, as credible research requires multiple method and data sources to enhance credibility.

David Hume

David Hume (1711–1776) was a philosopher and historian, who was influenced by Descartes. Hume was highly influential in the system of philosophical skepticism, empiricism, and naturalism. He believed that justice is not implicit in ethics; ethical standing depends on context (Eryılmaz, 2019). Simply stated, values are based on community standards, which can be just or unjust. Hume posited that sympathy is required in large societies to realize and reinforce the rules of justice, while believing that justice for all is not possible for all living beings in all cases. He set the stage for subtext in our pursuit of self-knowledge; the strong decide and benevolence will take care of the rest. Consequently, the state of necessity trumps the laws of justice and equity.

Immanual Kant

Immanual Kant (1724–1804) a philosopher in the Age of Enlightenment influenced Friedrich Nietzche (1844–1900) and Michel Foucault (1926–1984). Kant believed that ideas exist, yet the nature of existence is unknown. As such, our sensibility is passive and receptive, and the nature of understanding is active and spontaneous. The understanding is therefore self-determining (Shaddock, 2017).

Edmund Husserl

Edmund Husserl (1859–1938) was influenced by Hume and Kant, their skepticism and sensibility affected his ideology and he is known as the Father of Phenomenology. Born in the discipline of philosophy, Husserl's phenomenology suggested that the world should be bracketed. By removing the self, one might allow the phenomena of interest to be carefully portrayed as they were experienced in consciousness (Vagle, 2018). A student of Husserl, Heidegger's phenomenology stressed that phenomena are lived out interpretively in the world, therefore the researcher should be bracketed fully as a way to be fully engaged in the phenomenological inquiry. Husserl has had a dramatic impact on psychology with his phenomenological perspectives. The concept of bracketing one's experience is oriented toward client-centered practice (Englander, 2018).

DESCRIPTIVE PHENOMENOLOGY

Descriptive phenomenology is rooted in the 20th century philosophical traditions of Edmund Husserl (Reiners, 2012). Consistent with the essence of phenomenological research, Husserl believed that meaning could be derived from an individual's everyday experience. His stance, however, was grounded in the assumption that reality is objective and independent of context (Lopez & Willis, 2004). Accordingly, descriptive phenomenology is based on the premise that specific features of any lived experience (or phenomenon) are common to all people who have the shared experience, representing a universal essence or true nature of the phenomenon (Lopez & Willis, 2004; Wojnar & Swanson, 2007). As such, scholars suggest that descriptive phenomenology is nomothetic in nature. The focus is on the generality of the phenomenon wherein anyone with the specific experience should able to identify their own experience in the proposed description of the phenomenon of study (Englander, 2012; Wojnar & Swanson, 2007).

Husserl further proposed that the description of the phenomenon of study should be based on the research participants' lived experiences, as informed by their point of view (Wojnar & Swanson,

2007). In this sense, the researcher should abandon or suspend all suppositions, knowledge, preconceived opinions, and their own lived reality in relation to the phenomenon (Giorgi et al., 2017; Reiners, 2012; Wojnar & Swanson, 2007). The focus then is on the consciousness of the research participant rather than the researcher themselves, in which the description of the phenomenon is a result of information the participant directly presents (Giorgi et al., 2017; Wojnar & Swanson, 2007).

Procedures

When determining if descriptive phenomenology is the most appropriate approach for one's research study, researchers should ask themselves, "What is the purpose of this inquiry?" If the researcher wants to describe the phenomenon under study and set aside their own biases, knowledge, and suppositions, descriptive phenomenology is an appropriate method (Reiners, 2012). Consequently, some scholars suggest that the researcher should withhold engaging in a comprehensive literature review in an attempt to neutralize their personal biases, prior knowledge, and preconceptions (Lopez & Willis, 2004; Wojnar & Swanson, 2007). On the other hand, Wojnar and Swason (2007) explained that "the literature itself may even serve as a source to neutralize personal bias" (p. 173), which can then be followed by the researchers' quest to discover universal aspects of a phenomenon that were never conceptualized or incompletely conceptualized in prior research (Englander, 2012). From there, the research question(s) should be developed. As the first step in the inquiry process, the researcher must be careful to ensure that the main questions are consistent with the philosophy of descriptive phenomenology. According to Lopez and Willis (2004), this entails the inclusion of research questions that are consistent with the researcher's goal to only describe the participants' lived experiences in relation to the topic of study.

As an example, the first author and a group of colleagues conducted a qualitative study using descriptive phenomenology as the guiding methodology (Crumb et al., 2019). The purpose of the study was to explore the experiences of 15 professional counselors who worked with clients living in impoverished rural communities. After conducting a review of the literature in relation to the area of inquiry, the researchers determined that more information was needed to understand how counselors multicultural knowledge and awareness are applied to the practice of evidence-based social justice advocacy. As such, the purpose of the study was to develop an understanding of the participants' lived experiences as mental health counselors who work in rural, persistently poor communities and to identify how those counselors incorporated social justice advocacy into their counseling practices. The core research question was: What are the lived experiences of mental health counselors working in rural, persistently poor communities? As reflected in the research question, the researchers were only interested in describing the participants' experiences rather than interpreting how the participants' made sense of their experiences (see the section on Interpretative Phenomenological Analysis).

As is the case with most qualitative studies, the total number of participants is not the focus of studies grounded in descriptive phenomenology (Giorgi et al., 2017). Instead, the researcher should recruit and include individuals who have lived experiences that are consistent with the phenomenon of study. Using the aforementioned study conducted by Crumb et al. (2019) as an example, the researchers utilized purposeful criterion sampling (Patton, 2014). The fifteen participants were selected for the study based on their status as professional counselors who worked in persistently poor rural locales (this information was acquired through a pre-screening questionnaire).

Data Collection

Though researchers could collect descriptions of participants' experiences via written accounts (e.g., personal diaries), interviewing research participants remain to be the primary method of data collection when executing a descriptive phenomenological study (Englander, 2012; Giorgi, 2012). Englander (2012) suggests that unstructured interviews are suitable for studies grounded in this approach as long as the research participants are prompted to describe their experiences in relation to the phenomenon under study. Nevertheless, the researcher's use of a semi-structured interview protocol is a more common approach to interviewing research participants when utilizing descriptive phenomenology (Englander 2012; Giorgi et al., 2017). The number of interview questions can vary as well, as long as the questions are situated within the context of having the research participants describe their experiences. For example, Englander (2012) indicated that the first question interviewers should ask the participants is, "Can you please describe as detailed as possible a situation in which you experienced 'a phenomenon'[?]" (p. 26). The remaining questions should then prompt the participants to expand upon content shared with a focus on the phenomenon being studied.

Englander (2012) further suggested that researchers can use as few as five questions to explore the participants' lived experiences, though lengthier interview protocols are acceptable as well. Indeed, Crumb et al. (2019) created a 12-question semi-structured interview protocol to understand the participants' experiences with incorporating social justice advocacy into their professional practice. The questions were framed in such a way that prompted the participants to describe their (a) general experiences as counselors working in rural, poor communities and (b) specific experiences with employing social justice counseling using the Multicultural and Social Justice Counseling Competencies (MSJCC) as a basis for understanding the counselors' professional experiences. It is important to note that Englander (2012, p. 23) cautioned researchers to be careful with lengthier interview protocols in an attempt to be "overly prepared." In this sense, researchers may unintentionally lead the participants to specific answers instead of directing participants to share their lived experiences (Giorgi, 2009).

Data Analysis

Bracketing, used to neutralize the researcher, is a critical step in the data analysis process given that the researcher must withhold any preconceived notions and prior knowledge when seeking to understand the participants' experiences (Giorgi et al., 2017; Lopez & Willis, 2004; Wojnar & Swanson, 2007). Bracketing entails the researcher actively and consciously stripping away their prior knowledge and biases to avoid influencing the description of the phenomenon. According to Wojnar and Swanson (2007), bracketing may be accomplished by the investigator writing down their observations, assumptions, and confusions using a reflective diary (or field notes), or by maintaining ongoing caution about the role personal biases play when making sense of the data.

For instance, Crumb and colleagues explained that they bracketed their personal thoughts and feelings in relation to the research topic, discussed any biases they possessed that could have influenced their interpretation of the data, and strived to account for their assumptions and biases when describing their participants' experiences. As discussed in their article, Crumb et al. (2019) recognized that the frequent criminalization of poverty was a difficult finding to discuss with the participants. In turn, the researchers met as a team to express their thoughts about that particular finding, and they utilized a graduate research assistant who was less familiar with underserviced populations to assist with data collection and analysis to increase objectivity throughout the process.

Ultimately, data analysis should result in the emergence of themes that reflect the essential structure of the phenomenon (Giorgi, 2012; Giorgi et al., 2017; Reiners, 2012). The development of such themes can be carried out using a structured, step-by-step process (see Wojnar & Swanson, 2007 for a description of Colaizzi's [1978] process and Giorgi et al. [2017] for a description of their multistep process). We will briefly describe Giorgi et al.'s (2017) process and illustrate how it might manifest in practice using the Crumb et al. (2019) study as an example. Their process includes the following five steps:

- The researcher reads the entire transcription in order to grasp the basic sense of the whole description.

- The researcher assumes the attitude of the scientific phenomenological reduction. Meaning, the researcher sets aside "all knowledge not being directly presented to consciousness" and considers what is given as merely something present to consciousness. To accomplish this goal, Crumb and colleagues bracketed suppositions that might have influenced the data, such as the frustrations they experienced with respect to the deficit ideology that is all-to-often observed in research related to marginalized populations.

- Next, the researcher re-reads the description from the beginning and delineates parts of the data into meaningful units.

- The fourth step includes the use of "free imaginative variation" to transform the participants' expressions (implicit and explicit) into descriptions that highlight the meaningful, lifeworld experiences of the research participants. To this end, the investigator's intuition is "fed" through attentive listening and deep reflection about commonalities across all participants in a concentrated effort to imagine "what it might be like to live in the participants' skin" (Wojnar & Swanson, 2007, p. 176).

  - At this stage, Crumb et al. (2019) used free imaginative variation to determine the essence of the phenomenal structures and discussed any differences the researchers' experienced when seeking to understand the participants' invariant experiences.

- Finally, the researcher utilizes the meaning unit expressions as the basis for describing the phenomenon under study (see Table 11.1).

  - After identifying the interconnections and essential meanings of the meaning units within their data and coalescing their data, Crumb et al. (2019) identified four essential structures that represented the participants' descriptions of their experiences. The researchers then assigned a descriptive thematic label to each structure: (a) appreciating clients' worldviews and life experiences, (b) counseling relationships influencing service delivery, (c) engaging in individual and systems advocacy, and (d) utilizing professional support.

Because the data are derived from the participants' experiences alone, the researcher must refrain from adding to or subtracting from the presented information (Giorgi, 2012; Giorgi et al., 2017). Thus, if certain passages are unclear, the researcher can return to the participants for clarity to validate their findings (Englander, 2012; Reiners, 2012). Consequently, if aspects of the data are unclear and participants are no longer available to establish clarity, the researcher should acknowledge such, instead of trying to draw interpretations based on hypotheses, theories, or other existential assumptions (Englander, 2012).

TABLE 11.1 **Descriptive Phenomenology Meaning Units Coding Sample**

SIGNIFICANT STATEMENTS	FORMULATED MEANINGS
People have so little to fall back on, if they're chronically mentally ill or they have a family member who is, they're just out of resources, and they've maybe even burned their natural support. (Adele, p. 3, lines 14–17).	Understanding the client's positionality and lack of resources
With all the Medicaid changes...I've got to take every client into a financial conversation...So keeping myself educated...I can be a voice of support to them and have an understanding if they come to me. (Rene, p. 7, lines 23–25).	Educating self and using that knowledge to teach and support clients
I think [it's important] being willing to recognize that I'm not perfect... being willing to say here's a place where I need to improve (Sadie, p. 8, lines 8–9).	Being self-aware and understanding one's limitations

TRANSCENDENTAL PHENOMENOLOGY

Transcendental phenomenology originated with the work of Husserl in descriptive phenomenology. The concept of transcendental phenomenology was later expanded from theory to research application by Moustakas, who focused on Husserl's concept of epoche and bracketing. Moustakas drew greatly on Giorgi's work in phenomenological psychology (Giorgi, 1985) and the data analysis procedures of Van Kaam (1955) and Colaizzi (1978).

Procedures

Moustakas's (1994) procedures encompass the critical elements of conducting research with people. These aspects include valuing qualitative research, an emphasis on the wholeness of experience, search for meaning, and first-person accounts. These first person accounts reflect the interest and personal involvement of the researchers as well as highlight the inseparable relationship of the part from the whole. Consequently, this foundational framework guides the researcher in the first step of identifying the phenomenon to study and formulating the research question. The researcher intently selects a topic and examines it to ascertain if qualitative research is an ideal fit. Specific characteristics should be included in determining the research question:

- It reveals more fully the essences and meaning of the experience;
- It uncovers the qualitative factors in behavior and experience;
- It engages the self of the research participant, and maintains personal and passionate engagement;
- It does not predict or determine causal relationships; and
- It highlights rich and accurate presentations of the experiences.

After a determination is made that the essence of experience can be understood through narratives or observations, a researcher proceeds. Typically, transcendental phenomenology is useful in fields such as counseling, sociology, social work, psychology, health sciences, education, or any area field where the focus of the study will be on the experiences of participants (Creswell, 2013). Then they proceed to the next and primary step in the transcendental research process to set aside bias and judgment, called "epoche," a Greek word that means to abstain from judgment. This allows the researcher to be open to describe the experience in its entirety.

This process was evident in a study by Haskins et al. (2016) where the researchers explored the experiences of African American mothers on counselor education faculty, the selection of the topic clearly tied to their interests, their understanding of humanity, and the need to use first person accounts to illuminate an otherwise silent population. The authors also illustrated the epoche and discussed how they set aside their bias and engaged in the epoche process. During this experience they bracketed biases, judgments, and feelings related to the phenomenon (Moustakas, 1994). For example, they discussed personal values and interactions concerning their experiences as African Americans and mothers in counselor education. They also talked about potential findings based on their previous experiences and current literature related to mothering in higher education and the experiences of African American women in academic settings.

The next essential process is the transcendental-phenomenological reduction, which moves the experience beyond the everyday and into a fresh new way of seeing the phenomenon. The experience is dismantled and described in its totality in an open way. The imaginative variation phase follows, which focuses on understanding the structural essences of the experience to glean the elements of the experience and how they connect. These aspects were visible in the study, where Rivas and Hill (2018) explored counselor trainees' experiences with counseling disability. These structures of the experience encompassed the role of coursework, they described how coursework functioned in multiple ways to influence the experience and allowed the reader to more fully understand the phenomenon's structure.

Data Collection

Collect data from multiple individuals willing to discuss their experiences of the shared phenomenon. In transcendental phenomenology these individuals are called co-researchers. The primary researchers should typically consider age, race, ethnicity, religion, gender identity, sexual orientation, political and economic factors as well as any other cultural factors that may be relevant to the phenomenon (Moustakas, 1994). However, it is essential that participants have experienced the phenomenon, want to understand the experience, and are willing to take part in a lengthy interview that will be tape recorded (Moustakas, 1994).

In transcendental phenomenology the "long interview" is the method used to collect data on the topic and the question (Moustakas, 1994, p. 114). The interview utilizes open-ended comments and questions. The researcher typically comes to the interview with a list of questions but these questions may vary, be changed, or omitted as the co-researchers share their story during the interview. The interview begins with a social conversation to create a welcoming and trusting space. The researcher then asks that the co-researchers take a few moments to focus on the experience, reflecting on the impact, and then begin to describe the experience. The researcher should create a climate that is comfortable and displays unconditional positive regard (Moustakas, 1994). Once the initial data are collected the researcher can send the co-researchers a complete analysis of the research and request that they review the findings for accuracy. This type of engagement is critical in transcendental phenomenology and is visible in most published studies. For example, in Lonn and Junkhe's (2017) transcendental study where they explored nondisclosure in triadic supervision, they provided a copy of the transcript via e-mail to each participant for review. They then asked each participant to review them for accuracy.

Data Analysis

According to Moustakas (1994) phenomenological data follow a rigorous systematic procedure using a reduction strategy. First, the researchers described their own experiences with the

TABLE 11.2 Transcendental Phenomenological Transcript Coding Example

NEW HORIZON	CODE
I wrote about it a little bit, I grew up with a lot of strong Black women, I've written about the phenomenon of the strong Black woman. And I grew up with a lot of strong Black women,	Strong Black women models
my grandmothers, both of them were widows, um, at young ages like in their mid-40s, early 50s, um, they were left to raise families on their own with multiple children; and they just instilled in me to never give up,	Never give up
If you see a brother or sister in need you do something if you can do something. Don't sit there and be idle.	Don't sit and be idle
I have cousins who walked beside, literally beside Dr. King in marching.	Pride
I grew up in a in a home with women who were (laughing) had a voice.	A voice
My dad always instilled in me also because my dad was a motivating force behind me	Motivating force
He would say there will be nothing that you can't, that you can't do for yourself.	Encouragement

phenomenon (i.e., epoche). Next, the researchers identified significant statements and quotes using a horizontalization process then the researchers used these to develop the content into themes to create a textual description where the phenomenon is described (see Table 11.2 for an example of the horizontalization process).

Following, a structural description of the experiences is provided. Lastly, a composite of the textural and structural descriptions is presented to convey the overall essence of the experience. Moustakas specifically describes two data analysis processes that one can use when implementing his transcendental approach. Both the modification of the van Kaam method of analysis and the modification of the Stevick-Colaizzi-Keen Method of analysis encompass the preceding general data analysis processes, their individual criteria are presented in Table 11.3.

In a study by Pisarik et al. (2017), where they examined the career anxiety of college study, they specifically articulated the use of the Moustakas data analysis process. They analyzed each interview transcript and compiled a list of horizons that included co-researcher statements. The horizons were then collaboratively analyzed, and those that were overlapping and/or redundant and that did not sufficiently add to the understanding of the phenomenon were eliminated. Of the 88 horizons identified in the interviews, 25 were deemed necessary, sufficient, and nonredundant. These invariant constituents were clustered into seven themes: (a) general symptoms of anxiety, (b) existential concerns, (c) pressure, (d) lack of career guidance, (e) cognitive distortions, (f) social comparisons, and (g) economic/occupational uncertainty. The authors also included the textual-structural description, which described the "constellation of physical sensations, thoughts, and feelings that are associated with general anxiety" and how these present for college students (Pisarik et al., 2017, p. 347).

HERMENEUTIC PHENOMENOLOGY

The key figures exemplifying in hermeneutic phenomenology are Martin Heidegger (1889–1976), Hans-Georg Gadamer and Paul Ricoeur (Thompson, 1981). Phenomenology becomes hermeneutical when its method is focused on interpreting instead of describing. Heidegger's

TABLE 11.3 **Transcendental Phenomenological Data Analysis Processes**

MODIFICATION OF THE VANKAAM METHOD	MODIFICATION OF THE STEVICK-COLAIZZI-KEEN METHOD

1. Listing and Preliminary Grouping
List every expression relevant to the experience (Horizonalization)
2. Reduction and Elimination: To determine the Invariant Constituents: Teach each expression for two requirements
  a. Does it contain a moment of the experience that is a necessary and sufficient constituent for understanding it?
  b. Is it possible to abstract and label it?
3. Clustering and Thematizing the Invariant Constituents:
Cluster the invariant constituents of the experience that are related into the thematic label
4. Final Identification of the Invariant Constituents and Themes by Application: Validation—check the invariant constituents and their accompanying theme against the complete record of the research participant
5. Using the relevant, validated invariant constituents and themes, construct for each co-researcher an Individual Textual Description of the experience. Include verbatim examples
6. Construct for each co-researcher an Individual Structural Description of the experience based on the Individual Textural Description and Imaginative Variation
7. Construct for each research participant a Textural-Structural Description of the meanings and essences of the experience, incorporating the invariant constituents and themes
	1. Using a phenomenological approach, obtain a full description of your own experience of the phenomenon (epoche)
	2. From the verbatim transcript of your experience complete the following steps:
	  a. Consider each statement with respect to significance for description of the experiences
	  b. Record all relevant statements
	  c. List each nonrepetitive, nonoverlapping statement. These are the invariant horizons or meaning units of the experience
	  d. Relate and cluster the invariant meaning units into themes
	  e. Synthesize the invariant meaning units and themes into a description of the textures of the experience
	  f. Reflect on your own textural description. Through imaginative variation, construct a description of the structures of your experience
	  g. Construct a textual-structural description of the means and essences of your experience
	3. From the verbatim transcript of the experience of each of the other co-researchers, complete the above steps, a through g.
	4. From the individual textual-structural descriptions of all co-researchers' experiences, construct a composite textual-structural description of the meaning and essences of the experience, integrating all individual textural-structural descriptions into a universal description of the experience representing the group as a whole

later work specifically introduced poetry and art as ways of interpreting and understanding truth, language, and being. Hermeneutic phenomenology is concerned with human experience as it is lived and illuminating details, which may be viewed as trivial and unimportant aspects within the experience, with a aim of constructing meaning and attaining an understanding (Wilson & Hutchinson, 1991). Heidegger's student, Hans-Georg Gadamer, expanded hermeneutic phenomenology, in his work *Truth and Method* (1989), where he examined language, human conversation, the nature of questioning, and human understanding. Gadamer viewed hermeneutics as illuminating the situations where understanding happens: "Hermeneutics must start from the position that a person seeking to understand something has a bond to the subject matter that comes into language through the tradition text and has, or acquires, a connection with the tradition from which it speaks" (1960/1998, p. 295). Gadamer believed that language and its interpretation was the universal medium for understanding (1960/1998). Gadamer viewed understanding as occurring between interpreter's expectations and the text's meaning (Polkinghorne, 1983).

The hermeneutical circle described the constant process of trial and error, where individuals attempt to have the accurate anticipations, which arise out of our expectations and personal experiences. Openness came out of Heidegger's work and the construct of Dasien, which means already being. It captures the notion that one cannot be separate from what is already here within society. Consequently, one should reflect on their pre-understandings, beliefs, values, and expectations with openness (van Manen, 1990).

Procedures

Max van Manen developed a research approach that encompasses hermeneutic foundations and provides guidance for the phenomenological researcher. Paramount in this approach is the perspective that the focus is on lived experiences and the interpretation of texts that are produced throughout life. van Manen (1997) explained that conducting research from this perspective involves an interplay of six research activities: turning to a phenomenon that interests you, investigating experiences as we live it, reflecting on the themes which encompass the phenomenon, maintaining a strong and oriented pedagogical orientation to the phenomenon, and balancing the research context as it relates to the whole. These elements will be described in more detail over next two sections.

First, the researcher needs to determine an appropriate topic for phenomenological inquiry by questioning the nature of the lived experience. Focus carefully on the question of "what human experience is to be made topical for phenomenological investigation" (van Mahen, 1997, p. 40). Then one should orient oneselfs to the phenomenology, answering the question of how you are positioned in the world as it relates to the topic. For example, in a study about children who experienced trauma and the use of traditional and non-traditional healing practices, the researchers positioned themselves as allies and as individuals who had a strong perspective in terms of non-traditional healing practices (Dionne & Nixon, 2014). The development of the research question is a critical aspect of hermeneutics. One should live the question and become the question, it should come out of the lived experience of the researcher (van Mahen, 1990).

Data Collection

The data collection process begins with the researcher's own experiences related to the experience. The researcher should not bracket their beliefs as Husserl denotes but to make explicit what the perspectives, understandings, beliefs, judgments, assumptions, and theories are regarding the question based on their experiences. One should not try to forget these assumptions but to keep them at bay, while deliberately challenging them. The researcher should conduct a personal description of a lived experience related to the topic of study; this description should not include causal explanations or be interpreted into generalizations and is considered one of the first pieces of data that the researcher will analyze (van Mahen, 1990). Then reflect on how this description helps to add clarity to the question. Explore the etiological origins of the words that are being used, which may help to open up the topic and illuminate the past and current living ties of the word (van Mahen, 1997).

Obtaining experiential descriptions from others is typically the next step and takes place using a purposive criterion sampling process. This process is used to ensure that one can find information-rich cases (Merriam, 1998). Dionne and Nixon (2014) recruited their participants through referrals which were generated through trusted, established personal contacts. In hermeneutical phenomenology, multiple tools can be used to gather data: interview, observations, and written protocols. The interview can take two forms, the conversational interview (i.e., initial interview where the researcher collects information about the co-researchers perspective) and the hermeneutic interview (i.e., going back to the co-researcher to dialogue about the interview transcripts). In the conversational interview it is important to have the person explore specific situation, person, or events related to the topic, asking questions such as "what was it like" and "give me an example" (van Mahen, 1990). The hermeneutic interview is a part of the data collection and data analysis process.

Instead of a conversational interview the researcher can choose to have the co-research complete a writing protocol, where they respond to the statement, "Please write a direct account of a personal experience as you lived through it" (van Mahen, 1997, p. 65). The final way to collect data for hermeneutic phenomenology is close observation. Different than typical research observations (e.g., two-way mirror), the researcher attempts to enter the co-research's lifeworld by participating in it. In the observation, the researcher should intentionally observe and then step back and reflect on how the observed situation connects to the topic. After the anecdotes have been written from the observations, make sure to remove any extraneous information that does not relate to the topic (van Mahen, 1997). Experiential materials such as poetry, biography, diaries, art, and literature can be used to future explicate the topic and add nuance that may not be captured from the other data collection process. For example, if a researcher is exploring the experiences of Black women and their intersectionality in America, they may use the speech by Sojourner Truth "Ain't I Woman" where she explores the trials of being Black and the questioning of identity as a woman, to help illuminate the complexities.

Data Analysis

The goal of hermeneutic phenomenological data analysis is to ascertain the co-researchers' meanings from the combination of the primary researcher's understandings of the topic, co-researchers interview data, and any other relevant data sources. Reflection and writing are two specific processes that allow the researcher to make known the essence of lived experience. van Manen noted that "until we write, we do not really know what we knew because writing gives appearance and body to thought...Writing constantly seeks to make external what somehow is internal" (van Manen, 2015, p. 127). During the analysis process, the researchers must continue to have a strong relationship with the research topic, which helps the researcher to set aside preconceptions. The researcher needs to then balance the research context while also taking into consideration the parts and the whole. This process was exhibited by Kierski (2016); when he examined the anxiety experiences of male psychotherapists, he used van Manen's (1997) "principle of separating incidental from essential themes. This was achieved by creating a detailed in-depth understanding of the interviews (Langdridge, 2007) through reading the transcripts several times and in that way identifying the themes" (p. 113).

Consequently, Kierski as well as other hermeneutic phenomenological researchers' data analysis processes consist of a process called the hermeneutic circle, wherein the researcher's reading, reflective writing, and interpreting moves in a rigorous and cyclical manner (Laverty, 2003). This process is demonstrated in Figure 11.1.

Other researchers have devised composite methods based on hermeneutic tenets to analyze data (Benner, 1994; Diekelmann, Allen, & Tanner, 1989). For example, Diekelmann, Allen, and Tanner (1989), developed a method based on Heideggerian tenets, which is typically implemented by a research team and encompasses seven steps:

1.   Reading the interviews to obtain an overall understanding;
2.   Writing interpretive summaries and coding for emerging themes (see Table 11.4);

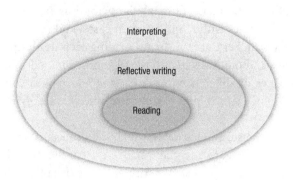

FIGURE 11.1 Hermeneutic Circle.

TABLE 11.4 Hermeneutic Phenomenology Coded Transcript Example

Student: Yeah I think um. And it's interesting while we are talking about this, I'm thinking maybe some of the reason…   we didn't specifically hone in on counseling White clients could be just an expression of privilege that we are assuming people know how to counsel white clients because that is quote unquote norm or majority.
Interest convergence
Interviewer: Right
Student: Um so I feel like specifically talking about it and specifically with   counselors who identify as people of color I think it would be helpful for us to process through what are our own what could our own reactions be in those counseling sessions counseling a client who is White.
Cultural sensitivity
Interviewer: Ok, can you say more about that?
Student: Yeah I'm thinking, like, so…   a lot of people don't know how I racially identify unless they blatantly ask. ***Personal experiences***   And especially, I'm in an elementary school. (laughs) So sometimes it's nice because they will blatantly ask because they are little. Personal experiences
Interviewer: Yeah
Student: Um But a lot of times, I think they just kind of guess and I'm thinking about if I were to counsel a student who was White and they are expressing um racist viewpoints towards people of color not knowing that that's how I'm going to identify. ***Comfort/self-efficacy***
Interviewer: Right

3. Analyzing selected transcripts as a group to identify themes;

4. Returning to the text or to the participants to clarify disagreements in interpretation and writing a composite analysis for each text;

5. Comparing and contrasting texts to identify and describe shared practices and common meanings;

6. Identifying patterns that link the themes; and

7. Eliciting responses and suggestions on a final draft from the interpretive team and from others who are familiar with the content or the methods of study.

Benner (1994) also outline a hermeneutic analysis method as (a) separating paradigm cases, (b) recognizing repetitive themes within and between cases, and (c) choosing exemplary quotes to illuminate themes. A researcher does this by (a) reading each transcription; some participants' experiences will quickly stand out as related to the phenomenon and others could be important because of their similarities or differences; each case should have a connection to the theme; (b) rereading and developing cases to pinpoint themes; and (c) classifying representative quotes to exemplify themes.

To ensure the quality of the study, Langdridge (2007) indicates that analytical rigor, persuasive account, and participant feedback are essential. Analytical rigor indicates that the researchers look at every case and determine if it is consistent with the theme or not. Feedback from participants is also critical to the developing a case and consequently themes. Researchers need to put forth accounts that are consistent with the lived experience. As the researchers attends to these three aspects, it is important to pay attention to the writing process and the written word.

INTERPRETATIVE PHENOMENOLOGY ANALYSIS

A modern method of conducting a phenomenological research is interpretative phenomenology analysis (IPA). The theoretical underpinnings of IPA primarily include: phenomenology, hermeneutics, and idiography. From a phenomenological perspective, IPA endeavors to glean the lived experience by integrating the works of four major phenomenological philosophers: Edmund Husserl, Martin Heidegger, Maurice Merleau-Ponty, and Paul Sartre to convey the phenomenology as one process that exists on a continuum. The next underpinning of IPA is hermeneutics. Hermeneutics in this process is considered constantly open to revision and reinterpretation. IPA employs four influential hermeneutic philosophers: Heidegger, Schleiermacher, Ricoeur and Gadamer. Interpretative phenomenology analysis is also viewed an idiographic approach compared to the nomothetic nature of descriptive phenomenology (Smith, 2004). Even when multiple participants are included in the study, the researcher seeks to understand how each individual's context, culture, language, and so forth give meaning to their lived experiences (Wojnar & Swanson, 2007).

Procedures

As previously discussed, Wojnar and Swanson (2007) explained that the main aim of interpretative phenomenology is to understand the contextual features of lived experiences as articulated by the participant *and* researcher. The researchers' knowledge of the literature leads them to realize that more research is needed in addition to generating specific ideas about how the inquiry needs to proceed. Consequently, the research question and overall study can be grounded in a theoretical orientation or conceptual framework that serves as the study's foundation (Lopez & Willis, 2004). For example, Pak (2018) utilized interpretative phenomenology to examine the lived experiences of Asian American and Pacific Islander men who played massively multiplayer online role-playing games (MMORPGs). Pak sought to gain insight into the participants' lived experiences relative to their race and gender, and the influence such experiences had on their engagement with the online games. Consistent with interpretative phenomenology, wherein an established theory can inform the research, Pak utilized critical race theory (Delgado & Stefancic, 2001) and hegemonic masculinity (Connell, 1982, 1983) as the guiding frameworks to answer his research question: What are the lived experiences of racism that Asian American and Pacific Islander men face playing

MMORPGs? As the researcher also needs to establish the contextual criteria when conducting an interpretative phenomenological study (Wojnar & Swanson, 2007), Pak focused on race and gender as the contextual features of interest in relation to the phenomenon of study.

Given the idiographic nature of IPA approach, a small number of research participants can be included in an interpretative study (as few as two to five participants; Alase, 2017; Smith, 2004). In this regard, the researcher is tasked with employing a detailed examination of each case (Alase, 2017; Smith, 2004). Irrespective of sample size, the sample of participants should be selected purposely and represent a homogeneous group (Alase, 2017). The research participants should share a similar sociocultural background, including having practical familiarity with the phenomenon of study based on their life experiences (Wojnar & Swanson, 2007).

Data Collection

Although data can be collected through focus group interviews, personal diaries/written autobiographical accounts, and photo elicitation (see Pak, 2018), in-depth semi-structured interviews are generally the primary method of data collection when utilizing interpretative phenomenology. In fact, Smith (2004) noted that a limitation in utilizing focus group interviews lies in the difficulty the researcher may experience with illuminating individual experiences in context. An in-depth semi-structured interview protocol can help researchers acquire the information they wish to obtain (Smith, 2004), and the guiding theory (or framework) informs the specific questions the researchers elect to ask (Lopez & Willis, 2004). For example, Pak's (2018) 17-interview protocol included specific questions relative to the participants' racial and gender identity and experience with playing MMORPGS (e.g., What MMORPGS do you play the most? How are Asian American and Pacific Islander men perceived in the gaming world? How do these racial or gender stereotypes impact your life?).

Data Analysis

Compared to descriptive phenomenology, bracketing is not a required component of interpretative phenomenology given that the interpretation of the participants' lived experiences as derived from the integration of meaning making from the researcher and participants (Reiners, 2012; Wojnar & Swanson, 2007). Thus, while Pak (2018) identified his efforts to bracket his own perspectives, he also acknowledged that his status as a Korean American male could impact his understanding and perception of the topic.

Data analysis for interpretative phenomenology can be described as a circular process, involving the interplay between deductive and inductive analysis (Smith, 2004; Wojnar & Swanson, 2007). Research findings can be discussed in relation to existing literature, theories, presuppositions and the researcher's expert knowledge, while also allowing for unanticipated topics and themes to emerge (Lopez & Willis, 2004; Smith, 2004; Wojnar & Swanson, 2007). Hence, though the ultimate goal is to create themes capturing key findings, a priori codes categories can be used in the beginning phases of data analysis.

With respect to the circular aspect of data analysis, Wojnar and Swanson (2007) indicated that the researcher should move back and forth between the whole and its parts. In particular, the researcher should closely examine all participants' individual experiences and relish in observed nuances and the uniqueness of their contextualized lived experiences. From there, a cross-case analysis should be employed to generate key themes based on the participants' collective experiences (Smith,

TABLE 11.5 Interpretative Phenomenology Analysis Coding Example

CODE/COMMON MEANINGS	PHRASES/QUOTES
Model minority stereotype	Uh. I believe we are perceived as the model minority. We kind of just do everything that is correct. Just succeed. We kind of blend in. We don't really worry about social issues. We are just worried about our own personal success. (Participant 1)
Model minority stereotype	I think it is a good stereotype to have but it also limits some of the things we can do. Like applying for colleges it is a bit harder for Asian men to apply to good colleges. You get rated against your race pretty much um that's one thing I thought was pretty bad about the college application experience. (Participant 2)
Model minority stereotype	Basically, the model minority is a tool used by mainstream society establishment to have Asian people perceived as industrious, hard working or what not so they should be so basically better than any race. (Participant 3)
Model minority stereotype	Like we are perceived to be this kind of like this race that isn't going to do bad or anything. Good goody two shoes. Like I've noticed several encounters with cops ended with just a warning or them giving me a lecture. They constantly telling me you look like a respectable young man. That differs drastically a lot cop stories from my friends who aren't Asian and White or African American. (Participant 4)
Model minority stereotype	Like how they say we are hard-working focus on academics and keep to ourselves that is based on how we were raised as children like the ethics and traditions down from our parents. I don't think it limits Asian Americans rather it is like a standard that most Asian traditions have. (Participant 5)

2004). Based on Alase (2017) and Wojnar and Swanson's (2007) literature review, the following steps should be employed when analyzing data using interpretative phenomenology (similar steps were conducted in Pak's [2018] study):

- First, the investigator should read through all interviews to obtain an overall understanding of the phenomenon under study. The investigator should begin to identify common themes and phrases that are repeated in the participants' responses, generate codes for the emerging themes, and write interpretative summaries for such themes. (See Table 11.5 for an example of the coding process.)

- The researcher then re-reads each transcript to clarify differences in interpretation and identify shared practices and common meanings.

- Finally, the researcher develops categories and themes based on the patterns of responses by the research participants. The researcher can also make formal theoretical connections after a close analysis of the data (Smith, 2004; themes are generated based on the researchers' interpretation, returning to the participants for response validation is not required).

POST-INTENTIONAL PHENOMENOLOGY

Post-intentional phenomenology was developed by Mark Vagle (2010) and is the most contemporary phenomenological approach presented here. It combines phenomenological and post-structural philosophies, with a focus on the multiple, varied, and partial realities of experience. Further, in comparison to other types of phenomenology approaches, post-intentional phenomenology sees phenomenon as based in context, ever changing, and being constructed. Vagle (2018) notes that post-intentional phenomenology also expands on the notion of reflexivity in that the study moves with the researcher and their intentional relationships with the phenomena.

Historical scholars in the area of phenomenological philosophy (Heidegger, 1998 [1927]; Husserl, 1970 [1954]; Merleau-Ponty, 1964 [1947]) used intentionality to describe how individuals connect meaningfully in the world. However, post-intentional phenomenology refuses notions of a stable intentionality or meaning, but incorporates intentionality as a means to understand being through individuals' relationships with others and with the world (Vagle, 2018). Vagle (2014) illuminates the flight away from traditional phenomenology. He notes that the first flight focuses on working the edges or margins, in an attempt to reconstitution of our understandings of intentional connection. The second flight embodies the move from subjectivity to existential, cultured, and gendered (Foucault, 1975; Ihde, 2003). The final flight involves the lack of a linear connection but an evolving and malleable or moving relationship among people that influences the experience constantly (Vagle, 2018).

Procedures

In post-intentional phenomenology, the researcher views the research process as malleable and non-linear, often shifting and changing (Vagle, 2014). Consequently, the researcher moves between and around the five-component research process outlined by Vagle (2014, p. 121):

- *Identify a phenomenon in its multiple, partial, and varied contexts.*
- *Devise a clear, yet flexible process for gathering data appropriate for the phenomenon under investigation.*
- *Make a post-reflexion plan.*
- *Read and write your way through your data in a systematic, responsive manner.*
- *Craft a text that captures tentative manifestations of the phenomenon in its multiple, partial, and varied contexts.*

Over the next two sections, these components will be described in detail. Vagle (2010, 2014) explained that to begin the process of conducting post-intentional phenomenological research one must first identify a phenomenon as it relates to how we find ourselves in relation with others and things in the world. He noted that during this process it is important to clearly state the research problem. In this statement, one should focus on the empirical, theoretical, personal, and practical value of the problem to determine why the study is important. Then conduct a partial literature review; the notion of partial is important for researchers conducting post-intentional phenomenology, as the study does not require the researcher to develop a case based on literature nor are existing theories used to explain or predict the phenomenon. It is also important to be able to dialogue about phenomenological philosophies that support the study; a clear and brief description of the philosophy is adequate in the proposal-drafting phase.

The development of post-intentional phenomenological research questions should emerge out of individuals' "intentional relationship with the world" (Vagle, 2014, p. 125). These research question stems should include one of the following: "What does it mean to…" "What is it like to…" or "What is it to find oneself…."The last aspect of component one is the necessity of situating the phenomenon in the multiple varied contexts based on the researchers' perspectives on where it currently resides. It is important to note that these may change as the research process unfolds; as such, it is necessary that the researchers remain open and continue to critique their own knowing and understanding of the phenomenon as varied encounters or performances and not as one distinct experience (St. Pierre, 1997; Vagle, 2014). For example, Smith and colleagues (2019) investigated therapists' experiences with the internalization process throughout the course of therapy, which allowed the researchers to explore their various interactions the therapists had with the clients and themselves.

Data Collection

The last aspect of the first component is participant selection. It is critical that the researcher selects participants that have an in-depth experience with the phenomenon that would allow them to provide a thorough description of the phenomenon. This will also allow the participants to fully represent the phenomenon collectively describing the multiple and varied contexts. The second component is devising a clear and flexible process for gathering appropriate data. In post-intentional phenomenology, the data collection methods can vary widely and belong to other research traditions (e.g., photo elicitation, writing, frequency counts). The most important aspect to remember is that all data collection methods are being used to analyze the units of analysis related to the intentionality of the relationships. For instance, the collection methods Smith and colleagues (2019) used included interviews and arts-based elicitation to answer the question, "What is it to find oneself, as a therapist, experiencing connections with/to clients outside of therapy sessions?"

It may be difficult to determine how much data you need; as a result, Vagle (2014) encourages researchers to collect more data than you think you may need. He also recommends that researchers conduct a short pilot to practice data collection techniques as it relates to the phenomenon being studied. In addition, the researcher will want to align each data source with each research question. The next component, creating a post-reflexion plan, which is essential to the post-intentional phenomenological study, will be described in this section as Vagle's post-reflexion strategies primarily occur during the data collection process. The post-reflexion plan should include: moments when the researcher instinctively connects with what they observe and moments in which they instinctively disconnect; the researchers' assumptions of normality; their bottom lines (e.g., beliefs, perceptions, perspectives, opinions that the researcher may refuse to shed); and moments in which they are shocked by what they observe (Vagle, 2014).

The post-reflexion journal should be used throughout the research process before the data collection and until the end of the writing of the text. Specifically, crafting an initial post-reflexion statement, similar to a subjectivity statement but extending further, as it requires the researcher to revisit it throughout the data collection and analysis process. Smith and colleagues (2019) discuss their use of the post-reflexion plan as a means to push the boundaries of their reflexivity. She described it a time where she reflected upon her own frame and conducted post-reflexion dialogues, which allowed her to engage with someone familiar with post-intentional phenomenology to ensure that she had adequately been immersed in the phenomenon being studied (Soule, 2013).

Data Analysis

The fourth component of post-intentional phenomenology moves the researcher fully into the data analysis process. During this component, the researcher reads and writes their way through their data in a systematic and responsive manner (Vagle, 2014). First, the researcher engages in two analytic "noticings" or looking for ways that knowledge "takes off" (Vagle, 2014, p.135). The researcher may consider what does not fit or what might they learn that is not yet thinkable? Next, the researcher will distinguish lines of flight from other lines operating on us and the phenomenon. This can be done by exploring the following questions and considerations:

- Question: Where might I have retreated to either/or thinking? Consideration: Consider alternative ways of thinking.

- Question: Where might I appear "certain" of what something means? Consideration: Think about where their certainty originates and seek to find uncertainties.

- Question: What have I considered creative and intriguing but moved away for a safer understanding?

- Question: Where might I appear uncertain of what something means?

Due to the nature of the post-intentional phenomenology analysis process, a sample description instead of a tabled example is provided. In her study, Smith and colleagues (2019) indicated that she explored these lines of flights, explaining "I tried to break up these binaries by posing alternative ways of thinking (e.g., poetry) … An example of this was present in the spontaneous composition of post-reflexion poetry. I reminded myself the importance of taking risks and retreating away from something that seemed more 'rational' and explanatory" (p. 68).

The fifth component of the post-intentional phenomenology is crafting a text that captures tentative manifestations of the phenomenon in its multiple, partial, and varied contexts. Before beginning the process, Vagle (2014) encourages researchers to apply two steps. First, restate the multiple and varied context and then brainstorm potential forms. These forms can take various textual expressions. They should also bring together all of your data, your post-reflexion journal, various theories, and different philosophies and constructs. The final text should be coherent and include tentative manifestations and creations that draw on phenomenological philosophy, is situated within the scholarly field of inquiry, and reflects the researchers post-reflexive process (Vagle, 2014, 2018).

INCREASING RIGOR IN PHENOMENOLOGY

To increase the rigor in phenomenological research studies, researchers should consider integrating prolonged engagement, triangulation, peer debriefing, consistent observation, thick description, and an audit trail (Creswell, 2014). Prolonged engagement involves taking the time to learn the culture and establish trust of the participants. Researchers can also use triangulation of data sources and researchers can significantly enhance the rigor and credibility of the study, it aids in confirming the findings (Lincoln & Guba, 1985). In addition, peer debriefing can allow an individual that is external to the study to examine the research process, review the findings, and expose a researcher's biases. Using consistent observation adds a deeper understanding of a situation and can help the researcher focus on a particular aspect of inquiry.

Moreover, using a thick description to detail as much of the findings as possible, the data collection and analysis process is a necessity in phenomenology research to ascertain the phenomenon and essence of the experience (Lincoln & Guba, 1985). Phenomenologists also strongly suggest that using an audit trail can increase the rigor of a study, as it requires the researcher to document each decision regarding data.

MULTICULTURAL ISSUES

Phenomenological researchers are encouraged to implement an open and curious stance toward participants in such a way that they appreciate the meanings each individual has attributed to their experiences (Finlay, 2014). This method requires that researchers intentionally synthesize the meaning and the descriptions that each participant provides about their unique experience (Giorgi, 2009). Yeh and Inman (2007) use the term "culture" to refer to the contextual meanings and interpretations that are rooted within the perspective of a particular group. By its nature, phenomenological research is a multicultural process steeped in the acknowledgment of intersectionality. For the phenomenological researcher, there is a continuous exploration of culture and its influence on self with comparisons and analyses of the participants. Moreover, cultural perspectives are critical to include in the construction and deconstruction of data and meaning (Yeh & Inman, 2007). Phenomenological research approaches work well to address social justice sensibilities when studying underserved communities

SOFTWARE APPLICATIONS

Over the last 25 years research has seen an increase in the use of Computer-Assisted Qualitative Data Analysis Software (CAQDAS; Goble et al., 2012; Paulus et al., 2017; Sànchez-Gomez et al., 2019). In general, CAQDAS programs are designed to *assist* with data storage and analysis, research management and organization, and in some cases theory development (Goble et al., 2012; Patton, 2002; Sànchez-Gomez et al., 2019). Though the use of such programs are not without critique, Goble et al. (2012) and Paulus et al. (2017) explained that some scholars view CAQDAS programs as beneficial because they can increase the speed of data analysis; they enable researchers to manage larger data sets; data can be stored in a convenient digital location; the researcher's decision-making process can be tracked through notes and memos; and they can strengthen the validity of data analysis.

On the other hand, skeptics of CAQDAS assert that the use of computer software packages can impose restrictions on the data analysis process. To be specific, one major identified shortcoming of CAQDAS includes the overall design of many programs. In this regard, scholars note that the structure of many programs implies that the data analysis process is synonymous across various qualitative methodologies (Goble et al., 2012; Paulus et al., 2017). Thus, the uniqueness of different approaches may not be taken into account. Second, because many programs reduce data analysis into a linear and numerical coding process, some argue that the richness and complexity of qualitative data analysis does not readily fit with the quantifying nature of data management, and thus lose meaning (Goble et al., 2012). In the same vein, because the development of codes is a primary feature of many CAQDAS programs, scholars have questioned their merit due to what appears to be an implicit assumption that coding is the only valid way to manage and interpret data (Goble et al., 2012; Zhao et al., 2016).

Considering the aforementioned criticisms, some scholars have questioned whether the use of the CAQDAS program is appropriate for phenomenological approaches (Goble et al., 2012; Paulus et al., 2017; Sohn, 2017). For example, Goble et al. (2012) and Sohn (2017) explained that a main goal of phenomenology is to create a rich and comprehensive account of how a phenomenon is experienced and capture the essence of the phenomenon of focus. Though coding is not necessarily prohibited when employing phenomenology, Goble and colleagues (2012) emphasized that the essence of a phenomenon is not codable because development of such occurs at a cognitive *and* intuitive levels. In other words, separating the data into multiple topics (or codes) may fail to reveal the essence of a phenomenon due to distracting the researcher from drawing upon their intuition and reflecting on the wholistic meaning of the phenomenon. In turn, the end result of data analysis could involve the creation of generic themes that are simply derived from written words (Goble et al., 2012). Consequently, after conducting a content analysis of 763 empirical articles published between 1994 and 2013, Woods, Paulus, Atkins, and Macklin (2015) found that researchers used generic qualitative and grounded theory approaches more often than phenomenology when using two popular CAQDAS programs: ATLAS.ti and NVivo. Indeed, coding is a major aspect of grounded theory research, and Sànchez-Gomez et al. (2019) indicated that most CAQDAS uses appear to be more aligned with grounded theory compared to other qualitative methods.

Because some phenomenology researchers may wish to use CAQDAS, we provide some general and specific tips as outlined in existing scholarship. First, it is important to remember that software programs should be used as tools that assist with data analysis rather than analyzing the data for the researcher (Patton, 2002; Zhao et al., 2016). Though there are a number of software programs available (see Patton [2002] and Sànchez et al. [2019] for a list of such programs), the programs are not designed to interpret the data for the researcher or influence the type of analysis they wish to pursue (Sànchez et al., 2019). Thus, the researcher must bring their creativity and intelligence to the process (Patton, 2002). Because coding and the general use of software programs can be a distracting and time-consuming process for new users (Goble et al., 2012; Sohn, 2017), it is paramount for users to become familiar with the specific software they choose to utilize (Paulus et al., 2017; Sànchez et al., 2019).

Researchers must also be careful how they utilize CAQDAS to avoid straying away from pre-identified goals (e.g., executing a specific methodological approach; Zhao et al., 2016). With respect to phenomenology, the researcher must take on the phenomenological attitude by moving toward a deeper understanding of the meaning of the data and refraining from limiting their focus to the development of code after code (Goble et al., 2012). Drawing from lessons Sohn (2017) learned when using MAXQDA to assist with data analysis for his phenomenological dissertation study, some additional suggestions include: (a) maintaining a reflective researcher's journal throughout the process to stay connected to the data, (b) manually coding some of the printed data/transcripts first to identify meaning units, (c) frequently recording memos and notes when using software to code data, (d) referring back to audio files/recordings to maintain a sense of humanity throughout the process, and (e) meeting with others to spark ideas, gain insight, discuss emerging findings, and so on instead of relying on the software alone.

LIMITATIONS TO PHENOMENOLOGICAL RESEARCH

While there are significant advantages to using phenomenology in the research process, it is important to be aware of the limitations that are associated with this method. First, this approach is reliant on individuals' ability to express themselves typically verbally. It may also be difficult for researchers to establish reliability and trustworthiness. The researchers' bias may be challenging for some to bracket or bridle, which may negatively influence the findings. In this regard, there is the question about the researchers' ability of purely bracketing. It is hard for researchers to determine what is typical for a particular phenomenon. Because the results are qualitative in nature it can be difficult to ascertain their utility. Lastly, the original works of Husserlian/Heideggerian texts were in German, and the translations may not be verbatim expressions; consequently, the meaning may not reflect the desires of Husserl and Heidegger.

Haskins, N. H., Whitfield, M., Shillingford, M. A., Singh, A., Moxley, R., & Ufauni, C. (2013). The experiences of Black master's counseling students: A phenomenological inquiry. *Counselor Education and Supervision, 52,* 162–178.

Several faculty members at a Southern university wanted to explore the experiences of Black master's students at a predominantly White university. The research team consisted of two faculty members with extensive expertise in qualitative methods, two faculty members with over 15 years of experience working with Black students at predominantly White universities, and two doctoral students. The conversation with several master's students and the growing body of research indicated a need for the counseling profession to further understand the experiences of Black graduate students in predominantly White counseling programs to gain an in-depth understanding of the potential challenges and injustices that exist within counseling programs for Black students.

After several discussions, the decision was made that a focus group interview structure would elicit the desired information. Focus group interviews are effective in gathering data based not only on an individual participant's experiences but also on the interaction among participants, which would otherwise be unavailable to the researcher (Krueger & Casey, 2009). Using this data source in phenomenology studies serves to enhance the credibility of the research by providing an environment that encourages interaction and clarification of dialogue among participants and researchers (Bradbury-Jones, Sambrook, & Irvine, 2009; Hays & Singh, 2012). Furthermore, the group approach to phenomenology promotes new viewpoints, enhances discussion, and enriches the dialogue (Palmer et al., 2010; Spiegelberg, 1975).

For this study, we used an exploratory single-category design by conducting multiple focus groups with one audience (Krueger & Casey, 2009). The following research question guided the study: What are the daily lived experiences of Black students enrolled in a master's counseling program in a predominantly White university?

RESEARCH PROCESS

We used a phenomenological approach to understand the essence of how Black master's counseling students experienced their counseling programs. To recruit participants, we utilized a purposive criterion sampling method. Our research team consisted of three Black women who developed the focus group discussion protocol and analyzed data. As researchers, we bracketed our positions before data were collected in an attempt to improve rigor and reduce bias. In addition, the research team explored predispositions and biases regarding Black students' experiences in predominantly White counseling programs. We developed the focus group protocol, using the review of the literature to operationalize the study's research question into focus group questions. After each focus group interview, participants were debriefed as a group and individually. The debriefing process gave the participants an opportunity to ask additional questions and allowed the facilitators to further discuss the purpose of the study. We compiled field notes and research memos from the focus group sessions.

This study adhered to the six components of van Manen's (1997) phenomenological research process. Specifically, the data collection and data analysis process included five steps. First, the audio recordings of the focus groups interviews were transcribed. Second, a thematic coding process was used, whereby the resulting transcripts (26 pages) were analyzed. This method involved two of the researchers (i.e., first and second authors) reading and rereading text, going back and forth between the text and code, coding, rereading, and recoding. Third, the researchers discussed inconsistencies regarding codes and reviewed the transcripts a second time in such cases and consulted with the remaining members of the research team until a consensus was reached. Fourth, a peer debriefer was employed to review the coded data, to control for researchers' biases, and to determine consistency of codes and identified themes. This process, which is indicative of phenomenological research, allowed the research team to derive five themes related to the experiences of Black counseling master's students at a predominantly White university. Fifth, the facilitators compiled field notes on participants' nonverbal behaviors, and general interpersonal dynamics were used to triangulate the data and document the group dynamics and individual idiosyncrasies (e.g., nonverbal behavior; Glesne, 2006).

To build trustworthiness we used triangulation of data sources and researchers, bracketing, member checking, prolonged engagement, and peer debriefing. Member checking took place on two levels. First, during the focus group interviews, the focus group facilitators asked participants questions to check for clarity in understanding, restating and summarizing information shared by participants. Second, at the end of each focus group interview, the research team presented participants individually with a summary of the focus group and asked them to correct any information that was incorrect and/or add any additional information to accurately reflect their experiences. Prolonged engagement and immersion in the data indicate that researchers spend time with data sources so that they are familiar with the intricacies of the phenomenon being studied (Glesne, 2006). We achieved this in the current study by having weekly research team meetings to examine and code the data. Lastly, a peer debriefing strategy was used throughout the process, which involved having the third author, who was familiar with the study, review and ask questions about the findings, the coding process, and authenticity aspects of the study to ensure that participants' accounts resonated with people other than the researchers (Hays & Singh, 2012).

DISCUSSION

We identified five themes of Black graduate counseling students' experiences in a PWI: (a) isolation as a Black student, (b) tokenization as a Black student, (c) lack of inclusion of Black counselor perspectives within course work, (d) differences between support received by faculty of color and support received by White faculty, and (e) access to support from people of color and White peers. The first three themes represented Black student experiences related to or labeled as microaggressions. The final two themes reflected the ways in which faculty of color and White faculty as well as peers provided support to the Black students.

Several limitations emerged from the study. The participants were primarily women. In addition, two focus groups were limited, and more data sources would be helpful in understanding the experience. Although there are limitations to transferability, the study's findings have the potential to benefit Black students in predominantly White counseling master's programs through stimulating discussion in the field of counseling about this area.

SUMMARY

- Phenomenological research is viewed as an ongoing dialogue, a way of living, and an encounter.
- Phenomenological research is rooted in philosophy and amplified in social justice and creativity.
- Phenomenological philosophers laid the ground work for what later became the phenomenological research which connected to how scholars and researchers have come to know how humans connect and engage with the world.
- Reflexivity is a shared construct found throughout all phenomenological traditions.
- The following traditions were described: hermeneutical, descriptive, transcendental, interpretative, phenomenological analysis, and post-intentional, highlighting the distinctiveness of phenomenological approaches.
- Rigorous phenomenology research includes prolonged engagement, triangulation, peer debriefing, consistent observation, thick description, and an audit trail.

STUDENT ACTIVITIES

Exercise 1: Bracket Yourself

Directions: Consider your values and beliefs as they relate to being a student. List your values, beliefs, preconceived notions, and experiences. Consider how these could influence how you engage in research related to students in higher education.

Exercise 2: Exploring the Essence

Directions: When one thinks about one's childhood, there are several poignant events, experiences, or beliefs that shape one. Describe your such experiences in detail and identify the essence and themes that permeate those experience. Now share those experiences with a classmate. Note the emotions and thoughts that you experience during this process.

Exercise 3: Post-Intentional Noticings

Directions: Consider a topic of interest on which you intend to conduct a qualitative study in the near future. Notice the following:

1. Alternative ways of thinking about the phenomenon;
2. Where your certainties originate about the phenomenon; and
3. How you can move away for a safer understanding.

Discuss your ponderings with a classmate. Document your response in your post-reflexion journal.

Exercise 4: Phenomenological Trustworthiness

Directions: Review the noted strategies to increase trustworthiness. Identify which strategies might be most challenging to implement. Explore why this difficulty exists and specify two ways to address this in the future.

Exercise 5: Methodological Triumphs

Directions: The case study provided highlights many aspects that are consistent with phenomenological research. Identify the aspects of the case study that demonstrate phenomenology and which approach is displayed. Identify the missed opportunities and specify two phenomenological strategies you would add to enhance the case study.

ADDITIONAL RESOURCES

Software Recommendations

NVivo Software (https://www.qsrinternational.com)

CAQDAS Software (https://www.maxqda.com)

ATLAS ti (https://atlasti.com)

Helpful Link

- https://plato.stanford.edu/entries/phenomenology/

Helpful Reading

Carroll, M. T., & Tafoya, E. (Eds.). (2000). *Phenomenological approaches to popular culture*. Popular Press.

Friesen, N., Henriksson, C., & Saevi, T. (Eds.). (2012). *Hermeneutic phenomenology in education: Method and practice* (Vol. 4). Springer Science & Business Media.

Colaizzi, P. F. (1978). *Psychological research as the phenomenologist views it*. In R. Vale & M. King (Eds.). Existential phenomenological alternatives for psychology (pp.48–71). Oxford University Press.

Giorgi, A. (Ed.). (1985). Phenomenology and psychological research. Duquesne University Press.

Groenewald, T. (2004). A phenomenological research design illustrated. *International journal of qualitative methods, 3(1)*, 42–55. https://doi.org/10.1177/160940690400300104

Heidegger, M. (1962). *Being and time*. (R. MacQuarrie & E. Robinson, Trans.). Harper & Row.

Hopkins, R. M., Regehr, G., & Pratt, D. D. (2017). A framework for negotiating positionality in phenomenological research. *Medical Teacher, 39(1)*, 20-25. https://doi.org/10.1080/0142159X.2017.1245854

Husserl, E. (1931). *Ideas: General introduction to pure phenomenology*. (D. Carr, Trans.). Northwestern University Press.

Husserl, E. (1970). *The crisis of European sciences and transcendental phenomenology*. (D. Carr, Trans.). Northwestern University Press.

Langdridge, D. (2007). *Phenomenological psychology: Theory, research and method*. Pearson Education.

LeVasseur, J. J. (2003). The problem with bracketing in phenomenology. *Qualitative Health Research, 31*, 408–420.

Lopez, K. A., & Willis, D. G. (2004). Descriptive versus interpretive phenomenology: Their contributions to nursing knowledge. *Qualitative Health Research, 14*, 726–735.

Merleau-Ponty, M. (1962). *Phenomenology of perception*. (C. Smith, Trans.). Routledge & Kegan Paul.

Moustakas, C. (1994). *Phenomenological research methods*. SAGE.

Natanson, M. (Ed.). (1973). *Phenomenology and the social sciences*. Northwestern University Press.

Peoples, K. (2020). *How to write a phenomenological dissertation: A step-by-step guide* (Vol. 56). SAGE.

Polkinghorne, D. E. (1989). Phenomenological research methods. In R. S. Valle & S. Halling (Eds.). *Existential phenomenological perspectives in psychology* (pp. 41–60). Plenum Press.

Van Kaam, A. (1966). *Existential foundations of psychology*. Duquesne University Press.

Van Manen, M. (1990). *Researching lived experience*. State University of New York Press.

Wertz, F. J. (2005). Phenomenological research methods for counseling psychology. *Journal of Counseling Psychology, 52,* 167–177.

Helpful Videos

▨ Study.com. (2020). "Phenomenological design: Definition, advantages, & limitations." Retreived from https://study.com/academy/lesson/phenomenological-design-definition-advantages-limitations.html

▨ Study.com. (2020). "Edmund Husserl & phenomenology." Retrieved from https://study.com/academy/lesson/edmund-husserl-phenomenology.html

KEY REFERENCES

Only key references appear in the print edition. The full reference list appears in the digital product found on http://connect.springerpub.com/content/book/978-0-8261-4385-3/part/part03/chapter/ch11

Benner, P. (1994). The tradition and skill of interpretive phenomenology in studying health, illness, and caring practices. In P. Benner, (Ed.). *Interpretative phenomenology, embodiment, caring, and ethics in health and illness* (pp. 99–127). SAGE. doi:10.4135/9781452204727.n6

Colaizzi, P. (1978). Psychological research as a phenomenologist views it. In Valle, R. S., & King, M. (1978). *Existential phenomenological alternatives for psychology.* Open University Press.

Creswell, J. W. (2014). *Research design: Qualitative, quantitative, and mixed methods approaches* (4th ed.). SAGE.

Delgado, R., & Stefancic, J. (2001). *Critical race theory: An introduction.* New York University Press.

Diekelman, N. L., Allen, D., & Tanner, C. (1989). *The NLN criteria for appraisal of baccalaureate programs: A critical hermeneutic analysis.* National League for Nursing.

Dionne, D., & Nixon, G. (2014). Moving beyond residential school trauma abuse: A phenomenological hermeneutic analysis. *International Journal of Mental Health Addiction* 12, 335–350. https://doi.org/10.1007/s11469-013-9457-y

Foucault, M. (1975). *Discipline and punish: The birth of the prison.* Pantheon Books.

Gadamer, H. G. (1989). *Truth and method.* Crossroad.

Glesne, C. (2006). *Becoming qualitative researchers: An introduction* (3rd ed.). Longman.

Guba, E. G., & Lincoln, Y. S. (1994). *Competing paradigms in qualitative research.* In N. K. Denzin & Y. S. Lincoln (Eds.), *Handbook of qualitative research* (pp. 105–117). SAGE.

Hays, D. G., & Singh, A. A. (2012). *Qualitative inquiry in clinical and educational settings.* Guilford.

Hill, C. E., Knox, S., Thompson, B. J., Williams, E. N., & Hess, S. A. (2005). Consensual qualitative research: An update. *Journal of Counseling Psychology, 52,* 1–30.

Ihde, D. (2003). If phenomenology is an albatross, is postphenomenology possible? In D. Ihde & E. Selinger (Eds.). *Chasing technoscience: Matrix for materiality.* Indiana University Press.

Kidd, S. A., & Kral, M. J. (2005). Practicing participatory action research. *Journal of Counseling Psychology, 52*(2), 187–195. https://doi.org/10.1037/0022-0167.52.2.187

Kierski, W. (2014). Anxiety experiences of male psychotherapists: A hermeneutic phenomenological study. *Counselling and Psychotherapy Research,* 14(2), 111–118. https://doi.org/10.1080/14733145.2013.779731

Krueger, R., & Casey, A. (2009). *Focus groups: A practical guide for applied research.* SAGE.

Langdridge, D. (2007). *Phenomenological psychology: Theory, research and method.* Pearson.

Laverty, S. M. (2003) Hermeneutic phenomenology: A comparison of historical and methodological considerations. *International Journal of Qualitative Methods,* 2, 1–29.

Lonn, M. R., & Juhnke, G. (2017). Nondisclosure in triadic supervision: A phenomenological study of counseling students. *Counselor Education & Supervision,* 56(2), 82–97. https://doi-org.libproxy.plymouth.edu/10.1002/ceas.12064

Palmer, M., Larkin, M., de Visser, R., & Fadden, G. (2010). Developing an interpretative phenomenological approach to focus group data. *Qualitative Research in Psychology*, 7, 99–121. http://dx.doi.org/10.1080/14780880802513194

Pisarik, C.T., Rowell, P. C., & Thompson, L. C. (2017). A phenomenological study of career anxiety among college students. *The Career Development Quarterly*, 65, 339–353.

Polkinghorne, D. (1983). *Methodology for the human sciences: Systems of inquiry*. State University of New York Press.

Rivas, M., & Hill, N. R. (2018). Counselor trainees' experiences counseling disability: A phenomenological study. *Counselor Education and Supervision*, 57, 116– 131. https://doi.org/10.1002/ceas.12097

Ruddle-Miyamoto, A.O. (2017). Regarding doubt and certainty in al-Ghazālī's *Deliverance from Error* and Descartes' *Meditations*. *Philosophy East and West*, 67(1), 160–176. https://doi.org/10.1353/pew.2017.0011.

Sohn, B. K. (2017). Phenomenology and qualitative data analysis software (QDAS): A careful reconciliation. *Forum Qualitative Sozialforschung / Forum: Qualitative Social Research*, 18(1), 1–18. https://doi.org/10.17169/fqs-18.1.2688

Soule, K. E. (2013). *Connected: A phenomenology of attachment parenting* (Unpublished dissertation). The University of Georgia.

Van Manen, M. (1990). *Researching lived experience: Human science for an action sensitive pedagogy*. SUNY Press.

Wojnar, D. M., & Swanson, K. M. (2007). Phenomenology: an exploration. *Journal of Holistic Nursing*, 25(3), 172–180. https://doi.org/10.1177/0898010106295172

CHAPTER 12

GROUNDED THEORY APPROACHES TO RESEARCH

Deborah J. Rubel, Ania Bartkowiak, Robert J. Cox, Danielle Render Turmaud, and Jeremy D. Shain

LEARNING OBJECTIVES

After reading this chapter, you will be able to:

- Identify three major types of grounded theory research
- Describe the general research process associated with grounded theory research
- Explain how to increase the rigor of grounded theory studies
- Discuss multicultural considerations for grounded theory research

INTRODUCTION TO GROUNDED THEORY

At its essence, grounded theory research is a pragmatic way to gain understanding of how people experience significant processes in the complex world in which they live. The target of grounded theory research is capturing how key individuals and communities experience the actions and interactions that are part of important problems in their lives. Building descriptions from those experiences, in the form of theory, may be useful in addressing those problems. According to Fassinger (2005) "The GT approach is so named because its ultimate aim is to produce innovative theory that is 'grounded' in data collected from participants on the basis of the complexities of their lived experiences in a social context" (p. 157).

The grounded theory approaches hold a unique place in the worlds of qualitative research and the behavioral sciences. Some of this unique valuing is due to grounded theory's ability to capture process systematically, which is not offered by other qualitative approaches (Corbin & Strauss, 2015). Grounded theory is also well-regarded by researchers, journal editors, and editorial boards due to its well-documented and sometimes prescriptive methods and raised the credibility of qualitative research with its inception. Charmaz (1996) states, "Furthermore, grounded theory methods undermine definitions of qualitative analysis as only intuitive and impressionistic and of quantitative analysis as exclusively rigorous and systematic" (p. 28). It is easy to see that well implemented grounded theory research, through its process and theory-focused nature, has the potential to fulfill the Council for Accreditation of Counseling and

Related Educational Program's (CACREP) emphasis on advancing the counseling profession and informing clinical practice (CACREP, 2016).

Further, while grounded theory research is widely celebrated, it sometimes evokes criticism within research, qualitative, and even grounded theory communities. For example, Charmaz (2008) states that in the 1900s, "For postmodernists, grounded theory epitomized distanced inquiry by objective experts who assumed their training licensed them to define and represent research participants" (p. 400). These reactions and its suitability for research in the behavioral sciences and professions are best understood in the context of the approach's history, philosophical foundations, multiplicity of methodologies, and current controversies. The following sections offer a general description of the grounded theory approaches, a comparison to other common qualitative approaches, and a brief history. Then the three main variants of grounded theory are described using examples and a focus on application. Finally, rigor, multicultural concerns, and limitations to the approach are described. Throughout these descriptions a single real-world example will be used to allow easy comparisons.

A BRIEF HISTORY OF GROUNDED THEORY

As with many qualitative approaches, the evolution of grounded theory is closely tied to its proponents and their relationships throughout time. American sociologists Barney Glaser and Ansel Strauss are universally referred to as the originators of grounded theory research. While doing their first grounded theory study, Glaser and Strauss became disenchanted with the typical processes of research (Kenny & Fourie, 2014). They believed that over-valuing theory *verification* limited discovery and that theory *generation* should be similarly valued. In collaboration they explored how theory can arise from systematically gathered interview and observation data. The result was a grounded theory study on death and dying, which informed compassionate care for terminal patients (Andrews, 2015). Following this publication, the pair coauthored *The Discovery of Grounded Theory* (1967) based on their methodological exploration. This publication served as the basis for Classic or Glaserian Grounded Theory (CGGT)and is seen as the beginning of a rich and diverse approach. Glaser continued on in this tradition, further refining CGGT through teaching, writing, and creating a journal specific to *his* variety of grounded theory (Kenny & Fourie, 2014).

Anselm Strauss, however, moved forward in a different direction, first publishing on his own, then joining forces with Juliet Corbin to publish *The Basics of Qualitative Research* in 1998. Strauss's revamping of the approach became known as Straussian Grounded Theory (SGT), which was characterized by increased systematization of data analysis and decreased focus on pure emergence of theory. Strauss's approach drew sharp criticism from Glaser, motivating him to further develop and defend CGGT. While Glaser remained steadfast in his commitment to CGGT, Strauss and Corbin approached SGT more flexibly, with more openness to variation and room for evolution and growth (Kenny & Fourie, 2014).

A third variant ofgrounded theory arose from the work of Kathy Charmaz, a student of both Glaser and Strauss. She moved the work of Glaser and Strauss, which was heavily influenced by the positivist and post-positivist trends of the 1960s, into the modern realm of constructivism. Although much had been made of the differences between CGGT and SGT, Charmaz characterized them similarly with respect to their veiled positivism/post-positivism influences. Charmaz's approach, Constructivist Grounded Theory (CGT) moved well beyond Strauss's changes, creating a more philosophically congruent methodology while retaining most methods from CGGT and SGT, but

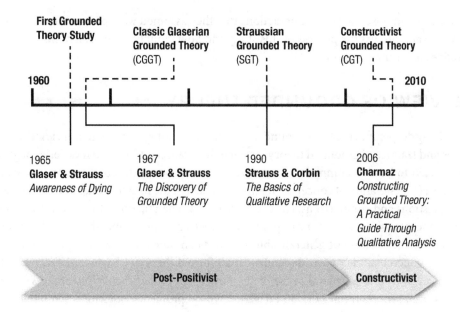

FIGURE 12.1 Grounded Theory Methodologies Timeline of Development.

predictably drew sharp criticism from Glaser (Kenny & Fourie, 2014). Figure 12.1 illustrates the timeline of the development of CGGT, SGT, and CGT.

As previously intimated, CGGT, SGT, and CGT are often positioned as distinctly different. Although the differences are important to understand, it is also important to understand their similarities and the evolving world of research, qualitative research, and grounded theory that gave rise to the methodologies. In the ensuing sections we explore how these three methodologies are similar and different as we simultaneously explore the process of planning and implementing a grounded theory study.

A CASE STUDY OF GROUNDED THEORY RESEARCH

The case we will use to illustrate chapter concepts is a grounded theory study the first author completed during her doctoral studies in counselor education. The study was completed in 2002 and published later (Rubel & Kline, 2008). Like many grounded theory studies, the published account represents only a small portion of the study's process and product. It also represents an early phase of the first author's development as a researcher and of the counseling profession's acceptance of qualitative research. Using this case allows us to report what was published and also critique the study based on motivations, intentions, thought processes, and challenges not apparent in the published account.

The study began with the first author's desire to better understand counseling and therapy group leadership and a sense that expert group leaders' experiences of the leadership process might provide useful insights. This curiosity was spurred by the overall problem that group leadership is intimidating and often difficult for newcomers due to its complexity and high emotional, cognitive, and behavioral demands. The first author and her dissertation chair determined that qualitative approaches were a good way to accommodate the complexity of the experience and provide a holistic account. Additionally, they decided that a grounded theory approach provided the best way to understand the actions and interactions that they assumed were part of the experience. We will describe and discuss the process of this study and how it might have been done from different perspectives in ensuing sections.

OVERVIEW OF GROUNDED THEORY

Before delving deeper into the three grounded theory methodologies, we will overview the common processes and features of grounded theory research that transcend "type." All varieties of grounded theory are said to have in common: (a) exploration of a process, (b) co-occuring data collection and analysis; (c) generation of concepts directly from data in the form of codes and categories using analytic questions and comparisons, (d) use of memos or analytic notes to explore and document tentative concepts and theory, (e) sampling to further conceptual and theoretical development rather than for the purpose of generalizability, and (f) an outcome of a theory grounded in data that is more concrete and context dependent than formal theory (Charmaz, 1996, p. 28; Reiger, 2019). However, to give a general sense of the flow of grounded theory research, we will use a general research process framework and describe typical problems, questions, sampling, and data collection, data analysis, and results along with key concepts common to all varieties of grounded theory. First, though, we will discuss the foundation upon which all research is built, the research paradigm, and in particular, the general paradigmatic hierarchy of grounded theory research.

THE PARADIGMATIC HIERARCHY OF GROUNDED THEORY RESEARCH

Crotty (1998) emphasized the importance of understanding the five nested aspects of research known as the paradigmatic hierarchy, which includes ontology, epistemology, theoretical perspective, methodology, and methods. The quality of grounded theory research depends upon purposefully connecting and making consistent these layers through careful planning and implementation (Ponterotto, 2005). The philosophical foundations of grounded theory are generally discussed in terms of its origins in symbolic interactionism and pragmatism and evolution from objectivism toward constructivism. However, the foundational writings on grounded theory can be unclear and inconsistent with respect to philosophical integration (Reigher, 2019). Thus, readers should be mindful that existing philosophical and methodological debate between different grounded theory camps is too extensive to cover exhaustively in this chapter. However, we will attempt to address the major influences and controversies.

The broadest aspect of the paradigmatic hierarchy is ontology. Ontology is the philosophical study of the nature of reality, truth, being, and existence. In terms of research, ontology impacts how researchers view the subject of their research (Ponterotto, 2005). That is, it concerns the very substance of what is being studied. As explained in earlier chapters two common ontological positions are realism and relativism. Both have been associated with different methodologies of grounded theory. Some grounded theory studies may be built on the belief that the researched subject exists separate from the participants and researchers, which is considered a realist ontology. Others can be built on the belief that the researched subject is not separate from the experiencing of the participants and researchers, which would be considered a relativist ontology.

Following directly from ontology is epistemology, which is the study of the nature of knowledge. It deals with what can be known and how that knowledge is justified. In terms of research, epistemology is the philosophical position on what can be known from the researchers' efforts and the means researchers must use to gain that knowledge (Ponterotto, 2005). Crotty (1998) states that epistemology is the theory of knowledge embedded in the theoretical perspective that informs the methodology. Typically, grounded theory epistemology can be either objectivist or constructivist. Objectivism corresponds to a realist ontology and is the position that a single truth exists and that this truth can be understood through logic (Crotty, 1998). Constructivism is not concerned with objective reality, focusing instead on multiple truths and knowledge constructed by the human mind and social interaction (Crotty, 1998). This corresponds to a relativist ontology.

Theoretical perspective is the next "layer" of the paradigmatic hierarchy. According to Crotty (1998), theoretical perspective is "the philosophical stance informing the methodology and thus providing a context for the process and grounding it in logic and criteria" (p. 11). This differs from epistemology in that the theoretical perspective is more specific, having more propositions, while remaining consistent with the underlying epistemology. The line between epistemology and theoretical perspective is sometimes unclear but every theoretical perspective has an epistemology. The theoretical perspectives most commonly associated with grounded theory include positivism, post-positivism, symbolic interactionism, and pragmatism. Several other theoretical perspectives such as feminism and critical theory have also been discussed in relationship to grounded theory (Fassinger, 2005).

Symbolic interactionism is often mentioned as influencing the development of grounded theory. It is considered a theoretical framework rather than a theory and focuses on the idea that humans *interpret* each other's actions rather than simply reacting to them (Blumer, 1969), thus symbolic interactionism can be considered ontologically relativist and epistemologically related to constructivism. Pragmatism also played a large role in grounded theory's inception and is viewed as not relying on any single philosophy. Rather it is focused on problems as they exist in the real world and research as a means to solve these problems. Pragmatism has been characterized as working with a changeable reality and knowledge created by human interaction and in this way aligns with relativism and constructivism. However, pragmatism's emphasis on philosophy-free problem-solving enables the uneasy and sloppy truce between the objectivist and constructivist methods sometimes seen in grounded theory studies.

Methodology is the next level in the paradigmatic hierarchy. According to Crotty (1998), a methodology is "the strategy, plan of action, process or design lying behind the choice and use of particular methods and linking the choice and use of methods to the desired outcomes" (p. 11). Methodology links epistemology and theoretical perspective to what is actually done in the study. Methodology not only includes the general approach taken to do the research, but also the reasoning behind the design choices. In this case, the methodology is grounded theory and its variants, CGGT, SGT, and CGT, which will be discussed more thoroughly later.

Methods are the final layer in the paradigmatic hierarchy. According to Crotty (1998), research methods are the "techniques or procedures used to gather and analyze data related to some research question or hypothesis" (p. 11). Methods are informed by the epistemology, theoretical perspective, and methodology. They are also informed by the purpose of the research as well as the context of the particular study. Grounded theory methods or techniques are distinctive. An example of a distinctive method is constant comparison, where the meanings of concepts are compared to the meaning of other concepts and the data associated with each to either further differentiate them or to coalesce them into a single concept (Corbin & Strauss, 2015). The methods or techniques of grounded theory will be further explicated as the general process and each of the variants are described. A summary of the paradigmatic hierarchy of grounded theory research is provided in Table 12.1.

TABLE 12.1 **Paradigmatic Hierarchy of Grounded Theory Research**

PARADIGM HIERARCHY LEVEL	DEFINITION	OBJECTIVIST ORIENTATION	CONSTRUCTIVIST ORIENTATION
Ontology	Philosophy of reality, truth, being, and existence	Realism—Researched subject exists separate from the participants and researchers	Relativism—Researched subject is not separate from participant and researcher experiences
Epistemology	Philosophy of knowledge and knowledge acquisition	Objectivist—A single truth exists and that this truth can be understood through logic	Constructivist—Multiple truths and knowledge constructed by the human mind and social interaction
Theoretical Perspective	Specific philosophical position informing methodology and methods.	Positivism, post-positivism, pragmatism	Symbolic interactionism, pragmatism critical
Methodology	General approach of research and reasoning for research design choices	Classic Glaserian Grounded Theory, Early Straussian Grounded Theory	Later Straussian Grounded Theory, Constructivist Grounded Theory
Methods	Strategies, protocols or techniques for collecting and analyzing data	Emergence, no literature review, etic and emic accounts, numeric/factual data, adherence to method controls subjectivity	Co-construction, literature review, emic accounts of experience, reflexivity controls subjectivity

RESEARCH PROBLEMS AND QUESTIONS SUITED FOR GROUNDED THEORY

Understanding what kind of questions are appropriate for qualitative research is important in counselor training (CACREP, 2016). So, what kinds of research questions are suited for grounded theory research? Glaser and Strauss, the creators of grounded theory might answer, "every kind" (Charmaz, 1996, p. 28). Like most qualitative approaches grounded theory is appropriate for *research problems* that are human, complex, and difficult to study using quantitative research (Corbin & Strauss, 2015). Grounded theory is used when a holistic understanding of an issue, phenomenon, or process is desired. Grounded theory research is particularly suited to problems that lack useful theory to test and require a process-focus or ability to account for interactions (Corbin & Strauss, 2015).

The **research question** narrows the focus of the research problem and translates that focus into a question that can be answered through a particular research approach (Creswell & Poth, 2018). The question will likely have the approach encoded in its language and, thus, will also imply epistemology and theoretical perspective. Thus, grounded theory research questions may hint at the approach's sensitivity to process and potential for theory generation. Grounded theory research questions may also sound different from study to study depending on the epistemology and theoretical perspective of the study. Studies based on more objectivist epistemologies or positivist or post-positivist theoretical frameworks may have research questions that refer to theory and explanation.

Case Study Example 12.1

Going back to the case study example, the first author's intent was to gain understanding of how expert group leaders experienced the process of leading groups. Her assumption was that this experience was multilayered, involving internal cognitive and emotional responses to a wide array of events that occur during the life of a group. While she was familiar with quantitative studies that explored isolated relationships between group leader behaviors and the functioning of their groups, this type of study seemed limited in its ability to capture a big picture of this process.

In terms of the case study example's research question, a post-positivist research question might have been, "What theory explains expert group leadership?" Conversely, studies reliant on a constructivist epistemology will have research questions that communicate valuing of individual experiences and perspectives. Using the case study example this might sound like, "How do expert group leaders experience the process of leading groups?" The research question actually used for the chapter's case study was closer to the second, constructivist example: "What do expert group leaders experience and perceive during the process of leading counseling and therapy groups?" (Rubel & Kline, 2008, p. 140).

SAMPLING AND DATA COLLECTION FOR GROUNDED THEORY RESEARCH

Like most qualitative methods, grounded theory studies often employ purposive sampling, which privileges use of participants or informants who have experienced the issue in question and also privileges data gathered directly from these informants (Polkinghorne, 2005). Because grounded theory research is capable of describing and explaining variation in processes and their outcomes, forms of maximum variation sampling might also be appropriate. This is where participants who have experienced the process in question differently or with different outcomes are selected (Patton, 2019). Other forms of data may include written data such as journal or survey answers from participants or observations made by secondary participants or researchers. Philosophical integration affects sampling and data collection. For example, while constructivist epistemologies will privilege first-hand accounts of participant perception and experience, objectivist epistemologies may also value non-participant observations and accounts as well as data sources that are numerical or purported to be factual.

Case Study Example 12.2

The case study for this chapter shows several of these features. The study focused on the perceptions and experiences of expert group counselors and therapists. Thus, a process of snowball sampling and peer-identification were used to recruit and purposefully sample expert group counselors and therapists. The process of snowball sampling started with contacting individuals listed as fellows of three influential group counseling and therapy organizations and these people were contacted to see if they fit the criteria and were willing to participate or if they could refer us to someone who did. Because we wanted a robust theory that might be applicable to more situations, maximum variation sampling was used. We could have chosen to sample based on the process under study (e.g., selecting for participants who had great experiences as well as poor experiences leading groups); we instead sampled across professions (social work, psychology, group psychotherapy, and counseling), across genders, and geographically across the United States. This sampling could be seen as closer to constructivist in epistemology than objectivist, in that the recruitment strategy was designed to elicit emic perspectives rather than etic. An emic stance emphasizes the voices of the people at the center of the studied experience to provide an intimate view of what is unique about the population and their experience. An etic perspective yields results that generalize beyond the participants by focusing on more universal behaviors and qualities (Ponterotto, 2005). Within grounded theory, an emic perspective aligns with a relativist ontology tieing the participant's experience to the subject of the study; while an etic perspective fits with a realist ontology, separating the studied phenomenon from the experience of the participants.

Data for grounded theory studies can include, among other things, interviews, surveys, observations, and existing documents (Corbin & Strauss, 2015). Most grounded theory studies rely heavily on interviews. Interviews for grounded theory research can be very open-ended or moderately structured depending on specific methodology and how much prior knowledge is allowed to guide the study (Charmaz, 2014; Glaser & Strauss, 1967). Even with studies that allow more prior knowledge to guide interviews, the questions will tend to be process-oriented with sufficient openness to allow and encourage participants to respond authentically (Creswell & Poth, 2018). Interview questions focusing on perceptions and experiences of participants are more indicative of a constructivist epistemology, while questions designed to elicit verifiable actions or occurrences indicate a more objectivist epistemology. As indicated in the discussion of sampling, an objectivist orientation might also include data from a variety of sources and a variety of types with a focus not only on rich description of emic perspectives but also on verification.

Case Study Example 12.3

For example, in this chapter's case study interview questions were quite broad but were based upon several very basic assumptions about group leaders' experiences, namely that all group leaders both think and feel during the leadership process, that they must make sense of the process somehow to lead, and that they relate in some way to multiple levels of group interaction. The questions were: (a) What thoughts and feelings do you experience while you lead a group, (b) describe how you make sense of the groups you lead, and (c) describe your relationships with the group as a whole and group members while you lead your groups (Rubel & Kline, 2008, p. 141). These interview questions could be characterized as constructivist due to their emic focus.

If the study had more of an objectivist epistemology, the questions might be phrased more openly with the assumption that "truth" would emerge with proper method or they might, particularly from a post-positivist theoretical perspective, be more structured, align with an verified theoretical perspective, and focus less on an emic and more on an etic perspective. A very open version of the questions might only have one question, such as, "How do you experience leading groups?" A more structured and theoretically based interview might include questions asking about specific theoretical constructs either in an open or confirmatory way. For instance, if we utilized an a priori expertise framework that included elements of intuition and confidence, we might ask, "How does your confidence as an expert group leader affect your group leadership?" and "How do you use intuition during your group leadership?"

A unique feature of grounded theory sampling and data collection is *theoretical sampling* where researchers actively seek data that further illuminate emerging theoretical concepts or relationships (Corbin & Strauss, 2015). This results in re-evaluation of existing data and engagement in multiple rounds of interviews. As data are analyzed, the researcher develops tentative propositions, in essence mini-theories, and then either samples existing data or, by constructing further interview questions, gathers more data to contradict, support, refine, or extend their propositions (Glaser, 1978).

Case Study Example 12.4

An example of theoretical sampling from the chapter case study involves a concept that emerged during first-round data collection and analysis. Participants described instances where they did not understand what was going on in their groups. However, further analysis with existing data did not illuminate what participants experienced or how they acted in this instance. Theoretical sampling is illustrated in the chapter case study when Rubel and Kline (2008) describe their response to a thin area in their theory related to what participants did when they did not understand their groups, "A general question was developed to further explore this area, 'What do you do when you don't understand what is going on in your group?' This question was presented during second round interviews and the data were collected, analyzed, and integrated into the theoretical structure" (p. 143).

DATA ANALYSIS AND GROUNDED THEORY RESEARCH

Data analysis methods distinguish grounded theory from other qualitative approaches. Grounded theory data analysis is largely inductive but can include deduction depending on methodology (Glaser, 1978). Inductive methods of inquiry start with concrete data and move to general conclusions abstract concepts such as theory. Deductive methods of inquiry move from the general ideas such as theories to the specific conclusions. An inductive process is when a person in Oregon, without prior knowledge, looks out the window, sees rain for 2 weeks in a row, and concludes that, "Oregon is rainy." A deductive process is when a person is warned by their meteorologist friend that Oregon is rainy, moves there anyway, and after looking out the window for 2 weeks concludes, "Yes, my friend was right; Oregon is rainy." While grounded theory data analysis can begin even as researchers listen to participants' interviews, typically it begins with transcribed first round interviews and continues in a recursive cycle of conceptualization, checking, theoretical sampling, and reconceptualization until saturation is achieved. Saturation is a point, based on the scope of the research, where sufficient data have been collected to support a rich, nuanced, and fully developed theory (Creswell & Poth, 2018) While the different grounded theory methodologies have differing analysis methods, several overlapping phases of analysis and characteristics are inherent to all grounded theory analysis.

During early analysis, researchers are not focused on theory. Rather, during this phase researchers are reading data with a more or less open mind, examining words, phrases, and lines of data for meaning in association with the research question, then assigning codes that are indicative of that meaning. Part of this process may involve different codes being condensed together into one code based on similarities with one another, or conversely one code may be differentiated into several concepts based on differences in the characteristics of the associated data. The exploration of similarities and differences is part of a signature technique in grounded theory, **constant comparison**. The product of this phase is usually a mixture of low and high abstraction-level concepts (Corbin & Strauss, 2008). While the researcher may have hunches about processes and relationships among these concepts, at this point the concepts are not formally related.

Case Study Example 12.5

To illustrate let's go back to the chapter case study and consider the following data concerning how a participant handles having a strong intuition about what to do while leading a group. Let's examine the meanings in light of the research question, "How do expert group leaders experience the process of leading groups?"

> *My experience is that over the years, I trust my intuition and I trust spontaneity. But there's also a filter . . . so I structure the spontaneity a little bit. I look at the questions of how is this going to affect the patients, and how it's going to affect the group, and how it's going to affect me . . . And if what I'm about to say is going to advance the progress of the group or is it somehow going to delay it. And even if it may delay it, I may say it anyway. . . . Then if I don't use that comment, I might use it later. (Rubel & Kline, 2008, p. 155)*

The entire paragraph might be coded as *using expertise to harness intuition* or the data might be initially coded in relatively small meaning units:

> *My experience is that over the years, I trust my intuition and I trust spontaneity* (**trusting self due to experience**) *But there's also a filter . . . so I structure the spontaneity a little bit* (**filtering intuition**). *I look at the questions of how is this going to affect the patients* (**anticipating effect of intuition on clients**), *and how it's going to affect the group* (**anticipating effect intuition on group**), *and how it's going to affect me* (**anticipating effect of intuition on self**). . .*And if what I'm about to say is going to advance the progress of the group or is it somehow going to delay it* (**weighing potential effect of intuition on group, anticipating a positive effect, anticipating a negative effect**). *And even if it may delay it, I may say it anyway* (**deciding to go with intuition**) . . . *Then if I don't use that comment, I might use it later* (**saving intuition for later**)

Constant comparison at this early stage might look like comparing and contrasting the codes *anticipating effect of intuition on group* and *weighing potential effect of intuition on group* and discovering that they both share a future orientation, evaluative quality, and group function focus. The difference in the codes could be characterized as the former is more general while the latter identifies two effects. The result of the constant comparison could be condensing these two codes into a more inclusive code *evaluating future effect of intuition on group*.

During the middle phase, grounded theory data analysis becomes more focused. Here concepts are further refined and clarified. The researcher will begin to relate concepts to each other functionally and conceptually as higher level "umbrella" concepts (e.g., categories) and lower-level concepts that describe some aspect of the higher-level concepts (e.g., subcategories, properties, or dimensions). Constant comparison is a common tool here also. During this phase the researcher continues to compare the characteristics of concepts and asks themselves key questions such as, "What are the necessary constituents of each concept?" and, "What do the similarities and differences between concepts say about their relationship to one another and the process in question?" At the end of this middle phase, the lower-level and higher-level concepts are more formally related to one another, with lower level concepts forming descriptive and/or functional clusters around higher level concepts. Researchers may have strong hunches about how the array of higher-level concepts connect with one another to form theory, but these relationships are not yet clear or formalized.

Case Study Example 12.6

Using the data and concepts from the chapter case study, let's use constant comparison to consider how to relate several codes to one another. The codes *anticipating effect of intuition on clients, evaluating future effect of intuition on group, and anticipating effect of intuition on self* all have a future-orientation and evaluative quality. However, their foci differ. Two of the foci, clients and self (leader), are parts of the group, though "group" can be thought of as all that composes a group or the group as a unique entity separate from its parts (e.g., group-as-a-whole). Regardless, the comparison might further condense all of the codes into *evaluating future effect of intuition on group*. Depending on type of grounded theory methodology, the varying foci of group-as-a-whole, client, and leader might be retained as three concepts that are part of a **property** (characteristic of a category) that has a **dimension** (variation in a property gives theory movement and interaction). Additionally, the codes of *anticipating a positive effect* and *anticipating a negative effect* can be seen as another dimension describing the outcome of the evaluation.

The last phases of coding in grounded theory data analysis involve organizing the clusters of concepts into theory. This involves the researcher evaluating the now more richly developed concepts and their relationships to find which high-level concept (category) seems to be central to the process or experience. Once this central concept is identified, the other high-level concepts are reconceptualized and reconnected around that central concept. Connections between the central concept and surrounding concepts are a product of relationships evident in the data and represented by interactions between the lower-level concepts associated with each. These relationships form theory and delineate process. This phase of analysis is about bringing together the pieces developed in prior steps to create a cohesive explanation or picture, and integrative tools such as storylines, "paradigm," and the conditional matrix are used to explore the holistic flow of the theory (Charmaz, 2014; Corbin & Strauss, 2015).

Case Study Example 12.7

While it is not possible to demonstrate theorizing fully with the preceding chapter case study data and concepts, we can see some of how codes of varying abstraction levels can be linked into bits of process or theory pieces. Following is a part of the coded data that contain some obvious variation and process as evidenced by contingent language such as "if," "when," and "then."

> . . .*And if what I'm about to say is going to advance the progress of the group or is it somehow going to delay it* (**weighing potential effect of intuition on group, anticipating a positive effect, anticipating a negative effect**). *And even if it may delay it, I may say it anyway* (**deciding to go with intuition**) . . . *Then if I don't use that comment, I might use it later* (**saving intuition for later**)

From this a storyline or process memo such as this could be written to help integrate theory: Expert group leaders evaluate the potential impacts of their intuition upon the group, group members, and themselves. If they see that the intuitive intervention will affect the group in a positive way they will likely go ahead and use the intervention. If they see that the intuitive intervention might delay group progress, they may not use it, but might under some circumstances. And even if they see that the intuitive intervention may be helpful, under certain circumstances they might save it and use it later.

For a fully developed and saturated theory, all parts and relationships within the storyline should be well-supported by data. In the preceding storyline, however, several contingencies such as *deciding to go with intuition* when *anticipating a positive effect* are implied or make theoretical sense but are not directly connected to the current data. Also, several interesting conditions are unknown or not a part of these data such as the conditions that might lead a group leader to implement an intuitive intervention even if they perceive it might slow group progress down. Both of these examples, if they were deemed important to the research question or participant experience, would indicate that the researcher should theoretically sample other data for instances supporting or contradicting the ideas or collect more data through further interviewing.

THE PRODUCTS OF GROUNDED THEORY

While many other qualitative approaches may co-opt grounded theory methods, the products and results of grounded theory studies should be distinctive. Obviously, the product of grounded theory methods should be theory. But what is theory? Backman and Kyngäs (1999) simply say that theory is, "… composed of concepts and their mutual connections. It is a systematic structure which describes, explains and/or controls phenomena" (p. 147). Backman and Kyngäs further explain that theory in grounded theory can be substantive or formal, which are designations originating from grounded theory's sociological beginnings. Substantive theory is theory that deals with a specific situation or setting and is applicable to that setting or potentially to similar settings, while formal theory is more abstract and developed and intended to have wider application. Some also mentioned midrange theory, also a sociological term, which describes the product of imperatives to tie empirical data to more abstract theory and to avoid searching for "grand theory" that is meant to explain very broad phenomena using few variables (Hassan & Lowery, 2015).

In grounded theory research the "type" of theory is determined by the philosophical integration of the study, the experience and skills of the researcher, and, potentially, the time and other resources available. With respect to philosophical integration, Charmaz (2014) indicated grounded theory research can produce positivist theory that, influenced by realist ontology and objectivist epistemology, makes generalizations about causation in an attempt to explain and predict. She indicates that grounded theory research can also produce interpretivist theory that, influenced by relativist ontology and constructivist epistemology, proposes tentative relationships between more or less abstract concepts. It may be useful to think of formal theory as more positivist, having a more etic focus, requiring larger more varied sampling, more time, and the ability to analytically discern and describe small differences in concepts and relationships on the part of the researcher. Similarly, substantive theory can be seen as more interpretivist. Substantive theory would have a more emic focus, rely on smaller more specific samples, and, thus, potentially require less time and fewer resources. Substantive, interpretivist theory can be seen as requiring the researcher to have the ability to describe more creatively to adequately convey less formulaic concepts and relationships.

In terms of what consumers of grounded theory will actually see in research reports, Glaser and Strauss (1967) indicated that, "grounded theory can be presented either as a well-codified set of propositions or in a running theoretical discussion, using conceptual categories and their properties" (p. 31). The propositions of formal or more positivist theory may resemble "paradigm," a method emphasized by Corbin and Strauss (2008), where theory is examined and delineated as contextual conditions, moderating conditions, and outcomes. Substantive or interpretive theory may take the shape of relationships and interactions that are narratively described and not reliant on formulaic presentation. In both cases, grounded theory results are often represented, in part, by diagrams that depict concepts, relationships between concepts, process, and overall participant experience. Charmaz (1996) stated that at that time most researchers using grounded theory did not produce theory, rather they emphasized producing "…analytic categories that synthesize and explicate process in the worlds they study rather than to constructing tightly framed theories that generate hypotheses and make explicit predictions" (p. 48).

Case Study Example 12.8

For this chapter's case (Rubel & Kline, 2008), the grounded theory products varied. The project's theoretical integration, like the status of grounded theory at the time, was somewhat unclear but in line with its primary methodological resource, Strauss and Corbin (1998). Thus, the study was influenced by the pragmatist and symbolic interactionist roots of SGT and showed both post-positivist and constructivist traits. Consistent with Strauss and Corbin (1998), the results consisted of densely developed categories, properties, and dimensions. Interactions between key categories via their varying properties and dimensions were illustrated in the resultant published manuscript through systematized descriptions using highly abstract language and several diagrams. In the original dissertation, these categories, properties, dimensions and their interactions were detailed even more extensively both narratively and via diagram. The constructivist influence was shown in the manuscript through provision of context and avoidance of generalizing language.

COMPARISON TO OTHER QUALITATIVE APPROACHES

To build on the general understanding of grounded theory process and products, it is useful to compare and contrast it to several other qualitative approaches. Grounded theory, while sharing many features of other qualitative methodologies, is distinct in a number of ways. Grounded theory methods will be differentiated from two common qualitative traditions, phenomenology and case study. Noteworthy differences in the intended purposes, sampling methods, data analysis, and end products exist between these approaches and grounded theory.

In terms of purpose, grounded theory research projects are conceived with the purpose of understanding a process (Corbin & Strauss, 2015). For example, Seward (2014) used grounded theory to examine the process of multicultural training for master's-level counseling students. To understand the process in question, researchers sought to develop a theory by immersing or grounding themselves in the data they collected. Conversely, phenomenology is concerned with the meaning people give to their experience of a phenomenon (Hays & Wood, 2011). While analysis of data may result in structural descriptions of the experience, no theory is developed in a phenomenological study. The purpose of case study research is to develop a thorough understanding of one or more cases (Strauss & Corbin, 1998). For example, one type of case study describes and analyzes a single instrumental case to provide a better understanding of the case and its implications.

Sampling and data collection are also distinguishing features of grounded theory research. Grounded theory, phenomenology, and case study all use purposive sampling, though its form may be different. Since grounded theory is designed to account for variation in processes and their outcomes, heterogeneous or maximum variation samples are often desirable (Patton, 2019). This is distinctly different from phenomenology where sample homogeneity with respect to the phenomenon is desirable (Creswell & Poth, 2018). Sampling in case study research is based on the purpose of the case study, how the boundaries of the case are defined, and the type of case study method, usually one (single case study), two (comparative), or several (multiple case study). The actual number of cases included are small (usually one to five) but each case might involve anything from one person to a more complex system or situation (e.g., an organization and all its internal and external interactions; Creswell & Poth, 2018).

However, grounded theory is the only approach to rely heavily on theoretical sampling. Theoretical sampling is used after the initial phase of data collection and analysis to identify data that will deepen or disprove the emerging theory. Theoretical sampling can involve reexamining existing data or collecting more data based on emerging concepts (Corbin & Strauss, 2015). This results in multiple rounds of interviews or data collection for grounded theory studies, while data collection is more likely to be a one-time event for the other approaches.

Grounded theory data analysis methods differ from those used for phenomenology and case study. Whereas in phenomenology and case studies data are generally collected once and then analyzed, in grounded theory research, theoretical sampling usually results in multiple rounds of data collection. Researchers will engross themselves in the first round of data and then based on their analysis, seek out additional data, through theoretical sampling, to refine their initial ideas and codes. This iterative cycle continues until saturation is achieved and the researcher is confident no new ideas or features of the process exist (Corbin & Strauss, 2015).

Grounded theory results are distinct from the results of case studies and phenomenology. It is largely accepted that the results of grounded theory should be theory of some kind (Charmaz, 2014; Corbin & Strauss, 2015; Glaser & Strauss, 1967). As stated, this might be more or less formal. Grounded theory usually does not result in themes, which are less distinct groupings of similar experiences than the concepts inherent to grounded theory, which are categories, properties, and dimensions (Corbin & Strauss, 2015). The results of phenomenology are generally in the form of themes or essences that describe the singular experience and the context in which the experience occurs (Creswell & Poth, 2018). Case study research can result in a wide variety of products depending on the type of case study. These might be themes, factors, and even interactions but the results generally provide a multifaceted view of the case in question that provides insight into critical aspects of the case.

THREE GROUNDED THEORY METHODOLOGIES

As indicated earlier, the three methodologies, Classic or Glaserian, Straussian, and Constructivist Grounded Theory continue to evolve. Their supporters and detractors may describe them in definitive ways, yet their very evolution indicates a flexibility that is consistent with the qualitative tradition. It is more practical and, likely, more accurate to view them as sharing many attributes and potentially overlapping in their philosophical integration and methods. Yet, as researchers emphasize a particular stance in their investigation, differences are evident. We will describe each in terms of their philosophical integration, preparation, data collection, data analysis and results emphasizing the distinctions.

CLASSIC GLASERIAN GROUNDED THEORY

As described earlier, Glaserian or Classic Glaserian Grounded Theory (CGGT) arose out of Glaser and Strauss's desire to move beyond existing research methods and promote theory generation rather than theory verification. Glaser has remained a proponent of the original incarnation of grounded theory, clarifying and deepening its implementation over the years while maintaining its essential form. Andrews (2015) indicates that at its essence CGGT should have a deep connection to the real world and that the theory produced from individuals' experiences should ultimately influence practitioners resulting in improved outcomes and best practices. For example, Glaser and Strauss's original work continues to impact how medical staff treat terminal illnesses (Andrews, 2015). Some of the unique characteristics of CGGT are its adherence to the principle of theory emergence, lack of a priori literature review or framework, two-phase data analysis, use of coding families later in analysis, and an end product of formal theory (Reiger, 2019).

Philosophical Integration of Glaserian Grounded Theory

Glaser asserted that grounded theory was flexible and could be applied using any research perspective. While Glaser himself did not claim a specific philosophical stance, authors note consistent trends in Glaser's discussion and implementation of his approach that indicate a stance. CGGT's early theoretical influences, through Strauss's involvement, include symbolic interactionism and pragmatism (Bryant, 2009). However, in terms of ontology, CGGT has been described by some as realist in orientation, implying a reality that lies separate from the perceptions and experiences of the researchers (Charmaz, 2008). This can be seen in Glaser's strong championing of the idea of emergence, the idea that the underlying theory exists and can be carefully uncovered or coaxed to emerge via CGGT methods (Charmaz, 2008). In terms of epistemology and theoretical perspective, CGGT is typically described as having objectivist and post-positivist leanings (Howard-Payne, 2016), which are consistent with the realist ontology. This is supported by Glaser's contention that by the rigorous use of constant comparison, "personal input by a researcher soon drops out as eccentric and the data become objectivist not constructionist" (Glaser, 2000, p. 6). This leaves the role of the researcher as that of an objective outsider whose experiences, knowledge, and beliefs are kept at bay to allow the participants'concerns to lead theory emergence (Glaser, 2000).

However, CGGT's origins in symbolic interactionism and pragmatism are somewhat at odds with this perceived realist/objectivist orientation. Bryant (2009) in critiquing SGT also critiques CGGT for this, describing an "epistemological fairytale" propagated by "naïve" adherence to an inductive ideal and lack of clear philosophical explanation and exploration in both methodologies. What is left is a tension in the philosophical integration of CGGT that must be resolved by individual researchers or left as a tension. Glaser seemed comfortable with this being resolved by the intent and action of those applying his method, while Strauss and Corbin resolved this by shifting increasingly toward constructivism.

Preparation

While most research, including qualitative research, begins with an extensive review of the literature, this is not the case for CGGT. Glaser does advocate reviewing literature in the area of research later in the research process (Heath & Cowley, 2004). The timing of the literature review, and the reasons for doing so, are one of the differences between Glaserian and Straussian Grounded Theory (Howard-Payne, 2016). This is connected to Glaser's promotion of a more purely inductive approach, which emphasizes moving from the specific to the general (data to theory) rather than a deductive approach (theory to specific application; Heath & Cowley, 2004). From this viewpoint, reviewing the literature extensively ahead of time is seen as interfering with unbiased data analysis and pure emergence of theory. Preparation, then, means that the researcher does not enter the process with pre-formed research questions. Instead, the researcher attempts to maintain a neutral position and view data objectively to allow participant concerns to emerge (Howard-Payne, 2016). In this first step, the researcher must trust the process that the theory will emerge from the data. This idea is somewhat controversial as some authors question researchers' ability to remove all theoretical influence (Bryant, 2009).

Sampling and Data Collection

As for other forms of grounded theory, interviews are the main form of data collection in CGGT, though Glaser himself has stated that his method is a general method and can also be applied to quantitative data (Glaser, 2009). Consistent with the idea of theory emergence, Glaserian data collection is associated with very open, unstructured interviews at the start of data collection such that the number and specificity of questions does not impose preconceived ideas (Simmons, 2010). For example, initial interview questions for the chapter case from a CGGT perspective may be limited to one general question, "How do you experience the process of leading groups?" with follow-up questions to clarify ideas expressed by the participants. Everything that comes out during the course of an interview is considered potentially useful information in the process of finding participants' main concerns and how they navigate through them.

Participant observation in an unstructured manner may also be part of the data collection process. Classic grounded theory will also use multiple rounds of data collection as a part of theoretical sampling, as other varieties of grounded theory do. Above all, it is imperative that the researcher bear in mind that the interview belongs to the participant, not to the researcher (Simmons, 2010). Throughout the interview process, the researcher is beginning to analyze the data that are gathered.

Data Analysis

Data analysis in CGGT utilizes two types of coding: substantive (open) and theoretical. This differs from the coding process of Strauss and Corbin, which involves three types of coding. In substantive coding, the researching is trying to identify sets of related ideas that may have theoretical value and give them conceptual names (Simmons, 2010). Codes are grouped conceptually into categories and categories are frequently refined and refitted during this process, and may become more abstract (Heath & Cowley, 2004). The codes are not predetermined. Rather as Kendall (1999) notes, "*emergence* is the process by which codes and categories of the theory fit the data, not the process of fitting the data to predetermined codes and categories" (p. 746). As coding moves forward, so does data collection. This continues until the point of "conceptual saturation"; that is, the point when no more unique codes can be determined (Kendall, 1999).

Following substantive coding, the researcher will move into theoretical coding. In theoretical coding, the researcher examines all of the previous coding in search of the "core variable" or category (Simmons, 2010). Simmons (2010) explains that this core variable helps the researcher to understand what the research is really about. Prior to this point, the researcher will have only had a general topic, but with this core variable, the formation of a theory will begin. Although data analysis focuses on emergence in CGGT, data analysis is not without structure. Glaser sometimes advocated for use of what he called "coding families" or sets of general, commonly acknowledged ideas in the field of sociology to spark organization of theory (Backman & Kyngäs, 1999). Glaser identified at least 18 coding families representing commonly accepted processes (Backman & Kyngäs, 1999; Reiger, 2019). An example of a coding family used by Glaser is Basic Psychological Process or BPP (Backman & Kyngäs). Additionally, a literature review may become appropriate as the theory emerges (Heath & Cowley, 2004). At this stage, the researcher may begin an initial outline of a research report, bearing in mind that additional memoing may still occur at this stage (Simmons, 2010). Outlines of a potential theory are written, which will eventually give way to a more formal research report.

Case Study Example 12.9

So how does coding used in CGGT compare to the earlier general coding examples in this chapter? In Case Study Example 12.4 the data were initially coded in a line-by-line way without a predetermined framework. One in vivo code was *filtering intuition*. The coding in Case Study Example 12.4 would largely be consistent with CGGT's substantive coding. In Case Study Example 12.5 the initial codes were refined, clarified, and, in one instance, made more abstract through the use of constant comparison. This is still consistent with CGGT's substantive coding phase. However, while CGGT coding might begin to hypothesize relationships between codes, terms such as property and dimension would not be used. In Case Study Example 12.6 the refined codes were integrated using a storyline to reflect a contingent relationship, for example, between *evaluating future effect of intuition on group, anticipating a positive effect,* and *deciding to go with intuition*. This differs from CGGT's theoretical coding phase in that no central variable or category was identified. In the actual study the data in the examples represent a small set of codes related to dealing with intuition and formulating interventions. However, a potential core variable is in part visible in the code *trusting self due to experience.* In Rubel and Kline (2008) the theory centered around the concept of *experiential influence* or knowledge, attitudes, and confidence derived from many years of practice. CGGT would place *experiential influence* in the center of the theory as the core variable. Then a coding family might be used to assist in relating other significant aspects of the process such as **understanding** the group, **formulating** interventions, and **evaluating** the effect of the interventions the core variable.

Results and Representation

The results of CGGT, similar to other grounded theory methodologies, usually consists of a theory united conceptually around a core category (Glaser, 1978); some features are distinctive. The grounded theory resulting from CGGT will tend to evidence the methodology's positivist/post-positivist influences (Charmaz, 2000). As Glaser (2002) indicated, CGGT "makes the generated theory as objective as humanly possible" (p. 5). Thus, the resulting grounded theory is expected to have some correspondence with reality, with consistent rigorous analysis producing some consistency of theory (Reiger, 2019). The resulting theory may give a sense of transcending the context of the location and research process, though without a declaration of generalizability. This characteristic along with Glaser's (1992) expectation that grounded theory should have explanatory and predictive power has drawn criticism from others such as Charmaz (2008).

STRAUSSIAN GROUNDED THEORY

Due to its use in numerous studies and the popularity of the texts published by Anselm Strauss and Juliet Corbin, Straussian Grounded Theory (SGT) is likely the version of grounded theory encountered first by budding researchers. While SGT continues to be criticized by Glaser due to its more structured data analysis approach and its non-rejection of a priori influences, these very elements often make it more accessible to novice researchers looking for guidance. Thus, the terminology of SGT has in some ways become the terminology of grounded theory for the masses. However, it is not a unitary approach and has evolved from Glaser and Strauss's early work, to the development of Strauss's own thoughts in collaboration with Juliet Corbin, to the increasingly prevalent voice of Corbin and overt constructivist influence after Strauss's death (Charmaz, 2014). Some of the unique characteristics of SGT are its shift to theory construction rather than emergence, acceptance of the role of researcher experience and literature in theoretical sensitivity, three phases of well-described data analysis, and use of a coding paradigm and conditional matrix during theory integration (Reiger, 2019).

Philosophical Integration of Straussian Grounded Theory

With its roots in his earlier work with Glaser, Strauss's grounded theory also evolved from the tradition of Chicago Interactionism and Pragmatism (Charmaz, 1996). However, Strauss broke away from the perceived positivist foundation of CGGT increasingly incorporating the concept of a fluid, ever-changing, and serendipitous world (Charmaz, 2000). What resulted over time in his collaboration with Juliet Corbin was a sometimes-uneasy mix of residual positivist and post-positivist influences, more overt nods to pragmatism and symbolic interactionism, and an ever-increasing association with constructivism. As with Glasser, this lack of clarity was compounded by Strauss and Corbin's early avoidance of discussing their epistemology in their works.

Ontologically, early SGT is characterized by various authors as having a realist ontology, an objectivist epistemology, and a positivist theoretical orientation because of its latent assumptions of an external reality, valuing of objective data collection, and use of linear research methods (Charmaz, 2000; Reiger, 2019). However, even in earlier texts Strauss and Corbin (1998) included references to the constructive nature of data and the multilayered nature of social truth (Reiger, 2019). In later texts Corbin began to share her increasingly constructivist leanings, while also representing Strauss's constructivist influenced post-positivist voice. With researchers utilizing all of Corbin's and Strauss's four texts, some preferring the more linear and cookbook nature of the earlier texts, the philosophical status of SGT remains a complex mixture that must be sorted and stated by the researcher to optimally inform their research. What is accepted is that SGT is not as realist in ontology or as objectivist as CGGT, placing the researcher more "in" the research and the research more in the context of the world surrounding it (Reiger, 2019).

Preparation

The shift from CGGT's strict stance on emergence to SGT's more flexible stance affects the preparation phase for SGT. The more flexible stance of SGT is related to increased acceptance of the researcher's role in theory construction, which removes the absolute restriction on a priori knowledge informing the research. While CGGT starts with no literature review and may not even have a defined research question at the outset, the process of SGT starts with articulating a research problem and research question and includes a literature browse as a way to inform the research problem and question. That part of Strauss's process differs from the tabula rasa approach of the CGGT approach. The next steps include framing the question with the context that will allow the calibration of the scope of the research question (Corbin & Strauss, 2015) and designing a data collection procedure.

Sampling and Data Collection

Sampling and data collection in SGT is similar to CGGT. Purposive sampling, relatively open interviews, and a recursive process of theoretical sampling also occur in SGT. Like CGGT, SGT may use data from a variety of sources—newspapers, pictures, journals, and so forth, to inform theory development. However, while CGGT relies heavily on unstructured interviews, SGT may include unstructured, semi-structured, and structured interviews (Corbin & Strauss, 2015). Typically, the opening question is designed to address the breadth and depth of the interviewees' experiences of the researched issue with minimal introjection from the researcher. Further questions, even in the initial interview, may be more specific and based on plausible general ideas from literature reviews and experience (Corbin & Strauss, 2015). As with CGGT, initial data and analysis will serve as the foundation for more specific questions as a part of theoretical sampling.

Data Analysis

While, SGT uses some of the basic concepts and operations of CGGT (Glasser & Strauss, 1967) key differences exist. For example, analysis of data can be informed by prior knowledge, something that Glasser fought against. As Dey (1993) notes, "…there is a difference between an open mind and an empty head. To analyze data, researchers draw upon accumulated knowledge. They don't dispense with it" (p. 63). With this freedom to become more personally involved in analysis, researchers are expected to engage reflexively to moderate the bias from prior knowledge.

More materially, while CGGT has data analysis phases of substantive and theoretical coding, SGT utilizes open, axial, selective coding stages. While open and axial coding correspond roughly to substantive coding and selective coding corresponds roughly to CGGT's theoretical coding, the procedures involved are much more minutely described and seemingly more complex. During these phases, SGT data analysis involves the use of analytical tools, which are largely types of questions and ways of thinking. These tools encourage the researcher to engage with the data in a disciplined and varied way that may diverge from the researcher's customary ways of thinking. This engagement with the data is characterized as more intensive than the engagement suggested by CGGT (Strauss & Corbin, 1998).

In terms of the specific stages of SGT data analysis, open coding occurs first and involves examining and coding raw data then refining and condensing codes to produce an uneven mixture of categories, properties, and dimensions of those properties (Strauss & Corbin, 1998). The next stage, axial coding, takes this mixture and begins to assemble the parts into the functional ingredients of theory. During this phase, categories that represent major components of process are further developed by refining their properties (characteristics) and dimensions (ways that properties vary). The properties and dimensions can be seen as conceptual "arms" that reach from the category and can interact with, influence, or be influenced by properties and dimensions associated with other significant categories. In this way, data that were broken into pieces during open coding are brought back together. A tool that is used during axial coding is the coding paradigm, a set of questions, similar to Glaser's coding families, that help functionally link categories by identifying patterns of conditions, inter/actions and emotions, and consequences (Corbin & Strauss, 2015).

During the third phase, selective coding, a core category is identified based on its centrality to all interactions and all other categories are related to this central category (Strauss & Corbin, 1998). During this phase tools and techniques that help with integration are used, such as storylines, diagrams, and the conditional matrix.

SGT's analysis process has been criticized as too complicated, "interrupt[ing] the true emergence" of theory (Glaser, 1992, p. 3–4) and as inflexible, which suppresses researchers' creativity (Charmaz, 2008). However, these criticism overlooked Strauss and Corbin's contention that their procedures should be used flexibly and in accordance with the research situation. Additionally, they defended their meticulously described and extensive techniques as helpful in moving past researchers' preconceived notions, in making theory generation systematic, and in producing dense, explanatory theory (Kenny & Fourie, 2015).

Case Study Example 12.10

The general data analysis case study examples described earlier in the chapter are very consistent with SGT data analysis. This is probably due to the heavy reliance on SGT methods in Rubel and Kline (2008). The coding in Case Study Example 12.4 is consistent with SGT's *open coding* as is some of the code refinement evident in the early part of Case Study Example 12.5. The latter parts of Case Study Example 12.5 that deal with identifying properties and related dimensions is very consistent with SGT's *axial coding*. Case Study Example 12.6 falls short of SGT's selective coding and theoretical integration because no central category was identified. However, the influence of SGT's coding paradigm is evident in the conditions and consequences outlined (e.g., the dependence of *deciding to go with intuition* upon the acts of *evaluating future effect of intuition on group* and *anticipating a positive effect*). The use of a storyline is also consistent with SGT's theoretical integration. In Rubel and Kline (2008), *experiential influence* served as the central category and it was related to four other categories via numerous properties and dimensions.

Results and Representation

Strauss shifted from the stance he shared with Glaser that the theory *emerges* or *is discovered* from the data. The foundation for the complex and specific structure of coding is that the theory is created by the researchers rather than exposed. The data do not contain dormant theories that await discovery. The theories are a product of intellectual labor and their accuracy and relevancy depend on the rigor that researchers are willing to hold themselves to (Mead, 1917; Kenny & Fourie, 2014, 2015). The theory for Strauss is, in the fewest words, to create a rich, comprehensive picture of the interaction between humans. It is about capturing the process in a systematic, cohesive, and explainable fashion (Corbin & Strauss, 1998). Similar to CGGT researchers, SGT researchers aim to identify a core category for the grounded theory (Corbin & Strauss, 2015).

The theory resulting from SGT research may have both positivist and interpretivist characteristics. The positivist characteristics are exemplified by descriptions of product of SGT as systematically related groups of categories where the connections are clearly described resulting in explanatory theory (Corbin & Strauss, 2008). The interpretivist characteristics, however, are exemplified by descriptions of the resultant theory being one of many possible interpretations that does not represent a unitary reality (Corbin & Strauss, 2015; Reiger, 2019)

CONSTRUCTIVIST GROUNDED THEORY

Charmaz intended to create an approach to grounded theory that is more relativist in orientation than Glaser or Strauss, who she critiqued as overly influenced by the positivist and post-positivist research cultures of the times (Charmaz, 2000). Novice researchers first encountering Charmaz's Constructivist Grounded Theory (CGT), may be struck by its overt embracing of constructivist principles, accessibility, focus on eliciting participant stories, and flexibility of both method and outcome. Other characteristics of CGT that distinguish it from CGGT and SGT include a clearly communicated and consistent philosophical integration, co-construction of data and analysis between researcher and participant, two-phase data analysis, clear articulation of inductive-abductive data analysis, and production of interpretivist theory (Reiger, 2019).

Philosophical Integration of Constructivist Grounded Theory

Charmaz's version of grounded theory is based upon the constructivist paradigm, which is associated with the ontological position of relativism and the epistemological position of constructivism. As Lincoln and Guba (1985) describe constructivist epistemology, "it is impossible to separate the inquirer from the inquired into. It is precisely their interactions that creates the data that will emerge from the inquiry" (p. 88). This paradigm offers the existence of multiple truths and realities instead of an absolute truth that can be discovered (Charmaz, 2014; Mills, Bonner, & Francis, 2006). A fundamental assumption in CGT is data and theories are not discovered, but instead are constructed through the interactions between people, perspectives, and research practices (Charmaz, 2014). Thus, the concepts of emergence and objectivity are rejected. This places the researcher firmly "in" the research, and similar to later versions of SGT, affects each aspect of the research process starting with preparation.

Preparation

Preparation for CGTy is distinct from preparation for CGGT and SGT due to its unambiguous reliance on co-construction of knowledge between researcher and participant. Both researcher and participant are affected. Charmaz (2008) indicates, "…when constructivist grounded theorists enter research sites and engage in their data, their perspectives may grow and/or change and thus permit the structure of inquiry, as well as its content, to be emergent" (p. 161). Thus, constructivist grounded theorists must recognize their privileges and preconceptions and how they impact the creation of theory (Charmaz, 2014). This requires researchers to analyze their role throughout the research and practice reflexivity even in the preparation stage (Mills, Bonner, and Francis, 2006). Additionally, theoretical sensitivity or prior knowledge of the phenomenon can help shape the research as long the knowledge is a starting rather than ending point for analysis (Charmaz, 2014, p. 30). In CGT, existing theories and literature can be used to develop theoretical sensitivity, which contrasts with CGGT but not SGT. Like SGT, CGT starts with a research question that is developed, in part, from theoretical sensitivity (Charmaz, 2014)

Sampling and Data Collection

Sampling and data collection in CGT research share similarities with other grounded theory methodologies. In terms of sampling, CGT values idiographic and local theories (Charmaz, 2014).

Thus, CGT researchers may not move beyond a community or specific location to build theory, valuing depth of understanding rather than breadth. Strategies like maximum variation sampling, which is intended to make the resultant theory more transferable, may not be seen as important in CGT research as they are in CGGT and SGT research.

Charmaz (2014) described the CGT data collection process as not being starkly different from those of CGGT and SGT. The differences rest more in how data collection and data are viewed. Interviews are the main form of data collection in CGT and should exhibit a "position of mutuality between researcher and participant in the research process" (Mills et al., 2006, p. 8). This contrasts with the latent power differential between researcher and participant in CGGT and SGT originating from their positivist and post-positivist roots. This relationship of mutuality is characterized by a careful building of rapport to minimize the power imbalance present between researcher and participant (Mills, Bonner, &Francis, 2006). Additionally, Charmaz (2014) emphasized the importance of interview recordings to ensure capturing the participant's voice and advised placing emphasis on the language used in interviews to promote co-construction of data. In terms of structure, CGT interviews tend to be semi-structured, with the researcher using their theoretical sensitivity to develop open and relevant interview questions. During these semi-structured interviews, CGT will be much more likely to follow the participant, adding thoughtful probes to deepen understanding of what the participant offers (Reiger, 2019).

Data Analysis

Where other grounded theory methodologies value, to varying degrees, objectivity, CGT researchers recognize objectivity as unobtainable and subjectivity as a certainty during data analysis (Charmaz, 2014). Charmaz contends that truly raw data do not exist in CGT since data arise from adapted language and meaning created with the researcher. Thus, data collection and data analysis are intertwined as products co-created and influenced by the both the researchers' sociocultural settings, academic training, and worldviews and those of the participants (Charmaz, 2018). As such, during data analysis CGT researchers do not pretend to be free from preconceptions but instead "engage in reflexivity and explicate their preconceptions during every phase of data collection and analysis" (Charmaz, 2018, p. 418). A prime tool of reflexivity is memo-writing. While memoing is used in all forms of grounded theory, in CGT it creates a space where researchers can converse with themselves not only about data and analytic ideas but also about their related experiences and assumptions (Charmaz, 2014).

According to Charmaz (2014), coding in grounded theory is "the pivotal link between collecting data and developing an emergent theory to explain these data" (p. 113). The CGT coding process is both similar to and different from that of CGGT and SGT. CGT shares the same general flow of first conceptualizing data into codes then integrating the codes into theory that is characteristic of CGGT and SGT (Charmaz, 2014) and also borrows techniques from both SGT and CGGT when appropriate (Charmaz, 2014). However, rather than the open, selective, and axial coding of SGT or the substantive and theoretical coding of CGGT, CGT involves two phases, initial coding and focused coding (Charmaz, 2018). Charmaz (2014) described initial coding as the process of studying the "fragments of data—words, lines, segments, and incidents—closely for their analytic import" then assigning codes (p. 109). Focused coding, then, is the phase where the "most significant and frequent initial codes" are sorted, synthesized, integrated, and organized (Charmaz, 2014, p. 113). These phases are not linear but interactive, with the researcher responding to the participants, data, and constructed meanings accordingly. The CGT researcher continuously refines and revises codes, concepts, and theory as they simultaneously try to understand the participants' worldview and their own influence (Charmaz, 2014).

After the researcher has analyzed the data to form some categories, concepts, and maybe tentative relationships but cannot easily move forward, Charmaz (2014) indicates that the researcher should engage in theoretical sampling. Theoretical sampling in the case of CGT is similar to theoretical sampling in CGGT and SG, but may involve less specificity in questioning to extend theory since relationships between concepts may be more general. The tools of CGT analysis are borrowed from CGGT and SGT but always evaluated and questioned for their suitability for constructivist processes and ends.

Case Study Example 12.11

Because CGT often borrows from the analytic methods of CGGT and SGT, the general Case Study Examples 12.4, 12.5, and 12.6 provided earlier can be viewed as consistent with CGT. However, some features of CGT analysis can be further distinguished using the examples. While a CGT researcher might easily produce the coding apparent in Case Study Example 12.4 as a part of initial coding, CGT analysis is particularly sensitive to the participants unique social situation. In this case the participants were experts in their scholarly and professional field, group counseling and therapy. Some reference is given in the example data of this position in the first line and is coded *trusting self due to experience*. With sensitivity to the participant's unique situation and identity as a expert this might be coded differently as *trusting self as an expert*. This emic lens of expertise might influence the remaining codes also, for example, flipping *evaluating future effects of intuition* to *using expertise to forecast effects*.

The use of constant comparison in both Case Study Examples 12.4 and 12.5 is consistent with CGT. However, the attention to properties and dimensions in Case Study Example 12.5 is less consistent with CGT. While axial coding methods might be borrowed by a CGT researcher if a strong rationale exists, CGT analysis tends to be more impressionistic and less detailed. For example, CGT analysis might stop at the most general code *evaluating future effects of intuition*. Then the codes included in its dimension (e.g., **a**nticipating *effects on group-as-a-whole, anticipating effects on client*, and *anticipating effects on self*) might be incorporated into the narrative description of *evaluating future effects of intuition* without being formalized.

Relating concepts to one another, which occurs at the end of Case Study Example 12.5, aligns with a transition from initial coding to focused coding. The use of the storyline for theory integration in Case Study Example 12.6 is also largely consistent with CGT analysis during the focused coding phase. However focused coding would rely more heavily on retaining unique features of the participant's story and less on precisely conceptualized relationships among codes. For example, the contingent relationship between *evaluating future effects of intuition, anticipating a positive effect*, and *deciding to go with intuition* might simply be presented as a theoretical memo about a single global concept code *using expertise to harness intuition*.

Results and Representation

In CGT, a foundational assumption is that the representation is inherently "problematic, relativistic, situational, and partial" because of the influence of the researcher's values, priorities, and actions (Charmaz, 2014, p. 236). The aim of CGT is to capture how the participants construct their meaning while also recognizing that analysis will be an interpretation that includes the researcher's view (Charmaz, 2014). In order to create a theory with this aim, the researcher must be willing to take a reflexive stance where the researcher attempts to "become aware of [their] presuppositions and to grapple with how they affect the research" (Charmaz, 2014, p. 240). With this stance, the researcher provides the reader with information on how they conducted the research, how they related to the participants, and other aspects that may have influenced the analysis (Charmaz, 2014). Doing this allows the reader to assess how the researcher may have influenced the process and the outcome. On the continuum of forms from positivist theory to interpretivist theory (Charmaz, 2014), CGT lies firmly on the interpretivist end. An interpretivist theory captures the studied phenomenon through abstract conceptualization and proposing relationships but does not explain causality. CGT theory should be identified as substantive theory rather than formal theory since it is derived from and applicable to a specific moment, population, and location (Reiger, 2019). Similarly, the theory should reflect its construction as an image of a reality, one option among many possible interpretations and not as a singular truth. In addition, some theory produced from CGT methodology may consist of theoretical concepts that are not organized around a core category (Reiger, 2019).

INCREASING RIGOR IN GROUNDED THEORY RESEARCH

Some authors (Cooney, 1991; Reynolds et al., 2011) indicate that quality in qualitative research encompasses two related but different areas, quality of output and quality of process. Rigor generally refers to the quality of the process and concerns how well researchers have utilized the specific principles of a qualitative research approach to design and implement their study (Gasson, 2004). Trustworthiness is the overall sense of trust research consumers develop when they encounter the strategies researchers use to promotes a study's credibility, transferability, dependability, confirmability, and authenticity (Morrow, 2005). Rigor's relationship to trustworthiness can be seen as mutual.

Rigor, in part, depends upon dedicated use of trustworthiness strategies, but also centers designing studies that are coherent with all parts relating smoothly to the research problem and question, philosophical assumptions, and chosen approach (Ponterotto, 2005). Rigor also means implementing the study's design with the integrity and intensity necessary to produce high-quality data and interpretations (Morrow, 2005). Additionally, part of rigorous implementation is remaining flexible (Corbin & Strauss, 2015) during the research process to adapt to newly perceived needs, unanticipated situations, and surprising results. Those changes could include changes in research questions, sampling, and interview strategies or reanalyzing data due to a newly realized bias.

Guidance on increasing rigor in grounded theory studies has evolved over time and across paradigms. In their early post-positivist-leaning grounded theory, Glaser and Strauss defined rigor narrowly, as a *methodological rigor* (Cooney, 2010). Beck (1993) and Chiovitti and Piran (2003) emphasize the *interpretive or analytic rigor* that extends beyond methodological rigor. From a post-positivist perspective, a rigorous study helps people make sense of a phenomenon while following research best practice (Glaser & Strauss, 1967). Some strategies to promote methodological rigor in post-positivist-leaning studies include using multiple sources of data including non-emic sources such as expert interviews and documents; multiple rounds of data collection over time with the same participants; and multiple qualitative trustworthiness procedures. Constructivist-leaning grounded theory studies may use similar strategies while maintaining an emic perspective (e.g., no expert triangulation or data or use of non-participant generated documents for data), however the focus stays on the trustworthiness of rigorous data collection and analysis. Adherence to the method is meant to increase the theory's connection to the data and participants' authentic experience, and all product and process criteria are seen as supportive of study quality (Morrow, 2005).

What does rigor look like in grounded theory research beyond general recommendations geared toward trustworthiness? Early criteria for the quality of grounded theory studies reflected its pragmatist roots with a focus on the quality of the outcome. Glaser and Strauss (1967) identified the criteria of (a) does the theory fit the situation and, (b) does the theory work to help the people in the situation? This pragmatic focus on outcome is also represented here by Corbin and Strauss (2015):

> *If it (theory or findings) fits and it is useful because it explains or describes things, then rigor and vigor and truth and everything else must have been built into the research process or the findings would not hold up to scrutiny, would not explain situations, and would be invalidated in practice. (pp. 345–346)*

Beyond quality outcomes, what are the conditions and actions that promote rigor in grounded theory research? Credibility, according to Beck (1993), ultimately comes down to how clear, evocative, and accurate the qualitative results are. Auditability, according to Beck, is when the researcher's decisions throughout the research process are clearly and deeply described enough so that other researchers are able to follow (Beck 1993). Fittingness, according to Beck (1993), describes how transferable the research results are to other contexts based on descriptions of research contexts and processes. Chiovitti and Piran's (2003) integration of grounded theory with Beck's (1993) conceptualization for rigor resulted in eight suggestions for achieving rigor in grounded theory. To promote *credibility* Chiovitti and Piran suggested:

1. Let participants lead the process as evidenced by revision of interview questions or conceptualizations based on participant response.
2. Check interpretations and theory against participant meaning as evidenced by reports of cross-checking with participants.
3. Use participants' words in the theory as evidenced by inclusion of quotes to support concepts and by explaining variations in participant wording.
4. Evidence researcher transparency by disclosing the researcher's experiences, views, and thinking. (p. 430)

To promote *auditability* Chiovitti and Piran suggested:

5. Specify the criteria inherent in the researcher's thinking as evidenced by disclosure of frameworks used to initiate and continue data analysis. Chiovitti and Piran (2003) specifically reference such frameworks as Strauss and Corbin's (1998) paradigm model for axial coding.
6. Describe the how and why of participant selection as evidenced by a thorough description of sampling rationale, criteria, and strategies (p. 430). We believe this should include a thorough description of the rationale for interview questions, interview strategy, and theoretical sampling.

To promote *fittingness* Chiovitti and Piran (2003) suggested:

7. Describe the scope of research in terms of sample, setting, and level of theory as evidenced by rich descriptions of participants and research location as well as disclosure of whether the theory is meant to be formal or substantive.
8. Cross-check categories and relationships between categories against the literature as evidenced by a thorough discussion of key theory points and similar and dissimilar phenomena in the literature. (p. 430)

Case Study Example 12.12

The chapter case study example Rubel and Kline (2008) exhibits strong methodological rigor in some ways but lacks rigor in others. The study evidences three full rounds of data collection over time with the same participants and utilized multiple trustworthiness procedures (e.g., member checking, negative case analysis, literature triangulation, and expert triangulation). Coherence was generally strong due to exclusive and detailed use of the methods outlined by Strauss and Corbin (1998). Coherence was not fully realized, however, due to lack of attention to the research paradigm, which in retrospect lay somewhere between post-positivism and constructivism. The study met all four of Chiovitti and Piran's (2003) criteria for promoting the credibility component of rigor. With respect to Chiovitti and Piran's auditability criteria, the chapter case study example did well in providing a thorough rationale for all methods used but was entirely missing discussions of the frameworks that informed the methods. Similarly, with respect to the fittingness criteria, the chapter case study example evidenced strong use of literature to cross-check conceptualizations and described the setting and participants well, but did not mention the intended level of the final theory.

MULTICULTURAL ISSUES AND GROUNDED THEORY RESEARCH

Ethical codes within many disciplines call for an acknowledgment of issues of diversity and multicultural considerations. For example, CACREP (2016) indicates that counselors and counselor educators should understand and use strategies for engaging in and reporting research that are culturally relevant and ethical. However, society is very different than it was in 1967 when Glaser and Strauss introduced grounded theory research to the world. So how do issues of multiculturalism and diversity relate to grounded theory research? To answer this question, it is important to consider the reasons for conducting qualitative research. Creswell and Poth (2018) note "We conduct qualitative research when we want to empower individuals to share their stories, hear their voices...when partial or inadequate theories exist for certain populations...or existing theories do not adequately capture the complexity of the problem" (pp. 45-46). These reasons speak directly to empowering the disenfranchised by amplifying their voices in research. Counseling researchers Merchant and Dupuy (1996) note that qualitative research shares a similar worldview to multicultural counseling: an awareness of personal assumptions and values, an understanding of worldviews that are different from one's own, and the use and development of culturally appropriate interventions. But how does grounded theory in particular deal with these issues?

Green, Shope, and Clark (2007) asserted that when researchers are mindful of issues of diversity, grounded theory holds great potential in creating new knowledge and theories surrounding these issues. However, this kind of mindfulness is not always present. Green et al. (2007) noted that the centrality of diversity in grounded theory research falls along a continuum: primary, complementary, peripheral, and absent. When grounded theory research places diversity in a position of primary importance, all phases of the research process are seen through a culturally and diversity sensitive lens. However, as the levels of importance lessen, issues of diversity may disappear entirely from the study (Green et al., 2007). They further note that while researchers should balance objectivity and sensitivity when responding to diversity as an emergent concept in GT, the dangers of under-sensitivity are much more common and dire than oversensitivity. In other words, being too theoretically sensitive to diversity is rarely an issue in grounded theory research.

From a practical standpoint, how does a researcher ensure that a grounded theory study includes and acknowledges issues of diversity? Self-reflection is one tool that may be helpful. Interviewer/ participant matching is another possibility, while ensuring that member checking includes a diversity of research participants and reading research from diverse scholars are also suggested (Green et al., 2007). As grounded theory has evolved since its initial conception, there has been a move toward more constructivist and post-modern approaches, which may be more fitting for research centered on multiculturalism and diversity. While purposefully exploring literature and research from diverse scholars may not align with Glaser's vision of grounded theory, this approach can promote greater sensitivity to issues of diversity (Olson, 2007). It follows that the original stance against the use of literature early in a grounded theory study may be counterproductive to the theoretical sensitivity needed for researchers to recognize their own privilege and worldview and begin to recognize the issues voiced by diverse participants.

LIMITATIONS OF GROUNDED THEORY RESEARCH

To choose the best approach for their research question, researchers need to be aware of both the advantages and limitations of the grounded theory approach (Hussein et al., 2014). While grounded theory research shares some of the limitations of other qualitative approaches, such as high levels of subjectivity and limited generalizability (Hussein et al., 2014), the literature on GT describes some unique limitations. These limitations are often related to grounded theory's strengths (Charmaz, 2006), which include a set of complex methods that are described in detail, an exhaustive approach that allows detailed understanding of social processes, and a set of subtly differing methodologies that can meet varying needs. These strengths can enhance grounded theory's limitations including the process being time and energy intensive and also being confusing and with a high potential for methodological error (Hussein et al., 2014).

One of the key advantages of the grounded theory approach is its potential for amassing rich and meaningful data resulting from multiple rounds of interviews (Charmaz, 2006). This large amount of data can lead to an extensive, complex, labor intensive process (Hussein et al., 2014). Grounded theory data collection and data analysis processes may take many months to complete, and the complexity of the methods may cause researchers to experience confusion during analysis (Creswell & Poth, 2018; Hussein et al., 2014).

An additional drawback to grounded theory research is the potential for methodological errors that may occur (Hussein et al., 2014). The potential methodological errors are not far different than errors that can be made in other qualitative studies such as making errors in sampling or incorrectly choosing methods (Charmaz, 2018). Additionally, Hussein et al. (2014) noted that an error, specifically harmful to grounded theory research, is the utilization of only one data source. This can limit the depth of the constructed theory.

As previously discussed, several approaches to grounded theory can be taken. Researchers may choose a Glasserian, Straussian, or constructivist approach, among other options. Each grounded theory approach differs in their path to arriving at theory (Hussein et al., 2014) and involve subtly different methods of data collection, data analysis, and writing. This may be confusing or overwhelming for novice researchers. Given the complex nature of GT, novice researchers may benefit from having a mentor throughout the process to assist with planning a study with a doable scope, to consult with about specific methods, and to help determine when to shift from one research phase to another.

SUMMARY

Grounded theory research is a robust and diverse collection of methodologies and methods that enable nuanced and credible research into human experiences and processes. Its diverse philosophical integration spans realist and relativist ontologies and objectivist and constructivist epistemologies and enables diversity within the approach but also can create some ambiguity and confusion. Key points to remember about grounded theory research include:

- Grounded theory is distinct from research approaches in its ability to account for process, its well-described analysis methods, and its final product of theory.
- Three major types of grounded theory research exist including CGGT, SGT, and CGT.
- The grounded theory research process begins with a process-oriented research problem and question and moves through a recursive data collection and analysis cycle driven by theoretical sampling. Collection and analysis continue until a theory is formed and saturated.
- The rigor of grounded theory research is intertwined with trustworthiness and relies upon procedures that align with methodological rigor and interpretive or analytic rigor.
- While grounded theory has great potential for researching diverse and multicultural experiences, researchers need to develop adequate sensitivity to the experiences and issues of the population. This may require more extensive than normal forays into literature.
- Grounded theory research has several limitations, including the complexity of the methods and intensity of the work.

STUDENT ACTIVITIES

Exercise 1: Creating a Grounded Theory Research Question

Directions: By linking all the chapter exercises you will get a taste of how grounded theory research flows. To start, these exercises will use a simplified problem common to most students using this text and use a constructivist stance for the exercises without sticking strictly to any one of the three methodologies described later. Think about the issue of studying on any given day for a research class. Study is seen as good thing, yet students both study and do not study when needed. Understanding how students in a research class decide to either study or not study could provide useful information for advisors, instructors, and students. This is your research problem. Now let's work on creating a research question.

Think about taking a constructivist stance for this study. The assumption is that the reality of this issue is complex, dependent on context, and based on how the participants think and feel during the process. You will be answering the question by valuing the participant's perspective of what is happening. How would you phrase the single core question you want to answer? Adapt it to the stem: How do *Y* experience the process of *Z*? Brainstorm more than one option if you have time. If you have a partner or classmate to discuss your research question(s) with, try to evaluate all your options. Which seems like the most succinct, yet broad and holistic question that aligns with what you want to understand? Pick or pick and revise the research question you feel is the best.

Exercise 2: Creating GT Interview Questions

Directions: Grounded theory interviews can be extremely opened ended and unstructured, very structured, or somewhere in between. For this exercise in creating grounded theory interview questions, you will create a semi-structured interview protocol. Creating good grounded theory interview questions relies upon having some understanding of the context around the researched case. For this exercise use the research question of, "How do students in research class experience the process of deciding to engage or not engage in studying?" or you can use the research question you constructed in Exercise 1.

Part 1: Developing a conceptual context normally involves a reflective process and a literature review. For this exercise, though, simply put yourself in the participants' shoes or think of your own experience. How have you or they experienced this process of deciding to engage or not engage in studying for research class over time? Brainstorm and list the (a) external systems or factors (e.g., school, home, work), (b) internal systems or factors (e.g., identifying as a procrastinator), and (c) historical factors (e.g., past experiences of failing) that might affect how they experience this process. Give yourself at least 15 minutes to brainstorm this list. When you are done, evaluate your ideas. Which seem most salient to the research question and outcomes? Can some be lumped together because they are more alike than different? Create a list of no more than four broad domains that cover the most important of these factors.

Part 2: Brainstorm up to five interview questions, one exploring the holistic process and the others exploring the domains identified in Part 1. For the holistic question simply rephrase your research question or ask for an example(s) of their process experiences. For all questions, focus on making them open ended, broad, and as free from bias as possible. Imagine your participant being encouraged to tell a story about their experience for each question. For example, if one of domains is "history with studying" you might write, "Tell me about your history with studying and how this affects your decision-making to engage or not engage in studying for research class?"

Once you have your five questions, evaluate them. If you have a learning partner or classmate, pair up to evaluate each other's interview questions. Do the questions focus on the process in question or some substantial part of the process? Are the questions open and likely to elicit a story? Are the questions relatively free of bias, that is, will they allow participants to talk about most or all outcomes and processes? When you have your interview protocol you can move on to Exercise 3.

Exercise 3: Gathering Data Through Interviews

Directions: For this exercise you will use the semi-structured interview protocol from Exercise 2. If you do not have an interview protocol use these questions: (a) Describe how you experience the process of deciding to engage or not engage in studying for your research class. (b) What are your thoughts and feelings as you decide to engage or not engage in studying for your research class? (c) If you can, describe some examples of how external factors have affected your experience of deciding to engage or not engage in studying for research class. (d) What makes you unique as a person and student and how does that affect your experience of deciding to engage or not engage in studying for research class? (e) Describe how your personal history or experiences in the past affect how you experience deciding to engage or not engage in studying for research class.

The goal here is to produce a small amount of data you can use in Exercises 5 and 6 and to give you a sense of interviewing without too much work. Using your own questions or the preceding questions, interview yourself or a classmate. Keep the interview to 10 minutes or less. Don't worry about getting very rich descriptions. However, feel free to ask a follow-up question or two such as, "Can you say more about that?" Record the interview using a digital device and transcribe it or use a voice-to-text recording app to save time. You or your interviewee can also write out the answers to the interview questions in a Word document or digital note.

Once you have your data in a digital document read it over. What seemed like the easiest parts of the interview for the participant? The most difficult? Think about the central research question. Where did the interviewee stay on track or stray? What seems important but needs more explanation? Where would you like to ask follow-up questions? What would you ask and why? Overall, would you change the interview questions, and if so, how? As you reflect on your own responses or the responses of your participant, can you identify any biases you might have? If you have a partner, trade transcripts and see if each of you can identify some potential biases from the interviews. Notes made as you answer these questions can be considered memos.

Exercise 4: Engaging in Initial or Open Coding

Directions: Coding for a grounded theory projects is rigorous and prolonged. However, the goal of this exercise is to get a feel for initial coding and to develop a set of codes to work with in Exercise 5. Start by reorienting yourself to the research question and conceptual context developed in Exercises 1 and 2. Then read slowly over the data thinking carefully about what the participant means. Assume that the data are a story of the process and are composed of parts or incidents. With this in mind, first try coding small pieces of data—a phrase or a sentence. Ask yourself, "What do these data mean to the participant?" and "What do they mean about their experience of the process of deciding to engage or not engage in studying?" Jot down some notes reflecting your thoughts on the meaning. When you have some sense of the meaning of the data bit, give this idea a name or code that is descriptive and action oriented.

Code *at least* the data produced by the first interview question. If you have time, code the whole interview. Keeping an action-orientation in your coding will facilitate theory formation later. One way to promote an action-orientation is to use gerund phrases for codes. Gerunds are nouns that are verbs with "ing" endings. Gerund phrases are gerunds that have modifiers and objects attached to them. For example, "run" is a verb and "running" is its gerund/noun form. "Running with scissors" is a gerund phrase. You can use the comment function in Microsoft Word to associate the codes with the data or any other method that works for you. Keep notes documenting your ideas and questions as you go along. Note also if you are starting to see patterns or see codes that are very similar or very different. For comparison you can also go back through the data you already coded and re-code multi-line pieces or whole paragraphs of data that seem to represent incidents in the process story, while maintaining your practice of memoing, questioning to uncover meaning related to the research question, and using an action-orientation.

When you have coded what you wish, take a step back and examine your codes. You may have coded some incidents that are similar using exactly the same code. You may also notice that some codes are not the same but may deal with very similar incidents. Comparing these similar codes to see if they share enough characteristics to be described by one code is a form of constant comparison. Using this comparison process, try to shrink your list of codes down to between 10 and 15 codes. This is an arbitrary number meant to make theorizing manageable for Exercise 5. In a real grounded theory study this condensation and clarification would still happen but would be extended and would not have a limit. List your 10 to 15 codes and make some notes about their definitions and meaning, what they are and are not, and how they seem to be related.

Exercise 5: Engaging in Theorizing and Theoretical Sampling

Directions: The purpose of this exercise is for you to get a sense of connecting concepts derived from data into theoretical propositions or relationships. We will continue analyzing using a constructivist perspective so we will not dig too deeply into identifying specific properties and dimensions. Look over your data for one paragraph that speaks cohesively about one aspect of the process of deciding to engage or not engage in studying. Pick a paragraph that seems to have a lot of process in it as evidenced by use of contingent language such as "if," "when," and "then" and seems to move the participant from one part of the process to another (e.g., "When I have to take care of my son and I have a headache, then I find it hard to study even if I know I have a test the next day").

You may already have codes assigned to this paragraph or you may recode it based on new ideas. Regardless, make sure to give the whole paragraph a code that reflects its overall meaning and also to code it at the level of phrases, sentences, or lines. Remember to use gerund phrases! Once you have the paragraph coded, rewrite the paragraph in the form of a storyline focusing on representing the codes or concepts you have created. You may need to back track and revise your codes to make them flow together and reflect the data. At this point is it okay to assume some obvious connections as we did in Case Study Example 12.6.

The goal here is to see if you can conceptualize your small amount of process-oriented data to reflect some kind of relationship among codes. It could be simply that the existence of one code seems to cause or trigger the action of another code or you might be able to find a longer and more clear relationship like the *evaluating future effect of intuition on group, anticipating a positive effect,* and *deciding to go with intuition* contingent relationship described in Case Study Examples 12.6 and 12.7. You may be able to conceptualize your line-by-line codes as parts of a process represented by your more general paragraph level code. If it helps, feel free to use drawings or diagrams to help the process along. Memoing while you think may also help by solidifying and making visual your thoughts and allowing you to analyze and evaluate them more easily. When you think you can articulate a solid relationship between concepts, double-check it against the data. You can also double check your thinking with a classmate. By yourself or with a partner reflect on:

1. What was it like to look for process?

ADDITIONAL RESOURCES

Software Recommendations

Corbin and Strauss (2015) recommend researchers, particularly novice researchers, use the simplest data analysis software they can find. A thorough review of many qualitative data analysis software packages can be found in Silver and Lewins (2014).

Helpful Links

- Website of The Grounded Theory Institute "The official website of Dr. Barney Glaser and Classic Grounded Theory" http://www.groundedtheory.com (Links to an external site.)

- Website of *Grounded Theory Review: An International Journal.* This journal publishes CGGT grounded theory studies and conceptual papers http://groundedtheoryreview.com

▨ A quick video tutorial on grounded theory by Kathy Charmaz. Prof. Charmaz talks about what she calls a "modern" version of GT, the Constructivist GT, as she was one of the main contributors to creating this framework. https://youtu.be/Es-PHU52qEE

▨ Notes on Grounded Theory from University of Amsterdam. This video provides an abbreviated history and key concepts on GT. https://youtu.be/Y6f1GHjD5JQ

▨ Notes on Grounded Theory from University of Amsterdam. This video focuses on different versions of GT. https://youtu.be/JX42ld18kao

Helpful Books

Charmaz, K. (2014). *Constructing grounded theory.* (2nd ed.). SAGE.
Corbin, J., & Strauss, A. (2015). *Basics of qualitative research: Techniques and procedures for developing grounded theory.* (3rd ed.). SAGE.
Glaser, B. G., & Strauss, A. L. (1967). *The discovery of grounded theory.* Aldine Publishing Company.

Helpful Videos

▨ https://www.youtube.com/watch?v=M2DyB-hGX-Q

▨ https://www.youtube.com/watch?v=lYzhgMZii3o

▨ https://www.youtube.com/watch?v=HXh7Y9yIE8E

KEY REFERENCES

Only key references appear in the print edition. The full reference list appears in the digital product found on http://connect.springerpub.com/content/book/978-0-8261-4385-3/part/part03/chapter/ch12

Beck C. T. (1993). Qualitative research: The evaluation of its credibility, fittingness, and auditability. *Western Journal of Nursing Research*, 15, 263–266.

Bryant, A. (2009). Grounded theory and pragmatism: The curious case of Anselm Strauss. *Forum Qualitative Sozialforschung*, 10(3), 1–37.

Cooney, A. (2010). Choosing between Glaser and Strauss: An example. *Nurse Researcher*, 17(4), 18–28.

Corbin, J., & Strauss, A. (2015). *Basics of qualitative research: Techniques and procedures for developing grounded theory* (3rd ed.). SAGE.

Creswell, J. W., & Poth, C. N. (2018). *Qualitative inquiry: Choosing among five approaches* (4th ed.). SAGE.

Glaser, B. G. (2009). J*argonizing: The use of the grounded theory vocabulary.* Sociology Press.

Glaser, B. G., & Strauss, A. L. (1967). *The discovery of grounded theory.* Aldine Publishing Company.

Patton, M. Q. (2019). *Qualitative research & evaluation methods integrating theory and practice* (5th ed.). Sage Publications.

Rubel, D. J., & Kline, W. B. (2008). An exploratory study of expert group leadership. *Journal for Specialists in Group Work*, 33(2), 138–160. https://doi.org/10.1080/01933920801977363

Strauss, A., & Corbin, J. (1998). *Basics of qualitative research: Techniques and procedures for developing grounded theory* (2nd ed.). SAGE.

CHAPTER 13

NARRATIVE RESEARCH

Heather Dahl and Wendy Hoskins

LEARNING OBJECTIVES

After reading this chapter, you will be able to:

- Classify narrative research as a tradition
- Recognize the process of data collection, procedure, and analysis using narrative and paradigmatic narrative strategies
- Identify qualitative rigor strategies in the narrative research tradition
- Recognize multicultural issues for narrative research

INTRODUCTION TO NARRATIVE RESEARCH

This chapter is your introduction to narrative research, a qualitative research tradition that is rich with stories and meaning. While many qualitative research traditions focus on meaning and experiences with participants, narrative researchers use the participants ability to be story tellers through lived and told experiences (Clandinin & Connelly, 2000; Creswell, 2018; Polkinghorne, 1995). Narrative research is a qualitative research tradition that aims to describe the story of those that are the focus of the research. In this tradition, researchers use a variety of data collection tools that are common across traditions in a way that allows the participant to be the author of their own experience.

It is a difficult task to distinguish narrative research from other research traditions when one of the most seminal pieces of work, *Narrative Inquiry* by Clandinin and Connelly (2000), specifically states that, "although this may be worthwhile for an understanding of the broad range of methodologies, it is of no great significance for narrative inquiry because...the place of theory in narrative inquiry differs from the place of theory in formalistic inquiries" (p. 128). These authors recognize similarities of narrative research to phenomenology and ethnography (e.g., participant lived experience), while also noting that the important distinguishing feature of narrative research is the narrative view of experience taken on by the researchers. Indeed, by distinguishing the unique aspects of each tradition, researchers have the ability to choose the tradition that is best suited to the research questions.

Narrative research has held many names as it has grown as a tradition. While we are using the term narrative research in this chapter (Creswell, 2018), other researchers use narratology (Hays & Wood, 2011, Hays and Singh, 2012) or narrative inquiry (Chase, 2005; Clandinin & Connelly, 2000, Polkinghorne, 1995), among others. In addition, the term narrative analysis is used in research as both a tradition and a data analysis term. All of these terms generally speak to the same tradition and practice and have been used interchangeably. In this chapter, we will use the term narrative research to describe the tradition.

Various disciplines have utilized narrative research in publications including counseling, education, anthropology, sociology, history, sociolinguistics, and literature since the early 1900s (Chase, 2005; Creswell, 2018). The origins of narrative research are grounded in the social sciences. One of the earliest known use of this tradition was with the Chicago School Sociologists who examined narratives of individuals across the 1900s. The first publication thought to exist was in 1918 with the publication of *The Polish Peasant*, a book written by Thomas and Znaniecki, sociologists at The Chicago School (Chase, 2005). Thomas and Znaniecki examined the life story of Wladek Wiszniewsky using personal life records that existed to paint a picture of him. This effort laid the groundwork for further use of narrative research within sociology as well as a multitude of other disciplines, including counseling.

As mentioned previously, a noted work in narrative research is Clandinin and Connelly's (2000) *Narrative Inquiry*. In this writing, the authors attempt to define narrative research in their view, while laying the groundwork from the conceptualization of research, data collection, analysis, and the report itself. The book explores the researcher–participant relationship and how to appropriately use this field of inquiry. The text is written from the perspective of their experience as researchers, and when speaking of the goal of the text stated, "Our intention is to come to the definition of narrative inquiry slowly by 'showing' rather than 'telling' what narrative inquirers do" (p. 20). This book is essential reading material for a narrative researcher.

While narrative research has similarities to other traditions such as phenomenology, ethnography, and heuristic inquiry, it is a unique and varied tradition. As described by Pollkinghorne (2005), narrative "refers to a discourse form in which events and happenings are configured into a temporal unity by means of a plot" (p. 5). While many different narrative researchers employ different approaches, at the core of the tradition, human experience is interpreted through the use of narrative data. Interpretation of the human experience may be through narrative stories, while others may use common elements of different items (e.g., documents) to describe a common-held narrative between the participants (Polkinghorne, 2005).

When understanding the undertaking of using narrative research as a tradition, Chase (2005) identified five contemporary strategies that narrative researchers employ when conducting research:

1. Treat inquiry as a form of discourse.
2. View narratives a verbal action—always emphasizing the narrator's voice in the work since they are the expert.
3. Stories are bounded by the context of those that the story is about and their surroundings and circumstances.
4. The experience described is not generalizable to those outside of the phenomenon.
5. Researchers are the narrators of the participant stories.

These five strategies are essential to the work of a narrative researcher, and most are unique to the tradition.

As mentioned earlier, narrative research is a natural fit for the counseling profession. When reviewing the Council for Accreditation of Counseling and Related Educational Programs (CACREP, 2016) standards, there are four that specifically stand out as relevant to the practice of narrative research:

- 2.f.a: The importance of research in advancing the counseling profession, including how to critique research to inform counseling practice.

- 2.f.f: Qualitative, quantitative and mixed research methods.

- 2.f.g: Designs used in research and program evaluation.

- 2.f.j: Ethical and culturally relevant strategies for conducting, interpreting, and reporting the results of research and/or program evaluation.

- 6.b.a: Research designs appropriate to quantitative and qualitative research questions.

- 6.b.c: Qualitative designs and approaches to qualitative data analysis.

- 6.b.g: Research questions appropriate for professional research and publication.

- 6.b.l: Ethical and culturally relevant strategies for conducting research.

Each of these standards are directly applicable to narrative research and apply across specialty. It is important to consider these standards as you continue to read through this chapter.

PARADIGMATIC HIERARCHY

An important distinguishing feature for narrative research is its unique paradigmatic hierarchy (Crotty, 2003). As with all qualitative research traditions, this hierarchy, identified by Crotty (2003), includes five levels: ontology, epistemology, theoretical stance, methodology, and method. Each level identifies pillars of narrative research design and are essential to understanding when to use this tradition.

The first level of the paradigmatic hierarchy is ontology, otherwise known as how reality is viewed in the research (Crotty, 2013; Hays & Singh, 2012). In narrative research, reality is placed in the hands of the participant's story, and the participant–researcher relationship (Clandinin & Connelly, 2000; Creswell, 2018). It is the intent of the researcher to tell the truths of those that are participating in the research, and not generalize to others. It is in this relativism that narrative research lives.

The second level of paradigmatic hierarchy is epistemology, or the way that knowledge is attained (Crotty, 2003). As Crotty (2003) noted, epistemology and ontology are often related and are identified together. In narrative research, the knowledge that can be gained in research is unlimited and constructed by those participating in the research process, otherwise known as constructionism. Constructionism is the view that "meaning is not discovered but constructed" (Crotty, 2003, p. 42). In narrative research, this is a central tenet of the interaction with participants. Interaction between the researcher and participant through multiple data sources is what drives meaning.

The third level of the paradigmatic hierarchy is theoretical stance, or the philosophical stance of the research. These paradigms are the underlying assumptions and interpretive frameworks that guide the research itself (Creswell, 2018; Hays & Singh, 2012). In the case of narrative research, social constructivism (i.e., interpretivism, postmodernism) is the paradigm that most appropriately forms its theoretical stance (Creswell, 2018; Hays & Singh, 2012; Patton, 2002;). Hays and Singh (2012) note that social constructivism "assumes that 'universal truth' cannot exist because there are multiple contextual perspectives and subjective voices that can label truth in scientific pursuit" (p. 41). Researchers using narrative inquiry understand that the participant and the researcher are biased and have their own perspectives, and it is the researcher's position to understand and work within this construct.

The fourth level of the paradigmatic hierarchy is methodology, or in this case the narrative research tradition itself (Crotty, 2003). Discussed in depth in this chapter, narrative research aims to describe the story of the participants, and capture the essence of their perspective (Chase, 2005; Clandinin, & Connelly, 2000; Creswell 2018).

The fifth and final level of the paradigmatic hierarchy is methods, or the tools used to collect, manage, and analyze data (Crotty, 2003). In narrative research, multiple methods are used to inform the story of the participant. Data collection includes sampling methods (e.g., purposeful, snowball), and the data collection itself using individual interviews, focus groups, oral statements, artifacts (e.g., symbols), and documents (e.g., written documents, personal journals, biographical information; Creswell, 2018; Hays & Wood, 2011; Polkinghorne, 1995). Data analysis includes both narrative analysis and paradigmatic narrative analysis and can include thematic coding.

DATA COLLECTION AND PROCEDURES

When working within the narrative research tradition, there are two different approaches that can be taken to tell the participant stories: narrative and paradigmatic narrative. In narrative, the researcher uses narrative reasoning to collect descriptions of events and synthesize them by means of a plot into a story or stories. Paradigmatic narrative in contrast uses multiple sources (e.g., stories, settings) to identify an overarching theme (Bruner, 1985; Polkinghorne, 1995). Polkinghorne (1995) succinctly described each method, stating that narrative "moves from elements to stories" while paradigmatic narrative "moves from stories to common elements" (p. 12). For the purposes of this chapter, both narrative and paradigmatic narrative data collection, procedures, and analysis will be described with the understanding that there are similarities and differences. Specifically, data collection and procedures will be described together, while data procedure and analysis will be described separately.

Research Question and Purpose

It is important to ponder the reason you have chosen narrative research as your qualitative research tradition. Your research question is a good place to begin. What is the question that you aim to answer? For narrative research, the purpose of the research could be one of two paths.

In narrative, the purpose of the research is to connect and synthesize information into a single story or stories (Creswell, Hanson, Plano Clark, & Morales, 2007; Polkinghorne, 1995). When deciding if this is the right procedure and analysis for a research topic, consider if the purpose of the study is to describe different data sources (e.g., documents, interviews) that occur over time to tell a story. In narrative, the purpose is to organize information collected into a singular story by linking data. In contrast, paradigmatic narrative is the better choice if the researcher will have multiple stories that have common elements across what can be identified as categories. Further, relationships can be identified and presented between the categories themselves.

Research questions should be written with the paradigmatic hierarchy of narrative research in mind. Hays and Singh (2012) recommend that all qualitative research questions should be coherent, have sound structure, and include relevant content. Further, the purpose statement should combine both the method and the theoretical foundations.

Sampling

When conducting qualitative research, participant sampling is a vital and sometimes overlooked step in the process. In narrative research, connection with the participant is essential, as their story being told is the purpose of the research itself (Patton, 2002). Different sample methods help accomplish this, some of which are outlined by Miles and Huberman (1994). Purposeful sampling, or sampling that specifically recruits those who have experienced what is being studied, is most often used with this tradition. Within this type of sample, criterion sampling, or sampling that recruits participants that meet a specific set of requirements, is one that is often used (Hays and Singh, 2012). For example, in criterion sampling a researcher may be wanting to interview participants who are licensed professional counselors that have taken a specific cognitive behavioral therapy training.

Another sampling method often used in narrative research is snowball sampling, or sampling that uses an initial participant to recommend the next participant. This sampling method can be used when it is difficult to recruit participants due to the nature of the study (Hays and Singh, 2012). An example of this sampling method could be a researcher wanting to interview participants that have been exposed to bullying in a middle school but is having difficulty finding participants to tell this narrative story. The researchers might ask students/teacher to identify key informants.

Data Sources

In narrative research, oral and written materials are used to compose the narrative or paradigmatic narrative. Chase (2005) stated that a narrative can be "oral or written and may be elicited or heard during fieldwork, an interview, or naturally occurring conversation" (p. 652). For the purposes of this chapter, we will focus on data sources most commonly used in narrative research (see Figure 13.1 for a concise overview of data sources).

INDIVIDUAL INTERVIEWS

As with the majority of qualitative research traditions, individual interviews are the most common form of data collection in narrative research (Creswell, 2018; Hays and Wood, 2011; Polkinghorne,

FIGURE 13.1 Data Sources.

2006). In narrative research, the researcher treats the participant as the expert in their own story. In narrative research, individual interviews are collected to tell a complete story of the interviewee (i.e., narrative analysis), or to connect multiple stories into a common theme (i.e., paradigmatic narrative; Polkinghorne, 1995). Interviews can be unstructured, semi-structured, or structured in nature. In narrative research, researchers tend to utilize all of these formats in different settings.

An unstructured interview is an interview that is guided by the research questions and purpose of the study, but the researcher does not go into the interview with an interview protocol. Hays and Singh (2012) stated that unstructured interviews "focus on the surrounding context at the time of the interview" and include participant observation (p. 240). An example of this is Chan et al. (2006) and their use of unstructured interviews to understand Hong Kong Chinese adults' perceptions of their health through cultural stories. The unstructured interviews in this study allowed the participants space to tell their own story with limited bias by the researchers.

In a semi-structured interview, the interviewer goes into the interview with an interview protocol that generally guides the interview process, but with flexibility in the process for additional probing questions that are guided by the interviewee's responses. This type of interview is ideal in narrative research because it allows the researcher to be prepared and guided by the research questions, while also allowing for new information by the interviewee that may take the interview in a new direction. Hannon et al. (2019) used semi-structured interviews as a component of their data collection investigating the narrative experience of school counselors who had experienced multiple student deaths in a school year.

Finally, in a structured interview, researchers come prepared with a strict interview protocol that is followed from start to finish, including any probing questions that may be included. In narrative research, structured interviews may be used in times when the researcher is collecting oral statements. Oral statements are a type of interview that is often used in narrative research. In oral statements, or oral history, the goal is to gather the participant's meaningful experience and perspective of their lived experience (Chase, 2005; Clandinin & Connelly, 2000). In this type of interview, the interviewer may choose to use a more structured interview format to allow the most autobiographical account by the interviewee as possible (Clandinin & Connelly, 2000). The interviewee is given the space to tell their personal narrative on the particular subject, with particular attention paid to the feelings and behaviors of the participant. An oral statement can also be a pre-recorded statement that is made by the subject of the research.

The interviewer/interviewee relationship is an essential part of narrative research. Location, degree of formality, time and date the interview takes place, confidentiality of the interview space, and so forth are conditions that are imperative to take into account when setting up an interview (Clandinin & Connelly, 2000). In narrative research, developing the researcher–participant relationship is imperative to the level of depth in the interview. The researcher understanding and minimizing the power dynamic greatly increases the chance of a successful interview with the participant (Clandinin & Connelly, 2000; Hays & Singh, 2012).

LIFE HISTORY

A life history is a data collection tool that is used when the interviewer is attempting to collect an extensive birth to present narrative of the participant. Multiple forms of data collection can be used for a life history, including interviews and documents (Chase, 2005). Additionally, a life story is similar, but the researcher may choose to focus on a specific bounded timeline to tell a particular story in the participant's life (Chase, 2005). One recent example is Spooner (2019) who explored the life history of place as a central character in place-based research.

Focus Groups

Although less common in narrative research, data can be collected using focus groups. In narrative research, a focus group could be used in conjunction with other data sources, or as a singular data method. Focus group interviews typically are conducted by one to two facilitators. Two or more participants are asked questions related to a singular phenomenon. For example, Norton and Early (2011) used focus groups to better understand the research identity of teachers using narrative research. In this study, the focus groups were used as an additional tool of data collection along with interviews and documents. The focus groups allowed those participating to have a dialogue with fellow teachers about the topic, and in this case allowed the participants space to tell their story.

Written Documents

Just like interviews, written documents are often used in data collection for narrative research (Clandinin & Connelly, 2000; Creswell, 2018; Hays & Singh, 2012; Polkinghorne, 2005). Many types of documents are used to best understand the shape of a narrative, and we will specifically delve into personal journals, artifacts, and biographical and/or autobiographical documents in this chapter.

Personal Journals

Personal journals, or diaries, are a well-used data collection strategy for narrative research. Personal journals can include journals that are kept throughout a study at the prompt of the researcher, or something that is shared with the researcher as an artifact. Mackrill (2008) investigated the use of personal journals in qualitative research of clients in psychotherapy sessions, and specifically noted its historical use in counseling history with prominent theorists. He noted that solicited personal journals can be structured as much or as little as the researcher desires. Some of the benefits of personal journaling as a data method include the longitudinal nature of a personal journal, providing more life context of the individual, reflective in nature, reveals concealed data that might not otherwise be accessed, and giving the participant an alternate form of expression (Mackrill, 2008). These are all benefits to narrative researchers who are attempting to fully describe the narrative of the participants.

Another form of personal journal that can be used in narrative research includes non-solicited personal journals. With non-solicited journals, participants present a personal journal that they have written to be used in data analysis. With unsolicited data like this, researchers have less control over what the participant is providing, and the data can vary among participants. Duchin and Wiseman (2019) used unsolicited journals in the form of memoir writing with survivors of the Holocaust. In addition to the personal journals, the authors utilized semi-structured interviews to understand the experience of the participants and their experience writing the personal journal. This example is especially relevant to counselors who want to better understand client experiences using personal journals as an additional form of data collection.

Artifacts

Artifacts are items that are provided by the participant and can be a symbol, picture, memory box, drawing, or other creative object (Clandinin & Connelly, 2000; Hays & Singh, 2012). This can be solicited or unsolicited by the researcher and are used in the data analysis process. Researchers can use artifacts as a supplement for discussion during the interview process (Hays & Singh, 2012). Additionally, Clandinin and Connelly (2000) noted that museums and archives are an important data collection method for narrative researchers and can provide a narrative of a community or specialized topic. For example, artifacts representing the culture of each participant were used in a narrative research study of six married couples engaging in premarital counseling (Stutzman, 2011).

Biographical and Autobiographical Documents

Biographical and autobiographical documents can be collected by the researchers for the purposes of narrative research. These documents can be written by the participant or those around the participant with direct knowledge about the participant. As noted earlier in this section, local museums or archives, memoirs, or autobiographies can be utilized as data collected for the purposes of narrative research. Ashby and Causten-Theoharis (2009) utilized autobiographies written by participants who identified as having a diagnosis of autism to better understand the narrative of the participants and their perception of competence.

TRUSTWORTHINESS STRATEGIES

An essential component of qualitative research is trustworthiness strategies. Research is only as strong as it is rigorous, and by employing trustworthiness strategies in the research design, your research is strengthened. Guba and Lincoln (1994) created five criteria of trustworthiness: credibility, transferability, dependability, confirmability, and authenticity. Each of these criteria have strategies that are generally accepted to increase rigor. In this section, we will provide suggested trustworthiness strategies for each criterion that relate to narrative research.

Within narrative research, there are many opportunities for trustworthiness using written tools that are natural to narrative work. Reflexive journaling, field notes, and memos are all trustworthiness strategies that are conducted in the field to increase credibility, confirmability, and authenticity (Clandinin & Connelly, 2000; Creswell, 2018; Hays & Wood, 2011; Hoshman, 2005). Member checking or checking in with the participant to make sure that what is transcribed or written about the participant matches their experience, is an essential component of the narrative research process, and is a strategy of confirmability authenticity, and dependability (Clandinin & Connelly, 2000).

Triangulation occurs when multiple data sources, data methods, and researchers are used to corroborate the findings. Triangulation is a strategy for credibility, transferability, dependability, confirmability, and authenticity. Thick description is another component of narrative research that is also a trustworthiness strategy for all of the criteria of trustworthiness (Clandinin & Connelly, 2000; Hays & Singh, 2012). Finally, researchers could create an audit trail, and have it audited. Audit trails include the entirety of the components of your research process (e.g., transcriptions, field memos, correspondence, research text, field text) kept together in one place meets the criteria for both credibility and confirmability.

While these trustworthiness strategies are not a requirement of all narrative research, they are components of rigorous qualitative research and should be included in narrative research.

ANALYSIS

There are many analysis methods in narrative research, which can be confusing for new researchers. Polkinghorne (1994) noted that earlier research in narrative research focused more on data collection than analysis. Because of this delay in general steps in the narrative analysis process, there are a multitude of options, but few clear-cut directions. For the purposes of this chapter, we will be focusing on two forms of analysis: narrative analysis and paradigmatic narrative analysis.

NARRATIVE ANALYSIS

Narrative analysis is a well-used form of analysis in narrative research, however, there is a lack of consensus on specific coding processes. Please see Figure 13.2 for a concise overview of the narrative data analysis process. With guidance from Clandinin and Connelly (2000), the following are six suggested steps in narrative analysis:

1. **Gather all field texts, materials to be analyzed (e.g., transcribed interviews, artifacts, documents) and data management texts (e.g., memos, fieldnotes).** In step one, researchers gather all of the materials that are going to be analyzed for the research study. Clandinin and Connelly (2000) call this composition the field text. If the researcher conducted interviews, focus groups, or recorded oral statements, this step would include transcribing these data sources.

2. **Read and re-read data collected, beginning the process of summarizing.** Read through all the collected data; spending time in the mindset of your participants is an important part of this process. Reviewing field notes, memos, and other data collected is an essential step in this process and is multidirectional (i.e., inward, outward, backward, forward).

3. **Narratively code data into clusters of information that make sense of the data using narrative analysis terms (e.g., names of characters, time, place, events, story lines, story gaps).** After feeling immersed in the data, begin to narratively code data, starting with sorting the data into information that makes sense of the data. This is also the time to begin to conceptualize the data into story form, thinking about different storytelling components. In this section you can begin to determine the main characters of the story, when the story takes place, critical events of the story, what story lines may be present, and what gaps are in the story. During this time, your focus is on clustering the data.

4. **Re-story by collapsing codes further and placing themes in chronological order.** Once the data have been clustered, it is time to begin reorganizing the story, otherwise known

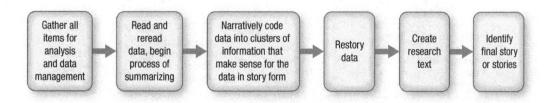

FIGURE 13.2 Narrative Analysis.

as re-storying (Creswell, 2018). During this time, themes are identified throughout the clusters of codes to begin to tell the story. While re-storying, it is important to make sure the story is in chronological order. This step is an important one, because participants often do not tell stories in chronological order, and that is the duty of the researcher.

5. **Creation of research text (i.e., codebook).** Taking the information from the previous steps, a research text, or codebook, is composed that is the final codebook of the process. This can be edited and revised as needed until the final story is written.

6. **Identification of final story or stories.** After the research text is finalized, the final story or stories of the research is co-constructed with the participants if possible.

The preceding summary is specific to narrative analysis and provides an overview of one of many different approaches to narrative analysis. Other suggested narrative analysis strategies in counseling and the social sciences were recognized in Avdi and Georgaca (2007) and include the following: (a) thematic analysis, (b) typological analysis, (c) dialogical analysis, (d) narrative process coding system, and (e) whole client narrative analysis.

PARADIGMATIC NARRATIVE ANALYSIS

In contradiction with narrative analysis, in paradigmatic narrative analysis, researchers are analyzing multiple stories into common themes (Bruner, 1985; Polkinghorne, 1995). Please see Figure 13.3 for a concise overview of paradigmatic narrative analysis. Polkinghorne (1995) wrote that this form of analysis can be represented in two cases: "(a) one in which the concepts are derived from previous theory or logical possibilities and are applied to the data to determine whether instances of these concepts are to be found; and (b) one in which concepts are inductively derived from the data" (p. 13).

In continuation of the proposed narrative analysis given previously and again with guidance from Clandinin and Connelly (2000), here are suggested steps for paradigmatic narrative analysis:

1. **Gather all field texts, materials to be analyzed (e.g., transcribed interviews, artifacts, documents) and data management texts (e.g., memos, fieldnotes).** In step one, researchers gather all of the materials that are going to be analyzed for the research study. Clandinin and Connelly (2000) call this composition of the field text. If the researcher conducted interviews, focus groups, or recorded oral statements, this step would include transcribing these data sources.

2. **Read and re-read data collected, beginning the process of summarizing.** Read through all the collected data; spending time in the mindset of your participants is an important part of this process. Reviewing field notes, memos, and other data collected is an essential step in this process and is multidirectional (i.e., inward, outward, backward, forward).

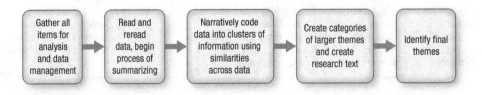

FIGURE 13.3 Paradigmatic Narrative Analysis.

3. **Narratively code data into clusters of information that appear to be similar across data sources.** After becoming immersed in the data, begin to code data, starting with sorting the data into information that makes sense to the data. In this step, researchers identify narrative similarities across participants or data sources.

4. **Create categories that hold codes across stories and create a research text.** In this step, researchers now create larger themes or categories to collapse codes into and to create the initial research text or codebook.

5. **Identification of final themes.** After the research text is finalized, the final themes or categories of the research are presented.

An example of this form of narrative analysis is well represented in Flynn and Black (2013) and their examination of altruism and self-interest archetypes. In this article, paradigmatic narrative analysis was utilized with multiple forms of data collected from 25 participants.

INCREASING RIGOR IN NARRATIVE RESEARCH

Narrative research is a valuable qualitative research tradition with many resources available to researchers. Increasing rigor in narrative research might sound difficult, but it means employing tools that are already available to researchers today. Hays, Wood, Dahl, & Kirk-Jenkins (2016) notes that rigor is the "systematic approach to research design and data analysis, interpretation, and presentation" (p. 173). In narrative research, we can examine each of these steps in the research process with suggestions for rigor.

During data collection, there are multiple processes researchers can utilize to increase rigor, including the following: (a) increase narrative through multiple in-depth interviews with the same individual(s); (b) increase narrative rigor through using multiple data collection points (e.g., interview, focus group, document analysis, journal analysis, artifact analysis); (c) employing multiple rounds of data collection over time with the same participants; and (d) using multiple qualitative trustworthiness procedures. Each of these strategies directly addresses methodical rigor in narrative research.

Rigor in narrative research design includes inclusion of a paradigm in the design process (e.g., social constructivism), clear and appropriate research questions, and must theoretically support methodological process (e.g., sampling methods, data sources). With data analysis, clear descriptions of how data will be analyzed and what type of narrative analysis the researcher is using is needed. Further, justification of procedure and analysis in the presentation of the data is important. In Hays et al. (2014), qualitative methodological rigor in the *Journal of Counseling and Development* was examined and found limited use or explicit description of use of trustworthiness strategies over a 15-year period. For narrative researchers, it is important to not only employ trustworthiness strategies that are essential to narrative research, but to be explicit in the procedural account of the use of trustworthiness strategies when writing the presentation of research.

MULTICULTURAL ISSUES

Narrative research has a tradition from its inception of being grounded in multicultural pluralism (Chase, 2005, Clandinin & Connelly, 2000). Narrative research uses the participant's voice to guide the story, which when used appropriately by the research, can be empowering for the participant. Co-constructing stories with the participants and ensuring that meaning is conveyed is an essential tenet of narrative research. Butana (2015) noted narrative research "has been used in many disciplines to learn more about the culture, historical experiences, identity, and lifestyle of the narrator" (p. 190).

A strength of narrative research is the applicability it has in a variety of settings. Duran and Firehammer (2015) discussed the power of narrative research in Indigenous methodology, stating that, "The power and value of story science lie in its capacity to reach deeper levels of understanding and uncover new knowledge.... By using narrative frameworks as devices of inquiry, story science evokes authentic information about human experiences" (p. 92). Narrative researchers using this methodology need to be mindful of the inherent power dynamics in research and work to minimize those dynamics as much as possible (Clandinin & Connelly, 2000).

LIMITATIONS

Narrative research is a long-standing tradition in the qualitative research field, but as with all areas of research there are limitations. The first and most glaring limitation is the inconsistency in the name of the tradition itself. Across disciplines, there is an inconsistent use of terminology that can confuse those using the tradition. Narrative research, narrative inquiry, narratology, and narrative analysis are just a few of the names that are used interchangeably. In fact, some use narrative analysis as a qualitative research tradition, and some use it exclusively as a method of analysis. Additionally, narrative research can often be confused with Narrative Therapy, a postmodern counseling theory.

Data analysis is another area of continued growth and opportunity for increased rigor in narrative research. More consistency in steps in methodology, use of paradigm, use of correct terminology, and more consistent presentation of narrative research design in publications is needed.

Case Study

BACKGROUND

After working in a clinical mental health setting in a suburb of a large West Coast city in recent years, Paul has noticed a specific older adult population coming in for services. Recently, he has been seeing clients who immigrated to the United States of America from the Azores islands as children and teenagers after a local volcanic eruption. Paul is interested in studying the experiences of these individuals. The research team consists of Paul and his fellow researcher Stefanie. Prior to beginning the study, Paul and Stefanie explore and reflect on their own personal experiences with immigration, knowledge of Portuguese and Azorean culture, and their perceptions of the experience. Paul reflects on his own experiences as a child of parents who immigrated from the Azores, and his own connection with his heritage.

Paul chose a narrative research tradition with a social constructivism paradigm to best describe the experiences of the population chosen. While Paul considered using phenomenology, he ultimately chose narrative research because he was most interested in the narrative story of the participants as opposed to the essence of the phenomenon. He chose to use narrative analysis as his chosen data analysis process. Since Paul is interested in the story of each individual participant and the chronological occurrence of the experience, narrative research appears to be the best fit. The purpose of this study was to better understand the immigration experience of individuals who immigrated to the United States of America from the Azores islands in the 1950s after a local volcano eruption and are now seeking clinical mental health services. The research question was as follows: What are the experiences of individuals who immigrated from the Azores islands in the 1950s after a local volcano eruption?

RESEARCH PROCESS

Paul reached out to a local Portuguese hall in the area whose membership included the participants needed for the study. Based on Paul's previous relationship with the hall, he was put in touch with the first participant of the study. Utilizing snowball and criterion sampling, after interviewing the first participant, Paul was put in touch with the remaining nine participants for the study. For this study, Paul utilized a semi-structured interview process, along with asking the participants to bring any artifacts that remind them of the immigration process. Paul and his research team utilized multiple strategies of trustworthiness, including member checking, triangulation of data sources, triangulation of research team, reflexive journaling, thick description, and an audit trail.

DISCUSSION, RESULTS, LIMITATIONS, ANDCONCLUSION

After completing data collection and analysis, Paul was able to put together a story that began in 1957 and ended in 1963. The story arc began with the volcanic explosion, the United States Azorean Refugee Act of 1958, and continued as the participants relocated to the United States. Identified themes included loss of home, happiness, logistics of moving, assimilation, and acculturation. Participants recognized that as they aged, they were reflecting on this experience more and more, and that may be a reason that they reached out for clinical mental health services. The strengths of this narrative research was the ability to allow the participants to describe their experience fully and process through feelings from their past. The limitation of this research method was the possible biases of the research team, and possible limits to the scope of the questions. Implications for clinical mental health counselors and school counselors include increased knowledge of immigration experiences of older adults and the lasting affects it may have on mental health.

SUMMARY

In this chapter, you were introduced to the narrative research tradition; specifically, the following:

- History of narrative research was discussed, as well as the paradigmatic hierarchy of this tradition.
- Data collection methods, trustworthiness strategies, and data analysis were discussed in depth, including increasing rigor.
- Multicultural issues were discussed, along with limitations of the research tradition.
- Software recommendations and resources were provided.

STUDENT ACTIVITIES

Exercise 1: Valuing Narrative Research

Directions: Review the list of contemporary strategies used by narrative researchers (Chase, 2005). Which of these strategies do you find most valuable when conducting narrative research in a counseling setting?

Exercise 2: Writing Your Narrative Research Question

Directions: Consider your research interests and how they interact with narrative research. Write down two or three potential research questions that may work in a narrative research design.

Exercise 3: Trustworthiness

Directions: Identify the unique trustworthiness strategies listed. Practice and write down how you might incorporate these strategies into your own research design.

Exercise 4: Data Analysis

Directions: Review the description of narrative analysis and paradigmatic narrative analysis. Write down the similarities and differences of each analysis, and think about when you might utilize each in your research designs.

Exercise 5: Article Review

Directions: Select a counseling article that uses narrative research. Read and analyze the article, looking for gaps in areas such as the research design, trustworthiness strategies, and/or paradigm.

ADDITIONAL RESOURCES

Software Recommendations

Nvivo 12: https://www.qsrinternational.com/nvivo/home

ATLAS.ti: https://atlasti.com/narrative-research/

Helpful Links

- https://www.keele.ac.uk/media/keeleuniversity/facnatsci/schpsych/documents/counselling/conference/5thannual/NarrativeApproachestoCaseStudies.pdf

- https://www.corwin.com/sites/default/files/upm-binaries/13550_Chapter17.pdf

- https://www.counseling.org/resources/library/Selected%20Topics/Multiculturalism/Narrative_Theory.htm

Helpful Reading

https://files.eric.ed.gov/fulltext/EJ881749.pdf

Chase, S. E. (2005). Narrative inquiry: Multiple lenses, approaches, voices. In N. K. Denzin and Y. S. Lincoln (Eds.), *The SAGE handbook of qualitative research* (3rd ed, pp. 507–536). SAGE.

Clandinin, D. J., & Connelly, F. M. (2000). *Narrative inquiry: Experience and story in qualitative research*. John Wiley and Sons.

Creswell, J. W. (2018). *Qualitative inquiry and research design: Choosing among five approaches* (5th ed.). SAGE.

Helpful Videos

- https://methods.sagepub.com/video/narrative-research-corrine-squire

- https://methods.sagepub.com/video/an-introduction-to-narrative-methods

- https://www.youtube.com/watch?v=7IDva7tzliA
- https://www.youtube.com/watch?v=Dfc-akqgNn8

KEY REFERENCES

Only key references appear in the print edition. The full reference list appears in the digital product found on http://connect.springerpub.com/content/book/978-0-8261-4385-3/part/part03/chapter/ch13

Chase, S. E. (2005). Narrative inquiry: Multiple lenses, approaches, voices. In N. K. Denzin and Y. S. Lincoln (Eds.), *The SAGE handbook of qualitative research* (3rd ed., pp. 507–536). SAGE.

Clandinin, D. J., & Connelly, F. M. (2000). *Narrative inquiry: Experience and story in qualitative research.* John Wiley and Sons.

Creswell, J. W. (2018). *Qualitative inquiry and research design: Choosing among five approaches* (5th ed.). SA.

Hays, D. G., & Wood, C. (2011). Infusing qualitative traditions in counseling research design. *Journal of Counseling & Development*, 89(3), 288–295. https://doi.org/10.1002/j.1556-6678.2011.tb00091.x

Hays, D. G., Wood, C., Dahl, H., & Kirk-Jenkins, A. (2016). Methodological rigor in Journal of Counseling & Development qualitative research articles: A 15-year review. *Journal of Counseling & Development*, 94(2), 172–183. https://doi.org/10.1002/jcad.12074

Polkinghorne, D. E. (1995). Narrative configuration in qualitative analysis. *International Journal of Qualitative Studies in Education*, 8(1), 5–24. https://doi.org/10.1080/0951839950080103

CHAPTER 14

CONSENSUAL QUALITATIVE RESEARCH

Katherine M. Murphy, Cody Dickson, and Stephen V. Flynn

LEARNING OBJECTIVES

After reading this chapter, you will be able to:

- Understand the Consensual Qualitative Research (CQR) process
- Comprehend the paradigmatic hierarchy of CQR
- Recognize variations of CQR
- Comprehend CQR rigor

DISTINGUISHING CONSENSUAL QUALITATIVE RESEARCH FROM OTHER APPROACHES

The concept of qualitative research goes at least as far back as Galileo Galilei (1564–1642), Isaac Newton (1642–1727), and John Locke (1632–1704; Brinkman et al., 2014). Researchers may refer to their studies as emphasizing a sense of quantity or quality. Others could refer to their investigations as being objective or subjective in nature (Crotty, 2003). While these perspectives are important, a central question that researchers ask themselves is, "What am I studying?" (Creswell, 2012). For the purpose of this chapter, researchers should consider their topic subjective in nature. This conclusion would likely lead a researcher to a qualitative methodology, but which one? Next they should consider employing consensual qualitative research (CQR). Let's consider this choice by first reviewing five qualitative research approaches.

PHENOMENOLOGY

Although Immanuel Kant (1724–1804) and George Wilhelm Friedrich Hegel (1770–1831) are often credited with the origin of phenomenology, Groenwald (2004) would argue it was German philosopher Edmund Husserl (1859-1938) who first argued the concept of making meaning. Husserl believed all individuals were capable of having an "internal experience of being conscious of something" (p. 4). A phenomenological approach seeks to answer what that something is, and how would the internal experience of it be described. The methods undertaken by the researcher are interview questions (open-ended) with some follow up, multi-interviews, and observations. The interviews are often digitally recorded and reproduced in the form of verbatim transcripts. As the data are sifted through, themes emerge (Creswell, 2012). These themes would be common concepts described with the individuals unique internal experience and language. The researcher highlights the unique language and descriptions of the participants to demonstrate the *essence* of a concept or pattern shared by the participants. Let's look at a fictitious study of adoptees seeking connection with their birth family. The phenomenon could be the connection adopted individuals seek from their birth family. The telling of that story, as it was experienced by the individual, would be the narrative of their experience. Phenomenology is one of the methodological frameworks that influenced the creation of CQR.

CASE STUDY

"A case study investigates a contemporary phenomenon (the 'case') in its real-world context, especially when boundaries between phenomenon and context may not be clearly evident" (Yin, 2018, p.15). Commonly, case study methodology is used by helping professionals, medical researchers, and legal scholars. Although this method uses in-depth interviews and observations, it also stresses the discovery of artifacts and documentation. The data are then analyzed, and descriptions are emphasized in both the individual case and any of the possible cross-cases. These descriptions are written up in detail.

NARRATIVE RESEARCH

Narrative research is an in-depth view into the life of individuals for whom you believe have detailed stories or life experiences that are relevant to your research question(s) (Creswell, 2012). The researcher devotes as much time as needed to collect these stories. The stories should not just be told by the participant but are collected from those in the participant's life (parents, friends, co-workers, etc.). The researcher may review a participant's written journals. Observations of the individual are noted by the researcher. Following the collection of stories from a variety of sources, a *restorying* or reorganization follows in order to understand perspective . The reorganization of stories can be placed in general context which involves a "negotiation of meaning" (Creswell, 2012, p. 57) with the participants. In the writing of a narrative study, it is hoped that insightful information will emerge that may clarify many important elements within the social circumstance.

GROUNDED THEORY

This approach is a departure from identifying rich context that other qualitative research offers. Grounded theory is centered on developing a theory grounded in data, collected from many participants (20 to 60 is not unusual), and utilizing a unique set of procedures that are easily adapted to various research questions (Creswell, 2017). The questions are to be answered in the study and will drive the development of a theory which emerges from the data following collection and a multi-step analysis of the data. The Straussian form of grounded theory analysis consists of the following steps: First, the data are categorized and sub-categorized in "open coding" (LaRossa, 2005, p. 148). Second, "axial coding" (p. 149) logically groups data by what appears to be these central concepts. Finally, the researcher attempts to connect data, using "selective coding" (p. 148) which integrates *open* and *axial* coding in a substantive manner that lends itself to theory (LaRossa, 2005). The researcher may then choose to create a visual representation to support understanding of these steps or the funneling of the data which should result in an applicable theory. Grounded theory was initially created in the 1960s and is a powerful form of qualitative methodology (McLeod, 2001). Grounded theory and CQR share the team process concept (Flynn et al., 2019).

ETHNOGRAPHY

Ethnographers focus on cultural groups and cultural context such as values, hierarchy, beliefs, messages, and patterns. The ethnographer becomes engrossed in the lives of the cultural group. Observations are made of any culturally driven pattern or behavior. The researcher makes determinations of themes based on their inside knowledge and experience of the culture. During this anthropological and systematic study of a culture, the ethnographer becomes the participant and engages in the cultural activities as a member.

Keep in mind that each of these approaches has their unique nuances when it comes to the collection of qualitative data. Back in Galileo's time, meaning was thought to be *subjective*. More recently, according to Merriam (2002) events in our daily lives, including shared events, will likely result in unique and individual meanings; these meanings are based on one's own socially constructed view. This concept is known as *constructivism*. Similarly, Michal Crotty (2003) described the process of subjectively gathering data "the making of meaning" (p. 42).

INTRODUCTION TO CONSENSUAL QUALITATIVE RESEARCH

The founder of CQR methodology is Dr. Clara E. Hill. A 2012 interview with Dr. Hill revealed her frustration with quantitative methodology. Early in her experience as a researcher she found that numbers alone could not capture the nuances and complexities of the human condition. Although qualitative research does a better job, Hill's frustrations were further realized in the clarity of how to properly understand and use qualitative methodology.

THE PARADIGMATIC HIERARCHY OF CONSENSUAL QUALITATIVE RESEARCH

The paradigmatic hierarchy of CQR envelopes the same five levels as described by Crotty (2003). CQR is constructivist in nature, meaning that this methodological framework proposes that individuals construct their own unique perspective of their life events. The researcher is tasked with discovery. Constructivism allows for individuals to have their own truths. The first author had a professor in a research course who referred to these constructs (individual meaning) as *truths*, truths with a small t and large T. Large T Ttruths are those that are universally true no matter who, what, where, or when; for example, gravity. Lower case truths are those that are only true for a specific individual and are constructed through the individual lens with which the subject views reality. The process of discovering each individual construct (truth), is referred to as ontology (i.e., the nature of reality). CQR is grounded in a relativistic ontological perspective.

When scholars and philosophers consider how an event or experience came to be, they are concerned with understanding its epistemology (Crotty, 2003). From an epistemological perspective, CQR is centered on constructivism (Hill et al., 2005). Speculation as to what and why a particular phenomenon has occurred is what we term theoretical stance. Theoretically speaking, CQR is post-positivistic in nature. Specifically, while considered a qualitative tradition, CQR utilizes a quasi-statistical approach to coding that emphasizes the consensus among multiple researchers and an external auditor. The manner in which the research goes about extracting answers is known as methodology (i.e., CQR). Finally, the process for gathering of and analyzing the data is the methods. CQR emphasizes the importance of consensus among researchers to construct results wrapped within the rich language of the participants rather than quantities to determine meaning within the data. The primary importance is placed on the consistency of data (words) explored. Hill (2012) believed traditional quantitative research could not address the complexities of the human condition. It lacked clarity in descriptions, comprehension and implementation. Consensual qualitative research was her rigorous response to these concerns.

CONSENSUAL QUALITATIVE RESEARCH

What is CQR? CQR is an inductive method that uses open-ended interview questions; is contextual; integrates the use of words, numbers, multiple viewpoints, descriptions of experiences; and has a team approach to analysis and for reaching consensus in addressing the research problem (Hill, 2012). As previously discussed, qualitative research is naturalistic and interpretative in its analysis of phenomenon;this is the tradition of CQR. CQR as a methodology is well-suited for studies that require thick, rich descriptions of individual and group experiences, attitudes, and beliefs. CQR is post-positivistic (theory) and constructivist (epistemology) oriented requiring researcher awareness of their constructed (truth) worldview (meaning) as it may influence observations and interpretations of the phenomenon (Flynn, et al., 2019; Hill, 2005, 2012). Finally, CQR uses a systemic approach to data analysis that examines information across participants, which ultimately allows for an inductive and collaborative process.

Simplistically stated, CQR is research utilizing a team(s) approach where discussion of differing views using open dialogue and cooperation concludes with consensus, a shared vision among researchers (Barden & Cashwell 2014; Flynn et al., 2018; Van den Berg & Struwig, 2017). Consensus by a team of researchers must occur in order to ensure accuracy and consistency in data analysis (van den Berg, 2017). Hill et al. (2005), described CQR as an amalgamation of "phenomenological, grounded theory, and comprehensive process analysis" (p. 3) with a large constructivist philosophy and a dollop of post-positivism blended in.

Within the CQR procedures a great deal of importance is placed on the concept of consensus, with considerable reliance on equity and respect among researchers (Hill, 1997). Furthermore Hill et al. (2005) identified five musts in CQR. These five critical elements are centered on the following: (a) the use of semi-structured open ended questioning, (b) the use of multiple judges throughout the data analysis phase of the investigation, (c) the frequent use of consensus and consensus meetings to attain agreement on the meaning of the findings, (d) the use of an auditor to examine the work of the primary team of judges, and (e) the use of a unique qualitative data analysis process (i.e., domains, core ideas, and cross analysis).

DATA COLLECTION

Consensual qualitative research data are often collected from interviews. These conversations are in depth and likely focused on participant experiences, viewpoints, values, and/or emotions.

Participants' verbal communications are often gathered in a variety of formats (i.e., individual interviews, focus groups, qualitative questionnaires). Similar to phenomenology and grounded theory methodologies, CQR researchers commonly use face-to-face and telephone interviews (Creswell, 2017; Groenwald, 2004; Hill, 2012) and qualitative journaling. Researchers will journal and reflect on their personal questions, insights, concerns, and biases. The researcher's journaling is also a method for the analysis of trustworthiness (Flynn et al., 2012; Merriam, 2002), which will be discussed later in this chapter. Frequently, the gathering of information comes from questionnaires (McLeod, 2001), especially if the sample size is extensive (Hill, 2012). Focus groups offer an alternative to the interview format that allows for the dynamic interaction of diverse individuals. Focus groups are defined as a group of diverse people, gathered by the researcher for the purpose of a discussion about a specific topic (Berg, 2007; Onwuegbuzie et al., 2009), which may be utilized in CQR. This data collection method is especially helpful when large sample size is recommended (Hill, 2012). While diverse data collection methods are allowed, Clara Hill (2012) described the gathering process as often being centered on the face-to-face process.

PROCEDURES AND EXAMPLES

As is true with most human subject research endeavors, institutional review board (IRB) approval must be obtained before a research study is initiated. However, a first step is understanding what your topic is and how you will proceed. Picking a topic that is important to you is a must, as you will be spending a great deal of time saturated in the research (Hill, 2005). For example, when the first author was in her counselor education doctoral program, she participated in a qualitative research course where we completed steps of a consensual qualitative research project. The research topic was completing the counseling dissertation process, a topic most of the doctoral students worried about. We spent an entire semester collecting and analyzing data, discussing the themes, breaking them down further, and finally coming to results. Following the completion of the course we completed the remaining CQR steps and finalized a scholarly manuscript for publication purposes the following semester. We spent approximately 12 months working on the research and the writing process; our hard work paid off with research expertise and a scholarly publication (see Flynn et al., 2012).

There are topics that are better suited to CQR. Some have referred to these topics under an umbrella entitled "special populations" (Flynn et al., 2019, p. 61). This umbrella allows for diverse possibilities. However, many researchers will undoubtedly choose topics with which they have personal experience. A note of caution is warranted here as researchers must work to remain neutral and bracket bias. With a team of researchers and auditors, one is likely to be confronted by their personal bias (Hill et al., 2005). While it is important to be cognizant of personal bias, it is also helpful to have true fervor for the topic as you will soon be immersed in it.

The team approach is signature of CQR. How the team is configured is flexible and may include set teams with specific tasks, or rotating teams where each team has input in one or all phases of the research. It is vital that the team is comprised of individuals with similar status, power, enthusiasm, and capability to ensure that all members of the team will voice their insights, concerns, differences, and biases in a trusting respectful atmosphere (Hill et al., 2005; Hill, 2012; van den Berg & Struwig, 2017). Consensus must be reached, therefore the team must have the ability to work through discourse (Hill, 2012).

DATA ANALYSIS AND EXAMPLES

Once you have chosen your topic and assembled the research teams (e.g., teams 1 and 2), your attention should turn to data collection. What question(s) are you attempting to answer? Why is it important to answer the question(s)? Reviewing current literature will be the conduit in navigating your research (Hill, 2012; van den Berg & Struwig, 2017). Drawing from the literature review and personal experience, researchers are now ready to develop their interview protocol. The interview process requires rapport between the researcher and the participant;open-ended queries that allow for detailed, descriptive narratives from each participant; prompts for further depth; and disclosure (Hill, 2012). The interview is a conversation, but that conversation can transpire in person, or over the phone (Hill et al., 2005; van den Berg & Struwig, 2017). Hill (2012) advises the use of two pilot interviews in order to assess the effectiveness of the questionnaire. Following the pilot interviews, researchers are encouraged to practice the interview process. This will ease the process of interviewing and create an interview context that is both comfortable and familiar.

The questionnaire itself should be succinct and scripted to provide consistency throughout the interview process across the team of interviewers. The semi-structured interview consists of open-ended questions paired with prompts, which resembles a genuineness in dialogue and increases likelihood of garnering detailed accounts and plentiful descriptions (Madill, 2011). The number of questions will vary but should roughly fill about an hour of time, somewhere around 12 questions is normative (Hill, 2012). It is important not to forget about the two pilot interviews.

Following a thorough review of the literature, IRB approval, and the development of the questionnaire, researchers begin the process of identifying the participants and how to go about accessing them. Berg (2007) identified purposive samples as a means of recruiting participants. With this sampling strategy researchers use their expertise, contacts, and knowledge base of persons associated with the given topic to be studied. Snowball sampling is frequently the sampling method applied in qualitative research (Noy, 2008). Further, Noy describes the snowball process as being repetitive in nature, as participants refer the researcher to another possible participant. The newly identified participants are contacted and interviewed, resulting in another referral, and on it goes. Convenient sampling is also an option for recruiting participants. This sampling method is centered on the accessibility of the participants as being convenient. Clearly, ease and/or access is the overarching concept with the aforementioned sampling strategies (Berg, 2007). Your sample size can vary depending on result consistency or what has been called saturation in other forms of qualitative methodology (grounded theory). You are no longer hearing new information, rather the information gathered is similar in theme, but perhaps described differently. If the researcher(s) use the example described previously with adopted individuals' experience of finding their birth family, each participant may describe their fears, worries, and concerns of further rejection. The details will likely vary, but the theme is one of fear of rejection. How many interviews will it take to reach this point is not concrete, however Hill (2007) suggests it may lie somewhere around 12 to 19. Hill et al. (2005) recommend applying frequency labels to each category to identify occurrence across cases. These labels can include general, typical, variant, and rare.

Data analysis begins with developing domains. It is possible that this began with the literature review, however the main thrust of domain related data will be made after reviewing the data collection points (e.g., transcripts; Hill, 2007). Once these areas have been identified, researchers can undertake a second round of interviews with Team 1 (primary researchers), to see if the domain remains accurate. At the end of this process, the team should have a consensus on what they believe are the domains, and they begin to assign a code to each identified domain (Hill et al.,

2005). A domain is simply one portion of the information gathered in a CQR study; there will be several phases, and they should be coded sequentially. Using our fictitious adoption study: Several participants may wonder why they were given away. This personal experience might be considered a domain, let's call it Domain A. Other participants sympathize with how difficult it must have been for their birth mother at that time; let's call this Domain B. Other participants are worried about their mother's current well-being, Domain C. Hopefully, the concept is becoming clearer.

Cross-analysis may very well be a third team, perhaps a combination of members from Team 1 and Team 2, or each researcher may individually create the categories, but a fresh set of eyes will review and analyze the data (Hill, 2007; Hill et al., 2005). During the cross-analysis phase, the researchers identify multiple categories (domains) and their sub-categories or "core ideas" (Hill, et al., 2005, p. 15). Often identifying the frequency is helpful at this point. The team will come to consensus on what constitutes *typical, variant, general ,or rare* frequency based on the sample size. Typically, when compared to other qualitative traditions, CQR has larger sample sizes (Flynn et al., 2019). Imagine a sample size of 17 in our adoptee study; if 13 or more fell into the category of wondering why they were given up for adoption, the team may identify this as *typical* in frequency, if eight individuals expressed concern for the birth moms' pregnancy experience resulting in giving up her child, the researchers may identify this as *variant in frequency.* Any responses under eight individuals may be determined as *general* or *rare.* There is no equation to determine frequency because every research sample size is different (Hill, 2012). To summarize, cross-analysis consists of (a) identifying domains, (b) breaking each domain down into core ideas, and (c) identifying the frequency of these responses (Barden & Craig, 2014). By now, you are hopefully well on your way to understanding and appreciating the concept of consensus in CQR. A team of auditors (Team 4) will now evaluate the domains, while centering their attention on the accuracy of the core ideas within each category. They will provide feedback to Team 1 with possible revisions to domains and core ideas (Hill, 2012).

A stability check is a technique used to verify the domains, categories, and frequencies. In looking at our sample size of 17 in our adoptee study, only 15 of those transcripts would be initially utilized to identify domains, core ideas, and frequencies. The two transcripts randomly withheld would now be evaluated and added. Would these two transcripts fit right in, or would they alter the domains, core ideas, and frequency (Hill et al., 2005)? In 2012, Hill noted that participants in qualitative methodology could vary from as little as three to as many as 97 and concluded that "it was unrealistic and perhaps fruitless to complete stability checks" (p. 129). Instead, CQR promotes the attainment of more cases, co-construction of larger teams, and additional auditors. This increase in scholarly participation allows for an increase in intensity and trustworthiness for the data analysis process as long as the study has a sufficient sample size (12 to 19 participants). As we consider the fictitious adoption study, is a stability check realistic or unrealistic?

Results should now be demonstrated through a written report, visual representation, or a combination of the two. If this sounds like a significant task, it is because it *is* a significant task (Berg, 2007; Creswell, 2017). Often in qualitative research, there is an abundance of data. Researchers must determine what data to collect, how to represent the data, and finalize the writing of a research report. The writer of a CQR research report is actively deciding what data to use as they proceed and, during the writing process, they are placing data intermittently throughout the results section. To simplify this process, ask yourself what findings speak directly to your research questions (Hill, 2012). Think back to the questionnaire used for interviewing purpose. The questionnaire was divided into rapport building, core questions, and closure. Answers connected to the core questions will provide the data that will likely find its way into the results section.

Organization can prove to be a complicated as well; however, once again, Hill (2012) suggests the stories of the participants, as they speak to the core ideas, will guide the way.

CONSENSUAL QUALITATIVE RESEARCH VARIANTS

As we noted, CQR takes a lot of effort and time, much like other qualitative research approaches, and for this reason there are other options. There are two variations of consensual qualitative research that have been developed since the inception of CQR. These two variations are consensual qualitative research-modified (CQR-M) and consensual qualitative research for case study (CQR-C; Hill, 2012; Jackson, Chui, & Hill, 2012; Spangler et al., 2012). In this section we briefly describe each and highlight how these two variations differ from the original CQR methodology.

CONSENSUAL QUALITATIVE RESEARCH—MODIFIED

We will first consider CQR-M as a means to conduct CQR with brief or simple qualitative data from large studies. This variation allows the researcher to reach consensus among judges to place data directly into categories (Spangler et al., 2012). CQR-M is a combination of original CQR, Mahrer's (1998) discovery-oriented research, and Hill's (1990) exploratory research. CQR, discovery-oriented and exploratory research, are considered bottom-up approaches by which the researchers form categories as opposed to pressing data into a fixed structure. These judges are used to code data and calculate interrater reliability. CQR-M unites conceptual and operational components of these three methodologies to create a method that accentuates interrater agreement. CQR-M team members share their expectations, personal biases, and team disagreements with one another to help keep fidelity of the data. CQR-M prioritizes this checks-and-balances approach to data.

When considering the use of CQR-M as your method for studying your selected phenomena, serious consideration should be placed on whether the study is exploring or describing the phenomena or for triangulating with other quantitative data. This will help you determine how many participants you will need for your study and how much data you will collect from them to address the topic of study. Traditionally, CQR uses small sample sizes (roughly 12 to 19 participants); however, CQR-M can adjust for larger samples. As with any methodology—qualitative, quantitative, or mixed—there is a need for a cost–benefit analysis. The larger the sample you collect with CQR-M could cost you in terms of the achievement of the rich depth offered with traditional CQR. However, the benefit of having a larger data set would equate to more participant consensus from the population of interest. Therefore, if your study is designed to collect a large amount of data with less descriptiveness, CQR-M may be a good option.

CQR-M is helpful with simple qualitative data collection, where the researcher relationship with the participant is less intimate and lacks the closeness of lengthy direct, face-to-face interviews. Data collection methods are typically in the form of written means and questionnaires. For this reason, the development of the questionnaire is crucial to the study. For example, the typical CQR-M questionnaire may include some 20 to 30 multiple choice questions with two to four short-answer questions requiring only a few lines of written response. If the researcher is using traditional CQR to describe or explore a phenomenon, then if they receive responses with some missing data they will likely be fine. However, in CQR-M studies that are analyzing qualitative and/or quantitative data for the purpose of triangulation, the researcher should approach with caution as you must determine if you can adjust for the omitted data or omit the participant all together.

CQR-M offers some variations in the development in coding teams. The CQR-M team should consider several factors such as amount of data, time requirements, and additional constraints that may make it more helpful to have two or more teams depending on the level of coding experience and knowledge of the phenomena. However, always keep in mind that training new coders/team members is beneficial to minimize possible biases and expectations. Like CQR, CQR-M team members also meet to discuss potential personal expectations and biases of the research phenomena. If you recall earlier in the CQR discussion of data collection and analysis, the CQR and CQR-M development of domains and categories is a bottom-up process. One team or a couple of individuals review transcripts and develop the domains. Then the teams meet to adjust domains for clarity, then begin the coding.

When using CQR-M, the researcher does not develop core ideas. Why no core ideas? Well, CQR-M data are less detailed, less complex, and less contextual than traditional CQR data. This allows the CQR-M researcher to immediately place data into categories (like CQR cross-analysis). For example, if in the fictitious adoption study, the researcher was interested in gathering data that was easily categorized as positive, negative, or neutral, then these categories would be utilized by the team. The reading of data is rotated among team members until consensus is reached on domains and category assignment. The determination of frequency is important in CQR-M when developing categories rather than labeling data general, typical, variant, or rare. Finally, the researcher looks at less frequent categories or categories that overlap and edits in an effort to combine smaller categories into larger, more abstract categories. At this point the data analysis is complete. Because CQR-M is a brief and less comprehensive process, auditing is not required. The simplicity and multiple team members appear adequate to adjust for and identify discrepancies. However, following the data analysis process a portion of the data may be submitted to a single auditor for checking.

The final step in a CQR or CQR-M research study, is the writing of the results and discussion. It is recommended that CQR-M researchers provide data in tables and provide the most common categories in the text of the results section, and, of course, CQR and CQR-M researchers encourage the use of quotations to highlight the participants' experiences of the phenomena (Hill, et al., 2005; Spangler et al., 2012). The discussion section should be utilized for deep elaborations of rich participant responses about the data that include descriptions of new and/or unexpected phenomena and how these new points relate to existing literature (Spangler et al., 2012). Additionally, the discussion sections are used to triangulate with quantitative data, how the results are consistent and/or inconsistent with other available qualitative or quantitative data, and how these new data expand our understanding of the phenomena.

CQR-M is a useful qualitative research approach that is well suited for large samples from which simple and brief data is collected by the researcher. CQR-M is adapted from the traditional CQR methodology with discovery-oriented and exploratory methods. However, CQR-M removed elements of traditional CQR to assist the researcher in managing larger samples for exploration, description of phenomena, and/or to triangulate quantitative data with qualitative findings. The second variation of traditional CQR, is referred to as Consensual Qualitative Research for Case Study (Hill, 2012; Jackson, Chui, & Hill, 2012), CQR-C will be discussed in the subsequent section.

CONSENSUAL QUALITATIVE RESEARCH FOR CASE STUDY

Consensual Qualitative Research for Case Study (CQR-C) was developed to address traditional CQR's primary purpose, that is for the use of research related to psychotherapy (Hill, et al., 2005).

Therefore, CQR-C was developed to address the need for CQR in psychotherapy case study research (Hill, 2012; Jackson et al., 2012). According to CQR-C authors, the definition of case study research in CQR is the investigation of a given phenomenon by analysis of a single or small number of cases within a psychotherapy context. Moreover, CQR-C is centered on the identification and description of relevant psychological phenomenon within the course of psychotherapy (e.g., termination session, trauma-based therapy). This new system allows for researchers to move away from quantitative methods, such as time series, to obtain richer, unique, and novel aspects of the phenomenon of study and to help make the findings more dynamic. In this section, we highlight the differences between traditional CQR and CQR-C.

The initial steps in CQR-C are very similar to traditional CQR. For review of these steps see Chapter 18 of Hill's (2012) text, *Consensual Qualitative Research: A Practical Resource for Investigating Social Science Phenomena*. Here we focus on the differences in CQR-C for psychotherapy case study research as opposed to the two other CQR and CQR-M methodologies discussed in this section. There is no significant departure in selecting a topic for CQR-C compared with the other CQR methodological frameworks; however, when choosing your team of judges, it is important to have those with experience with psychotherapy training and practice. This psychotherapy practice and training should include knowledge of techniques, interventions, theory, and knowledge of the topic.

When using CQR-C there are two options for obtaining the case or cases. The first option is to utilize a case(s) that is already complete with proper documentation, preferably digitally recorded sessions, and completed intake, assessments, and progress notes. The second option is to recruit client(s) and psychotherapist(s) that fits the topic and purpose of the study. For example, if you want to study adults who were adopted as children that are currently in psychotherapy for recurring relationship issues, you could locate those reports through a therapist, or recruit a therapeutic dyad who are presently addressing this topic. Initially, you will need to define the event you are studying. The event under investigation is the aspect of the therapeutic sessions or process where the topic of study appears and ends. The next phase of CQR-C is to define the domains and view the case material to identify the event. The research team then prepares the narrative of the event and codes according to the domains with repetition of these steps until all events, related notations, and coding have been made and consensus via the research team has been reached. Now that the team has reached the end of the data collection stage, the team moves toward cross-analysis by developing summary tables and categories within the domains and triangulating other case data with the event data. The CQR-C team then develops the "story" provided by the case with a written narrative. This narrative is to provide a synopsis of the case and attempts to answer the original research questions. The narrative is built by having individual team members write up their conceptualization of the case. After this, the team works together to develop a final conceptualization, which leads to writing the manuscript.

As has been described through the CQR and CQR-M formats, writing the manuscript involves clarifying and revising all aspects of the research process. This write up should include demographic data and specific notes on the psychotherapist's orientation. Consensus is important throughout the CQR-C process, including in the writing and revising of the manuscript. CQR-C does not utilize auditors because the process calls for large teams of four to six researchers. Furthermore, the repetitive viewing of the case study data for coding purposes provides a second layer of consistency.

CQR-C remains relatively new and is in need of continued use to assist in the standardization of the process. CQR-C developers (Hill, 2012; Jackson et al., 2012) note that CQR-C is a means to analyze case study data in the context of psychotherapy so that therapists may continue to research phenomenon that arise in therapy. Research remains the key to revision or development of new therapeutic techniques and/or better understanding of phenomena. The authors encourage innovation and input to continue to improve all CQR methods.

INCREASING RIGOR IN CONSENSUAL QUALITATIVE RESEARCH

Rigor, credibility, scientific merit, objectivity, and relevance are all terms associated with research and are of importance to qualitative researchers as we face what Denzin and Lincoln (2015) called the "double-faced ghost" (Denzin & Lincoln, 2005; Stahl et al., 2012). The double-faced ghost refers to qualitative research's ability to find balance between rigor and relevance. Stahl, Taylor, and Hill (2012) discussed the richness of deep qualitative responses with the need for objectivity that has plagued qualitative research from the beginning. CQR developers believe that the strength of CQR is in the design. CQR was designed to implement more rigorous methodology and remain qualitatively relevant.

The key to maintaining rigor is through the methods the researcher uses to investigate their chosen phenomenon (Flynn et al., 2019). Some important factors to consider include consistency in the procedures and process, diversity of data and sample, member and team checking, auditing, triangulation of data sources, means and procedures of data collection, and ensuring trustworthiness through defined procedures. CQR is quite rigorous as has been pointed out; however, all methodologies have space to improve and increase rigor. We identify three areas of caution in CQR that could impact and potentially increase rigor.

First, CQR relies heavily on adherence to the process with well-defined steps. However, the assumption is that the researchers will maintain procedural consistency and not make modifications to the procedures outside of the prescribed methodology. For example, selecting the wrong CQR methodology for the study type or adjusting the number of team members where more members are expected but fewer members are utilized. Another example would be the lack of a pilot study for the interview questions, resulting in the researcher asking question irrelevant to the topic. To ensure and continually improve rigor in CQR, the methods the researcher uses must remain centered on the appropriate procedures and researchers must be willing to follow trustworthiness steps as expected in a rigorous qualitative research study.

A second method for improving rigor within CQR methods is related to trustworthiness (Williams & Hill, 2012). As an approach that emphasizes a post-positivism theoretical perspective, CQR relies on detailed methods, triangulation of consistent and reliable data, and efforts to control for generalizability and transferability. However, generalizability has continued to be a struggle for qualitative research. This is primarily due to small samples and a lack of representativeness of the sample to the population. In addition, CQR relies on thick and rich descriptions to build a story told by the data that represents the phenomenon in a broader sense to a related population (i.e., transferability). CQR researcher should make efforts to select participants randomly from a homogeneous population. For CQR researchers, finding areas to improve trustworthiness would increase its credibility, transferability, dependability, and confirmability (Flynn et al., 2019; Hill, 2012).

Finally, CQR procedures weigh heavily on the writing of the manuscript. CQR lays out detailed steps on how to write and revise as well as clearly communicate the findings. However, this requires individual researchers to demonstrate fidelity to CQR procedures; as Hill (2012) indicated several times in descriptions of CQR, CQR requires researchers and team members who are committed to the study, knowledgeable of the topic, and who remain aware of personal and professional biases. These points, made by Hill, are important during the write-up of the study. The researchers must clearly communicate the findings, link the findings to theory, provide well-defined limitations, be willing to adjust the procedures to improve rigor, and make continual efforts to maintain frequent communication between researchers and participants (Williams & Hill, 2012). CQR's original intent was to increase the standing of qualitative research in the scientific community by delineating defined steps for exploring qualitative data. There are few processes indicated to improve rigor in the CQR process other than to provide significant procedural consistency, keep a close eye on trustworthiness, and write as descriptively and transparently as possible.

MULTICULTURAL ISSUES

Inman, Howard, and Hill (2012), commit a book chapter to the cultural considerations inherent to CQR. The authors provide a list of seven steps and recommendations for taking culture into consideration when using CQR. These steps include contextual framework, construction and function of the research team, developing your research questions, selecting your sample, data collection considerations, understanding the data as presented by the participants, and trustworthiness. The authors provided a few recommendations at each step to ensure cultural considerations and address multicultural issues in a manner that is ethical and procedurally sound. One key recommendation is for the researcher to frame the research within the appropriate cultural context while acknowledging the perspectives of the participant and researcher as well as the self-awareness of the researcher regarding the cultural context. Second, by including members from diverse cultural, methodological, educational, and experiential backgrounds with awareness of power differentials, multicultural issues can be more easily considered. A third consideration is to be purposeful and contemplate theoretical components when sampling and developing the research questions. The researcher should also consider cultural norms and values and be reflective of the population that is being studied. The researcher should be aware of culturally specific meanings and responses while collecting the data, particularly during interviews. Finally, the issues of trustworthiness are important when making cultural considerations. The researcher must demonstrate an immersive participation in the culture of study to develop rapport. This includes directly asking participants or members of the participants' community what could be implemented to ensure trustworthiness, which may include the use of quotations to remain close to the data and true to the culture without implied interpretations. CQR developers acknowledged, early in CQR development, that they are committed to multicultural issues and considerations (Hill et al., 2005; Hill, 2012).

LIMITATIONS TO CONSENSUAL QUALITATIVE RESEARCH

There are a handful of limitations acknowledged by CQR researchers. The most apparent limitation is the time commitment that is needed in a CQR study. Hill (2012) stated that a research study can take several years with communication between members being as often as several times a week. This is one reason why CQR researchers stress the commitment level of team members. The next significant limitation is the repetition of the tasks in CQR studies where constant reanalysis, rereading, revising, and rewriting are expected for procedural consistency. The developers of

CQR also acknowledge, rather ironically, that there is a lack of precision in the guidelines in some steps. This can be seen in the issues of saturation and consensus. The process often leaves novice researchers with questions on how to precisely follow the defined CQR steps, then find themselves looking for further guidance. The final limitation of CQR is in the difficulty of meta-analysis and the combination of across study findings. Flynn et al. (2019) completed a content analysis of three qualitative methods, including CQR, grounded theory, and phenomenological studies in the counseling profession. This analysis showed that for studies between 2002 and 2016 there were only 14 CQR studies compared to 44 and 25 studies using phenomenology and grounded theory, respectively. There are simply so few CQR studies that a full analysis would be difficult, even more so if the researcher were looking for triangulation data on a specific topic.

Case Study

Flynn, S. V., Chasek, T., Harper, I., Murphy, K., & Jorgensen, M. (2012). Counselor preparation: A qualitative inquiry of the counseling dissertation process. *Counselor Education and Supervision*, *51*, 242–255.

BACKGROUND

Project-based learning (PBL) is an important pedagogical practice for increasing student mastery of complicated topics (Hattie, 2008). The first author had the opportunity to engage with an intensive PBL project during her doctoral program. The goal of this project was to use a doctoral-level counselor education research course as the platform for conducting a CQR investigation on the counseling dissertation process. The overarching objectives of this PBL were to deeply understand CQR by engaging in an investigation that would assist emerging counselor educators in understanding the dissertation process, experience working together as collaborative rotating research teams, and understand the peer-review scholarly publication process (see Flynn et al., 2012).

The full research team decided to use a CQR approach to research the counseling dissertation process. Specifically, the group desired a set of procedures that would allow for defining a homogeneous sample (doctoral level counselor education graduates) and use a singular agreed upon protocol for all participants. In addition, the class reached consensus that the use of qualitative rotating teams was an optimal framework as this would allow for an in-depth, inductive, and iterative process.

Using a criterion-based and snowball sampling procedure to identify and select participants, the research team interviewed 42 counselor education graduates from four midwestern states about their experience with the counseling dissertation process. The researchers used two rotating teams. Team A comprised of 12 researchers while Team B had four researchers. The following overarching research questions guided this study: (a) What is the dissertation process for counselor education students? (b) What are sources of support during the dissertation? (c) What are sources of need during the dissertation? and (d) How do interpersonal factors relate, if at all, to the dissertation process?

RESEARCH PROCESS

Prior to initiating the investigation, the first author (principal investigator) of the project met with the entire group and discussed the research team member's roles during the CQR process. During

TABLE 14.1 **Counseling Dissertation Process Interview Protocol**

1.	What was your dissertation topic?
2.	Describe your process during the dissertation.
3.	How did you stay motivated throughout the dissertation process?
4.	How did you set up your research design?
5.	How were you supported through the dissertation process?
6.	In what ways were you challenged throughout the dissertation process?
7.	What were your scholarly obligations during your dissertation process?
8.	How did you choose your dissertation committee?
9.	How did you choose your dissertation chair?
10.	How did your dissertation impact your future publications and career?
11.	What advice do you wish you had received when you started your dissertation?
12.	How did you handle positive or negative experiences during the dissertation process?
13.	Describe your feelings and thoughts following the completion of your dissertation.

NOTE: Questions are listed in order of delivery.

this conversation the first author attempted to create a safe atmosphere and differentiate this process from roles traditionally used within the program (e.g., faculty and doctoral students). In addition, all researchers involved in this study received CQR training from the primary author prior to the beginning of the investigation. Next, the entire research team collaborated on the procedures, interview protocol, email messages/solicitations, composition of rotating teams, and purposefully choosing potential participants. Once the protocols were created, the first author created and submitted the institutional review board (IRB) application. This research study received full approval from the University IRB. The co-created interview protocol questions are listed in Table 14.1.

After participants signed and discussed the informed consent document and completed a demographic questionnaire, Team A conducted a single digitally recorded interview with all 42 participants. Following the individual interviews, the digital data were transcribed by Team A members. The research teams followed CQR data analysis standards. During the initial coding process, all transcripts were concurrently coded by two members of Team A. All dual-coded transcripts were analyzed by Team A members for discrepancies and initial codes and emerging clusters were recorded within a code book. The initial coding and codebook were reanalyzed by the auditor for further divergences. Team A uncovered 47 domains from the initial coding procedure.

Through a process of reformulating the 47 domains into concise and assumption-free ideas that align with the participant's words, the four members of Team B reformulated the initial 47 domains into 21 core ideas. Next, two members of Team B created a table containing 47 domains and 21 core ideas. Team B conducted a full cross-analysis which concluded in the identification of the six categories and applied a frequency label to each category. These categories were entitled impact of environment, competing influences, personal traits, chair influence, committee function, and barriers to completion. The frequency labels were as follows: general (G; 41 of 42 cases), typical (T; 22 to 40 cases), variant (V; three to 21 cases), and rare (R; one to 2 cases). To maximize trustworthiness of the findings, all researchers undertook the following procedures: researcher reflexivity, reflexive journaling, triangulation, member checking, thick description, data saturation, dependability audits (audit trail), and frequent consensus meetings; Teams A and B created a researcher epoch.

DISCUSSION

The emergent categories were interrelated across three factors, including: relational factors, professional factors, and internal factors. While this integrated theory provides a framework, the findings are made more meaningful when considered pragmatically. Faculty members can use this theory to understand the perspective of the dissertation student. This perspective can bring forth important infrastructure within counselor education doctoral programs, including dissertation study groups, honoring the various factors (e.g., childcare) affecting a student's life during the dissertation process, and providing an open and autonomous dissertation framework.

Understanding the personality and internal factors of the dissertation student is a second finding that translates well to counselor education doctoral programs. Recognizing traits and skills in emerging counselor educators is key to helping them maximize their dissertation process. A few important factors include level of scholarly writing self-efficacy, internal motivation, sense of destiny, and level of personal ambition. Counselor educators could consider the traits and skills and tailor the dissertation process to the unique needs of each doctoral candidate. For example, the dissertation chair and committee members could model some of the writing behaviors and study habits that could be helpful for a particular student.

SUMMARY

In this chapter CQR was reviewed and examples of CQR methodology were provided, including data collection, procedures, and data analysis. CQR is an inductive method that uses small sample sizes and open-ended interview questions; is contextual;integrates the use of words, numbers, multiple viewpoints, descriptions of experiences; and has a team approach to analysis for reaching consensus in addressing the research problem (Hill, 2012). You may also recall that qualitative research is naturalistic and interpretative in its analysis of phenomenon, this is also apparent within the tradition of CQR. CQR, as a methodology, is compatible with studies that require thick and rich descriptions of individual and group experiences, attitudes, and beliefs. It is important to recall that CQR is often utilized in analysis of multicultural issues and embeds ethical decision-making into its methodological approach. In addition to the traditional CQR, this chapter highlighted the two primary variations CQR-M and CQR-C. All three of these approaches are developed to assist the researcher in meeting their individual project needs. CQR-M is identified for use with small chucks of data from larger studies, while CQR-C was developed for case study research specific to psychotherapy. As you finish this textbook and move on to developing your own studies or you are using this text for a current study, we hope that the information provided on CQR is helpful in your determination of a research methodology.

STUDENT ACTIVITIES

Exercise 1: Pick a Qualitative Methodology

Directions: After reviewing the five qualitative research approaches, pick the method you feel best fits you. Answer the following questions:

Which method did you select?

What is it about this approach you favored over the others?

What do you feel are the limitations and strengths of the method you selected?

Exercise 2: Consider Your Worldview

Directions: Think about your own life. List at least five biases, beliefs, assumptions, or "small t truths" you are aware that you hold about your life and lives of others. Now consider these five concepts in analyzing the phenomenon of adoption. How could the biases, beliefs, assumptions, or "small t truths" influence your research?

Exercise 3: Research Topic and Pilot Interview Questions

Directions: Assume you and a group of researchers are interested in the overall topic of adoptions in the United States from the perspective of the adoptees. First, formulate a more concise topic sentence. Then identify at least five questions you want answered on the topic you have developed. Finally, consider with whom you would conduct your one to two pilot interviews in order to prepare your interview protocol.

Exercise 4: The Results Are in

Directions: Now that you have completed your adoption interviews from our fictitious adoption case study, imagine several core ideas that the team discovered from the participants' stories. List three to five core ideas you will use in writing up your study.

Exercise 5: Three CQR Methods — Preliminary Study

Directions: Now that you have learned about the three methods of CQR it is time to develop your own short case or cases and pick the method you would utilize. Think of a topic you would like to study. Pick the population and how you will select the sample. Then determine which CQR method you would use to investigate your topic. Explain why you chose this method and how you would build your research team.

ADDITIONAL RESOURCES

Software Recommendations

Thompson, Vivino, and Hill (2012) briefly discussed CQR software platform recommendations. At this point, no software has been created or discovered that could be used when designing a CQR study. Furthermore, CQR researchers may prefer to remain intimate with the data and utilize no more than Microsoft Office processing software. CQR researchers place significant value on organization of the data unit and assignment to the appropriate domains. Furthermore, CQR researchers focus on remaining close to the original data source and moving toward the consensus process linking the transcribed data by line number to what has been discovered during the analysis process. CQR researchers may find any number of Computer-Assisted Qualitative Data Analysis

(CAQDA) software programs useful; however, fidelity to CQR would dictate what moving forward in this manner should be done with significant caution.

- NVivo Software (https://www.qsrinternational.com)
- ATLAS ti (https://atlasti.com)

Helpful Links

- https://vimeo.com/77135380
- https://tpcjournal.nbcc.org/professional-identity-development-of-counselor-education-doctoral-students-a-qualitative-investigation/

Helpful Books

Hill C. E. (2012) *Consensual qualitative research: A practical resource for investigating, social science phenomena.* American Psychological Association.
Saldaña, J. (2015). *The coding manual for qualitative researchers.* Sage.

Helpful Videos

- https://www.apa.org/pubs/books/interviews/4313031-hill
- https://prezi.com/7waqtbgmcvab/consensual-qualitative-research/

KEY REFERENCES

Only key references appear in the print edition. The full reference list appears in the digital product found on http://connect.springerpub.com/content/book/978-0-8261-4385-3/part/part03/chapter/ch14

Denzin, N. K., & Lincoln, Y. S. (eds). (2005). *The SAGE handbook of qualitative research* (3rd ed.). SAGE.
Flynn, S. V., Chasek, T., Harper, I., Murphy, K., & Jorgensen, M. (2012). Counselor preparation: A qualitative inquiry of the counseling dissertation process. *Counselor Education and Supervision*, 51, 242–255.
Flynn, S. V., Korcska, J. S., Brady, N. V., & Hays, D. G. (2019). A 15-year content analysis of Three qualitative research traditions. *Counselor Education and Supervision*, 58, 49–63.
Hill, C. E. (2012). *Consensual qualitative research: A practical resource for investigation social science phenomena.* American Psychological Association.
Hill, C. E., Knox, S., Thompson, B. J., Williams, E. N., & Hess, S. A. (2005). Consensual qualitative research: An update. *Journal of Counseling Psychology*, 52, 1–30.

PART IV

MIXED METHODS
RESEARCH

ACTION RESEARCH

Eric S. Thompson

After reading this chapter, you will be able to:

- Describe the history and key concepts of action research
- Recognize various action research models
- Gain competency in applying action research to diverse groups and uses
- Describe evidence-based practices and the data decision-making process in action research

INTRODUCTION TO ACTION RESEARCH

As a practicing counselor or counselor educator, you are likely to eventually ask, "How can I use data to improve my practice as a therapist or educator? What can I do to help my community with an issue?" These types of questions are common in the action research (AR) process. The AR process provides a means for answering these questions in a way that is capable of being rigorous and immediately relevant.

AR is a "form of collective, self-reflective enquiry undertaken by participants in social situations in order to improve the rationality, coherence, adequacy or justice of their own social or educational practices, as well as the understanding of these practices and the situations in which these practices are carried out" (Kemmis & McTaggart 1988, p. 5). AR is a rich methodology and is a powerful approach for counselors to consider while improving their personal lives, counseling practice, and work with communities. The methodology of AR emphasizes the improvement of practice, or lived experience, by following a repetitive series of cycles (see Box 15.1) that include identifying a problem or series of problems, designing an intervention, implementing the intervention, gathering data, and using that feedback to change practice. Next, the process is repeated by identifying additional issues and intervening. AR enables practitioners with various research backgrounds and exposure to engage in meaningful research practices. In addition, AR is versatile and flexible. It covers a range of professional activities from individual improvement, to working with others, to working with communities and third parties.

BOX 15.1

SEVEN QUESTIONS COMMON TO THE ACTION RESEARCH CYCLE

1. What is your focus or problem area for the project?
2. What are the data and how will you collect and analyze them?
3. How will you interpret results and disseminate the findings?
4. Reflect on the results—what do the results mean?
5. How will you utilize the results to revise the action plan?
6. What new action will you take based on the feedback?
7. How will I take new action and repeat the cycle?

AR can be defined by the four key processes of the AR cycle, including planning, implementing the plan, gathering and analyzing data as the plan is implemented, and reflecting on the results (Rowell et al., 2015). Key processes of ARinclude critical reflection on action and reflexive writing about professional belief systems, and reflection on the broader contexts including the organization and society in general.

MAJOR FORMS OF ACTION RESEARCH

The purpose of this chapter is to introduce counselors to historical influences, key concepts, and essential approaches to AR. We discuss various approaches to inquiry in AR including first, second and third person approaches, participatory AR, and practitioner AR. First-person inquiry is a uniquely reflective process of inquiry. Through first-person inquiry one can develop their personal lives or professional practice through cycles of reflection, action, and evaluation. If you are interested in helping a community on an issue, third-person participatory action research may be the best fit. The reasons for these decisions will be discussed in the following.

This chapter will encourage you to consider what type of inquiry can be used to improve your practice as well as the type of AR-influenced design that fits with your research goals. Furthermore, this chapter includes examples and steps to help you complete an AR project and includes a case study to illustrate the AR process.

APPLICATIONS OF ACTION RESEARCH

The processes of AR seeks to bridge a gap between scientific rigor and relevance in the field (Guiffrida et al., 2011). The practice of AR has been used in business, education, counseling, and community organizations that focus mostly on enhancing practice and enriching the context in which one works or lives. AR can combine a rigorous mixed methods research approach informed by experience. The behavioral sciences can benefit from AR due to its focus on meaningful change in solving problems (Guiffrida et al., 2011). AR can be applied in many areas:

1. *Counselor education*: For example, improving one teaching method with another approach and evaluating its outcome.

2. *Evaluation*: For example, improving one's process of continuous assessment of students.

3. *Climate*: For example, creating positive attitudes at work or helping to develop value systems that help improve an area in life.

4. *Administrative processes*: For example, increasing efficacy related to some aspect of administrative life.

5. *Community change*: For example, helping to improve social justice advocacy regarding a community issue or initiative.

While there are many forms of AR, AR has a few essential distinguishing principles and methods. AR is a type of research that is presented as a cyclical process, where one identifies an area for improvement, plans, takes exploratory action, evaluates the outcome of the action, and finds more information that will be relevant to a desired outcome. The process is then repeated and refined until the problem is solved or there is consensus that the project goals have been met. There are many models that depict the cyclical nature of AR (Bargal, 2008; McNiff & Whitehead, 2011; Rowell et al., 2015; Stringer, 2010; Watkins et al., 2016) but each one contains the following basic steps summarized in Figure 15.1:

During step one, action researchers begin by identifying a problem and designing the research questions. In this first step, one uses first, second, or third person reflection to consider a problem or issue to address. In counseling, one may identify how to make a community agency more inclusive to a more diverse population. In counseling practice, one may develop their practice further by identifying an issue (e.g., declining client return rate), considering the usefulness of a specific intervention, or set of skills.

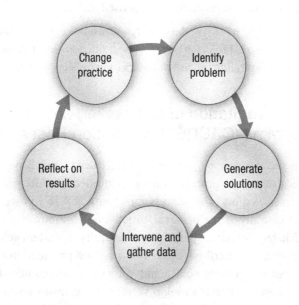

FIGURE 15.1 An Example of a Common Action Research Cycle.

The second step includes generating solutions by planning the research and identifying a design for the research. In this step you determine which methodology and which, if any, interventions you will use to complete the study. If a mental health agency is struggling to increase client attendance, it may consider solutions such as changing its hours of operation, increasing the diversity of counselors, and offering additional community services.

The third step includes the intervention and data collection stage. This chapter covers data collection methods in detail, but a major emphasis in AR is to use triangulation. Triangulation is the process of using multiple sources of data to observe an outcome. For example, in a mental health agency, one might address the problem of diversity and client engagement, so one intervenes by using the previously mentioned solutions (more diversity, more inclusive hours of operation, additional community services). To measure the impact by gathering the results, the researchers might conduct focus groups, implement surveys, and observe how many sessions the clients attend. Using these three methods is triangulation and gathers a more thorough and in-depth amount of data than each method individually.

The fourth step involves the analysis and reflection on data. This type of reflection can include first-, second-, or third-person types of reflection and analysis. In the example of the community agency, perhaps the data suggested that changing the hours of operation helped clients feel that the center was more accessible and that the increased diversity of the counselors made them feel more welcome. The data also revealed that two of the three community initiatives were successful but the third one was unnecessary. In addition, the reflection process includes considering ways to use the data to change the approach or practice.

In step five you will initiate the changes based on the reflection stage. In our community agency example, the agency administrators continued to refine the hours of operation and include counselors of diverse backgrounds and expertise. They removed the third, unsuccessful program and directed the funds to other outreach activities. The two programs were refined with more feedback from the community. The cycle is then repeated, and the practice shifts based on the cycle of action, feedback, reflection, and revised action.

When deciding which model to follow, the best recommendation is to follow the model that makes the most sense for your project. Many of these models are extensions of the same underlying ideas of a cyclical and spiraling process of observation, reflection, action, and reevaluation.

The Council for Accreditation of Counseling and Related Educational Programs (CACREP) and Action Research

AR has strong roots in social justice beginning with Kurt Lewin and Paolo Freire. The CACREP 2016 standard 1.e. indicates that advocacy processes are needed to address institutional and social barriers that impede access, equity, and success for clients. AR is a powerful research method that addresses issues of inequity at the personal, group, and community levels. Likewise, School Counseling Standard 5.k. requires strategies to promote equity in student achievement and college access. The reflection processes described in the following and provided in the exercises can help you to consider strategies to promote equity and student achievement. AR, with an emphasis on equity, can help a school counselor develop various strategies to promote equitable student outcomes. AR is also a useful method to address ethical practice. Interdisciplinary community outreach (F.5.d.) can be enhanced through many of the third-person action research approaches.

TABLE 15.1 **Type of Inquiries, Methods, and Description**

TYPE OF ACTION RESEARCH	METHOD	CONCISE DESCRIPTION
First-person inquiry	Inquiry, reflexive journaling, cooperative inquiry	Development of practitioner and of learning
Second-person inquiry	Focus groups, casual and emergent co-inquiry, action learning sets, collaborative inquiry and dialogue groups	More than one person working together to inquire about a mutual concern or issue
Third-person inquiry	Mixed methods, quantitative methods	Working with larger groups or communities to create equitable change
Participatory/ community	Mixed methods	Type of AR that emphasizes participation and action from groups or communities
Practitioner	Focus groups, participant observation, interviews, field notes Photovoice, examining	Type of action research that emphasize the development of practice through the action research cycles

DISTINGUISHING ACTION RESEARCH FROM OTHER TRADITIONS

When conducting AR, researchers often utilize mixed methods to observe their professional practice and determine current processes, identify areas that need change, and use data and stakeholder information to change the problem (McNiff & Whitehead, 2011). The use of AR shifts the focus from a scientist conducting research on subjects to the researcher becoming the subject of inquiry (see Table 15.1) with a focus on improving practice. AR is vast and has many methodologies making the use of action available to counselors and other helping professionals with diverse experiences and abilities. The action research inquiry process empowers researchers by helping them investigate their practice and develop their skills as a professional.

Action research can be considered a unique application of the scientist–practitioner model with a rich history and wide variety of approaches. As discussed, there are two major types of AR— participatory and practitioner. Both approaches utilize quantitative and qualitative methods as well as first-, second-, and third-person levels of inquiry. The type of AR is determined by the goals and resources available for the project. Participatory AR is a form of social research that is completed as a team. It includes a research team and stakeholders who want to improve a problem within a social context (e.g., work or community). Practitioner AR is geared toward addressing social problems, while participatory action research focuses on developing an individual's, group's, or organization's practice. Practitioner research is also frequently cited in the education literature and in school counseling journals (Rowell et al., 2015)

LEVELS OF INTERACTION

According to Chandler and Torbert (2003), there is a tripartite typology of practice and interaction that includes first-person, second-person, and third-person dynamics. The first-person dynamics include intrapsychic or intrapersonal issues, including feelings, thoughts, personal practice, and so forth. Second-person practice focuses on interpersonal or intrapsychic phenomena. Third-person practice emphasizes external level issues; for example, community or institutional matters.

If one wants to research how to better develop empathy with diverse clients, improve interpersonal climate among peers, or any relational activity, second-person practice is a useful application. Each practice can be used separately or together; however, Bradbury and Reason (2002) recommended that researchers use all three together in a study. Once you determine which level or combination of levels of practice in which you would like to engage, you will generate a plan for which qualitative, qualitative, or mixed method traditions you would like to use for your study.

Bryden-Miller and Coghlan (2018) used first-, second-, and third-person inquiry to explore values in the process of generating knowledge. The authors utilized first-person inquiry to articulate a personal set of values that informed their practice through a structured ethical reflection process.

An example of a first-person inquiry might include a personal exploration of how a counselor educator might improve wellness and burnout prevention in preservice counseling students. The researcher may ask students and other faculty to reflect on their wellness and burnout experiences and concerns in a practicum and internship course. From the findings, the action researcher can discover patterns of responses that address student and faculty concerns about wellness, burnout prevention, and practicum/internship. From these data, the researcher can begin a small wellness program for practicum and internship students to take throughout the semester and collect narrative data on the process.

In the same case, I might decide to build on my first-person inquiry by reaching out to other faculty to gather their input on how to better establish wellness and burnout prevention in practicum and internship coursework. This inquiry could take the form of focus groups or research meetings with a small group of faculty and students with an intention to learn more about themselves. Perhaps in this case, I would work with faculty from other departments who also have preservice students to start a pilot wellness program for the practicum and internship courses. In these groups we would design an appropriate wellness program that fits with the goals of each respective profession and implement the program. As an inquiry group, we would meet to discuss concerns and ideas regarding the progress of the wellness programs.

In our example study, Brydon-Miller and Coghlan (2018) used a inquiry group process and generated a shared set of values within the groups. The values were aligned with co-researchers to points in their collaborative research process. The authors utilized collaborative inquiry through face-to-face dialogue and began to take coordinated action. A list of values was developed for the ethical reflection process. The participants named and defined their core values. The values list became a living document that evolved and guided their behavior throughout the research process. The participants reflected on the following areas and asked questions about each element. I have paraphrased in the following the areas of focus that they addressed in the second person reflection process:

- Values—Participants listed their values; for example, helping the community, taking risks.
- Constructing the research question—For example, how might this question help the community or push my own limits?
- Planning project and identifying sources of data—For example, how will this impact the community; how do I create a supportive environment to take risks?
- Participant recruitment—For example, who in the community should be represented? How do we know participants are safe while taking a risk?
- Data collection and acting— For example, How will the data collection process impact the community? How can I provide a safe environment to share risky content?

- Analyzing data and evaluating the actions—For example, how do we accurately approach the data from a community needs focus? What are the qualities and dimensions of risk-taking behaviors in my data?

- Member checking—For example, how does this process of looking at the results bring together the community? How can we encourage honest feedback which might be risky at time?

- Disseminating the research—For example, how will the project strengthen the community? How can I share risks that were taken in a supportive environment?

Third-person processes were used to develop a framework to develop a public dialogue concerning values-based ethics for conducting AR. They expanded from a research group inquiry to develop a model for dialogue. An example of the third-person process that the authors pointed out was the dissemination of their article. Throughout the first and second exploration process they developed a model for first- and second-person ethical exploration.

A third-person inquiry expands further into an organization or community. In the example of a wellness program, we might begin to expand the program to the rest of the college or find ways to implement principles of wellness into a community that needs it. The inquiry groups would begin to look more like research groups with procedures using surveys to collect data from larger numbers of people. We might survey the students in the college to address any other wellness concerns or needs and begin to develop a larger more comprehensive program. We would gather multiple sources of data to triangulate on the progress of students involved in the wellness program. Perhaps the results would be presented at an AR conference or stakeholder meeting to receive feedback and direction from other stakeholders. From these presentations and conferences additional projects might emerge. Ideally, these conferences would promote an enhanced culture of inquiry within the college.

McNiff and Whitehead (2011) emphasized how defining AR is simple, the challenge is for an action researcher to have a cohesive underlying theory that directs human inquiry as an objective process or as a living subjective process. The challenge of choosing a cohesive underlying approach brings forth a rich environment for mixed methods and unique approaches to conducting research that improves one's context. There are three major characteristics of AR that help shape the methods and the overall action research process. The first is that the situation is typically included in a local context focusing on local, not general, issues. Second, consistent with a scientist–practitioner model, the research tends to be conducted by the practitioner and for the practitioner or environment. Third, AR results in a change that is generated and implemented within the context of the study (Mertler, 2010).

AR differs from formal research in that it requires less training than formal research, the focus is more localized, and the interventions are meant to improve practice or resolve an unresolved situation. Unlike research that utilizes randomization and comparison groups for the purposes of generalizing the results, AR focuses on practical significance for the local context.

In a Delphi study that attempted to locate the distinguishing factors of AR, Rowell, Polush et al. (2015) found numerous perspectives about what distinguishes AR from other approaches. First, they looked at the nature of AR and found that AR provides four major functions:

- Mix of action and inquiry that enables practitioner reflection on their, beliefs, assumptions, and activities to improve practice and influence the institution

- Democratic intent and contribution to knowledge
- Improve quality of life, not to just generate knowledge
- Inquire, collect, and reflect on data to change practice

Next, they examined the various processes involved in AR. These included:

- Focus on practice and improving understanding of practice and conditions under which the practice occurs
- Iterative, cyclic, and reflective
- Vigorous and purposeful, ends with problem-centered action or solution, not just more information as the essence of the research
- Linked through critical reflections
- Participants involved at all stages of inquiry
- Authentic collaboration with participants

Finally, they noted the types of practices that distinguished AR from other methods of research. These practices included:

- Reflecting on the next steps
- Use of action reflection cycles
- Dependent on a question, dilemma, or nature of practice situation
- Requires multiple research methods through the process (data collection, through interpretation) to create actionable knowledge relevant to stakeholders/participants

As you can see, AR is a rich and diverse field that utilizes qualitative, quantitative, and mixed methods to effect change in one's practice, group, or community.

THE PARADIGMATIC HIERARCHY OF ACTION RESEARCH

A paradigm is the philosophical integration of a research tradition. AR has a unique combination of philosophical integration. Of note in this philosophical integration is that AR is value laden and morally committed to positive change (see Table 15.2). Knowledge is not seen as a static discoverable phenomenon, but as a changing and uncertain process. The research methods tend to be open

TABLE 15.2 **Differences in Ontology and Epistemology Between Positivist and Action Research**

	POSITIVISM	ACTION RESEARCH
Ontology	No values	Value laden
	Understand other	Understand what I/we are doing
	Researcher is independent	Researcher is in relation with others
Epistemology	Focus on other	Focus on "I" or "we"
	Knowledge is certain	Knowledge is uncertain
	Knowledge is discoverable	Knowledge is created

ended and developmental as they go through the research cycles. The researcher's role is to be an agent of change.

Ontology

AR has many ontologies that underpin the research process (McNiff & Whitehead, 2011). First, AR is value laden and morally committed. Essentially, when you choose to do an AR project you are committing to creating some form of change. In a sense, AR is like the counseling of the research world. Both approaches seek to generate meaningful, beneficial, and lasting change in an individual, group, or community through problem identification, intervention, reflection, revision of action, and taking new action. Action researchers acknowledge interrelationships between each other and social contexts instead of independent observers removed from participants. In positivist research, a researcher attempts to be free of values and biases in hopes not to impact the results. This is even evidenced in the third-person writing style of many research papers. Alternatively, people who conduct AR articulate values and are aware of them and the influence of their values. As action researchers choose which values to attend to, it is important to explain one's commitments. For example, if you seek to improve a process in the community or an area of your practice, there is a reason for that change. A first-person inquiry may help you elaborate further on what you would like to change. Finally, action researchers work hard to develop relational and inclusive values. McNiff et al. (2011) postulate that it is not enough to consider ourselves as just socially connected, but that we are also connected through our "mental world" or world of ideas. Think of how social media and other Internet-related activities exemplify how ideas can spread.

As opposed to a positivistic or objectivist view that seeks an objective view of reality and generalizes across time and context, reality in AR is co-created, based on context, and relationships (Ozanne & Saatcioglu, 2008). Thus, many approaches and methods in action research are related to qualitative and mixed methods research practices. Additionally, AR is more relativistic than its positivist counterpart. Another assumption is that various historical interests impact social practices. Thus, historical-, reflective-, and change-focused methods of research and intervention are favored since they provide insight into current social practices, demonstrating that social practices have a cause, are malleable, can be critiqued and changed with a more inclusive focus (Ozanne & Saatcioglu, 2008). An inclusive focus includes ideas, other perspectives, feedback from practice, and practices/programs that focus on expanding services to marginalized populations. Additionally, AR provides methods and tools that focus on consciousness raising and reflection to help individuals and groups increase their ability to challenge unjust power structures.

Epistemology

The way that knowledge is generated in action research is through an assumption that social reality is based on context and is socially constructed. Thus, instead of generalizing results across contexts, meaningful descriptions are based on these contexts and knowledge is generated within these contexts. Action researchers solve problems through negotiating the interests of stakeholders with varying degrees of power and resources and assume that knowledge is changing, lacks certainty, is directed by values, and is highly contextual.

AR can be traced back to Kurt Lewin (1890–1947) during the pre-World War II era. The purpose of AR is to apply social theories and interventions with the intent of evaluating their effectiveness using experimental methods (Tekin & Kotaman, 2013). The process of AR was designed to link the scholarly theories and to apply them to real-life scenarios. In education, during the 1970s, AR focused on increasing education effectiveness through teachers developing a research identity. Paolo Freire (1921–1997), a founder of action research, taught critical consciousness and argued that knowledge is gained by a focus not just on the world nor just on humans, but the interaction between person and environment. Freire focused on dialogue between humanity and the worlds they experience. Thus, according to Crotty (1998), many of the founding principles of AR are a rejection of the extremes of mechanistic objectivism (i.e., an objective and God's eye view) and solipsism (i.e., a focus completely on subjectivity or extreme phenomenology). Alternatively, the philosophical underpinnings emphasize a unity or interdependence between subjective reality and the objectivity not entirely rejecting one approach over the other.

Freire's approach differed from positivistic methods in that he focused on practical improvements over objective knowledge. Freire's understanding of praxis is considered a mode of acting on the world and reflecting on the consequences of such action (Freire, 1997). Three unique epistemological assumptions occur in AR. First is that the object of inquiry is the "I," knowledge is uncertain, and knowledge creation is a collaborative process. In AR, the major focus is on you and your development. In practitioner AR, you ask questions that focus on how to improve your practice.

A participatory action researcher may emphasize a mindset that focuses on what can be done to improve an issue and what can we do to improve the overarching problem. Alternatively, in positivist methods, knowledge is true, certain, and discoverable. The answers to questions are set for the rest of time (McNiff & Whitehead, 2011). For example, a child may misbehave in class. In AR an approach would be to observe, gather feedback from many perspectives, and intervene with the child's behavior in mind, and also with consideration of the child's home environment. Perhaps a combination of financial and family stressors combined with a missed breakfast and a poor relationship with a teacher created the appropriate conditions for that child to behave more impulsively that day. An action researcher would begin to observe and assess where the problem starts, locate student and family needs and resources, provide appropriate intervention, collect data, and revise the intervention based on the feedback.

AR is flexible and has many ways of knowing. The AR process can be a quantitative or qualitative dominant approach, depending on the needs of the research and the context of the research. A researcher using AR may use empirical methods to complete the research goals, but AR can be distinguished from an objective focus of positivist research. One major distinction is that an empirical research epistemology attempts to isolate variables and create a clean environment to find links between a few dependent and independent variables. In comparison, AR focuses on subjectivity as its epistemological core.

The theoretical perspective in AR emphasizes symbolic interactionism and critical inquiry. Action researchers tend to focus on group needs, what needs to be changed, and work with stakeholders to begin acting on change. An action researcher might ask, "How do I improve the living conditions of those living homeless," "How can we modify a treatment approach to improve counseling outcomes in diverse populations"?"Alternatively, a quantitative researcher may ask about the statistically significant predictors of homelessness or explore whether the modification of a treatment plan differs across socioeconomic status or ethnicity. Thus, the methods used in AR can be drawn from qualitative and/or quantitative approaches.

AR principles utilize post positivist and interpretivist methodologies. In addition, there is an emphasis on pragmatism in AR. AR challenged social sciences by deviating from the contemporary positivistic methodological norm. The principles of AR blur boundaries between research and practices and sets up a process where practices inform research and research informs practices to generate social change.

Axiology

Axiology focuses on the core values in the AR process. AR starts with experiences or challenges within a group of people. Goals of AR include practical solutions to pressing concerns and development of human abilities and potential. For example, AR was used to explore the impact of an emotional issue, White supremacy identity. Through the inquiry process, the individuals who held a harmful White supremacy identity began to develop a capacity to engage in critical inquiry, practice new behaviors, unlearn old behaviors, reflect on the action, and stay open to emotional responses (Collaborative, 2005).

Methodological Assumptions and Methods

Action researchers have a few key methodological assumptions in how they conduct research. First, AR is completed by those who see themselves as agents of change. Second, AR's methodology is open ended and developmental. In comparison, once a quantitative research project is completed, the data are final and future research expands on the results. AR projects become more refined over time and the focus of AR is to improve practice or learning with a social justice focus (McNiff & Whitehead, 2011).

One of the distinguishing factors of AR is the intention of the research. As discussed, the emphasis in AR is on change using iterative cycles of reflection and action. Therefore, one can use quantitative, qualitative, and mixed methods to accomplish the aims of AR. As you read this book, you can revisit the qualitative, quantitative, and mixed methods sections through an AR lens and consider which methods would be helpful for any given AR project. Generally, first- and second-person inquiry would use qualitative methods given the small sample size and one-on-one nature of the research. Third-person inquiry may utilize more quantitative methods to show objective and generalizable data about the community or organization involved in the AR process. These methods are discussed in more detail in the following section.

Kurt Lewin

Kurt Lewin was born in 1890 in Mogilno, Poland and moved to Berlin, Germany, when he was 14. Lewin developed an interest in Gestalt psychology while at the University of Berlin. He moved to Stanford as visiting professor in 1933 after hearing of Hitler's rise to power. Lewin wrote to his mentors about the discrimination and injustice in Germany, and his sadness about leaving Germany to go to the United States. He continued his role as professor and began teaching at the Massachusetts Institute of Technology and established the Research Center for Group Dynamics. A central focus of this Center was to solve social problems. His experiences of discrimination stayed with him and led him to focus on social justice focused research in minority and majority groups. He formulated the concepts of action research between 1945 and 1947 and unfortunately passed away in 1947, before he had a chance to expand on his action research principles (Bargal, 2006).

Lewin described action research as a type of comparative research on any conditions and effects of social action and research that produces social action (Adelman, 1993). Action research emphasizes the link between social action that includes planning, implementation of the plan, gathering and analyzing the data while the plan is being implemented, and then reflecting on the results (Rowell et al., 2015). Lewin further developed the formula $B = f (P,E)$ that illustrates that behavior is the result of an individual person and the external conditions and context in which that person exists (Lewin, 1946). Contrast this concept to an isolated experimental lab, the goal of which is to isolate and account for as many variables as possible. Rather, AR uses the information from the surrounding environment as essential to the research environment. In this formula, *B* represents observable behavior. The letter *P* represents the person or personal factors what reside within an individual, including traits, attitudes, and behavioral dispositions; and *E* represents the external world, and context, including social roles, weather, physical surroundings, neighborhood, family, peers, and so forth. Finally, the *f* means function (Kihlstrom, 2014).

The formula means that behavior is a function of person and environment. Many counseling theories emphasize changing the person (e.g., Rational Emotive Behavior Therapy's focus on changing irrational beliefs), while others emphasize a conducive environment for change and growth (Adlerian Therapy, Person-Centered Therapy). In Lewin's formula, a person's behavior is a function of the individual and the environment in which they live. In a stressful environment (*E*), a person with Posttraumatic Stress Disorder may be more likely to experience a behavioral trigger (e.g., drinking), whereas in a less stressful environment one may be less likely to be triggered. Thus, a person's behavior (*B*) is a function of person (*P*), in this case the person has PTSD, and environment (*E*) is the level of contextual stress. This formula contributes to AR by considering the interaction between a person and their context.

Paulo Freire

Paulo Freire was a Brazilian educator and philosopher born in 1921. He used core elements of action research to transform education. Although born in Brazil, Freire moved to Chile after the military coup of 1964 (Freire, 1997). Freire began research as a form of social action and generated themes of how important it is to consider the issues and concerns from stakeholders. One of Freire's contributions is designing a methodology to enable those who were previously illiterate to comprehend and develop a critical view of the world. This type of critical analysis is known as critical pedagogy and is published in his well-known work *Pedagogy of the Oppressed* (Freire, 1970).

Freire's work on oppression and critical pedagogy led to a powerful method of understanding and to challenging oppressive forces. Freire argued that educational goals should emphasize reflection and action in an effort to transform the context in which one operates for the better (Seider et al., 2017). Critical consciousness was divided into three components: analyzing oppression, navigating oppression, and challenging oppression (Seider et al., 2017). The ability to develop skills to analyze oppressive forces leads to the development of critical thinking that is purposeful and self-aware, and enables one to provide an analysis of a complex issue. The second dimension of critical consciousness is navigating the impact of the oppressive social forces. This includes recognizing how biases and prejudices help one to cope with the impact of oppressive forces. Freire helped students develop additional adaptive strategies that cultivated social intelligence and awareness of other motives, feelings, and managing social contexts. Finally, challenging oppressive forces sharpens civic character and strengths associated with activism and other social action. Such concepts lead nicely into the various levels of interaction within action research. Freire emphasized three main concepts for social transformation: education, politics, and humanization. Such concepts informed the practice of participatory action research, a type of research detailed in the following. While Freire rarely used the term "participatory AR," his ideas and presentations inspired the creation of participatory AR. Freire's focus was to use research to address social injustices. He argued that education of citizens can impact issues of social justice in many ways. Specifically, through education, politics, and humanitarian communities, individuals can use the liberation approaches laid out by Freire to rise out of oppressive circumstances. According to Freire, people have the right to be creators of knowledge.

Freire emphasized, in the *Pedagogy of the Oppressed*, that people are knowers and creators of their world, where they are aware of oppression and have commitment to end it. Individuals can reflect, conceptualize, think critically, and have a social capacity for collective community and social planning. Freire concluded that research cannot be neutral and objective because knowledge and power are naturally intertwined. Research is not neutral as it can be used to reduce social injustice and oppression or to increase it. He argued that through investigating reality, people feel ownership of their knowing process, which increases self-efficacy in relationship to increased community action. The research focus is simultaneously liberating and collaborative to promote critical awareness, to construct knowledge (Freire, 1997), and to inform transformative action.

PRACTITIONER ACTION RESEARCH

AR has many facets that tend to emphasize generating change in individual, group, and community practice. AR generally requires participation from co-researchers and participants which makes it participatory. Practitioner AR developed by Lewin (1946) emphasized the development of practitioners. While participatory AR is intended for community involvement, practitioner AR is intended for improving an individual's or group's practice. The practitioner AR approach focuses on person–environment interactions that help explain relations between individual and environment. An example of this person–environment interaction is included in a brief case study example, which follows, where an individual engaged in reflection on her practices, the organizational culture, and how each impacts the other. Essentially, like many qualitative research traditions, participatory action researchers often utilize three methods: focus groups, participant observation, and interviews (MacDonald, 2012).

First-Person Practice

First-person AR emphasizes the development of the practitioner and their process of learning. One way to consider action research is to ask yourself if you are emphasizing the development of practice or the development of a community or organization. Practitioner AR uses AR to develop one's practice while participatory AR develops a community or organization. First-person inquiry and practice are more likely to focus around one's practice, while third-person appears to emphasize community participatory AR At the first-person level, one develops the ability to engage with and respond to the world with awareness and monitor the impact of behavior (Reason & Bradbury, 2007). An application for a counselor can include "How do I engage in therapeutic lifestyle changes to become a more therapeutic person and improve client outcomes?"

First-person practice means that the inquirer's values, beliefs, schemas, and behavior are essential to the generation of knowledge and change. First-person practice means that subjective inquiry and learning from our direct actions and internal drives lead to awareness and knowledge of a phenomenon. First-person practice requires that one be active and receptive in the process of action and reflection and that each person creates an individualized practice. This practice is centered on maintaining and improving quality through various forms of action, evaluation, and reflection (Coghlan, 2008). Ultimately, this process of inquiry leads to insight. The development of insight was described by Lonergan (2008) as self-appropriation. The process of inquiry included basic principles such as attention to observable data, imagining potential explanations of the data, and preference for explanations that account for the most data (Coghlan, 2008). Following are examples of questions related to first-person inquiry.

- What am I doing in my practice?
- What am I thinking about my practice?
- What am I feeling in this context?
- What inspired these thoughts?
- What motivated these feelings?
- What experience prompted me to think about this issue?
- Did my thinking conclude or resolve?
- Did I learn anything in the thinking process?
- Am I sure I learned something?
- How do I know I am sure?
- What are the differences between the thoughts and the feelings I experienced?
- How were they related to each other?
- Did my feelings lead to a thought?
- Did my thoughts lead to a feeling? (Adapted from Coghlan, 2008)

In addition to the these questions, living education theory can provide a useful process to first-person inquiry. Like the preceding questions, living education theory emphasizes introspection processes on the importance and intentionality of your practice. Such questions are related to context, concern, describing experiences, one's ability to act and to specify a particular action to take, how to gather data and evaluate potential influences, how to come to fair conclusions, validity of personal perception of learning, and how to modify practice in response to evaluation (McNiff & Whitehead, 2011).

Brief Case Study Example

Kidd, S., Kenny, A., & McKinstry, C. (2014). From experience to action in recovery-oriented mental health practice: A first person inquiry. *Action Research*, 12(4), 357–373. https://doi.org/10.1177/1476750314534997

In one example of first-person practice, Kidd et al. (2014) looked at recovery oriented mental health services to use AR as an application for organizational cultural change. A process called cooperative inquiry was utilized and is a reflexive process where a researcher records how they make meaning of their experiences in connection with themselves, others, the environment, and the universe in general. It implies that meaning is effected by a person's interactions with the world, people, or environment (Kidd et al., 2014). The researcher recorded experiences and used first-person inquiry to reflect on changing practices, ways of thinking, and quality of attention. The author focused on four types of knowing: **experiential knowing**experiences of life; **presentational knowing**-the way one conveys lived experiences; **propositional knowing**-use of theory and concepts to conceptualize the meaning making process, and **practical knowing**-the way one applies what one knows. By using these four types of knowing, Kidd et al, (2014), asserted that one's practice can become more intentional. In this study, the authors illustrate how subjective experiences were excluded in favor of a more dominant biomedical epistemology. As the researcher continued to participate in the research process, she became more critical of her biases and the biases of the organizational culture. By becoming increasingly reflective on her practice and the culture in the organization, new dialogues occurred. She discussed becoming more articulate about her own practice, even challenges around involuntary treatment and hospitalization.

Second Person Practice

Second person action research involves more than one person working together to inquire about a mutual concern. The two or more individuals work together to conceptualize and develop inquiry questions to determine how the information will be gathered, analyzed, interpreted, and acted upon. The process of second person inquiry covers a variety of practices, from face to face conversations to large group inquiry (Coghlan & Brydon-Miller, 2014).

There are many methods in second person inquiry. Second person inquiry focuses on the relational aspect of research and moves toward a humanistic approach of validating the person as opposed to observing an object. Second person inquiry can be likened to focus groups, but with differences. Focus groups utilize a third party and generate the topic of discussion, usually without input of the group. Second person inquiry allows for more control by involving stakeholders in the process of developing the questions and topics of discussion. The topics of discussion and questions focus on meeting the needs of the group under investigation, while focus groups tend to meet the needs of the researchers. Second person inquiry methods include casual and emergent co-inquiry through conversation to formal group interactions that negotiate the questions for inquiry with each other.

The second person practice was developed to describe a type of interaction. One interesting aspect of second person practice is that it focuses on relational knowledge. Second person practice emphasizes how researchers work with participants as opposed to on the participants. Self-determination and autonomy are respected and valued in second person practice and in action research. This approach also values subjective experience as opposed to objective and removed experience. In second person practice, the individual inquire knows self-experience with its distortions and the process of inquiry challenges those distortions. Thus, validity focuses less on ending up on objective truth, but validity is negotiated and tested in its usefulness and practicality in changing the problem. Chandler and Torbert (2003) suggested four approaches to communicating about an issue with someone: framing, advocating, illustrating, and inquiring (see Table 15.3). Framing includes setting up an agenda or setting the stage for what will be discussed. Counselors may use framing to define the parameters of a group meeting, setting the meeting purpose, goals, and consider objections or additional matters. Advocating includes stating emphasizing a stance or argument and includes feelings, plans, goals, and other strategic recommendations. Illustrating is a process of presenting the topic or idea in concrete terms potentially using analogy, phrases, or words within a given community to make the topic more relatable and interesting. Finally, inquiry refers to a feedback process including questions, probing, and information seeking. The inquiry is useful as it helps one clarify and strengthen assumptions.

Co-operative inquiry, developed by Heron and Reason (1997), utilizes a small group ranging from 5 to 15 people who work with questions of group concern through cycles of action and reflection. They meet over a period of months or years, and the researchers and participants are simultaneously co-researchers and subjects.

TABLE 15.3 **Habermas's Types of Communication**

SPEECH FORM	INVOLVES	WHY USE	EXAMPLE
Framing/reframing	Others do not have the same frame of reference as you	Increase awareness of shared questions, vision, or mission	What does social justice advocacy mean to you?
Advocating	Explicitly asserting opinion, suggestion, feeling, plan, claim, goal, or strategy	Propose a way forward	A certain theoretical perspective will certainly help with this issue
Illustrating	Present topic in more concrete terms by sharing analogy or story	Makes the process more meaningful and relatable	For example, previously this theory was used on this population to… improve emotion regulation
Inquiry	Inviting feedback from others by asking questions, probing, seeking information	Helps you notice if your assumptions are valid or need to be refined	As your role as counselor, how do you adapt your approach to those with various levels of emotional regulation?

NOTE: Making sure that no issue or argument has been prematurely dismissed (inspired by Kakabadse et al., 2007).

Action learning is comprised of small groups that meet with a facilitator to pursue the questions connected to their work and practice. Participants are generally invited by someone in their shared work area (e.g., administrators). A facilitator will guide the group through a process of disciplined questions and reflection of the work of the group (Mertier, 2019)

COLLABORATIVE INQUIRY AND DIALOGUE GROUPS

The process of collaborative inquiry groups is less formal with fewer than 40 members. The group operates as an open group where the group membership is more fluid than the aforementioned groups. The focus of this group is to generate a collaborative awareness of knowing within the groups. Knowing takes the form of group conversation and inquiring interaction. The purpose of the facilitator is to help with the group inquiry process.

Among the many topics that second person inquiry can be useful for, working in groups requires many practical skills. Many of these skills are developed in the group classes. First person practice focuses on one's self reflection and development, while second person research focuses on validating congruence between our own frameworks, behaviors, and outcomes. Consider working with a diverse population where there are uncommunicated assumptions about indirect communication as a preferred way to solve a conflict. While indirect communication is promoted by some, others in the group strongly believe direct communication is a better approach. Third person research or practice focuses on objective inquiry; as emphasizing third person objects.

Brief Case Study Example

Petre, D. A. (2019). Constructing a safer space for queer aesthetics in psychotherapy: A cooperative inquiry approach. *Journal of Experiential Psychotherapy* (Vol. 22). Retrieved from https://osf.io/83w6z.

In Romania, collaborative inquiry was used in a psychotherapy office to ensure a safe place for queer aesthetics for clients and therapists (Petre, 2019). Queer aesthetics are aesthetics related to LGBTQ imagery and may include men or women with non-traditional hair, makeup, and/or clothing. Aggressive behaviors, including microaggressions, murder, and assault, towards queer aesthetics in society, remains a problem and these researchers wanted to investigate how to make their practice offices a safer space for queer aesthetics. Such aggressions include individuals being left out of the intervention processes because they perceive it as an aggressive space for them. When attending therapy sessions, those who cross dressed or men who wore makeup, would be marginalized through the process of empathic failure. The psychotherapists gathered during five meetings to complete a cooperative inquiry on creating a safer space for queer aesthetics. Between the sessions, researchers engaged in reflection and action based on the topic of inquiry. The author described his process of going through the inquiries and reflected on dynamics in the meeting. For example, the first author was expected to lead the group, struggled with transitioning to be a participant, but then gave up and stayed as the leader.

In this study, six therapists or therapists in training participated in meetings spanning 6 weeks. The method used was cooperative inquiry. Purposive sampling was used to select participants. Participants were determined by a need to work with typical psychotherapists and those who wanted to work with atypical psychotherapists (those interested in gender studies and clothing). They selected co-researchers based on the training in psychotherapy. The authors also mentioned that they used convenience and snowball sampling. Four women and two men were selected with ages ranging from 22-30 years. All were cis gender. One participant was bisexual, one was gay, and one identified as heteroflexible.

The inquiry included five meetings that were each two hours long. Each meeting was held online, transcribed, and coded. According to the authors, the only data that is written down in cooperative inquiries is the researchers work diaries. The report is considered another part of the cooperative inquiry. The authors reported the cycles of reflection and action. In summary, the first cycle consisted of the group compiling examples of social attitudes towards queer aesthetics. The examples were shared in the groups and transcribed. One example centered around aggressions against trans persons. During the meetings, the researchers tried to agree on what queer aesthetics was. The definition was based on experience or on their knowledge of the topic. A list of definitions and impressions were made. In another meeting they reflected on the sources of knowledge of queerness and what influenced their decisions about disclosing their orientation.

The third session consisted of multiple self-analyses that included their level of queerness and the course of their development, when they acted with microaggressions towards the queerness of others, moments when microaggressions occurred in therapy. Questions about when they were micro-aggressed, by whom, how, and if they can use their knowledge and experiences to transform offices into a safer space.

The authors investigated how their psychotherapy office, a micro symbol of society, can be more supportive and safer for clients and therapists with queer aesthetics. They engaged in cycles of reflection and action of how to construct a safer space for queer aesthetics in the office. The fourth session emphasized nonverbal self-disclosure and courage. It began with an observation of a co-researcher with a new haircut that did not conform to traditional norms. Disclosing the haircut was an important topic in self-disclosure. The cooperative inquiry showed that his previous decisions to hide his queer aesthetics was based on fear of losing clients and position as a therapist. He asked himself how he could help someone affirm their queer self when he hides his own. As a result, other employees began to share their queer aesthetic. The fifth group focused on creating safer spaces for the therapist's queerness. They shared stories of being pressured by employers to hide their aesthetics. Four themes emerged: therapist courage, the disguise, a male researcher discussed how he conducted a therapy session wearing bold red lipstick, which encouraged other therapists to disclose more as well.

The authors concluded that their psychotherapy office was not considered a safe space for queer aesthetics by clients or therapists. Therapeutic safe space was investigated at the clothing decision level to address microaggressions acted by therapists and by institutions. The authors concluded that there is a need for more integration of gender studies in psychotherapy training. They particularly focused on addressing attitudes towards queer clothing as part of the therapeutic alliance and a common factor in therapy.

Third Person Practice

Third person practice emphasizes a type of inquiry on objects or third person objects (Coghlan & Brydon-Miller, 2014). The third person approach emphasizes objectivity more than first- and second-person action research. In the third person approach, objective methods become more relevant and compelling. Such methods include descriptive and inferential statistics. Third person research has its origins in Reason and Bradbury (2007) who focused on broad social issues where the main approach was to use face to face groups and close contact. It was difficult to expand beyond the small group that worked together. Lewin wanted to generalize his results but ran into difficulty using first and second person approaches. Instead, using third person approaches to action research, action research groups and researchers began to disseminate face to face projects and meetings through text. Another approach used to disseminate information was to run an action research project repeatedly until it hit a "critical mass" of participants and data. Next, large scale interventions could be used. For example, planning an alcohol screening intervention at a festival, providing face masks in public settings during a public health crisis, or work with a community agency to cope with PTSD. The emphasis of the third person practice is to take smaller scale projects and upscale it to create an impact on a community, ideally creating a culture of inquiry within the community in which the action research is being performed. Third-person strategies aim to create a wider community of inquiry involving persons who, because they cannot be known to each other face-to-face (say, in a large, geographically dispersed corporation), have an impersonal quality. Writing and other methods of reporting the process and outcomes of inquiries can also be an important form of third-person inquiry (Reason & Bradbury, 2007, p.6).

While third person action research is compelling, the most rigorous forms of action research utilize all three forms of practice and inquiry: first, second, and third (Reason & Bradbury, 2007). Ideally a researcher would utilize all three approaches as they can build on each other. First person inquiry helps to organize and clarify what is most meaningful for you to research. Stemming from the results of first-person inquiry, one can interview someone who experiences similar issues. Finally, based off of the results of the first- and second-person inquiry, one may introduce a third person perspective that includes outreach to a community or group.

Brief Case Study Example

Sheikhattari, P., Apata, J., Kamangar, F., Schutzman, C., O'Keefe, & Buccheri, W. (2016). Examining smoking cessation in a community-based versus clinic-based interv...: EBSCOhost. *Journal of Community Health2, 41*(1), 1146–1152.

Third person action research focused on the community can utilize mixed methods to accomplish the task. In this case study example, action research was used to develop, implement, and evaluate a collaborative community-based action research project for smoking cessation.

Third person community based action research was utilized on a smoking cessation program within a community (Sheikhattari et al., 2016). In this study, 965 participants were enrolled in a smoking cessation intervention. The participants were 18 years or older, current smokers who smoked at least three cigarettes per day in the past week. In this 12-week program, participants were given access to nicotine replacement therapy and/or medications. Participants were given counseling in community venues and worked with peer mentors/motivators from the communities in which the interventions took place. In this second phase the curriculum included 6-week smoking cessation modules and followed up with a 6-week relapse prevention module. There was a three and six month follow up after completion of the program as well. Phase three included more flexibility and was implemented in recovery centers, mental health clinics and at organizations that served the homeless. There were six cessation classes and six optional relapse prevention courses with follow up at 3 and six months.

Participants were recruited through word of mouth, referrals, peer mentors, community organization collaborations. Participants were given a baseline questionnaire that included demographics, overall health, smoking history, obstacles to quitting, change stages, etc. An exit form at the end of each session was administered to participants. Participants were measured with a measure of physical addiction to nicotine called the Fagerstrom Test. This measure ranges from 0 (low) to 10 (high dependence). Smoking status was also assessed at the end of each program and at each follow up session. The self-report of smoking abstinence was verified by carbon monoxide levels in participants' expired air. Various statistical analyses were sued including univariate, bivariate, Chi square tests of independence for categorical variables, and Student's t test. Multivariate logistic regression model was employed to compare odds of quitting in each phase. The study identified intervention setting as a major factor associated with smoking cessation. Quitting smoking odds increased when the setting of the program was moved from the health center and into the community. The researchers used participant feedback to introduce changes in the third phase of the project which lead to an even greater reduction of smoking in the community. The use of peer motivators to help with the intervention who were former smokers increased compliance with the program. The quit rates at phase one was 9.4%, at the 12-week follow-up from the community-based trial was 21%, and phase three was 30%. According to the results and after controlling for confounding variables, the most significant predictor of smoking cessation was the service delivery in community settings. This study provided support for community-based interventions to increase the effectiveness of smoking cessation services in low income urban populations. The authors also suggest that the community-based programs increase participant engagement and retention.

PARTICIPATORY ACTION RESEARCH

Participatory action research tends to focus on generating social change in surrounding contexts, while practitioner action research tends to focus on improving one's practice. A practitioner action research project might focus on the best approach to work with individuals with PTSD given any context, while participatory action researchers might collaborate with community partners to reduce traumatic exposure to citizens in the surrounding environment.

The practice of participatory action research empowers people through multiple voices speaking together on a certain issue or problem. Participatory action research (PAR) or critical participatory action research is a reflective process of self-reflective cycles of planning for change, acting, reflecting, revising the plan, act/observe, and reflect in a cycle. It is "an approach to research in which local perspectives, needs, and knowledge are prioritized through collaborations with community member throughout the research process" (Smith et al., 2010, p. 1116). As mentioned above, action researchers may struggle with what theoretical approach to use. Participatory action researchers are highly involved and participate in the research process working with and collaborating with participants. In participatory action research, participants are encouraged to explore the environmental conditions that lead to their dilemma, a self-study of practices of what can be done to improve issue and thus work in a series of cycles of planning, acting, observing, and reflecting (Kemmis et al., 2014).

Freire used PAR to encourage communities in poverty to understand the reasons for theory poverty and oppression, including structural reasons (Freire, 1997). PAR emphasizes reflection and questioning about the nature of reality and the construction of knowledge. It looks at how experience can be a basis of knowing, experience is valid, and power influences ones lived experience. PAR practices were developed to improve practice by changing it. It is a collective and self-reflective inquiry process undertaken with participants in an egalitarian way. There is an emphasis on empowerment in PAR and an overall arc towards increased control over their lives and environment (Baum et al., 2006)

Since the primary focus of PAR is to change one's practice, the process and perspective of research differs from many other types of research because it is focused on changing practice. The participatory action research process is reflexive and dialectical that looks at both the subjective and objective relations and connections. Additionally, participatory action research practice is created and recreated by human agency and social action. It combines multiple methodological frameworks for research including mixed methods. There are a few reasons to change practice through participatory action research. Among these reasons is that an element of practice has become irrational or unreasonable, the practice is unsustainable or ineffective because it limits self-development, or the practice is unjust where the practice serves the interests of some at the expense of others (Ozanne & Saatcioglu, 2008; White et al., 2004).

Participatory action research explores one's life, community, and concerns. Since every PAR activity is different, participants, methods, and data collection techniques will be unique to the context in which the project occurs. Since PAR specifically and action research in general are so dependent on the context; qualitative, quantitative, and mixed methods are used to generate knowledge. In addition to traditional methods like surveys, interviews, and concept mapping, other creative methods are used including photovoice, dramatization, and symbolic art. Analytical methods also range from project to project including photographs, collages, and group dialogue.

In participatory action research, the researcher has an equal part in a group that intends to study and improve practice. The researcher acts more as a project manager who gathers information, implements changes, listens to feedback, etc. Alternatively, a strictly quantitative researcher's role would be more as the expert in charge who collects and analyzes the data gathered from the research subjects.

Participatory action research application is geared towards developing, applying, and testing new interventions, processes, or procedures while an action researcher emphasizes the development of new solutions and increasing the development of the participants. In contract, the application for a strictly quantitative researcher is to develop new knowledge.

McIntyre, (2008) suggest the following questions to ask yourself while developing a PAR project. Consider how you might use these questions to guide the development of an PAR project.

- What do you perceive as a problem or an issue in your community that needs to be addressed?

- How does it relate to your life? To the community's life?

- Why do these issues/problems exist?

- What can we do about them?

- What do we need to know?

- What do we already know?

- What resources do we need to proceed with the project?

- How will this project benefit the participants and the rest of the community?

- What are the common themes that have been generated in the research process?

- How do we summarize these themes in ways that benefit those involved?

- Who will control the research project? Make the decisions? Decide how to disseminate information to others?

- How will we address issues of confidentiality and privacy in the dissemination of the information we gather in the project?

- How will we inform others about the project?

- Will our research represent only the realities of those involved or those of other members of the community/group as well?

- What are the criteria we will use to assess the adequacy and efficacy of the project? (p. 50)

Now that you have an action research project topic and a plan, recruitment is another important consideration. The recruitment process in PAR follows a similar path as many qualitative methodologies. White et al, (2004) identified seven activities recommended for implementing a recruitment process. First, one identifies potential team members. This might include colleagues, students, and the participants in the project. The next step is advertising AR opportunities to participate in the project. These advertisements can be placed in flyers, bulletins, periodicals, and online. The opportunities to participate in the process may include seeking peers to develop the research agenda. Additional participation opportunities may include research assistantships, data analyses, facilitator of focus groups, and supporting the writing process. The third step is to enter a setting or group. This can have challenges if you plan to work with vulnerable populations or if there are few resources to assist you. Once in the setting or group, the researcher begins to focus on developing the participatory relations and orienting potential team members to the study goals, procedures, and intentions. Following the orientations, it is time to recruit team members to participate in the study. Finally, through the continued development of meaningful relationships, the researchers focus on retaining the team members. White (2004) illustrates these processes in more detail.

Participatory action research has similar procedures as ethnographic discovery (Reason & Bradbury, 2007) in terms of an emphasis on allowing the research team time to develop rapport with community members. A main difference between PAR and ethnographic discovery is the level of participant involvement. In PAR the participant and researcher involvement is high, while ethnographies typically have low researcher involvement. Since the PAR process is mostly focused on working with individuals or groups, there are few recommended procedures and principles for PAR (Greenwood et al., 1993).

ACTION RESEARCH DATA COLLECTION METHODS AND EXAMPLES

The data collection methods in action research are akin to those used in traditional mixed methods approaches. Much of the data comes from interviews, various perceptual and outcome data, interviewing stakeholders. Additional methods include field notes, recording sheets and observation schedules, sociometric analysis, written accounts, personal logs, questionnaires, surveys and interviews (McNiff & Whitehead, 2011). Many of these methods have been discussed in other chapters. Remember that while AR uses qualitative and quantitative methods, one of the distinguishing features of AR is that the intended outcome to affect change in a practice, group, or community.

The methods used in AR are chosen for the situation and context from which the research is conducted. Many data collection methods are selected in collaboration with the group or community. As mentioned in other chapters, **Triangulation** will generate stronger evidence by utilizing multiple forms of data collection. Triangulation is the process of using multiple data points or sources of data to corroborate findings.

A **focus group** generally consists of six to 12 individuals where a facilitator provides an environment for optimal communication among participants. Collaboration among the facilitators and participants to decide the topic for the focus group is encouraged and all involved in the research process are considered active participants in the process. (MacDonald, 2012). A three stage model of focus groups in Participatory AR, presented by Chiu (2003), suggested the first group emphasize problem identification and facilitate experiential knowledge in preparation for the second group. The second group emphasizes solution generation and facilitates practical knowledge. The third group explores how to implement and evaluate the process and facilitates critical reflection on change and consolidate the various ways of knowing.

Participant observation is the systematic recording of behaviors, interactions, objects, and events in the research setting. Observation provides first person knowledge of social behavior as it occurs through time and the researcher gains a more inclusive perspective of implicit and contextual dynamics that occur in the research context.

Interviews are one on one meetings and interactions with participants. There are generally three types of interviews: structured, semi-structured and unstructured. An unstructured interview takes place with little structure or set list of questions. The interview progresses in a similar way that a conversation would progress, but the focus of the interview is on the research topic. These interviews can be useful for establishing rapport with the participants. The flexible structure enables the interview to probe more freely around the issue. Semi-structured interviews use interview protocols to guide the researcher, but it is more guided than an unstructured interview. In semi-structured interviews, there may be a few preset questions or general ideas of what to discuss, but there is also flexibility built into the process so the researcher can probe and ask questions that may be more suited for the moment or immediate response from the participant. Finally, structured interviews are less flexible and utilize a more rigid protocol. Only the questions included in the original interview sheet are used. Thus, there are fewer opportunities to probe and explore topics. It is useful, however, because it helps target specific phenomena and sets up an efficient data collection process.

Enquiring is another approach that asks participants to respond to a prompt in one form or another. Interviews and focus groups are very common action research strategies for collecting enquiry data. A type of questioning can be used at the beginning of interviews called grand tour questions that enable participants to discuss an issue in their own way. For example, a researcher might ask a participant to open up with "Please tell me about your experiences working with this agency"(Stringer, 2010). Additional considerations with enquiring include broad questions seeking a description about a process (e.g. describe a typical day at work). More specific questions or probes can be used as follow-up (e.g. Tell me more specifically about what happened at work that caused this concern). Finally, the guided tour questions can ask the participants to provide details about people and activities in the various settings (e.g. please describe your work environment).

One may gather data through one's own personal experience. This data is collected in the form of field notes. Such experience can be recorded through field nots. Field notes include descriptions of the field, places, people, actions, activities, intentions, purposes, and any other data that is observable.

Photovoice is a popular approach where participants take photographs and voice their experiences, perspectives and analyses through the photos(Coghlan & Brydon-Miller, 2014). A good example of photovoice can be found in a youth participatory action research project (Foster-Fishman, Law, Lichty, & Aoun, 2010). A new AR approach called the ReACT Method was implemented using photovoice to promote local knowledge and critical consciousness by going through an action research process. Additionally, the case study of this chapter reviews an action research project that utilizes photovoice.

Examining is also used by collecting artifacts, materials, and other items that already exist or are collected in the setting. For example, one may collect local community poetry, periodicals and flyers, cloth, symbolic statues, etc. In terms of putting it all together, a person conducting an action research project could start with experiencing. As a beginning researcher you could begin taking field notes on issues you see in your agency. internship site, or community. Once you notice something worthy of inquiry, you can begin to enquire. Perhaps you can begin with a few informal interviews

Participatory action research has a focus on equity, social justice, and community perspectives. Counselors have an ethical imperative to promote the dignity and welfare of clients and social justice (American Counseling Association [ACA], 2014, code A.1., Preamble 3.). Action research methods have a history of empowering individuals and communities to take action towards equitable outcomes in their local environments and communities (Lewin, 1946; Masters, 1995). While PAR is rich in methodologies and initiating social change, PAR has a lack of defined procedures which make it difficult to systematically apply and replicate (White et al., 2004).

PRACTITIONER ACTION RESEARCH DATA ANALYSIS AND EXAMPLES

Once you have gathered data the next step will be to organize and make meaning out of the data. Like many quantitative methods, data can be converted to percentages, one can take baseline data and use graphs to demonstrate results. Data analysis in AR includes obtaining data and may include analyzing a person's behavior or poem. Analyses is also defined as interpreting the data and may include transcript analysis. Finally, analysis can be viewed as the result of an analytical process (Snyder, 2009). Snyder (2009) recommends continuing to ask throughout the process how the analysis assists in the answer to the research question and whether it help plan the next action in the research cycle.

Data analysis can follow three main process. First, label the data with information. For example, when the data was gathered, anonymize the data with pseudonyms, and create an archive for your data. This archive is intended to include various details relating to each data item collected. Such

---

Bullying survey

1. On a scale of 1-10 (10 is highest) I am concerned about bullying in my school

2. Where have you seen bullying occur (circle one)

       Hallways   Cafeteria   In class   Bus Area   Other___

3. When do you most see bullying?

       8–10   10–12   12–2   2–4

4. On a scale of 1–10 (10 is excellent), how would you rate our current bullying prevention program?

5. I would like to speak to a counselor about bullying YES   NO

FIGURE 15.2 Example of a Brief Bullying Questionnaire.

items can include the coding scheme, various types of data collected and the labels, how the data was collected, who was involved and were they consulted and anonymized, whether the data is primary or transformed, and any additional field notes.

An example data collection process is illustrated below. A group of school counselors were concerned about a rise in bullying in their middle school. To investigate, they distributed anonymous questionnaires (see Figure 15.2) for students, faculty, and administrators to complete over the course of a semester. They collected and collated the data. Once they collected the data, they realized that:

- bullying occurs most frequently near the cafeteria right after lunch
- Some teachers did not receive the bullying prevention toolkits and fliers
- Most individuals said that bullying is a major concern
- Attempts to stop bullying were rated as very poor by students.

Once the data was collected, they were able to setup meetings to address the concerns and revise their interventions.

It is important to consider the various components of data collected which include ideas, issues that come up, questions and doubts about the project, any dilemmas or difficult choices, significant events, emotions, relationships, shared values or discourse. You may not be able to address all these items, but you can select a few when expecting to work with a population. For example, if you ask a client about a type of medication, the response may include ideas, decisions, emotions, and dilemmas. While analyzing the narratives you can code whether a person is expressing an opinion, dilemma, and so forth. As the data is collected and coded you can begin to look for themes and patterns running through the data. If you have qualitative and quantitative data, you can use triangulation to gain stronger evidence.

INCREASING RIGOR IN ACTION RESEARCH

Rigor in action research is not always as clear as rigor in quantitative approaches to research. Audiences for AR include other practitioners, specialists on a subject, communities, among others. Many of the readers will read it for interest, while others will read the research as a peer and will want to understand the level of rigor involved in the research. Rigor can be seen as synonymous as validity where validity is the, "accuracy and trustworthiness of instruments data, and research findings?" (Melrose, 2001).

Action research is a constantly improving process so one cycle is generally not enough to provide enough evidence to pass as a rigorous study. Action researchers typically utilize multiple cycles to act and reflect and take revised action in order to demonstrate rigor. The cycles provide a process of refinement that is not easily found in other areas of research. The cycles are used early on to collect data and change course while the later cycles are dependent on the decisions made in the first cycles. Frequently, the first cycle is an exploration of a phenomenon or concern, the second cycle may provide a stronger intervention and the third cycle provides a stronger focus on the evaluation of the intervention. For example, a school counselor might utilize the first cycle to conduct a needs assessment to identify pressing concerns in the school. The second cycle could prioritize the interventions and begin collecting data on these interventions. Perhaps the committee discovered that the school needs a bullying program and the program gets started. The third cycle would evaluate the prevention program and refine based on the needs and feedback of stakeholders. Using reflection in each cycle enables the intervention and data to integrate into the research.

Another useful approach to developing rigor in action research is to utilize a process of member checking. In member checking, participants are provided with a chance to review the data analyses, and reports at any stage of the process to provide their feedback. Rigor is enhanced because it enables participants to verify aspects of the research process and to provide an opportunity to further explain information provided or that is unclear to the researcher. In the example of a school needs assessment, the team developing the action research project would analyze the needs assessment and then meet with participants in person to check out with the participants and stakeholders to verify the results of the needs assessment indicating that bullying is the most pressing concern. Participants may agree, disagree, or be mixed about the results.

Member checking verifies the facts of the study. Alternatively, participant debriefing focuses on additional feedback. The process of participant debriefing (Stringer, 2010) is a chance for participants to provide feedback and additional insights. Instead of focusing on factual data, the emphasis is on affective domain. In this case, the debriefing may help participants address any concerns that have impacted memories of events. In the school counseling example, participant checking might ask a few students to individually describe their recent memories of being bullied or witnessing bulling at the school. This data will help inform the development of the bullying program.

Credibility is also a way of increasing rigor. According to Melrose (2001) rigor can also refer to a constant. For example, the rigor in an AR project can be increased by the constancy of those associated with the project. For example, one may ask if the group has stayed together or has there been a high degree of turnover? Is there agreement between participants and researchers about the results? Have the researchers created a flexible plan and appropriately carried out the plan? At the beginning of an AR project, a project team will include an action researcher who has skills with facilitating group processes. Counselors in training are equipped with such research and group facilitation skills so you already have many of the tools you need to begin an AR project! As with good counseling, building a strong relationship with participants increases the credibility of the researcher which also increase the rigor of the research.

While AR may not be entirely quantitative or modernist in nature, it is a rigorous and empirical process that requires individuals to clearly define and observe the phenomena being investigated. To demonstrate rigor you will need to spend time with the community or group to demonstrate that you are credible, can offer accurate observations, and are able to listen accurately. Time spent engaging with the group will develop your sensitivity to the various micro dynamics in the culture. Enhanced sensitivity to the group or culture provides cues that you would not otherwise pickup if you had not been immersed in that group. Developing this type of sensitivity is like learning a language. One can learn Spanish from a textbook but will miss the nuanced cues that can only be gained by immersing yourself into a Spanish speaking culture. In terms of phenomenological experience, community, organizational, and institutional contexts each ascribe different meaning and symbols to information and phenomenon. A researcher who has developed a relationship with AR participants will more likely be immersed in the culture and understand cues and concepts that a foreigner may not follow as easily. This level of understanding and acceptance from the culture of interest is a sign of rigor. For example, if you wanted to conduct an AR project at the veteran's affairs, it may take a little while to simply get used to the new acronyms let alone the underlying cultural contexts and dynamics.

Research in AR projects require appropriate methods of data collection. These methods need to be suitable for the paradigm that the research project requires. Action research does not impose the research questions onto the participants but are negotiated with those involved in the research process, including the participants (see Table 15.4). When collecting data, the recommended approach is to be inclusive and informative to those providing the information. Instead of gathering information to test a series of hypotheses, the data and research questions are practical and likely to result in novel and useful information for practice or community.

Rigor and validity are separate constructs in the AR framework. The constructivist qualitive paradigms found in action research are used to guide thinking to views of multiple perspectives and changing circumstances (Watkins et al., 2016). In action research one attempts to change habitual practices by exploring more effective alternative actions. While empirical positivism seeks to find validity, generalizability, and answering pre-designed questions, action research focuses on mutual, voluntary, and transformative action from moment to moment. As (Watkins et al., 2016) explained, AR is a shift away from one single underlying truth towards critical inquiry in action by individuals, groups, and communities.

Qualitive research may focus on rigor by detailing a thorough and deep account of a few cases. Quantitative research focuses on rigor through the experimental methods and generating statistically significant and generalizable results. Action research emphasizes methods used to obtain first person data that is subjective about self while taking action to behave differently at the same time. Action research also utilizes second person data from AR team members to understand and appreciate multiple perspectives (Watkins et al., 2016). At the core of AR is a simultaneous emphasis on research and practice, among others.

Action research differs from empirical positivism. Empirical positivism focuses of two areas of experience—the outside world of data, and the cognitive world. The cognitive world emphasizes theory and systematic methods for testing the validity of the fit between data and theory (Watkins

TABLE 15.4 Generating Research Questions Using First, Second, and Third Person Sources

RESEARCH QUESTION	FIRST DATA SOURCE	SECOND DATA SOURCE	THIRD DATA SOURCE
How do I improve participation in class?	personal reflections	student focus groups	observation log of classroom participation
How can I make multicultural/diversity conversations in class more meaningful?	personal assessment about covert bias	student feedback	feedback from community groups
Are students comfortable discussing multi-cultural issues in class?	student interviews	student surveys	online discussions about comfort levels

et al., 2016). Action research alternatively utilizes multiple perspectives from participants in the AR team, descriptions of experiences with power and hegemony. Action research participants explore relationships to power and empowerment. For example

MULTICULTURAL ISSUES AND ACTION RESEARCH

The ACA code of ethics emphasizes that counselors have an ethical mandate to, "honor... diversity and embrace... a multicultural approach in support of the worth, dignity, potential, and uniqueness of people within their social and cultural contexts; 3. Promot(e)... social justice" (ACA Code of Ethics, 2014). Counselors who seek to conduct action research have the basic ethical mandates as any researcher and more importantly, because one will work with various communities and populations, understanding one's biases (covert and overt) and a capacity to empathize with those from different contexts will support stronger partnerships with the research partners and lead to more accurate findings.

The Association of Multicultural Counseling and Development (AMCD) lists three major competencies related to the practice of action research. Counselors are to have awareness of own cultural values and biases; awareness of the client's world view; counselors use appropriate intervention strategies. Action research is uniquely suited for multicultural issues. Practitioner action research is powerful because it gives tools a practitioner (e.g. teacher or counselor) to evaluate and change his/her practice. For example, if a counselor in practice in a highly collectivistic population, who comes from a more individualistic background placing greater importance on individualism over the family, they could conduct a practitioner research project to understand how much their clients believe the counselor is biased towards individualistic messages as opposed to more collectivistic approaches to working with individuals and family involvement.

The ACA recognizes these counseling competencies and each competency contains a series of attitudes and beliefs, knowledge, and skills to be acquired to be considered multiculturally competent. The multicultural competencies are generally oriented towards practitioner focused endeavors, these competencies can be applied to the practice of action research. In fact, the practice of action research provides a powerful vehicle for those with a multicultural focus to conduct research. Researchers conducting a community action research project for example have an ethical imperative to be aware of the impacts of their privilege and power play a role in working with diverse and underserved populations. Showing up as a researcher, facilitating a group puts you in a place of power and may elicit different responses.

Likewise, counselors conducting action research may run into issues with an emic or etic perspective and its relationship to generalizability and pluralism. An etic perspective is essentially color blindness. It is an approach that emphasizes universal approaches and between group differences. Counselors conducting action research are to carefully consider a participant's background, cultural norms, and expectations, and be familiar with even the artifacts and periodical. An emic perspective emphasizes within group differences. For example, any culture has many levels and within group differences (Sue, Sue, & Neville, 2019). Black ethnicity makes up a rich and diverse background of African, Caribbean, and many other types of subgroups. Likewise, being "Whiteness" is not simply one ethnicity, but there are many groups within the White" designation including, Irish, German, and so forth. Many ascribe to an etic view of race that upholds colorblindness about ethnicity and culture. A color-blind approach provides comfort in that one can simply say that they are non-racist because they do not focus on race. Indeed, it is not enough in our profession to be non-racist. As leaders in our field working towards equitable therapeutic outcomes an anti-racist approach is more consistent with our profession's stances on social justice and multicultural competencies.

LIMITATIONS TO ACTION RESEARCH

Despite the many strengths of AR, there are also limitations to the process. Action research is highly context dependent, so it can be challenging to gather the data and make sense of it all. Action research can be considered too subjective and lacking rigor. The researcher may become too involved in the study and introduce personal bias as well. Like other qualitative methods, AR is time consuming as one must go through the many cycles, analyzing and reporting the data during each iteration. The end of an action research is when the problem resolved, so if one adhered strictly to that rule they might be in the for longer than expected. Likewise, the results with AR are intended to be limited to the specific context in which the research occurred.

A further limitation of action research is that the method itself emphasizes problem solving and intervention from the researchers. Those from a more positivist perspective who prefer objectivity and detached observation might find the results to be tainted by subjectivity and bias. While Action research has many methods to increase rigor, scientific rigor, objectivity, and generalizability can be among the most persistent criticisms and limitations.

The action research process is value laden and is inherently biased towards helping those it researches. Thus, the questions are more subjective in nature and would not stand up to the scrutiny of most experimental research designs. Many of the goals of positivist approaches is to gather an objective or God's eye point of view. This level of objectivity is incompatible with the goals and processes of action research.

On the other hand, the push to intervene, reflect and refine the intervention, and take action to help a community, person, or practice, makes action research so unique. Action researchers collect evidence to evaluate an intervention and subsequently refine the intervention in a series of cycles. The evidence collected is not intended to be generalized to other populations or groups, it is intended to help the context in which the problem emerged. The dissemination of action research sheds light into how the action research process helped a certain group or case. Consumers of action research can use the information from published studies to reflect and intervene on their practice or community issues.

Case Study

Sackett, C. R., & Dogan, J. N. (2019). An Exploration of Black Teens' Experiences of Their Own Racial Identity Through Photovoice: Implications for Counselors. *Journal of Multicultural Counseling and Development, 47*(3), 172–189. https://doi.org/10.1002/jmcd.12140

BACKGROUND

The study highlighted below (Sackett & Dogan, 2019) provides an example of a qualitatively focused participatory action research project using photovoice. The topic of research is on Black teens' experiences of racial identity. I chose this topic because further multicultural competencies surrounding the experiences of marginalized populations and the calls for empathy and anti-racist responses are louder more now than ever. As I write this case study, the United States (U.S.) is experiencing multiple outbreaks of the COVID-19 virus and nationwide protests in response to a series of tragic events including the death of George Floyd in police custody. The combination of environmental stressors appears to have the nation at an unusually high tension and the nation appears polarized. A study that intends to increase empathy, inform others of experiences with racial identity development models, and decrease racial polarization is a perfect counterbalance for the beginning of Summer of 2020.

Sackett and Dogan (2019) explored how the racial identity of Black teens is a salient and pressing issue in the United States. Many in the U.S. are involved in a nationwide social movement towards equity and social justice. A dominant expression of these social activities is the Black Lives Matter Movement. Black Lives Matter is an anti-racist and social justice movement designed to bring about equitable treatment and outcomes for Black people in America. The authors further elaborated on how the departure of Barack Obama and the rise of Donald Trump gave way to increased overt and covert racism throughout the United States. A key underlying emphasis of Sackett and Dogan's study is that through an "increase in empathy and understanding around the painful history of Black people and other marginalized groups in this country, it may be possible to break the cycle of polarization around race. Again, it is imperative to hear the voices of marginalized groups on their experiences of racial identity which is why we sought to understand the experiences of black teens..." (p.174). The emphasis on breaking the polarization around race signals that participatory action research is an appropriate method of inquiry and action.

The study focused on the development of racial identity. Racial identity is a process that involves one's thoughts, perceptions, and level of investment in one's racial group's cultural patterns. As one goes through the racial identity development process, not only does one begin to ask questions surrounding identity, but one also begins to ask questions related to their racial identity. Not only do Black American adolescents ask common questions (e.g., who am I?), additional questions centered around racial identity emerge that may not be present for their privileged or White counterparts (e.g., "Who am I as a racial being"?). These questions are useful because a developed racial identity is linked to increased community support when experiencing discrimination from other groups. The more one identifies with their race, the more their sense of community protects them from the diverse effects of racism and oppression.

BACKGROUND AND CONTEXT

Sackett and Dogan conducted the study to fill the many gaps in the counseling literature concerning Black adolescent experiences of racial identity. The study was also conducted to provide information on racial identity development, a process that enables counselors to relate to those who might be in a transition through various stages of their racial development. Participants included adolescents in rural southeastern United States.

Corrine Sackett is an Associate Professor at Clemson University. Her research interests include counseling process, supervision, counseling experiences, and advocacy. Jardin Dogan is a second-year doctoral student in Counseling Psychology at the University of Kentucky. I reached out to the authors for additional thoughts about this article and action research in general. They responded, "we feel we need more action research in our field". Dr. Sackett and Ms. Dogan were award the inaugural 2019 *Journal of Multicultural Counseling and Development* – Patricia Arrendondo Outstanding Article Award for the paper, which they found "very exciting...and speaks to the impact of and need for action research on societal issues" (C S. Dr. personal communication, 6/30/2020).

The authors intended to explore the racial identity experiences of Black teens. The overarching research question included "what are Black teens' experiences of their own racial identity?". The goals the authors stated, were to answer the above question in a way that would provide in depth answers and provide an empowering experience. An additional emphasis was on transforming real-world issues by providing a platform to amplify the voices of and to empower vulnerable populations. Action research is very suitable for this research question and the intentions of this research project. In addition, the emphasis on transformative change and exploring one's racial identity make action research an appropriate vehicle for this research. Photovoice is a qualitative tool used in action research to help share the perspective of those affected and wanting to influence social policy.

As mentioned above, action research can utilize quantitative, qualitative, or mixed methods to accomplish change. This study aimed to generate empathy and awareness about the experiences of Black adolescents. If the sole goal of the study were to gain a deep inquiry into one's experiences, a phenomenological qualitative approach would be a more appropriate method. The current study had an additional emphasis on social change, which opened the doors for participatory action research. Given the intentions of the authors, the emphasis of qualitative methods to pursue outcomes connected to the process of action research appeared appropriate.

DATA ANALYSIS

The participatory action research data analysis method was a collaborative and reflective process. In this case, the participants discussed concerns, experiences, and anticipated actions. Photovoice was used to help participants codify the data that emerged from the photos taken. Participants were asked to discuss their photographs and then to reflect on the themes and patterns discussed in the stories related to their photos. Once the group gained consensus on the themes, they reached saturation when they could no longer identify further themes. The second photovoice session was analyzed by the first author with a constant comparative method to make sure that the relevant content was covered.

PARTICIPANTS

Participants were Black adolescents, between 14 and 18 years of age. While the sample began with ten participants, two could not attend the final photovoice session leaving eight participants. Of the eight, five were female and three were male. Six participants identified as Black or African American, one as mixed race, and another as Native American and Black. Participants were awarded gift cards for participation.

SAMPLING METHOD

Participants were recruited from three Black churches in the community. The groups met for two photovoice sessions over two weeks. The authors co-facilitated the photovoice sessions. In the first session, the focus of discussion was the racial identity of Black teens. Many issues were covered including power and ethics in the study, camera use, and emphasized Black teen racial identity. The authors chose to brainstorm with the participants what it meant to be a Black teen all the while emphasizing that the researchers wanted to hear from the participants who were uplifted as experts. Participants were subsequently asked to photograph "people, places and things" that would showcase their perspective on the issue. The participants were given disposable cameras and one week to take the pictures and drop them off.

The second photovoice session occurred two weeks after the first session and involved selecting the photographs, contextualize and codify the themes that emerge. The photos were returned to the participants and shown how to the most meaningful or favorite photo and then asked to write a title, and an explanatory caption. Participants shared their photos using a method called the SHOWeD framework. The questions asked in this method were

1. "See here?
2. What is really happening here?
3. How does this relate to our lives?
4. Why does this situation, concern, or strength exist?
5. What can we do about it?
6. what do WE see here? —to allow for group analysis of the photos" (p. 178).

Finally, the session was recorded and transcribed.

The research team worked together to enhance rigor of the study. One way was to focus on credibility. Sackett and Dogan clearly stated their roles and that they were researchers of the study. Together the researchers approached the sites for recruitment and facilitated the sessions. They maintained awareness of their authority as researchers in the room, in terms of age and social position. The authors clearly identified their identities (White and African American) and maintained awareness of their identities as they discussed racial identity with the groups. They emphasized frequently that the participants were the experts. In addition to these emphases, the authors also provided peer debriefings and reflexivity throughout the project.

The data was presented at the same church community in which the photovoice sessions were conducted. The participants in the study developed a slide show and presented the results with the church community two months after the final photovoice session.

RESULTS

The two photovoice sessions generated three themes. These themes included "the places you don't belong", "comfort places" and "strengths/concerns". The first theme demonstrated that the teens believed there are places where they are not welcome or cannot access. The article provided many examples of the narratives and are worth reading.

The patterns that emerged from "places where they do not belong" included an area in the school parking lot where they and others were harassed. Another perspective related to where students sat on the bus. White students would generally sit up front, while non-White students would sit in the back of the bus. The narrative explains why she thinks this dynamic occurs. Another issue emerged where a student pointed out how advanced level courses are mostly populated by White students. The Black students may have received the message that they do not belong in the advanced level courses.

The comfort places pattern described the places the students went to for strength, safety, and comfort. The places were physical, spiritual, natural, and applied to their relationships. One student described his church as his comfort place while another emphasized the comfort derived from looking up at the moon. In terms of places where they exhibited strength, one student focused on the track sports that she was involved in, while another participant discussed the meaning derived from relationships by sharing a picture of prom dress shopping with her friend.

Finally, the theme of strengths and concerns highlighted the teens' views of strengths and concerns related to Black racial identity. In addition to strengths and concerns, the conversation also focused on the manner in which individuals act that lead to stereotyping, out grouping, and many forms of ignorance. One student shared a concern about his front yard and how he wanted to see his "stuff" in a better place. Another student expressed a concern about other Black teens behaving in a way that might reinforce stereotypes. Strengths portrayed included hopes about college. Another participant shared a photo of her mother as an inspiration.

The authors utilized Cross's Nigrescence model to discuss the findings of the research. In the sample, teens were aware of racial discrimination and experienced it daily. The authors suggested that many of the participants were in the Encounter Stage of their racial identity development. This stage is when they begin to realize they are part of a racial minority and have been subject to racism in school. In this study, the teens wanted to be seen in a way that avoided negative stereotyping. Teens were able to identify strengths and weaknesses about their racial identity. Some participants appeared to be in the Pre-Encounter Stage where they have internalized and aligned with many beliefs of the dominant culture. Some of these beliefs may be acting ignorantly, having "poor attitudes," or a need to better themselves. Relationships were discussed as a source of strength and the participants perceived other Black teens as hanging out in homogenous groups. Other participants shared stories where someone understood negative racial messages but did not respond with concern. Other findings demonstrated that teens were concerned that their Black peers did not challenge themselves academically by taking more challenging courses. This paragraph served to highlight some of the findings and discussions found in the study. With these meaningful findings in mind, the study had many merits and limitations.

REFLECTIONS ON THE STRENGTHS AND WEAKNESSES OF THE APPROACH

The study recruited participants from two Black churches. Involvement in these churches may represent the values and teachings of those churches. Action research is a values laden approach, so it was appropriate for this context. The transferability of the findings is limited because of the rural area in which the study took place. Action research does not typically rely on generalizing the results, but the concept of whether the results could be transferred to other settings is unlikely. It is possible that these results and experiences may have transferability to other Black adolescents in rural communities.

IMPLICATIONS FOR THE FIELD

The study concluded with numerous implications for the field of counseling. First, it provided further evidence that action research is a useful method for gaining insight into Black adolescents racial identity development and generating change. Another implication is that simply understanding worldviews of diverse clients is not enough. Instead the authors suggest that counselors engage in an ongoing process of awareness into their own values, beliefs, and bias. Increase internal awareness of your beliefs and potential bias provide a basis for a stronger therapeutic relationship. In addition, using insights from these multicultural competencies enable counselors to work with clients who struggle with their own racial development process.

Another implication is that counselors in schools would benefit from awareness and insight into the racial identity development processes that students of color experience daily. According to the results, the teens felt that there were places at school where they believed they did not belong. The action research process used here provided opportunities of Black teens to share stories of how they experience race and what makes race salient in life. The teens' experiences of racial identity development were mixed: pleasant and painful. The study reiterated the insight that adolescents were aware of and impacted by the sociopolitical tension in our country. A discussion about this tension and how it might impact their daily lives are all useful avenues to pursue. Additional insights gained from this study include:

- Schools may benefit minority students by providing opportunities to engage together to cope with the psychological and emotionally unsafe areas.
- Use these experiences to develop resiliency and character.
- Recognize the academic potential of Black teens and barriers to involvement in advanced courses.
- Address interventions that help Black adolescents navigate painful racial identity issues by understanding the cognitive dissonance caused by the conflicting cultural and societal values and the promotion of self-acceptance.
- Counselors can do more to create relationships with Black churches in student communities to promote trust and even referrals from the church.
- Strengths-based counseling approaches can be enhanced by acknowledging the role of spirituality and religion in Black communities.
- Enhanced knowledge of Nigrescence and facilitation of conversations about race with adolescents is important.
- Acknowledge and discuss the saliency for and impact of race on teenagers.

SUMMARY

This chapter covered many approaches to AR , including its founders, and various philosophical underpinnings. This chapter described the ontology, epistemology, axiology, methodology, and methods associated with AR. This chapter described the various levels of AR inquiry: first person, second person, and third person and the focus of AR researchers on creating meaningful change through their research. Furthermore, this chapter explored how quantitative, qualitative, and mixed methods approaches can be used in AR studies. This chapter distinguishes AR from other forms of research inquiry that may use similar methods. Brief examples, activities, and various tables were used to enhance the learning experience and consolidate this series of complex yet meaningful research skills.

STUDENT ACTIVITIES

Exercise 1: Discussing an Action Research Article

Directions: Read the following article and identify at least five elements of Participatory Action Research: Roxas, K. C., Gabriel, M. L. & Becker, K. (2017). "Mexicans Are Like Thieves and Bad People, and We're Not Really Like That": Immigrant youth use photovoice to counter racism and discrimination. *Journal of School Counseling*, 15(19). Justify how these criteria relate or do not relate to the article.

Exercise 2: Finding an Action Research Topic

Directions: Please utilize the below form to develop your action research topic. Share it with a partner and discuss what you find meaningful.

FINDING AN AR TOPIC (PRACTITIONER FOCUS)	
What social practice or personal practice could be improved:	
1	
2	
3	
Which is the most important one to me:	I would like to know more about...
What bothers me about this practice:	What dreams, desire, and hope could be different...
What do I usually do about this practice:	I would like to change...
What I would never do about this practice is:	My AR project will be...
The best way to resolve my problem through action research is to:	

Exercise 3: Reflection Questions for Action Research Projects

Directions: Utilize the following questions to develop your own first-person inquiry into a participatory AR project. Write a short reflexive journal in response to each of these questions.

- What do you perceive as a problem or an issue in your community that needs to be addressed?
- How does it relate to your life? To the community's life?
- Why do these issues/problems exist?
- What can we do about them?
- What do we need to know?
- What do we already know?
- What resources do we need to proceed with the project?
- How will this project benefit the participants and the rest of the community?
- What are the common themes that have been generated in the research process?
- How do we summarize these themes in ways that benefit those involved?
- Who will control the research project? Make the decisions? Decide how to disseminate information to others?
- How will we address issues of confidentiality and privacy in the dissemination of the information we gather in the project?
- How will we inform others about the project?
- Will our research represent only the realities of those involved or those of other members of the community/group as well?
- What are the criteria we will use to assess the adequacy and efficacy of the project? (McIntyre, 2008, p. 50)

Exercise 4: Questions to Ask While Developing a Literature Review

Describe the nature of the problem that you would like to address. Look for articles that have various opinions on these issues and use various research methodologies. Find which approach works best for you. Begin by thinking about the outcome that you are looking to improve and then investigate issues or variables that might impact that outcome. Make a list of the outcomes that you would like to see happen and what will the boosters and barriers be to making that outcome happen.

In your narrative have the various authors debate with each other. Discuss how some findings support your position and others do not. Complete the list below to detail some of the findings

AUTHOR	POSITION	ADDITIONAL THOUGHTS AND FINDINGS FROM ARTICLE
1		
2		
3		

Exercise 5: Logic Model Template

Based on Exercise 4, begin to think about the various activities and outputs that you would like to see happen. See https://files.eric.ed.gov/fulltext/EJ1063200.pdf and generate a logic model based on the the reflections in Exercise 4 using the logic model template.

INPUTS	ACTIVITIES	OUTPUTS	OUTCOMES	

ADDITIONAL RESOURCES

Software Recommendations

IBM SPSS Statistics for Windows, Version 21.0

NCSS: Statistical Software

Nvivo 12 for Windows is a qualitative analysis software.

Helpful Links

- http://yparhub.berkeley.edu/
- https://learningforsustainability.net/action-research/
- http://www.edfutures.net/Practitioner_Research

Helpful Reading

- https://www.equinetafrica.org/par/sections/participatory-action-research-training-resources
- https://www.ial.edu.sg/content/dam/projects/tms/ial/Find-resources/Learning-resource-and-tools/Tools-for-Re-imagining-Learning/Research/Practitioner%20Research%20Resource_Final.pdf

Helpful Videos

- https://www.youtube.com/watch?v=6D492AP9JP4
- https://www.youtube.com/watch?v=dhIlgSpVk78
- https://www.youtube.com/watch?v=0Zng5AoMvVA
- https://www.youtube.com/watch?v=vuXoKKXp6QM
- https://www.youtube.com/watch?v=tP4dPiAmt9g
- https://www.youtube.com/watch?v=TOrQ-sVTuE0
- https://www.youtube.com/watch?v=oUMDhgQJmi4

KEY REFERENCE

Only key references appear in the print edition. The full reference list appears in the digital product found on http://connect.springerpub.com/content/book/978-0-8261-4385-3/part/part04/chapter/ch15

Adelman, C. (1993). Kurt Lewin and the origins of action research. *Educational Action Research*, 1(1), 7–24. https://doi.org/10.1080/0965079930010102

CHAPTER 16

MIXED METHODS RESEARCH: CONVERGENT AND EMBEDDED DESIGNS

Stephen V. Flynn and Nicole V. Brady

LEARNING OBJECTIVES

After reading this chapter, you will be able to:

- Distinguish the basics of mixed methods research
- Describe the philosophical integration of convergent and embedded research design
- Illustrate how to maximize the rigor of embedded and convergent research design
- Recognize how mixed methods traditions can enhance multicultural competency

INTRODUCTION TO CONVERGENT AND EMBEDDED DESIGNS

No matter the tradition of research methodology one embarks from, the intention is the same. To open the hatch, test the waters, set your compass, explore the seas, and venture toward new sands and settings to see what can be discovered and brought back to share. We, as pioneers of deeper understanding of the human condition, are pilgrims in a land we still do not fully grasp; meaning that there are innumerable research questions yet unanswered, methodological frameworks unused, and even yet formulated. Thus, there are countless horizons of realization upon which to rise. Within the behavioral sciences, we have at our fingertips many uncharted frontiers of human psychological functioning that can drive the desire to delve into the remaining mysteries of human cognition, emotion, and behavior. Why do we act the way we do? What factors motivate us to act or mitigate our behaviors and choices? How do we differ from one another and why? In what ways might we be of best service to our fellow human and help the collective evolution, one person at a time, one treatment at a time, and one counseling session at a time? The questions are endless. Now that you have gained a basic understanding of quantitative and qualitative approaches in research, let's dive in by moving into a common mode of utilizing the best of both worlds in the aptly titled methodological framework of mixed methods research.

The present chapter, and remainder of this textbook, is centered on mixed methods research traditions. We will assume that you have an adequate understanding of the previously presented chapters and will build on this understanding by describing pertinent mixed methods information. As you start to get acclimated to the world of mixed methods research design, you will experience a barrage of new nomenclature and ideas that seemingly expand the methodological possibilities of what was presented in the previous chapters. To make this process more manageable Chapters 16, 17, and 18 provide a progressive information building and scaffolding process. In other words, while new mixed methods traditions will be presented in each chapter, there will also be a sequential construction of general and advanced mixed methods concepts, methods, and procedures throughout the remainder of the book.

Quantitative, Qualitative, and Mixed Methods

While the quantification of data has been evidenced since the beginning of civilization, as discussed in Chapter 2, in 1848 Auguste Comte created the initial philosophy of positivism through his book entitled: *A General View of Positivism* (Comte, 1884). Quantitative research and methodology formally grew out of the philosophy of positivism. Quantitative research is a deductive approach to inquiry that utilizes statistical formulations to generalize the results to particular populations and predict events (Scotland, 2012). Quantitative researchers rely on probability theory and random sampling due to the philosophical notion that chance and uncertainty can create data that are generalizable to a population (Hurlburt, 2017).

As noted in earlier chapters, qualitative methodology was cultivated through the latter portion of the 20th century in response to the growing realization that "many processes of human interaction cannot easily be reduced to observable or objectively measurable behaviors" (Buckley, 2010, p. 115). Qualitative research is not centered on the results being due to the independent variable's effect on the dependent variable. Furthermore, qualitative researchers do not believe social events can be generalized/transferred to other populations or situations (Merriam, 1998). They maintain a naturalistic approach to research and are purposeful with directly attaining participants who have a relationship with a particular phenomenon or who are conveniently accessible. As such, qualitative researchers reject probability theory and philosophical notions that chance and uncertainty accurately generalize social phenomena.

Often using pragmatism as a research paradigm, mixed methods researchers utilize an inductive and pluralistic philosophy to data collection and analysis. As the researcher considers the research question(s), they take action in collecting the type of data that seems most relevant and meaningful to the research question(s) and, from these data, create the most robust understanding of the phenomenon under analysis. Mixed methods researchers engage in a sense of pluralism due to needing to use qualitative, quantitative, and mixed data analyses and validation procedures (Hall, 2013). Onwuegbuzie and Johnson (2006) aptly labeled the outcomes of the mixed methods multiple validation procedures *multiple validities legitimation*. Mixed method designs legitimize a sense of understanding by exploring data through the use of diverse modalities (qualitative, quantitative, and mixing). According to Johnson et al. (2007) mixed methods research is defined as:

> ... *the type of research in which a researcher or team of researchers combines elements of qualitative and quantitative research approaches (e.g., use of qualitative and quantitative viewpoints, data collection, analysis, inference techniques) for the broad purposes of breadth and depth of understanding and corroboration. (p. 123)*

Understanding Mixed Methods

Consider this philosophical question: "If you had to choose which pair of appendages to use for today, your arms or your legs, which would it be?" Well, both are very important and have different strengths and purposes, so why decide on just one? What if you had to settle on a choice between indelible daylight and a ceaseless starry night? Both have their purpose and appeal and it would feel almost impossible to take sides, although you might have a *leaning* in one direction or other, depending on what kind of activities you envisioned or what you were setting out to accomplish. You might argue that if you had to choose between two situations, settings, or, say, research approaches, it would depend on the context and the intentions. This is where mixed methods research comes in. A mixed methods design is more intentional than a haphazard mixing of qualitative and quantitative methods, and instead could be likened to the general meaning of a gestalt. The ultimate goal of this approach to research is to synthesize the two distinct quantitative and qualitative elements into a richer whole that is greater than the sum of either or all parts. Meaningful synthesis of qualitative and quatitative strands to effectively answer the research question(s) is the essence of a valid and trustworthy mixed methods research endeavor (Creswell & Plano-Clark, 2017).

On the surface, it seems advantageous to combine the best of both methodological worlds to fully answer the research question(s) (i.e., mixed methods research); however, the existence of any transition to a "non-purist" method has historically led to debate and conflict for those married to the idea that one tried and true tradition should be upheld and adhered to no matter what (e.g., the paradigm wars, paradigm debate; Gage, 1989). Let's consider some of the particular uses and benefits of both quantitative and qualitative research. Quantitative researchers effectively use measured and operationalized constructs, enabling the creation of empirical data for comparisons within and between groups. Furthermore, quantitatively, researchers in the behavioral sciences have the ability to explore and to determine the degree of correlation and association between variables (Castro et al., 2010). Qualitative traditions offer the benefits of preserving the context and lived experience of a phenomenon and, in so doing, create rich and thick data that take into account the holistic experience of the human subject. Qualitative research also affords the capacity for deeply examining contextual elements, such as family, social status, culture, personal relationships, and other social or systemic factors (Castro et al., 2010).

According to Tashakkori and Teddlie (2003), over 15 years ago there were nearly 40 different types of mixed methods research approaches. As you can imagine, today there are many more. Mixed methods research has been referred to as the third methodological movement (i.e., following qualitative and quantitative traditions). In combining both qualitative and quantitative traditions, mixed methods designs create greater depth and breadth. From a data collection and analysis perspective, behavioral science researchers using mixed methods designs can mix, integrate, and/ or link data to achieve a richer and fuller understanding of a construct. The two mixed method approaches explored within this chapter include convergent and embedded designs. A researcher using a convergent approach collects the qualitative and quantitative data simultaneously, merges the data, and utilizes the results to more fully answer the research questions. Researchers using an embedded design will put either the qualitative or quantitative approach as the primary data collection method, and use the other (i.e., qualitative or quantitative data collection method) in a less significant manner.

THE PHILOSOPHICAL INTEGRATION OF CONVERGENT AND EMBEDDED DESIGNS

Many mixed methods research traditions reject the traditional philosophical integration (i.e., ontology, epistemology, theoretical perspective, methodology, and methods) in favor of an action-oriented approach that is centered on paradigm and methods. Convergent and embedded mixed methods designs integrate the elements of both qualitative and quantitative approaches, under the aegis that the two can complement each other and can help to illustrate and explain unusual variance that otherwise may be overlooked or attributed to the method used instead of the subject being studied (Hanson, Plano-Clark, Petska, Creswell, & Creswell, 2005). Mixed methods researchers, using a convergent or embedded design, integrate the inductive, subjective, and contextual elements of qualitative research with the deductive, objective, and generalizing elements of quantitative research (Morgan, 2007).

Pragmatism is the philosophy that is most relevant to the convergent design. For the purpose of this textbook, we will refer to pragmatism as a research paradigm. A paradigm has been defined as a "set of interrelated assumptions about the social world which provides a philosophical and conceptual framework for the organized study of that world" (Filstead, 1979, p. 34). If you review the philosophical literature on pragmatism as it relates to mixed methods research, you will immediately notice that its nature is referred to in a number of ways, including (but not limited to) paradigm, culture, ideology, worldview, doctrine of meaning, philosophy, and theory of truth. You may now be asking yourself, "Which one is it?" In short, it depends on what literature one reads and which argument one finds evidence to support. While the convergent design is often philosophically integrated with pragmatism, the embedded design often displays a paradigmatic hierarchy in line with the primary thread (i.e., qualitative or quantitative). This is due to the secondary data set being subservient and supportive within the embedded research framework (Creswell & Plano Clark, 2017). Table 16.1 provides information on the purpose, thread emphasis, sequence, and paradigm of the prominent mixed methods approaches. The approaches described in this chapter are bolded and aspects of each tradition are explicated using Morse's notation system. When designing a mixed method study, this notation can assist in describing the components, primacy of components, and the implementation sequence. Morse's notation includes the following: QUAL and QUAN to emphasize the primacy, *qual* and *quan* indicating the secondary emphasis, plus (+) to indicate the concurrent use of components, and arrows (→) indicating the sequential implementation (Morse & Niehaus, 2009). Table 16.1, with the chapter-based bolded traditions, is repeated throughout the three mixed methods chapters.

While there is more than one "right" way to design the paradigmatic hierarchy of a study, certain philosophical combinations and/or methods are incompatible with one another. For example, if a researcher considers an embedded qualitative design to be based solely on the epistemology of positivism, they would likely be making a mistake in their interpretation of the philosophical nesting. In the case of an embedded qualitative design, the epistemology is most often related to constructionism, constructivism, or subjectivism. Overall, for mixed methods research, the best procedure may be considering the research methods themselves, instead of the paradigmatic hierarchy behind the method; in other words, using what is practical or pragmatic; using what works best in a given study (Hanson et al., 2005).

In Figure 16.1 we compare the paradigm of mixed methods research with a traditional qualitative/quantitative paradigm. Notice the integration is much simpler for mixed methods research. Within the mixed methods paradigm, the methods and overarching paradigm are the only two elements

TABLE 16.1 **The Nature of Prominent Mixed Method Traditions**

NAME	PURPOSE	THREAD EMPHASIS	SEQUENCE	PARADIGM
Convergent	**Compare qual and quan data**	**QUAL + QUAN**	**Concurrent**	**Pragmatism**
Embedded	**Embed a smaller qual/quan into a larger design**	**QUAN + *qual*, QUAL + *quan*, QUAN → *qual*, QUAL → *quan***	**Single phase, sequential**	**Traditional paradigmatic hierarchy**
Explanatory	Use qual results to explain quan results	QUAN → *qual*	Sequential	Traditional paradigmatic hierarchy
Exploratory	Use quan results to explain qual results	QUAL → *quan*	Sequential	Traditional paradigmatic hierarchy
Transformative	Uses qual and quan methods to advance social justice causes	QUAN + qual, QUAL +quan, QUAL + QUAN, QUAN + QUAL QUAL → Quan, QUAN → qual	Concurrent, sequential, single phase	Transformative paradigm, pragmatism
Multiphase	Uses separate studies and multiple phases for large projects	QUAL + QUAN, QUAN + QUAL QUAL → Quan, QUAN → qual	Sequential, Concurrent	Pragmatism

NOTE: Bolded, the emphasis of the chapter; qual, qualitative; quan, quantitative; QUAL + QUAN, qualitative and quantitative have equal emphasis in a study; QUAN + *qual*, embedding a smaller qualitative thread into a quantitative design; QUAL + *quan*, embedding a smaller quantitative thread into a qualitative design; QUAN → *qual*, a smaller qualitative thread follows a quantitative phase; QUAL → *quan*, a smaller quantitative thread follows a qualitative phase.

interacting, while the qualitative and quantitative paradigm provides the traditional paradigmatic hierarchy. While this model is accurate for many mixed methods methodological designs, it does not accurately reflect the embedded approach to mixed methods research. As described earlier, embedded designs follow the philosophical integration of primary research thread (e.g., survey research relates to positivism or post-positivism).

Pragmatism is based, in part, on the writings of late 19th and early 20th century philosophers, including (but not limited to): Charles Pierce (1839–1914), William James (1842–1910), John Dewey (1859–1952), and George Mead (1863–1931). It is our belief that researchers in the behavioral sciences are attracted to this philosophy due to its emphasis on action and the contextual factors of the problem (e.g., social and historical contexts; Morgan, 2014). Pragmatists promote the notion of action determining thinking in research. Researchers, operating from a pragmatist philosophy, will frequently incorporate action and reflection into their exploration of a construct. Morgan (2014) described pragmatism as being based on the notion that the meaning of an experience cannot be understood prior to action. For example, while the research team's initial thinking was to solve the research problem using survey research methods due to the need to integrate the voices of marginalized participants (i.e., advocacy), they soon realized the additional need to gather data using in-depth semi-structured interviews.

The philosophy of pragmatism integrates *how to* questions with that of *why to* questions. The pluralistic action (i.e., *how to*) of pragmatism includes the iterative creation of knowledge that,

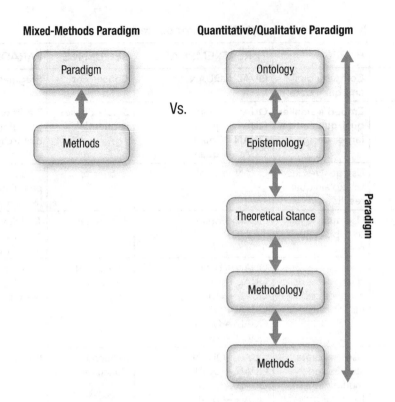

FIGURE 16.1 Mixed Methods Paradigm Compared to Qualitative and Quantitative Paradigms.
NOTE: Double ended arrows equals interaction; large vertical double-ended arrow underneath the word paradigm demonstrates that paradigm is encompassing of ontology, epistemology, theoretical stance, methodology, and methods.

methodologically speaking, provides a philosophical platform for both deduction and induction (i.e., mixed methods research; James, 1995). While *how to* questions involve the philosophy and technical requirements of choosing a particular direction when answering research questions, researchers answering the *why to* questions are directed to consider why their values, ethics, politics, and personal choices influence their research goals (Denzin, 2012; Morgan, 2014). For example, a researcher who was a refugee, politically and personally supports liberal issues on immigration. Because of the researcher's personal/political leanings, the researcher is engaging in a mixed methods research study on the felt experiences of Mexican refugees being detained at the southern border of the United States.

Distinguishing Convergent and Embedded Designs

Mixed methods research studies using a convergent design are aiming to simultaneously use diverse methodological frameworks, which complement each other, to converge on a richer understanding of a phenomenon. Each strand (i.e., qualitative and quantitative) of the convergent approach has equal strength (i.e., one is not primary or secondary). Through using both qualitative and quantitative methods concurrently, the researcher eliminates the weaknesses of only using one framework, and the synthesis of diverse data creates a more robust understanding of the findings. Because this is a singular phase approach, the convergent design (also referred to as *triangulation* or *concurrent triangulation design*) is very efficient in nature.

The term *triangulation* itself was adopted from military terminology to describe the science of using more than one reference point to determine a precise position (Hanson, Plano-Clark, Petska, Creswell, & Creswell, 2005). Within the convergent methodological group, there are variations to the general approach. Three of the main variates include the parallel data base model, the data transformation model, and the data validation model (Creswell & Plano-Clark, 2017). Within all of the convergent frameworks, the researcher(s) generally collects the data separately and brings both data sets together during the analysis or will wait until after the separate analyses are complete to interpret the data sets holistically. As you can imagine, this data collection and analysis approach is ideal for research teams that have members with strong qualitative and quantitative expertise.

The embedded methodological design does not have two, qualitative and quantitative, aspects completed separately. Instead, researchers using this approach, will have a primary methodological framework (i.e., quantitative/quantitative) and second supportive thread that is embedded into the main approach. Similar to other mixed methods approaches, the embedded design is needed when a singular methodology is insufficient in answering all of the research questions, however with this framework, one of the strands plays a supplemental role. The embedded tradition can be a one-phase or two-phase design. Two common variants to the main model include the embedded correlational model and the embedded experimental model. This design is ideal for individuals and organizations that do not have sufficient time or resources to complete two separate primary threads (Creswell & Plano Clark, 2017).

CONVERGENT (TRIANGULATION) DESIGN

The use of convergent mixed methods design has substantially increased over the past 10 years. Operationalizing the convergent mixed methods design through rigorous and innovative research created to better understand contemporary behavioral science issues is important to the evolution of the convergent approach. A sample of recent scholarship highlights the use of a convergent design in the execution of (a) a pilot convergent mixed methods study aimed at understanding the social validity of an autism intervention through the use of parallel in-depth, semi-structured interviews and a quantitative questionnaire (i.e., TARF-R questionnaire; Ogilvie & McCrudden, 2017); (b) applying individual semi-structured interviews and survey protocol in understanding posttraumatic growth following the participant's first episode of psychosis (Jordan et al., 2016); and (c) combining the results of a cross-sectional survey and a self-report questionnaire to better understand the sexual counseling process for patients with heart failure (Kolbe et al., 2016).

Convergent or triangulation mixed methods designs offer the full complexity of qualitative understanding with the scope and power of quantitative methods. According to Kroll and Neri (2009) convergent mixed methods designs support the researcher(s) in corroborating the analyzed data, validity, and interpretation of results. Using a single phase, researcher(s) use qualitative and quantitative approaches to gather data that confirm and expand the understanding and credibility/validity of the findings generated by each method. As described earlier in the chapter, most variants of the convergent methodology have phases of equal strength. According to Creswell and Plano Clark (2017) "This design is used when the researcher wants to triangulate the methods by directly comparing and contrasting quantitative statistical results with qualitative findings for corroboration and validation purposes" (p. 77). For example, students taking part in a convergent mixed methods research study centered on student retention were asked to answer 10 in-depth, semi-structured interview questions and to concurrently take part in a 55-question validated

FIGURE 16.2 Convergent Mixed Methods Research Process.
NOTE: Arrows, convergence toward the integration of results and discussion.

retention-based survey. Figure 16.2 provides a basic description of the data-merging process indicative of convergent mixed methods designs.

The Parallel-Databases Variant

This variant of the convergent approach requires the researcher(s) to gather two separate data sets, analyze them separately, and integrate the divergent findings within the discussion (Creswell & Plano Clark, 2017). This one-time, simultaneous collection and analysis of both qualitative and quantitative data is used to examine different elements of a single construct; however, the findings are usually mixed during the discussion of the research.

The Data-Validation Variant

The data-validation variant is centered on the nature of the questions asked during the research process. The researcher includes both open- and closed-ended questions to confirm their findings. Specifically, the qualitative open-ended questions are used to confirm the initial closed-ended survey questions (Creswell & Plano Clark, 2017). This model has a major quantitative strand that is embellished and validated by the qualitative findings.

The Data-Transformation Variant

The data transformation variant is when there is a greater weight given to the quantitative strand. Following the analysis of qualitative and quantitative data, the qualitative data are quantified. The process of quantitizing qualitative data usually involves assigning a number to qualitative data. This transformation of data converges the qualitative data directly with the larger quantitative data iteratively during the analysis (Creswell & Plano Clark, 2017). Clearly, this is very similar to the embedded design discussed later in this chapter. Figure 16.3 describes the five-step data merging process associated with the data-transformation model.

EMBEDDED DESIGN

The innovative use of embedded mixed methods design has substantially increased over the past 10 years. Operationalizing and enhancing the embedded mixed methods design through rigorous and innovative research design is important to the evolution of the embedded mixed methods approach. Recent scholarship highlights the use of an embedded design in the execution of IT virtual teams (Yu, 2013), applying a smaller qualitative component to a full quantitative instrument

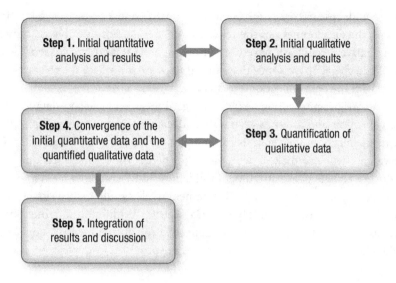

FIGURE 16.3 Convergent Data-Transformation Variant.

NOTE: Single direction arrows, describing the next step in the process; double directional arrows, describing the convergence of data.

validation effort (e.g., Comprehensive Counseling Skills Rubric; Flynn & Hays, 2015), embedding a qualitative component into a full experimental research design centered on Tibetan yoga practice on lymphoma patients (Leal et al., 2018), and embedding a qualitative component into a quasi-experimental design aimed at understanding self-regulated learning through a language portfolio (Ziegler, 2014).

According to Creswell and Plano Clark (2017) embedded designs organize and scaffold data and research pragmatics in a manner that gives more weight to either the qualitative or quantitative elements of the study. The additional smaller qualitative/quantitative strand is embedded into the central tradition to enhance the overall research design. The way embedded designs differ from the various mixed methods traditions is the unique nature of the research procedures, the researcher(s) intentions, and the way the data are synthesized. Embedded mixed methods research experiences often use a variety of data collection methods, research procedures, and protocols for analyzing and synthesizing the qualitative and quantitative data; however, as previously stated, the distinguishing feature of this tradition is the emphasis applied to the qualitative and quantitative aspects of the investigation.

When designing an embedded mixed methods study, it is critical to go through the proper procedures. First, there must be consideration given to the overarching purpose of the study (i.e., what scholarly gaps it intends to fill), the research question(s), what kind of data to collect, and in what order (Hanson et al., 2005). Researchers utilizing an embedded design approach have created research questions that cannot be sufficiently answered by one single data set. Each question requires a different type of data and each strand has different emphasis and research weight within the context of the study.

Next, the embedded design researcher(s) will begin sculpting their research focus. They could be motivated by a number of factors, including (but not limited to) investigating a problem, advocating for an underrepresented population, creating new knowledge, or emphasizing and clarifying the nature of a phenomenon. This step is often described as emerging sequentially after the development of the research question;however, for many researchers, this task is timed directly with, or precedes, the development of the research question(s). For example, a study that uses an embedded quantitative design will have a main quantitative thread and a secondary qualitative thread used within a single phase. Once these initial steps are solidified, the researcher then begins moving forward with the data collection process.

The embedded design approach is flexible in regard to how and when data are collected and analyzed. The collection and analysis of the second data set may occur before, during, and/or following the data collection and analysis of the main research thread (Creswell & Plano Clark, 2017). The researcher will also make a decision as to whether the research has one or two phases. For example, during a single phase instrument validation study, a research team may quantitatively evaluate the strength of various items on the instrument while simultaneously gathering qualitative feedback to further enhance each item (Flynn & Hays, 2015). Within the aforementioned example, the embedded qualitative data set provides a supportive role in the investigation. The secondary qualitative data is helpful to the research team as they are provided in-depth feedback on their new instrument.

Embedded Experimental Variant

Authors suggest that the embedded experimental variant may be the most frequently used embedded model (Creswell & Plano Clark, 2017). The major thread within this design is the quantitatively based experimental methodology. The qualitative thread can be used when a researcher needs data prior to the intervention, to explain the results of the intervention, or to follow up with certain participants.

Embedded Instrument Development and Validation Variant

This model embeds qualitative data into a quantitative instrument development and validation design. The qualitative data are collected to further enhance the instrument. Similar to other embedded approaches, the qualitative data can be collected before, during, or following the quantitative data collection and analysis. In addition, the design itself can be multi-phase in nature (Flynn & Hays, 2015).

CONVERGENT AND EMBEDDED DATA COLLECTION AND ANALYSIS

The researcher(s) employing a mixed methods approach must determine data *implementation*, *priority*, and the context of data analysis. Implementation has to do with the order in which quantitative and qualitative data are collected or if both data strands will be collected simultaneously. Priority is in reference to the weight or emphasis of a particular data strand. Equal and balanced emphasis on the quantitative and qualitative data leads to designs like convergent, whereas an imbalanced emphasis in the data collection or how those data are analyzed/interpreted, leads to unequal priority, which is what the embedded design is centered on. The structure of the embedded designs have a differential balance of priority, as well as a sequential process of data collection, while convergent designs are most often single phase designs in which all data are collected simultaneously, with equal priority given to qualitative and quantitative threads. It should be noted that the data transformation convergent variant does not follow this rule (Hanson et al., 2005).

Sampling in Mixed Methods Research

Sampling is the process where researchers select a subsection of participants from a larger population of interest. A main sampling goal is to fully answer the research question. When conducting convergent or embedded studies, researchers must adopt a strategy to select the participants (i.e., sampling scheme) and choose the appropriate sample size. Within any mixed methods study, a *sampling framework* encompasses the sampling strategy and the sample sizes. Due to the multiple phases, sequence, and the use of both qualitative and quantitative threads, the mixed methods sampling framework is often far more complex than a normal research study (Collins, 2010).

As described in Chapter 1, researchers employing a quantitative scheme often utilize probability sampling, while researchers employing a qualitative scheme typically use a non-probability purposive or convenience sampling scheme. Review Table 16.2 for additional information on probability and non-probability sampling methods. In the context of a mixed methods research study, the researchers must choose a sampling scheme for the qualitative and quantitative phases, and these decisions affect the power, validity, and trustworthiness of the findings and emergent meta-inferences. If an investigation has an inadequate sample, faulty sample size, or inappropriate strategy, the merit of the investigation is aptly called into question. For example, a small quantitative sample size reduces the statistical power of the investigation and limits the generalizability of the findings. Qualitatively, inappropriate sample size limits the saturation and ability of the researchers to provide an in-depth exploration of the phenomenon. Lastly, from a mixed methods perspective, inadequate sample size decreases the researcher's ability to make meta-inferences, which are based on the conclusions of both qualitative and quantitative aspects of the investigation (Collins, 2010).

Quantitative Analysis in Mixed Methods Research

We now turn our attention to mixed methods data analysis. Whether a researcher is using a convergent, embedded, or alternative mixed methods design, for many researchers, analyzing mixed methods data is the most challenging aspect of the research process. One of the main benefits of combining both qualitative and quantitative threads is the creation of an inclusive framework; however, a framework inclusive of multiple research threads creates a more complicated and sophisticated research framework. The benefits of a mixed methods framework, include an accessible structure for both qualitative and quantitative researchers, establishment of a common methodological language, a platform from which researchers can develop similar strategies, and an accountability framework (i.e., analysis audit; Onwuegbuzie & Combs, 2010).

When designing convergent and embedded mixed methods designs, researchers follow particular steps to ensure they are analyzing the data in an appropriate manner. All mixed methods research teams should consist of a qualitative and a quantitative research expert. Note that at times one researcher can have both expertise. The research team must also be proficient in mixing the findings from both strands to create a meaningful whole. As stated earlier, oftentimes the consequence of the mixing level of analysis are the creation of coherent qualitized and quantitized meta-inferences (Onwuegbuzie & Combs, 2010).

Whether the quantitative aspect of the investigation is the primary or secondary thread, one of the first analysis decisions a researcher must make is whether they are using descriptive statistics, inferential statistics, or both. Because most research studies involving human participants have a demographic analysis, most investigations analyze demographics with descriptive statistics. If descriptive statistics are needed, the researcher(s) must decide if they are using the

TABLE 16.2 Common Probability and Non-Probability Sampling Methods

	NAME OF SAMPLING METHOD	PROBABILITY OR NON-PROBABILITY	DESCRIPTION
1	Simple Random Sampling	Probability	This method of sampling is randomized. Randomization could involve using a randomized number generator in order to select numbers.
2	Stratified Random Sampling	Probability	This method of sampling divides a population into smaller sub-groups and then uses simple random sampling to choose subjects from the groups to select the sample.
3	Systemic Sampling	Probability	This method of sampling required selecting every "*nth*" participant from the population to complete your sample.
4	Cluster Random Sampling	Probability	In cluster random sampling, the researchers will select a cluster to sample from instead of the entire population.
5	Multi-Stage Random Sampling	Probability	This method of sampling uses a mixture of all sampling techniques.
6	Convenience Sampling	Non-probability	This method of sampling uses participants that are conveniently accessibly to the researcher.
7	Purposive Sampling	Non-probability	This method of sampling uses the researchers own judgment to select what they feel will be the most suitable sample for the study.
8	Expert Sampling	Non-probability	This method of sampling uses experts from the field related to the study, selected by the researcher.
9	Heterogeneity Sampling	Non-probability	This method of sampling purposefully selects participants to represent all perspectives in the sample.
10	Modal Instance Sampling	Non-probability	This method of sampling takes the most "common" participants for the sample.
11	Quota Sampling	Non-probability	This method of sampling represents demographics proportionally.
12	Snowball Sampling	Non-probability	This method of sampling allows participants to recruit further participants for the sample.
13	Maximum Variation Sampling	Non-probability	This method of sampling allows for the selection of individual, group, and setting to maximize the diversity of perspective.
14	Theory Based Sampling	Non-probability	This method of sampling allows for the inclusion of participants that help a theory develop.
15	Extreme Case	Non-probability	This method of sampling allows for the selection of outlying cases.

NOTE: This table contains 15 concise sampling descriptions. Further reading is necessary to fully understand each approach.

single-quantity-based statistics, including measures of central tendency, variability, position/ relative standing, or distributional shape. Alternatively, the researcher(s) may want to use exploratory-based statistics, including multidimensional scaling, correspondence analysis, exploratory factor analysis, and cluster analysis. If the quantitative side of the investigation requires inferential statistics, the researcher(s) must decide if they are going to use a parametric or non-parametric analysis. If a parametric analysis is deemed appropriate for the study, the researcher(s) will choose among the various parametric approaches to data analysis (e.g., multiple regression, independent samples *t* test, analysis of variance). Alternatively, if the researcher(s) decide to use a non-parametric analysis, they would analyze information through measures of association and population tests (Onwuegbuzie & Combs, 2010).

Qualitative Analysis in Mixed Methods Research

According to Onwuegbuzie and Combs (2010), there are four groupings of qualitative data collection points, including observations, talk, drawing and other media, and documents. Once the qualitative researcher(s) have completed the data collection process, they will decide if they are going to conduct a cross-case or within-case analysis. Note, at times, researcher(s) will conduct both cross- and within-case analyses within a single investigation. The within-case analysis process is when a researcher codes the data one case at a time. The cross-case analysis involves the researcher analyzing data across multiple cases simultaneously (Miles & Huberman, 1994).

Next, the qualitative researcher(s) will determine the coding process they will use to analyze data. Coding is a meticulous line-by-line process of sifting through a transcribed narrative to discover the latent meaning of the data. Researchers continuously compare codes until nothing new is found and there is agreement among other coders on the research team (i.e., consensus). Following the line-by-line coding analysis, researchers create clusters of similar codes. These emergent clusters of codes are grouped and regrouped into primary themes and secondary themes. Themes are connected (i.e., domains) to create a meaningful interpretation of the findings (i.e., the phenomenon, the grounded theory). Researchers can code data and come up with unique patterns (i.e., inductive coding), create codes from the scholarly literature and examine the raw data for instances of their existence (i.e., deductive coding), and use both inductive and deductive coding (i.e., abductive coding; Creswell, 2012). The last step is choosing a formal data analysis procedure (e.g., constant comparison analysis, classical content analysis, discourse analysis). These procedures are often associated with a particular qualitative tradition and are multi-step processes that systematically organize, sort, and describe the data.

Mixed Analysis

The analysis of both strands, or mixed methods analysis, has to do with combining qualitative and quantitative elements of a study to better understand the phenomenon under investigation. When beginning the mixed methods analysis portion of the investigation, researcher(s) consider *time sequence, priority*, and the creation of *meta-inferences*. Regarding time sequence, the researcher(s) can conduct the analysis of both strands concurrently, chronologically (i.e., sequentially), and in no chronological order. As described earlier in the chapter, if a researcher follows the convergent design, embedded design, or one of the convergent/embedded variants, they are committing to a particular time sequence. When a concurrent analysis is employed there is no prescribed order to the integration of qualitative and quantitative strands. When a chronological analysis occurs, the researcher alternates the qualitative and quantitative phases in a sequential order. Specifically, either a qualitative or quantitative phase is conducted first which informs the results of the other thread within second phase. Lastly, at times, the researcher(s) will employ more than two phases in a sequential arrangement (Onwuegbuzie & Combs, 2010).

During the mixing stage of the mixed methods process, the researcher(s) will often give priority to one of the analytical strands. Researchers using a mixed methods model will notice if there is a priority given to the qualitative and quantitative strands. Convergent designs tend to place equal priority within both stands, while embedded frameworks are designed to prioritize one of the methodological traditions. The prioritization of a particular thread is initially reflected in the research questions. For example, a mixed methods design that used the qualitative themes and subthemes to inform the creation of survey questions would prioritize the qualitative thread and conceptualize the quantitative-based survey as supportive (Onwuegbuzie & Combs, 2010). Once the analysis of both qualitative and quantitative data is complete, the researcher(s) will attempt to blend the findings into a holistic account of the phenomenon. This synthesis of threads creates convergent and divergent meta-inferences. Meta-inferences demonstrate how the two strands link and integrate with each another (Onwuegbuzie & Combs, 2010).

RIGOR IN MIXED METHODS RESEARCH

It is necessary and critical when designing and publishing a research study to define for the readers how you have conducted a rigorous and well thought out research design. Rigor itself can be conceptualized as trustworthiness, goodness, validity, and the sound systematic approach to a study's design, analysis of data, interpretation/synthesis, and reporting or presenting of results (Hays, et al., 2016). Regardless of the time sequence, emphasis, or mixed methods approach employed, each method must be respected and conducted in a valid/trustworthy manner. To ensure rigor, all qualitative (e.g., diversity in data collection methods, iterations of the same data collection method, foundational criteria for trustworthiness) and quantitative (e.g., internal validity, external validity, and replicability) principles must be thoroughly adhered to until the point of interface (Hurlburt, 2017; Lincoln & Guba, 1985). In addition, within any mixed methods research process there could be instances where the researcher(s) simply is not doing enough. From a quantitative standpoint, it is inadequate to have a small purposeful sample. If the researcher(s) does not have a large enough sample or utilizes a random sampling method, the researcher(s) will have limited statistical power (i.e., limited probability of rejecting the null hypothesis when the null hypothesis is false). Due to the importance of probabilities, researchers utilizing a quantitative approach need enough *power* to run tests (e.g., *t*-test, ANOVA, MANCOVA) and they need the appropriate *effect size* to determine the impact the independent variables have on the dependent variables (Kelley & Preacher, 2012). From a qualitative vantage point, researchers must use enough methods to deeply uncover the essence of the phenomenon. If the qualitative analysis is not thick and rich (e.g., multiple data collection methods, multiple trustworthiness procedures, multiple interviews with the same sample) it will fail to provide an in-depth and rigorous review of the data (Flynn & Korcuska, 2018a,b; Flynn et al., 2019).

According to Morse (2010) there are two main designs in which qualitative and quantitative threads are analyzed together (i.e., mixed). The first design is when there is a primary quantitative thread and secondary/supportive qualitative element. Within this design, the qualitative information is transformed into numerical data and the data are combined with core quantitative/

statistical data corpus. To ensure rigor, this method is only performed if the qualitative information is equivalent in regard to sample size and the qualitative data have been collected from all participants. The second design is when a primary qualitative thread has a supportive/secondary quantitative component. All individuals involved in the initial qualitative aspect of the study will have answered a question that sorts the data set into groups. The researchers will use a quantitative analysis method (e.g., chi-square analysis) to determine the significant differences. Within this, or any mixed methods design, it is important to combine results from both data sets into one multifaceted results and/or discussion section.

A method for enhancing the rigor of any research study is to conduct a pilot or feasibility study. Pilot studies are essentially smaller versions of a large study. Pilot studies are conducted to support the overarching project by testing all of the methods (e.g., sampling, instrumentation, statistical procedure, data collection methods). Within a mixed methods context, pilot studies should be conducted on all elements for which the researcher needs confirmation on feasibility (Ismail et al., 2017).

Increasing Rigor in Convergent and Embedded Designs

Convergent mixed methods design employs a single phase (i.e., qualitative and quantitative) of equal strength to enhance the understanding of the construct under investigation. Because there are no primary and secondary/supportive research threads, the qualitative and quantitative aspects of the investigation each must be rigorous, procedurally coherent, and valid/trustworthy, and research principles must be thoroughly adhered to. Quantitatively, the convergent mixed methods design should use a random (i.e., based on probability theory) sampling strategy (e.g., simple random sampling, stratified random sampling, cluster random sampling) and have an adequate sample size so the results generalize to a population of interest (Bhattacherjee, 2012). Since qualitative investigations are not centered on generalizing the results to a particular population, the qualitative thread, within a convergent investigation, should employ non-probability sampling procedures to uncover rich and thick information regarding the population of interest. For example, purposeful and/or convenience sampling procedures are often used when qualitatively exploring constructs (see Chapter 1 for further review).

Embedded mixed methods designs employ a main research phase that is either qualitative or quantitative in nature and the other design plays a subservient/supportive role within the study. The additional, smaller, qualitative/quantitative strand is embedded into the primary tradition to more thoroughly understand the emergent findings. The embedded philosophical integration is not based on pragmatism; instead, this tradition touts a paradigmatic hierarchy associated with the main approach (i.e., quantitative or qualitative research). This points to the importance of executing the main thread in a rigorous, valid/trustworthy, and coherent manner, and supporting the smaller thread as it relates to the overall study.

MULTICULTURAL ISSUES

The presence, consideration, and empowerment of disadvantaged groups is at the forefront of research in the behavioral sciences. We live in a world where justice and equity are not always upheld as inalienable, therefore certain research-based platforms create conduits for social advocacy, individual and systemic change, improved cultural awareness, and enhanced equality in the interpersonal social ecosystem in which we learn and live. While there are many social justice areas where research and scholarship are being used to better understand disadvantaged groups, research within the behavioral sciences, as a whole, has historically reflected an inadequate representation of minority groups, leaning largely toward the participant populations of educated middle-class White individuals (Prictor et al., 2018). This focus on White, educated, middle-class participants is even more concerning given that, according to the 2013 U.S. Census Bureau, non-Hispanic White individuals only make up 62.6% of the U.S. population.

Supporting research processes that protect diverse, minority, and vulnerable groups has been promoted by federal guidelines and legislation. For example, the 1993 National Institutes of Health (NIH) Revitalization Act (PL 103-43; 42 USC 298a-1) mandated the inclusion of racial/ethnic minorities and women in research to better understand the needs of these groups (NIH, 2001). Furthermore, the Common Rule (45 CFR 46.111(b)) effected institutional review boards (IRBs) safeguards for particular populations. Specifically, the populations that were considered vulnerable included children, prisoners, pregnant women, those with mental disabilities, and economically or educationally disadvantaged persons. IRBs now carefully scrutinize the research design and participant selection processes for these particular groups to ensure their safe and ethical treatment (U.S. Department of Health and Human Services, 2016).

Multicultural and Social Justice Research

Multicultural research focuses on the counseling relationship, including approaching practice with cultural understanding, attaining cultural knowledge to better understand client issues, and awareness and skill in delivering effective and sensitive treatment/interventions (Lyons & Bike, 2013). Multiculturallyoriented researchers approach participants and the research process through a variety of worldviews. While all individuals and researchers have personal values and bias, the multiculturallysound researcher is able to keep these personal views from having precedence over their professional judgment.

Social justice is an action-oriented construct related to helping disadvantaged group's access resources, achieve equity, and aims to empower oppressed individuals to participate in the various entities governing their lives. Often the individuals empowered through social justice causes and multiculturallyoriented research are marginalized and minority populations. Minority groups can include sexual orientation, gender identification, religious affiliation, elderly individuals, and various racial and ethnic minorities (Kim, 2006). Social justice research is a form of inquiry that promotes human development and the common and collective good by exploring the issues and challenges related to personal and distributable justice (Nash, 2008). This form of research is centered on the macrocosm. Specifically, social justice research explores constructs that will benefit the specific or explicit needs of a culture or underrepresented group. Furthermore, researchers seek to use their results to advocate for these groups and their needs, to ultimately fill the gap of inequity at a systemic level (Lyons & Bike, 2013).

As culturally competent, multiculturally sensitive, and socially just researchers, you are charged to advocate for the voices of minorities and disadvantaged groups who may go underrepresented and underserved. Through avoiding convenience in methodology, sampling, theorizing, and reporting, we can elevate research to higher standards and send our clinical practice soaring to higher states of quality and rigor. In qualitative and mixed methods research, we have the added benefit of the position of researcher-as-instrument to ensure advocacy and adequacy of multicultural competence. Among other things, this position encourages us to bracket assumptions and own our idiosyncratic bias during the research process. It is imperative that we take the required time and care to be able to exhibit that our study and our sampling selection is truly representative and generalizable of and to the population we wish to study and to serve (O'Hara et al., 2016; Scotland, 2012).

Mixed Methods Designs

Multicultural and social justice-oriented mixed methods investigations engage and empower marginalized groups, minority populations, and those who face discrimination and oppression (O'Hara et al., 2016). Mixed methods research has the potential to empower and support disadvantaged groups through the combination of in-depth, thick, and rich qualitative findings, and powerful quantitative research that generalizes descriptive and inferential results to a particular disadvantaged group. While quantitative data have the potential to garner grant-based and political support (Lyons et al., 2012; Ponterotto et al., 2013) due to its individualistic focus, there are instances when a singular post-positivistic quantitative approach can be at odds with collectivist cultures. This can unfortunately result in the continued oppression of a disadvantaged group (Ponterotto et al., 2013). Mixing a major qualitative thread with a quantitative approach can provide an in-depth voice which moves beyond generalizability and probability through capturing the essence of the participant's day-to-day life and collective group experiences. Furthermore, methods like focus groups and individual interviews have a remarkable capacity to create an in-depth narrative of the experiences of the participants and also the groups with which they might identify or associate.

As previously discussed, the single phase convergent mixed methods model offers the full complexity of qualitative and quantitative research methods, while the embedded mixed methods model gives priority to either the qualitative or quantitative thread of the study and embeds the smaller supportive thread into the central tradition. The embedded model relies on the paradigmatic hierarchy of the primary approach, while pragmatism philosophically informs the convergent design. Both of these approaches to research could be multiculturally challenging if a/the primary thread is incompatible with the ideology of the culture under investigation. Alternatively, the combination of quantitative and qualitative methodology has the potential to create a holistic and comprehensive understanding of the social justice/multicultural issue under investigation. According to Ponterotto et al. (2013) "the use of carefully sequenced diverse methods can provide researchers with multiple windows into the lives of the less empowered and historically silenced within our society" (p. 47).

There is a distinction in behavioral science research between the etic and emic approaches. Etic is a broad approach that emphasizes generalizability and the vantage point of the observer. To many researchers, this etic approach appears to echo the goals of quantitative research. Specifically, a goal of quantitative research and the etic approach would be to sample and apply the results to a very broad and diverse cross-section of a population or society. Emic approaches, on the other hand, are more akin to using a microscope or magnifying glass to examine the details and nuances of a specific population, or to create interventions that may be tailored to a certain group. Etic approaches are often conceptualized and used to make between-group comparisons or draw large-scale conclusions, whereas emic approaches tend to focus more on within-group differences and experiences (Chang et al., 2010). Therefore, when using a mixed methods research design, we have the opportunity to increase our scope of multicultural competence and relevance by combining both etic and emic approaches through the nature of the quantitative (etic) and qualitative (emic) integration.

LIMITATIONS OF CONVERGENT AND EMBEDDED APPROACHES

Mixed methods research is a major methodological framework that aims to answer the research question(s) through mixing qualitative and quantitative data in a single or multiphase investigation. While there are obvious benefits associated with blending diverse methods to holistically and deeply answer research questions/hypotheses, there are also multiple challenges and limitations to mixed methods design. A major challenge to conducting mixed methods research is the need for expertise. First, not only must quantitative and qualitative data be collected, analyzed, and integrated, but the hypotheses and research questions must also be integrated. The appropriate integration of both threads requires foresight, tools, expertise, and experience. Whether someone is conducting a convergent or embedded mixed methods design, every aspect of the research project is improved if the researcher or research team has expertise and experience in conducting qualitative, quantitative, and mixed methods research designs. If the individual or team conducting the investigation is lacking expertise and experience in one or more areas, the study will likely be flawed or take an enormous amount of time to complete. Examples of where the flaw could emerge include (but are not limited to) poorly formulated research questions and hypotheses; faulty analysis; faulty trustworthiness, reliability, and validity procedures; and inability to accurately interpret the results.

A second major limitation to any mixed methods investigation is the danger in trying to do too many things in the context of a single study. Mixed methods research design has the potential to incorporate multiple phases of data garnered from the use of diverse and expansive qualitative, quantitative, and mixed methods research frameworks. While there are clear benefits to having in-depth and diverse data mixed together, researchers also risk having too much information that does not lend itself to a synergistic integration (Creswell & Plano-Clark, 2017).

Third, if the researcher is conducting multicultural or social justice–oriented mixed methods research there are considerations. Whether the qualitative is the main or supportive thread, the individual conducting the investigation is the human instrument who attempts to give voice to the marginalized and/or disadvantaged group(s). From a multicultural perspective, if the researcher does not have high levels of multicultural competence and awareness, they could fail to deliver an ethical and/or multiculturally sound analysis of the data. In fact, evidence suggests they could risk causing further oppression and marginalization if they are unaware of the multicultural issues at work during the investigation (Nagata et al., 2012).

A fourth limitation in conducting mixed methods research, is the time and effort involved in gathering and analyzing the data. This holds especially true for the convergent and multi-phase mixed methods designs. Convergent designs require concurrent data collection and involves the use of multiple, full, and complete qualitative and quantitative research threads. This is more significant than most other mixed methods frameworks because the researcher(s) must meet the full scholarly expectations of qualitative, quantitative, and mixed methods research (e.g., sample design/size, data analysis, validity, and trustworthiness procedures) within a single investigation. The convergent data-transformation variant would likely be the most time/resource consuming of the convergent frameworks. Embedded designs are also energy and time consuming because the researchers must collect and analyze qualitative and quantitative information and effectively mix the data; however, a main difference between convergent and embedded designs is the researcher(s) using an embedded approach are collecting one of the data threads as part of the larger and more prominent thread. Thus, the subservient data thread takes less time and effort.

Lastly, it should be noted that time and work commitment is contingent and dependent on the number of individuals on the research team and the level of expertise for the given approach to research. For example, a research team with multiple qualitative and quantitative researchers who have experience and expertise in the traditions being utilized, could conduct a convergent design in a relatively expedient manner.

Timing and merging are two important elements to effectively strategize when conducting convergent and embedded mixed methods designs. Researchers conducting convergent designs will no doubt ask themselves the following, "What happens if my sample sizes are different for each thread?," "How do I merge and interpret the threads that have different sample sizes?" First, it is common for convergent design researchers to have different sample sizes due to the nature of each methodological framework. Qualitative researchers generally seek in-depth information from a purposefully selected sample of participants, while quantitative researchers generally seek a large random sample of participants for the purpose of generalizing the results to a population of interest. Because qualitative researchers seek quality and in-depth data, there is an emphasis on deeply exploring the participants' thoughts, feelings, and experiences through multiple data collection methods aimed at producing thick accounts of the participants' perceptions (e.g., individual interview, focus group). Alternatively, quantitative researchers seek large samples that exemplify quantity and have enough statistical power to generalize to the targeted population. In short, it is normal to both have more quantitative participants and it is considered rigorous for qualitative researchers to use a larger number of methods to deeply explore a small sample of participants. Lastly, within a convergent design framework, there are often separate and unique qualitative, quantitative, and mixed research questions. Answering each of these research questions will create a context for unique methodological elements (Creswell & Plano-Clark, 2017).

Researchers conducting embedded mixed method designs do not necessarily merge two different data sets collected to answer one research question. Instead they purposefully collect and analyze one main data set and include the second data thread as part of the larger study. The researcher using this approach must match the primary and secondary data set with particular research questions and decide when they want to collect the secondary data point (e.g., before, during, after, or some combination). While this timing is important to understand, it is essential to appreciate that researchers do not need to mix the results. The two sets of results could remain separate within the research report/manuscript (Creswell & Plano-Clark, 2017).

Case Study: Convergent Design

Jordan, G., Malla, A., & Iyer, S. N. (2020). Perceived facilitators and predictors of positive change and posttraumatic growth following a first episode of psychosis: A mixed methods study using a convergent design. *BMC Psychiatry, 20(1),* 1-16. doi: 10.1186/s12888-020-02693-y

BACKGROUND

Jordan et al.'s (2016; 2020) mixed methods protocol (2016) and investigation (2020) explored posttraumatic growth (PTG) following a first episode of psychosis (FEP). Our interpretation of this case is based solely on our review of the 2016 and 2020 articles and may not fully reflect the research team's complete efforts.

Posttraumatic growth is when positive client change happens following a first episode psychosis. Instead of feeling alienated or disturbed, some individuals experience PTG and develop better interpersonal and/or intrapersonal skills (e.g., enhanced ability to handle stressful situations). The literature has described PTG as being a part of the recovery process and a transformational form of recovery (Jacobson & Greenley, 2001). The overarching goal of the present investigation was to use a convergent mixed methods approach to explore two aspects of PTG, including: (a) better relationships and (b) enhanced facilitators of PTG (e.g., coping skills).

The research team used a convergent mixed methods approach for two primary reasons: (a) to objectively capture the extent to which PTG were endorsed by individuals with FEP and (b) to understand how PTG is subjectively experienced by following individuals purporting to experience it. The researchers closely followed the convergent mixed methods approach by simultaneously mixing qualitative and qualitative information during the formulation of the research questions, when choosing the data collection methods, designing and implementing the data analysis, and when interpreting the results.

RESEARCH PROCESS

The overarching qualitative research questions that were utilized with this study were (a) What are the aspects of PTG service-users experience following a FEP? and (b) What do service-users perceive as facilitating aspects of PTG following FEP? The quantitative research questions that were utilized with this investigation were (1) What aspects of PTG are most frequently endorsed by service-users following FEP? and (2) Which factors predict PTG following a FEP?

Participants included service-users and case managers being offered treatment for FEP at a specialized early intervention service. The qualitative strand was rigorous in scope and participation. Using a maximum variation strategy, researchers recruited 12 participants who met the criteria of experiencing some degree of growth after their FEP. The qualitative procedures included the primary author administering a one-hour semi-structured qualitative interview to service-users exploring their subjective experience of PTG and understanding what they thought enabled them to grow. The primary author developed and validated the semi-structured interview guide through feedback from service-users, their family, research evaluators, and psychiatrists.

In addition to the qualitative methods, the research team used a cross-sectional survey design which included seven separate quantitative questionnaires to analyze service users and case managers perceptions on the impact of FEP on their lives (service users) or the lives of their clients (case managers). Ninety-four participants completed assessments related to PTG and five hypothesized predictors of PTG. The questionnaire measuring PTG was the Posttraumatic Growth Inventory (Tedeschi & Calhoun, 1996). A second inventory measured the impact of psychosis with the Subjective Experiences of Psychosis Scale. A third questionnaire measured coping with the Brief COPE Scale (Carver, 1997). A fourth questionnaire assessed social support with the Multidimensional Scale of Perceived Social Support (Zimet, Dahlem, Zimet, & Farley, 1988). The recovery process was measured using the Recovery Assessment Scale (Corrigan, Salzer, Ralph, Sangster, & Keck, 2004). Resilience was measured with two separate inventories, including: The Child and Youth Resilience Measure—Youth version and the adult version of the Child and Youth Resilience Measure (Jacobson, McGarrigle, & Unger, 2019).

The research team initially engaged in separate qualitative and quantitative data analyses. After analyzing both threads, the researchers merged the results of both methods. Using multiple coders, transcripts were qualitatively analyzed using a descriptive analysis. Specifically, researchers analyzed the qualitative transcripts for initial codes, themes, and a thematic map among themes. Quantitative questionnaires were scored, and the researchers used descriptive statistics to analyze for patterns across measures and respondents. The PTG inventory scores, within the service-user and case managers groups, were computed along with any potential covariates using a multiple stepwise regression.

After completing separate qualitative and quantitative analyses, the researchers began the mixing of threads. The mixed methods analysis consisted of qualitative and quantitative results being examined side-by-side with the associated research question. The mixed results were organized by level of convergence (similar qualitative/quantitative findings) and divergence (contradictory qualitative/quantitative findings).

DISCUSSION

The results indicated that person-environment interactions facilitated PTG following a FEP. The results specify that spiritual coping and positive reframing appeared to facilitate positive change. Spirituality and positive reframing both seemed to create new constructive meaning to the adversity participants experienced. Third, qualitative and quantitative results identified subjective recovery as a factor that created positive change. This could be in the form of a belief that the "voices" a participant experienced served a purpose. Lastly, seeking help and eventually being hospitalized for FEP appeared to produce a positive change.

When treated for a FEP, PTG was also facilitated by engaging in treatment and receiving medication. Medication was seen as positive and helpful in achieving a sense of recovery and healing for individuals experiencing a FEP. Lastly, an important finding was the notion that engaging with a personal meaning making process post-FEP was key to PTG. If counselors facilitate a search for meaning, future clients will likely find it helpful.

Case Study: Embedded Design

Field, T. A., Beeson, E. T., Luke, C., Ghoston, M., & Golubovic, N. (2019). Counselors' neuroscience conceptualization of depression. *Journal of Mental Health Counseling, 41*(3), 260–279. https://doi-org.libproxy.plymouth.edu/10.7744/mehc.41.3.05.

BACKGROUND

Field et al.'s (2019) investigation entitled "Counselors' neuroscience conceptualizations of depression" was used as our case study for the embedded mixed methods approach. Our interpretation of this case is based solely on our review of the 2019 article and may not fully reflect the research team's complete efforts.

A team of five counselor education faculty members, from various universities around the United States, set out to conduct a study into how mental health clinicians incorporate neuroscience into their work with clients. The overarching goals of this group were to conceptualize client problems/symptoms using a neuroscience lens, explore how counselors conceptualize cases from this perspective, and to help clientele through neuroeducation. The impetus for this project was partly due to the American Counseling Association's ethical imperative that professionals within the field maintain a working knowledge of new scientific research and incorporate this knowledge into practice. A second motivating factor was in response to a growing trend for counselors to use neuroscience to understand mental health issues and to educate their clients.

The research team decided to use an embedded mixed methods approach to research how counselors conceptualize client depression from a neuroscience perspective. Specifically, the group aimed to gather quantitative and qualitative survey data. After the collection of qualitative data, the team transformed the emergent codes into quantitative data. To collect and use both types of data, the team used a survey tool which collected demographic information, questions related to neuroscience, and, through the survey platform, posed an open-ended question to obtain the qualitative data. The qualitative responses were then categorized, clustered and then converted into frequency counts so that the resulting empirical data could be merged with the quantitative data already obtained. The embedded design format was chosen due to the need to gather specific statistical data and rich and thick qualitative data that would fill a gap in the scholarly literature.

The authors began their process by discerning and examining the top five neuroscience theories used in understanding and explaining major depressive disorder. The commonly referenced neuroscience theories included monoamine theory, neuroplasticity theory, glutamate theory, a theory that postulated that certain types of depression are being linked to the physiological process and structural damage or abnormalities within the brain, and a fifth theory that viewed medical conditions as the leading cause of depression, such as hormonal issues or vitamin deficiencies linked to particular medical conditions or diseases. Contradictory to the newly emerging neuroscience theories around the causes and treatments for depression, there is a paucity of research describing how counselors are using and applying this knowledge in their work with clients, including a dearth of research related to how counselors are using neuroscience in the treatment and conceptualization of depression. The researchers' purpose, therefore, was to explore how professional counselors are conceptualizing and treating depression from a neuroscience standpoint and to determine how they are conveying this information to clients.

Using a post-positivistic framework, the research team collected a large sample ($N = 334$) in order to convert qualitative material into quantitative data. Due to the complexity of various neuroscience findings and perceived causes and contributors to depression, the research team chose a research format that could accommodate this complex material in as much depth as possible, guided by the question: How are counselors currently conceptualizing client depression in a neuroscience perspective?

RESEARCH PROCESS

All data were collected via an online survey that included an open-ended (qualitative) question about counselor conceptualization of client depression in a neuroscience context. The survey questions (quantitative) were based on the five aforementioned theories of neuroscience conceptualization of depression, including monoamine theory, neuroplasticity theory, glutamate theory, a theory that postulated that certain types of depression are being linked to the physiological process and structural damage or abnormalities within the brain, and a fifth theory that viewed medical conditions as the leading cause of depression.

After receiving IRB approval, the research team piloted the survey. Following the pilot phase, the finalized research survey was then open for 6 weeks. Researchers recruited a large convenience/ snowball sample of participants enrolled to target a population of counselors with varying backgrounds and experience levels. The study was an embedded design, due to the fact that the authors converted qualitative data into frequency counts of themed responses, and placed more emphasis on the quantitative element of the investigation.

Upon completion of qualitative and quantitative data collection, the research team analyzed qualitative findings with a constant comparative analysis. The research team then engaged in the qualitative data analysis process. Specifically, the team of researchers met for several months developing a codebook and using a grounded theory coding scheme. The team analyzed the data with both an a priori coding scheme (based on the five neuroscience theories presented) and a new emergent coding process. Emergent codes were identified but not categorized; however, the a priori codes were tallied. Next, the team used descriptive statistics to present findings on the frequency of responses that fell within the five categories. In addition, the team computed the interrater reliability for the coding process. This statistical analysis was completed to better understand the relative frequency of response themes.

To ensure and enhance the validity, credibility, transferability, and trustworthiness of their study, the research team was comprised of members with diverse ages, racial and gender backgrounds, and varying levels of research and neuroscience expertise. This diversity in the research team helped avoid potential bias in coding. Additionally, to ensure the credibility and triangulation of data, the researchers engaged in memo-writing, and conducted two phases of coding. Quantitatively, the authors followed inter-coder consistency guidelines related to percentage of agreement and the kappa cutoff, exceeding the criteria for reliability.

DISCUSSION

For participants categorized as conceptualizing their depressed clients within the neuroscience context and theories, the results indicate that the monoamine theory was the most common, emphasizing serotonin, and the neuroplasticity theory was second most commonly cited. Surprisingly, the glutamate theory was not mentioned by any participants. Other results with which the research team expressed some shared concern were that only one third of participants cited a neuroscience theory in their qualitative responses, and less than a quarter of participants mentioned more than one neuroscience theory in the explanation of symptomology.

The outcomes of this study indicate that the advised multidimensional approach to understanding and addressing client symptoms, per the National Institute of Mental Health, is perhaps falling short of what is actually being understood, conceptualized, and practiced by counselors. The research team thought it was positive to see a more recent theory being discussed in participant responses (i.e., the neuroplasticity theory), but were also aware of the inaccurate information in participant responses and therefore expressed cautious and emphatic recommendation that those in the counseling profession stay up to date with evolving and emerging neuroscience in the context of mental maladies and depressive disorders.

The limitations acknowledged by the researchers included the nature of a hypothetical case for the survey question, and the possible bias in participant response, self-selection, and the written versus verbal format of response. Additionally, it was noted that there was an overrepresentation of White, female participants and therefore might not adequately or accurately represent the collective counselors in the field.

Further research was suggested by the authors in the areas of neuro case, client, symptom conceptualization and the use of neuroscience in explaining and treating client symptomology. It was recommended, via the results and discussion, that more training and deeper understanding are needed among the practicing counselor population to adequately use information to address and treat clients. Lastly, the authors recommended that emerging counselors be well-versed in treatment options so as not to misdiagnose or mismedicate clientele. Lastly, the authors note that counselors should not forget the non-therapeutic personal lifestyle changes that can have a positive influence upon client neurological functioning.

SUMMARY

Throughout this chapter you were introduced to the philosophical, pragmatic, and contextual aspects to convergent and embedded mixed methods research design. In addition, we took some time to re-introduce you to a number of general mixed methods considerations. As you continue your journey with mixed methods research design, please remember there is no short-cut to having a strong research team and, for early career professionals, there is no substitute for an effective training program and a good research mentor. It is our hope that the information outlined within this chapter will provide you with enough information to begin to initiate a convergent and/or embedded mixed methods research project. At this point, you have a basic blueprint for designing these two important mixed methods traditions. Good luck in your future work as mixed methods researchers; we hope you use this chapter as a platform to create dynamic and innovative research.

STUDENT ACTIVITIES

Exercise 1: Understanding Mixed Methods Research

Directions: Within this section of the chapter, the philosophical integration of mixed methods research design was explored. In the following we provide two questions related to mixed methods research. Using the Internet and your university's library online database (Academic Search Premier), answer the following questions.

- Explain the purpose and nature of mixed methods research design, and articulate two key benefits to mixed methods approaches, along with two key limitations a researcher may encounter.
- The philosophical/paradigmatic stance from which scientist–practitioners typically approach the mixed methods style of research, linking both qualitative and quantitative research camps, is essential to understand. Explain this philosophical stance and how a research team may use it during their research process.

Exercise 2: Phases and Research Questions

Directions: Answer the following questions. Can you think of a circumstance in which a research team might opt for a concurrent mixed methods design, and a situation in which a sequential mixed method design may be better suited? Can you expand on this by considering a research question which may be best suited to a convergent design, and a question which might align best with an embedded design? Consider contextual factors in your response.

Exercise 3: Compare and Contrast

Directions: Throughout this chapter the salient differences between convergent and embedded mixed methods research designs were explored. Describe the similarities and differences between convergent and embedded designs. Review the following convergent and embedded design articles and describe the main differences you found in the following areas:

- Purpose statement
- Research questions
- Procedures

- Data analysis
- Trustworthiness/validation procedures

CONVERGENT DESIGN ARTICLE

Ponton, R., Brown, T., McDonnell, B., Clark, C., Pepe, J., & Deykerhoff, M. (2014). Vocational perception: A mixed-method investigation of calling. *The Psychologist-Manager Journal, 17*(3), 182–204.

EMBEDDED DESIGN ARTICLE

Flynn, S. V., & Hays, D. G. (2015). the development and validation of the comprehensive counseling skills rubric. *Counseling Outcome Research and Evaluation, 6*(2), 87–99. https://doi.org/ 10.1177/ 2150137815592216

Exercise 4: Hallmarks of Rigor

Directions: Answer these questions. What are the hallmarks of a rigorous mixed methods study? How can a researcher or a research team convey that they have demonstrated rigor in their research endeavor?

Exercise 5: Multicultural and Social Justice Issues in Mixed Methods Research

Directions: Within this section of the chapter the multicultural and social justice issues relative to mixed methods research design were explored. In the following we provide three questions related to mixed methods research. Using the Internet and your university's library online database, answer the following questions.

- How is mixed methods research particularly appropriate for multicultural research?
- What is the difference between multicultural competency and social justice proficiency in research?
- Do you believe that quality research can enhance multicultural competency in the field of counseling research and practice? Why? Do you feel that multicultural competency can increase the rigor of a research investigation? Why?

ADDITIONAL RESOURCES

Software Recommendations

NVivo Software (https://www.qsrinternational.com)

CAQDAS Software (https://www.maxqda.com)

ATLAS ti (https://atlasti.com)

MaxQDA (https://maxda.com)

Helpful Links

- https://www.ncbi.nlm.nih.gov/pmc/articles/PMC5602001/
- https://pcmh.ahrq.gov/page/mixed-methods-integrating-quantitative-and-qualitative-data-collection-and-analysis-while

- https://soundleisure.com/base/embedded-design-mixed-methods-research\
- http://www.annfammed.org/content/13/6/554.full
- https://link.springer.com/article/10.1007/s11577-017-0454-1

Helpful Books

Creswell, J. W. (2012). *Educational research: Planning, conducting, and evaluating quantitative and qualitative research* (4th ed.). Pearson.

Creswell, J., & Plano Clark, V. (2017). *Designing and conducting mixed methods research* (3rd ed.). SAGE.

Greene, J. C. (2007). *Mixed methods in social inquiry*. Jossey-Bass.

Morrow, S. L., & Smith, M. L. (2000). Qualitative research for counseling psychology. In S. D. Brown & R. W. Lent (Eds.), *Handbook of Counseling Psychology* (3rd ed., pp. 199–230). Wiley.

Robson, C., & McCartan, K. (2016). *Real world research* (4th ed.). Wiley.

Tashakkori, A., & Teddlie, C. (Eds.). (2010). *Handbook of mixed methods in social and behavioral research*. SAGE.

Teddlie, C., & Tashakkori, A. (2009). *Foundations of mixed methods research: Integrating quantitative and qualitative approaches in the social and behavioral sciences*. SAGE.

Helpful Videos

- https://www.youtube.com/watch?v=1OaNiTlpyX8
- https://www.youtube.com/watch?v=XynPxWSLjZY
- https://www.youtube.com/watch?v=PSVsD9fAx38
- https://www.youtube.com/watch?v=A7YYA9qQjJA
- https://www.youtube.com/watch?v=oO3cspRrq4E
- https://www.youtube.com/watch?v=D0h85FtRYLc
- https://www.youtube.com/watch?v=0CRwUYsNVwU

KEY REFERENCE

Only key references appear in the print edition. The full reference list appears in the digital product found on http://connect.springerpub.com/content/book/978-0-8261-4385-3/part/part04/chapter/ch16

Onwuegbuzie, A. J., & Johnson, R. B. (2006). The validity issue in mixed research. *Research in the Schools*, 13, 48–63.

CHAPTER 17

MIXED METHODS RESEARCH: EXPLANATORY AND EXPLORATORY DESIGNS

Stephen V. Flynn and Clarissa M. Uttley

LEARNING OBJECTIVES

After reading this chapter, you will be able to:

- Describe the philosophical underpinnings of explanatory and exploratory research designs
- Explain how to maximize the rigor of explanatory and exploratory research designs
- Recognize which data analysis methods are suited to explanatory and exploratory research designs
- Interpret how explanatory and exploratory research design traditions can enhance multicultural competency

INTRODUCTION TO EXPLANATORY AND EXPLORATORY DESIGNS

Many researchers undoubtedly consider the ideal nature of having qualitative data that enhances the understanding of quantitative data or having quantitative data that further develops qualitative data. Likewise, when conducting a literature review, researchers often look to qualitative data when designing a quantitative investigation or to quantitative research when designing a qualitative investigation. While there are instances when this process is deserving of two separate investigations, mixed methods researchers will often design a study that employs a framework that touts a major methodological emphasis (qualitative or quantitative) and a secondary framework that enhances and supplements the main strand. This type of mixed methods research is known as either sequential explanatory or sequential exploratory research design.

At times, researchers are interested in quantitatively assessing a construct and then attaining additional qualitative data (i.e., sequential explanatory design). One example of this could be a researcher using a quantitatively based survey to attain initial results and then following up with a qualitative interview protocol that addresses any unique findings. Alternatively, there are times a researcher may decide to gather qualitative information and further explore a phenomenon through receiving secondary quantitative feedback (i.e., sequential exploratory design). One example could be a researcher asking a purposefully selected group of participants a variety of questions around a construct of interest, and using the emergent qualitative themes to create a quantitatively based survey to be randomly disseminated to the population. A major emphasis with these two mixed methods frameworks is to use either a qualitative or quantitative approach to better understand the initial research thread. The word "sequential" refers to a research study that employs a two-phased approach that begins either quantitatively or qualitatively. Since greater importance is typically placed on the first phase of the investigation, this important first phase dictates whether the researcher is using an explanatory (QUANTITATIVE → *qualitative*) design or an exploratory (QUALITATIVE → *quantitative*) design.

DISTINGUISHING EXPLANATORY AND EXPLORATORY DESIGNS

Within this section, we attempt to differentiate the sequential explanatory and exploratory mixed methods framework from other related mixed methods traditions. Researchers most often use a sequential explanatory design framework when they want to analyze data quantitatively (i.e., main thread) and explore the associated trends and contextual variables qualitatively (i.e., secondary thread). Researchers use a sequential exploratory design framework when they are interested in quantitatively testing or assessing emergent qualitative findings across a random sample. Both exploratory and explanatory methodological frameworks use separate sequential phases for each thread. In comparison, the embedded mixed methods approach is most similar. The emphasis with embedded mixed methods design is to collect a primary data set, analyzed either qualitatively or quantitatively, and a secondary data set from a different methodological tradition, that provides a smaller supportive role. The embedded approach can also be completed in a single phase. For example, a researcher could have a qualitative interview protocol embedded within a quantitative analysis document. The participants would review and complete both quantitative and qualitative elements in one sitting.

Researchers engaging in convergent mixed methods designs, are attempting to utilize diverse methodological frameworks, which complement each other, to converge on a richer understanding of a phenomenon. Unlike explanatory, exploratory, and embedded designs, each strand (i.e., qualitative and quantitative) of the convergent approach has equal strength. In comparison, the transformative approach can use many different mixed methods structures (e.g., QUALITATIVE → *quantitative*, QUANTITATIVE → *qualitative*, QUALITATIVE + QUANTITATIVE, QUANTITATIVE + QUALITATIVE, QUALITATIVE + *quantitative*, QUANTITATIVE + *qualitative*) and sequence (i.e., concurrent, sequential, single phase), however its distinguishing feature is that the researcher uses a theoretically based framework to support marginalized and underrepresented populations. A multiphase mixed methods design would contain multiple separate investigations within the same study. Each qualitative and quantitative element would have a shared purpose; however, they would be conducted separately, and the researcher would have distinct findings. Table 17.1 provides information on the purpose, thread emphasis, sequence, and paradigm of the various mixed methods approaches. This table uses Morse's notation system (see Chapter 16 for a review; Morse & Niehaus, 2009).

TABLE 17.1 **The Nature of Prominent Mixed Method Traditions**

NAME	PURPOSE	THREAD EMPHASIS	SEQUENCE	PARADIGM
Convergent	Compare qual and quan data	QUAL + QUAN	Concurrent	Pragmatism
Embedded	Embed a smaller qual/quan into a larger design	QUAN + *qual,* QUAL + *quan,* QUAN → *qual,* QUAL → *quan*	Single phase, sequential	Traditional paradigmatic hierarchy
Explanatory	**Use qual results to explain quan results**	**QUAN → *qual***	**Sequential**	**Traditional paradigmatic hierarchy**
Exploratory	**Use quan results to explain qual results**	**QUAL → *quan***	**Sequential**	**Traditional paradigmatic hierarchy**
Transformative	Uses qual and quan methods to advance social justice causes	QUAN + qual, QUAL + quan, QUAL + QUAN, QUAN + QUAL QUAL → Quan, QUAN → qual	Concurrent, sequential, single phase	Transformative paradigm, pragmatism
Multiphase	Uses separate studies and multiple phases for large projects	QUAL + QUAN, QUAN + QUAL QUAL → Quan, QUAN → qual	Sequential, Concurrent	Pragmatism

NOTE: Bolded, the emphasis of the chapter; qual, qualitative; quan, quantitative; QUAL + QUAN, qualitative and quantitative have equal emphasis in a study; QUAN + *qual,* embedding a smaller qualitative thread into a quantitative design; QUAL +*quan,* embedding a smaller quantitative thread into a qualitative design; QUAN → *qual,* a smaller qualitative thread follows a quantitative phase; QUAL → *quan,* a smaller quantitative thread follows a qualitative phase.

THE PHILOSOPHICAL INTEGRATION OF EXPLANATORY AND EXPLORATORY DESIGN

The philosophical integration of the sequential explanatory and exploratory mixed methods traditions is directed by the first thread's approach to research (i.e., qualitative, quantitative). The explanatory approach has a strong initial dominant quantitative phase followed by a supportive qualitative thread, while the exploratory approach has an initial qualitative phase followed by a secondary quantitative thread. While the two phases are separate and adhere to the full procedures and rigor of each paradigm, most of the time the explanatory approach's dominant quantitative thread guides the study (Figure 17.1). Similarly, the qualitative thread of the exploratory approach directs the design (Figure 17.2). While the entire complexity of each paradigmatic hierarchy is incorporated into each phase of an explanatory and exploratory investigation, the overarching approach to resolving the research problem is influenced by pragmatism (Morgan, 2014). For example, pragmatically, researchers using an explanatory approach make a decision on what they believe would be the best qualitative tradition (e.g., case study, phenomenology, grounded theory), data collection points (e.g., interviews, documents), and sampling method (e.g., criterion, snowball, convenient) to enhance their quantitative phase (e.g., survey, experimental design, single subjects design).

Ontologically, the explanatory mixed methodology tradition has a realism emphasis and the exploratory mixed methods tradition is centered on relativism. You may be wondering how a

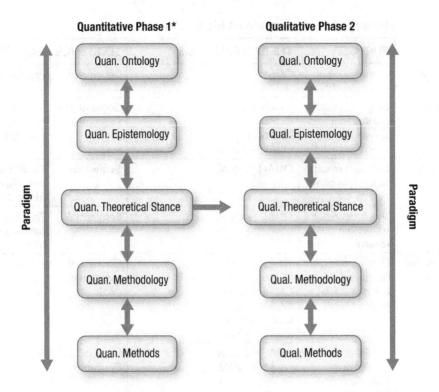

FIGURE 17.1 Explanatory Mixed Methods Research Paradigm.

NOTE: Double-ended arrows, interaction; large vertical double-ended arrow underneath the word paradigm, demonstrating that paradigm is encompassing of ontology, epistemology, theoretical stance, methodology, and methods; single right arrow in the center, phase 1 to phase 2 flow. An asterisk indicates the dominant phase in most cases.

research study can have an overall emphasis and simultaneously capture the procedural coherence of a tradition (i.e., qualitative or quantitative). This has to do with the strength and prominence of the first phase of an explanatory/exploratory investigation. Because of this initial emphasis, there will be an overall ontological leaning to that form of reality. For example, if a researcher was conducting an exploratory design that utilized a rigorous phenomenological approach within the first phase and the emergent themes were converted into a quantitative survey within the second phase, the origins and emphasis of the investigation would be relativistic in nature (i.e., qualitative).

When an explanatory or exploratory mixed methods researcher begins to consider their study's theory of knowledge (i.e., epistemology) they begin to fully meet the expectations of both a qualitative and quantitative paradigm. From an epistemological perspective, explanatory mixed methodology is grounded in objectivism, while exploratory mixed methodology is centered on subjectivism or constructionism. There will essentially be two epistemological approaches to any exploratory or explanatory mixed methods design. Theoretically, the philosophical stance of each phase will be considered. If the study is explanatory in nature, there will likely be an initial positivistic or post-positivistic theoretical leaning followed by a qualitative emphasis (e.g., symbolic interactionism, phenomenological, feminism). Exploratory investigations will have a similar coordinated effort; however, exploratory researchers will begin with a qualitative theory and follow-up with a quantitative theory (Crotty, 2003).

Methodology is more practical when compared to the macro guiding philosophical assumptions because the methodology provides a blueprint for discovering what is knowable (Crotty, 2003).

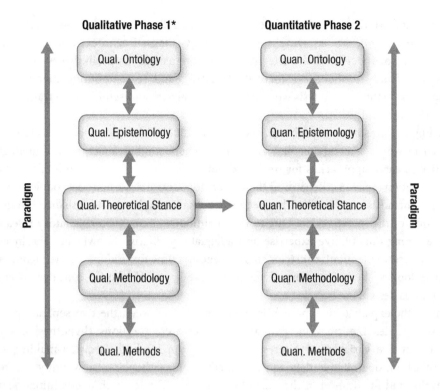

FIGURE 17.2 Exploratory Mixed Methods Research Paradigm.

NOTE: Double-ended arrows, interaction; large vertical double-ended arrow underneath the word paradigm, demonstrating that paradigm is encompassing of ontology, epistemology, theoretical stance, methodology, and methods; single right arrow in the center, phase 1 to phase 2 flow.

* The dominant phase in most cases; qual, qualitative; quan, quantitative.

The methodology utilized within each phase of explanatory or exploratory design will meet the rigorous demands of each tradition. Common qualitative and quantitative approaches to research were reviewed within Chapters 5 through 14 of this text. Now that the researcher's entire paradigm has been considered, the investigators will determine the methods they will be using to gather and analyze their data. Quantitatively and qualitatively based research paradigms each have a plethora of methods to choose from; however, it is essential that researchers ground and justify all their methodological decisions in the research paradigm they are utilizing. Regarding the explanatory/exploratory traditions, the supportive thread should be appropriate and enhance and augment the main (initial) thread.

EXPLANATORY DESIGN

The rigorous use of sequential explanatory mixed methods design has substantially increased over the past 15 years. Operationalizing the explanatory mixed methods design through rigorous and innovative research created to better understand contemporary behavioral science issues is important to fully understanding complex issues in the social sciences. Recent research details the use of explanatory mixed methods research in (a) understanding the process of mandatory counseling through the integration of multiple quantitative self-report questionnaires (i.e., WAI,

Hope Scale, and Motivation of Treatment Scale) and follow up qualitative interview process (Razzhavaikina, 2008); (b) applying a sequential questionnaire, interview, observation, and documentation to understand the effectiveness of premarital counseling service on marriage harmony and family resilience (Samad et al., 2016); and (c) combining hierarchical linear modeling and a qualitative analysis when comparing walk-in counseling with a traditional model of service (Stalker et al. 2016).

According to Johnson, Onwuegbuzie, and Turner (2007): "Mixed methods research is the type of research in which a researcher or team of researchers combines elements of qualitative and quantitative research approaches for the broad purposes of breadth and depth of understanding and corroboration" (p. 123). Regarding the explanatory research design methodology, the initial quantitative thread is combined with a secondary qualitative thread to enhance the depth and corroboration of the investigation. Due to the quantitative focus, the explanatory research team must have strong quantitative expertise and adequate qualitative knowledge. The investigators must have access to quantitative instruments and enough time to conduct the two rigorous phases. Researchers looking for a more expedient one-phase approach should consider an embedded mixed methods design.

Salient to the explanatory approach is the distinction between the two separate phases. The first phase includes the creation of quantitative research questions (hypothesis), a decision on the quantitative variables of interest, data collection methods decision-making, sampling method selection, quantitative data analysis, methods for enhancing the validity and reliability of the results, and finalization of the quantitative results. The research team's initial quantitative findings will provide guidance for the second phase (i.e., qualitative research phase). The areas for further qualitative inquiry are often aspects of the quantitative results that require clarity, further elaboration, and/or corroboration. The qualitative phase begins with a thorough review of quantitative results and simultaneous shaping of the overarching qualitative methodology, research questions, interview protocol, sampling method(s), data collection methods, trustworthiness procedures, and qualitative analysis. This qualitative alignment with the quantitative findings symbolizes the sequential nature of the explanatory approach.

The mixing of qualitative and quantitative results is the final step in the explanatory research design. According to Creswell and Plano-Clark (2017), the goal of the explanatory approach, and most mixed methods designs, is the synthesis of the two separate quantitative and qualitative threads. The research team, comprised of qualitative and quantitative experts, will collaborate on the meaningful synthesis of qualitative and quantitative aspects of the study. The overall goal of this mixing of results is to provide the most accurate and comprehensive answers to the research question(s). Researchers will quite literally interpret the extent and the way the qualitative findings augment the quantitative results.

Follow-Up Explanation and Participant-Selections Variants

According to Creswell and Plano-Clark (2017), the follow-up explanation variant is a common variant of the explanatory approach that places the dominance within the initial quantitative thread. The qualitative phase is mainly used for clarifying and explaining the results of the quantitative phase. This model can be extremely helpful if the researcher(s) want to qualitatively explore unique or unanticipated quantitative findings uncovered in the first phase.

The participant variant design is a significant deviation to the original intention of explanatory mixed methods design. Within this variation the prominent thread is the second qualitative phase.

The initial quantitative section is used to identify and secure pertinent qualitative (i.e., second phase) participants (for a review see Creswell & Plano-Clark, 2017).

EXPLORATORY DESIGN

The innovative use of a sequential exploratory mixed methods design has substantially increased over the past 10 years. Operationalizing the exploratory mixed methods approach in exploring contemporary issues is important to fully understand issues in the behavioral sciences. Recent research details (a) the use of a three-phase (qualitative-quantitative-qualitative) sequential exploratory approach to understand strategies for empowering adolescent girls in the area of reproductive health (Allahverizadeh et al., 2018); (b) sequentially combining the results of semi-structured interview groups, three separate quantitative measures, and a modified version of the Psychosocial Treatments Interview (Steketee et al., 1997) to understand a peer advocate model aimed at supporting rural gender and sexual minorities (Willging et al., 2018); and (c) qualitatively and quantitatively exploring a mindfulness-based stress reduction curriculum on middle-aged and older adults with memory complaints (Berk et al., 2018).

The sequential exploratory design is a two-phase mixed methodology approach to research. Exploratory mixed methods design is different from explanatory research due to the researcher/research team beginning with a rigorous qualitative phase and following up with a supportive quantitative phase. The intent of the first phase is to collect a small purposive qualitative sample, analyze the data, and determine the findings. The primary purpose of the second phase is to gather a larger probability sample and conduct a quantitative research study designed to validate and generalize the qualitative findings (Creswell & Plano-Clark, 2017).

As the name suggests, an initial qualitative exploration is needed to ensure a primary understanding of the construct or because there are no instruments available to measure a phenomenon. According to Creswell and Plano-Clark (2017) this design is very helpful when researchers want to do one of the following: (a) develop and test new instruments that examine unique constructs, (b) rigorously explore qualitative research questions with a mixed design, and (c) the researcher discovers new qualitative information (phase 1) that are best answered with a quantitative approach (phase 2). In addition to the aforementioned information, in many ways the behavioral sciences are still exploring new psychological frontiers. At times, there are few empirically based measures for assessing pertinent psychological constructs (e.g., adult attachment styles, learned helplessness, altruism, partner abuse potential). A major benefit of the exploratory approach is the production of a new instrument that is designed to measure a unique construct.

Like explanatory designs, priority, sequence, and purpose are paramount with the exploratory mixed methods approach. It is important to note that a full sequentially based qualitative and quantitative methodological approach must be adhered to when utilizing this approach. For researchers looking for a one-phase approach, they are encouraged to review convergent and embedded designs. Once the researcher has decided upon the exploratory approach, they initiate the qualitative phase (phase 1). Once the entire qualitative phase has been completed (e.g., research question, purpose, participant sampling, data collection, data analysis, trustworthiness engagement), the research team begins mixing the qualitative findings with an emergent quantitative instrument. This essentially connects the qualitative and quantitative threads. Following this, the research team engages fully in the quantitative phase (phase 2) with a new quantitative sample. Lastly, the research team attempts to enhance and corroborate the initial qualitative findings with the quantitative results.

Theory Development and Instrument Development Variants

When using the theory development variant, researchers put the emphasis and rigor on the initial qualitative findings. Based on those findings, researchers will follow up with a quantitative analysis. The quantitative phase is used primarily to demonstrate the existence, prevalence, and/or to test the qualitative information with a larger sample. This is a common method of qualitatively deconstructing the nature of a construct and quantitatively testing its existence.

The instrument development framework places the procedural emphasis on the second quantitative phase of the methodology. The first phase is secondary due to the primary purpose being the collection of data to construct the initial iteration of an instrument. The second phase is the prominent one due to the extensive instrument validation effort that takes place.

EXPLANATORY AND EXPLORATORY DATA COLLECTION AND ANALYSIS

According to Morgan (2007), quantitative data collection and analysis emphasize the deductive, objective, and generalizable elements, while qualitative research is centered on inductive, subjective, and contextual influences that form sophisticated patterns. Ideally, the research team using an explanatory or exploratory approach will have quantitative and qualitative expertise. The optimal composition of a mixed methods research team is for each member to have both qualitative and quantitative expertise. This is because decisions about methodological justification, points of interface, and consensus are dependent on team members' expertise. *Implementation priority* is an important facet of explanatory and exploratory mixed methods research. Consequently, a first step in the data collection process is determining the order in which qualitative and quantitative data are collected. As previously stated, the implantation priority of explanatory design is quantitative followed by qualitative (i.e., QUAN → *qual)*, while the exploratory design priority is qualitative followed by quantitative (i.e., QUAL → *quan*). A second important decision is understanding what, if any, phase is given more priority. While both explanatory and exploratory designs use a full sequential qualitative and quantitative methodological framework, the emphasis in an explanatory design is quantitative while the emphasis in exploratory design is qualitative. This priority comes to life when considering the order of methodology and the rigor in which the methodology is implemented (i.e., more rigor with the prominent thread; Onwuegbuzie & Combs, 2010).

Once the research team, priority, sequence, and purpose are determined, the researcher or research team must consider the best methodological approaches to utilize. Depending on the purpose, explanatory and exploratory researchers can choose from a wide range of deductive quantitative approaches, including (but not limited to) experimental design, survey research, single subject design, and quantitative content analysis. Similarly, there are quite a few inductive qualitative traditions to choose from, including ethnography, phenomenology, case study, grounded theory, narrative inquiry, and consensual qualitative research. At this point, it should hopefully be clear that researchers must align the purpose of their investigation with the overarching emphasis of the qualitative/quantitative methodological tradition. Following this alignment, a variety of additional decisions must be made and justified, including (but not limited to) data collection methods, appropriate sampling methods, screening of participants, and validity and trustworthiness procedures.

The Purpose

Following the creation of research question(s), the researcher(s) will decide upon a purpose for their mixed methods study. Ultimately, the purpose of any mixed methods study is about enhancing the potential investigatory power and validity of a design. While this may be an overarching goal of mixed methods research, researchers have more specific reasons for combining multiple threads for the eventual enhancement of the conclusions. The purpose of the mixed methods investigation should adhere to inclusivity, which assumes that the purpose will affect and must integrate with the various phases of the research process. Greene et al. (1989, p. 259), distinguished the following five purposes for mixed methods research:

1. *Triangulation* seeks convergence, corroboration, correspondence of results from different methods;

2. *Complementarity* seeks elaboration, enhancement, illustration, clarification of the results from one method with the results from the other method;

3. *Development* seeks to use the results from one method to help develop or inform the other method, where development is broadly construed to include sampling and implementation, as well as measurement decisions;

4. *Initiation* seeks the discovery of paradox and contradiction, new perspectives of frameworks, the recasting of questions or results from one method with questions or results from the other method;

5. *Expansion* seeks to extend the breadth and range of inquiry by using different methods for different inquiry components. an analysis of published mixed methods studies.

Researchers using explanatory and exploratory mixed methods designs could use the aforementioned purposes to justify their use of a design, however these traditions are often used because the use of both qualitative and quantitative methods would greatly enhance the integrity of the results (Bryman, 2006) and because qualitative findings can corroborate quantitative results and quantitative results can generalize qualitative findings.

Sampling

Prior to the implantation of each phase, mixed methods researchers must decide on a sampling design and a population to sample. According to Tashakkori and Teddlie (2003) sampling is the procedure researchers use to collect a portion of participants from a larger population to use as a subset to answer the research question(s). A sampling design encompasses the methodology, population of interest, sequence, and number of phases. Mixed methods researchers using an explanatory or exploratory approach must ensure that their sampling goal is fully meeting the research question(s). Chapter 16 provides a probability and non-probability sampling method table. Please review this information for an easy-to-access guide to common qualitative (non-probability) and quantitative (probability) sampling methods, noting that both probability and non-probability will likely be necessary for a mixed methods study.

Mixed methods researchers must go beyond a basic understanding of various sampling approaches. Specifically, they must use an *inclusive approach* to select a sampling design. An inclusive approach to sampling is centered on the understanding that sampling decisions influence and are influenced by the various phases of the research process (e.g., purpose, research questions, procedures, data analysis). Because there are two sequential threads, the explanatory/exploratory sampling framework becomes much more complex when compared to a non-mixed methods study. Furthermore, the inclusive approach to sampling decisions assumes that the choices made by a researcher partly reflects their values and assumptions about what constitutes credible, rigorous, and appropriate sampling methods (Collins, 2010). For example, while some qualitative researchers may think snowball sampling is a perfectly reasonable technique, others may question the rigor of such an approach (Morse, 2010; Onwuegbuzie & Combs, 2010).

Once a researcher selects a methodological framework to explore their construct(s) of interest, they will consider possible sampling schemes for different phases of the project. Mixed methods researchers typically have two sampling schemes. These schemes are associated with the nature of the phase of an investigation. For example, a probability sampling scheme is associated with a quantitative phase(s) of the investigation and a purposeful scheme is associated with the qualitative phase(s). Sampling schemes will have a parameter based on the sampling method employed (Table 16.2). For example, a purposive sampling scheme would have boundaries that delimit the specific participant characteristics (e.g., multicultural group, gender, sexual identity, socio-economic status). Similarly, a probability sampling scheme would have parameters based on a predetermined number of participants and this scheme would have an overall goal of ensuring that every member of the population of interest has an equal chance of being selected (Collins, 2010).

Qualitative and Quantitative Analysis

The data analysis portion of any mixed methods study can seem extremely daunting. To effectively conduct a mixed methods study, the researcher and/or their research team need to have a deep understanding of qualitative and quantitative data analysis. Within this section we breakdown a few basic aspects of qualitative and quantitative data analysis. Please note, this is meant to be a basic blueprint, not a guide for every qualitative and quantitative tradition. For a more in-depth review of statistics Chapter 4 provides an in-depth review of descriptive, inferential, and Bayesian models and procedures.

QUALITATIVE ANALYSIS

Given the sequential nature of explanatory and exploratory approaches, researchers will begin their investigations with either a full qualitative or quantitative approach. If the researcher is using an exploratory approach, they will begin with qualitative data analysis. One way to distinguish qualitative analyses approaches is to differentiate whether the researcher(s) are using a within-case or a cross-case analysis. Within-case analysis is when a qualitative researcher analyzes one case at a time (i.e., one participant at a time). In comparison, cross-case analysis investigates all cases simultaneously. Event listing is an example of a time-ordered within-case analysis. Event listing is a flow chart that organizes events by time periods and sorts them into categories. In comparison, a case-ordered descriptive meta-matrix is an example of a cross-case analysis. A case-ordered descriptive meta-matrix contains descriptive data from all cases, and the cases are ordered by the main construct of interest (Morse, 2010).

Once the style and order of qualitative analysis is chosen, most qualitative analysis techniques can be organized around four types of data, including: talk (e.g., constant comparison analysis), observation (e.g., conversation analysis), drawings/photographs/videos (e.g., domain analysis), and documents (e.g., text mining; Leech & Onwuegbuzie, 2008). While soft boundaries lie between qualitative coding strategies and a data analysis framework, researchers can generally choose from a plethora of coding processes, including descriptive coding, numerical coding, open coding, process coding, theoretical coding, in vivo coding, focused coding, axial coding, and selective coding. Though the intricacies vary among qualitative data analysis techniques, the objective of most is to attempt to achieve a sense of saturation or in-depth understanding of a construct.

The next aspect of the qualitative analysis process involves transforming the coded information into clusters of meaning and, through a theming process that is idiosyncratic to the methodological approach, separate yet connected primary and secondary themes are described. The themes are housed within a structural description that shares the themes collective meaning and narrative (e.g., the phenomenon, the grounded theory). At this point in the process, the themes and structural description will be carefully integrated with the quantitative information (i.e., point of interface) to determine meta-inferences (Onwuegbuzie & Combs, 2010).

QUANTITATIVE ANALYSIS

Quantitatively, once researchers collect numerical data, they must decide if they are going to be conducting a descriptive or inferential analysis. A descriptive analysis can be in the form of an exploratory analysis (e.g., exploratory factor analysis, cluster analysis, correspondence analysis). Descriptive analysis can also be in the form of measures of central tendency, variability position, and distributional shape. Generally, researchers conducting an inferential analysis of the quantitative data must make two initial decisions, parametric analysis or nonparametric analysis. Investigations requiring a parametric analysis will use either general linear model analysis or non-general linear analysis (e.g., predictive discriminant analysis). Researchers engaging in nonparametric analysis use measures of association, single-population tests, two-population comparisons, and several-population comparisons (Morse, 2010).

Eventually the descriptive data analysis will turn the numerical information into descriptive statistics and the researcher and/or research team will determine the significance of the findings. Similarly, all inferential analyses will be transformed into inferential statistics and the researcher and/or research team will work to determine the significance of the findings. At this point in the process, the inferential and/or descriptive information will be carefully integrated with the qualitative information (i.e., point of interface) to determine meta-inferences.

The Point of Interface

While every mixed methods study has at least one point of interface (i.e., point in which qualitative and quantitative results are integrated), generally speaking, the points of interface can be at any and/or all of the following stages: research questions, purposes, methods, methodology, philosophical integration, data analysis, and findings (Schoonenboom & Johnson, 2017). This is essentially where the "mixed" in mixed methods research was derived from. Mixing has to do with carefully integrating the various qualitative and quantitative components of an investigation. Determining and justifying how and when the results will be integrated is one of the most important decisions that mixed methods researchers must make. In addition to the careful consideration of the point of interface, mixed methods researchers using the explanatory and exploratory designs must remember to fully complete each phase and consider the separate qualitative and quantitative results. Following the analysis and interpretation of the phase-based results, researchers begin to consider the ways qualitative findings help to explain the quantitative results (explanatory) and vice versa (exploratory).

At this point, regarding explanatory and exploratory designs, it should clear that the full qualitative and quantitative phases must be completed sequentially and then merged at strategic points. In addition, the qualitative, quantitative, and mixed findings are always connected to one or more of the research questions outlined at the beginning of the investigation. Both exploratory and explanatory traditions require that the researchers connect the analysis of the initial data set to the collection of the second data set and provide a final merging of both results. For example, an exploratory researcher would use the results of the initial qualitative analysis to create a point of interface that would result in the creation of a quantitative protocol. Similarly, an explanatory research team would use the initial quantitative results as the point of interface to determine what results needed deeper exploration during the qualitative phase. The qualitative product that would be produced during interface is often in the form of interview questions. Following the completion of phase two of the explanatory/exploratory study, the research team would carefully merge the findings of both threads. This merging can take many forms. For example, it could be in the form of a meta-inference and/or a detailed narrative of the convergent and divergent results.

INCREASING THE RIGOR OF EXPLANATORY AND EXPLORATORY APPROACHES

One method for increasing the rigor of the explanatory and exploratory approaches is keeping the qualitative and quantitative threads separate and, while conducting each separate methodology, following the separate methodological principles and assumptions closely (i.e., inclusivity). For example, when using the explanatory approach (QUAN → qual) the principles and assumptions of the secondary qualitative methodology must be completely followed even though the qualitative framework is less prominent than the quantitative thread. Similarly, when using an exploratory approach (QUAL → quan) the principles and assumptions of both frameworks must be followed.

Sampling

One aspect of mixed methods rigor that deserves special attention is sampling. Attending to the principles and assumption of qualitative and quantitative sampling is essential for attaining rigor. For example, it invalidates the exploratory project to use the qualitative sampling strategy and population for the secondary quantitative phase. Remember, a quantitative researcher would consider a qualitative sample to be too small (i.e., lacking statistical power) and if the sample were collected in a purposeful manner, a quantitative researcher would label it as being biased (i.e., selection bias; Morse, 2010). Instead of using the same strategy or population, the supplemental quantitative phase would gather a new random sample from the population. Similarly, while the explanatory approach begins with a quantitative sampling method, it would switch to a qualitative sampling method during the second phase. Qualitative researchers would see a quantitative sample as being too large and inappropriate due to its being based on random sampling principles and assumptions. The second phase of an explanatory framework would use a non-probability sampling method to capture a qualitative sample based on qualitative assumptions.

Points of Interface

Eventually the researcher(s) will need to increase the mixed methods rigor through integrating the secondary thread into the primary thread. As previously mentioned, this can and should happen at multiple procedural points; however, the rigor of the explanatory and exploratory approach is greatly enhanced when the analysis and results are carefully integrated. Explanatory mixed methods design utilizes an *analytic point of interface* by using the quantitative results to construct the qualitative protocol (e.g., questionnaire), while exploratory researchers can use the initial qualitative results to inform the creation of a quantitative measure (e.g., survey). Following the completion of both threads, both explanatory and exploratory researchers will engage in the *results point of interface*. To increase rigor, the results section is presented with the combined findings of both threads. This combination could be in the form of a narrative, table(s), and/or figure(s) (Morse, 2010; Onwuegbuzie & Combs, 2010).

Respecting Philosophical Integration

Wrestling with the intricacies of two paradigmatic hierarchies can seem intimidating; however, being mentally prepared for the unique expectations of each methodology reminds researchers of the overall direction of the project, the philosophical assumptions, procedures, theory, and the methods that are driving each phase. The inductive nature of qualitative inquiry and the deductive spirit of quantitative inquiry are great starting points when developing a mental model of a phase. From an inductive perspective, the researcher is focused on drawing information from new emergent data (e.g., patterns, clusters, themes). Deductive-based research is centered on developing and testing hypotheses that are based on previously established theory. Whether the researcher is operating from a qualitative (inductive) or quantitative (deductive) framework, this very general philosophy provides an overall direction.

When engaging in the various aspects of the philosophical integration, it is essential to maintain consistency with the entire paradigm and to provide clear justification for decisions. Of critical importance is the adherence to the pragmatics of the theory, methodology, and methods of a phase. These three levels demonstrate to your audience the pragmatics of your adherence to a rigorous methodology. For example, if an exploratory researcher follows an initial phenomenological framework for the first phase of the investigation, they will need to adhere to the theory of phenomenology (i.e., subcategory of interpretivism), decide on a phenomenological methodology (e.g., descriptive, Hermeneutic, transcendental), and the associated methods (e.g., horizontalization, theming, descriptive coding). In addition, the researcher(s) will provide justifications for various aspects of the research process. This careful management and jurying of decisions will create a strong sense of procedural adherence, which is a common element of qualitative rigor (Flynn et al., 2019).

Increasing Rigor Through Validity and Trustworthiness

Depending on the quantitative methodology being used, there will be different methods for enhancing the rigor of a study. Generally, the degree of internal and external and internal validity in a quantitative investigation equates to a higher degree of rigor. Regarding quantitative sampling, studies are generally considered more valid if there is a higher degree of representation between the sample and the population that is targeted for generalization. In a similar respect, the sample size will impact the external validity of the study and, if the sample is too small, the statistical power will be limited. Table 17.2 provides information on minimum sample size recommendations.

While it is helpful to understand minimum standards, it is important to remember that rigorous quantitative studies provide more than the bare minimum. The fewer participants the lower the statistical power and the fewer statistically significant relationships and differences will be

TABLE 17.2 **Sample Size Minimums**

THEORETICAL NATURE	RESEARCH DESIGN	MINIMUM SAMPLE SIZE	CITATION
Deductive	Experimental	21 part. per group	(Onwuegbuie et al., 2004)
Deductive	Correlational	64 part. one-tailed, 82 part. two-tailed	(Onwuegbuie et al., 2004)
Deductive	Causal comparative	51 part. per group one-tailed, 64 part. two-tailed	(Onwuegbuie et al., 2004)
Inductive	Case study	3–5 part.	(Creswell, 2005)
Inductive	Grounded theory	15 part.	(Creswell, 2005)
Inductive	Phenomenology	10 part.	(Creswell, 2005)

NOTE: part., participants.

identified. Quantitative researchers utilizing inferential statistics are interested in having enough statistical significance to reject the null hypothesis when the null hypothesis is false. In order to do this efficiently, quantitative researchers need enough participants to achieve an adequate amount of power and a large enough effect size to determine the power of the intervention. This power ensures the researcher that the statistically significant effect is not due to chance or error. Effect size is a related concept that determines the extent of the impact the independent variable has on the dependent variable (see Chapter 4 for a review).

In addition to quantitative sample representation and size, selection bias can symbolize a significant threat to internal validity and rigor. In the context of an experimental study, selection bias is evident if non-comparable participants in a study are assigned to treatment groups. This skews the results since certain predispositions may make participants more predisposed to a treatment response. For example, if non-depressed individuals are placed in the experimental treatment sample for a study on the effects of a treatment on participant depression level, they will likely have favorable outcomes because they were not depressed to begin with.

From a qualitative perspective, there is evidence (Flynn & Korcuska, 2018a; Flynn & Korcuska, 2018b) that rigor is increased when researchers collect multiple data collection points (e.g., interviews, focus group, documents) and triangulate this diversity of data on the comprehensive understanding of a construct. Similarly, qualitative rigor is enhanced through conducting multiple rounds of high quality interviews with the same individuals (Flynn et al., 2019). This additional interviewing provides clarification and a deeper understanding of the construct(s) being explored (i.e., rigor). For example, consider the exploration of a sensitive topic such as the cognitive process of women who have sought an abortion. Whereas one interview with a participant may scrape the surface, through conducting multiple in-depth semi-structured interviews with the same person, the participant(s) may start to feel comfortable enough to share their true thoughts around the process. This in-depth expression of the participants' thoughts and feelings illustrates the "quality" in qualitative research and is important to the creation of rigorous findings.

As described throughout this textbook (Chapters 1, 10, 11, 12, 13, and 16), the employment of qualitative trustworthiness strategies greatly enhances the rigor of qualitative research. Lincoln and Guba's (1985) trustworthiness criteria includescredibility, dependability, transferability, and confirmability. *Credibility* ensures the quality of the qualitative investigation. An example of a trustworthiness strategy centered on credibility includes reflexivity (e.g., field journaling).

Reflexivity is important because the researcher's subjective experiences always affects what and how they write. *Dependability* ensures that the qualitative process of inquiry was traceable, documented, and logical. One method for ensuring dependability is triangulation. Triangulation ensures dependability through taking data from a variety of sources and converging on a deep and consistent understanding of the process. *Transferability* is a type of qualitative external validity and is primarily centered on ensuring that a phenomenon is transferable from case to case. Thick and rich descriptions of the data is one method for ensuring some level of transferability. The thickness and richness can be achieved through recording participant's intentions, circumstances, motivations, and strategies related to the action being explored. *Confirmability* demonstrates the accuracy of the findings and reveals that the conclusions were not created by the researcher. Member checks are a common method for ensuring confirmability. During the member checking process, participants are sent their transcript, codes, emergent themes, and associated quotes. Following the dissemination of this information, participants are invited to negotiate and/or confirm the researcher's interpretation of their interview (Creswell, 2005).

MULTICULTURAL CONSIDERATIONS

Human subjects research, multiculturalism, and social justice issues are closely intertwined. In the world of research, the lines around these issues become gray as multiculturally competent research has begun to acknowledge the definition and aims of socially just research and practice; namely, the deliberate effort to eliminate inequity and inequality (Lyons & Bike, 2013). While multicultural competency, skills, and awareness are centered on attaining knowledge, skills, sensitivity, acceptance, and context, social justice promotes dissemination of power, access, privilege, and justice at the system level. We live in a world where justice and equity are not always upheld as inalienable, and therefore certain avenues of service and study can be conduits for social advocacy, individual and systemic change, improved cultural awareness, and enhanced equality in the interpersonal social environment in which we learn and live. Given the multicultural and social justice emphasis in the behavioral sciences, it only seems normal for researchers in these fields to seek approaches that combine the generalizability of quantitative studies with the in-depth, contextually nuanced essence of qualitative research. This powerful combination has the ability to help others understand the interpersonal and intrapersonal narratives of various cultures (i.e., multiculturalism), while providing enough statistical power to generalize and create change (i.e., social justice).

The accreditation of graduate programs provides standards for research-based competency. As with the American Psychological Association (APA), the Commission on Accreditation for Marriage and Family Therapy Education (COAMFTE), and the Council on Social Work Education (CSWE), the Council for Accreditation of Counseling and Related Education Programs (CACREP) emphasizes multicultural research considerations (CACREP, 2016). Counseling trainees are expected to learn culturally pertinent techniques for conducting research. Explanatory and exploratory research approaches use the strength of quantitative validation methods (e.g., rigor of internal/external validity, care with participant selection, reduction of bias, attention to the validity and reliability of instruments) to ensure results are accurate and unbiased. Similarly, through deeply exploring the cultural and personal experiences of participants, qualitative research is uniquely situated to empower participants in research in the behavioral sciences to understand multicultural issues and actions. Ideally, every qualitative phase of inquiry adheres to rigorous trustworthiness and multicultural standards through all phases of the research process.

Challenges can come up because qualitative research is subjective in nature and, by design, qualitative results are not generalizable to a population. Researchers using qualitative designs cannot ethically describe their findings as generalizing to a larger sample. Similarly, quantitative investigations are subject to researcher bias and error, and without the correct power and effect size, the results can lack accuracy. While qualitative findings do not generalize to a population and are more focused on the emergent nature of in-depth thematic results, quantitative results may inaccurately generalize results to a population or compare those from the dominant cultural to minority groups for malicious purposes.

Though there are strengths and weaknesses associated with each thread, a key component to being an ethical, multiculturally sensitive, and competent researcher, is the researcher's own level of sensitivity to social justice and multicultural issues. Maintaining multicultural competence requires the frequent and continuous exploration of culture (e.g., literature, research, professional development), social justice issues (e.g., keeping up with world events, advocating for fair and just cultural behavior), one's own beliefs (e.g., personal reflection, taking part in counseling), and how those personal and professional phenomena intersect with the research-oriented analysis of the participants.

LIMITATIONS TO EXPLANATORY AND EXPLORATORY MIXED METHODS RESEARCH

While there are many positive and important aspects to mixed methods research (e.g., rigor, enhancement of pertinent multicultural issues, analysis confirmation, enhanced validity, and trustworthiness), explanatory and exploratory mixed methods design have limitations that are deserving of consideration. First, the sequential nature of these designs sets the stage for a very lengthy and potentially expensive research effort. While the qualitative design may take more overall time, it can be difficult, at times, to collect a large enough quantitative sample. Furthermore, while some research teams may be supported by a grant, others will need to secure the appropriate personnel to conduct the study. This can often come at an actual fiscal cost or it can be interpreted when considering the time spent in the research process.

Another limitation to explanatory and exploratory mixed methods research, and perhaps all mixed methods research, includes the expertise needed on the research team. Once the research traditions have been specified, it is ideal if every member of the research team has expertise in the relevant qualitative and quantitative research traditions. If this optimal condition is not available, it is important to have separate members with the relevant expertise and a continuous research team consensus process.

From an ethical vantage point, all research designs employing multiple and unique phases can run into issues with their respective institutional review board (IRB). Due to the relevance of the first phase in creating the second phase, it can be difficult, if not impossible, to predict what will take place and what will be needed until after the first iteration is complete. This usually requires multiple IRB applications relevant for the given phase. While it is ethical and extremely helpful to have oversight, it can take extra time, resources, and finances to go through multiple IRB reviews (Creswell & Plano-Clark, 2017).

A final limitation is the need to have a large enough quantitative phase to produce non-bias results and the in-depth data needed to ensure the qualitative phase has enough data collection points to create in-depth trustworthy findings. Table 17.2 provides cited minimum sample sizes explicated in the literature for major qualitative and quantitative approaches; however, the correct sample size for a particular qualitative and quantitative research thread is ultimately decided during the investigation. These decisions are bound to particular processes, such as the research tradition, population of interest, research team consensus, principles of probability theory, and the expertise of the principal investigator.

Case Study: Exploratory Design

Bibbo, J., & Proulx, C. M. (2019). The impact of a care recipient's pet on caregiving burden, satisfaction, and mastery: A pilot investigation. *Human-Animal Interaction Bulletin, 7*(2), 81–102.

BACKGROUND

The field of Human-Animal Interaction has been anecdotally studied since humans began keeping records (hieroglyphic drawings in caves in Australia and Egypt, for example) and has evolved to include empirical, rigorous studies designed to examine relationships between pets and their people across the life span. Research in this field has expanded to include studies on the value of companion animals in various environments from early childhood classrooms (Uttley, 2013) to hospitals and nursing homes (Souter & Miller, 2007). Specific developmental domains are also being examined, mostly focusing on social–emotional and physical health (see Purewal et al., 2017) and loneliness and cognitive abilities (see Valiyamattam, 2013).

The study by Bibbo and Proulx (2019) addresses a gap in the research literature by examining the relationship between a human caretaker and their clients (care recipient) pet as an extension of the studies focusing on the direct relationship older adult (care recipient) and their pets. Dr. Bibbo is a research scientist at the Benjamin Rose Institute on Aging in Ohio where her studies center on healthy aging. Dr. Proulx is an associate professor at the University of Missouri in the Human Development and Family Science program. Her research focuses on the well-being of adults within various roles adopted throughout adulthood and their close relationships.

Bibbo and Proulx (2019) developed this pilot study with the framework of Role Theory and understanding that multiple roles exist in individuals' lives. Role Theory is commonly utilized when characterizing caregiving relationships and can be applied when exploring both negative and positive impacts of these relationships. Examples of caregiving topics that have been studied include caregiver burden, caregiver satisfaction, and caregiver mastery. Our interpretation of this case is based solely on our review of the 2019 article and may not fully reflect the research team's complete efforts.

While the caregiving topics mentioned previously have been examined in numerous studies, the relationship between caregivers and their clients' companion animal has not been. Therefore, Bibbo and Proulx (2019) designed a pilot study with an exploratory paradigm to answer the research questions: (a) To what extent were caregiver outcomes associated with pet care tasks and perceived costs of care recipients pet care, and (b) are the associations moderated by the relationships among the caregiver, care recipient, and pet?

RESEARCH PROCESS

Participants for this study were recruited through online and in-person support groups and caregiving organizations that provided flyers and links to the study for their members. Study participants were self-identified as meeting the following criteria: over the age of 18 years; caring for an adult over the age of 50 who lived with at least one dog or cat; did not consider themselves as the owner or co-owner of the pet; had provided care for a minimum of 6 months; was not paid for the care; and had an established relationship with the care recipient.

The researchers opted to design the study to allow both dog and cat owners to participate based on the similarity of tasks related to the care of the two species. However, study participants were instructed to respond to survey items based on the work they did for a specific pet, not all or each of the pets in the household. The online survey was designed as an anonymous survey taking approximately 40 minutes to complete. The researchers provided participants an opportunity to enter a drawing for a $25 VISA gift card.

Data were collected only from the caregivers; no care recipients participated in the survey. In addition to collected demographic variables, the online survey items included questions concerning the following constructs: caregiver burden, satisfaction, and mastery; pet caregiving tasks; costs of and emotional closeness to the pet; care recipients emotional bond with the pet; mutuality with care recipients; and inadequate help. The majority of these constructs were measured through specific pre-developed tools with Cronbach alpha levels of 0.76 to 0.94, ensuring that the study had a solid level of reliability.

DISCUSSION

The majority of participants were adult females who were taking care of a relative, most commonly with the primary diagnosis of Alzheimer's disease. Results from this study showed that the type of relationship that the caregiver had with care recipients' pets had a significant impact to the relationship with the care recipient. In other words, if the caregivers' relationship with the pet was positive the care recipients' outcomes were generally improved. One unexpected finding was that if the caregiver perceived the associated financial costs of having a pet as high, this stressor had more of a negative outcome for the care recipient.

As an exploratory study, the sample size was small, and results are not generalizable. However, participants provided insights that may help future research but also support caregivers. Caregivers with stronger emotional connections to the care recipients' pets reported greater mastery in their caregiving skills and indicated less stress. This finding supports previous research that pets provide emotional support to owners and others that they interact with regardless of the relationship.

While the results only provide subjective experiences, they show the importance of the interconnectedness of several relationships to the care of older adults. Further research to quantify the effects of the relationships and the specific impacts of the pet relationship on the emotional and physical wellness of the caregiver is needed in order to make policy and practice recommendations.

Khalid, A., & Dildar, S. (2019). Effect of pet interaction on stress reduction and positive mood enhancement among pet-owners and non-owners. *Human-Animal Interaction Bulletin, 7*(1), 77–104.

BACKGROUND

Decades of research in the field of Human-Animal Interaction have shown that humans have strong, emotional attachments to companion animals based on the caregiver relationship. Recent experiments have shown that companion animals may have an impact on physiological aspects in humans. The study by Khalid and Dildar (2019) was designed to further explore the impact of companion animals on the specific areas of human stress and mood through an explanatory design. Our interpretation of this case is based solely on our review of the 2019 article and may not fully reflect the research team's complete efforts.

Aliya Khalid was a consulting psychiatrist in Pakistan and Saadia Dildar was an Assistant Professor at the Government College University also in Pakistan. In their article, Khalid and Dildar present a review of the cross-cultural aspects of and research in the field of human–animal interaction, specifically as applied to experimental studies showing the benefits of interacting with companion animals. To expand on the existing body of research, the authors designed an experiment based on the qualitative results of how interacting with companion animals reduces stress levels and improves mood as evidenced through quantitative measures.

This study employed an experimental design with five distinct groups (four experimental groups and one control group). Each of the experimental groups was given a different intervention: pet owners were given an interaction time-period with a dog; non-pet owners were given an interaction time-period with a dog; pet owners were given an interaction time-period with a cat; and non-pet owners were given an interaction time-period with a cat. The control group contained both pet owners and non-pet owners who were assigned to read magazines during the same amount of interaction time. Research goals included examining the effect of pet interaction on stress reduction and positive mood enhancement and to investigate if the amount of time spent engaged in pet interactions impacted stress and mood.

RESEARCH PROCESS

Study participants included 180 university students ranging in age from 18 to 26 years. Participants completed a survey protocol that included a demographic survey and two survey instruments for a total of 52 items for the pre-intervention data collection period. The post-intervention data collection included only the two measures (40 items). Participants, based on random selection, were assigned to intervention groups and interventions lasted no longer than 5 minutes.

The researchers conducted reliability analyses on the measures, and ANOVAs and Independent Sample *t*-tests on data collected. These analyses ensured that the measures had acceptable psychometric properties, thus, results could be deemed valid and reliable. The ANOVAs and *t*-tests compared pre- and post-intervention data to measure any change attributed to the intervention experienced.

DISCUSSION

Results from this study provided evidence that interactions with animals can positively affect stress and mood in humans. A major finding from this study was the amount of time that the interactions needed to be in order to effect a difference. Previous research had found that a minimum of 5 minutes was required to effect change; however, this study found that interaction times of under 5 minutes spent with an animal had similar influence on stress levels and perceived mood.

This study was the first empirical study to examine the influence of interactions with pets on stress levels and perceived mood in a Pakistani sample. Including samples from culturally diverse populations and geographical locations is necessary to fully understand the impact of animals on human development. Additional research should be conducted with other types of pets (reptiles, birds), in conjunction with data regarding the type of relationships or feelings that people have toward that animal (attachment scales).

SUMMARY

This chapter introduced you to the explanatory and exploratory mixed methods research designs. Readers explored the philosophical, pragmatic, and contextual aspects to explanatory and exploratory mixed methods design. This chapter explored, deeply, the fundamental elements of each approach and the specific blueprints for enhancing mixed methods rigor. As you consider the various elements of mixed methods research design it is important to remember that, in many ways, mixed methods research symbolizes a new frontier for research in the behavioral sciences. It is helpful to engage mixed methods research projects with a comprehensive and knowledgeable research team and to take careful steps to thoughtfully integrate all of the various steps, procedures, areas for interface, and ethical considerations. Working closely with a mixed methods research mentor, taking foundational coursework, and collaborating with your IRB are important initial steps for graduate students new to mixed methods research. Good luck in your future work with the explanatory and exploratory approaches; we hope you use this chapter as a platform to create groundbreaking research.

STUDENT ACTIVITIES

Exercise 1: Understanding How Paradigms Connect

Directions: Review the below information and answer/respond to the reflection questions.

The notion that qualitative and quantitative traditions are distinct is centered on different philosophical principles that are integrated into their respective paradigms. When considering the various integration principles, qualitative and quantitative research paradigms are viewed as having very different philosophical assumptions (i.e., paradigm debate; see Gage, 1989). Kuhn (1970) capitalized on this consideration when describing paradigms as incommensurable. While it may be helpful to consider differences between qualitative and quantitative paradigms, it may be equally helpful to consider how they are connected and similar.

- Describe how quantitative and qualitative sampling methods are similar
- Consider the epistemology of objectivism and subjectivism. How are these two philosophies relatable?

■ Consider the semantics around qualitative interview questions and survey questions. Go online and look up the intricacies of each approach. How are they similar?

Exercise 2: Develop a Survey Based on Qualitative Themes

Directions: Review the following instructions and answer the follow-up questions.

Exploratory mixed methods research includes a survey development variant in which initial qualitative themes are transformed into survey questions. Review the Flynn and Black (2011) article:

Flynn, S. V., & Black, L. L. (2011). An emergent theory of altruism and self-interest. *Journal of Counseling & Development, 89,* 459–469. https://doi.org/10.1002/j.1556-6676.2011.tb02843.x

Next, consider the emergent qualitative themes that are reviewed in the results section. Next, review the following online resources for designing effective survey questions: https://www.uxbooth.com/articles/the-essential-guide-to-writing-effective-survey-questions/.

Using both resources, turn all of the emergent themes in the article into effective survey questions.

Exercise 3: Article Review

Directions: Review the below instructions and answer the questions.

Go to your university's online EBSCO Data Base and find Academic Search Premier. Search and find a mixed methods article that displays an explanatory or exploratory mixed methods design. Review the article in its entirety and answer the following questions related to mixed methods integration.

1. Is the rationale for a mixed method approach clearly specified?
2. Are the qualitative and quantitative data systematically integrated in such a way that maximizes the strengths and minimizes the weaknesses of each approach?
3. Is the form of data integration clearly specified?
4. Do the authors clearly identify how they integrate quantitative and qualitative data either through merging, connecting, or embedding data?
5. At what phase of the study was the mixed methods approach introduced (e.g., pilot phase, program evaluation, embedded in longitudinal study? (Weisner & Fiese, 2011, p. 797)

Exercise 4: Increasing the Rigor of Mixed Methods Research

Directions: Follow the instructions and respond to the related questions.

Go to your university's online EBSCO Data Base and find Academic Search Premier. Find an article that uses an explanatory or exploratory approach. Review the entire article and answer the following questions related to rigor.

1. Do the explicated qualitative and quantitative samples seem rigorous and/or meet the minimum sample size standards for the approach?
2. Do the authors justify their approach, population, validation, and trustworthiness procedures?

3. How many data collection points does the qualitative phase have? Does this seem rigorous?

4. Do the authors describe the areas of interface? Does the study appear to be rigorously conducted?

ADDITIONAL RESOURCES

Software Recommendations

NVivo Software (https://www.qsrinternational.com)

CAQDAS Software (https://www.maxqda.com)

ATLAS ti (https://atlasti.com)

MaxQDA (https://maxda.com)

Statistical Package for the Social Sciences (SPSS): (https://www.ibm.com/analytics/spss-statistics-software)

R: (https://www.r-project.org/)

SAS: (https://www.sas.com/en_us/software/stat.html)

Mplus: (https://www.statmodel.com/)

Helpful Links

- http://salmapatel.co.uk/academia/the-research-paradigm-methodology-epistemology-and-ontology-explained-in-simple-language/

- https://www.ncbi.nlm.nih.gov/pmc/articles/PMC4485510/

- https://libguides.usc.edu/writingguide/quantitative

- https://www.ncbi.nlm.nih.gov/pmc/articles/PMC5602001/

- https://link.springer.com/article/10.1007/s11186-019-09345-5

- http://coalition4evidence.org/468-2/publications/

Helpful Books

Creswell, J. W. (2012). *Educational research: Planning, conducting, and evaluating quantitative and qualitative research* (4th ed.). Pearson.

Creswell, J., & Plano Clark, V. (2017). *Designing and conducting mixed methods research* (3rd ed.). SAGE.

Cohen, J. (1988). *Statistical power analysis for the behavioral sciences* (2nd ed.). Erlbaum.

Cozby, P. C. (2009). *Methods in behavioral research* (10th ed.). McGraw-Hill.

Greene, J. C. (2007). *Mixed methods in social inquiry*. Jossey-Bass.

Morrow, S. L., & Smith, M. L. (2000). Qualitative research for counseling psychology. In S. D. Brown & R. W. Lent (Eds.), *Handbook of counseling psychology* (3rd ed., pp. 199–230). Wiley.

Robson, C., & McCartan, K. (2016). *Real world research* (4th ed.). Wiley.

Tashakkori, A., & Teddlie, C. (Eds.). (2010). *Handbook of mixed methods in social and behavioral research*. SAGE.

Teddlie, C., & Tashakkori, A. (2009). *Foundations of mixed methods research: Integrating quantitative and qualitative approaches in the social and behavioral sciences*. SAGE.

Helpful Videos

- https://www.youtube.com/watch?v=kdhGFdPWQyI

- https://www.youtube.com/watch?v=jlol_bG6kAQ

- https://www.youtube.com/watch?v=_dFePs6Th00

- https://www.youtube.com/watch?v=jjrfLCdE9Ws

KEY REFERENCES

Only key references appear in the print edition. The full reference list appears in the digital product found on http://connect.springerpub.com/content/book/978-0-8261-4385-3/part/part04/chapter/ch17

Creswell, J., & Plano Clark, V. (2017). *Designing and conducting mixed methods research* (3rd ed.). SAGE.

Crotty, M. (2003). *The foundations of social research: Meaning and perspective in the research process.* SAGE.

Flynn, S. V., & Korcuska, J. S. (2018a). Credible phenomenological research: A mixed methods study. *Counselor Education & Supervision, 57*, 34–50. https://doi.org/10.1002/ceas.12092

Flynn, S. V., & Korcuska, J. S. (2018b). Grounded theory research design: An investigation into practices and procedures. *Counseling Outcome Research and Evaluation, 9*, 102–116. https://doi.org/10.1080/21 501378.2017.1403849

Flynn, S. V., Korcuska, J. S., Brady, N. V., & Hays, D. G. (2019). A 15-year content analysis of three qualitative research traditions. *Counselor Education & Supervision, 58*, 49–63. https://doi.org/10.1002/ ceas.12123

Lincoln, Y. S. & Guba, E. G. (1985). *Naturalistic inquiry.* SAGE.

Morgan, D. L. (2014). Pragmatism as a paradigm for social research. *Qualitative Inquiry, 20*, 1045–1053. https://doi.org/10.1177/1077800413513733

Tashakkori, A., & Teddlie, C. (2003). *Handbook of mixed methods in social and behavioral research.* SAGE.

CHAPTER 18

MIXED METHODS RESEARCH: TRANSFORMATIVE AND MULTIPHASE DESIGNS

Stephen V. Flynn and Samantha Waterhouse

LEARNING OBJECTIVES

After reading this chapter, you will be able to:

- Comprehend the philosophical integration of transformative and multiphase research design
- Recognize how to maximize the rigor of transformative and multiphase design
- Define the data analysis process for transformative and multiphase designs
- Explain how mixed methods traditions can enhance multicultural competency

INTRODUCTION TO TRANSFORMATIVE AND MULTIPHASE DESIGNS

This chapter emphasizes two different approaches to mixed methods research. The transformative mixed methods approach creates new social justice–oriented research by employing qualitative and quantitative methods within a single phase, sequential phases, or concurrently. Typically, there is a stronger/main thread within this approach and all relevant transformative procedures (e.g., research questions, sampling strategies) are aligned to be social justice and action oriented. The multiphase mixed methods tradition is specifically designed for large-scale investigations that employ separate and equally emphasized qualitative and quantitative methodological frameworks. The order of data collection and analysis can either be sequential or concurrent, and each phase builds on the previous thread culminating in a fuller understanding of the overall project objectives.

Behavioral science researchers are often interested in investigating a variety of social justice issues, including (but not limited to) privilege, poverty, disease, war, discrimination, and power imbalances (Sweetman et al., 2010). In order to help those in need, researchers employ methodologies that are sensitive to marginalized and disadvantaged groups. The transformative mixed methods approach accomplishes this by providing a platform for generalizing social justice–oriented quantitative data and using qualitative data to explore the voices and lived experiences of participants. The transformative framework emphasizes social justice and change by engaging the research process in a manner that thoroughly incorporates this ideology into all relevant methodological procedures and research design phases. This allows researchers to use a social justice lens when defining the problem, creating research questions, searching the literature, sampling participants, conducting and interpreting the data analysis, and reporting the results in a manner that creates social change.

The transformative theoretical framework is the overarching research philosophical stance within the paradigm. Often scholars refer to this approach as having a transformative paradigm, however, the transformative approach is also influenced by the philosophy of pragmatism. Pragmatism, based on the writings of late 19th and early 20th century philosophers, is relevant to this action-oriented approach to research (Morgan, 2014). Figure 18.1 describes the transformative mixed methods research process. The two large curved arrows around the perimeter of the figure demonstrate the overarching transformative theory and paradigm of pragmatism. Within the curved arrows is a three-sided arrow indicating the importance of the qualitative, quantitative, and mixing data collection and mixing components.

Although most mixed methods frameworks promote separate yet interrelated aspects of the research process, the multiphase mixed methods design is intended to examine research questions on a large scale (i.e., multiple separate interconnected studies conducted over many years). Multiphase research studies use an iterative, sequential, and connected series of separate qualitative and quantitative investigations that progressively respond to the overall purpose of the investigation. After the distinct, large scale, qualitative and quantitative studies are used to fully answer the separate research questions, researcher can mix the results or tie the studies together within the write up of the discussion and implications sections of the manuscript (Creswell & Plano-Clark, 2017). For example, to determine the student retention issues at a university, the multiphase research team initially conducted qualitative semi-structured individual interviews with stakeholders and students. The next phase involved a campus-wide survey aiming to determine the students' experience of campus life and student affairs. The third phase involved qualitative focus groups with at-risk students including: students of color, first generation college students, and those from low socio-economic status to determine their experience of the learning atmosphere.

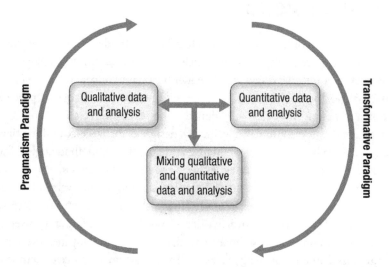

FIGURE 18.1 The Transformative Design Research Process.

NOTE: Three directional arrows, interconnection of the mixed methods process; large outer arrows, the larger philosophical integration.

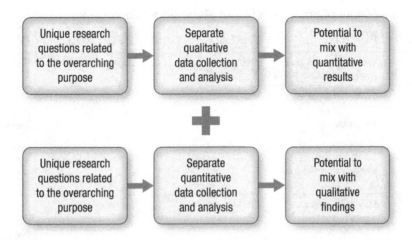

FIGURE 18.2 The Multiphase Mixed Methods Process.

NOTE: Arrows, direction of research action; addition symbol, addition of the separate research process.

Figure 18.2 describes the multiphase mixed methods research process. The two separate qualitative and quantitative threads symbolize the independent nature of the process. The figure could add additional phases and accompanying threads if needed. The final box of each research thread provides the option of allowing the research to mix the findings or to keep them separate. The addition symbol indicates the interconnectedness of the separate studies in answering the phase-based research questions, overall research objectives, and purpose. If both symbolic threads were completed simultaneously, they would be concurrent. If they were completed one after the other, they would be sequential in nature. Once the multiphase sequencing is complete, researchers mix the data at different points (e.g., data collection, interpretation of analysis) in order to elaborate on the results from one phase to the next. Lastly, multiphase researchers often triangulate the overall phase conclusions to ascertain a complete understanding of the study (Bryman, 2006).

The example promoted within Figure 18.2 would be the first phase of a convergent multiphase design. While the figure demonstrates a symbolic representation of the approach, there are many possibilities for multiphase thread configuration. While phase variability exists, all mixed methods studies involve the eventual mixing of qualitative and quantitative threads. For example, if data were sequentially linked in three phases, a research team could utilize a more traditional quantitative (phase 1), qualitative (phase 2), and quantitative (phase 3) format. Two alternative arrangements could be a quantitative (phase 1), quantitative (phase 2), and qualitative (phase 3) arrangement, or a qualitative (phase 1), qualitative (phase 2), and quantitative (phase 3) setup.

When comparing transformative and multiphase mixed methods approaches to other traditions, there is a lot of variability. The emphasis with embedded mixed methods design is to collect and analyze a primary data set and a smaller supportive data set within a single phase. Similarly, the explanatory and exploratory mixed methods research design is also centered on starting with a main thread (initial qualitative = exploratory, initial quantitative = explanatory), however it *sequentially* incorporates a less prominent secondary thread into an additional phase instead of embedding the less prominent thread within the same phase (i.e., embedded). Convergent mixed methods design has two threads of equal strength, concurrently converging on each other in an effort to thoroughly understand a construct. Table 18.1 provides information on the purpose,

TABLE 18.1 **The Nature of Prominent Mixed Method Traditions**

NAME	PURPOSE	THREAD EMPHASIS	SEQUENCE	PARADIGM
Convergent	Compare qual and quan data	QUAL + QUAN	Concurrent	Pragmatism
Embedded	Embed a smaller qual/quan into a larger design	QUAN + *qual,* QUAL + *quan,* QUAN → *qual,* QUAL → *quan*	Single phase, sequential	Traditional paradigmatic hierarchy
Explanatory	Use qual results to explain quan results	QUAN → *qual*	Sequential	Traditional paradigmatic hierarchy
Exploratory	Use quan results to explain qual results	QUAL → *quan*	Sequential	Traditional paradigmatic hierarchy
Transformative	Uses qual and quan methods to advance social justice causes	QUAN + qual, QUAL + quan, QUAL + QUAN, QUAN + QUAL QUAL → Quan, QUAN → qual	Concurrent, sequential, single phase	**Transformative paradigm,** pragmatism
Multiphase	Uses separate studies and multiple phases for large projects	QUAL + QUAN, QUAN + QUAL QUAL → Quan, QUAN → qual	Sequential, Concurrent	Pragmatism

NOTE: Bolded, the emphasis of the chapter; qual, qualitative; quan, quantitative; QUAL + QUAN, qualitative and quantitative have equal emphasis in a study; QUAN + *qual,* embedding a smaller qualitative thread into a quantitative design; QUAL + *quan,* embedding a smaller quantitative thread into a qualitative design; QUAN → *qual,* a smaller qualitative thread follows a quantitative phase; QUAL → *quan,* a smaller quantitative thread follows a qualitative phase.

thread emphasis, sequence, and paradigm of the various mixed methods approaches. This table uses Morse's notation system (see Chapter 16 for a review; Morse & Niehaus, 2009).

TRANSFORMATIVE AND MULTIPHASE PHILOSOPHICAL INTEGRATION

Researchers in the behavioral sciences approach their work with a theoretically defined worldview, called a paradigm, which is comprised of a philosophical integration describing how and why knowledge and, in this case, research results are ascertained. Within the context of a paradigm, scholars describe ontology, epistemology, theory, methodology, and methods (Leavy, 2017). Unique to mixed methods designs is pragmatism. Pragmatists promote the notion of action prior to developing in-depth strategies in research. Specifically, classic pragmatism equates equal importance to the research goals, priorities, and the research questions that are driving the project.

According to Onwuegbuzie and Johnson (2006) mixed methods scholars examine their qualitative, quantitative, and mixed methods research paradigmatic beliefs and expressions through an integration of ontological, epistemological, axiological, theoretical, and rhetorical beliefs. Onwuegbuzie and Johnson entitled this process the *paradigmatic mixing legitimation*. In comparison, pragmatism would operate from a more action- and experience-based framework.

John Dewey (1859–1952), a pioneer of pragmatism, postulated two relevant questions that are salient to his (1938) definition of experience. These questions include: (a) What are the sources of our beliefs? and (b) What are the meanings of our actions? Dewey's questions are important to mixed methods research and should be considered when incorporating a pragmatist lens. Because the transformative and multiphase models are based fully (multiphase) and partly (transformative) on pragmatism, researchers will frequently incorporate reflection, journaling, and action into their research procedures to evidence practical adherence to their mixing legitimation (Morgan, 2014; Onwuegbuzie & Johnson, 2006).

Transformative Integration. Transformative mixed method design, including emancipatory and community-based participatory action research (for a review of these two methodologies, see Seedat et al., 2017), is centered on creating research that is change oriented and that advances social justice issues (Mertens, 2009). The mixing of methods in transformative designs is for ideological and value-based reasons. The transformative ontological assumption is centered on exploring the nature of reality based on the different lenses of privilege with which participants and researchers view a phenomenon. Given the emphasis on creating social change, participant opinions about different versions of reality will encompass different levels of legitimacy. For example, if researchers were analyzing the conditions of Haitian immigrant's acculturation process, they would likely prioritize the vantage point of the Haitian immigrant. The researcher(s) bias and opinions about the construct under investigation would be fully explored and, whenever relevant, integrated with the results.

From an epistemological position, a trusting relationship must be formed with the community of interest. According to Mertens (2012), "To understand differing versions of reality and how they are synergistically related to power issues, the researcher needs to establish an interactive link with community members" (p. 807). Epistemological positions like endarkened feminist epistemology (see Dillard, 2000) and the building of coalitions (see Johnson et al., 2009) provide helpful epistemological frameworks.

While embedded, convergent (triangulation), exploratory, explanatory, and multiphase mixed methods research designs use the procedures, sequence, and qualitative/quantitative emphasis as the major defining criterion of their approach, mixed methods researchers using a transformative design apply a theoretical framework as the central organizing feature. The transformative framework affects almost every aspect of the research process (Mertens, 2009), which equates to the researcher taking a social justice position to support the marginalized population(s) under investigation (i.e., action).

The transformative methodological perspective is centered on creating research that is change oriented and that advances social justice issues (Mertens, 2009). The researcher intentionally uses the methods that allow for the most authentic and comprehensive understanding of the social justice issues being explored (Creswell & Plano-Clark, 2017). According to Mertens (2012) "transformative methodological assumptions suggest that researchers start with qualitative data collection methods to learn about the community and begin to establish trusting relationships" (p. 809). For example, after conducting six focus group interviews with a tribal-based American Indian population, the research team developed a survey to quantify supports and barriers participants felt while attending school on the reservation. After completing the research process, the authors would write implications for increasing government support of tribal-based grade schools.

A transformative framework can combine various traditions, use any relevant sequence, and emphasize either qualitative or quantitative threads; however, as previously stated, the key requirement is the maintenance of a social justice theoretical lens throughout the process. Methods are chosen that are best suited for advancing social justice issues in a change-oriented manner

(Martens, 2012). In this sense, concepts like procedural consistency and generalizability are a secondary consideration to the implementation of culturally sound and engaging recruitment strategies, research goals, and purpose.

Multiphase Integration. This textbook considers three common research paradigms, including: (a) pragmatism (Morgan, 2014), (b) a philosophical model that integrates ontology (i.e., form and nature of reality), epistemology (i.e., theory of knowledge acquisition), theoretical stance (i.e., philosophical stance), methodology (i.e., process for discovering what is knowable), and method (i.e., procedures for gathering and analyzing data (Flynn & Korcuska, 2018a, 2018b; Flynn et al., 2019); and (c) the transformative paradigm (Mertens, 2009). When using a multiphase approach, pragmatism guides the mixed methods design (Creswell & Plano Clark, 2017). The pragmatist rejects the traditional paradigmatic hierarchical model and promotes the notion that reality is true as far as it assists individuals in understanding other aspects of an experience. Similarly, truth, pragmatically, equates to what has stood up to scrutiny over time (Baker & Schaltegger, 2015). Larger philosophical discussions are not practical since they represent theoretical arguments that can never be solved (Dillon et al., 2000). For example, pragmatism encourages researchers to engage in empiricism and avoid the forced dichotomies (i.e., dualism) including objectivity versussubjectivity and postpositivist versus constructivism (Kaushik & Walsh, 2019).

According to Kauchik and Walsh (2019), pragmatists view knowledge as having a basis in experience. Everyone's knowledge is unique as it is shaped by their unique experiences. As such, knowledge could also be called "social knowledge." The paradigm of pragmatism is very closely related to the notion that methodology should connect philosophical concepts to concrete methods. In short, the essence of pragmatism includes grounding philosophical threads with the pragmatics of a research design.

Multiphase designs are defined pragmatically by methodological procedures rather than a specific type of paradigmatic hierarchy. They are distinguished by optimizing the rigor of quantitative and qualitative methodological adherence for exploring a single research query. Additionally, multiphase mixed method research design provides a methodological framework for a large-scale multiyear and multiphased program of research. There are always more than two phases to the multiphase research process and the strands can be executed in a sequential or concurrent manner.

TRANSFORMATIVE DESIGN AND DATA COLLECTION

The transformative mixed methods research design is an important approach that has been frequently utilized over the past decade. The transformative tradition has been used with a variety of populations in numerous contexts. A few recent scholarly examples highlight the diverse uses of the transformative mixed methods approach, including: (a) the combination of queer theory and transformative mixed methods design in understanding the relationship between locus of control and the college experience for queer spectrum and trans-spectrum students (Bell, 2018); (b) the role of cultural and social capital in encouraging Latino parents with guiding their children toward post-secondary education (Silva Diaz, 2016); and (c) exploration of the HIV-associated drug abuse related sexual behaviors and aggression among female IV drug users in Puerto Rico (Collazo, 2016).

According to Mertens (2009) the transformative mixed methods design is a valid approach to understanding and exploring power structures that perpetuate social inequities. Leavy (2017) added that the transformative approach is a metaphysical umbrella for research of theoretical perspectives that have a culturally responsive, democratic, and inclusive oriented framework, including (but not limited to) critical race theory, feminist theory, and participatory action research. At least three theoretically based variants of transformative approach have been identified, including the feminist lens transformative variant, disability lens transformative variant, and the socioeconomic class lens transformative variant (Creswell & Plano-Clark, 2017).

The transformative approach is both action-oriented and participatory in nature. The participation is often reflected by the level of community integration by the researcher(s). Transformative researchers should be respectfully integrating into the community of interest to the extent that is possible. Continuous introspection, reflexivity, and research team debriefings are key to enhancing the overall validity and trustworthiness of the approach. Researchers will often form partnerships with the relevant marginalized group(s) and develop unique methods for ensuring within-group participation in the research process. This is typically beyond simply being a participant in the investigation. Common examples include entering and engaging with the community, creating a rigorous trustworthiness experience (member checks, peer debriefing, confirmability and dependability audits), creating authorship experiences for representative contributors, use of an expert panel, and diversifying/triangulating relevant data collection points with the pertinent group members (e.g., survey, focus groups, interviews; Leavy, 2017; Mertens, 2009).

Transformative Data Collection

According to Mertens (2009), data collection methods for a transformative mixed methods research study would primarily include personal reflections, interviews, focus groups, gender analysis, document and artifact review, visual data collection, surveys, tests, and observation. These techniques are similar to those used in most mixed methods traditions, but the difference when used with transformative research is the choice, development, and implementation of the data-collection strategies so that they are grounded in the community and the advancement of human rights. When working together, the community and the researcher(s) make decisions with regard to a data-collection method that is culturally appropriate, reflects a deep understanding of the cultural issues involved, builds trust to obtain valid data, makes modifications that may be necessary to collect data from various groups, and links the data collected to social action.

An avoidance of bias and an acknowledgment of power differential are key factors in data collection for transformative researchers. When conducting this type of mixed method research, researchers begin with the acknowledgment that there is a power differential between themselves and the people in the study. This declaration can be written, spoken, or both. Furthermore, the choice of language is a critical decision for researchers. Being aware of which languages are in use within the communities involved in the research study is crucial. For example, using back translation (i.e., translation of a previously translated document) is a common validation practice when using document data collection methods (Mertens, 2009). The overarching steps for planning the data-collection strategies to use within a transformative mixed methods research study include:

1. Working with community members to determine which data collection strategies will work best for the researchers and the participants of the study. Finding out if any accommodations will be necessary while collecting data, such as interpreters, a person recording interviews, or any visual aids.

2. Planning a pilot test with the chosen data collection strategies before conducting research with actual participants.

3. Determining the frequency that the research team plans to meet with participants during the research process.

4. Planning and confirming with community members on what will be said to participants when making first contact, to set up data collection, and to establish informed consent.

5. Determining how the data will be recorded, whether through self-report, audio recording, digital recording, or taking notes.

6. Thinking about questions or issues that will need to be explored during the data collection process and considering how these may vary for different participants.

7. Ensuring quality in data collection by completing notes and reflections immediately after data collection or checking recordings for clarity post-session.

8. Preparing for how to end the data collection process through reviewing data and findings with participants or providing them with a report (Mertens, 2009).

The Interview. A central data collection method for the transformative approach is the interview. There are many types of interviews that can be used in a transformative approach, such as general qualitative interviews, in-depth interviews, phenomenological interviews, focus groups, oral histories, and ethnographic interviews (Mertens, 2009). Each type of interview has its own procedure that a researcher would have to become comfortable with before using it as a data collection method. It is also important to keep in mind that there can be a number of challenges involved with interviewing, such as having to respond to unexpected participant behaviors during an interview, dealing with the consequences of the researcher's own actions during an interview, having to phrase and negotiate questions during an interview, and dealing with sensitive issues within a community (Mertens, 2009). Before conducting interviews within a community of interest, it would best help the researcher to become familiar with cultural norms and assess how to work within them during the interview process. For example, during a qualitative study (Flynn et al., 2014) focusing on the Native American acculturation process from tribal lands to predominately White culture, the first author consulted with an elder of the tribal-based community under investigation. During this consultation, he was encouraged to have a drink of water prepared prior to the interview and to provide Native American participants some level of compensation for their participation.

Observations, Documents, and Artifacts. Observation and document/artifact review are data collection strategies that are very commonly used within transformative research studies. Observations can be conducted formally or informally, can be made by using a field notes approach or by noting specific behaviors that are of interest, and the researcher can hold different roles as an observer, such as becoming fully or peripherally involved in the community. Document and artifact review can include written, electronic, or hard-copy items ranging from official documents to those created for personal reasons, such as diaries. It is important that the researcher keep in mind issues of power or privilege that can result in the preservation of what a group may consider to be an essential document, where other documents may have been deemed less important and may not have been preserved or could have even been destroyed (Mertens, 2009).

Surveys. Surveys can be used in various ways and can be a support of social transformation or a tool of oppression. The delivery process for a survey can vary, such as over the phone, in person, in the mail, or electronic. When developing a survey it is important to keep in mind how the meaning of the items will be interpreted by the community it is intended for. This is a necessary concern because the developer may not have access to the community they wish to survey while creating the items, and it is critical that the target population be able to understand the concepts being asked about in the same way that the survey developer does (Mertens, 2009). To ensure the questions are well-developed, ethically sound, and to confirm the influence of the community of interest in the creation of the survey, researchers will invite individuals within the community being explored to serve in an important role such as expert panel member, auditor, or coauthor.

MULTIPHASE DESIGN

The innovative use of multiphase mixed methods design has substantially increased over the past 10 years. Operationalizing the multiphase approach through diverse rigorous procedures and processes is important to its evolution. Recent scholarship highlights the use of a pilot study in the enhancement of the multiphase design (Williams-McBean, 2019). The multiphase mixed methods approach has recently been used in the instrument development process. One investigation used a multiphase framework to psychometrically evaluate the Counseling Training Environment Scale (CTES; Lau et al., 2019). In addition to the aforementioned innovative uses of the multiphase approach, presently there is an ongoing large-scale multiphase research project entitled the Campus Sexual Violence Elimination Act Bystander Program. The goal of this three phase (qualitative-quantitative-qualitative) multi-year investigation is to reduce sexual and intimate partner violence in American college communities (Davidov et al., 2019).

The multiphase design is a team approach within the scope of a large scale, multiple phase, mixed methods research project. This approach strategically incorporates sequential and concurrent mixed methods phases to effectively answer research questions and achieve the overarching program objectives. While each phase is somewhat mutually exclusive from the others, the interconnectedness of each research phase and the corresponding research questions is carefully considered throughout the project. Each phase and research question build upon each other, each contributing to a fuller more robust understanding of the constructs in question (Creswell & Plano-Clark, 2017). While the overarching research goal is moving the project toward overall completion, specific research questions and associated study phases allow for the creation of multiple scholarly publications.

While careful strategy is a necessity for the multiphase approach, equal importance is given to project and researcher team flexibility. Given multiphase design's multiyear outlook, frequent vacillation between concurrent and sequential sequence, multiple research questions, and the evolving accumulation of various researchers with diverse skillsets, flexibility may be the most important trait a multiphase research team can bring to the project. This form of research is an evolving, iterative, and systematic endeavor that requires considerable expertise (Creswell & Plano-Clark, 2017).

Large-Scale and Statewide Variants

There are many potential variants to the multiphase approach. As previously described, the multiphase process can combine both concurrent and sequential phases and is generally considered a type of mixed methods research project that incorporates multiple separate (i.e., full procedural blueprints of each approach), yet connected (i.e., sharing common purpose and overarching research goals), research phases. Within this paragraph we outline two variants. The large-scale program development and evaluation variant of the multiphase design is centered on very large, multiphase, federally funded investigations within education and health services. These investigations have multiple levels of analysis (e.g., initial exploration, feasibility study, program development). See Haneuse and Chen (2011) for a relevant example. The second common variant is the multilevel statewide approach that uses an iterative combination of sequences and phases to answer research questions addressing large-scale statewide issues. For a relevant example see Teddlie and Yu (2007). Typically, this variant will research the local, state, and national levels (Creswell & Plano-Clark, 2017).

DATA ANALYSIS IN TRANSFORMATIVE AND MULTIPHASE APPROACHES

As discussed in Chapters 1, 16, and 17, mixed methods research can have several foci, including qualitative dominant (i.e., researcher(s) rely heavily on a qualitative paradigm and allow for quantitative enhancement); quantitative dominant (i.e., researcher(s) rely heavily on a quantitative paradigm and allow for qualitative enhancement); and equal status (i.e., researcher(s) rely on both qualitative and quantitative threads to enhance the research process; Johnson et al., 2007). Once a researcher determines the research questions and purpose statement, they will decide on their paradigm, methodology, sequence, and the timing of their data collection and analysis. Those utilizing a transformative approach will have a pre-determined social justice-oriented paradigm, while multiphase researchers must very carefully consider how the research questions build on one another and relate to both the multiple mixed methods investigations and the overarching project goals and purpose.

Mixed Methods Research Problem, Questions, and Purpose

In considering what type of research tradition to use, scholars will typically begin with a scholarly problem. An example of a problem might be, "What facilitates motivation for designing a research study for beginning researchers?" The motivation for designing a research study would be the social object that researcher(s) would apply qualitative, quantitative, and mixed characteristics to. Next, the researcher(s) would start to create their research questions. When creating research questions, researchers are careful to not ask what is already known. To ensure questions are relevant, researchers will deeply review the literature to find gaps in a field's scholarly knowledgebase. In addition to ensuring the research questions have not already been answered, scholars will break down research questions, so they are not too broad or too general. Taking this problem and breaking it down to a clear researchable question might look like the following, "What situational factors can stimulate master's level professional counseling students to engage in initial research design efforts?" Once the research questions have been developed, the researcher(s) will begin considering two things: (a) What is the purpose of their study; and (b) What methodology fits the goals and research questions? (Teddlie & Tashakkori, 2010).

Whether one chooses a transformative or a multiphase mixed method tradition, creating the qualitative, quantitative, and mixed methods research questions are an initial consideration. There is an order to mixed methods research questions and/or hypotheses. Generally, the sequence in which a researcher conducts the various phases of a mixed methods study is the order in which the research questions are written and answered. For example, in a two-phase exploratory study the qualitative research question would come first, and the quantitative research question would come second. In a single-phase convergent study, the order of questions is in relation to the size of a research thread (i.e., the larger thread comes first). Mixed methods projects must include a mixed question. A mixed question is one that demonstrates the mixed nature of the study. Specifically, the mixed question must demonstrate the mixing of qualitative and quantitative strands of the project. The mixing phase of the research typically takes place after the qualitative and quantitative elements have been complete; consequently, the mixed research question often appears last within an article (Tashakkori & Teddlie, 2010).

An example of all three styles of questions (qualitative, quantitative, mixed) might help clarify how to create a series of mixed methods research questions. In an unpublished exploratory mixed methods investigation that sought to understand the external influences that function as supports and barriers for rural college students, the first author used the following overarching mixed research question: "Are the emergent qualitative themes, derived from small college stakeholders, regarding the supports and barriers for at-risk rural college students, generalizable to a sample of students attending a rural college?" Within the same investigation, the qualitative research question that guided the investigation was, "What are the supports and barriers for at-risk student populations residing in a rural college setting?" Lastly, the research questions that guided the quantitative aspect of this investigation were: (a) "To what extent do the emergent environmental supports and barriers effect a sample of rural university students?" and (b) "Is there a relationship between survey questions and the corresponding survey response?"

While the initial problem and research questions are being considered and constructed, you will start to consider the purpose of the investigation and if one of the established mixed methods traditions (e.g., embedded, convergent, exploratory, explanatory, transformative, multiphase) best suits your needs. According to Shoonenboom and Johnson (2017), a universal purpose for incorporating mixed methods is to expand and strengthen the analysis and results of an investigation in order to make a meaningful contribution to the literature. Regardless of the chosen design, a mixed methods purpose statement incorporates a rationale for using both qualitative and quantitative strands and the purpose section should set a framework for answering the various research questions. An example purpose statement, taken from the previously described rural college student study, could be, "The purpose of this investigation was to identify the environmental supports and barriers for at-risk students in a rural college setting. Through creating survey questions based on qualitative primary themes and meaning units, the researchers developed a survey to measure student agreement and to facilitate a shared understanding across both qualitative and quantitative methods."

Sequence and Dependence

As described in Chapters 16 and 17, some mixed methods designs are either concurrent, single phase, or sequential (Table 18.1 outlines these possibilities). The present chapter focuses two mixed methods designs that allow for various sequence timing options. Transformative mixed methods research design is theoretically centered on creating a more just and democratic society and, consequently, the entire research process uses a pragmatic philosophy to accomplish this mission. As such, transformative researchers use a concurrent, single, and sequential timing process to accomplish the overarching theoretical mission. The multiphase mixed methods research design is centered on engaging in multiple research projects conducted over time that build on each other and contribute to an inclusive program goal. These separate yet connected studies use pragmatism to determine if they will use a sequential or concurrent data collection/analysis method.

An important distinction is the notion that mixed methods research projects can be either *dependent* or *independent*. Dependent mixed methods research has to do with the second component being dependent on the results of the first mixed methods component. Sequential mixed methods research is dependent in nature and allows for redirection within the second phase. For example, if a sequential/dependent transformative mixed methods research project uses a phenomenological qualitative research approach within the first phase, the researcher can build on this phase and choose to do something that is uniquely tailored to enhance the results of the second phase. In comparison, independent mixed methods research does not depend on the results or data analysis in the other components. The concurrent sequence is in line with an independent approach because the data collection and data analysis are theorized to occur simultaneously and independently. For example, the first phase of a concurrent/independent multiphase mixed methods research project includes a simultaneous grounded theory and survey research design (Shoonenboom & Johnson, 2017; Tashakkori & Teddlie, 2010).

Qualitative Analysis

Qualitative inquiry is a holistic method that is subjective in nature and is somewhat dependent on participant openness and collaboration. The qualitative data collection and analysis processes are designed to be in-depth (e.g., multiple interviews with the same participants); encompass multiple data collection points (e.g., individual interview, focus group, artifact analysis, journal analysis); and must demonstrate a level of trustworthiness (i.e., credibility, confirmability, dependability, transferability, and authenticity). Given this level of depth, qualitative data sets can be large, and the analysis process can be extremely time-consuming. Fortunately, the analysis is made more manageable with the assistance of platforms such as ATLAS.ti and NVivo.

While there are certain factors that cut across all qualitative approaches, including trustworthiness strategies, qualitative sampling, qualitative data collection methods, and researcher reflexivity (Flynn, et al. 2019), researchers conducting a rigorous mixed methods study will incorporate the full procedures and standards of a qualitative research tradition. Hays and Singh (2012) postulated five separate categories of qualitative traditions, including the *universal tradition* (e.g., case study); *experience and theory formulation* (e.g., grounded theory, phenomenology, heuristic inquiry, and consensual qualitative research); the *meaning of symbol and text* (e.g., biography, symbolic Interaction, semiotics, life history, hermeneutics, and narratology); *cultural expressions of process and experience* (e.g., ethnography, ethnomethodology, and autoethnography); and *research as a change agent* (e.g., participatory action research). According to Hays and Singh (2012) these clusters "may overlap and be combined depending on the purpose of the qualitative inquiry" (p. 44). See Table 18.2 for a more comprehensive review.

Qualitative analysis is a rich and expansive process with unique analytic methods prescribed to qualitative traditions (e.g., grounded theory's constant comparative process). While there is differentiation between qualitative analytic approaches, there is much overlap and use of standard terms (e.g., open coding, theme, codebook, member check). The analysis of qualitative data is centered on coding data (e.g., interview transcripts, texts, and artifacts), engaging in the clustering of raw codes, indication and labeling overarching themes, and the designing of a macro dimensional structure (e.g., phenomenon, grounded theory). While researchers occasionally adjust and add different elements to a research tradition, they typically do so with a credible justification. This textbook provides in-depth and pragmatic reviews of a variety of applicable qualitative traditions,

TABLE 18.2 **The Categories of Qualitative Research**

QUALITATIVE CATEGORY	THE NATURE OF THE CATEGORY	QUALITATIVE TRADITIONS
The Universal Tradition	Case study offers an in-depth case description and is considered universal due to its applicability to other traditions (i.e., many qualitative traditions use cases).	Case study
Experience and Theory Formation	The traditions within this cluster derive information from participant experience and create theories based on human experience.	Grounded theory, phenomenology, heuristic inquiry, consensual qualitative research (CQR)
The Meaning of Symbol and Text	Researchers use traditions from this cluster to derive meaning from texts and verbal and non-verbal communication.	Biography, symbolic interaction, semiotics, life history, hermeneutics, narratology
Cultural Expressions of Process and Experience	This cluster emphasizes traditions that explore social and cultural behaviors and norms.	Ethnography, ethnomethodology, autoethnography
Research as a Change Agent	This cluster is centered on the advocacy of research as an agent for change.	Participatory action research

including content analysis, case study, grounded theory, phenomenology, consensual qualitative research, and narrative inquiry.

Quantitative Analysis

The structure for a quantitative design is centered on the scientific method. Quantitative researchers use deductive reasoning to form a hypothesis, collect numerical data, and then use the data to conduct systematic statistical analysis that attempts to answer the research question(s) and hypothesis. As discussed thoroughly in Chapters 4 and 5, there are four main types of quantitative research: descriptive, correlational, causal comparative/quasi-experimental, and experimental research. Descriptive research is based on describing identified variables through systematic quantitative process. Correlational studies statistically determine the degree of a relationship between multiple variables. Researchers using causal-comparative and quasi-experimental approaches attempt to determine a cause-and-effect relationship among variables, however, there is no random assignment, the variables are not manipulated, and the participants are in the form of pre-existing groups. Lastly, experimental research (i.e., the true experiment) is a research study that determines cause and effect through randomly assigning participants and controlling variables (Hurlburt, 2017).

Quantitative analysis is a set of techniques that use mathematical equations, statistics, and other forms of measurement to represent behavior numerically. Quantitative information is any data that are transformed into numerical form such as statistics, percentages, z-scores, and t-scores. Scientific investigations use statistical techniques to measure variables in isolation or in the context of variables influence. Variables are assigned a numerical value to quantify how they differ. Quantitative data sets can be analyzed with the assistance of platforms such as SPSS and SASSI.

Descriptive, inferential, and Bayesian statistics are used to analyze data in the behavioral sciences. Descriptive statistics allow one to organize, summarize, and understand data sets.

Inferential statistics are based on the central limit theorem and use statistics to randomly select participants to infer the probability of results generalizing to a population. Bayesian statistics are based on the Bayes' theorem and use previous knowledge to compute conditional probabilities. In the behavioral sciences, these three forms of statistics are often used together when conducting the quantitative portion of mixed methods research. For example, a researcher using an inferential test (e.g., *t*-test, chi squared, ANOVA, MANOVA, ANCOVA, regression) will also analyze descriptive statistics (e.g., mean, standard deviation) gathered from a demographic questionnaire.

Mixed Method Points-of-Interface

According to Schooneneboom and Johnson (2017) all mixed methods investigations have a point in which the qualitative and quantitative procedures are integrated. Examples of possible areas for interface include research questions, purposes, methods, methodology, philosophical integration, data analysis, and findings. While all points should be considered, most mixed methods research integrates the threads into the results (i.e., *results point of integration*) and many have an integrative point in the data analysis section (i.e., *analytical point integration*).

In addition to general considerations regarding the point of interface, mixed methods researchers using the transformative approach must remember to fully complete each phase with the overarching social-justice oriented theoretical component implemented. Regarding the sampling framework, qualitative researchers using a transformative design will purposefully select participants that fall within the group that is being explored. During the sampling process, researchers give themselves permission to change their opinion, adjust their strategy, and invite diverse participants that will encourage a fuller more inclusive level of understanding. Similarly, a transformative quantitative sample will have a level of flexibility and may engage in parametric practices that involve dividing the population into smaller subgroups (i.e., stratified random sampling). In comparison, given the vast and differentiated nature of the multiphase approach, researchers may follow their initial objective or engage in a large consensus meeting prior to changing any of the methodological components.

Meta-Inferences

Meta-inferences are the cohesively integrated inferences that are grounded in the results of the qualitative and quantitative threads of a mixed methods investigation (Teddlie & Tashakkori, 2006). During the meta-inference creation process, mixed methods researchers integrate qualitative and quantitative inferences to the point that they have a third vantage point that incorporates both qualitative and quantitative standpoints. Onwuegbuzie and Johnson (2006) refer to this viewpoint as *commensurability legitimation*. The commensurability legitimation process is meant to go beyond information provided in either qualitative or quantitative threads. Within the next section, we discuss the process of quantitizing and qualitizing data. It is important for you to know that the measure of commensurability legitimation is whether the quantitizing and qualitizing process leads to interpretable meta-inferences.

While generating meta-inferences is essential to the notion of mixing and creating an integrated outlook of the data, it is critical to thoroughly validate the qualitative and quantitative threads separately to ensure a legitimate, valid, and robust mixing phase. Onwuegbuzie and Johnson (2006) describe the process of thoroughly validating the qualitative, quantitative, and mixed phases of an investigation *multiple validities legitimation*. When researchers thoroughly enhance their investigation through multiple validity procedures, they ensure high-quality meta-inferences.

Tashakkori and Teddlie (2003) took this notion of multiple validities legitimation a step further when they introduced the notion of *inference quality*. This was essentially a critique on how accurately the inductive and deductive aspects were created. This echoed support for the gestalt of mixed methods research design, as it went beyond the legitimation of separate threads and conceptualized a mixed methods study as being created by the whole of a mixed methods research study. Tashakkori and Teddlie describe assigning *design quality* and *interpretive quality* to ensure both the rigor of the methodological design and the rigor of interpretation of the study conclusions (i.e., meta-inferences).

Quantitizing Qualitative Data. If researchers are considering a transformative or multiphase approach to mixed methods research, one method for synthesizing the data is engaging in the quantitization of qualitative data (i.e., qualitative frequency counting). Quantitizing has been defined as "the process of assigning numerical values (nominal or ordinal) to data conceived as not numerical" (Sandelowski et al., 2009; pp. 209–210). A benefit of quantitized qualitative data is they can be used in statistical comparisons with quantitative data and in the eventual creation of meta-inferences. There are many ways in which researchers can quantitize qualitative data. This is a method in which qualitative researcher's count the number of times a qualitative code occurs. Quantitized frequencies are helpful because they can indicate how influential codes are. Another method for quantitizing qualitative data is tallying the frequency of themes in a sample. In other words, the researcher(s) would separately break down the frequency in which a theme is associated with the participants taking part in the various data collection methods (e.g., focus group, individual interviews, journal analysis). Lastly, counting the percentage of people selecting a certain theme has been used to quantitize qualitative data (Driscoll, Appiah-Yeboah, Salib, & Rupert, 2007; Onwuegbuzie & Teddlie 2003).

Qualitizing Quantitative Data. Qualitizing is the process of converting quantitative data into qualitative data. Quantitative data is converted into the emergent qualitative themes (Leal, Engebretson, & Cohen, 2016). According to Nzabonima (2018) "The qualitizing process is not confined to turning numbers into words, but it is about finding or imposing an underlying conceptual qualitative representation of the items that make up the factor or the denominator concept which is shared among the items loading together" (p. 3). Qualitizing also includes participant profiling, which theoretically groups participants based on their quantitative scores. These scores are derived from quantitative data collection points. According to Nzabonima (2018), qualitative profiling includes taking a participant's or a group of participants' Likert scale scores and applying their level of agreement and disagreement to the emergent qualitative themes. For example, the resultant participant scores from a 5-point Likert scale that are relevant to a particular qualitative theme would be indicated within the theme description. The researchers would then indicate quantitative trends. If respondents were in high agreement, item scores would be closer to 5. If they were mostly in disagreement, the respondents would be low (e.g., a score of 1 or 2). Lastly, participants' quantitative reactions would be labeled as in agreement or in disagreement with the qualitative theme.

INCREASING RIGOR OF TRANSFORMATIVE AND MULTIPHASE APPROACHES

Mixed methods research designs naturally enhance the rigor of an investigation due to combining the power of quantitative procedures and the in-depth nature of qualitative methods. In addition to enhancing the rigor of the investigation, they also offset weaknesses (e.g., quantitative lack of depth, qualitative inability to generalize to a population) of each approach. Lastly, the integration (i.e., mixing) of both qualitative and quantitative traditions has the potential to provide more rigorous comprehensive and nuanced results when compared to using one approach (Brown et al., 2015).

Rigor in Transformative Mixed Methods Research

Standards for transformative rigor in research include the assertion that the researcher should know the community "well enough" to link the research to positive action within that community (Lincoln, 1995). You may be wondering what it meant to know a community "well enough." Awareness and knowledge of a community of people is dependent on the community's present and historical cultural context, the level of integration committed by the researcher, what is deemed important within the community, what values the community holds, and the researcher's personal understanding of the community (Mertens, 2009). To increase the rigor of transformative research, it is essential for the researcher to embed themselves in the focused community, to be able to work respectfully with and within them, which ultimately enhances their ability to work with them during the research process. By embedding themselves at any level, the researchers experience an aspect of the communities that they would not otherwise have access to, which would consequently enhance the validity of their research.

An aspect of transformative rigor is the extent to which the researcher and members of the community collaborate on the creation of the research design. The research design should respond to the practical and cultural needs of marginalized subgroups. Common variables explored through a transformative lens include disability, culture, language, gender, class, race, ethnicity, and other contextually dependent dimensions of diversity (Mertens, 2009). To enhance the rigor of understanding these variables, researchers often recruit community members to serve in the roles of expert panel member, coauthor, or auditor.

As previously stated, it is possible to further enhance transformative methodological rigor through the development of partnerships. A partnership is when a member or members of the community of interest supports the researcher or research team. This support could include collaboration on the research design, understanding cultural norms, and supporting the researcher(s) with the cultural integration process. Partnerships are centered on a researcher's level of cultural awareness, knowledge, and competence. Furthermore, it is essential to be respectful when entering a community to conduct research. Within the context of respect, researchers need to be aware that there are different cultural views of what respect looks like. Reciprocity is an additional element in establishing research partnerships. How can a researcher or a research team enhance the participant's quality of life, even for a short period of time? Reciprocity addresses power differentials between the researcher(s) and the members of a marginalized community of interest. By enhancing someone (e.g., personal compensation) or someplace (e.g., creation of a needed community resource) researchers can, at times, witness the secondary effect of an increase in participant willingness to share cultural or life experiences in an open manner (Mertens, 2009).

Rigor in Multiphase Mixed Methods Research

Researchers using the multiphase approach to mixed methods research will essentially be conducting multiple separate investigations (i.e., multiphase) that share common methodological frameworks (e.g., research goals, hypotheses, and purpose). These separate and large-scale research studies must fully meet the rigor and standards of both qualitative and quantitative approaches and build on the findings gathered within the previous phase. According to Creswell and Plano-Clark (2011), researchers using a multiphase design "examine a problem or topic through an iteration of connected quantitative and qualitative studies that are sequentially aligned, with each new approach building on what was learned previously to address a central program objective" (p. 100).

From a rigor vantage point, multiphase approaches have many strengths. The essence of the multiphase approach is to essentially maximize the rigor of each phase to answer large-scale, multifaceted, multiphase, multiyear projects aimed at working on complex research endeavors. This is the methodological framework of choice for research teams aiming at conducting multiple mixed methods studies for one overarching project. Central to the question of multiphase rigor is ensuring that qualitative and quantitative rigor standards are maximized.

Qualitative rigor is assessed much differently when compared to quantitative rigor. Whereas quantitative research assesses rigor in validity (e.g., construct validity), reliability (e.g., test-retest validity), generalizability (e.g., external validity), and replicability (e.g., independent researchers), qualitative researchers are interested in credibility (e.g., triangulation), transferability (e.g., thick descriptions), confirmability (e.g., research journal), dependability (e.g., dependability audit), and authenticity (e.g., section on researcher bias; Lincoln & Guba, 1985; Polit & Beck, 2014). Table 18.3 provides a breakdown of elements related to rigor in quantitative research and Table 18.4 provides a concise breakdown of qualitative standards of rigor and methods for ensuring trustworthiness.

Given the differentiation of the phases within a multiphase project, researchers and consumers of research will analyze the rigor of qualitative and quantitative phases separately. While it is essential to consider the strengths of both qualitative and quantitative threads, Bryman et al. (2008) argue for the need to assess the quality and the justification of mixing the approaches. An example of

TABLE 18.3 Quantitative Rigor Standard, Description, and Example

STANDARD OF RIGOR	DESCRIPTION	EXAMPLES
Validity	*Validity* in research is the degree to which your findings represent the construct you are claiming to measure.	Construct validity, content validity, criterion related validity, predictive validity, concurrent validity, convergent validity, discriminant validity
Reliability	*Reliability* in research is the degree to which researchers produce stable and consistent results	Test–retest reliability, parallel forms reliability, inter-rater reliability, internal consistency reliability
Replicability	*Replicability* in research is when a separate group of researchers copy the procedures with a similar population and arrive at similar results as the original study	The independent group, diverse methods across studies
Generalizability	*Generalizability* involves making broad inferences from observations from a study	Large sample, representativeness of the sample

NOTE: This table contains four standards of quantitative rigor, their descriptions, and examples. Further reading is necessary to fully understand each standard of rigor.

TABLE 18.4 **Qualitative Rigor Standard, Description, and Example**

STANDARD OF RIGOR	DESCRIPTION	EXAMPLES
Credibility	*Credibility* is the leve of confidence in the accuracy of the study procedures and findings. This form of qualitative trustworthiness is similar to the quantitative research process of internal validity	Member checking, triangulation, peer debriefing
Confirmability	*Confirmability* demonstrates qualitative objectivity and neutrality of the findings. This demonstrates that the conclusions derived from a study were not developed by the researcher	Memo, audit trail, research journal
Dependability	*Dependability* demonstrates that the findings are traceable, logical, and documented. This ensures the data are stable over time and are similar to the quantitative construct of reliability	Process logs, dependability audits
Transferability	*Transferability* is the qualitative version of external validity and attempts to see if phenomena can be transferred from case-to-case	Thick and rich descriptions
Authenticity	*Authenticity* is the degree to which the researcher accurately portrays the participant's life	Description of researcher bias, deep and contextually accurate descriptions of all elements of the research process

NOTE: This table contains five standards of qualitative rigor, their descriptions, and examples. Further reading is necessary to fully understand each standard of rigor.

this level of rigor is to provide a transparent description of the research, research team interaction, and clear justification of methodological decision-making (Brown, et al., 2015). Within the mixing process researchers will provide clear blueprints for the outcomes and process of the mixing. This could be in the form of qualitizing, quantitizing, and/or meta-inferences.

Multicultural Issues

Helpers conducting multicultural and social justice-oriented research in the behavioral sciences often want to incorporate a mixed methods research design within their work. Mixed methods mimics the process that many helpers use in their clinical practice when they merge quantitative assessments (e.g., empirically based instruments, outcome questionnaires, satisfaction surveys) with qualitative information about a client's experience (e.g., psychosocial documentation, treatment plan, case notes, and intake narrative responses; Plano-Clark & Wang, 2010). Furthermore, mixed methods approaches are well suited for research conducted with diverse populations because the approach includes the qualitative strength of understanding the in-depth thoughts and feelings of diverse individuals and simultaneously develops culturally sensitive relationships within their communities (Plano-Clark & Wang, 2010). These approaches can be collaborative, meeting the needs of distinct participants, and produce results that are useful for promoting change.

The transformative paradigm is particularly applicable to people who have experienced discrimination and oppression within their lives, including (but not limited to) race, ethnicity, disability, immigrant status, political conflict, sexual orientation, poverty, gender, age, or any of the other characteristics that can be associated with less access to socially just treatment and provisions (Mertens, 2009). As previously described in this chapter, the transformative paradigm is centered on culturally appropriate strategies to facilitate understandings that will create sustainable social change. Understanding the dynamics of power and privilege and how they can be challenged in the set circumstances is also a priority for researchers using this approach (Creswell & Plano-Clark, 2017).

When working with various communities, it is important to remember that different cultural groups hold contrasting values and expectations. Each community is intricate and complex. While it is important to use research methods to enhance the challenging aspects to various cultures (e.g., substance abuse, acculturation difficulties), there can be an over adherence to a *deficit perspective* which can be a limitation because it does not integrate a full perspective of a culture (Mertens, 2009; Plano-Clark & Wang, 2010). Researchers must be able to present a balanced report that identifies strengths and challenges within the community of interest, treats participants with respect, engages in propriety and social action, while avoiding harming community members and increasing discriminatory beliefs when evaluating possible cultural problems.

LIMITATIONS TO TRANSFORMATIVE AND MULTIPHASE DESIGNS

The concept of a transformative paradigm is vague and can be viewed as a theoretical *umbrella term* that includes emancipatory, anti-discriminatory, participatory, and Freirean approaches demonstrated within feminist, racial/ethnic minority, disability, and research on behalf of other disparaged groups (Mertens, 1999). With such a broadly encompassing paradigm, there are many ways in which to interpret the application of this paradigm in research studies (Sweetman et al., 2010).

The transformative theoretical perspective has been referred to as a paradigm, theoretical perspective, and worldview. The notion that an entire mixed method approach is guided by a single theoretical perspective has caused more than a little confusion. Creswell and Plano-Clark (2017) add that very little structure has been provided within the literature to guide researchers in executing their mixed methods study in a transformative way. In response to this potential limitation, researchers utilizing the transformative approach might use a method similar to grounded theory's inductive reasoning (Glaser, 1967). This process allows researchers to use a social construction procedure to create and recreate unique human phenomena. The difference is that the transformative framework creates and recreates the structure, methods, and points of interface to work within the unique contextual conditions of a community of interest. From a transformative perspective, the more trust the researcher builds with the participants (i.e., community), the more they will likely share information and allow the researcher to access pertinent cultural artifacts and documents. The process of the researcher attaining quality data following increased levels of participant trust can challenge research teams due to sudden changes in the scope of the project. This inductive process may require the researchers to define and redefine their research process and procedures.

The multiphase mixed methods tradition is a team approach and, while not considered solely a team approach, the transformative approach can be difficult for a single researcher, especially when the design is concurrent. We recommend using a full team for both approaches; however, the use of additional researchers can add time and cost to a project. Furthermore, if a research team with diverse research skills is not available, a transformative or multiphase mixed methods study may require that the researchers spend significant time learning new research methods, defending/justifying the use of these methods, and learning to use and integrate them correctly (Cronholm & Hialmarsson, 2011). This is a limitation because the project timeframe would include both executing the research methods and the researcher(s) learning how to execute them.

Sequential and concurrent methodological frameworks bring their share of challenges. When conducting a sequential transformative or multiphase investigation, the main weakness is the length of time that is involved in data collection due to the two separate phases required. Researchers will have to make key decisions about which findings from the initial phase will be focused on within the following phase. Concurrent studies require great effort and expertise to simultaneously study a phenomenon with two separate threads. It can be difficult to compare and interface the results of two analyses/results using different approaches. When the two data phases are compared, discrepancies may arise that need to be deciphered by an experienced mixed methods researcher (Creswell & Plano-Clark, 2017).

Transformative Research Design Case Study

Lucero, J., Wallerstein, N., Duran, B., Alegria, M., Greene-Moton, E., Israel, B., Kastelic, S., Magarati, M., Oetzel, J., Person, C., Shulz, A., Villegas, M., & White Hat, E. R. (2018). Development of a mixed methods investigation of processes and outcomes of community-based participatory research. *Journal of Mixed Methods Research, 12*(1), 55–74. https://doi-org.libproxy.plymouth.edu/10.1177/1558689816633309

BACKGROUND

This investigation represents a large-scale National Institutes of Health (NIH) funded project aimed at understanding how community-based participatory research (CBPR) processes and community participation add value to health disparity research in American Indian/Alaska Native communities (Lucero, et al., 2018). Given the large-scale nature of the project, we are only reviewing a portion of the work within this case study. Furthermore, this review will only cover what could be determined from the Lucero et al. (2018) article; as such, many of the phases, procedures, and details are not fully presented.

According to Israel et al. (1998) CBPR is an action-oriented approach to research that directly (e.g., expert panel, auditor, co-author, editor) and indirectly (e.g., conversations, email communication) involves community members, representatives of interest, researchers with diverse expertise, and experts in all aspects of the research process. Once the construct(s) of interest have been fully deliberated with the various communities of interest, the data are used to create social and policy change (i.e., action).

A major methodological trend over the past 20 years has been incorporating CBPR partnership practices into transformative mixed methods investigations (Creswell & Plano-Clark, 2017). Examples of CBPR practices include (but are not limited to) community member assistance with research decision-making, conflict mediation, and resource sharing (Lucero, et al. 2018). While theory and research exist, best practice for CBPR is largely unknown.

Authors of the present investigation used a CBPR conceptual model and indigenous transformative theory to guide their mixed methods framework. The initial phase of this investigation was a Research for Improved Health (RIH) mixed methods pilot study. Next, the mixed methods design transformed from a convergent parallel design to a sequential (dependent) approach (qualitative [phase 2], and quantitative [phase 3]). The research questions that guided Lucero et al.'s (2018) investigation, included:

1. How much variability is there in characteristics of CBPR projects?
2. How much congruence or divergence is there among partners on perceptions of context, group dynamics, research design, and outcomes?
3. How does the concept of CBPR differ across partnership contexts?
4. How do group dynamics develop over time? (p. 63)

RESEARCH PROCESS

The initial phase of the investigation was a grant funded RIH pilot study. This pilot study was specifically developed to create and test a conceptual model for successful CBPR relationships. The authors conducted an extant literature review, met and deliberated with an advisory council comprised of community and academic CBPR experts, used a web-based survey to critique the appropriateness of the emergent model, and further enhanced and critiqued the model with six qualitative community focus groups. The CBPR principles developed within the pilot study influenced the main mixed methods investigation.

Next, the full mixed methods investigation began. The study was entitled "RIH: A Study of Community-Academic Partnerships." A main goal of the RIH study was partly to use mixed methods, within every phase of the investigation, to understand the variability of CBPR health researcher partnerships across the nation. The National Congress of American Indians Policy Research Center collaborated with a Scientific Community Advisory Council composed of a diverse group of scholars, to contrast and compare partnership procedures. Researchers recruited 200 federally funded and diverse CBPR partnerships for a cross-sectional Internet survey. While this was taking place, researchers executed eight diverse qualitative case studies and conducted 80 individual interviews and six focus groups.

The data analysis was focused on triangulation. The research team compared qualitative and quantitative strands to confirm the findings. Researchers analyzed the quantitative data with community and academic partners and used the qualitative findings to discuss alignment of data. In addition, researchers explored the role and variability of governance in CBPR projects. Researchers used quantitative and qualitative methods to determine the nature of agreements that were developed. While priority was given to the quantitative data, the qualitative data provided illustrative governance strategies within tribal communities.

DISCUSSION

This large-scale mixed method transformative study utilized an indigenous theoretical perspective and CBPR model to deeply understand context and relational dynamics among health disparities in American Indian/Alaska Native and other diverse groups. The quantitative data provided evidence of links between CBPR dynamics and the qualitative data proved the contextual analysis for how and why individual partnering constructs may or may not be important. The authors suggest that embedding CBPR within a mixed methods design framework is critical for understanding the lived realities of indigenous communities.

Multiphase Research Design Case Study

Duron, J. F. (2018). Legal decision-making in child sexual abuse investigations: A mixed-methods study of factors that influence prosecution. *Child Abuse & Neglect, 79,* 302–314. https://doi-org. librporxy.plymouth.edu/10.1016/j.chiabu.2018.02.022

BACKGROUND

The legal protection of children and prosecution of child sexual abuse perpetrators are essential aspects of a community's response to the sexual violation of children. According to Finkelhor and Jones (2012) between 1992 and 2010 there was a reported decline in substantiated child sexual abuse (CSA) cases, with disclosure rates reflecting 10% of sexually abused children (Lyon & Ahern, 2011). Salient to understanding CSA case reports are the factors influencing the decision to prosecute. The present multiphase study sought to understand how prosecutors evaluate cases and decide which CSA cases rise to the level of trial. Our interpretation of this case is based solely on our review of the 2018 article and may not fully reflect the researcher's complete efforts.

Specifically, Duron (2018) sought to understand the factors that differentiate CSA cases that rise to the level of criminal prosecution of alleged perpetrator(s) from those that do not. To accomplish this, Duron designed a three-phase sequential multiphase study (qualitative [first phase], quantitative [second phase], qualitative [third phase]). Five multiphase research questions guided this investigation, including:

1. What is the prosecutors' process for pursuing prosecution? What influences the decision to pursue prosecution?
2. What case factors are associated with the prosecution of child sexual abuse cases?
3. How do prosecutors make decisions? What characteristics of each case led to prosecution? (Duron, 2018, p. 304)

RESEARCH PROCESS

There were three sequential (dependent) phases. The first phase qualitatively explored the perceptions of four prosecutors purposefully selected from a district attorney's Child Abuse Division in the southern United States. Participants were four (three females, one male) White prosecutors, 30–49 years of age, with service records ranging from 6 months to 10 years. Individual interview questions were centered on understanding how the prosecutors handled and processed CSA cases, and what case features affected charging potential.

The phase one qualitative analysis process consisted of a research team conducting an iterative content analysis procedure. Duron and her research assistant independently read and coded transcripts related to the four interviews. Coding consensus meetings were conducted, and a final juried codebook was used to further independently code the four transcripts. Final themes were determined after the second round of independent coding and an in-depth research team consensus meeting.

The second (quantitative) phase randomly selected 100 child advocacy center (CAC) files (2009-2013) related to CSA. These CAC cases were in the form of documented closed legal outcomes and video recorded interviews. These files were analyzed in order to develop a prediction model. The researcher determined factors associated with prosecution of sexual offenders through logistic regression modeling.

The phase two quantitative analysis process consisted of using descriptive statistics to describe the sample. Further data related to the case record and forensic interview were quantified. This information was statistically analyzed with the dependent variable of whether the CSA case was prosecuted. The researcher created a prediction model building procedure (Hosmer & Lemeshow, 2000), utilized a square root transformation, and used a univariate logistic regression analysis to identify correlates of risk for the baseline multivariable model (Duron, 2018).

The third (qualitative) phase was centered on the in-depth interviewing of three prosecutors and 10 prosecuted cases. The cases were determined through choosing every third case available for each of the three prosecutors. This phase sought to expand and confirm upon the factors contributing to prosecution uncovered in phase two.

The phase two qualitative analysis process consisted of the author and a research associate analyzing interview transcripts using a framework analysis. According to Duron (2018), the "five stages of analysis included: familiarization, identifying a thematic framework, indexing (coding), charting, and mapping and interpretation." (p. 307). Throughout the aforementioned qualitative stages research team consensus, jurying, and negotiation meetings were conducted prior to arriving at finalized code and theme meanings. To ensure phase three trustworthiness, member checking was conducted.

DISCUSSION

Results from this study provided evidence that CSA prosecution is most strongly predicted through availability of corroborating accounts, evidence, and caregiver support. The results suggest that the quality of evidence and the careful accounting of details surrounding the investigations are extremely important factors in achieving a positive outcome (i.e., accurate prosecution of the perpetrator of CSA). The most important stated evidence was the childs' (victims) disclosures of the criminal behavior. In relation to this disclosure, was the caregiver(s) support. Caregiver support was conceptualized as non-offending parents and safe family members assisting the child with discussing the sexual abuse.

SUMMARY

This chapter introduced you to the transformative and multiphase mixed methods research traditions. These two traditions were created to provide support to specific research endeavors. The transformative design's infusion of social justice ideology into all relevant aspects of the methodology and the multiphase design's emphasis on supporting large-scale research projects, provide emerging researchers with an important guide for research problems and questions that are well-suited to these approaches. Please remember, researchers using either of these traditions require a supportive research environment including mentoring, a research team with relevant expertise, and physical and financial resources to support an intensive research project.

Throughout this chapter you were informed about the various aspects of the transformative and multiphase research process, including research questions, mixed methods purpose statement, qualitative strand standards, quantitative strand standards, data analysis, multicultural issues, and a guide for enhancing rigor. These two approaches require research experience and thoughtfulness at each phase of the project. For example, given the goal of carefully integrating a social justice emphasis into the various transformative mixed methods phases and procedures, you should consider working collaboratively with one or all of the following: a thoughtful research team, an experienced mentor, or a group of participant researchers with relevant life-experience and/or knowledge about the social justice issue being explored. Similarly, researchers using the multiphase approach are engaging in a complicated large-scale investigation. As such, you should only consider leading this type of investigation if you have a large research team with relevant experience and knowledge. Furthermore, given the strategic and complex nature of the multiphase approach, this is not a good fit for novice researchers with little research team experience. If your research questions and purpose are relevant, we hope you consider these powerful and innovative approaches to research.

STUDENT ACTIVITIES

Exercise 1: Developing Interview Questions for a Transformative Research Study

Directions: Review the following scenario and develop interview questions for a transformative mixed methods research study.

Researchers are looking to conduct a mixed methods study examining the lived experiences of members within a small, closed-off religious community. The focus of the study is on how religion impacts the culture of the community, and how deep this impact runs. The researchers will be conducting a focus group interview with 10 individuals from the community. The goal of the interview is to learn more about the practice of religion within this community.

Develop five questions that could be used in this focus group. Keep in mind the multicultural issues surrounding the development of interview questions.

Exercise 2: Understanding Differences in Mixed Methods Design

Directions: Review the following information and respond to the reflection questions.

Within mixed methods research studies, concurrent and sequential designs are used for different reasons. The sequence may be a choice made by the researcher or the nature of the research tradition may seem to require a design. When considering the various mixed methods frameworks, consider the rationale for deciding to use a concurrent design and/or a sequential design. Respond to the below prompts:

- Describe the main differences between concurrent and sequential studies.
- What are the main strengths and weaknesses of each sequence?
- Consider the discussion on independence and dependence: Are concurrent designs always independent and are sequential studies always dependent? Go to your university's EBSCO Data Base and find Academic Search Premier, use the search function to find examples in current literature that do not follow this trend.

Exercise 3: Understanding Data Collection Methods

Directions: Review the following information and determine which data collection methods would work best for the given research study.

Researchers are looking to conduct a study utilizing a mixed methods design examining how women are treated in current male-dominant fields, such as engineering or finance. The focus of the study is on the culture surrounding these fields and how this culture may affect the women working within them. The researchers plan on conducting their research with everyone within predetermined workplaces, not just working with the female employees.

- What qualitative data collection methods would work best with this study? Justify your answer.
- What quantitative data collection methods would work best with this study? Justify your answer.

Exercise 4: Understanding Multicultural Issues Within Mixed Methods Research

Directions: Follow the below instructions and answer the following questions.

Go to your university's online EBSCO Data Base and find Academic Search Premier. Search and find a mixed methods article that focuses on a multicultural phenomenon. Review the article in its entirety and answer the following questions related to issues surrounding multicultural mixed methods research.

- Describe, in detail, the methodological framework of this study.
- What multicultural/social justice are reflected with this particular methodology?
- What multicultural issues came up during this research study?
- What impact do the multicultural issues have on the study?
- How did the authors attempt to reduce the impact of these issues?

ADDITIONAL RESOURCES

Software Recommendations

NVivo Software (https://www.qsrinternational.com)

CAQDAS Software (https://www.maxqda.com)

ATLAS ti (https://atlasti.com)

MaxQDA (https://maxda.com)

Statistical Package for the Social Sciences (SPSS): (https://www.ibm.com/analytics/spss-statistics-software)

R: (https://www.r-project.org/)

SAS: (https://www.sas.com/en_us/software/stat.html)

Mplus: (https://www.statmodel.com/)

Helpful Links

- http://salmapatel.co.uk/academia/the-research-paradigm-methodology-epistemology-and-ontology-explained-in-simple-language/
- https://www.ncbi.nlm.nih.gov/pmc/articles/PMC4485510/
- https://libguides.usc.edu/writingguide/quantitative

- https://www.ncbi.nlm.nih.gov/pmc/articles/PMC5602001/

- https://link.springer.com/article/10.1007/s11186-019-09345-5

- http://coalition4evidence.org/468-2/publications/

Helpful Books

Creswell, J., & Plano Clark, V. (2017). *Designing and conducting mixed methods research* (3rd ed.). SAGE.

Crotty, M. (2003). *The foundations of social research: Meaning and perspective in the research process.* SAGE.

Hays, D. G., & Singh, A. A. (2012). *Qualitative inquiry in clinical and educational settings.* Guilford.

Lincoln, Y. S. & Guba, E. G. (1985). *Naturalistic inquiry.* SAGE.

Mertens, D. M. (2009). *Transformative research and evaluation.* Guilford

Morse, J.M., & Niehaus, L. (2009). *Mixed method design: Principles and procedures.* Left Coast Press.

Tashakkori, A., & Teddlie, C. (Eds.). (2010). *Handbook of mixed methods in social and behavioral research.* SAGE.

Teddlie, C., & Tashakkori, A. (2009). *Foundations of mixed methods research: Integrating quantitative and qualitative approaches in the social and behavioral sciences.* SAGE.

Helpful Videos

- https://www.youtube.com/watch?v=1P-6zy6ahlc

- https://www.youtube.com/watch?v=A3-AFup3nzM&t=23s

- https://www.youtube.com/watch?v=XynPxWSLjZY&t=5s

- https://www.youtube.com/watch?v=T5HOpyJJmjQ

- https://www.youtube.com/watch?v=A3-AFup3nzM

- https://www.youtube.com/watch?v=DK54BERZejA

KEY REFERENCES

Only key references appear in the print edition. The full reference list appears in the digital product found on http://connect.springerpub.com/content/book/978-0-8261-4385-3/part/part04/chapter/ch18

Flynn, S. V., Korcuska, J. S., Brady, N. V., & Hays, D. G. (2019). A 15-year content analysis of three qualitative research traditions. *Counselor Education & Supervision*, 58, 49–63. https://doi.org/10.1002/ceas.12123

Hays, D. G., & Singh, A. A. (2012). *Qualitative inquiry in clinical and educational settings.* Guilford.

Mertens, D. M. (2009). *Transformative research and evaluation.* Guilford.

Morgan, D. L. (2014). Pragmatism as a paradigm for social research. *Qualitative Inquiry*, 20, 1045–1053. https://doi.org/10.1177/1077800413513733

Onwuegbuzie, A. J., & Combs, J. P. (2010). Emergent data analysis techniques in mixed methods research: A synthesis. In A. Tashakkori & C. Teddlie (Eds.), *Handbook of mixed methods in social and behavioral research* (2nd ed., pp. 397–430). SAGE.

Onwuegbuzie, A. J., & Johnson, R. B. (2006). The validity issue in mixed research. *Research in the Schools*, 13, 48–63.

Onwuegbuzie, A. J., & Teddlie, C. (2003). A framework for analyzing data in mixed methods research. In A. Tashakkori & C. Teddlie (Eds.), *Handbook of mixed methods in social and behavioral research* (pp. 351–383). SAGE.

Schoonenboom, J., & Johnson, R.B. (2017). How to construct a mixed methods research design. *Köln Z Soziol*, 69, 107–131. https://doi.org/10.1007/s11577-017-0454-1

Tashakkori, A., & Teddlie, C. (2003). The past and future of mixed methods research: From data triangulation to mixed model designs. In A. Tashakkori & C. Teddlie (Eds.), *Handbook of mixed methods in the social & behavioral research* (pp. 671–701). SAGE.

Teddlie, C., & Tashakkori, A. (2006). A general typology of research designs featuring mixed methods. *Research in the Schools*, 13, 12–28.

INDEX

CPSIA information can be obtained
at www.ICGtesting.com
Printed in the USA
BVHW020923100123
655921BV00022B/269